"SUSANNA," "JEANIE," AND "THE OLD FOLKS AT HOME"

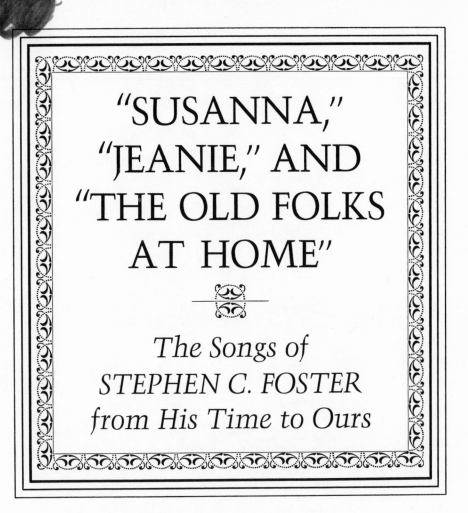

"SUSANNA," "JEANIE," AND "THE OLD FOLKS AT HOME"

The Songs of STEPHEN C. FOSTER from His Time to Ours

William W. Austin

MACMILLAN PUBLISHING CO., INC.

NEW YORK

COLLIER MACMILLAN PUBLISHERS

LONDON

76-2655

Macmillan Publishing Co., Inc.
866 Third Avenue, New York, N.Y. 10022
Collier Macmillan Canada, Ltd.

Library of Congress Cataloging in Publication Data

Austin, William W.

Susanna, Jeanie, and The old folks at home.
Includes index.
1. Foster, Stephen Collins, 1826–1864. Songs.
I. Title.
ML410.F78A9   784'.092'4   75-17635
ISBN 0-02-504500-8

FIRST PRINTING 1975

Printed in the United States of America

Contents

[v]

PART THREE: "THE OLD FOLKS AT HOME" AND OTHER "PATHETIC PLANTATION SONGS"—What They Meant to

Acknowledgments

Many people in many places have helped me explore the songs of Stephen Foster and what they mean. "Everywhere I roam" I find facts and insights that can fit together to illuminate each other. So many people have provided these facts and insights that, even when the contributions were enormous, I can make only a token acknowledgment. Each of the friends named here has given something indispensable: Robert M. Adams, Richard B. Allen, Elizabeth J. Austin, James C. Austin, Lee H. Austin, Margery J. Austin, William M. Austin, Malcolm Bilson, Richard O. Boyer, Phyllis Brodhead, Jack Carruth, Gilbert Chase, William Crowder, Mary Cullen, Steve Drews, Richard F. French, Jane Garrett, Charles Hamm, H. Wiley Hitchcock, John Hsu, Martha Hsu, Alfred E. Kahn, Michael Kammen, Barbara Kaplan, Leo Marx, Henry Pleasants, Saunders Redding, Steve Reich, Harold E. Samuel, Grigori Shneerson, Earl Hobson Smith, Ann Smock, William H. Smock, Eileen Southern, Curtis Benjamin Taylor, Victor Ullman. I am grateful to each one.

At the sumptuous archive of the Foster Hall Collection at the University of Pittsburgh, the curator, Fletcher Hodges, Jr., welcomed me to study Foster's manuscript notebook. He read an embryonic draft of my ideas. Then, years later, he read the whole book and corrected my mistakes of biographical fact. His own interpretations, naturally different from mine on some points, did not interfere with his generosity.

At the New York Public Library's Music Division, Lincoln Center, the head of the Americana collection, Richard Jackson, edited the *Stephen Foster Song Book* (New York: Dover, 1974) in time to make it a fine companion to my study. When he read my draft he kindly chided me for having taken so long with it. Then in January 1975 he discovered the manuscript copy of Dvořák's arrangement of "Old Folks at Home" and promptly sent a xerox so that I could squeeze in my description of it here. I owe thanks to all the staff at Lincoln Center, but most to Jackson.

John Kirkpatrick, during many years as Professor of Music at Cornell and then as professor and curator of the Ives Collection at Yale, taught me much about music and "all the world." For instance, his performance of Foster's "Anadolia," soon after we became colleagues in 1947, surprised me and greatly extended the range of my thoughts. His loan of the set of Foster Hall Reproductions that he had inherited from Ann Luckey of the Princeton Conservatory of Music greatly facilitated my work. Kirkpatrick's meticulous scholarship and his unique perspectives helped me refine what had begun as a very crude interpretation. If even now my perspectives differ from his, they overlap more and more, and where they do so, I trust they coincide.

Richard K. Winslow, Professor of Music at Wesleyan University and chief animator of the "world music" program there, was among the first to respond to the combination of concerns that motivated my exploration. He effectively urged me on. Now, just as galley proofs are being corrected, he sends an exciting composition— variations for violin, unaccompanied, on Foster's "Hard Times, Come Again No More," written this spring. If Winslow's variations win the attention they deserve, they may require a whole new chapter on continually changing meanings of Foster's songs through "all the world."

W. A.
Ithaca
May 1975

Introduction:
Three types of song,
their writer
and their meanings

Stephen C. Foster resists traditional biography, and his songs elude mere musical description or analysis. Though some elements of biography and some account of his simple musical techniques are important in this book, they fit into a pattern that gives more emphasis to poetry, to history, and to cultural contrasts and connections. Foster's songs combine words and music—often his own words, often words that later singers chose to put with his tunes, occasionally words of earlier poets that Foster set to music. Therefore the songs invite us to study words and music through the generations of his parents, his brothers and sisters and friends, his daughter, his granddaughter, his great-grand nieces and nephews. Such a study is somewhat novel.

Like many American products, Foster's songs are not exclusively American, nor equally cherished by all Americans. In a serious study of Foster, English and German cultural history are as important as American, and the question "what is Black culture?" looms as large as "what is American?" or "bourgeois?" or "proletarian?" or "folk?" Foster's songs offer a focus of study useful to anyone striving to clarify these issues. Such a study is risky. But risks well calculated can be exhilarating.

The songs of Foster mean many things to a great many people. Whistle the tune of "Oh! Susanna" or "Camptown Races" almost anywhere in the world: you will find someone to join you in finishing it, but he is likely to twist the details of rhythm or of pitch a little from the details you know, and if he supplies any words to the tune they may surprise you; they may be German words or Greek or Chinese or, if they are English, they may still be new and strange. Try humming the slower, sweeter tune of "Jeanie with the Light Brown Hair": you may not so surely get a response with "Jeanie" as with "Susanna," but anyone who can name the tune is likely to know a few words of the same poem. What this means to him may range from a sentiment more serious than your own to a joke or an annoyance. Finally, if you dare, try "Old Black Joe" or "Old Folks at Home" (Way down upon the Swanee River); you may be in for a fight or a law suit. These tunes, almost as widely known as "Susanna," mean what their words mean, as does the tune of "Jeanie," but the words of "Old Folks" can be interpreted not just variously but in ways quite opposed to each other.

"Susanna," "Jeanie," and the "Old Folks" represent three types of song. Foster himself labeled "Susanna" comic, "Jeanie" poetic, and "Old Folks" pathetic, that is, expressing pathos. These labels help as much as any others to distinguish the types. All three types are to be fully studied in this book, to be used as an organizing framework.

Readers interested in Foster's songs, naturally enough, are likely to think first of the most controversial type. "Old Folks," "Old Black Joe," "My Old Kentucky Home," and "Massa's in de Cold Ground" all share the pathos—whether we like it or resent it or laugh it off. "Susanna" and "Jeanie" and the hundred odd songs less famous than these interest us, if at all, in some relation to the "Old Folks" type, though that relation may be unspoken or even unconscious. Differences and similarities among the three types can become interesting to anyone whose interest in "Old Folks" is admiring or indignant or ambivalent or indulgent, providing only that it is a somewhat sustained interest.

If we pause to think about all three types together and the permutations of responses they may meet from various people, we recognize that there is probably no other composer's work that can match this variety. Foster is peculiar, not in the mere fact that a dozen of his songs are widely popular, nor in the fact that the four "pathetic" songs are so densely ambiguous, but in the combination of these facts.

To explore the various meanings of Foster's songs in their social and historical contexts is the purpose of this study. The combination of popularity and ambiguity peculiar to these songs calls for a wide-ranging exploration. It has fascinated me for a long time. I cannot take the songs for granted. I cannot forget them. I cannot be content with any of the one-sided discussions of them that I have encountered. So I gather here all the facts and interpretations that seem to me relevant, to enable anyone who shares my uneasy fascination to join in the exploring.

The goal of the study is not some one interpretation of the songs, new or old, but a clarification of the whole range of meanings in relation to each other. Not even Foster's own intentions, though we wish to probe as close to them as we can, need compel us to agree, for one or another of us may argue that Foster unintentionally brought forth great good or evil. All we need try to do together is to disentangle attitudes sufficiently to permit a more intelligent choice than can be made in confusion and ignorance. If, after some exploring, we choose to disagree about the present and potential value of the songs, we may at least understand our disagreement. We can use and enjoy the songs if we choose, or at last dismiss them, knowing why we do so. But however we may be able to apply our discoveries, the exploration itself is our joint concern. We could, of course, continue exploring indefinitely. But again, without clearing up every ambiguity, we can approach the goal of clarity by means of a comprehensive critical survey.

Among the interpretations that attract most attention, those in the words and music of several composers and composer-performers are outstanding. Antonín Dvořák, Charles Ives, Ray Charles, and Ornette Coleman have all been concerned with Foster's songs. Dvořák's praise for them, and his recommendation of them alongside the Negro Spirituals as likely themes for American symphonies, contributed much to the prestige that Foster enjoyed in many quarters from the 1890s on. Dvořák's symphonic arrangement of "Old Folks at Home" awaits attention. Charles Ives in the decade before World War I made use of Foster's songs, or rather of motifs from them, in symphonies and other compositions that would have shocked Dvořák. Ives' music began to win increasing recognition only shortly before he died in 1954, but since then it has aroused more curiosity about Foster than Dvořák did for me and my contemporaries. More than either Ives or Dvořák, Ray Charles, converting "Old Folks" into his "Swanee River Rock," 1957, surprised me and motivated me to pursue my exploration of Foster's many meanings. Ornette Coleman's "free jazz" version of "Old Black Joe," which I heard in 1967, challenged me anew. I am far from confident that my explorations suffice to meet Coleman's challenge, but they help me, at least, to try. All these musical interpretations of Foster's songs are more than subsidiary to the originals. Each of them merits unprejudiced study in the whole historical context.

Interesting as each interpretation may be in itself, the juxtaposition of all of them interests me still more. Each composer mentioned —Dvořák, Ives, Charles, and Coleman—appeals to his own audience, and all these audiences meet in the far larger audience of Foster. While each of the four composers may interest his own audience more intensely than Foster does, only through Foster are all four special audiences likely to meet, for too many devotees of Dvořák doubt that the others are artists at all; too many enthusiasts of Ives think the others are banal or tame; too many fans of Charles have no access to any of the others; too many partisans of Coleman, perhaps, are committed to an exclusiveness of their own. No musical audience of the 20th century can come so close to representing a whole society as can the huge population that knows Foster's songs. Therefore a study of what his songs mean to each of the composers may rightly be subordinated to a comprehensive and comparative study.

There is another living musician whose interpretation of Foster is invaluable. He is a composer too, though seldom recognized as such, because his songs are not nearly so elaborate as the works of Dvořák, Ives, Charles, and Coleman. Pete Seeger brings the Foster songs to life, not just for listening audiences but for thousands of people to join in singing, while he inspires them with his banjo or guitar. Seeger is well aware of the variety of meanings the songs communicate. He chooses among them, naturally. He respects the intentions of Foster himself, as far as they can be known. Yet he does not hesitate to discard some of those intentions, or to modify the ones he is fulfilling by the shrewd way he places the songs in his programs. He contributes new meanings. His work cannot be neglected in our survey. It may elucidate the work of Foster, Ives, and Charles and help us see them all in one context.

Besides composers and performers, others interpret Foster's songs: more than any musician it is the poets, critics, and historians who teach us to call such songs "folksongs" or "American." They are the sources of our image of Foster himself, and of the world he knew. They continually reshape for us the meanings of the words he used and the words we use to think about him. Even if we care more for his tunes than for his words, yet when we ask about the significance of his songs we need the help of the professional masters of words. The tunes rather than the words are what I have known by heart from childhood; the tunes, or even the accompanying chords as they feel in the fingers on the keyboard, come to my mind more readily than any words when I think of Foster. (Foster himself, according to his friend John Mahon, remembered all his tunes and forgot the words for all but one—"Hard Times.") Yet with the tunes and chords come the confused meanings, and these impel me to look to the poets, critics, and historians for interpretation. Before I had decided to make music my life's work, I had begun studying the great contemporaries of Foster—Thoreau, Melville, Whitman, Mark Twain—under the guidance of two great teachers—F. O. Matthiessen and Perry Miller. Those writers' prophetic visions of America set me on my way exploring the meanings of the Foster songs, and any reader familiar with Matthiessen and Miller will recognize their influence more often than I acknowledge it. More recently Ralph Ellison, James Baldwin, and Imamu Amiri Baraka (LeRoi Jones) have taught me much that was neglected by Matthiessen and Miller; all three of these writers treat music from first-hand knowledge, and I am indebted to them for insights into music as well as for their mastery of words and meanings. Readers familiar with them will recognize their influence, too, as pervading this study. If these influences have been sufficiently absorbed, perhaps this study can contribute something to continuing discussions of "the mind of America" and "the Black soul."

The issues of Americanism and Blackness are connected chiefly with "Old Folks at Home" and the three other famous "pathetic" songs most nearly resembling it: "Massa's in de Cold Ground," "My Old Kentucky Home," and "Old Black Joe." The analysis of multiple meanings can proceed most efficiently by leaving these till last. There are enough complications to deal with in the case of the "comic" "Susanna," "Camptown Races," and "Nelly Bly"; considering these will introduce the issues gradually and help prepare us for tackling the final group. In between, there are the "poetic" songs that Foster himself would have insisted were central: "Jeanie with the Light Brown Hair" and about sixty more, among which some readers will recognize "Come, Where My Love Lies Dreaming," "Old Dog Tray," "Gentle Annie," and "Beautiful Dreamer"; connoisseurs of Foster's whole work will anticipate the inclusion in this central group of the little-known Sunday-school songs and the theatrical songs with texts by Foster's friend George Cooper, though some of these are more comic than "Susanna." Our three divisions should be regarded not as mutually exclusive, but as somewhat overlapping. Several songs will be considered from different points of view in different contexts. But the three typical songs—"Susanna," "Jeanie," and "Old Folks"—serve as main landmarks for our labyrinthine exploration.

Possibly short-cuts through the labyrinth will appeal to some readers. The organization of the book makes cuts possible, though not without sacrifice. If you, for instance, are impatient to learn what the survey reveals in relation to current questions of music and race, nation, class, culture, and commerce, you may begin with Chapter 9, about the publicity surrounding Foster from his own time to ours; go on through Chapter 10, about the "Old Folks" type in Foster's time; and the remaining chapters, about musical and literary interpretations of "Old Folks" in later generations. (You will not find a pat "conclusion" even at the end of Chapter 14.) If you are fond of Foster's songs and an image of the man, but impatient with his antecedents and his musical techniques, you may prefer to begin with Chapter 6, about his family, and go on to Chapter 8, about his friends. In these two chapters many little-known songs are studied in relation to Foster's life and character. In these chapters and Chapter 10, a portrait of the man emerges, more complex and more thoroughly sympathetic than that of earlier studies, though less heroic.

If your interest in American history and literature is keener than your concern for music or for biography, your attention is directed to chapters 3 and 4, which present some fresh findings and new interpretations of works by Melville and Whitman among others. Then you may take the route beginning with Chapter 9. If your interest in America is subordinate to concern for international perplexities about *Kitsch* or *Trivialmusik* and *Rezeptionsgeschichte* of music in general—even Beethoven's—then chapters 2, 4, and 7 may attract you first, then 10 to 14. The material in the earlier chapters is relevant to some current arguments among German musicologists in particular.

If musical techniques seem to you the chief proper focus for our exploration, you may begin with Chapter 5, jump to 13 and 14, and then leaf through other parts of the book.

Since the author has friends with all these divergent interests, he trusts them to be tolerant, if not always patient, with each other's claims on the conduct of the study. All the interests converge, for me. The possible convergence is the book's main concern. Therefore a reading of the whole book in sequence should serve every interest better than any short-cut.

Chronology contributes to the sequence, but less than the logic of the three types of song. Each type has its own history. Each history leads us back to Foster's childhood and adolescence, 1826–46; each shows its distinctive chronological pattern in the course of his career down to his death in 1864; and each continues differently after his death, as successive adaptations of the "Old Folks" type affect the other types in their different surroundings. Rather than throwing together all three types in a single chronological narrative (as most earlier writers on Foster have done) we can risk exaggerating the distinctions among the types that help clarify meanings. When we trace a preliminary outline of Foster's obscure life and subsequent fame, this chronological core opens questions about his talent and character that we can hold in suspense. For our interest in Foster as man and writer is aroused by our concerns with the various things the songs mean to us. Our concerns lead to a number of histories; we expect no single history to unite us all. What may unite us, and unite the several histories, is the exploration of meanings.

The Songwriter

Stephen Collins Foster enjoyed no great personal celebrity during his thirty-seven and a half years of life, 1826–64. Millions of people sang "Oh! Susanna" (first publicly performed in 1847) and "Old Folks at Home" (1851) without knowing who wrote these songs. If a singer or listener was reminded of any source, it would be not the author but rather one of the Christy Minstrels who had sung "Susanna" and introduced "Old Folks" on the stage in New York and London. In 1854, at the peak of Foster's career, when his principal publishers in New York issued "Jeanie with the Light Brown Hair," they advertised in vain to admirers of the best sellers "Old Folks," "My Old Kentucky Home," "Massa's in de Cold Ground," and "Old Dog Tray," recommending the new production of "THE SONGWRITER OF AMERICA." In the next ten years "Jeanie" and all the rest of his new songs sold too few copies to maintain Foster with his wife and child in the way they had lived for the few years 1851–54. When Foster died, alone in New York, in 1864, his publishers paid little attention. Newspapers and music journals copied their obituaries from one or two sources. If reporters asked questions of the widow or of Stephen's brother Morrison, who arranged the funeral in Pittsburgh, they were satisfied with brief answers. Seven lines in the London *Musical World* omit the best sellers and include, as final examples, two songs not Foster's at all, so that the opening tribute is hard to believe:

> His loss will be equally lamented in England, where his songs were more successful than those of any composer during the last ten years. The following are some of Mr. Foster's most favorite ballads: "Willie, we have missed you," "Come, where my love lies dreaming," "Hard times, come again no more," "Camptown races," "Gentle Annie," "Lucy Long," "Cheer up, Sam."

The inaccuracy of the anonymous writer's information is as significant as the praise. But this praise from London is as genuine as any from New York or Pittsburgh.

Through the next decades the persistent fame of the handful of songs like "Old Folks" gradually aroused some curiosity about the author. Were these folksongs? Or was their author a composer for Americans to celebrate? In 1896, to correct the legends that were forming around his name, Morrison Foster published Stephen's collected works, with a short biography. Then Morrison's daughter, Evelyn Morneweck, continued for a lifetime collecting and sifting family records, which she published in two volumes in 1944. Like most other writers on Foster, both Morrison and his daughter present their factual matter in a context of unqualified praise for the famous songs and hasty apologies for some of the others. The writers look back fondly at the quaint times when Stephen lived. They pardon his foibles, as understandable in those times, and as a small price to pay for his inspired works. Evelyn Foster Morneweck traces facts about the Foster family into more minute detail than most readers want to remember, for these facts are only vaguely or indirectly related to "Old Folks" or any other famous song, whereas many questions that might naturally occur to us about Stephen's schooling, his friends, his detailed musical experience, and his intellectual response to the social changes of his time remain unanswered. Family details, to be sure, can lure us into explorations of his psyche in relation to "Jeanie" and other less-known songs of the "Jeanie" type. But we need select only the most essential facts about the family as equipment for the study of "Susanna."

The Foster family was big. Stephen was the ninth child of his parents. Before he was three years old, in 1829, a tenth and last baby was born. That summer the two lived through the whooping cough, but next winter the youngest died, leaving Stephen to be doubly babied by his older brothers and sisters and their aging parents. He grew up, like many a 19th-century child, amid the agitations of frequent partings and reunions and final bereavements of his big family.

The family lived in some comfort, if precariously, setting itself above the average level of the population, but never forgetting how easily a straying member of the family could fall below the average, never forgetting that slavery marked off a lower level still. When Stephen was born, there was a full-time servant, Olivia Pise; Morrison remembered her and filled out his memories in 1896 with a plausible guess about her taking Stephen to church. We should like to know much more about her, but we may suspend judgment of Morrison's guess until we can see his motives, as well as all relevant facts. William B. Foster, father of the family, was a Democratic member of the Pennsylvania State Legislature, traveling often between the capitol at Harrisburg and the suburban cottage at Lawrenceville, east of Pittsburgh, where he had settled ten years before. The oldest son, William Jr., was beginning a rather brilliant career as an engineer; in 1828 he presented his mother and sisters with a piano.

In 1830 the family began a series of moves. The piano was abandoned, as was the servant Olivia. Had the toddling Stephen noticed either enough to remember them, we wonder? In 1832 his mother, Eliza, writes about the five-year-old's marching with a drum and whistling "Auld Lang Syne." Her wistful memories of the years at Lawrenceville pervade her letters from now on.

In the course of the 1830s two more brothers left home to follow brother William into business. Two sisters left to marry—when they returned for visits they brought along a stream of children. The family spread out as far as Paradise, Pennsylvania; Youngstown and Cincinnati, Ohio. Old Mr. Foster, running for the State Legislature again, went down to defeat with the whole Jackson party. For a year he tried to manage a store in Pittsburgh, but this endeavor was caught in the banking crisis of 1837. In 1839 the sixteen-year-old Morrison started to work in stores and offices, leaving thirteen-year-old Stephen more solitary hours than before. In 1841, if Morrison's memory was correct, Stephen composed a "Tioga Waltz" for piano, rather like a yodeling song. In 1841 his father reported to brother William that Stephen's "leisure hours are all devoted to music, for which he possesses a strange talent." Six weeks later his mother wrote, "He is not so much devoted to music as he was: other studies seem to be elevated in his opinion. He reads a great deal, and fools about none at all." The question of whether he might aspire to a college education was nervously considered, never explicitly decided.

Family fortunes began a brief rally in 1841. Brother William provided a fine house on the East Common in Allegheny, and the father was elected mayor of this town, a populous residential suburb of Pittsburgh. Here Stephen and Morrison enjoyed some happy times with the sons and daughters of neighboring doctors, lawyers, and a successful brewer. Stephen's desultory lessons with various tutors and his vague ambition of attending the newly opened Naval Academy at Annapolis were not pursued very seriously. His verse writing and flute playing were indulged, but of course these were not serious either—they were suitable diversions for a young man of good family. Stephen's musical setting of the poem by George P. Morris, "Open Thy Lattice, Love," was published in Philadelphia, 1844, doubtless with family subsidy.

Toward the end of 1846 came Stephen's turn to leave home, a few months before he was twenty-one. By now he had a little experience as a clerk in Allegheny and Pittsburgh. He went to join his brother

Dunning in Cincinnati. In the next three years he traveled back and forth many times between Cincinnati and Pittsburgh. Though he did not advance in business as his brothers had done, he fulfilled his responsibilities, apparently without complaint. Though he did not become quite independent of his family, much less contribute to their support, still his progress seemed to satisfy them as adequate.

Cincinnati and Pittsburgh were rival cities throughout the lifetime of Foster. Both cities grew at an amazing rate, ever accelerating. By 1830 Pittsburgh was famous for its manufactures and its polluted air and water. By 1840 Cincinnati excelled as a shipping and railroad center, and also as a place where music and poetry were noticed more than anywhere else in the West. In greater Pittsburgh, while Stephen Foster was going to school, there were only one or two men trying to earn a living from music—by running music stores and playing and singing at the most prosperous churches. Nobody published music in Pittsburgh, though one of the storekeepers, a few years before Stephen, composed songs and dances that were published in New York. Cincinnati, by contrast, had several music publishers, one of them the able English immigrant bandsman William C. Peters, who published one Foster song in 1846, two more in 1847, and then, in 1848, made what Morrison called a fortune from "Oh! Susanna" and "Old Uncle Ned." Peters later owned a chain of stores from Baltimore to Chicago. In Baltimore, 1849 and 1850, he published one more Foster song and a polka for piano. How well did Stephen know Peters? We can only guess. If Stephen resented his exploitation of "Susanna" and "Uncle Ned," as Morrison did, he was too much the gentleman to say so. But probably resentment, if any, was crowded out of his mind in those years, 1847 to 1850, when he was twenty-one to twenty-four, speeding from novelty to success to uncertainty to new excitement every few days. Cincinnati, though it meant an expansion of Stephen's world, was not to be his home. Pittsburgh and New York were the centers of his mature life, from 1850 on.

He made his first contact with the New York publisher Firth and Pond in 1849. This agent—officially Firth, Pond, and Company—at once helped him to learn to deal with performers like the Christys. Firth and Pond accepted everything he sent them, including the great success of 1850, "Nelly Bly." In 1852 they commissioned Thomas Hicks to paint his portrait. In 1853 they gave him an exclusive contract, with generous advances. Thereafter, in 1854, 1857, and 1858, they made similar contracts, which modern biographers have analyzed thoroughly, with no discredit to Firth and Pond. Their whole account with Foster was trifling compared with the money their piano factory earned, or what it lost after 1854 when the rival manufacturer Steinway began to win prizes. In 1860 the last agreement with Foster expired, but Firth and Pond continued to publish some of his best new works to the very end. Altogether they issued over seventy of his pieces. In the peak years 1853–54 there were nine songs, including "My Old Kentucky Home" and "Jeanie with the Light Brown Hair," and seven dances, four of which first appeared in a collection arranged by Foster under the title *The Social Orchestra*. The publishers' efficiency and reliability were evident to Foster in 1849. Relying on them, he left his dull work in Cincinnati and from 1850 on devoted all his time to songwriting.

Besides the family documents and the files of Firth and Pond, there is a prime source of information in the manuscript notebook that Foster kept from June 26, 1851, to the summer of 1860. Here we can see him polishing his verses and writing out with assurance the simple scores of the songs. There is no sign here, however, of an arranger's craftsmanship.

How much did Foster play any instrument? How far did he know the capabilities of professional instrumentalists? Evidence is sadly lacking. Brother Morrison—responding in 1896 to hints that Stephen might have needed to employ hacks to write out his vague inspirations, or else that he might have written as a crude hack himself, exploiting the inspirations of some unknown illiterate genius— naturally laid emphasis on Stephen's deep study of "musical science." Morrison names no textbook or teacher. And just when, where, or how Stephen played what notes—Morrison does not tell, nor does anyone. His friends and relatives refer casually to his playing the flute, violin, guitar, and piano, but they never mention speed or loudness or any other characteristic. More often they refer to his singing, in a sweet gentle baritone, with a girl playing his accompaniment at the piano while he looks over her shoulder at the notes on the rack. A somewhat close study of his music may warrant a few more guesses about his performing abilities. But guesses based on naively biased interpretations of only a few of his songs add no verisimilitude to a portrait of him. Most important, whatever the extent of his performing abilities, is the fact that he performed only as an amateur. The career of professional song writer, as he saw it, was quite distinct from the career of performer on the public stage.

What music did Stephen play, or even hear, before he went to New York in 1853? Morrison, in 1896, refers solemnly to Beethoven, Mozart, and Weber as his models. These names were known in Pittsburgh, and more so in Cincinnati, in the 1840s, but they were not yet revered as they were beginning to be in Boston and Concord. Opportunities to hear any symphonies were excessively rare before 1850. Foster was probably ignorant of Beethoven's and equally ignorant of those of Father Anton P. Heinrich, "the Beethoven of Kentucky," which were beginning to make a stir in Boston and New York. Weber was more accessible. In fact Foster possessed, by 1850, a copy of Weber's "Invitation to the Waltz." Tunes from Weber's *Freischütz* (1821) were old favorites, played and sung in all sorts of arrangements and parodies, alongside tunes from Rossini's last opera, *William Tell* (1829), and Donizetti's *Lucia* (1835). These were the strongest attractions in the musical world for most city people sensitive to music, and Foster did not escape them. We can cite enough facts about what he heard in concerts to prove this point, if not to satisfy all possible curiosity. But, unlike his Philadelphia contemporary William Henry Fry (1813–64) or the New Yorker George Frederick Bristow (1825–98), the Westerner, Foster, never dreamed of composing an opera. It is not certain that he heard a whole opera even in New York, though his letters mention attending at least one. But in his *Social Orchestra* he included his arrangements of nine tunes by Donizetti and one attributed to Beethoven.

All this music was somewhat remote from Foster's home, but not so remote that it would not be recognized by his mother and his sisters as a proper object of family aspirations. What sounded at home was typified by "Auld Lang Syne"—a very old, anonymous song polished to classic form by Robert Burns (1788)—and "Home, Sweet Home"—a synthetic product typical of its time (1823), words by the American dramatist John Howard Payne, with a tune by the eminent English composer Henry Bishop, hurriedly derived from a "Sicilian air" he had learned from a publisher. When Donizetti included "Home, Sweet Home" in his opera *Anna Bolena* (1830), this too became "classic." For Stephen such favorites of his family were at least among the important models.

Was music from the theater more important than music from the church? Did the family attend church? The mother's and sisters' letters are full of pious exclamations and exhortations, but it seems that most male members of the family, including Stephen and his father, never joined. In the fashionable Episcopal church of the ladies, smooth organ music and quasi-operatic vocal quartets were heard without making very deep impressions. Once more, we may well wish for more facts than we can find, and we may eventually allow ourselves some guesses rather different from those of Morrison Foster or any other interpreter of Stephen's songs. But to start with we may well emphasize the negative fact that Stephen never sought a career as church musician, such as hundreds of his contemporaries found most open to their talents, no matter whether they were pious or not.

Was new music from the theater more important than any classic? Morrison and Stephen learned to sing the tunes that black-faced actors made popular, one after another, in the 1830s and '40s; first George Washington Dixon's "Long-tail Blue" and "Coal-black Rose," which had been introduced in 1827 and 1828; then Thomas D. Rice's "Jim Crow," of about 1830; then Dixon's "Zip Coon" ("Turkey in the Straw"), of 1834. Morrison remembered these songs in particular when he told how, in 1835, the nine-year-old Stephen was the star of a troupe of boys in the Fosters' carriage house, singing and dancing these new pieces. In the next decade the boys surely kept up with Billy Whitlock's "Miss Lucy Long" (1842), Dan Myers' "Dandy Jim of Caroline" (1843), Dan Emmett's "Boatmen's Dance" (1843), and Cool White's "Lubbly Fan," or "Buffalo Gals, Won't You Come Out Tonight" (1844). Stephen's "Susanna" (1847) takes a place alongside these, as we shall see. His productions of the next few years coincide with the rise of the "minstrel show" as supreme theatrical form, and it was to be through the blackface minstrels that Foster's works won their first popularity. His attitude toward them changed in the course of these years—his letters to Christy show something of that change. Exactly what his attitude was at each moment, we can never know as well as we should wish, but in our spiralling study of the songs—popular and unpopular—we can understand more and more the ambivalence and the change.

What books did Foster read? What besides song shaped his mind? Walter Scott and Tom Moore were among his favorites and they were also models for a good many of the younger authors he knew. He was enthusiastic about certain stanzas of Tennyson, Longfellow, and Poe. He liked Irving, Captain Marryatt, and Dickens. He was aware of Shakespeare and Milton and William Cowper but there is no evidence that he studied them much. Judging from the poems he chose to set to music, by men whose names are little known to posterity, we can be fairly sure that his literary culture never advanced to the point where he could appreciate, say, Browning or Whitman or Melville. But if we revive a little of the contemporary fame of Charles Mackay or George P. Morris, we can see Foster's aims more clearly and we can judge the bulk of his work more in accordance with his aims. If we investigate the literary works of his Pittsburgh friend Charles Shiras, we can come closer still to Foster's developing mind, and we can raise more fresh questions than we can answer. Shiras began a hopeful literary career in 1847, editing two new weekly journals. In 1850 he wrote his most famous poem, "The Popular Credo." In 1852 he published a book of poems. In 1853 Shiras and Foster wrote a song together, "Annie, My Own Love." Later that year Foster supplied music for a play by Shiras, *The Invisible Prince*. What sort of music was this? Alas, it is not extant. In 1854 Shiras died. How must his death have affected Foster? How might Foster have developed if Shiras had lived a few more years? Finally, we wonder about the influence of Harriet Beecher Stowe's *Uncle Tom's Cabin*, which appeared in 1852. Foster's notebook shows that "My Old Kentucky Home" started out as a song for Uncle Tom. But why was this connection suppressed? What did Foster think of Uncle Tom?

Was Foster's personal experience more important than any books? Soon after Foster came home to Pittsburgh to be a full-time songwriter, he was married. The date was July 22, 1850. He was twenty-four and the bride, Jane McDowell, was nineteen. Her sister Agnes, writing next day to another sister Marion, described the pair as "pretty much frightened. Steve quite pale." On April 18, 1851, a daughter Marion was born. In 1852 the couple joined several old friends on a month's cruise to New Orleans and back. Did they hear any slave choruses? The friends on the trip recalled nothing of the sort—rather they remembered Stephen's new duet with words from *Romeo and Juliet*, which they sang while he and Jane listened. In 1853 Jane and the baby were left behind in Pittsburgh while Stephen went to New York; just how long he stayed away is uncertain. In the summer of 1854 the three were together in a rented house in Hoboken, New Jersey. In the fall Stephen suddenly decided to sell the furniture and go back to Allegheny. He was still there when his parents died in 1855. Thereafter he paid brother William a nominal rent, while Morrison from time to time paid board to Stephen and Jane. But now the comfortable house was too expensive. From April 1857 to April 1858 Stephen and Jane lived at the Eagle Hotel in Pittsburgh, then in a series of boarding houses. In 1860 they were in a hotel at Warren, Ohio, where Stephen's sister lived. A little later that year they went to New York, where Stephen stayed the rest of his life, while Jane took the little girl to the home of her sister Agnes in Lewistown, Pennsylvania. At some point Jane earned their living as a telegrapher. The last meeting of Stephen and Jane was in 1862. Then, in 1864, Jane came with Morrison to claim the dead body. What was Jane like? How did Stephen love her, day by day, year after year? How were their relations connected with his work? The facts just surveyed, not enough to answer these questions, still must have some bearing on the texts of songs like "Molly, Do You Love Me?" (May 1850), "Mother, Thou'rt Faithful" (March 1851), "Fondly Old Memories" (1853), "Comrades, Fill No Glass for Me" (1855), "I See Her Still in My Dreams" (1856), "Lula Is Gone" (1858), "Thou Art the Queen of My Song" (1859), "Belle of the Allegheny, I'm Coming Home" (unfinished, 1860), "The Wife" (1860), "Why Have My Loved Ones Gone?" (1861), "A Dream of My Mother" (1862), "The Love I Bear to Thee" (1863), and "Beautiful Dreamer" (1864). And all these songs, with their personal connotations, must have some bearing on the more famous, more problematic ones, like "Old Folks."

Does the chronology of Foster's work indicate something about the relations among the three types of song? In the list of the "Old Folks" type, unlike the "Jeanie" type, there is a gap of several years. After "My Old Kentucky Home" (January 1853) no new song extends the list until 1860, when the two final contributions appear—"Old Black Joe" and "Down Among the Canebrakes."

The "Susanna" type, surveyed chronologically, shows an even wider gap. "Ring de Banjo" (1851) marks the end of continuous production. Then in 1860 there is a pale revival with "The Glendy Burk" and "Don't Bet Your Money on de Shanghai."

After 1860 all the varied production is more like "Jeanie" than either "Susanna" or "Old Folks." The sheer fact that Foster's interest in the "Old Folks" and "Susanna" types underwent such fluctuations, while his interest in the "Jeanie" type was constant, has never been sufficiently noticed. The fact that he dropped his most successful types so soon after beginning his full-time commitment to songwriting and returned to them only briefly at the moment when he could no longer command an exclusive contract—this has not been noticed at all. These facts, though irrelevant to some interpretations of the songs, serve at least to disprove some interpretations of Foster's personality. Can we explain them? Not without patient study of all his works.

In 1862 Foster began to collaborate with a new young friend, George Cooper (1840–1927). In the last eighteen months or so before Foster died, he wrote at least twenty-one songs to words by Cooper. Cooper's account of their joint "song factory," as given to Foster's biographer Harold V. Milligan, is vivid:

> He wrote with great facility and without the aid of a piano. If no music-paper was handy, he would take whatever paper he could find, and ruling the lines on it, proceed without hesitation to write. He seemed never at a loss for a melody, and the simple accompaniment caused him no trouble. These first drafts were taken out and sold to a publisher or theatre manager, practically without correction. To this habit is evidently due the "brown wrapping paper" legend, as Cooper says that he would use brown wrapping paper if he couldn't find anything else.

Was this way of composing very different from the way Stephen had worked earlier? Was every song of the last year or two composed in the same way? Was even every Cooper song composed quite so casually, or so desperately? Evidence is not conclusive, but sufficient to modify the image of Foster that is presented in many books of reference, as well as in popular accounts.

In 1863 Foster also published twenty new songs in the collections of hymns and Sunday School pieces edited by Horace Waters. Were these, too, products of a "factory" industry? Or was Foster awakened to religious concerns he had never previously sung about? Evidence tends to support the latter possibility.

The Cooper songs, the Sunday School songs, and a few miscellaneous ones of the last year or so all fit more nearly with the "Jeanie" type than with "Susanna" or "Old Folks." Even if they were regarded as a separate type altogether, the "Jeanie" type would still be the largest, represented by at least one song in every year from 1846 on down to 1864, and including over a hundred songs altogether. If the last year's varied production is counted along with "Jeanie," then that class constitutes about three-fourths of Foster's whole work.

Keeping in mind the facts we have surveyed, we can now inquire more deeply into the meanings, for Foster himself and for others in his time and later, of each of the three main types of song.

PART ONE

"SUSANNA"
AND OTHER
"COMIC, ETHIOPIAN
SONGS"

CHAPTER 1

Foster,
the young
amateur,
1847

"OH! SUSANNA" came to mean much to Foster himself. At first it was only a piece of boyish fun, then it showed him the way to his vocation. When it was first performed in public, at Andrews' Ice Cream Saloon in Pittsburgh, on September 11, 1847, the meaning of the song began to change. The twenty-one-year-old composer changed with it. We can picture him first singing "Oh! Susanna" with his friends and then, when strangers had begun to sing it, coming to the decision about his career.

In 1847 Foster was undecided about many things. He was still dependent on his parents and his four older brothers, who were all busy in the commerce of the Ohio River, the Pennsylvania State Canal, and the projected Pennsylvania Railroad. Would Stephen follow a similar career? Or would he have to interrupt his business, as two of the brothers did, to serve in the Mexican War? Brother Dunning, twenty-six, was off in Mexico now, on leave from his partnership in a Cincinnati shipping agency where he left Stephen working as a clerk. Brother Morrison, twenty-three, having served a few months in the army without seeing combat, was now back at his job as agent for the Hope Cotton Mills of Pittsburgh, where Stephen had worked briefly in 1845 before he went to Cincinnati. Dunning and Morrison both worried about Stephen. But they also shared— Morrison especially—Stephen's love of books, plays, and songs. Morrison led an active social life. He kept Stephen in touch with all their Allegheny and Pittsburgh friends. When Morrison first saw or heard "Susanna," he recognized it readily as a diversion from work and worry, a fine reinforcement of the brothers' convivial friendships.

Stephen and Morrison's closest friends had already inspired something similar. In 1845, not long before Stephen left home for Cincinnati, he wrote a set of verses about them, "The Five 'Nice Young Men.' " Though music is mentioned here only once, in the last stanza, the whole poem is worth reading, for the sake of at least three features. First, the poem introduces us to the friends, whose interests aside from singing are relevant to Stephen's character and his later work. Next, the tone of the poem combines a degree of genteel propriety with a lively sense of the ridiculous—a combination characteristic of "Susanna" and some favorite later songs. Finally, the verse technique, though crude, is agreeably free from convention, a creditable performance for an eighteen-year-old. Here then are Foster's "Nice Young Men," as he teased them in verse:

> First, there's Charley the elder, the Sunday-school teacher
>> Who laughs with a groan,
>> In an unearthly tone,
>> Without moving a bone
>>> Or a feature.

> Then Charley the younger, the Illinois screecher,
>> Who never gets mad,
>> But always seems glad
>> While others are sad:
> Though his face is so long that it wouldn't look bad
>> On a methodist preacher.

> There's Andy, who used to be great on a spree,
> Whose *duds* (as he calls them) all fit to a T:
>> But people do tell us
>> He's got just as jealous
>>> Of Latimer as he can be.
>> They say that he wishes
>> The sharks and the *fishes*
> Would catch him and eat him when he gets out to sea.

> And Bob, that smokes seventeen *tobies* a day,
> He's liberal, however, and gives some away.
>> Bob's been to college
>> Picking up knowledge
> But now he's got home and I hope he will stay.

> We will wind up with Harvey, the *bluffer*, the gay.
> He can play on the fiddle (or thinks he can play).

Harvey's mind
Is inclined
To all that's refined,
With a count'nance so bright
That it rivals the light
Of the sun that now cheers us in this sweet month of May.

Charles Shiras, Charles Rahm, Andrew Robinson, Robert Mc-
Dowell, and Harvey Davis all turn up often in Morrison Foster's
correspondence and scrapbooks as members of a club called, apparently, The Knights of the Square Table. They sometimes carried
their mock chivalry to absurd lengths. These young men had evidently read the novels of Sir Walter Scott, recognizing in them something apt for playful parody. Stephen's kind of fun is similar. He
mocks the religiosity of both Charleys, the learning of Bob, and
the musical exertions of Harvey. His point in the verse on Andy
may need some explanation: George Latimer was a fugitive slave
whose rescue in Boston from the agent of his Southern master had
made a stir in the newspapers of 1842; the Robinson family, well-
to-do neighbors of the Fosters across the common in Allegheny,
were more strongly inclined to antislavery sentiments than some
others of their circle. No more so, however, than the unsmiling
Charles Shiras, Stephen's closest friend of all, who in 1847 was to
edit an abolitionist magazine. He was the son of Pittsburgh's leading brewer, able to afford literary ambitions and political radicalism.
The later collaboration of Shiras and Foster on a song and a play
depended on their childhood and adolescent friendship. Never were
the Foster brothers so affluent, so well read, nor so imprudent as
their friend Shiras. He seems to have laughed at their jokes, however; if he maintained his Sunday-school face, he still took part in
their pleasures.

Music was a pleasure for the young ladies these "knights" courted,
as well as for themselves. For instance, the family next door to the
Fosters in Allegheny, that of the attorney Ephraim Pentland, had a
daughter Susan, who in 1849 was to marry Andy Robinson, the
well-dressed young man said to be jealous of Latimer. Susan sang
and played the piano. To her, in 1844, Stephen Foster had dedicated
his first extant song, "Open Thy Lattice, Love." "Oh! Susanna"
could serve the young men as a serenading song, or it might be
sung with a mixed quartet joining in the chorus, as the printed
music indicates. Although it was not quite the thing to dedicate
to a lady, it contained nothing to offend one. Its humor was simple
nonsense, and its theme was a "nice" mockery of courtly love:

I come from Alabama with my banjo on my knee;
I'se guine to Lou'siana my true lub for to see.

It rain'd all night de day I left, De wedder it was dry,
The sun so hot I froze to def, Susanna, don't you cry.
CHORUS: Oh! Susanna, do not cry for me;
       I come from Alabama, Wid my banjo on my knee.

I had a dream de udder night, when ebryting was still;
I thought I saw Susanna dear, a coming down de hill.
De buckwheat cake was in her mouf, de tear was in her eye;
I says, I'se coming from de souf, Susanna don't you cry.

Chorus

I soon will be in New Orleans, And den I'll look all 'round,
And when I find Susanna, I'll fall upon de ground.
But if I do not find her, Dis darkey'll surely die,
And when I'm dead and buried, Susanna don't you cry.

Chorus

This song was appropriate for the music making of the "Nice Young Men."

Shiras or Robinson might possibly have called Foster's attention to a "slave ballad" to which "Susanna" bears some slight resemblance. The "ballad" was printed in the *Journal* of Edward S. Abdy, an English abolitionist who toured the United States in 1833–34. Abdy said he had learned the ballad in Philadelphia, where his black informant's honesty was attested by several friends:

I born in Sout Calina, fine country ebber seen,
I guine from Sout Calina, I guine to New Orlean.
Old boss, he discontentum—He take de mare, black Fanny,
He buy a pedlar wagon, And he boun' for Lousy-Anny.
CHORUS: He boun' for Lousy-Anny,
       Old Debble, Lousy-Anny!

He gone five day in Georgy, Fine place for egg and ham:
When he get among the Ingens, And he push for Alabam.
He look 'bout 'pon de prairie, Where de hear de cotton grow:
But he spirit still contrary, And he must fudder go.

Chorus

He look at Mrs. Seapy, Good lady 'nough dey say;
But he tink de State look sleepy, and so he 'fuse to stay.
When once he leff Calina, and on he mare, black Fanny,
He not take off he bridle-bit till he get to Lousy-Anny.

Chorus

Old debble, Lousy-Anny, dat scarecrow for poor nigger,
Where de sugar-cane grow to pine-tree, and de pine-tree turn to sugar.

Abdy's text breaks off here, but this is enough to show both similarities and differences in relation to "Susanna." Rhythm, rhyme, and diction are similar; themes and geography are different. The humor of the slave is pointed at the master, whose westward trip is followed accurately, whereas Foster's humor involves a romantic quest that no Black man could have undertaken, and he seems to suppose that Alabama is south of New Orleans. But if any of Foster's friends stopped to think of the map, or to think of what they had read in Abdy's *Journal* and other antislavery literature, they did not stop long enough to spoil the irresponsible fun of "Susanna."

"Susanna" and some of Foster's later songs revived an episode from the utterly irresponsible childhood of his neighborhood group, including Andy Robinson and, of course, Morrison Foster, who remembered it well. The Foster family's carriage house was fitted up as a theater for the boys. There they performed, three evenings a week for some weeks, to an audience of their families, earning pennies which they needed to buy tickets for the real theater in Pittsburgh on Saturdays. Morrison tells how nine-year-old Stephen was "a star performer, and was guaranteed a certain sum weekly. It was a very small sum, but it was sufficient to mark his superiority over the rest of the company." The performances included songs, and Morrison lists four of them, which he identifies as "the only Ethiopian songs then known."

"Ethiopian songs"—by the time Morrison wrote the name sounded quaint. In the 1830s it was newly fashionable. It was a euphemism for "nigger songs," permitting an inference that the songs came from Africa, for "Ethiopia" and "Africa" had been interchangeable vague names in ancient Latin. By the 1850s there was a tendency to distinguish the theatrical "Ethiopian songs" from the songs actually sung by slaves on the Southern plantations, but the four songs that Morrison remembered were still widely popular. Two of the four had made the fame of the singing actor George Washington Dixon in 1827 and 1828: "My Long-tail Blue" and "Coal-black Rose." Though by no means the first Negro impersonator on the stage, Dixon was the first to win great popularity for such dialect songs. Another piece in the boys' repertory was "Jim Crow," with which Thomas D. Rice had surpassed Dixon, beginning about 1830 in Cincinnati or Pittsburgh, with his staging of a song and dance that he said he had copied from a Black street-clown. Throughout the next decade "Daddy" Rice prospered in New York, London, and elsewhere with his Jim Crow dance expanded to a whole act, and then to whole evenings of "Ethiopian opera." The last of the four songs was "Zip Coon," or "Turkey in the Straw," the latest hit of 1834; its authorship is disputed among half a dozen actors. The performances in the Fosters' carriage house, about 1835, were up-to-date with "Jim Crow" and "Zip Coon." Now, in 1847, Stephen was adapting his childhood skills to the purposes of his grown-up friends. "Susanna" was a more delicate, more adult burlesque. None of the friends could have imagined that "Susanna" would be tough enough to compete with "Jim Crow" or "Zip Coon" in the real theater.

"Susanna" more adult? The lines about dry rain and freezing sun are unique in Foster's verse. Do they indicate a consciousness of distance between the character who sings "I" and the actual singer on the stage or among his friends? Do they anticipate 20th-century surrealistic songs? Do they prolong childishness in association with courtship? Do they proclaim adolescence as a status distinct from both childhood and responsible adulthood? This was in fact the status of Stephen and his friends in 1847.

The young men's interest in the theater and theatrical music set them a little apart from their parents, who had grown up before there were steamboats to take actors on regular tours west of the Allegheny Mountains. Perhaps recalling the crude singing schools that had flourished in Pittsburgh in the 1820s, which their urbane sons had never known, the parents may have smiled indulgently at the new songs. They did not join in. Some of them may have frowned, instead of smiling, at the nonsense and the dialect. In any case, they recognized the contrast between this novel style and that of "Yankee Doodle" or of their favorite patriotic songs from the War of 1812, or of the ballad "In Good Old Colony Times" that Morrison remembered his father singing. Times were changing. The young people's music fitted their lives as no older music could fit.

The musical rhythm of "Susanna" was especially up-to-date. It was that of the polka, the latest fashionable dance from Paris, London, and New York. To be sure, it was not so different from the good old reels and quadrilles as the waltz, but its movements were more strenuous and more suggestive, and it had a new accent, distorting the words a little:

> I come from Al—abama with—my banjo on my knee.

Stephen Foster's alertness to the polka shows up in his words for another song of 1847, "Lou'siana Belle," in which he imagines Dandy Jim of Caroline dancing "the polka pigeon-wing." Within the next year, the polka rhythm of "Susanna" was recognized by several arrangers and publishers, though others labeled it a quickstep or quadrille, and its connection with the polka has seldom been noticed since. In 1850 Foster published two wordless polkas for piano, "Soirée Polka" and "Village Bells." For him, "Susanna" was a very similar novelty.

Does every generation need a new rhythm? The polka of the 1840s fitted conspicuous representatives of the generation growing up then in the cities of Europe and America. The lively polka set young people apart from parents and teachers, whose smooth gliding waltz had dominated the ballrooms since 1815 when Talleyrand and Metternich, in Vienna, had organized peace and legitimacy. Now, for the fighters of 1848, the polka fitted exuberant hopes for national freedom—no matter whether the nation was Polish, Bohemian, German, French, Irish, or American. The polka protested with a stomp, in the name of rising youth, somewhat as the Charleston of the 1920s flaunted the rebellion of "flaming youth," as rock 'n' roll in the 1950s screamed the defiance of the "greasy kids" and the "folk" and "rock" of the 1960s identified the hairy "drop-outs." The polka, of course, came to seem stodgy when its generation grew old. By 1870 the military marches of the new German, Italian, and American empires, with their swaggering 6/8 rhythms animating the boom of drum and cymbal, were the most representative of the young. In 20th-century perspective, waltz and march and polka blend together as antiques, but each of them once belonged to a new generation.

Does the local origin of a dance affect its meaning as it spreads around the world? Does the popular image of an exotic origin matter more than documented facts? Surely the polka fits an image of brave Slavic peasants viewed from the overcrowded cities in the West. While historians of dance trace the earliest polka to Czech villages rather than to the Polish home of the mazurka—which had made its lesser wave of fashion in Paris and London around 1830—still French, English, and American enthusiasm for Polish strivings against the Russian czars contributed to the polka's popularity. In 20th-century America the polka carries connotations of the "dumb Polak" of popular jokes. It seems as remote as a waltz from any Afro-American dance. Yet for Foster and his contemporaries the combination of polka and "Zip Coon" was natural: the "polka pigeon-wing" was easy to recognize as an endearing, hopeful, comic, exotic novelty, fit for restless young Blacks as well as for the restless young whites hoping to make their fortunes in Pittsburgh or Cincinnati or a bigger city.

Does the adoption of a new, foreign rhythm by a group of young friends constitute a typical event in music history? It seems to me not far-fetched to compare Foster's polka with Beethoven's waltz. Beethoven and his friends in provincial Bonn, around 1790, adopted a new Viennese rhythm to set themselves apart from the minuet long associated with French decadence and its petty imitators, including the young men's teachers and patrons. Likewise Stockhausen and his friends, in Darmstadt around 1950, adopted the new rhythms they found in Bartók, Messiaen, and Cage, to set themselves apart from the outworn squareness of their elders. The connections of distinctive rhythms with times and places, in short, are more than popular fashions.

Are the discontinuities of generations and of migrations especially characteristic of America? The English poet Stephen Spender, reflecting in 1972 on a lifetime's concern with "Americanization," claims this is so. "Each American transformation," he writes, "cut off from previous ones by completely changed circumstances, has been walled within its one or two generations." Spender exaggerates, but the discontinuities he feels so strongly do require us to seek continuities in hidden places.

Deprived of its rhythm, smoothed out to sober steady motion, the melody of "Susanna" resembles a famous hymn by Lowell Mason (1792–1872), his first and perhaps most famous composition, the "Missionary Hymn" (From Greenland's Icy Mountains) that he wrote when he was a bank clerk and choir leader in Savannah, Georgia, and that he took with him when he went to Boston in 1827 to begin his career as foremost American musician in churches, schools, and publishing. The first seven notes of the hymn match the main notes of "Susanna's" first line, and the whole form of the hymn matches "Susanna's," with pairs of lines making up the four phrases, A A' B A', and with an emphasis in the B phrase on the chord of the fourth scale-degree, the "Amen" chord. The resemblance might be mere coincidence, or it might point to some earlier common source, but probably Foster had absorbed Mason's melody from the singing of his mother and sisters; now he fused its firm shape of pitches with the new rhythm and the comic words.

The idea of publishing "Susanna" and "Lou'siana Belle" seems to have occurred to Foster only after the songs had circulated throughout his circle of friends. Even then he was not eager. This boyish fun was not meant for the public. Print could not dignify it, as print had presumably enhanced the tribute to Susan Pentland in 1844 and "The Good Time Coming" that Foster wrote for another neighborhood beauty, Mary Keller, in 1846. Publicity for "Susanna" might even embarrass the author. The publisher to whom he finally gave the new songs omitted Foster's name, as did most other publishers of various arrangements of it.

But if the song was originally a private matter, that soon changed. The theatrical singer Nelson Kneass introduced it to wider audiences in Pittsburgh and elsewhere. The Christy Minstrels soon picked it up; they were currently breaking all records in the New York theater with their show, and their performances of "Susanna" doubtless spread it farther than anyone else's. It was published first in New York "as sung by G. N. Christy." The Cincinnati publisher W. C. Peters, to whom Foster had given a copy, listed it "as sung by Mr.

Tichnor of the Sable Harmonists." Counting all the known musical arrangements, but not trying to count the reprintings of words alone in pocket songsters, there were twenty editions by 1851. Long before that, "Susanna" and "Uncle Ned" ranked with "Zip Coon" as nationwide favorites.

Foster was surprised, according to the recollections of Morrison and of a Pittsburgh friend, the druggist and amateur singer R. P. Nevin. In Nevin's account, first printed in a newspaper in 1858, the publisher Peters requested the manuscript, received it free, and then gave Foster a fee. As Peters' copyright claim dates from December 1848, his gift was probably made about then. "Imagine my delight," Foster wrote Nevin, probably closer to 1858 than to 1848, "in receiving one hundred dollars in cash!" And he goes on, "It had the effect of starting me on my present vocation as songwriter."

Morrison's version of the change, not so swift or so simple as R. P. Nevin's, is naturally more colorful and more plausible, for Morrison plays a considerable part in it himself. He acted as Stephen's business agent in Pittsburgh. He attended a concert by Nelson Kneass' company at the Andrews Ice Cream Saloon, where a lady sang Stephen's latest ladylike piece, "What Must a Fairy's Dream Be?" Kneass himself sang something in blackface, with impressive success. Morrison recalled Stephen's comic songs and began to calculate. Soon he read in the newspaper that Mr. Andrews was offering a prize for the best new "Ethiopian song," to be performed by Kneass' company during an extended engagement. Morrison lost no time in obtaining from Stephen a copy of "Away Down South," evidently brand new. It was sung, with great approval by singers and audience, but the prize was awarded to a composer in the Kneass company. The next day at the court house, where Morrison had just filed a copy of "Away Down South" for copyright, Morrison found Kneass with *his* copy, claiming it as his own composition. Business indeed! Morrison foiled him, but alas, the new song was never a prizewinner like "Susanna," which Stephen had given away. Kneass sang "Susanna" the next week, as if thumbing his nose at the Foster brothers. Morrison watched with amazement. Later he came to believe that the Cincinnati publisher Peters had made a profit of $10,000 from "Susanna." When he heard about the gift of a hundred, he must have snorted in indignation.

In the spring of 1848, soon after "Susanna" had been published in New York, "Old Uncle Ned" was published simultaneously there and in Cincinnati; by the end of the year it had also appeared in Baltimore. According to Morrison's recollections, this song, like "Lou'siana Belle," had been written for the "nice young men." It is different from either "Lou'siana Belle" or "Susanna" in its elegiac mood, and slightly different in form, though similar in basic structure as are most of Foster's later songs. The sad mood of "Uncle Ned" anticipates "Old Folks at Home."

During 1849, while Stephen continued to work for Dunning in Cincinnati, Morrison helped him negotiate with several publishers. It was not until early in 1850, when the most prominent firm in New York, Firth and Pond, signed a fair contract, that Stephen returned to Allegheny to stay and to "make a business of songwriting."

In these years just after "Susanna," Stephen wrote five more songs of a similar sort. Published in 1849 was "My Brudder Gum," in 1850 "Camptown Races," "Dolly Day," and "Nelly Bly," and in 1851 "Ring de Banjo." The success of "Susanna" was almost matched by two of these—"Camptown" and "Nelly Bly"—and the thought of the market must have entered into the composition of all of them. The new songs were not primarily for the "nice young men" and they were not to be given away to any stranger who asked for a copy: they were a kind of property whose value might soar in the marketplace. The motive of sheer fun, though doubtless alive and important, was not strong enough to produce so much work. It was now mixed with a more urgent motive. Stephen hoped that he had discovered a respectable business that could be fun too. "Susanna" encouraged that hope.

CHAPTER 2

Foster
and his rivals in
the international
music business
around 1850

"SUSANNA" meant business to hundreds of people whose lives, skills, and attitudes were barely glimpsed or dimly imagined by Stephen Foster. The business they carried on, in fact, was an intricate, impersonal, risky competition for public patronage, no more congenial for a "nice young man" than the shipping business he had left behind in Cincinnati. Their business was not his proposed business of songwriting. Writing was normally incidental to public performing, and, for the publishers, a writer's name was less useful than a performer's in selling the product. Among the performers and publishers who exploited "Susanna" and "Uncle Ned," some paid no attention to Foster's later work, but others worked with him perhaps as closely as he was willing to work. There were still other performers who had some influence on his view of the business. Their careers enable us to see, now, better than Foster himself saw, what a risk he was undertaking when he gave up the steady job in his brother's office to become a full-time songwriter. The somewhat fragmentary verifiable details of his connections with the music business provide a vivid picture of that business at the moment he approached it. From this picture we can derive an understanding of the basis of his subsequent successes and failures, as well as a range of connotations for all his songs somewhat richer than the mere sociological label of "commercial popular music."

Besides exploring the careers of men whose names we have already encountered—the singers Kneass and Christy, and the publishers Peters of Cincinnati and Firth and Pond of New York—we shall trace Foster's connections with nearly a dozen other individuals, including some performer-composers whose work may hold as much interest as Foster's for some of us: Henry Russell, Dan Emmett, Henri Herz, and Louis Moreau Gottschalk. All these men were at least as famous as Foster among their contemporaries, and they worked successfully for longer periods than he did. The fact that Foster, after his death in 1864, was to become more intensely interesting than any of them to more and more people depended on later developments of the music business and the wider culture, and it depended on "Old Folks at Home." But in the few years between "Susanna" (1847) and "Old Folks" (1851), Foster's songs like "Camptown Races" and "Nelly Bly," for all their success, showed no indication of outlasting their rivals. The successful Foster songs were assimilated into a generally booming music business whose nature we can understand by considering, one by one, the businesslike people who played some part in Foster's early career.

Nelson Kneass' connection with Foster, though crucial, ended swiftly and unpleasantly, as we have seen. Until shortly before the time when Kneass sang "Away Down South" and "Susanna," he had been a member of the Sable Harmonists in Cincinnati. There Foster surely knew him, but how well is not known. From 1849 to 1853 Kneass was a leading member of the troupe of Samuel S. Sanford, whose memoirs are a unique record of the minstrel business. Kneass and Sanford performed "Camptown Races" when it was new in 1850. They did "Old Folks" and "Massa's in de Cold Ground" promptly in 1852. Sanford claimed that Kneass was not only an outstanding singer but also "among the greatest minstrel composers . . . above Stephen F. [sic] Foster in his overall influence on minstrel music." But Sanford's opinion, if ever widely shared, was not destined to win out in the long run. If Kneass is remembered in the 20th century at all, it is for the song he composed—or perhaps arranged from a German tune—to fit the words of a poem by Thomas Dunn English, "Do You Remember Sweet Alice, Ben Bolt?" From 1848, when Kneass introduced "Ben Bolt," it was a parlor favorite. In Kneass' stage performances "Ben Bolt" and "Susanna" fit comfortably together.

More closely connected to Foster than Kneass was the star member of the Sable Harmonists in Cincinnati, William Roark. Indeed, Roark was, aside from Edwin Christy, Foster's closest known connection with the "minstrels." Foster gave Roark a copy of "Uncle Ned" before it was published in May 1848. This we know from a letter of Foster's to the New York publisher William Millet, dated May 25, 1849. Now, a year or more later, Foster cannot recall whether anything was said about exclusive rights of performance; he expects to see Roark again and check up about this. The letter is tantalizing. On its evidence we may surmise that in 1846–47 Foster heard Roark on the stage singing Billy Whitlock's "Miss Lucy Long" (1842), Dan Myers' "Dandy Jim of Caroline" (1843), Dan Emmett's "Boatmen's Dance" (1843), and Cool White's "Lubbly Fan" or "Buffalo Gals, Won't You Come Out Tonight" (1844). Whether or not Roark himself played an important part in Foster's development, he represents the provincial, second-hand but up-to-date sample of the music-theater business that Foster knew best.

Foster had some acquaintance with the chief precursor of the "minstrels," the "Jim Crow" impersonator Thomas "Daddy" Rice (1808–60). So it was held, at least in the Rice family, after the death of both men. A publication of 1931 revealed two previously unknown songs that Foster had sold to Rice around 1850, "Long Ago Day" and "This Rose Will Remind You." In a preface, D. J. Rice says that when his grandfather performed in Pittsburgh sometime before 1845, the boy Foster brought him "some farcical negro songs" of his own "with the hope of their acceptance." Rice was not interested in the songs, but became a friend for life. By the time of "Susanna," apparently, he could no longer refuse Foster's offers even if he had no use for them.

Besides "Jim Crow," one song of Rice's surely stuck in Foster's memory, whether or not he knew the singer personally. This was Rice's hit of 1832, "Clare de Kitchen, Old Folks, Young Folks," whose words come closer than any other song to Foster's most distinctive work. The last stanza is closest of all:

> I wish I was back in old Kentuck,
> For since I left it I had no luck;
> De gals so proud dey wont eat mush,
> And wen you go to court 'em day say O hush.
>> Its clare de kitchen, etc.

Musically this tune, like "Jim Crow," has an attractive unconventional phrasing. Further, it avoids the normal symmetry of popular songs by a surprising repetition of its third phrase, a sequential development of its fourth, and a tiny coda. Foster must have admired it; no tune of his own showed such a combination of originality and successful craftsmanship.

If Foster had enrolled as an apprentice of Rice, he might have learned how to achieve something more than he ever achieved. But his success with "Susanna" at twenty-one led him to think that he could make a business of song-writing without demeaning himself to the routines of performance in public.

Four extant letters of 1850–52 from Foster to Edwin Pearce Christy show a relation of businesslike formality between them. Three of these letters will concern us in connection with Foster's conduct of his business, but the first letter is interesting chiefly for the sake of its tone and its date. It was written very soon after Foster had resigned his clerkship in Cincinnati, knowing that Christy had performed "Susanna" in New York.

Pittsburgh, Feb. 23, 1850

Dear Sir:

Herewith I send you copies of two of my late songs "Gwine to run all night," and "Dolly Day." I regret that the title-page had been ordered, and probably cut before I was informed of your desire that your name should not be used in connection with other bands. I have accordingly ordered my publisher in Baltimore to have a new title page cut bearing the name of your band alone like that used by Messrs. Firth, Pond and Co. N.Y. as I wish to unite with you in every effort to encourage a taste for this style of music so cried down by opera mongers. I hope to be in New York in the Spring when I will probably have an opportunity to gratify the desire which I have to hear your band. Please inform me how you are pleased with the accompanying songs. Very respectfully yours,

Stephen C. Foster.

E. P. Christy Esq.

Sheer reputation commanded the deferential tone. Before Foster had seen or heard the Christy show, he had heard and read enough about it to be confident that his publishers would yield to the order of a new title page. The name of the Christys was worth more than those of all other minstrel troupes combined. Their shows had come to New York from the West in 1846, having got started about four years earlier in Buffalo and having toured successfully as far as London. They were now established as a permanent feature of the city, where they were to maintain their preeminence over some ten rival troupes that likewise occupied New York theaters permanently through the 1850s, not to mention Western touring companies. The Christy Minstrels were so famous that their name became, as acknowledged by the Oxford English Dictionary, almost a single word.

Edwin P. Christy himself was more manager than musician. Although he sang and played the banjo a little, and took credit for composing, or at least arranging, "Good Night, Ladies," 1847, his chief role on the stage was as interlocutor—master of ceremonies, monologist, and straight man for the jokes of the "tambo and bones" players at the ends of the line. His featured singer, the one who took credit for introducing "Susanna" to New York, used the stage name G. N. Christy. Then, along with four minor members of the troupe, there were E. P. Christy's two sons, about ten and eleven years old at the time of Foster's first letter. Unlike some of the earlier black-face acts, theirs was a family show, suitable for a family audience, as "Good Night, Ladies" might suggest. E. P. Christy was concerned with taste—that is, with decorous words—but as far as is known he was less concerned with musical details than with words and business.

Success was fleeting for Christy personally, though his troupe continued for decades to spread his name and Foster's; in 1854 he had to retire at the age of thirty-nine, exhausted and half mad. He suffered delusions of bankruptcy. Finally, in 1862, he jumped from a hotel window and killed himself.

If Foster had fulfilled his hope of seeing Christy in New York in 1850, rather than putting it off until 1853, he could have worked with Christy at the height of his career. Foster could have heard his own songs performed with the utmost theatrical effect, observing the audience response to various songs in variously modified performances. He could have learned, in short, a more complex craft than in fact he ever learned. When he showed up in 1853 there was less chance to learn. By then Foster was established as author of several phenomenally popular songs; Christy was approaching his retirement. Did Foster even then attempt to learn what Christy had to teach him? There is no evidence that he did beyond the polite expression of hope in his 1850 letter. There is no evidence that the two men met at all, though it is hard to imagine that they failed to. Foster's career benefitted from Christy's sponsorship of "Susanna," "Old Folks," and a dozen other songs, but he looked elsewhere for models of his own "business" of songwriting.

The quite different singer-composer who inspired Foster more than the Christys or any minstrel troupe was Henry Russell. Russell was born in London, in 1812, into a poor Jewish theatrical family; he went on the stage at the age of four, and by the time he was seven he played the piano well enough to accompany adult singers. At fifteen he went off to Italy to study singing under the international theater's reigning masters, including Rossini and Bellini. Back in London, Russell made his adult debut in Weber's opera *Abu Hassan*, under the direction of Henry Rowley Bishop. But, impatient with his prospects, he emigrated to America in 1833. While working as an organist in Rochester, New York, he listened with a sensitive ear to the spellbinding spread-eagle oratory of Henry Clay and to the extraordinary singing of some Negro congregations. Soon he

developed the novel style of dramatic concert singing, at once ora-
torical and democratic, that was to make his fame. Accompanying
himself on a little portable piano, so that he faced his audience,
he used his big operatic voice to dramatize scenes of "A Ship on
Fire" and "The Maniac," and then to draw tears with the sentimental verses of G. P. Morris' "Woodman, Spare that Tree" and
"My Mother's Bible." He also included in his programs a few Negro
dialect songs. In 1847 Russell was connected with Samuel Sanford's
troupe. In the 1850s his repertory included "Susanna," "Old Folks,"
and five more of Foster's "plantation songs." But in 1843, when the
sixteen-year-old Foster heard Russell in Pittsburgh, what impressed
him was not the dialect songs so much as the sentimental ones and
the balance of the whole program with its effective variety. When
Foster began, about five years later, to think of himself as a songwriter, his hope was to supply songs for Russell and his imitators,
English and American.

There is a more concrete indication of Russell's influence on
Foster. In 1846—not long before, or possibly just after, "Susanna"—
Foster made his own musical setting of one of the poems he had
heard Russell sing, Charles Mackay's vision of social and moral
progress, "The Good Time Coming." Without quoting all eight stanzas, we may sample this poem, the most famous work of Mackay:

> There's a good time coming, boys,
>   A good time coming.
> The pen shall supersede the sword.
> And Right, not Might, shall be the lord
>   In the good time coming.
> Worth, not Birth, shall rule mankind
>   And be acknowledged stronger:
> The proper impulse has been given;—
>   Wait a little longer.
>
> There's a good time coming . . .
> Hateful rivalries of creed
> Shall not make their martyrs bleed
>   In the good time coming.
> Religion shall be shorn of pride
>   And flourish all the stronger . . .
>
> War in all men's eyes shall be
> A monster of iniquity
>   In the good time coming.

Mackay's sentiments, in Russell's musical setting, stirred many listeners; the refrain of "The good time coming" was often used in
political talk and journalism to sum up the whole ideology of con-

fident liberalism fighting every aristocratic, clerical, and military privilege. Such sentiments were endorsed by the Foster family, all staunch Jacksonian Democrats. When the brothers Morrison and Stephen heard Russell's song, they could applaud it whole-heartedly. They probably sang it themselves at home in the next few years, perhaps often enough to get tired of Russell's simple setting. Stephen, at any rate, set the Mackay poem and had it published in 1846 in Cincinnati with a dedication to Mary Keller of Allegheny; his tune differs from Russell's enough to be distinct, but the style is the same simple one. For title, Stephen used the whole first line, "There's a Good Time Coming." To connect "Susanna" with "The Good Time Coming" would have been no easier for Russell than for a 20th-century investigator. To foresee the time when Russell himself would be obscure, investigated for the sake of Foster, might have been impossible. But for Foster, on the other hand, the generous idea of "The good time" might perfectly well mingle with the hope of personal success that "Susanna" had aroused, the hope that he, like Russell, could find a market for both inspiring songs and amusing ones.

When Charles Mackay published a collection of his lyrics in 1850, his preface included some words of advice that Foster may have taken to heart:

> . . . Noble words set to the music which stirs the blood will never want listeners. The poets who do that have an arduous but noble task . . . if they be but in earnest with it, and will not make it their pastime, but the business and recompense of their lives.

A "noble task" as well as a business, Foster hoped, could develop for him from what had been a pastime.

Daniel Decatur Emmett, the composer of "Dixie," was as versatile as Henry Russell—more so than Foster—though Emmett's range of interests, in part overlapping theirs, extended in quite different directions. He played the fiddle and banjo, and sometimes the fife and drum; he sang, he probably danced, he acted in skits, he took all the roles in the minstrel shows. He disputed Christy's claim to be the originator of the minstrel show format, and though the dispute may never be settled, Emmett's claims have been enormously strengthened by the meticulous researches of the musicologist Hans Nathan: Emmett joined early in 1843 with three other capable performers in New York to make up the Virginia Minstrels; their full evening programs had an effective pattern that became the norm, replacing Rice's "Ethiopian operas"; their singing and playing blended in time and tone, and emphasized the four-part "chorus" harmony, comparable to that of the then-recently-successful Tyrolese Family Rainer, who had called themselves Tyrolese Minstrels. The Virginia Minstrels won great success immediately in New York, Boston, and London. They disbanded the next year, however, and through the following decade, while Christy established his fame, Emmett was associated with various less prominent companies in New York and on tours. From 1858 to 1866 he was part of a large stable troupe under the direction of three brothers, The Bryants' Minstrels, for whom "His main task was to write the tune and the words for walk-arounds, the finale and high point of their shows." Such a high point was "Dixie" (1859). Emmett's manuscript collection of all his walk-arounds has a preface, quoted by Nathan, in which Emmett claims to have "always strictly confined myself to the habits and crude ideas of the slaves of the South." Nathan shows that though he actually utilized a wide variety of sources, and though the text of "Dixie" was calculated to appeal to questionable New York political sentiments, indeed Emmett and the Bryants were more consistently close to oral musical traditions, including those of some Negroes, than the Christys and Foster were. Emmett's earlier published collections of banjo tunes (1843–44) seem to Nathan equally valuable for their genuine rootedness in backcountry traditions. Nathan sees the banjo style of Emmett and others, with its characteristic syncopation, as furnishing a basic element for the later development of ragtime and jazz.

Unlike Foster, Emmett never played the piano and never aspired to write parlor songs. He was "an indifferent reader." He was born in the little town of Mt. Vernon, Ohio, and died there in 1896 when he was eighty-eight. Foster's posthumous recognition in genteel magazines and books probably never bothered Emmett.

At least once, in 1853, Emmett's work touched Foster's: he took part in a skit called "Old Uncle Ned or Effusions from Lord Byron." No doubt he picked out on his banjo the Foster tune of "Uncle Ned." Almost certainly he had similar occasions to play "Susanna" as well.

The theatrical business of Emmett, Christy, and the other minstrels, whether it derived much or little from slave music and dance, systematically excluded Black performers. This exclusion, unnecessary in Europe, was a matter of course throughout the United States. Several Black performers who grew up on the fringes of the American theater made careers in Europe; their work contributed in the long run, ironically, to the fame of Foster's songs. The most important of them was the dancer William Henry Lane, known as Juba, born about the same time as Foster. From 1848 until he died in 1852, Juba was a chief representative of the minstrel theater in London. A reviewer in the London *Theatrical Times* found "an *ideality* in what he does that makes his efforts at once *grotesque* and *poetical.*"

But if business often observed segregation by class and race, the music business also frequently exploited the desire to cross boundaries and integrate contrasting styles. So, for example, "The Popular Melody Oh! Susanna, Arranged with Introduction and Brilliant Variations by Henri Herz" was the first Foster publication of Firth and Pond, 1849, before Foster was in touch with them. Henri Herz had their respect as one of the world's leading concert pianists; professor at the Paris Conservatory 1842–74, he was on tour in America 1845–51. His compositions included eight piano concertos, numerous respected studies, and a stream of brilliant arrangements for piano of the favorite tunes from the theater—mostly, that is, from operas by Bellini, Donizetti, Boieldieu, Auber, Halévy, and Meyerbeer. Liszt called them "derangements." Schumann never tired of berating Herz as the arch-Philistine in music. He was, indeed, a businessman more than a composer, though of course he was an outstanding craftsman and pedagogue first. Like two earlier piano virtuosos, Clementi and Pleyel, Herz went into the business of manufacturing pianos. When this enterprise faltered in 1845, he resorted to his American tour to raise money to invest in the factory. Back in Paris, Herz wrote his most amusing anecdotes about *Mes Voyages en Amérique*. They provide a colorful background for his "Susanna" "derangement," a view of the music business that Foster never attained.

For the tour Herz hired a manager named Ullman. In the memoir he blames Ullman for the invention of "financial music," explaining that this meant

> music arranged for eight or ten pianos, which everywhere in America had the gift of drawing crowds, especially when the theme of the concert consisted of national airs.

Herz himself, of course, was the arranger. He only pretends to be shocked at Ullman's cynicism in order to give his anecdotes some dramatic excitement. His best story is about a charitable benefit concert in New Orleans, where he stayed some weeks after his initial successes in the Eastern cities. At the New Orleans concert he supervised two players at each of the eight pianos, sixteen "fashionable ladies, all of them pretty." When one of the sixteen took sick, Herz replaced her with a pretty lady who could not play at all; he told her simply to wave her hands over the top of the keys, persuading her with all sorts of French gallantry that she was doing a good deed for the poor and, for the audience, making "music for the eyes." Another day in New Orleans, as Herz tells it, he was visited by a delegation of colored citizens requesting him to play a special concert for them, at any fee he might name. He says he was persuaded by the manager Ullman that to grant this request would mean to lose all future white audiences. He declined. These stories, never mentioning "Susanna," nevertheless indicate what that tune meant to Herz: a popular song, a bit of raw material for his "financial music."

In Paris Herz heard a boy from New Orleans who studied there in 1841–46: Louis Moreau Gottschalk, the first native American to win international renown as pianist and composer. Gottschalk earned the praise of Chopin both for his mastery of pianistic techniques and for his intelligent use of Creole dance rhythms, corresponding to Chopin's use of Polish materials in his mazurkas and polonaises. In 1853 Gottschalk returned to America, following in the footsteps of Herz on the concert circuit and surpassing him in public acclaim. He brought along a composition that he had produced in Madrid, an arrangement for ten pianos of "national airs" with the addition of cannon-fire effects, to represent *The Siege of Saragossa;* in America it was transformed into the *Grand National Symphony: Bunker Hill.* When Gottschalk revised this work as a solo, he called it *American Reminiscence,* or *National Glory,* and included in it quotations of "Oh! Susanna" and "Old Folks at Home." Gottschalk's *Columbia: caprice américaine,* op. 34, 1859, is an elaborate version of Foster's "My Old Kentucky Home," with "elegant" accompaniment ranging over the whole keyboard and a "misterioso" interlude between stanzas. Gottschalk's "derangement" is as far from Foster's original as many a 20th-century version. Yet it was a characteristic part of the world of music in which Foster tried to compete.

If the concert pianists, the minstrels, and Henry Russell represent various aspects of the music business to which Foster aspired without knowing enough about them, he knew at least one musical businessman a little better: Henry Kleber of Pittsburgh. Kleber was versatile enough to represent several aspects at once: he was a tenor; played the piano and organ; led a choir; organized and led a wind band that was to become the nucleus of the Pittsburgh Symphony; taught; composed songs, piano pieces, and arrangements; and established a store to sell music and instruments. Kleber's father had gone to Pittsburgh from Darmstadt in 1830; when he sent for the family to follow him two years later, Henry was perhaps fifteen years old—surely between ten and twenty. He arrived, then, with an incomplete German education. Around 1840 he supplemented his craft with some vocal lessons from an old pupil of Rossini named Giamboni, who had become a chocolate maker in Pittsburgh. Kleber opened his music store in 1846, bringing better pianos to town than the older store of John Mellor, stationer, and organist at the Episcopal church. In 1850 Kleber moved to a larger store. He was Pittsburgh's representative of the publishers Firth and Pond, with his name on their title pages. In 1856 he became agent for Steinway pianos.

The evidence of Foster's connection with Kleber is considerable. By 1850, if not before, Foster and Kleber were acquainted. That year, back from his four-year stint in Cincinnati, Foster dedicated his "Village Bells Polka" to Kleber. At about the same time Foster had a bookbinder sew together his own nine published compositions and a dozen piano pieces by various composers, including a waltz by Kleber that was published in 1848. Then in 1851 Foster provided the English translation of a German song that Kleber arranged for publication. In 1854, when Foster compiled for publication his volume of instrumental arrangements, *The Social Orchestra*, he included four pieces by Kleber, among which the "Rainbow Schottische" and "Coral Schottische" were the most popular works of Kleber's whole life. In 1857 Kleber organized a concert performance of the "Anvil Chorus" from Verdi's *Il Trovatore*. Kleber asked Foster to play the anvil, but, as Foster wrote to his friend Billy Hamilton, clerk on a river steamboat, he was "unwilling to go through the course of training and dieting requisite for the undertaking," and therefore declined. Kleber, he continued in the same facetious tone, "has sent to Europe for a 'first anvil.'" When Foster died in 1864, Kleber provided music for the funeral. On the basis of these facts, biographers assume that the two men were friendly and that Foster learned from Kleber his rudimentary craft of notewriting and instrumentation.

If their relations were close, however, it is strange that Kleber, living until 1897, never claimed credit for teaching or even befriending Foster. (At some later date his daughter, Ida Kleber Todd, stated that Kleber had helped revise "Come, Where My Love Lies Dreaming," 1855.) The lack of evidence connecting them at the time of Foster's first song (1844) suggests that they may not have met before the Kleber store opened, when Foster was already in Cincinnati. Then, two facts about the year 1850, when they did at least exchange favors, raise doubts as to the extent of their collaboration: it was just then that Kleber was moving to his bigger store, and it was then too that one day he took offense at a newspaper criticism of his piano playing, chased the critic down the street with a cowhide whip, and was haled into court and fined. He was not yet the model of business success and decorum for Foster to look up to. The letter to Billy Hamilton suggests that in 1857 Foster rather looked down on Kleber.

It was no local business that lured Foster, any more than it was a touring performer's craft. Rather it was the vaguely imagined nation-wide business, with worldwide connections, whose direction was concentrated increasingly in New York, and whose chief commodity was the printed page—"sheet music." From 1844 onward Foster was learning about this business. By 1850, when his contract with Firth and Pond emboldened him to leave Cincinnati, he thought he was well meshed with it. His songs were published in Philadelphia and Baltimore, even in Boston. He learned that these cities, like Pitts-burgh and Cincinnati, were coming into the commercial empire of New York. New York was eventually to be his headquarters.

His first publisher was George Willig of Philadelphia and Balti-more, a respected veteran of the music trades. Back in 1844 Willig had accepted the boy's "Open Thy Lattice, Love." Philadelphia, rather than New York, was the metropolis of commerce, politics, and culture for the elder Fosters. Willig brought out a "Susanna Polka" in 1849, a piano arrangement that the title page claimed was "composed" by one J. E. Miller—no mention of Foster at all.

Willig's successor and protégé in Baltimore, F. D. Benteen, brought out at least three different arrangements of "Susanna," all without Foster's name. Then, between 1849 and 1851, Benteen published over a dozen Foster songs, giving him due credit and paying him royalties.

The Cincinnati publisher William C. Peters, whose surprising hundred-dollar fee for "Susanna" meant so much to Foster, was an English immigrant. He had gone to America as a boy in 1820, had played clarinet in a military band in Canada, and had settled in Pittsburgh about 1823 to 1830. There he ran the first music store, which he sold out to Smith and Mellor, the later rivals of Kleber. Morrison Foster recalled that Peters had given some piano lessons to the Foster girls. In the 1830s Peters was active as teacher and store-keeper in Louisville, prospering enough by 1839 to establish the branch in Cincinnati where Stephen met him. Peters' profits on "Susanna," according to Morrison, were the foundation of his later successes, which included a branch in Baltimore and a magazine, *The Musical Olio*. In 1857 Peters himself told a Cincinnati reporter, John B. Russell, that "Uncle Ned" in his edition had sold even more copies than "Susanna." Peters claimed to have been Foster's "firm friend and adviser," but imagined that Foster was still a clerk and, as composer, still an amateur. Peters was not aware, then, that he had spurred Foster to think of songwriting as a vocation. It was true, of course, that Foster never became so able a craftsman or so rich a businessman as Peters. But with his later publishers Foster did learn to be businesslike. By that time, when he recalled his naive dealings with Peters, he had left them far behind.

In New York several publishers issued "Susanna." Two of them besides Firth and Pond may be noted briefly. C. Holt, Jr., brought out the earliest edition February 25, 1848, attributing the song to the Christy Minstrels; Holt also published at least four arrangements of "Susanna" in 1850, but nothing more of Foster's. Then there was William E. Millet, who issued "Susanna" and "Uncle Ned." He evidently wrote to Foster to secure permission; it is Foster's reply to him that informs us about the Cincinnati singer William Roark.

Firth and Pond had the biggest music business in New York. An account of their trade in the *New York Musical Review* (1854) divides it into four departments. The work of engraving and printing an annual output of some 225 pieces of music occupied twenty men. Selling these pieces in the store occupied another ten, and brought a revenue of $70,000. The manufacture of instruments, including flute and guitar, employed twenty-two men and earned $30,000. Finally, manufacturing pianos occupied forty and earned $50,000; about 300 pianos per week were turned out, selling at an average price of $300; this was the most important branch of the business until the Steinweg family (later spelled Steinway), whose factory had been founded in New York in 1853, began to win prizes with their novel combination of the "overstrung system" and the cast-iron frame. Firth and Pond occupied the Walter Franklin mansion, which had been George Washington's presidential residence in 1789.

The first negotiations between this august organization and the young songwriter concerned a song he had sent first, in manuscript, to a New York minstrel singer, and then to Firth and Pond: "Nelly Was a Lady." He had also offered to send shortly a song he had not quite finished, "Brudder Gum." The firm's reply tactfully advises Foster to learn the rules of the business:

New York
September 12, 1849

S. C. Foster, Esq.
Dear Sir

Your favor of 8th inst. is received and we hasten to reply.

We will accept the proposition therein made, viz. to allow you two cents upon every copy of your future publications issued by our house, after the expenses of publication are paid. Of course it is always our interest to push them as widely as possible. From your acquaintance with the proprietors or managers of the different bands of "minstrels," and from your known reputation, you can undoubtedly arrange with them to sing them and thus introduce them to the public in that way, but in order to secure the copyright exclusively for our house, it is safe to hand such persons printed copies only, of the pieces, for if manuscript copies are issued particularly by the author, the market will be flooded with spurious issues in a short time.

It is also advisable to compose only such pieces as are likely both in the sentiment and melody to take the public taste. Numerous instances can be cited of composers whose reputation has greatly depreciated,

from the fact of their music becoming too popular, and as a conse-
quence they write too much and too fast, and in a short time others
supercede [sic] them.

As soon as "Brother Gum" makes his appearance he shall be joined
to pretty "Nelly," and your interest in the two favorites duly forwarded
to your address, say 50 copies of each.

We remain . . .

The advice was sound, and Foster followed it. Firth and Pond issued
"My Brudder Gum" the next month, "Dolcy Jones" six weeks later.
In 1850 they published five pieces of Foster, including "Nelly Bly."
By September 22, 1851, though he had not yet visited them in New
York, the tone of the correspondence had become less formal. The
firm then wrote: " 'Nelly Bly' goes like hot cakes. . . . Christy has
not yet sung 'Old folks at home'. . ."

When Foster did go to New York, in 1853, a contract was signed
whereby Firth and Pond were to publish all of his works thereafter.
In 1854 the firm's advertisement in the *New York Musical Review*
boasted that Foster was "the most successful 'American composer'
of the day." This accolade was doubtless read with a lifted eyebrow
by Henry Kleber, who had had some piano pieces of his published
by Firth and Pond too. But Foster himself, for a moment, doubtless
believed in his supreme success. "Nelly Bly," "Camptown Races,"
and now "Old Folks" and three more recent hits were bringing him
enough to live on, and were justifying Firth and Pond in risking
such different titles as "Eulalie" and "Jeanie with the Light Brown
Hair." His success, if not complete or secure, was still unprecedent-
edly great. Although he was still essentially the "nice young man"
of Allegheny, escaping from the drudgery of the shipping business,
connected quite loosely with his performers and publishers, and
amazingly ignorant of his rivals, still his songs were part of their
booming business.

In the early 1850s the several kinds of music business represented
by Christy, Russell, Emmett, Herz, and the publishers all boomed
beyond any previous heights of success. Their markets were expanding rapidly as cities grew and transportation speeded up. This
expansion was worldwide, and was especially swift in the United
States. Foster's commercial success was a phenomenon of the changing times. To his associates and rivals his successful songs had
connotations of good times for business. "Susanna," "Camptown
Races," and "Nelly Bly" carry those expansive connotations still,
though they carry so many more that those are largely forgotten.
Reviving these connotations, in terms of particular events of the
1840s and 50s, helps to prepare us for a critical exploration of the
later-accumulated meanings of the songs.

CHAPTER 3

Working singers

THE MUSIC business thrives only because music means more than business. For many people, music is neither a livelihood nor a diversion from the serious business of life, but rather a natural accompaniment—almost a necessary part—of work, worship, and social and political intercourse. Especially for people who seldom or never attend the theater, who read few or no books, whose musical instruments if any are homemade, music fills these functions. And though, in the middle of the 19th century, cities were growing fast, still the great majority of the population was rural, in America and Europe, as in Asia and Africa. England was the vanguard of urbanization, with its overseas empire feeding its rapid growth. Books and newspapers circulated more widely than ever before, schools expanded, and national copyright laws were more and more refined, but a large minority still was illiterate. The music business, through its customers in the theaters and sheet-music stores, reached the bigger groups only indirectly, but music like Foster's, especially "Oh! Susanna," reached many illiterate folk, who put it to work in many ways.

The tunes of "Susanna," "Uncle Ned," "Camptown Races," and "Nelly Bly" became much more than commercial successes. The tunes were used, often with no words at all, or with new words to fit new functions. These four tunes in particular were so used, alongside other men's tunes like "Zip Coon" and "The Arkansas Traveller" (1840, anonymous). Foster's "Old Folks" and his subsequent more distinctive songs did not fit so well as "Susanna" into so many contexts.

Before we examine the evidence for these generalizations, however, we should acknowledge connections as well as the contrast between commercial music and functional music. The contrast is easily exaggerated and oversimplified. Between the suave and unscrupulous Professor Henri Herz and some illiterate rustic mother lulling her baby while she cooks a pot of greens, there are gradations and endless variants. For instance, people go not only to big-city theaters but also to ice-cream "saloons" and small-town dance halls, and their attendance may be frequent or only very occasional. People read many sorts of print, more or less of it, more or less studiously. People move from the countryside to the cities, from East to West. People make music for money, more or less, sometimes or often. For example, on the keelboats that still plied some tributaries of the Ohio and the Mississippi in the 1840s, boatmen who could afford it hired a fiddler to travel with them or gave free passage in exchange for musical entertainment while they rowed. On many plantations in the South a slave who played for his master's dancing party could expect a gift of money at the end of the evening, or at least a bonus of food and drink beyond the regular ration of the slave quarters; in some cases a good fiddler was hired out to neighboring plantations for his master's profit. In a few cases a slave might earn enough to "hire his time" from the master. In one case, Solomon Northrup, a New Yorker of African ancestry who played the fiddle well, was kidnapped and held as a slave for twelve years before friends won his release through the courts; his fiddle was an instrument of his oppression, his resistance, and his consolation. There was no sharp division between the music business and the rest of music.

Bayard Taylor, the brilliant young reporter for Horace Greeley's New York *Tribune*, heard "Susanna" far from home in 1849, when he traveled to California, and he described the interesting social context vividly on at least two occasions. The first time was on his way out, going over the Isthmus of Panama, up the Changres River in a canoe. One of the paddlers was Juan Bega, a man of "the lowest class, almost entirely of negro blood." His paddling kept time with the "Ethiopian melodies he had picked up from the emigrants," including "Susanna." Presumably the song helped coordinate Bega's paddling with that of his boss, Ambrosio Mendez "of the mixed Indian and Spanish race." At the same time, it was meant to please the American passengers, for Bega looked around at them at the end of a song "with a grin of satisfaction at his skill," and when the trip was ended he sang for them again, one of the "native songs" that Taylor had liked especially. Moreover, as Taylor notes, "Singing begets thirst, and perhaps Juan sang the more that he might have a more frequent claim on the brandy." Juan Bega was doubtless typical, in his multiple uses of "Susanna," of many another musical boatman.

It was in Sacramento that Bayard Taylor was most impressed by the uses of "Susanna" and similar songs. His description and his reflections on it, cited fleetingly by several later writers, deserve to be read in full:

> The door of many a gambling-hell on the levee, and in J and K streets, stands invitingly open; the wail of torture from innumerable musical instruments peals from all quarters through the fog and darkness. Full bands, each playing different tunes discordantly, are stationed in front of the principal establishments, and as these happen to be near together, the mingling of the sounds in one horrid, ear-splitting, brazen chaos, would drive frantic a man of delicate nerve. All one's old acquaintances in the amateur-music line, seem to have followed him. The gentleman who played the flute in the next room to yours, at home, has been hired at an ounce [of gold] a night to perform in the drinking-tent across the way; the very French horn whose lamentations used to awake you dismally from the first sweet snooze, now greets you at some corner; and all the squeaking violins, grumbling violincellos [sic] and rowdy trumpets which have severally plagued you in other times, are congregated here, in loving proximity. The very strength, loudness, and confusion of the noises, which, heard at a little distance, have the effect of one great scattering performance, marvellously takes the fancy of the rough mountain men.
>
> Some of the establishments have small companies of Ethiopian melodists, who nightly call upon "Susanna!" and entreat to be carried back to Old Virginny. These songs are universally popular, and the crowd of listeners is often so great as to embarrass the player at the monte tables and injure the business of the gamblers. I confess to a strong liking for the Ethiopian airs, and used to spend half an hour every night in listening to them and watching the curious expressions of satisfaction and delight in the faces of the overland emigrants, who always attended in a body. The spirit of the music was always encouraging; even its most doleful passages had a grotesque touch of cheerfulness—a mingling of sincere pathos and whimsical consolation, which somehow took hold of all moods in which it might be heard, raising them to the same notch of careless good-humor. The Ethiopian melodies well deserve to be called, as they are in fact, the national airs of America. Their quaint, mock-sentimental cadences, so well suited to the broad absurdity of the words —their reckless gaiety and irreverent familiarity with serious subjects— and their spirit of antagonism and perseverance—are true expressions of the more popular sides of the national character. They follow the American race in all its emigrations, colonizations and conquests, as certainly

as the Fourth of July and Thanksgiving Day. The penniless and half despairing emigrant is stimulated to try again by the sound of "It'll never do to give it up so!" and feels a pang of home-sickness at the burthen of the "Old Virginia Shore."

Taylor's concluding thoughts anticipate our concerns with meaning attributed to Foster's songs by other literary interpreters. That Taylor developed such thoughts in response to the colorful scene at Sacramento, which he observed for some weeks, is our concern now. Thanks largely to his reporting, "Oh! Susanna" came to be widely associated with the '49ers in California. "Susanna" could indeed unite virtually the whole society of boom towns like Sacramento, a fragmentary, temporary society of men without women, children, or old folks, a society of men assembled from many origins, looking to many different destinations, uniting only with difficulty, loosely and temporarily. Such a society exaggerated some traits of the American society of which it was part, or of the developing world-wide urban industrial society in which England was dominant. Bayard Taylor thought it "natural that California should be the most democratic country in the world." Without explicitly connecting this thought with his observations on music or on the limitations of the society, he insisted on its democracy: "The practical equality of all the members of a community, whatever might be the wealth, intelligence, or profession of each, was never before thoroughly demonstrated." He overlooked the racism of the majority that was already agitating to expel all Negroes from California. Whether such a society is rightly designated by Taylor's term "community" is questionable. Yet it is something more than either Foster's circle of "nice young men" or the audience of a "minstrel show." The California '49ers typify the changing times in which Foster's work went around the world.

Books of song texts published in California in the 1850s included many new stanzas to fit the tune of "Susanna." A typical one goes:

> The white folks all am crazy
> With nuffin' in der mouth
> But de mines of California.
> Who's agwan Souff?

The repertory of the songsters referred not only to Foster's tune, of course, but also to some of Emmett's and the other minstrels', and to older favorites like "Home, Sweet Home." But because "Susanna" was the new hit tune in 1849, and because no remarkable new tune sprang up in California itself, the association of "Susanna" with California was especially noted.

But the fact that California contributed a special connotation to the tune did not hinder at all its acquiring other meanings elsewhere in the world, among quite different societies. It was reported in some astonishingly remote places, and in some of them it entered traditional repertories in which it seemed to fit securely for a century or more. Bayard Taylor himself, in 1853, heard "Susanna" sung by a Hindu in Delhi. Later he heard "Uncle Ned" among Arabs in North Africa. An anonymous Boston reporter heard the tune of "Susanna" whistled in a Paris street. Various German versions and parodies are recorded, and, in 1950, when an American radio program in Germany used "Susanna" as a theme song, listeners complained that this was a German tune—they would prefer something more American. A Swedish collector of sea chanties in 1935 found "Susanna visan" a favorite. The collectors of Mormon traditional songs found three versions of a lively text for "Susanna": "Zack the Mormon Engineer," in 1933, 1945, and 1959. A folklore scholar in 1959 marveled at a "Susanita" from New Mexico, still recognizable as the Foster melody though its polka rhythm had been displaced by a languorous 6/8 time. While any one of these reports might be a freakish accident, the accumulation of them (and many more that could be cited from intermediary accounts) is convincing evidence that "Susanna" belongs no more to California than to Louisiana: its uses are world wide.

More than anywhere else, whether in America or abroad, it is in England that detailed contemporary evidence shows the process of dissemination from theater to countryside for "Susanna." In the 1850s the pioneer investigator Henry Mayhew was compiling his four-volume study of *London Labour and the London Poor*, which includes fascinating interviews with street singers, players, clowns, and beggars, several of whom mention "Susanna" and "Uncle Ned" in particular. One of Mayhew's informants estimated that some fifty men managed to eke out a living in London as "Ethiopian serenaders" on the streets; this man had been at it for eight years, and was a member of the best such band. He recalled watching the dancer Juba and starting his own career by imitating Juba just outside the theater where Juba performed. The street musician listed his repertory of the first years, when "Buffalo Gals" was liked best. Then the newer favorites, including the two Foster songs. He told how his band, at Christmas time, put aside its banjos and bones, washed off the burnt-cork blacking, and proceeded to "go out as waits," singing traditional Christmas songs. One of Mayhew's street-singers or "chaunters" testified that some twenty years earlier there had been trios of glee singers on the streets year round, but now that tradition was chiefly confined to the provinces. "Many of the glee-singers have given up the business, and taken to the street Ethiopians instead." Among some 250 ballad singers and a thousand performers on various instruments, a good many were blind, and some of these candidly told Mayhew that they used music not "as a means of pleasing, but rather as a mode of soliciting attention." One such blind beggar was a woman who played the hurdy-gurdy, which she called a "cymbal." Her honesty, pluck, and good cheer won Mayhew's admiration, and he recorded her whole life story. Her musical repertory was slender, beginning with "God Save the King," and including six or eight songs, of which "Susanna" was the newest. She explained, "I learnt it myself by hearing it on the horgan. I always try and listen to a new tune when I am in the street, and get it off if I can: it's my bread." Yet another of Mayhew's informants was a "whistling man" who specialized in whistling as he danced; his tunes included "Lucy Neal" and "Ben Bolt." Finally there was a Punch-and-Judy team whose act was diversified by a Jim Crow character singing snatches of four or five "Ethiopian" songs in the midst of his dialogue with Punch. The Foster songs took their place in this very English atmosphere just as readily as in California. And from the London street singers they went on to the provincial cities and towns and villages. In 1855 a reporter for *Putnam's Monthly Magazine* heard "Susanna" "whistled by a yellow headed Somersetshire lout, under the broken noses of battered saints in the antique archway of a Norman church hidden in the green heart of western England."

Back in America, at the middle of the century, street musicians were not yet so common as in England. One English traveler in 1859, John MacGregor, noted their absence. When, by exception, he heard a serenading band playing some "negro melody music," he listened with delight. Describing it in his journal, MacGregor went on to give his explanation for the rarity of music in America: "Dollar, dollar, dollar! This is the ringing music of the West." When, later in the century, street singers and organ grinders became more common, they were largely, like most learned musicians of this time, recent immigrants. Thus it is quite possible that a Pittsburgh steelworker of the 1880s might have learned "Susanna" in his childhood in England or Ireland and taken it to the streets of Foster's home town along with his repertory of ballads.

In mid-century America more than in England, the dissemination of tunes depended on organizations and on print, if available evidence adequately reflects the reality. Military bands, political clubs, temperance clubs, and all the other associations of that "age of reform" in America made popular tunes more popular by using them for topical words. In the presidential campaign of 1840, Horace Greeley had given great impetus to this process by printing in every issue of the *Tribune* a new set of words to go with some popular tune. The Mexican War was an occasion for speeding up the process, as can be seen by a glance at the compilation of William McCarty: he had published in 1842 a three-volume *National Song Book* with the aim of including all the American songs he could find, patriotic, naval, and military. In 1846 he brought out a supplement, *National Songs, Ballads, and Other Patriotic Poetry, Chiefly Relating to the War of 1846*, in which a high proportion of the tunes were those of the early minstrels, "Dan Tucker" and "Lucy Neal" especially being used again and again. In 1851 Foster himself wrote a campaign song to the tune of "Camptown Races," in support of the Bigler brothers—William, who was to be governor of Pennsylvania, and John, governor of California; the tune fixes the pronunciation of "hurrah" as "hoo-rah," like "doo-dah." The third and fifth stanzas of this text are as exciting as the horserace described in the original:

> The Constitution is our theme, Hurrah! Hurrah!
> And Union is our cherished dream,
> > Hurrah for the Bigler boys!
> If South Carolina makes a fuss, Hurrah! Hurrah!
> Oh, why should *we* be in the muss?
> > Hurrah for the Bigler boys!
> We've let the Whigs elect an ass, Hurrah! Hurrah!
> But now we'll turn him out to grass,
> > Hurrah for the Bigler boys!
> For when the tug of war is over, Hurrah! Hurrah!
> The Democrats will live in the clover,
> > Hurrah for the Bigler boys!
> CHORUS: Going to run again? Johnston, your [sic] insane!
> > I'll bet my money on the Bigler boys
> > For the Whigs have had their reign!

For the election of 1856 the Democrats of Allegheny formed a "Buchanan Glee Club," with Morrison Foster as treasurer and Stephen as musical director. One member of the club, Billy Hamilton, recalled later that Foster had supplied many songs for this club. Two texts have been identified, of which one fits the tune that Foster later published as "The Merry Month of May," and the other goes to the anonymous tune "Villikins and his Dinah." (The tune links Foster once more with the London author Henry Mayhew, the earliest recorded use of it being in Mayhew's farce of 1834, *The Wandering Minstrel*.) In the 1850s "Villikins" was as great a favorite for new texts as "Susanna"; it survived into the 20th century, especially with the words "On Top of Old Smokey." Foster's use of "Villikins" and "Camptown Races" for similar purposes shows something of his own attitudes not just to immediate political issues, but also to the significance of his melodies in general and their relation to society. His text for "Villikins" is an antiabolitionist satire—"The Great Baby Show." His text for his own tune in 1856 is a more solemn anthem, "The White House Chair," beginning

> Let all our hearts for Union be,
> For the North and South are one . . .

This solemnity too shows something of Foster's general attitude. Satire was not, he thought, so appropriate to his melodies as to "Villikins." But in the varied programs of the Buchanan Glee Club his satire and his solemnity made a good balance. Unfortunately the solemn text never won popularity for his new tune. Political texts, perhaps, can only enhance a popularity already established. In 1860 the best Foster campaign song of all was one to the tune of "Nelly Bly," which appeared, probably without Foster's approval, in the Republican Songster:

> Hi! Lincoln, Ho! Lincoln! An honest man for me:
> I'll sing for you—I'll shout for you, the People's nominee.

By this time, on the other hand, "Camptown Races" and "Old Dog Tray" were being sung in a medley that climaxed with "Dixie," put together by Harry McCarthy, the English immigrant concert singer who was to be the "national poet of the South" during the Civil War, and the author of the Confederate anthem, "The Bonnie Blue Flag." The political texts were attached to Foster's melodies too loosely to stick, and contradictory meanings could help spread his tunes among people who read the newspapers and attended the rallies though they might not read sheet music or attend a minstrel show.

The editor of the Republican Songster, John W. Hutchinson, was the foremost member of the famous singing Hutchinson family from New Hampshire, whose whole career illuminates the meanings of Foster's songs at several points. From 1842 until 1863 the Hutchinsons were presenting concerts and performing at meetings of antislavery societies all over the northern United States and in England and Scotland; down to the end of the century the concerts were continued by a second and third generation of the family. They kept their home on a farm in New Hampshire; their concerts paid traveling expenses, but they depended on the family farm, and contributed their most characteristic singing as a gift to the cause of freedom. They spread many kinds of music to audiences that never went to concerts or theaters. Foster's "Nelly Bly," though not his only tune that they sang, was the only perennially popular one that they put to political use, as far as is known. They used his "Ellen Bayne" tune for a more sentimental appeal, "Hope for the Slave." Their singing, with Foster's own words, of his "Gentle Annie," "Old Folks," and at least two more songs will bring the Hutchinsons to our attention again later. But their repertory included two songs by other composers that concern us now for two reasons: they are connected with Foster and they are veritable theme songs of the antislavery movement. One of these is "The Good Time Coming," Mackay's poem, sometimes extended with topical stanzas, in a musical setting by Jesse Hutchinson. Like Foster, Hutchinson had been inspired by Henry Russell's setting of "The Good Time" to make one of his own. The other song is "Get Off the Track! a Song for Emancipation," with words by Jesse Hutchinson, 1844, to the minstrel tune "Old Dan Tucker," whose hero Foster mentioned in the text of his "Away Down South in Alabama." The Hutchinson chorus goes

> Ho! the car Emancipation
> Rides majestic thro' our Nation,
> Bearing on its train the story,
> Liberty! a nation's glory.

That the idea of nationwide emancipation, extremely radical in 1844, could fit a tune from the blackface theater may seem ironic. The Hutchinsons did not use many tunes from that source, but they used "Dan Tucker" and "Nelly Bly" well. They helped to extend and preserve the tunes in social contexts where they might otherwise have been ignored or repudiated. The Hutchinsons sang in Cincinnati at the very time when "Susanna" was published there by Peters: December 1848. Foster probably heard them, certainly heard about them. They probably picked up "Susanna" then and there.

The antislavery movement made use of many singers less famous than the Hutchinsons and produced several interesting songbooks in which "The Good Time Coming" and "Get Off the Track!" appeared regularly; in one of them Foster's "Nelly Bly" appears once more, with a still different text, and in another there is a fine text for "Oh! Susanna." The books of two different editors, George Whitfield Clark and William Wells Brown, each went through several editions. Clark's *Liberty Minstrel* came out first in 1844, reached a seventh edition in 1850, and in 1856 was expanded with a new title, *The Harp of Freedom*. Clark's tunes at first were mostly solemn old-fashioned hymns and compositions of his own, resembling hymns, but in the expanded edition he included several minstrel tunes: "Nelly Bly" and "Old Folks" are among them. The original words of "Old Folks" are altered only in a few lines, in an attempt to redirect its sad and weary longing:

> When will de day of 'Mancipation
> Bring all de darkies home?

"Nelly Bly's" original text, on the contrary, is forgotten; the distinctive rhythm of the tune controls the new idea, an appeal to join the guerrilla warfare of John Brown against the extension of slavery in the West:

> Ho! brothers! come, brothers! hasten all with me;
> We'll sing upon the Kansas plains a song of liberty.

Clark's songster, like the Hutchinsons', helped make the tune of "Nelly Bly" a favorite of some 20th-century singers.

It is "Susanna," in the version of the Black writer William Wells Brown, that most certainly entered the repertory of illiterate singers, including the two great heroines of the antislavery movement, Sojourner Truth and Harriet Tubman. Brown's *Anti-Slavery Harp* included "Susanna" in its second and third editions, 1849 and 1851, as tune for "The Northern Star"; the chorus goes:

> Oh! Star of Freedom, 'Tis the star for me;
> 'Twill lead me off to Canada, There I will be free.

Brown probably wrote these words, for he had been born a slave, had escaped to freedom in Illinois, and had helped many others escape to Canada while working as a boatman on Lake Erie, about 1834 to 1843. Now, in 1849, at the age of thirty-five, he was a paid lecturer for the antislavery movement, esteemed author of a *Narrative* of his life (1847), as well as editor of the songster. Eventually, after the War, Brown became the foremost Black historian, best known for his volume on *The Negro in the American Rebellion*. Both his literary skill and his experience on Lake Erie qualified him to write "The Northern Star." In Brown's collection there are texts for other tunes from the minstrels' repertory, including "Dandy Jim," along with a much older tune, used several times, "Auld Lang Syne," and a single more elaborate tune, something from *Il Trovatore* (the "anvil chorus"?—Brown's book, unlike Clark's, merely names the tunes, printing no notes). The most tantalizing item is a "Song of the Coffle Gang" "said to be sung by slaves"; its chorus seems to owe something to Mackay's "Good Time":

> There's a better day acoming, will you go along with me?
> There's a better day acoming, go sound the jubilee.

"Susanna," as "The Northern Star," fitted here perhaps even better than "Nelly Bly" fitted in the contexts of Clark and the Hutchinsons. At any rate, it was "The Northern Star" that was sung in triumph by successful ex-slaves.

Sojourner Truth was a domestic slave in the final years of slavery in New York State. She believed that she had been brought from Africa as a child. She was converted to Christianity as an adult, and in 1843 began her career as "lecturer" at a camp meeting revival in Brooklyn. She discovered that she could attract a crowd by singing and then hold them for her sermon and prayer. She took the name Sojourner and wandered from one such meeting to another. Eventually she learned to organize meetings of her own. But also she found her way to the antislavery meetings, to which she devoted most of her time through the 1850s; it was then that she asked God for a second name, and was inspired with the name Truth. She told Harriet Beecher Stowe, who met her in 1863, that "the Lord has made me a sign unto this nation." Stowe described her vividly, a regal woman more than six feet tall, singing "with those indescribable upward turns and those deep gutturals which give such a wild, peculiar power to the negro singing—but above all, with such an overwhelming energy of personal appropriation that the hymn seemed to be fused in the furnace of her feelings and come out recrystallized as a production of her own." She sang mostly hymns "whose burden was 'O glory, glory, glory, won't you come along with me?'" But she also sang "The Northern Star," and Stowe recorded her text, though without the title and without mention of the tune:

> I'm on my way to Canada, That cold but happy land;
> The dire effects of slavery I can no longer stand.
> O righteous Father, Do look down on me,
> And help me on to Canada, Where colored folks are free.

After the war, Sojourner Truth continued to lecture on behalf of rights for the freedmen, and now she used her songs as a finale. She composed a text of her own for the tune of "John Brown's Body," in honor of the Michigan regiment of colored soldiers, with reference to a favorite line of the minstrels:

> The possum up the gum tree couldn't keep it still
> As we went climbing on.

Sojourner Truth wrote another text—the tune is unknown—which was partly recorded by a listener at Lisbon, Ohio, in about 1871:

> I am pleading for my people, A poor down-trodden race,
> Who dwell in freedom's boasted land, With no abiding place.

It is tempting to add a chorus to these lines, to complete the tune of "Susanna" once more. But the words of Sojourner Truth are hard to match.

Harriet Tubman was born about 1820 on a plantation in Maryland. She rebelled in childhood, refused to serve as a domestic, and became a tough field worker, despised by her master because a hideous injury had made her subject to sleeping fits. She escaped in 1849. She then took domestic jobs just long enough to prepare for the almost incredible return trips to bring her friends and relatives out to freedom. Through the 1850s she made some fifteen or twenty trips. When she met John Brown in 1858, he called her "General" and counted on her collaboration in his plan. She fell sick in 1859, and Brown went to Harper's Ferry without her. When the war came, she was put to work as nurse, scout, and spy, with fabulous effectiveness. She retired to Auburn, New York, where she lived until 1913.

According to Earl Conrad, Harriet Tubman's biographer, she made regular use of songs as signals, codes, and disguises. Her repertory included "Go Down, Moses," and she herself was Moses, going down to "Egypt" to rescue "my people." It included "Swing Low, Sweet Chariot," and Harriet was "Old Chariot." It included "Steal Away to Jesus," with the meaning "away to freedom." And it included "The Northern Star," with the tune of "Susanna"; the sole account of a song on a particular occasion is an account of this song, six stanzas of it, sung at Niagara Falls in 1856 by a whole party led by Harriet Tubman, rejoicing at their escape to Canada.

> Farewell, old master, don't think hard of me.
> I'm on my way to Canada, where all the slaves are free.

Here, more than in the California gambling halls or on the streets of London, not to speak of any theater or any family parlor, the tune of "Susanna" expressed and confirmed the solidarity of a group of people, mostly illiterate, working together and celebrating their common effort. Here "Susanna" was a folksong, in the honorific sense of that word. But a "national air of America," as Bayard Taylor called it? When the group of people singing were escaping from the United States? When escape was their common work and the theme of their song? No, this use of the tune contradicts Taylor's interpretation at the same time that it confirms the most general point of his observations, the point that "Susanna" and other "Ethiopian melodies" were shared by an extremely widespread and extremely mobile population. The tune was shared far more widely than the words Foster had given it, more widely than any one meaning. It served all sorts of groups, enhancing their internal unity, but among the groups, in relation to each other, the tune established no unity of will or understanding. The tune was adaptable to the functions of many separate "folks." What it meant to each of them depended on them more than on the music.

It would be a mistake to imagine that "Susanna" and other songs like it were adopted at once throughout the slave population or among the free Negroes, North and South. There is at least one bit of evidence that some singers resisted the spread of these songs. The slaves first freed by Northern conquest, at Port Royal, South Carolina, in 1862, had a marvelous repertory of work songs and "Spirituals." The contrast between their repertory and the lively minstrel songs struck observers forcibly. According to one of the earliest reporters, H. G. Spaulding, 1863, the Sea Islanders never sang "the joyous, merry strains which have been associated in the minds of many with the Southern negro." Spaulding indicates that they heard "Uncle Ned" and "Susanna" in particular, and considered such songs "highly improper." Spaulding tells how a group of Charleston Negroes, on the other hand, in their time off duty as officers' servants, formed the "Charleston Minstrels" and gave a concert in the Episcopal Church for the benefit of the sick and wounded soldiers. Their program, excluding all comic songs, nevertheless was far from the Sea Islanders' repertory; "Uncle Ned" may well have fitted it, along with patriotic songs and "half-mournful" ballads.

Later in the detailed *Atlantic Monthly* article about spirituals by Colonel Thomas Wentworth Higginson (1867), there is a similar observation relevant to our present concern:

> A few youths from Savannah, who were comparatively men of the world, had learned some of the "Ethiopian Minstrel" ditties, imported from the North. These took no hold upon the mass.

The wordly youths from the city were foreign to the coherent group of rural natives who sang "Deep River." Higginson, like Spaulding, appreciated the contrast. He believed that the "indigenous" repertory reflected the continuity of generations, as well as the immediate solidarity of the group, and that generations would have to pass before "Uncle Ned" and "Susanna" could take on many of the values that he prized in the spirituals.

By 1915, however, when the scholarly folklorist Newman White collected Negro folksongs in Georgia and North Carolina, he found "Susanna" in the repertory of at least one rural worker, who believed that it had been a "slave song." White found five versions of "Uncle Ned," and one song with a reference to "Camptown Races." He noted that he did not find "Old Folks" or any other Foster song, but those three seemed firmly fixed in the tradition that he studied.

By 1960 a far more sophisticated student of folksong throughout the world, Alan Lomax, lists "Susanna" along with "Turkey in the Straw," "Old Dan Tucker," "Buffalo Gals," and "The Blue-tail Fly," as one of the best pieces of the "minstrel composers," which were close enough to "the ring games and animal jingles of the slaves" to have "proved themselves by going back into wide oral circulation." "Susanna" is the only one of Foster's songs that Lomax includes in his list.

"Folksong" is a notoriously ambiguous label. Its history in Europe and America needs to be traced before we can apply it usefully to "Old Folks." But here we may let it stand as a summary of what we have learned about the many functions and meanings of "Susanna."

Our exploration of "Susanna's" meanings has taken us far from the composer himself, the "nice young man" about to begin a career in the booming music business. "Susanna" did not unite him personally with the groups of people who sang the tune. The meanings they gave his tune were independent of his intentions. To find a true relation between the accumulated meanings and the ascertainable facts about his life, his personality, and his intentions, is no easy task. Understandably, most students of his life, motivated by a regard for some few of the meanings of some of his songs, have contrived images of him that are not convincing. If we feel a growing curiosity about the whole range of meanings, we will continue to be patient with the slow, gradual emergence of a complex portrait of the man, which in turn will contribute to our grasp of the interrelated meanings of his several kinds of songs. "Susanna" reveals less of Foster than "Jeanie" or "Old Folks"; "Susanna" is closer than the others to more "folk," and by that very fact more detached from him.

The great variety of functions filled by "Susanna" and the persistence of this song in oral tradition through several generations, alongside "Turkey in the Straw" and "Buffalo Gals," as well as "Uncle Ned," "Camptown Races," and "Nelly Bly," affect the meaning of the music for 20th-century singers and listeners more than the commercial-theater context in which the songs had their initial success. The whole history of the minstrel shows would be rightly forgotten if it were not for these tunes, which functioned and survived so far beyond the shows. The commercial connotations of the songs, though they can be revived and sorted out with a little effort, are ordinarily assimilated to the hopeful connotations of folksong.

⟨ CHAPTER 4 ⟩

Contemporary critics

"SUSANNA'S" meanings troubled some people who heard the song when it was newly popular around 1850. Among them, a few articulate thinkers criticized it, along with other similar songs that had spread from the theater to wider uses. Though most people who felt a twinge of trouble probably tried simply to ignore these songs, there were many recorded reflections besides those of Bayard Taylor, the young journalist whose reports and interpretations we have seen. The questions that were raised must have troubled Foster himself, though almost none of the critics knew his name.

Did songs like "Susanna" express a national character? A distinctive American energy, as Bayard Taylor thought? Or did they appeal to Americans and Englishmen and others because of an exotic African quality? Did they indicate an innate musicality among people of African descent? An innate destiny to become the very soul of America? Or the soul of the modern world? Or, rather, did these songs exploit and degrade Afro-Americans with a stereotype of childish innocence or monkey shines? More urgent questions: did these songs show Blacks content with slavery, or did they show up the false claims of white apologists for slavery?

Such questions were discussed in the 1840s and '50s largely without use of the terms "folklore" and "folksong," which were to come into English only in the 1860s and '70s. At least one German writer, the journalist Moritz Busch, was ready in 1852 to apply the term *Volkslied* to "Susanna" and "Uncle Ned"; with the help of this term he discussed some of the troubling questions at length. His ideas, though not his terms, were shared to some extent by English and American writers, including the heroic champion of English letters, Thomas Carlyle, and the most eminent New York poet, William Cullen Bryant; German ideas were further assimilated by the pioneer Bostonian critic of music, John Sullivan Dwight, and his friends like Lowell, Whittier, Thoreau, and Thomas Wentworth Higginson. Two younger Bostonians were in Germany in 1850—Alexander Wheelock Thayer, beginning studies toward his Beethoven biography, and Francis James Child, acquiring scientific disciplines of research into the words of the oldest *Volklieder;* both of them at least mentioned the current "minstrel" songs. Walt Whitman's eloquent enthusiasm for music and for America make his notice of the "minstrels" important. And Herman Melville's ambiguities reflect a light on the minstrel songs unique among contemporaries. Moreover, the questions about the songs concerned the Black abolitionist leaders Frederick Douglass and Martin Delany. Each of these men answered the troubling questions in his own way. Some of them, in the course of a few years, changed their opinions. The whole range of their opinions is interesting.

Though Foster himself could not survey the range of opinion as we can, his own changes of attitude indicate that the range is relevant to our attempt to understand him. He was not faced with a simple choice between scorning the minstrel songs and defending them; a good many later accounts of his life make such a supposed choice melodramatic. We can imagine more plausibly that he groped his way among many shades of opinion. If he did not read the particular opinions that we can read, still he read and heard more than two neatly opposed views. To understand his changing attitudes we can benefit from acquaintance with selected varied views of his contemporaries.

Moritz Busch heard "Susanna" many times and gave it more study than any American who wrote about it. He heard it first in 1851 on board the ship bringing him to America. During the next year he heard memorable performances in a New York City waterfront dance hall; on a street-corner in the village of Dunkirk, New York; somewhere in backwoods Pennsylvania; and somewhere on the prairie in Illinois. He must have heard countless forgettable performances in "Susanna's" own Cincinnati, where Busch spent several months. He ranked it the supreme popular favorite, as well as one of the very best of the thirteen "Negro songs" he chose for translation and commentary from about 200 he had collected.

Busch was thirty in 1851. Only five years older than Foster, he was far more learned and experienced. He had earned the doctorate in theology at Leipzig, had read and spoken English, had taken part in the vain uprising of 1849 at Dresden. He doubtless considered emigrating to America for good, but instead he wrote a two-volume book for prospective German immigrants, *Wanderungen zwischen Hudson und Mississippi, 1851 und 1852,* published at Stuttgart, 1854. (An English translation, incomplete but useful for its notes, appeared only in 1971.) Later Busch went on to write many books and articles, of which the most famous were memoirs of his work as press officer for Bismarck, 1870–73.

Throughout the book there are references to music or the lack of music, which enhance the value of the sixth chapter, devoted entirely to "Thirteen Songs and a Picture of Negro Character." In general Busch observes that Americans sing less than Germans; he notes the worst music of his trip, however, in a German Lutheran church in Cincinnati, where a miserable organ accompanies a congregation he regards as stupid. He is delighted when he finds an exceptional group of Anglo-Americans in the hills of Kentucky, singing old folksongs he hoped to find more often, comparable to those of the Scottish highlands. He thinks Methodist camp-meeting tunes resemble German student songs. He is amused at the tune used for a hymn of the Mormons, which he recognizes as "Du, du liegst mir im Herzen," a pseudo-Tyrolese waltz recently popular in Germany. He is moved by the songs and dances of the Shaker worshippers in Ohio; he studies their manuscript hymnbook; and among them he observes particularly a tall old "Negress" leading a circle dance in a song of jubilation, not to be found in the book. He remarks on a town crier with a bell; a thirty-man band, marching in a procession that includes fewer than thirty nonmusicians; a reel in a hotel bar that reminds him of the new Parisian can-can; and, by all means, the new organ of 2700 pipes, built by a German master for the Catholic cathedral in Cincinnati, largest church in America. He hears a choir of 95 prisoners in a Methodist Sunday School at Columbus, and notes that the proportion of Black singers is higher than the proportion of Blacks in the prison, which officials tell him is one in thirteen. (The proportion of Blacks in the population of Cincinnati in 1850 is about one in thirty; the proportion of Germans more than one in three.) He is overwhelmed at the Cincinnati African Methodist Church, where he hears a congregation of 200 sing, hears them respond continually to the sermon, and sees them move in religious excitement. He hears Black choruses outdoors, workers returning from the field to their cabins, and firemen on a steamboat. Among white Americans he notices that the pious disapprove "Negro songs" while the wordly are "attached" to them, perhaps especially to those of the "pseudo-Negroes" who "have now almost monopolized this industry in the North." Thus Busch's study of the thirteen songs rests on far more than hearsay.

He begins his chapter on the songs with a careful exposition of his purpose. He tries to clear away any presuppositions his readers may have about the African character. He proposes that to judge a people, a *Volk*, when it lacks historical records and works of litera-ture, its songs are "among the most important considerations and indicative of its inner attitude." He regrets that white Americans have produced no genuine *Volkslied*, despite the worthy poetry of Dana, Longfellow, and, especially, Bryant. He speculates that the Blacks may be providing the "indicative" songs for the whole American *Volk*, who find in these songs "far more pleasure than Jenny Lind, Ole Bull, and Fanny Elssler together." He mentions three of the minstrel companies, White's, Christy's, and Dumble-ton's, of which one branch may be found in every larger city. Naturally he does not trace the precedents for these groups back to the "Jim Crow" shows of the 1830s or to any earlier theatrical sources. Rather, he assumes that the minstrels have copied whatever is genuine from their Black models. What is genuine? He assumes that his own taste is a sufficient criterion. And this taste, though somehow affected by the sounds of fiddle and banjo, tambourine and bones, is directed mainly to the words of the songs.

In the sound and rhythm of "Susanna" Busch recognizes the polka, but he is more interested in the words. When the tune is used at Dunkirk, New York, for a long comic-fantastic narrative ballad designed to sell soap, Busch refers to the tune as a *"volkstümliche Negermelodie"* rather than a *Volkslied*. (*Volkstümlich* has not yet got an English equivalent, though "folkish" or, in the 1960s and '70s, simply "folk" may carry a similar meaning of the imitation in literate, urban groups of some form and spirit attributed to rural tradition.) Busch enjoys the commercial ballad enough to translate it complete, but he likes Foster's words better, supposing them to be genuinely Negro. He likes the wit. Seven of his thirteen songs are comical, like "Susanna." The rest illustrate three types: one is a hymn of battle and glory, heard at the Cincinnati church; two are narrative ballads connected with the execution of Gabriel Prosser, leader of a slave revolt at Richmond, Virginia, in 1800; three are songs of love or death, and here Foster's "Uncle Ned" turns up. For Busch, these thirteen song-texts show that Negroes have more intelligence, wit, courage, and sensitivity than some readers are ready to grant them. But despite this praise, he concludes his chapter with the provisional judgment that Negroes are inferior to people of European and Asian descent with respect to rationality, especially in religion. He does not attach his opinion to any argument for or against slavery; his detachment from that burning issue enables him to consider the broader issues of "race" coolly, and even to wonder for a moment whether America is eventually to be the scene of a thorough mixing of all the races of the world. The songs he judges to be both distinctively American and worthy of comparison with folksongs around the world.

Another European traveler, the facile writer Frederika Bremer of Stockholm, made similar judgments. Her mention of "Susanna" and "Uncle Ned" in her widely read book of informal letters, *The Homes of the New World*, 1853, has gone unnoticed by some readers who value her testimony about slave boatmen and worshippers. At Columbia, South Carolina, on May 25, 1850, she listens to a program sung for her and her hosts by a "young negro who was not so evangelical." His songs remind her

> . . . of Haydn's and Mozart's simple, naive melodies; for example, "Rosa Lee," "Oh, Susannah," "Dearest May," "Carry me back to old Virginny," "Uncle Ned," and "Mary Blane," all of which are full of the most touching pathos, both in words and melody.

Despite the pathos, Bremer is impressed with the fact that "there is no bitterness, no gloomy spirit in these songs." She supposes the songs all originated as

> improvisations, which have taken root in the mind of the people, and are listened to and sung by the whites, who, possessed of a knowledge of music, have caught and noted them down.

She regards both sacred and secular songs as "the only original people's songs which the New World possesses."

Bremer's enthusiasm, though less convincing than Busch's for lack of any questioning, still complements his observations. Her testimony reinforces the point that listeners for whom "folksong" was a familiar concept took "Susanna" and "Uncle Ned" seriously.

Nearly a century earlier the concept of folksong had been vastly enriched, if not originated or transformed, by Johann Gottfried Herder, who had proposed to find songs among German-speaking people that would help unite them into a nation-state. Such songs were worth more to them than any artificial, professional product rivaling the arts of France and Italy, gratifying the elite minority of Germans or their crude snobbish imitators in the cities. To rival not just the French and Italians but the ancient Hebrews and Greeks, all modern nations must draw on their own distinctive peasant traditions. Herder envisaged a worldwide exchange of genuine folksong, not merely a German liberation from foreign cultural hegemony. He admired the discoveries of English and Scottish antiquarians, particularly Thomas Percy, and even the fake-antiquity of James MacPherson, *Ossian*. But Herder was no antiquarian. Rather he was a prophet and educator, and his concept of folksong was directed to the future more than the past. His hope for German political unity was only partially fulfilled in 1871, and then hardly in the way Herder hoped for.

Herder's idea had inspired many kinds of activity in the generations between his own and that of Busch and Foster. From Herder, for example, Goethe had learned to appreciate Robert Burns. The brothers Grimm had devoted their lives to finding and publishing folktales. Hans Christian Andersen had invented convincing *volkstümliche Märchen*. The Romantic poets Brentano and Arnim had published the collection of song-texts, *Des Knaben Wunderhorn*. Erk and Irmer, 1838–45, had published the first big scholarly collection of melodies. Through schools, through journalism, through adaptations in professional music and verse, Herder's idea had now become accepted, almost taken for granted in Germany and Scandinavia.

An outstanding propagator of German ideas to the English-speaking world was Thomas Carlyle; before his *Sartor Resartus*, 1834, he had won some fame for his translations, and his *Essay on Burns* had won the praise of Goethe. In this essay Carlyle hailed the songs as Burns' best work, and hailed their emphasis on nationality as their greatest feature. Though Carlyle did not concern himself much with music, nor with America, he wrote two characteristic short articles that brought these subjects together. For the annual publication *Keepsake*, in 1852, he wrote on "The Opera," attributing his piece to "Professor Ezechiel Peasemeal, a distinguished American friend . . . crowned by the Phi Beta Kappa Society of Buncombe." For *Fraser's Magazine*, in 1849, Carlyle wrote, as the work of "Dr. Phelim McQuirk, absconded reporter, submitted by his respectable unfortunate landlady" an "Occasional Discourse on the Nigger Question," soon reprinted as a pamphlet with his own name. Part of this discourse is a reply to the inquiries of "the Honorable Hickory Buckskin, Senator of Carolina."

According to Carlyle, music testifies to the corruption and confusion of modern society. In the Italian opera he has heard at London,

> . . . the Modern Aristocracy of men brought the divinest of its Arts, heavenly Music itself; and, piling all the upholsteries and ingenuities that other human art could do, had lighted them into a bonfire to illuminate an hour's flirtation . . .

Much as he admires the talent and ingenuity of the leading singer, Carlyle deplores the song and its motive.

Wretched spiritual Nigger, O, if you *had* some genius, and were not a born Nigger with mere appetite for pumpkin, should you have endured such a lot?

In his peroration Carlyle qualifies his judgment momentarily, to prepare for his final thrusts.

Good sirs, surely I by no means expect the Opera will abolish itself this year or the next. But if you ask me, why heroes are not born now, why heroisms are not done now? I will answer you: It is a world all calculated for strangling heroisms. To its Hells of sweating tailors, distressed needle-women and the like, this Opera of yours is the appropriate Heaven!

If he had hoped, when he was younger, writing about Burns, that music could help reform society, no such hope survived his experience of opera. Needless to say, he was annoyed at every organ-grinder. When the organ-grinders played "Susanna," Carlyle must have been driven to fury. For the "Nigger Question" was another instance of the pervading social confusion. His discourse is a sarcastic attack on the glib self-righteous advocates of the abolition of slavery.

. . . You cannot abolish slavery by an act of parliament, but can only abolish the *name* of it, which is very little! . . . To save men's bodies, and fill them with pumpkins and rum, is a poor task for human benevolence, if you have to kill their soul, what soul there was, in the business!

Carlyle defends American slavery, conditionally. He provokes its opponents, charging them with hypocrisy; he reminds them of the "sweating tailors" and "distressed needlewomen" in their own cities, and more vigorously he reminds the English liberals of Ireland. Their recent parliamentary victory—the legal, verbal abolition of all British slavery—he predicts will prove "to have 'emancipated' the West Indies into a *Black* Ireland." His argument, despite its subtlety and penetration, never specifies what he means by "Black" or "Negro" or "Nigger." He personifies an undefined group with a resourceful, musical type.

Do I, then, hate the Negro? No; except when the soul is killed out of him. . . . A swift, supple fellow, a merry-hearted, grinning, dancing, singing, affectionate kind of creature, with a great deal of melody and amenability in his composition. This certainly is a notable fact: The black African, alone of wild men, can live among men civilized. While all manner of Caribs and others pine into annihilation in presence of the pale faces, he contrives to continue; does not die of rage, of rum, of brutish laziness and darkness, and fated incompatibility with his new place.

Among the necessary conditions Carlyle prescribes for just slavery is a nationwide law whereby any individual can earn his freedom for a set sum. His typical "Nigger" will prefer the permanent contract with his master. Men who choose freedom and its risks are no "Niggers." But what might happen to the free Black's music and dance? Carlyle does not say. He does not claim complete wisdom. But he insists on a further question, which is implicit in the songs of Foster:

> What are the true relations between Negro and White, their mutual duties under the sight of the Maker of them both; what human laws will assist both to comply more and more with these? . . . the solution is perhaps still distant . . . this of declaring that Negro and White are unrelated, loose from one another, on a footing of perfect equality, and subject to no law but that of supply and demand according to the Dismal Science; this, which contradicts the palpablest facts, is clearly no solution.

Carlyle's discourse so shocked and appalled his American friends like Emerson and Whittier that they could not bring their intelligence and generous feeling to bear on the hardest questions. Whitman and Melville, a bit removed, and younger, took them to heart. While Foster himself was probably unaware of Carlyle's ideas, those ideas affected the reception of his songs by his contemporaries and for many generations later.

The authority of Carlyle may have emboldened some men like Charles Mackay to express their less rational and less sympathetic opinions more casually. Mackay had often been invited to America. When he came at last in 1857–58, he was lionized, for he was editor of the *Illustrated News,* as well as author of popular songs. On his return to England he published his sketches of *Life and Liberty in America,* including the concise and unqualified statement that the United States

> . . . have as yet done nothing in music. England, erroneously and stupidly said to be a non-musical country until Mr. Chappell, in his painstaking and highly valuable work, "The popular music of the olden time," knocked the absurdity on the head and killed it forever, seems to have transmitted no portion of her musical genius to her children in America. . . . The airs called "negro melodies," concocted for the most part in New York, . . . [are] rifacimenti of old English, Scotch, and Irish melodies altered in time and character.

Mackay did not bother to specify what the alterations were. His statement, however, carried for some readers more authority than Carlyle's questions. Whereas Carlyle perhaps never came to Foster's attention, Mackay did, as we know, and his expression of contempt probably hurt. In any case, Foster was familiar with this contempt from various sources throughout his life.

William Cullen Bryant, as editor of the New York *Evening Post* and author of slim volumes of poetry respected everywhere, was known to Foster at least by name. In 1850 Bryant published an essay based on his diary of "A Tour in the Old South" that he made in 1843. It formed a chapter in the volume of *Letters of a Traveller*. In this essay he describes four songs and their singers, with extraordinary precision. Neither here nor elsewhere does he venture any explicit opinions in answer to the generalized questions about "Negro music." On immediate political issues, as they arose, he came forward with firm opinions, moving eventually from the Free-Soil wing of the Democratic Party to the new Republican Party of 1856; Foster probably followed Bryant's moves closely in 1850–53, though in '56 he stuck with his brother Morrison in supporting Buchanan. If Foster looked into Bryant's *Letters* he must have read the "Tour in the Old South" with special interest and noted the reference to "John Crow" instead of "Jim Crow," and "Dan, de Dandy" rather than "Susanna." At Richmond, in 1843, Bryant visited a tobacco factory, where the Black workers often sang Baptist hymns, sometimes all day long. In his report he notes that they "work better while singing" and that "they must sing wholly of their own accord, it is of no use to bid them do it." Bryant learns, on inquiring of his guides, that most of the workers are members of a Baptist church—the "best choir in all Richmond, I heard somebody say." (Mixed with them are a few Methodists; Methodist music was more famous than Baptist to readers who might be Unitarian or Episcopalian.) A few weeks later, in the Barnwell District of South Carolina, Bryant records the texts of two "corn-shucking" songs and a "monkey-song, probably African," and he describes the dances that followed, in the kitchen, with accompaniment by a man beating two sticks on the floor. On both occasions, Bryant makes clear his respectful interest in his subject. He assumes that his readers will respect his objective report, no matter how they may interpret its meaning. His guess that a particular song has come from Africa is an extremely rare testimony from the period. His publication of such a guess in 1850 is more remarkable than it would have been in 1843. All these features of his report make its brevity tantalizing—anyone interested in music must wish that Bryant had reported on it more often and at length. But his only other essay about music indicates that he could never have found much time for it. He writes, in 1856, to support "Music in the Public Schools" as an innocent relaxation from serious academic work: "A tune," he argues, "is certainly better than a cigar." If he knew that some teachers by 1856 were using Foster tunes, presumably Bryant had no objection. He was not, like the younger New England poets, concerned to uplift taste or forge a national unity through music.

Among his contemporaries in New England, the poet and critic whose views Foster could hardly have escaped was the witty James Russell Lowell. The second number of Lowell's *Biglow Papers*, purporting to be a letter from Mexico by Private Birdofredum Sawin to his family in a Massachusetts village, was typical of Lowell's best work; both its timely subject and its novel style must have attracted Foster when it appeared in Cincinnati reprints.

> . . . Afore I come away from hum I hed a strong persuasion
> Thet Mexicans worn't human beans,—an ourangoutang nation,
> A sort o' folks a chap could kill an' never dream on't arter,
> No more'n a feller'd dream o' pigs that he hed hed to slarter.
> I'd an idee thet they were built arter the darkie fashion all,
> An' kickin' colored folks about, you know, 's a kind o' national;
> But wen I jined I worn't so wise ez thet air queen o' Sheby,
> Fer come to look at 'em, they ain't much diff'rent from wut we be,
> An' here we air ascourgin' 'em out o' thir own dominions,
> Ashelterin' 'em, ez Caleb sez, under our eagle's pinions. . . .
> Wal, it doos seem a curus way, but then hooraw fer Jackson!
> It must be right, fer Caleb sez, it's reg'lar Anglo-saxon. . . .
> Thet our nation's bigger'n theirn an' so its rights air bigger,
> An' thet it's all to make 'em free thet we air pullin' trigger,
> Thet Anglo-Saxondom's idee's abreakin' 'em to pieces,
> An' thet idee's thet every man doos jest wut he damn pleases;
> Ef I don't make his meanin' clear, perhaps in some respex I can,
> I know thet 'every man' don't mean a nigger or a Mexican.

Lowell's irony, gentler and funnier than Carlyle's, was not so prominent when he discussed music, as he did on many occasions. In 1843, before he was famous, he wrote on "Song Writing" for the ambitious new magazine that he edited, *The Pioneer*. If Foster read this, he may have found in it the definition of the career he wished to follow:

> The song-writer must take his place somewhere between the poet and the musician, and must form a distinct class by himself. . . . His words bring solace to the lowest ranks of men. . . . Perhaps the mission of the song-writer may herein be deemed loftier and diviner than any other.

Lowell shows his acquaintance with the ideas of Herder when he begins this essay by characterizing "the songs of a nation" as "wild flowers pressed, as it were, by chance, between the blood-stained pages of a history." He refers, of course, to Burns as the greatest songwriter of recent times, rooted in the wild songs of his own nation.

The possible connection between "national song" and "the niggers" claimed Lowell's attention in "The Power of Sound, a Rhymed Lecture," delivered in 1857 (not printed until 1896, and then only privately). Here, after treating traditional topics of music in the

Bible and in Greek mythology, he undertakes a history of music in America, with appropriate lines on the 16th-century psalm-tune "Old Hundred," on Burns and Moore, on "Yankee Doodle," Handel and Haydn, Beethoven, and Italian opera. Then be bursts out:

> But have we nothing that is wholly ours?
> No songs commensurate with our growing powers?
> Answer, whose ears have felt the torturing blows
> Of lays like "Jump Jim Crow" or "Coal-black Rose,"
> The pioneers, from nightly lampblacked jaws,
> Of all those tunes that set our teeth like saws!
> Answer, ye patient victims, doomed to hear
> The white man's Ethiop doggerel by the year. . . .
>   Music, thou keystone of Creation's arch . . .
> What a descent to banjo strains like these!
> No sin more base than thus to vulgarize
> The Arts, which, rightly used, make great and wise. . . .
> These to degrade, through want of thought or pelf,
> Is to debase the coin of God himself!
> But I am preaching: ah me! what's the use,
> Not they who teach please most, but who amuse.

Lowell's accurate reference to the "pioneer" tunes makes his indignation about the whole "Ethiopian business" very different from Mackay's mere contempt. Though Foster could hardly have read these lines of Lowell, he probably encountered more than once the opinions to which they give an almost classic expression. Not quite classic, to be sure, for Lowell's lines sag with the weakness that he confessed, characteristically, in his *Fable for Critics:*

> There is Lowell, who's striving Parnassus to climb
> With a whole bale of *isms* tied together with rhyme. . . .
> The top of the hill he will ne'er come nigh reaching
> Till he learns the distinction 'twixt singing and preaching;
> His lyre has some chords that would ring pretty well,
> But he'd rather by half make a drum of the shell,
> And rattle away till he's old as Methusalem,
> At the head of a march to the last new Jerusalem.

Lowell's statements assembled here are valuable not merely as representing an attitude, but also as showing the development of opinion from 1843 to 1857, from grand fresh hope for popular national song, through struggle and irony, to a brittle bitterness. Lowell was by no means the only man whose views changed in just this way. His hope was part of a remarkable wave of musical progress in Boston; his bitterness was part of the national drift to war. His attitude toward the "nigger minstrels" was incidental to the broader movement of thought.

John Greenleaf Whittier's "isms" were more famous in 1850 than his love of music. Quakerism allowed no music in worship. Abolitionism filled his verses with "Duty's rugged march through storm and strife," at the cost of "mystic beauty, dreamy grace," as he apologized in his "Proem," 1847. Moreover, invalidism kept him from traveling to hear the music of the Blacks, which he admired from a distance and imitated in several poems, climaxing with the one called "At Port Royal, 1861," whose central four stanzas are the "Song of the Negro Boatmen." Whittier's masterpiece, "Snowbound," was not to come until 1866, a fulfillment of lifelong emulation of Burns, whose "Cotter's Saturday Night" no one else could rival so well. If around 1850 Whittier heard the Hutchinson family's version of "Susanna" or "Uncle Ned," he may not have recognized its theatrical associations. If Foster read Whittier—as his abolitionist friend Charles Shiras must have recommended—Foster may not have recognized any common ground. Whittier can represent for us an attitude that Foster knew, among some of his ablest and most earnest neighbors, for whom songs like "Susanna" were beneath the indignant notice of a Lowell or even the contempt of a Mackay.

One of Boston's Congressmen in 1850, on leave from his post as treasurer of Harvard College (1842–53), was Samuel Atkins Eliot, father of the future Harvard president Charles William Eliot, and, according to Daniel Webster, "the impersonation of Boston." Samuel Eliot in his thirties had been the chief founder and first president of the Academy of Music and had delivered a memorable address at the opening of the Odeon, 1835, in which he almost officially set aside the Puritans' "slight tinge of cruelty" toward the arts; modern enlightenment could guard against "the dangerous attractions of the theatre, or the bacchanalian festivity" and foster pure music in concerts, schools, and homes. In 1837, when he was mayor of Boston, Eliot found time to lead the choir at King's Chapel. In 1841 he contributed to the *North American* magazine an article on "Music in America" that Lowell and Whittier doubtless knew and applauded, and which perhaps encouraged Foster too.

> A great revolution in the musical character of the American people has begun, and is, we trust, to go forward, like other revolutions, until its ultimate object be attained.

Eliot's "revolution" was beginning in schools and homes, not in theaters. His trust, if he maintained it until he died in 1862, would have to contend with complications he did not foresee in 1841. His later musical interests kept up with those of his protégés Lowell Mason and John Sullivan Dwight, who worked at a process too slow and laborious to be called a "revolution." Eliot was also a chief patron of the Black Methodist preacher Josiah Henson; in 1849 Eliot took dictation from Henson to write the story of his marvellous life as slave, as overseer, as earner of his own freedom and kidnapper of his wife and children, and at last as leader of the Black community in Colchester and Camden, Ontario. Then Eliot helped Father Henson sell his black walnut lumber to the piano maker Jonas Chickering and take a sample of it to London where he was the only Black exhibitor at the Crystal Palace, "though there were negroes from Africa brought to be exhibited." Henson's accolades from Queen Victoria and Prime Minister Lord Russell probably brought Eliot's name to Foster's attention.

A younger Harvard man, Henry R. Cleveland, wrote on "National Music" in the *North American*, 1840, in a way that makes the high hopes of those years in Boston seem closer to Foster. When Cleveland died, in 1842, only thirty-four years old, his essay was published with other writings in a little book; then it was reprinted in various magazines up to 1853, so that Foster may have read it more than once. Cleveland, in contrast to Mackay, insists that there is no true "national music" in England to compare with that of Scotland or Germany. He analyzes the reasons for the lack: England's greater division of labor, greater emphasis on commerce, greater dependence on importations of many kinds. He sees a better chance for national music

> . . . in a country where the laborers sing at their toil, or join in chorus as they return from the fields, than in that which devotes millions to the building of opera-houses, and the importation of performers.

He sees the quest for an American national music as difficult:

> We have received nothing of this kind from England and we shall bequeath nothing to our posterity; unless a future age shall be polite enough to dignify the great national airs of *Yankee Doodle* and *Hail Columbia* with the title of traditionary music. . . . American music, if it ever exists in the true sense of the word, must be as various, as copious, and as comprehensive, as the character of the people growing up under such widely differing influences. . . . There is more hope, far more hope, that a national music will grow out of the rude but fervent hymns, with which the overflowing congregations of the Wesleyan Methodists rend the heavens, than that it will ever be reared by the opera, or the costly concerts of the nobility.
>
> In America, music must be in a considerable degree popular. . . . Music in America must be surrendered to the people, must be domiciled among them, must grow up among them, or it cannot exist at all.

Cleveland's "surrender" is not so different, however, from Eliot's "revolution." For he continues:

> . . . Music must be made popular, not by debasing the art, but by elevating the people.

Like Eliot, Cleveland looks to churches, schools, and homes (not theaters) to fulfill his hope. But Cleveland never mentions the "dangerous attractions of the theatre" and if Foster read his essay he might easily suppose that even theaters could contribute to "elevating the people."

The hopes of Lowell, Eliot, and Cleveland met derision in 1845 from a New Hampshire writer, J. Kennard, Jr., in the *Knickerbocker Magazine;* he asks in his title, "Who Are Our National Poets?" He answers his own question:

> the Jim Crows, the Zip Coons, and Dandy Jims, who have electrified the world. From them proceed our ONLY TRULY NATIONAL POETS.

Bryant, Halleck, and Longfellow he has dismissed as "too universal." They are neither distinctive nor popular as Burns is both. He proceeds to condemn

> . . . those miserable counterfeits, "Lucy Long," and "Old Dan Tucker," [which] have secured a large share of favor, on the supposition that they were genuine negro songs. With the music, no great fault can be found; that may be pure negro, though some people declare it to be Italian. Be that as it may, the words are far beneath the genius of our American poets.

The words from the 1830s—"Jim Crow" perhaps above all—are what Kennard proposes as characteristically American.

> *African* melodists! As well might the Hutchinsons call themselves *English* melodists . . . They are *American* melodists, *par excellence*. Is not Sambo the incarnation of the taste, intellect, and heart of America, the ladies being the judge? Do not shrink from the answer, most beautiful, accomplished, delicate and refined lady-reader! You cannot hold yourself above him, for you imitate him.

The relation between words and music, with dance also an essential component, Kennard finds distinctive in the genuine "negro song."

> The blacks themselves leave out old stanzas and introduce new ones at pleasure. . . . Elasticity of form is peculiar to the negro song.

His study of the subject has clearly gone farther than most of his contemporaries' study, though no farther than that of Moritz Busch a few years later. And in contrast to Busch's, Kennard's study is no open-minded inquiry but a polemical use of the idea of "national song" for a motive that remains obscure. His conclusion is that since "the national poet" in every country remains anonymous in his lowly working life, "America asks praise for bringing him up, with infinite pains, in the only way in which a true poet should go." This veiled excuse for slavery indicates that if Kennard lived to read Lowell or Whittier a year or two after his essay, their antislavery passion probably blinded him to their lyrical mastery.

All these thinkers and writers, despite their individual differences, contributed to shaping a climate of opinion in which "Susanna" could become a folksong.

Much more was contributed to the gradually prevailing climate for American music by a specialist in music criticism, a constant reader of German poetry and thought, a translator of the musical writings of Heinrich Heine—the Bostonian J. S. Dwight.

John Sullivan Dwight graduated from Harvard in 1832, barely nineteen years old. In 1852, at thirty-nine, he founded his *Journal of Music,* which he edited until 1881. His writings in various magazines before the *Journal* and in its first few volumes naturally show more of a comprehensive developing thought about music than the essays of Lowell, Eliot, Cleveland, and Kennard, all of which Dwight must have studied thoroughly, together with much German writing on music, much German poetry, and everything of Emerson and his friend Thoreau. The young man recorded his Transcendental thoughts "On Music" in 1835, in a manuscript, and in 1841 he began to publish them. Music, he affirmed, was the "natural language" of all impulses toward the harmony of the human race. Music at its grandest height, in the symphonies of Beethoven, was at the center of a worldwide movement for freedom and brotherhood, in which America was or ought to be leading the way; therefore to perform Beethoven decently in America was the most urgent work, and to spread the gospel of Beethoven through interpretive essays, reviews, and critiques was Dwight's vocation, calling him away from the Unitarian ministry in which he served for a few years. In 1843, after a season with Thoreau at the Transcendentalists' "Brook Farm" community, Dwight became a full-time musical journalist: he reported on Beethoven's Second and Fifth Symphonies in Lowell's journal, *The Pioneer.* In 1845 he began regular contributions to the new Transcendentalist journal, *The Harbinger,* and here the next year he reported on the first American performance of Beethoven's Ninth, in New York.

Seeing that the *serious* occupations of our nation are so damnable; that the so called earnest business of politicians and rulers is altogether worse than idle, since it is neither more nor less than the business of establishing the supremacy of the bad passions among men (whatever paradoxes may be held up, about "conquering peace"); seeing too that all this war is only the ultimate cutaneous eruption of a strife continually raging in the veins of a competitive commercial society, which dignifies its paper warfare by the name of *"business,"* we confess to a certain pride in giving ourselves to what these self-styled serious people may deem "lighter matters." . . . the music understood all that, and in its way was solving the same problem bearing up the weight of a world-wide sympathetic sadness, on its waves of an indomitable wise faith.

Dwight surveyed all kinds of musical activity and judged it by the criterion of Beethoven's Ninth: opera, church music, school music, and every kind of popular music he measured by this standard—not a merely technical one but also a Transcendental one. In 1846 Dwight looked at the efforts of Lowell Mason in churches and schools as a subordinate channel for the "deepening, purifying, and blending influence to our national character."

In 1851 he took note of the "minstrels". Now writing a regular column for the fashionable *Sartain's Magazine,* he included a parenthesis in the midst of his account of Boston's concert season:

(Of course there has been no lack, at the same time, of "music for the million." The simple, and often truly beautiful melodies of "negro Minstrels," "Harmoneans," "Aeoleans," &c.—which shun the *artificial* on the side of nature, as the classic music shuns it on the side of art, and therefore are a part of our genuine musical growth,—have always had their audiences.)

He concludes this report with a sense of encouragement "to those who long to have Americans become a musical people." In 1852, now writing in his own *Journal,* Dwight protested the use of both "negro melodies" and operatic airs by the military bands on parade. He would have preferred simple old-fashioned fife-and-drum marches, if the recently expanded and diversified corps of bandsmen could have been content to play them; "It is a pity that our bands should lose in the character of the music which they play, what they have gained in skill of playing." A few weeks later he is complaining that the good old songs of Tom Moore

. . . have been almost supplanted and made obsolete by the fashionable airs of Italian opera, by the romantic German songs, and by the popular "Negro melodies."

But still in 1852, he prints in the *Journal* a report from Alexander Wheelock Thayer, rusticating in a New England village:

. . . What magnificent basses and tenors may be heard among our firemen, when making merry together and singing "Uncle Ned," "Old Dan Tucker," or "Lovely May!" There is real feeling in some of these songs.

In 1853 Dwight prints news about the "Negro melodies" from an anonymous teacher who has spent two years in Georgia:

Although first published at the North, you know nothing of the power and pathos given them here. The whites first learn them—the negroes catch the air and words from once hearing, after which wood and fields resound with their strains—the whites catch the expression from these sable minstrels—thus Negro Melodies have an effect here not dreamed of at the north. . . .

An old favorite of all is said to be "Home, Sweet Home." Then:

"Old folks at home," as I hear it shouted from house to house, from the fields and in the vallies, has an effect scarcely inferior. I find myself often humming the chorus. . . . This has little to do with musical education in the main, but much in effect. A thing that speaks so to the heart is hard to be reasoned down. . . . Beethoven's sonatas are not entirely unknown here, but I confess they are by no means daily companions.

By 1853 Dwight is resisting the fashion:

. . . We are glad to see that our City fathers are taking action with regard to music on the Common and Copps Hill this summer. Only let it be *music,* and not the "Oh Susanna" sort of jingle. Let it refine and educate the millions, and not merely tickle up the idle old whistling, drumming, foot-lifting habit, which is a mere chronic irritation of the rhythmic nerves.

When he hears the "jingles" invade the concert room, he is not amused:

. . . Strakosch, the "unrivalled pianist," played banjo tunes and "Old Folks at Home," with extraordinary variations, naturally followed by vollies of senseless hand-clapping.

But Dwight's most severe reprimands go to indigenous types of music business:

. . . the namby-pamby song and psalm-book making, the ceaseless publication of vile "variations" and "arrangements," and much of the teaching and "professorizing" . . .

Dwight rails on:

Your sharp-set, speculating Yankee is as ready to profess fine arts as scissors-grinding, if there be money to be made by it; and our goodly land is overrun by musical "professors," who are simply peddling speculators. . . . The market-brawl and tumult of this music *trade* must be swept away, before the sweet, sincere tones of the heavenly Cecilia can become appreciable to the general ear.

He persists in his hope for a democratic music:

. . . humanity is all in motion, with a quicker *tempo,* and a vaster field and object than ever before. . . . In proportion to this incalculable amount of new movement of Humanity, shall be, must be, the out-gush of a new musical inspiration, the up-heaval of new and mightier than Handelian mountain-chains of sublime works of musical Art, here, in this practical, utilitarian, unaesthetic world.

Now, at a band concert, he is willing to tolerate some proportion of vulgarity in the hope that a Mozart minuet on the program is gradually elevating individual tastes:

> Of course, the quicksteps and the Ethiopians elicited most clapping, because addressed most to the *clapping classes,* who must not always be taken as the thermometer of the whole musical audience. . . . No one can reasonably complain of the light and humdrum pieces, so long as there is a fair sampling of what is good.

But at the concert of Jullien's orchestra, Dwight cannot excuse the mixture. He blames the solo singer:

> . . . Anna Zerr, who (shame to say) stopped to pick up one night and sing "Old Folks at Home," for the b'hoys; one would as soon think of picking up an apple-core in the street.

Poor Dwight! This bit of vivid writing has been turned against him by many admirers of Foster. In the context provided here, it does not impugn Dwight's democratic faith. A few weeks after Anna Zerr, it is Louis Gottschalk who puts Dwight's faith to the test with a medley of "American Reminiscences." Gottschalk has won applause, says Dwight, by

> . . . allusions to "Old Folks at Home," and then by that homely tune, (which seems to be a sort of catching, melodic *itch* of the times) fully developed, and then varied in divers difficult and astounding ways. Also "O [sic] Susanna (if we remember rightly) in the same fashion . . . to see an artist so little in earnest with his Art and to find the dilettant public still so ready to extol as Art what properly is little more than sleight of hand!

Dwight's objection is not to the "itchy" tune itself, but to the bogus pretensions of "artiste" and "refined" audience. When Jullien, at another concert the same season, plays his "American Quadrille," based on "Yankee Doodle," Dwight is carried away with the whole audience in spite of his scruples:

> This is making a colossal toy of the orchestra, as we have said! but the effect is most ingeniously and most triumphantly managed.

When he hears Gottschalk once more, he proceeds to meditate on this exemplification of national character:

> We Yankees are said to be the most go-aheaditive, curious, ingenious people on earth, and so we must needs produce a pianist that can play the fastest, the most ingeniously, the most wonderfully of any that ever

lived; who leaves a world of beauty and sublimity in the background, while he pinches, torments, and pulls the hair of the "Old Folks at Home," and plays "puss in the corner" with "Oh! Susanna."

Though Dwight never deigns to analyze or applaud "Susanna" as he does "Yankee Doodle," he has learned, we may note, Foster's own spelling and punctuation.

By 1855 Dwight has another characterization of Americans in relation to "Popular Amusements":

> We are an anxious people, uncomfortably demonized and ridden, night-mare-like, by that which gives us power.

Therefore he does not wish to censor programs:

> Privation is not temperance. Prohibition may be even as great an evil as intemperance.

So, when the touring virtuoso pianist Sigismond Thalberg, in 1857, plays "Susanna" on the banjo, Dwight merely notes the fact. And when Dwight makes his first trip to Europe, in 1860, "Susanna" on the streets of Southampton only bemuses him:

> The strangest thing about it was to hear familiar Ethiopian melodies.

In later years he still occasionally refers to his high hopes; he mutes them but never gives them up:

> We, as a democratic people, a great mixed people of *all* races, overrunning a vast continent, need music even more than others.

This reference sounds a bit wistful in the *Atlantic Monthly* of 1870, where Dwight's subject is "Music as a Means of Culture." The autumnal essay ends by recommending music as the panacea for loneliness. Dwight's taste has been challenged by Wagner, bolstered by Brahms, baffled by America. About Foster's tunes he has no more to say.

Throughout the years of his *Journal* Dwight must have missed his Brook Farm friend Margaret Fuller, who died in 1850, for she was the most articulate music critic among the Transcendentalists next to Dwight himself. In 1842, reviewing "Entertainments of the Past Winter" in *The Dial*, Fuller discussed "national music" as well as opera, oratorio, ballet, and the Beethoven symphonies II and V. By way of introduction, she identified "the lecture" as "the only entertainment we have truly expressive of New England *as it is* in its transition state." Then she came to the popular song:

> Our only national melody, *Yankee Doodle*, is shrewdly suggested to be a scion from British art. All symptoms of invention are confined to the African race, who, like the German literati, are relieved by their position

from the cares of government. "Jump Jim Crow," is a dance native to this country, and one which we plead guilty to seeing with pleasure, not on the stage, where we have not seen it, but as danced by children of an ebon hue in the street. Such of the African melodies as we have heard are beautiful. But the Caucasian race have yet their railroads to make. . . .

If Margaret Fuller had lived to take account of "Susanna," the cause of "American music" might have advanced more swiftly than Dwight saw it advance.

But neither Dwight nor Fuller could have satisfied the Transcendental yearning for music of their friend Henry David Thoreau. No doubt he advised them both to learn to play the flute, as he did, and to forget the newspapers and magazines, if not the concerts as well. In 1851 he wrote in his *Journal:*

> One will lose no music by not attending the oratorios and operas. . . . All Vienna cannot serve me more than the Italian boy who seeks my door with his organ.

And in 1853:

> Many an irksome sound in our neighborhood, go a long distance off, is heard as music and a proud sweet satire on the meanness of our life. Not a music to dance to, but to live by.

Thoreau's thoughts on music pervade his *Journal* all through the 1840s and '50s, rarely with any concrete reference to a particular piece of music or style, but never with mere cliché. Some of his thoughts will be useful when we come to Foster's "Old Folks at Home." The organ grinder is his closest link with "Susanna."

Thomas Wentworth Higginson was a friend of all these New England neighbors. He was especially close to Lowell in 1842, to Whittier in 1848, to Thoreau in 1858. He was storing up experience that would make him ready, in 1863, to help "discover" and, in 1867, to name the repertory of songs at Port Royal "Negro spirituals."

If any of the New Englanders had been asked about Stephen Foster, no song would have come to mind. They were all more or less cautious friends of Higginson's neighbor Stephen Symonds Foster, the most devoted uncompromising activist of the age, along with his wife Abby Kelley. These Fosters attacked Northern prejudice and especially church collusion with slavery more fanatically than they opposed Southern policy. S. S. Foster's book of 1843, *The Brotherhood of Thieves: or, A True Picture of the American Church and Clergy*, spread his notoriety across the nation. In 1846 and 1847 he lectured at Oberlin. In 1850 his lectures stressed the prostitution of slave women by their masters. By 1855 he proclaimed *Revolution the Only Remedy for Slavery*. In 1863 he led the demand for equal pay for Black troops. Throughout these years he often shared platforms with the Hutchinson Family singers; doubtless he heard "Susanna"; but, as far as his biographers can tell, he may have been tone-deaf. On the other hand, Stephen Collins Foster surely knew the reputation of Stephen Symonds Foster. The coincidence of their names must have worried S. C. Foster, his family, and the family of his bride in 1850; might he not need a pseudonym to avoid confusion and make his own career? Or was he doomed a victim of the rampant, desperate confusion about Blacks in American life and American arts?

No New Englander was more earnest in the search for "national song" than the Brooklyn poet Walt Whitman, whose *Leaves of Grass* appeared in its first edition in 1855 when he was thirty-six. Whitman's searching, through the preceding decade, led him from the antislavery songs of the Hutchinsons, through a gradual development of enormous enthusiasm for Italian opera, to his characteristic eclectic appreciation of the whole world's music and his subordination of music to language, of song to the seminal truth of "The Answerer," "the poet." Along the way he referred to "negro singing" several times. In 1845, for the *Broadway Journal*, Whitman wrote an article on "Art Singing and Heart Singing," exalting the Hutchinsons at the expense of artificial imported operas; he affirmed the principle that Herder, Carlyle, and the Transcendentalists had advocated:

> The subtlest spirit of a nation is expressed through its music—and the music acts reciprocally on the nation's very soul.

In January 1846, in the Brooklyn *Evening Star*, Whitman reports on a similar singing group, the Harmoneons, under the heading "True American Singing":

> . . . their Ethiopian singing is wonderfully pure, if we may apply that word, and less exceptionable than any we ever heard before. . . . Indeed, their negro singing altogether proves how shiningly golden talent can be spread over a subject generally considered "low." "Nigger" singing with them is a subject from obscure life in the hands of a divine painter: rags, patches and coarseness are imbued with the genius of the artist. . . .

Whitman's friends, in these years, often heard him sing the "Ethiopian" tunes, according to the researches of Joseph Rubin. But his taste expanded and changed steadily.

Through 1846 and 1847 Whitman's reports for the *Star* and the Brooklyn *Eagle* are full of praise for every musical exercise in the public schools, the Sunday Schools, the Blind Asylum, and the Orphan Asylum. He is thrilled by the thousand-voiced children's choirs assembled by William Bradbury to sing hymns, anthems, and simple cantatas. He still finds a professional performance of Mendelssohn's *Elijah* "too heavy," but now, in 1847, he is swayed by Rossini's *Barber;* in 1851 Donizetti's *Favorita* and by 1853 Verdi's *Rigoletto* and all the other operas he hears inspire rapture to which he will testify in many poems and in his autobiographical *Specimen Days.* In 1848 he recognizes "Old Dan Tucker" on the streets of New Orleans. In 1850, back in Brooklyn, he buys a guitar, a melodeon, and a piano. In 1851 he writes in the New York *Evening Post* about two paintings—one of a boy with a flute, by Walter Libbey, that he prefers to the one of a Long Island Negro with a goose, by William Sidney Mount:

> Mount's negro may be said to have a character of Americanism, too; but I must be pardoned for saying, that I never could, and never will, admire the exemplifying of our national attributes with Ethiopian minstrelsy . . .

In a manuscript fragment of about 1852 he tries to bring his musical ideas together:

> American Opera.—put three banjos (or more?) in the orchestra. . . .

A paragraph in the *American Primer* that Whitman brought to a state near completion in 1855 expands on the idea of the future American opera:

> The nigger dialect furnishes hundreds of outré words, many of them adopted into the common speech of the mass of the people.—Curiously, these words show the old English instinct for wide open pronunciations, as *yallah* for yellow— *massah* for master—and for rounding off all the corners of words. The nigger dialect has hints of the future theory of the modification of all the words of the English language, for musical purposes, for a native grand opera in America, leaving the words just as they are for writing and speaking, but the same words so modified as to answer for musical purposes, on grand and simple principles.—Then we should have two sets of words, male and female as they should be, in these states, both equally understood by the people, giving a fit much-needed medium to that passion for music, which is deeper and purer in America than in any other land in the world.—The music of America is to adopt the Italian method, and expand it to vaster, simpler, far superber effects.—It is not to be satisfied till it comprehends the people and is comprehended by them.

A manuscript of 1855 shows that he has abandoned this touching amateurish project, to find more objective, historical relations among the kinds of music he loves:

> The English opera, the tunes of the ballads, &c. sung by the various bands of "minstrels," and indeed all modern musical performances and compositions are, to all intents and purposes, but driblets from Italian music. —True there are bequeathed to us, from other quarters, some fresh and

original tunes, as the native songs of Scotland, Ireland, and one or two other lands.

With this insight, Whitman is free to make his own poetic use of allusions to music that he has perhaps only read about, from all times and places. In his long "Salut au Monde," as it appears in editions of *Leaves* from 1856 to 1876, a catalogue of musics includes

> . . . the Virginia plantation chorus of negroes of a harvest night, in the glare of pineknots. I heard the strong baritone of the 'long-shoremen of Manahatta—I hear the stevedores unlading the cargoes, and singing.

(These lines are cut out in the final version of the poem, to make clearer the relation between America and the other continents, which is the poem's theme.) What Whitman learned from the "Ethiopian minstrels" has been transmuted into his kind of truth. Again, in "Our Old Feuillage," 1860, a few lines put the banjo in its true place:

> On rivers boatmen safely moor'd . . .
> Some of the younger men dance to the sound of the banjo or fiddle.

When at last, in 1865, Whitman makes music the theme of a major poem, "Proud Music of the Storm," he omits banjos and Black singers. But the understanding of this poem by a 20th-century reader can benefit from having traced the poet's development in relation to the most popular songs of his youth. And a 20th-century picture of Stephen C. Foster can be sharpened by reference to the all-embracing figure of Whitman in the background.

The fiction of Herman Melville, Whitman's exact contemporary, uses music like Foster's in ways characteristic of Melville's subtle and powerful mind, ways that touch all the troubling questions raised by this music. In Melville's masterpiece, *Moby Dick* (1851), the character of Pip, the Black cabin boy, ends the exciting chapter on "The Doubloon" with a minstrel song, "Jenny Git Yer Hoe-cake," which perfectly symbolizes Pip's perspective on the lurid events of the plot. In two novels just before *Moby Dick* and two short stories soon after, Melville speaks more explicitly about our questions. *Redburn*, of 1849, has a chapter devoted to the young organ grinder, Carlo, who plays

> sad airs to the merry, and merry airs to the sad; and most always the rich best fancy the sad airs, and the poor best fancy the merry.

The author-narrator, enchanted by Carlo's grace, reflects:

> There is no humble thing with music in it, not a fife, not a negro-fiddle, that is not to be reverenced as much as the grandest architectural organ.

Whitejacket, of 1850, develops almost a subplot devoted to the

ship's cook, Old Coffee, and "his assistants, negroes also," called
Sunshine, Rose-water, and May-day, like a whole minstrel band.
Sunshine is chief singer. Rose-water and May-day are contrasting
types—Rose-water slim and pale, May-day brawny and proudly
black. The narrator borrows a songbook from Rose-water: Moore's
Loves of the Angels. He borrows from an old sheet-anchor-man
(white) a "Negro Song-book, containing Sittin' on a Rail, Gumbo
Squash, and Jim Along Josey." Then he explains, with multiple
layers of irony:

> The sad taste of this old tar, in admiring such vulgar stuff, was much
> denounced by Rose-water, whose own predilections were of a more
> elegant nature, as evinced by his exalted opinion of the literary merits of
> the "Loves of the Angels."

But Rose-water, by Melville's further irony, becomes a sympathetic
hero; the ship's captain requires him to put on a display of head-
bumping with his tough colleague May-day; he endures his regular
defeats without complaint until

> May-day confidentially told Rose-water that he considered him a"*nigger*,"
> which, among some blacks, is held a great term of reproach.

Rose-water resents the insult and fights back; the captain punishes
the fighting, but tempers his punishment in order to be able to resume the show-fights; at this, Rose-water is insulted more than by
May-day's epithet, not to mention the original head-bumping:

> Of all insults, the temporary condescension of a master to a slave is the
> most outrageous and galling. That potentate who most condescends, mark
> him well; for that potentate, if occasion come, will prove your uttermost
> tyrant.

So Rose-water's opinion of the minstrel song-book should be taken
seriously after all.

In the fall of 1849 Melville took the proofs of his new novels to
England to arrange for their publication there. With his German
traveling companion, Dr. Adler, he attended theaters and concert-
halls; in one week he noted in his *Journal* Donizetti's *Don Pasquale,*
a program by Jullien's orchestra, and, briefly, on a Saturday night,
a Penny Theater, which frightened Adler while Melville found it
"very comical." His knowledge and critical appreciation of all sorts
of music all through his mature life may be represented by this
week's array. In 1851, writing to Nathaniel Hawthorne in response
to Hawthorne's unique appreciation of his work, Melville imagines
that if the two friends meet in Paradise

> . . . Then shall songs be composed as when wars are over; humorous,
> comic songs.—"Oh, when I lived in that queer little hole called the

world," or, "Oh, when I toiled and sweated below," or "Oh, when I knocked and was knocked in the fight"—yes, let us look forward to such things.

In 1854 Melville published his story "The Fiddler." The narrator is a frustrated writer, Helmstone, whose glib friend Standard takes him to visit the old musician Hautboy, who "played away right merrily at 'Yankee Doodle' and other off-handed, dashing, and disdainfully carefree airs." Helmstone envies Hautboy's serenity; shares his disdain for the world represented by Standard; resolves to study the violin. But readers are free to wonder how far Melville identifies himself with Helmstone; for one careful reader, W. R. Thompson, in 1961, Hautboy is "a symbol of the unconditional surrender of artistic integrity" rather than humane wisdom. Such an ambiguity is typical of Melville. A similar ambiguity hangs heavy on the story of 1855 in which Melville dramatizes the questions of slavery and Blackness, "Benito Cereno." Don Benito, the sick (or hypochondriac?) captain of a Spanish slave ship, seems to be a decadent aristocrat, an indulgent tyrant, a pitiable victim. The chief Black character, Babo, seems obsequiously devoted to Don Benito, yet independent of him in command of fellow Blacks. Babo never tells his side of the story; he ends with his severed head on a stake, staring out at the world. Don Benito, released shortly before, has written a long legal indictment of Babo as mutineer, but Benito dies "under the shadow" without revealing to the reader any truth. The benevolent but obtuse Captain Delano from New England, dupe of both Babo and Benito down to some unknown level of deceit, is sometimes frightened by the crowd of Blacks playing rhythmically with the hatchets they are sharpening, sometimes cheered by their singing at work on the hawsers, and most characteristically musing about them, when Babo shaves Benito, in their relation to music:

> Most negroes are natural valets and hair-dressers, taking to the comb and brush congenially as to the castanets. . . . [Their] tact [is] pleasing to behold, and still more so to be the manipulated subject of. And above all is the great gift of good humour. Not the mere grin or laugh is here meant. Those were unsuitable. But a certain easy cheerfulness, harmonious in every glance and gesture; as though God had set the whole negro to some pleasant tune.

Here is Melville's final criticism of the "negro melodies" of the mid-century. Every reader's estimate of Captain Delano and his "pleasant tune" betrays Melville's judgment of the reader. The more a reader knows of the whole background of "Susanna," the better he can cope with Melville, and the more he knows of Melville, the better he can picture Stephen C. Foster embarking on his "business of song-writing."

Frederick Douglass escaped slavery in 1838. He had grown up on a plantation in Maryland where, in 1841, Stephen Foster's mother, Eliza, was a guest with her Maryand relatives, so it is possible that the Foster family heard of Douglass before he became a famous antislavery orator and published his *Narrative* in 1845. In the *Narrative* Douglass writes the most comprehensive and fully credible descriptions of slave music by anyone before the 20th century. He himself sings and plays the violin. He takes part in music at churches, Sunday Schools, camp meetings, Christmas dances, and clandestine meetings to plot escape. When he becomes a dock worker at New Bedford, Massachusetts, he notices that the other workers do not sing. When he goes with the Hutchinson family on his first fund-raising trip to England, in 1846, he makes a pilgrimage to Scotland to pay tribute to Robert Burns, and sends a letter about it to the New York *Tribune*. When he returns to America and establishes his weekly newspaper at Rochester, New York, in 1847, he finds room in nearly every issue for some notice of musical events: local choir programs, traveling soloists and groups, the piano provided by Chickering to an antislavery rally. In the issue for March 3, 1848, he prints the testimony of another fugitive slave, Charity Bowery, about the use of Charles Mackay's verses in connection with the Nat Turner rebellion:

> They wouldn't let us sing that. They thought we was going to *rise*, because we sung "better days are coming."

On June 2, 1848, he has a letter from a member of the free Black community in Kingston, Ontario, reporting that "Music is a favorite study," with students busy at the guitar, flute, piano, and drums (no banjo).

On September 8, 1848, Douglass has a report from the Eagle Saloon at Pittsburgh, where just a year earlier "Susanna" had its first known public performance. Now the Sable Brothers of the Smoky City have attracted a full house, and their songs attract Douglass's wrath:

> Men who can devote themselves to the cowardly purpose of sporting over the miseries and misfortunes of an oppressed people [are] contemptible.

On October 27 he attacks an unnamed rival editor who

> . . . does not object to the "Virginia Minstrels," "Christy's Minstrels," the "Ethiopian Serenaders," or any of the filthy scum of white society, who have stolen from us a complexion denied to them by nature, in which to make money, and pander to the corrupt taste of their white fellow citizens. . . . [with] "Ole Zip Coon," "Jim Crow," "Ole Dan Tucker," "Jim along Josey," and a few other of such specimens of *American* musical genius.

Douglass' paper was renamed in 1849, *The North Star*. Here, on June 29, he announces the forthcoming appearance of

> . . . Gavitt's Original Ethiopian Serenaders, said to be composed entirely of colored people, and it may be so. . . . We are not sure that our readers will approve of our mention of those persons, so strong must be their dislike to everything that seems to feed the flame of American prejudice against colored people, and in this they may be right; but we think otherwise. It is something gained, when the colored man in any form can appear before a white audience; and we think that even this company, with industry, application, and a proper cultivation of their taste, may yet be instrumental in removing the prejudice against our race. But they must cease to exaggerate the exaggerations of our enemies; and represent the colored man rather as he is, than as Ethiopian Minstrels usually represent him to be. They will *then* command the respect of both races . . . relying more on the refinement of the public than its vulgarity.

Did Foster read such opinions as these? Probably not in 1849 unless, on one of his visits home from Cincinnati, his friend Charles Shiras showed it to him. Between 1850 and 1853, however, when Foster and Shiras were often collaborating, opinions like Douglass' almost surely reached his ears.

Every musical notice in Douglass' paper is interesting. Especially so are the reports of many concerts by the singer Elizabeth Greenfield, "The Black Swan," beginning October 23, 1851.

> We are happy to see the musical talent of the Black Swan thus appreciated, and hail it as one indication of the "good time coming."

Miss Greenfield's programs of music by Handel, Bellini, Donizetti, Sir Henry Bishop, and others, accompanied alternately by piano, harp, and guitar, sometimes ended with "Old Hundred" for the sake of familiarity to her mixed audience; two years later in England she gave a similar place to "Old Folks at Home." In Boston, February 1852, Miss Greenfield is said to have "submitted to excluding Negroes" from her audience, and several correspondents worry about this.

At the first Convention of Colored People, Rochester, July 1853, Douglass sings a hymn in which the whole convention joins:

> From all that dwell beneath the skies
> Let the Creator's praise arise.

By now in Rochester the variety of music in which Black people participate is so conspicuous that no distinctive unifying type or stereotype calls for Douglass' attention. His two eldest children, Rosetta and Lewis Henry, aged fourteen and thirteen, are learning to play the violin. But at the same time his work is founded on the

affirmation of unity among Black people, which he put beautifully
in an address at Cleveland, 1848, and always adhered to:

> . . . we are as a people, chained together. We are one people—one in gen-
> eral complexion, one in a common degradation, one in popular estima-
> tion. . . . Every one of us should be ashamed to consider himself free,
> while his brother is a slave. . . . Although it may seem to conflict with
> our views of human brotherhood, we shall undoubtedly for many years
> be compelled to have institutions of a complexionary character, in order
> to attain this very idea of human brotherhood.

Within the antislavery movement Douglass was not exempt from
the degrading "popular estimation"; the convention he organized
was more than a part of that movement. For him music was part of
both the movement and the degradation.

Douglass visited Pittsburgh in August 1847 and enlisted the thirty-
five-year-old Martin Delany as correspondent there and on tour for
his newspaper. Delany had come to Pittsburgh in 1831, the nineteen-year-old son of a couple who had escaped from slavery in
Charles Town, Virginia, to Chambersburg, Pennsylvania. About 1835
he was among the founders of the Pittsburgh Anti-Slavery Society,
along with John Bathan Vashon, keeper of public baths. Delany became a "cupper, leecher, and bleeder" and an apprentice of Dr.
Andrew McDowell, whose daughter Jane was to be the wife of
Stephen C. Foster. In 1839 he traveled through the Southwest. Back
in Pittsburgh from 1843 to 1846, he edited a weekly magazine, *The
Mystery*. Now, from 1847 to 1849, he collaborated with Douglass.
In 1848 he debated the Mexican War with Vashon's son George,
who had won his A.B. at Oberlin and was working there toward
his A.M. in theology. In the fall of 1849 Delany entered Harvard to
continue his study of medicine until student protests caused him to
leave. In 1850 he was back at Pittsburgh, working as a doctor and
again contributing to Douglass' paper. With the support of William
Robinson, father of Foster's friend Andrew, Delany organized a
protest of the Fugitive Slave Law. In 1852 he published his first
book, in Philadelphia, *The Condition, Elevation, Emigration, and
Destiny of the Colored People of the United States, Politically Considered*, in which he praised the achievements of Elizabeth Greenfield
and other Black musicians. In 1853 Delany participated in the
Rochester Convention; he began to disagree with Douglass about the
hopes for Blacks in the United States and to work on a series of
plans for mass emigration, perhaps to Canada, or to Nebraska, or to
South America, or to Africa. In 1858 he drafted a novel, *Blake; or the
Huts of America*, which was partially published serially in the
Anglo-African Magazine, 1859, and again in the *Weekly Afro-American*, 1861–62, and finally as a book, over a century later, in 1970.

In 1859–60 he explored and negotiated in Africa. In 1861 he spent seven months in England, lecturing to raise money for his emigration plans. In 1865 he became a major in the United States Army.

Douglass described Delany in 1862:

> He stands up so straight that he leans back a little. . . . He is the intensest embodiment of black Nationality to be met with outside the valley of the Niger.

There is no report of Delany's singing or playing with Douglass or anyone else. But he paid attention to music, and in his novel he used it copiously.

Among Delany's first reports to Douglass, two are concerned with Cincinnati. On May 26, 1848, he describes the rich society of colored people there; "anti-slavery is but a beggarly element," evidently contrasting with Pittsburgh. On June 16 Delany has attended a "musical soirée" by a newly organized "band of colored artists" who play for "all benevolent occasions." What they play, or how, Delany does not report. On July 6 and 13, 1849, he reports on a change among the "colored citizens of Pittsburgh" within the past year and a half: prosperity is leading to extravagance and loose morals, including "low dances, a custom unknown to Pittsburgh for the last fourteen years."

Unless further evidence of Delany's thought from the years 1850–58 is yet to be found, we must suppose that he was too busy to comment on the career of his fellow Pittsburgher Foster. But in the novel he shows that he has not ignored Foster's songs.

There are about thirty songs in *Blake*, scattered through the 310 pages extant. The singers and players represent a panorama of Black people in a dozen States and in Cuba. Fourteen songs are religious; six are explicit protest songs and one is a patriotic hymn of Black triumph; four are laments or farewells; three are, roughly, comic. Most of them are choral songs, sometimes connected with dance; a few that are sung by solitary individuals are all the lonelier because they should ideally be choral. Instruments appear only in Cuba: "the African bango," the guitar, the piano, and a drum and gourd. "Susanna," with the words of William Brown's songbook, "I'm on my way to Canada," has an appropriate place on the march of a group escaping from Kentucky across Indiana; the hero, Blake, joins in the chorus. An exuberant parody of "Old Uncle Ned" is sung by a minor character who has just heard of the plan for escape:

> . . . Hang up the shovel and the hoe-o-o-o!
> I don't care whether I work or no!
> Old master's gone to the slaveholders rest—
> He's gone where they all ought to go!

("Uncle Ned" goes unrecognized by the 20th-century editor of *Blake*.) In New Orleans the hero hears boatmen singing a variant of "Old Folks at Home." (See below p. 252.) The fact that Delany gave the three most famous of Foster's songs to Black singers is a remarkable tribute. If Delany, this "intensest embodiment of black Nationality," had left Foster to "the scum of white society," there would have been no reason for surprise.

Delany's attitude as represented in *Blake* is as favorable toward Foster's songs as any of the American attitudes we have surveyed, if not quite so favorable as the praise of Moritz Busch or Frederika Bremer. Douglass' attitude in 1848, moderated in 1849, goes beyond the contempt of Charles Mackay. Together Douglass and Delany may sum up the range of attitudes that Foster faced when he undertook to follow "Susanna" and "Uncle Ned" with a whole repertory for the minstrels.

All the critics of the "minstrel" songs find their various meanings more in the words than in the music. Some critics treat the music as a mere neutral vehicle for the words; a single tune can serve opposed meanings. But some critics recognize more or less explicitly that music affects the meanings of sung words too; a single epithet or sentence or narrative can serve opposed meanings in accordance with the rhythm and intonation provided by tunes, with the timbre of voices alone and in chorus, with the cultural associations of instrumental sounds that accompany the tunes. Further, the situation of a performance contributes meanings, which may elude the most careful student, like Busch, when he works over a text at his desk; such meanings may be most intensively vivid for a singer like Douglass on a political platform; they may be woven into complex structures of meaning by an artist like Melville, to go on troubling many generations.

CHAPTER 5

Foster,
the craftsman,
1849-51

BETWEEN the fall of 1848 and the spring of 1851, Foster sold to his various publishers twelve songs similar to "Susanna," together with three piano pieces and sixteen songs that belong with the "Jeanie" group. The publishers distinguished the "Susanna" type by labels on the title page: "Ethiopian" or "Plantation melodies." The label "Plantation" would apply also to the "Old Folks" type that began only in 1851. "Ethiopian" carried a connotation of comic purpose. The dozen songs, simpler than "Old Folks," with which Foster established himself in the business world, include "Camptown Races" and "Nelly Bly," worthy rivals of "Susanna" in the use of various groups of singers for over a century, though not so prominent as to have attracted comment by contemporary critics. The last published song of the group, "Ring de Banjo," includes the words, "Come again, Susanna." This makes it seem possible that Foster himself regarded the group as belonging together, and that he thought of it as ending in 1851, though he was to return to the type after a long interval with "The Glendy Burk" and "Don't Bet Your Money."

How similar to "Susanna" are these twelve songs? So much so, in their rhythm, melody, chords, and simple structure of phrases, that some commentators have suspected Foster of writing them by formula. Indeed, some modern students have devised a formula that could program a computer to turn out more songs similar to these. But, within the narrow limits of the style, there are of course subtle differences. A musician can recognize the computer products, though he may be unable to specify why. There is a striking lack of standardization in one important respect: an essential feature of the songs is the alternation of solo voice and chorus, but none of them has as many choral voices as "Susanna," none has such independent voices in the chorus as "Uncle Ned" (a product of 1847, like "Susanna"), and no two of the songs have their choral parts named in the same way in the first editions. This variety of treatment of the chorus is worth study, as a clue to Foster's mind. Though it is easy enough for anyone to study, none of Foster's admirers seems to have taken the trouble.

The chorus in "Susanna," as printed by C. Holt in 1848, copyright February 25, has four staves. The main melody is on top, marked "first voice." Next comes "second voice." Next "tenor," with two parts on the same staff. Finally "bass." The five voices all pronounce the words together. They make up chords, like the chords of the piano accompaniment, but not merely duplicating it. The bass comes up the scale in contrary motion to the downward broken-chord notes of the tune. The other three voices are "filler," with a few parallel motions that J. S. Dwight would have marked "incorrect." The two tenors are fairly surely meant to read their parts an octave lower than written; this use of the G clef was gradually spreading throughout the 19th century, not yet firmly established anywhere by 1850. If the "first voice" and "second voice" are taken by males, they too will read an octave lower, leaving the tenor pitched above them; they will not, in "Susanna," drop below the bass, so the total effect may be very satisfactory. Whether Foster's names for the parts imply that he would prefer male or female voices here, or whether he might like a chorus in which these parts were doubled at both octaves, there is insufficient evidence to decide.

(The slightly later edition of "Susanna" that W. C. Peters copyrighted December 30, 1848, preferred by some students as likely to be closer to Foster's manuscript, has only four voices in the chorus, no "errors" of voice-leading, no melodic interest in the bass, and a variant in the tune at the beginning of the chorus that disappoints everyone who knows the tune by ear.)

The chorus of "Uncle Ned" has only three voices, with no names for them. The upper two, on the treble clef, might be assigned to males or females; males would seem likely here, because the upper voice is a continuation, after a rest, of the solo in the verses, which was sung on the stage by William Roark. During the rest, the bass enters alone, marked fortissimo. The middle voice, alas, if sung by a male, drops below the bass at the end; this suggests that Foster may have composed not so much for Roark and his Sable Harmonists as for the female friends of the "nice young men." The uncertainty suggests that Foster was not fussy about his choruses, but rather expected performers to adjust the parts in many ways.

In the third song of 1847 associated with the "nice young men," "Lou'siana Belle," which Peters published "as sung by Joseph Murphy of the Sable Harmonists," there is a four-part chorus, marked "1st Tenore, 2nd Tenore, Alto, and Bass." The "alto" part needs to be read an octave low; indeed it could be read two octaves low without undermining the bass until the last chord, in which the alto is strangely divided, implying that at least two singers are assigned to this part. The two "tenor" parts, if sung an octave low, make good sense, but if sung at the written pitch the 2nd tenor is easy and even the first is not too high for some male voices. What is best? Arrangers have to decide.

A table can show the various dispositions of choral parts in the dozen songs from "Away Down South" (which Peters copyrighted together with "Susanna" and "Uncle Ned" at the end of 1848) to "Ring de Banjo" (published by Firth and Pond in New York in 1851).

"Away Down South"	Soprano 1 & 2, on one staff; could be read either 8ve. Tenor & Bass, on one staff
"Nelly Was a Lady"	Four parts unmarked; might be SAAB or TTTB
"My Brudder Gum"	Alto, Tenor 1, T 2, B; tune in T 1, A best 8ve low
"Dolcy Jones"	Unmarked; SSBB or TTBB
"Nelly Bly"	Only two parts, S 1 & 2; "S" does not rule out low 8ve
"Gwine to Run All Night" ("Camptown Races")	Air, Alto, T, B; Alto must be 8ve low
"Dolly Day"	T 1 & 2, Alto, B; like "Lou'siana Belle"
"Oh! Lemuel"	Air, Alto, T, B; Alto must read in 8ve written
"Way Down in Cairo"	Unmarked; SAAB or TTTB
"Angelina Baker"	Unmarked; STAB or TTTB
"Melinda May"	Air, Alto, T, B; Alto best in same 8ve as Air
"Ring de Banjo"	Unison chorus

In his songs later than these, Foster continued to vacillate with respect to the number of voices, the names for them, and the order of their staves on the page. "Old Folks," "Massa's in de Cold Ground," and "The Glendy Burk" have unison choruses; "My Old Kentucky Home" has four voices, called "Tenor, 1st Soprano (Air), 2nd Soprano, and Bass." "Old Black Joe" (1860) has three voices, unmarked; they make a fine effect assigned to tenor, baritone, and bass.

Foster's most elaborate part-writing, not for chorus at all, but explicitly marked *"per voce sole,"* is in "Come, Where My Love Lies Dreaming: Quartette" (1855). Here the parts labelled "Soprano, Tenor, Contralto, and Bass" seem still uncertain as to octave register: if the soprano and alto are sung in the written octave, the tenor too sounds best there, but it can never relax in the lower part of the range normally called tenor; if, on the other hand, the soprano is assigned to a second tenor and the alto to a baritone, there are a few moments when the bass might better drop to its low octave too.

The array of various treatments of the chorus indicates that Foster was no slick master of a formula, but rather a singer who often imagined a chorus supporting him with its vague chords. His imagination was based on what he had heard from the stage, what he heard in the amateur groups he belonged to, and perhaps what he heard in choruses of workers or worshippers that might have baffled the practiced ear of a Mozart. His songs, as he wrote them, invite choruses to arrange themselves spontaneously if they can, to "harmonize" without inhibition from the notes on the page.

The words of the twelve "Susanna"-like songs fit this picture of Foster in relation to his choruses. In every song there is an individual singer who refers to himself. Again and again "I sing." In "Susanna" he is "dis darkey." In "Dolly Day" he identifies himself as the same character: he reminds us that he has told about Susanna's banjo and Uncle Ned's shovel and hoe. But he now avoids such nonsense as "The sun so hot I froze to death" and such lugubrious piety as "where all de good niggas go." In one verse of "Way Down in Cairo" he generalizes about "de nigga's life" and identifies himself with it. In "Angelina Baker" he introduces himself as born "way down on de old plantation." In "Away Down South" he invites, "Chime in niggas. . . Come along to Cuba." In "My Brudder Gum" he offers, "White folks I'll sing for you," and points out "All de yaller gals runnin' round." In "Nelly Bly" he sings to Nelly in the kitchen and presumably gets her to join his song. In "Gwine to Run All Night" he echoes the Camptown ladies' song, "Doodah." In "Oh! Lemuel" he asks Lemuel to "bring de boys . . . de Nigga boys all" from the field to a ball. In "Way Down in Cairo" he predicts:

> All de ladies in de land,
>   And all de gemmen too
> Am guine to hear de darkey band
>   And see what dey can do.

The singer praises Angelina Baker for her unusual relation to the group:

> Angelina likes de boys
>> As far as she can see dem,
> She used to run old Massa round
>> To ax him for to free dem.

But Angelina is gone, nobody knows where, and the singer has to weep. In "Melinda May" the singer asks for a smile from his love, and in his last verse he wishes to exalt her over the vague crowd:

> If I was a hero and people would fall
>> Where ebber I'd tell dem to lie,
> I'd make my Melinda de queen ob dem al,
>> And lib on de light ob her eye.

This singer is clearly the same fellow who keeps comforting Susanna, "don't you cry." He is not the grotesque clown of "Jim Crow," not the affected dandy of "Zip Coon." In "Ring de Banjo" he defines his position in society more than anywhere else:

> De time is nebber dreary
>> If de darkey nebber groans;
> De ladies nebber weary.
>> Wid de rattle ob de bones.
> Den come again Susanna
>> By de gaslight ob de moon;
> We'll tum de old Piano
>> When de banjo's out ob tune.
>>> Ring, ring de banjo! &c.

> De darkey hab no troubles
>> While he's got dis song to sing. . . .

> I roam de old plantation
>> Wid my true lub on my arm. . . .

> Once I was so lucky,
>> My massa set me free,
> I went to old Kentucky
>> To see what I could see:
> I could not go no farder,
>> I turn to massa's door,
> I lub him all de harder,
>> I'll go away no more.
>>> Ring, ring de banjo! &c.

> Early in de morning
>> Ob a lubly summer day,
> My massa send me warning
>> He'd like to hear me play.
> On de banjo tapping,
>> I come wid dulcem strain;
> Massa fall a napping—

He'll nebber wake again.
Ring, ring de banjo! &c.

My lub, I'll hab to leabe you
While de ribber's running high:
But I nebber can deceibe you—
So dont you wipe your eye.
I's guine to make some money;
But I'll come anodder day—
I'll come again my honey,
If I hab to work my way.
Ring, ring de banjo!
I like dat good old song,
Come again my true lub,
Oh! wha you been so long.

The ladies who listen, never tiring, are invited to identify themselves with Susanna and the rhyming piano. The singer won't deceive these listeners, if they don't take him too seriously. He is going to leave them, though he once rejected freedom to return to his beloved master, now dead. Where is he going next? To earn money with his good old song. Let the ladies, and gentlemen too, join this cheerful character in a chorus; let them forget all the troubles that made them groan like a "darkey" before the start of the song. The tune of the chorus is identical with the repeated couplets of the soloist's verses, except for the first line, which is a childlike chant, the simplest possible, and if it is out of tune, no matter.

Foster's most explicit cheerful poem may be too subtle for success on the stage. How often any of the minstrels sang "Ring de Banjo" is not known; the Firth and Pond title page is silent about it, whereas nearly every other song is advertised with the name of Christy. In 1857 the total royalties paid for "Ring de Banjo" by Firth and Pond, according to Foster's manuscript memorandum, were $35.24, and his estimate of its future value was $1.00, the same as he estimated for "Dolcy Jones" and several songs of the "Jeanie" type. (He hoped that "Old Folks," which had brought him the maximum amount, $1647.47, was good for another $100, and that "Jeanie," which had earned so far $217.80, might go on to make $350.) "Ring de Banjo" was not taken too seriously by Foster himself. Though it was unlike "Susanna" in its self-conscious address to a market, it still was like "Susanna" in its predominating spirit of casual entertainment. It reveals the songwriter still a "nice young man," who pretends to be a "darkey" more to amuse the ladies than to command a big rough audience in a theater, much less to instruct anyone about Blacks as they really are, or to persuade anyone to help them.

Foster imagined the chorus of characters evoked by the words of all these songs as vaguely as he imagined the actual chorus of minstrel performers. His spokesman, the solo singer and narrator, like Foster himself early in 1850, was loosely connected with the people surrounding him. The individuals he sang about—six ladies whose names appear in the titles of the songs, and only two men—Foster portrayed with more variety than he gave the singer, but with no more vividness than the singer of "Ring de Banjo." The anonymous larger group of "niggers" referred to in most of the songs were working for "massa" in the fields. Fields of corn (in three songs), of cane (in four), of cotton (two), and of 'bacco (one). But their work was never brought to the center of the stage. Their solidarity was not strengthened by the individual singer and his ladies. The group was only a dim background.

The instrumental accompaniments, like the chorus, testify to Foster's persisting attachment to his circle of young friends, his distance from both theaters and real slave plantations.

All the twelve songs resemble "Susanna" in preceding the first stanza with a phrase or two for the piano. All but one have a piano phrase or two for conclusion; in "Lou'siana Belle" Foster calls this bit by the quaint name "symphony," which he does not use again in any publication. The notes of the "symphony" are exactly the same as the introduction, almost the same as the opening eight measures of the tune itself. But the introductions and conclusions of the twelve songs are no more standardized than the treatment of the chorus. Their variety is enough to indicate that Foster took some interest in them.

"Away Down South," "Camptown Races," and "Melinda May" all use the same pair of phrases for beginning and end, and all these phrases are slight variants of the tune. "Nelly Was a Lady" has a distinctive phrase for introduction and another one for conclusion— a solemn, hymnlike coda. "My Brudder Gum" also has distinctive bits of melody, the introduction two phrases and the conclusion only one. "Uncle Ned," "Dolcy Jones," and "Angelina Baker" all have conclusions of just one phrase, adequately balancing introductions of two; their phrases are all variants of the tune. "Way Down in Cairo" stands out because it lacks any conclusion, but more so because its introduction varies the tune with a banjo figuration. "Ring de Banjo" is one of the simplest songs in this respect, with its introduction matching the first phrases of the tune, its conclusion echoing the chorus.

When Foster sent to E. P. Christy copies of "Camptown Races" and "Dolly Day," in February 1850, he did not know whether Christy's band used a piano, for he mentions this ignorance in the letter of June 20, 1851 (p. 85 below). He doubtless expected Christy's band to improvise its own arrangement with banjo, tambourine, and bones. He had probably heard pianists accompany William Roark, Nelson Kneass, and the other singers of the Sable Harmonists in Cincinnati; this group, according to the recollections of Samuel Sanford, used no banjo. Foster was probably accustomed to the pianists' introducing and concluding the songs, while the singer preened. The modest variety of the introductions and conclusions published with Foster's songs fits with such a theatrical situation. There is no need to prefer the written introductions and conclusions to whatever an accompanist wishes to improvise.

While the piano is mentioned in no other song than "Ring de Banjo," the banjo itself is named in five of the twelve. The jawbone has an important place in "Angelina Baker" and is mentioned in three more of the twelve. "Oh! Lemuel" mentions a drum. Both "Oh! Lemuel" and "Dolly Day" mention the fiddle, though not so prominently as "Uncle Ned." Foster seems not to know or not to care that fiddles are more common on real Southern plantations of his time than banjos. He seems not to know or care that Dan Emmett and others have developed a distinctive style of playing the banjo, and are adding a fifth string to the instrument. No song mentions the guitar, though several of his songs were published in a version with guitar accompaniment, simultaneously with the piano version. For Foster, all the instruments are like the chorus, loosely associated with the solo singer.

Dancing too is only loosely associated with these songs. According to Sanford again, the Sable Harmonists lacked dance, so perhaps Foster never observed anything like the antics of Dan Emmett and William Diamond. Seven of the twelve songs have the polka bounce of "Susanna." "Camptown" has a rare racy stomp. The others are slow, though none need be slower than the dirge for "Uncle Ned." "Oh! Lemuel" recalls the ball of "Lou'siana Belle," with a grotesque touch in Lemuel's big feet. More characteristic are the "fairy footsteps" of "Dolly Day" and the swinging walk of "Nelly Bly":

> De way she walks, she lifts her foot
> And den she brings it down,
> And when it lights, der's music dah
> In dat part ob de town.

Most tantalizing is the line in the chorus of "Away Down South":

> Den come along to Cuba and we'll dance de polka-juba,
> Way down souf, where de corn grow.

What did "juba" mean to Foster? Did he know about Juba on the London stage? Did he read the words of *"Juba,* the great Banjo Solo, as Sung by George Christy and Wood's Minstrels," in *White's New Illustrated Melodeon Song Book* (New York: 1848)? Or did he know something of the practice of "clapping juber," described in 1838 by William B. Smith in the *Farmer's Register* of Petersburg, Virginia? Smith had attended a "beer dance" authorized by the master of a neighboring plantation and had seen

> . . . two athletic blacks, with open mouth and pearl-white teeth, clapping *Juber* to the notes of the banjor.

Smith was reminded of Burns' "Tam O'Shanter." He recorded the words of a dance-song with the refrain,

> Hoe corn, hill tobacco,
> Get over double trouble.
> Juber boys, Juber.

Even better, Smith recorded some fragments of conversation among the Blacks:

> "Sal *does* put her foot good." "Molly look like a kildee; she move like handsaw—see how she shake herself." . . . "Lor see how Aggy shake her foot; she *ken* pull the whip-saw down." . . . "See Ben cross hi' bow-legs!"

Foster's dancers are not so vivid as Smith's. Their "juba" is predominantly a polka. But perhaps Foster's dancers are no less realistic, for Smith concludes his article with the moral observation that "Virginia slaves were the happiest of the human race," a claim that Foster's songs never make. The transient happiness of his singers depends on the uncertain favor of their ladies more than on any boisterous dance.

Foster's singers are more inclined to weep than to dance. In six of the twelve songs there are cries or tears or weeping. The most doleful is "Nelly Was a Lady." Even "Ring de Banjo" has to ward off the "groans."

The tempo markings of the songs show Foster's tendency toward moping, as well as a concern to avoid extremes. Only two songs lack any indication of tempo. Six of the twelve are marked "moderato." This is the direction even for "Camptown Races." "Oh! Lemuel" is "not too fast"; "Away Down South" "not too slow." "Melinda May" is "poco adagio." For the lament, "Nelly Was a Lady," outright "adagio" is appropriate.

More significant than the tempo markings are the deviations from the regular beat of the dance or slow march: in the closing phrase of either verse or chorus of nearly every song, as in the verse of "Susanna," there is a *fermata,* calling for the singer to hold out a syllable beyond the time that a steady series of beats would allow. The dance must surrender to the expression of the words, if performers observe this characteristic *fermata*. With "Uncle Ned" they are almost sure to do so, for the *fermata* is on the high note of the melody and the slow pulse is not strong enough to pull through this note. There are similar high notes in "Dolcy Jones," "Melinda May," "Away Down in Cairo," and "Ring de Banjo," though singers may be more likely to ignore the *fermata* in these brisker tunes, as in "Susanna." Foster's *fermata* distinguishes his songs from most of the earlier minstrel tunes and later walk-arounds like "Dixie." A rare precedent is "Clare de Kitchen."

The song with greatest rhythmic interest is "My Brudder Gum," in which the title words are set off at the beginning of the chorus, followed by a rest—a whole measure—in all parts. The word "Brudder" fits naturally here on an upbeat, but this gives an extraordinary accent to "My" because each verse has ended with a syncopated figure for "Hay! Brudder Gum"—the "Hay!" fills a whole measure, with a *fermata*, the "Brudder" gets a fresh downbeat accent and seems surprisingly fast, and the "Gum" is a short note on the upbeat, followed by a silent beat.

Rhythmic details are varied in the several verses of each song, so as to allow natural syllabic accents, speeds, and groupings. But of course the lines of text are never run on across the musical phrase-endings. The variants of detail seem finicky. Probably they authorize singers to vary the syllabic values freely, somewhat further than Foster's notation.

Syncopation is a frequent result of natural accenting of the words, as in "Comin' Through the Rye" and many other Scottish songs. Never does Foster use the distinctive banjo syncopation of Dan Emmett, with silence on the downbeat amid a rapid flow of notes subdividing the beats.

All the traits we have observed reflect an emphasis on the individual singer and his melody, moving against the vague background of chorus, instruments, and rhythmic beats. Sweet melody—"dulcem melody"—predominates over rhythm and all variable details of sound. This appropriate name for Foster's kind of melody occurs in "Nelly Bly." The "dulcem strain" of the instrument we have noticed in "Ring de Banjo." The sweetness is more important to Foster than the ringing, rhythmic stroke. Melody is supreme.

The twelve tunes all have a larger range of pitch than "Susanna" and "Uncle Ned," which rise only six steps up the major scale from a solid tonic note. "Camptown Races" and "Ring de Banjo" are similar to "Susanna," but they include one higher note, the octave above the tonic, and they emphasize this note. They avoid the seventh note of the scale, which in tunes like "Villikins" and "Du, du liegst mir im Herzen" has an important function binding the whole scale together. "Away Down South" lies mostly in the six-note range, but extends it downward with an unemphasized note on the lower fifth of the scale. The two songs with the biggest range simply combine both upward and downward extensions, keeping most of the time within the easy middle range: "Brudder Gum" and "Dolcy Jones." A subgroup of four songs uses a range of an octave or less with the keynote near the center of the range, instead of being near the bottom: "Dolly Day," "Oh! Lemuel," "Way Down in Cairo," and "Angelina Baker." Their pitch-structure is like that of "Yankee Doodle," never stretching so far as "Auld Lang Syne." These four similar songs were published between January and April 1850; they seem to hint at an effort to depart from the model of "Susanna," but then "Ring de Banjo," in 1851, returns to that model, with the extension characteristic of "Camptown." The two most interesting melodies from the point of view of pitch are "Nelly Bly" and "Melinda May." Both range through ten notes of the scale, touching the low keynote with discretion rather than resting on it frequently. "Nelly Bly" ends an important phrase on the low second degree of the scale, and then soars in the answering phrase to end on the high tonic. "Melinda May" ends its first phrase on the high tonic, then modulates to the key of the fifth, with a very graceful phrase, making the chorus a fulfillment and return and yet a novelty when it finally leads down to the low tonic. "Melinda May" seems excessively elaborate for an "Ethiopian song." "Nelly Bly" is an almost freakish success.

"Nelly Bly" has another melodic aspect: the phrases are composed of a three-note motif, repeated and then developed in a little sequence. This feature holds the tune together in spite of the unusual balancing of high and low notes in the range. Also the three-note motif helps keep away from the sheer repetition of one or two notes that is characteristic of "Susanna" and many earlier minstrel tunes. In the view of Hans Nathan, such repetitions are the foremost feature of the "indigenous vocabulary" established by "Zip Coon" ("Turkey in the Straw") with its "firm, noncantabile intervals, operating vigorously within an unlyrical context," and corresponding to "a heavy-footed motion, partly resulting from accentuated endings of brief phrases, which has nothing in common with old world dances." "Nelly Bly" is a "dulcem melody." And its peculiar sweetness only carries to an extreme a quality that distinguishes most of Foster's tunes from those of his rivals in the minstrel tradition.

None of the twelve songs follow up "Uncle Ned" with respect to the use of chromatic half-steps between the normal notes of the major scale. Their accompaniments occasionally use some chromatic notes, enough perhaps to warrant an arranger's adding a few more, though the rhythms and the words tend to hold back any such tendency. The precedent of "Uncle Ned" is more related to "Jeanie" and "Old Folks."

None of the "Susanna"-type songs departs from the major scale in the direction of the minor (which Foster did venture to use in a few other pieces) or the Mixolydian, with its flat seventh, which may have puzzled him when he heard it in anonymous tunes like "The Ole Grey Goose," "Ole Pee Dee," and "Who's Dat Nigga Dar a Peepin'," all published in 1844, as sung by the early minstrels. Foster's attachment to the major scale seems firmer than that of anyone else who gave so much time to music.

With respect to the relations between tune and chords, most of the songs are a bit more complicated than "Susanna" or any composing-formula yet devised for a computer. "Susanna's" tune clearly implies the three major chords of the major scale—if the tune is in C, then the chords of C and G alternate, with an emphatic F-chord at the beginning of the chorus. The implications are so strong that a very unskilled player can pick them out by ear correctly. A subtler player can use an occasional G_7-chord, or even a D_7-chord, as in the first edition, though these refinements are not necessary. But in most of the other songs, until "Ring de Banjo" calls "come again, Susanna," there are a few melody-notes that make important dissonant intervals with the chords. A clear example is in the "Doodah" of "Camptown Races," where only a dull accompanist will provide the consonant tonic chord for the syllable "doo"; in lively performances, as in the noted score, the accent on this syllable is enhanced by the mild dissonance. In "Nelly Was a Lady" and "Melinda May" the effect of dissonant notes is more bittersweet. In "Nelly's" introduction and conclusion such notes are as profuse as in Mozart, if not Weber or Donizetti. Then there are examples of a different kind, in which a sustained or repeated melody-note belongs to a rich 7th-chord or even a 9th-chord; these can be found in "Brudder Gum," "Dolcy Jones," "Oh! Lemuel," and "Way Down in Cairo." Best of all, there are some exceptional phrases in which a tonic note in the melody clashes with the chord of the fifth degree approaching the final tonic: "Nelly Was a Lady" and "Angelina Baker" both have these pungent dissonances.

On the other hand, Foster rarely uses as great a variety of chords as Dan Emmett. The minor chord on the sixth degree of the scale, in "Angelina Baker," is exceptional. Foster sticks close to the three major chords that suffice for "Susanna."

The limitations of the style are so narrow that our observations risk pedantry. Yet these observations of various details show that the songs are no mechanical repetitions of a type, but individual hand-crafted products. The narrow limits and the slight, unpredictable variations within the limits help to place Foster's work in its historical context; they help us imagine him at work, a "nice young man" in a changing world that he is very little acquainted with. His musical craftsmanship and style fit all we know about his personality in its actual environment.

One minstrel singer, J. William Pope, wrote for the Pittsburgh *Press* in 1895 what he recalled of Foster's personality and musicianship around 1850. Pope's vignette adds nothing to our picture, but confirms it, especially with respect to melody and harmony:

> In 1849, I was proprietor and manager of a minstrel company of the old school. We were playing at the historic old Lafayette Hall, when one day Stephen Foster brought me the original manuscript for "Nelly Was a Lady," also the score. My company gave the song its first rendition in public, at Lafayette Hall, and we sang it every night there for three weeks. It was a success from the start, and the people went fairly wild over it.
>
> I knew Foster well, and we were great friends. He showed me the manuscript of many of his melodies before they were sent to the publishers. Foster's ear was correct as to melody, but he sometimes made amusing mistakes in trying to produce the harmonies. On one occasion, I heard him singing a song in one key and playing it on the piano in another. I presume his mind was so wrapped up in the melody he was singing, that he paid no attention to the accompaniment. He was certainly a genius for producing melodies.

More than any detail of melody, rhythm, or harmony, it is the pattern of phrases constituting a whole tune that may seem stereotyped to a hasty student of Foster's songs, but that reveals some variety on more patient inspection. Does this variety testify to spontaneity or to striving? A tabular representation of the phrases can save some time:

	VERSE	CHORUS
"Susanna"	a a' a a'	b a'
"Uncle Ned"	a a'	b c c'
"Away Down South"	a a'	b c
"Nelly Was a Lady"	a a	b (unusually long phrases)
"Brudder Gum"	a b	c d
"Dolcy Jones"	a a' a a''	b c
"Nelly Bly"	a b a b	c b c b
"Camptown Races"	a a' a a'	b a'
	(chorus within each phrase)	
"Dolly Day"	a b a b'	b b'
"Oh! Lemuel"	a a b	c
"Way Down in Cairo"	a a'	b a'
"Angelina Baker"	a a' a a'	b a'
"Melinda May"	a a' (modulation)	b c
"Ring de Banjo"	a b a b	c b

A glance at the table indicates that the pattern of "Susanna" is matched only in "Angelina Baker" and in "Camptown Races," but in "Camptown" there is the biggest discrepancy of all in the use of the "Doodah" choral fragments to end each line, before the "chorus" proper—Dan Emmett's walk-arounds develop this device regularly, as Foster never does again. Each of the other songs has its unique form; though the differences may seem trivial, they provide more complexity than any music theorist has yet taught to a computer.

In every song except "Dolly Day" the chorus begins with a new phrase. Yet there is something elusive about the way this phrase fits into the whole. In half the songs the new phrase leads to a return of a phrase from the verse, but in the other songs the unity of the whole seems just as strong. In four songs the chorus phrases balance the verse phrases with equal length; "Uncle Ned" is unique in having a longer chorus; the rest have shorter choruses, yet they seem to make a satisfactory asymmetrical balance too, even when the chorus is relatively so short as in "Oh! Lemuel."

Rhymes link phrases, but not often in the same way as musical repetition. Quatrains like those of "Ring de Banjo" are the most elaborate rhyme schemes; "Dolcy Jones" is the only matching song in this respect, and its musical pattern is quite different. "Nelly Bly" and "Camptown" have simple couplets, and again their musical patterns are contrasting.

Soon after "Ring de Banjo," in 1851, Foster composed another lament, "Oh! Boys, Carry Me 'Long," which makes a transition to "Old Folks at Home." The rhythm and the words have important novel features, while the range of melody, chords, and phrase pattern are still much like those of "Susanna" and "Ring de Banjo." Foster offered to send a copy of "Oh! Boys" to Christy ahead of publication. The letter containing the offer and another letter responding to Christy's prompt payment provide a unique technical discussion of his work by the composer himself:

Allegheny City, June 12, 1851

Dear Sir:

   I have just received a letter from Messrs. Firth, Pond & Co. stating that they have copy-righted a new song of mine ("Oh! boys, carry me 'long") but will not be able to issue it for some little time yet, owing to other engagements. This will give me time to send you the m.s. and allow you the privilege of singing it for at least two weeks, and probably a month before it is issued, or before any other band gets it (unless they catch it up from you). If you will send me 10$ immediately for this privilege I pledge myself, as a gentleman of the old school, to give you the m.s. I have written to F.P.&Co. not to publish till they hear from me again. This song is certain to become popular, as I have taken great pains with it. If you accept my proposition I will make it a point to notify you hereafter when I have a new song and send you the m.s. on the same terms, reserving to myself in all cases the exclusive privilege of publishing. Thus it will become notorious that your band brings out all the new songs. You can state in the papers that the song was composed expressly for you. I make this proposition because I am sure of the song's popularity.

> Very Respectfully Yours,
> S. C. Foster

Christy's reply is not preserved, but the next letter from the composer shows that Christy snapped up the opportunity.

> June 20, 1851

Your favor of the 12th inst., inclosing ten dollars for the privilege of singing "Oh! boys, carry me 'long" is received. Accept my thanks. Herewith, I send you the m.s. according to agreement. I am not certain that you use a piano in your band; but I have arranged an accompaniment for that instrument at a venture. If you have a tenor voice in the company that can sing up to "g" with ease (which is probable) it will be better to sing the song in the key of "g" [rather than the written F]. Thus you will not carry the bass voice quite so low. I hope that you will preserve the harmony in the chorus just as I have written it, and practise the song well before you bring it out. It is especially necessary that the person who sings the verses should know all the words perfectly, as the least hesitation in singing will damn any song—but this you of course know as well as anyone. Remember it should be sung in a pathetic, not a comic style. You will find the last three verses on another page of this letter. I regret that it is too late to have the name of your band on the title page, but I will endeavor to place it (alone) on future songs, and will cheerfully do anything else in my humble way to advance your interest.

> Very Respectfully Yours,
> S. C. Foster

These letters, from the author of "Susanna," "Camptown," "Nelly Bly," and "Ring de Banjo," seem, like the new song, more pathetic than comic. Foster's "great pains" over the years 1849–51 might have been more rewarding if he had gone to stay in New York, as he hoped to do in 1850, and had found out about the piano and the tenor and many other things. Yet his "dulcem melody" with all its limitations, its little variations, its adaptability, and, in some instances, its durability, might not have developed from "Susanna" so well in New York as it did in Cincinnati and Pittsburgh. The shy, proud, hopeful tone of the letters matches the qualities of the songs. Foster's "business of song-writing" is shown by the combination of the songs and the letters to be a peculiar and tenuous business.

The minstrel theater and its questionable use of images of the Blacks were not the whole of Foster's "business," nor the central, determining part of it. While his letters to Christy show him at his most businesslike, and his "Susanna"-type songs show his conscientious working within the limitations of the minstrel tradition, we remember that he was writing at the same time a greater number of songs of a slightly different type. These demand some attention before we shall understand his new pathos in "Oh! Boys, Carry Me 'Long" and "Old Folks at Home." And in connection with the big central group of songs, typified by "Jeanie," we need to approach him as closely as we can from the point of view of his closest personal society—his family. If he sang mainly for friends and family when he pretended to be a "darkey," how much more directly might he sing without this mask? Can we learn to recognize his true face behind other masks? Or to pick out certain songs as naked expressions of his personal feelings?

PART TWO

"JEANIE"
AND OTHER
"POETIC SONGS"
AND BALLADS

CHAPTER 6

Foster
and his family

ABOUT the meaning of "Jeanie with the Light Brown Hair," Morrison Foster knew more than he wrote for the public. He sang the song to his daughter Evelyn, but, in the fifty-five page biographical sketch he wrote about Stephen, he never mentions "Jeanie." He does discuss eighteen songs, ten of them "plantation melodies" including "Susanna" and "Old Folks"; the remaining eight are distinguished by Morrison as "sentimental songs," with the observation that Stephen himself preferred these to the others. Omitting "Jeanie" must have been deliberate. Evelyn remembered Morrison's pronouncing it "Jennie." He explained that Jane Denny McDowell, Stephen's wife, was called "Jennie." He suggested that the song might have helped bring Jane back to Stephen when it was new, in 1854; they had been married in 1850, temporarily separated in 1853. The words of the song fit this conjectural interpretation:

> I dream of Jeanie . . .
> I long for Jeanie . . .
> I hear her melodies, like joys gone by,
> Sighing 'round my heart o'er the fond hopes that die . . .
> I sigh for Jeanie . . .
> Her smiles have vanished and her sweet songs flown,
> Flitting like the dreams that have cheered us and gone.
> Now the nodding wild flow'rs may wither on the shore

> While her gentle fingers will cull them no more:
> Oh! I sigh for Jeanie with the light brown hair,
> Floating, like a vapor, on the soft summer air.

"Jeanie" meant Jane—Jane's often-admired hair floating, Jane's smiles flitting—and Stephen's sighs for the fond hopes that died. If hopes revived for a while, they soon died again. Morrison wished to call no attention to "Jeanie."

Morrison's interpretation of his brother's life, work, and character, as prepared for the public in 1896, naturally needs to be supplemented and even corrected on many points. But since Morrison was the only witness (except for their elder brother Henry) throughout Stephen's life, since he was a friend of Jane's before Stephen met her, and continued to befriend her until she died in 1903, since he knew and loved many of the songs, his interpretations carry great weight. They make an appropriate starting point for our exploration of Foster's personal life. Much of the supplementary material about the family, collected by Evelyn Foster Morneweck, is connected with the songs so remotely that it will not concern us, whereas her father's statements—and his silences—are all helpful. If he is silent not for lack of information but for some other reason, the information that he leaves out allows us to focus on Stephen with a stereoscopic view. It provides clues to the reasons for Morrison's silence, which can contribute to a clearer view of Stephen. Morrison was too strong a father for such circuitous procedures as ours to have occurred to his daughter Evelyn. But anyone who cares about the complex truth of Stephen's life and its bearing on the meaning of his songs will profit from the comparative procedure.

Morrison's reasons for saying almost nothing about Henry Baldwin Foster, the eldest brother to survive Stephen, could have been innocent. Within the limits of fifty-five pages, more mention of Henry would have cluttered the picture for readers to whom all the names were new. Henry's knowledge of Stephen was less than that of the eldest brother, William, who died in 1860, or of the middle brother, Dunning, who died in 1855, as well as of Morrison himself, the closest brother. And by the time Morrison wrote, Henry had been dead for twenty-five years; he left no memoirs. For these reasons, at any rate, we may set aside Henry's perspective until we have put together Morrison's account and the evidence from Dunning and their sisters, Ann Eliza and Henrietta. There is enough without Henry's contribution to arrive at richer meanings of "Jeanie" than the one Morrison suggested to his daughter.

Morrison remembered Stephen's gathering the best singers among his friends and neighbors to "assist him in singing the choruses of his songs while they were in course of preparation." He names four ladies in particular, but not Jane. He tells how Stephen "delighted in playing accompaniments on the flute to the singing and playing on the piano of his sister or one of his lady friends." Not Jane. According to Evelyn, Jane had no voice and hardly an ear for music; she talked through concerts. When Evelyn met her as an old lady, long remarried, Jane seemed "sweet and kind," but Evelyn believed she had been, as a girl, "exceedingly pretty . . . spoiled and petted at home." Jane's granddaughter, when she in turn was an old lady, in 1926, recalled that Jane had recognized "Old Black Joe" and asked the young people not to sing it. In Morrison's book, to fill up a brief paragraph about Jane, he falls back on a letter that her grandfather had preserved from George Washington. Morrison's omission of "Jeanie" is part of his generally tight-lipped treatment of Jane. His suggestion to his daughter about how "Jeanie" might have worked on Jane seems improbable; if Jane paid attention to it once, it made no lasting impression on her.

No letters to or from Jane before 1861 survive. But she is mentioned in several letters of the Foster family. First, from brother Dunning, in Cincinnati, January 13, 1849, Morrison heard about Jane's visit there, while Stephen was visiting at home in Pittsburgh. Dunning wished he could arrange more parties for her. He said she often sighed over friends at Pittsburgh. But still, "she appears to enjoy herself very well, and does not complain in any way. She is, by the way, a very sensible and interesting young lady." Dunning himself never married.

Stephen's first testimony explicitly about Jane is his letter announcing their marriage to his sister Ann Eliza Buchanan:

Pittsburgh, July 16, 1850

My dear Sister

I write to say that I am to be married on Monday next to Miss Jane, daughter of the late Dr. McDowell of this place [her father died suddenly in 1849, leaving six daughters], and that we will start on the same evening for Baltimore and New York. The trip will be on business as well as for pleasure, as I wish to see my publishers in the east as soon as possible, therefore I regret that I cannot, to my own advantage, pay you a visit in going, although I will pass very near your house. We will however endeavor to give you a call in returning, but this may not be for several months. We are to have but a small wedding. With love to Mr. Buchanan and the dear children,

Your Affectionate Brother
Stephen

The trip seemed to be on Foster's mind more than the small wedding. He had been planning the trip since no later than February, when he wrote to Christy about "Camptown Races." But if he got to

New York at all, he missed Christy as we know. He was back with Jane at his parents' house in Allegheny by September 8. In the following spring, April 18, 1851, the baby daughter, Marion, was born. That summer Stephen rented an office in which to do his work. From August 4 until Christmas the three lived with Jane's mother. Then they returned to the Fosters' house. By now the office was abandoned. From February 20 to March 21, 1852, they were part of a cruise party of ten or twelve friends aboard Dunning's steamboat, down the Ohio and the Mississippi to New Orleans and back. Morrison joined the party toward the end. He joined in singing many songs, and again his account omits Jane from the singing. Perhaps the baby kept her busy. They returned to the Foster house, where they seem to have stayed until the separation of 1853. Morrison evidently reported this to his sister Henrietta Thornton, for she replied with an outpouring of sympathy on June 20, 1853:

> . . . How sorry I feel for dear Stephy, though when I read your letter, I was not at all surprised at the news it contained with regard to him and [illegibly expunged]. I last winter felt convinced that she would either have to change her course of conduct, or a separation was inevitable. Though I never wrote a word of the kind to Stephy, for I thought he had trouble enough already. Tell him to come out and stay a while with me, we have a delightful house, well shaded by trees, and I know it must be pleasanter than in Pitts. this hot weather. You did not tell me what he had done with little Marion, dear little lamb, who is she with? Give much love to Stephy for me, and tell him to feel assured that he has the prayers and sincere sympathy of his sister Etty, dear boy, may God lead him in the ways of peace, and fill his heart with that love which alone is satisfying, and which *never* disappoints. a love that will (by seeking it) take such complete possession of the Soul, as to make all other loves but matters of small importance.

Henrietta's pity for "dear Stephy" was shared by all the brothers and sisters, not to mention their ailing parents. Henrietta's censure of Jane, however, she soon retracted to some degree, when she learned that Jane took good care of the baby and that Stephen's troubles had led him to seek solace in rum more often than religion. Henrietta's concern for the baby was doubtless paramount: she herself was mother of seven, and always more motherly than sisterly toward Stephen. When Stephen brought his wife and child to Ohio for an extended visit in 1860, Henrietta often mothered Jane and the nine-year-old Marion too.

A letter from Dunning to Morrison indicates the family's revised attitude. This was written on March 3, 1854, mainly about various contracts and projects; the reference to Stephen, now in New York (longing and sighing for Jane?), is all too brief:

... Have you heard anything from Stephen lately? It is a subject of much anxiety to me, notwithstanding his foolish and unaccountable course.—I hope he will continue to make a comfortable living for himself.

Stephen's "foolish and unaccountable course," wavering between his duties to Jane and his other interests, concerned the brothers and sisters increasingly all the rest of his life.

In 1855, when Stephen and Jane were back together at Allegheny, mourning the death of the mother and nursing the father who was to die that summer, Stephen wrote to Henrietta one of his longest letters:

March 19, 1855

My dear Sister

You will be delighted to hear that I have received a letter from Dunning written at New Orleans conveying cheering news with regard to his health. He says that he is so much improved in health as to feel that he will ultimately overcome his complaint entirely, at the same time saying that he has suffered a great deal both in body and mind. His letter is full of kindness and affection expressed towards us all and of deep feeling on the subject of our dear mother's death. he hopes to visit us all in the summer, nameing in this connection Youngstown, Allegheny City & Philada.

Pa's health has been excellent ever since you left us. I have taken great care to see that he is treated with regularity and system. . . . [Five lines are devoted to servants.] I hope dear Mary's health [Henrietta's older daughter] is firmly established by this time. Mit is in Philada. With love to all

Your affectionate brother
Stephen

Jane sends her love.
She is making summer dresses for Marion.
Please let me hear from you.

The postscript about Jane matches the tone of the whole letter— not quite false, but a tone of exaggerated cheer in circumstances very dismal. If Jane had taken a moment away from household duties to write, her tone might have been more realistic than dreamy Stephen's.

The main concern of both Henrietta and Dunning was for Stephen's health, happiness, and responsible conduct. If they were concerned for his work as songwriter, they left no evidence of that. Yet Morrison, in his book, generalized that the whole family had regarded Stephen's "poetic and musical genius" with pride. Morrison himself, fond of singing and of all sorts of theater, as well as proud of his whole family's good repute, may have felt a more complex concern for his wayward brother than the others could feel.

He may, to be sure, have attributed his own feelings to them all. He may, in the 1890s, have revised his own judgment with wider allowance for the dead "genius" than he had given "dear Stephy" at some critical moments. Or he may have waited until he was the last survivor of his generation before writing his memoir, lest one of the pious sisters should dispute a point and insist on expressing more sympathy than he felt for Jane. Families are complicated. But no matter whether Henrietta and her elder sister, Ann Eliza, could have approved Morrison's extreme reserve about Jane, the sisters would never have demanded that he give a place to "Jeanie."

Both sisters wrote poetry themselves, which Morrison doubtless called "sentimental." Henrietta even published some of her work in newspapers and magazines in 1862–64. Perhaps she thought her own share of the family "genius" as great as Stephen's; surely she meant her work to be more edifying than his, less lyrical, and not a bit amusing, for it dealt with the war, its griefs, and its religious overtones. Ann Eliza, modestly, kept her poetry in manuscript and kept its themes within the family. Two examples survive in which Stephen is mentioned. One is an elegy "written at the time of my brother Stephen's death," in six quatrains. Ann Eliza sends this to Pittsburgh because she cannot be there herself for the funeral. In the first stanzas she pictures the tombs of the parents and the siblings already dead, then she proceeds:

> And now, ye bring to our blest Mother's side
>   With bursting hearts, & reverential care,
> Her latest born, her darling & her pride;
>   And with meet Holy rites ye leave him there.
>
> Me—desolate mourner in my faroff home,
>   Alike by sickness & by sorrow prest,
> Can but in heart & mourning spirit come,
>   To bear our brother to his final rest.

Ann Eliza goes on to anticipate the deaths of all the mourners, and their souls' "bliss unending," in lines more to the taste of her clergyman husband than of Morrison. She has no message for Jane. Some years later Ann Eliza writes about the family again, in a long poem called "My Three Worlds." Here she evokes her happy childhood in Lawrenceville, where Stephen was born when she was a girl of twelve:

> What wealth of summer pastimes and of winter sports were ours,
> What frolics in our wandering for Springtime's earliest flowers.
> What gambols on the hillside where the old log schoolhouse stood,
> What strolls along the river bank, what rambles in the wood. . . .

Married in 1833, when Stephen was only six, Ann Eliza bore ten

children in the next two decades. She saw Stephen and Jane less
often than Henrietta, much less than Morrison. But by the time of
her long poem, if not before, she has come to feel pride in Stephen,
like Morrison's pride. Her lines about Stephen, following her tributes
to the departed older brothers, make a little climax in the poem:

> . . . How the infant boy, who filled the cradle then
> Grew up to weave a magic spell of melody for men:
> And when the world was fully waked to listen to his strain,
> Yielded his life, and gift of song, to Him who gave, again.

Did Ann Eliza sing any of Stephen's songs? If she did, it was more
likely the Sunday School songs of his last years than "Susanna" or
"Jeanie" or "Old Folks."

The sisters, if they knew "Jeanie" at all, knew it as one of Stephen's
efforts to rise above the almost unmentionable "nigger songs" that
earned his precarious living. If they called any of Stephen's work
"sentimental," they implied a regret that it was not more orthodox
in its sentiment. Both Stephen and Morrison, in their efforts to be
"gentlemen of the old school," fell short of the Christian chivalry
that was the ideal of Henrietta and Ann Eliza. If the sisters connected any of Stephen's songs with Jane they were astute enough to
see that Stephen's dreamy image of her was never much like the real
woman with a baby to care for.

The seven extant letters from Stephen to Morrison, 1853 to 1860,
include only two perfunctory references to Jane. On November 11,
1858, a trip to Cincinnati is planned, for Stephen, Jane, Marion, and
Mary Wick, Henrietta's twenty-one-year-old daughter. On April 27,
1860, from Warren, Ohio: "Jane and Marion are well, also Etty's
family." These letters, full of negotiations with publishers and miscellaneous information, suggest that Stephen did not confide his
marital troubles to Morrison.

Beginning in 1861, Jane did confide. She needed help. Her four
letters to Morrison show both of them coping with whatever is still
"strange and unaccountable" in Stephen's conduct. Jane uses the
family nickname for Morrison, "Mit."

September 30, 1861

Dear Mit:

I have been spending a couple of months here [at Lewistown, Pennsylvania, with her sister Agnes], and I am now beginning to feel very
uneasy about Steve, and he has not at present the money to send me.
I concluded to ask you to lend me ten dollars as I wish to go back
to him immediately, and indeed it is very necessary that I should be
with him. You will oblige me very much if you can send it, do so as
soon as possible. I would not ask you, Mit, for I know you have your
own family to take care of.

October 5, 1861

I received your letter yesterday, enclosing ten dollars and I assure you that I am very much obliged indeed. When I arrive in New York, I will deliver your message to Steve. Marion is well and sends her love to you. She goes to school every day; she is very attentive to her studies and is a most excellent child in every respect.

The delicacy, speed, and scope of this exchange go far toward filling the gap left by Morrison's silence in his book. The next letter is calmer:

June 30, 1862

I received a few days ago your very kind letter. You have my best and warmest thanks for your kindness. Marion is no worse, but she is still very delicate. I left Steve in New York; he was well, and publishes once in a long while with Pond. The clothing you sent him he was very much obliged to you & he told me that he would write and thank you.

Jane's way of referring to the songwriting business is distant, but respectful. Her outlook on the future is no longer anxious. But her last letter, sometime in October 1863, is only wistful in its hope:

You do not know, dear Mit, how much relieved I felt about Steve when I read your letter. If you can persuade him to return to Cleveland with you, I am sure that all will soon be well with him again.

Three months later, January 13, 1864, Stephen died. Morrison, called to New York to take charge, brought Jane to join him. They went together to Pittsburgh for the funeral.

When the copyrights came up for renewal in 1879, Morrison helped Jane draw up contracts so that she and Marion could receive the royalties. In 1891 "Jeanie" earned seventy-five cents. Between 1880 and 1898 royalties for all the songs together came to $3,815.49, but there was no more for "Jeanie." These facts, like Jane's letters, help to fill in the gaps of Morrison's book. Possibly, for anyone concerned about Jane, they modify the meaning of "Jeanie."

In her last years, around 1900 (after reading Morrison's book?), Jane reminisced about Stephen as often as her granddaughter, Jessie Welsh Rose, would listen. These reminiscences remained unwritten until the Foster centennial year, 1926, when Mrs. Rose published some of them in the Pittsburgh *Post*. In 1934 she expanded them for the *Foster Hall Bulletin*. They describe Stephen as an impulsive young suitor, as a convivial escort to a New Year's Ball in New York soon after "Jeanie," and as a shabby dresser in his last few years, but not as husband and father, not as songwriter. One surprising but plausible detail is worth extracting: Jane regarded Stephen as not so handsome as one of her taller beaux. But, she told her young listener, she never regretted that she had married him. Had kind Morrison's book convinced her that her little husband was a genius?

Morrison altogether omitted the "excellent child" Marion from his book. He never introduced his daughter to her cousin Marion, as he had done to her aunt Jane. He wished the world to forget that Stephen had failed in his role as provider for a child, whereas he gave eleven of his fifty-five pages to Stephen's own childhood.

Marion Foster was finally interviewed by an anonymous reporter for the Pittsburgh *Press* in 1900, and by a biographer of her father, John Tasker Howard, in 1933. The reporter quoted her recollections:

> I was his pet. He took me everywhere with him, and I was the only one allowed to invade the sanctity of his den where he wrote his songs. I could not quite understand his sudden change from my gay, almost child-like companion of the street, to the thoughtful preoccupied, almost stern man in the study. He could not bear the slightest noise or interruption in his work. I soon learned to respect his "composing moods" and not to interrupt him while at work.
>
> He took us constantly to the theaters, but his love for good music and his execration of indifferent music made it often very uncomfortable for the rest of us. It was not uncommon for him to jump up and bolt right out of the theatre if some unusually vile break in the orchestra or vocalization disgusted him.

The details make Marion's testimony convincing, and the emphasis on Stephen's sudden changes and his "almost childlike" character are worth remembering. J. T. Howard found the eighty-two-year-old lady not so articulate, but still emphasizing the same points. Repeatedly she said that her father always wanted her to have a good time; he loved to watch her dance. And she pictured him suddenly, after long days in his room at work, rushing out to the music store. It seems fair to say that for Marion he was more like a grown-up brother than a parent.

Since Marion was only about ten years old when she last saw her father, she was doubtless protected from any first-hand knowledge of his shortcomings and from much insight into her mother's "flitting" relations with him. Neither interviewer asked her about Jane. Neither asked about "Jeanie" or any other particular song. Her daughter, Jessie Welsh Rose, recalled that Marion's favorite composer was Tchaikovsky.

But if "Jeanie" means Jane, then another song must mean Marion. In December, 1853—that is, during the first separation—Foster's "Little Ella" was copyrighted. It has the rhythm of a waltz, rare among his songs, and words most appropriate for the father of a prattling two-year-old:

> Little Ella, fairest, dearest
>   Unto me and unto mine,
> Earthly cherub coming nearest
>   To my dreams of forms divine:
> Her brief absence frets and pains me,
>   Her bright presence solace brings,
> Her spontaneous love restrains me
>   From a thousand selfish things. . . .
> Little Ella brings a blessing
>   With her bright and winning smile,
> With her frank and fond caressing
>   And her prattle free from guile.
> When I hear her footsteps bounding,
>   In the hall or through the grove,
> And her voice with joy resounding,
>   'Tis the music that I love.

Juxtaposed with Marion's memories of her father, these lines sound sincere. They modify, for at least one reader, the meaning of "Jeanie," which was written so soon after "Ella." They sharpen a picture of the songwriter as a complicated man responding to his actual world, and organizing his response with the help of rhythm and rhyme. They intensify the sadness of Morrison's omissions.

Morrison's interpretation balances Stephen's "genius" with certain manly virtues, leaving aside not only parental responsibilities but also any question of faith, which to Morrison was a concern more of mothers than of gentlemen. Morrison describes Stephen's physique in a paragraph near the beginning of his book, and alternates the praise for sensitivity with praise for justice and bravery and frugality:

> In person he was slender, in height not over five feet seven inches. His figure was handsome; exceedingly well proportioned. His feet were small, as were his hands, which were soft and delicate. His head was large and well proportioned. The features of his face were regular and striking. His nose was straight, inclined to aquiline; his nostrils full and dilated. His mouth was regular in form and the lips full. His most remarkable feature were his eyes. They were very dark and very large, and lit up with unusual intelligence. His hair was dark, nearly black. . . . At times tears could be seen on his cheeks as he sang this song [the "May Queen" by Tennyson, as set to music by Dempster], so sensitive was his nature to the influence of true poetry combined with music. . . . And yet this sensitive man had the nerve and courage of a lion physically. From earliest childhood he was noted for his courage, coolness and skill in the combats which continually occur among boys of the same town. As he grew up, no odds ever seemed to awe him. . . . He was very simple in his tastes, and no matter how well his income justified it, he shrank from everything like display. . . . His love for his mother amounted to adoration. She was to him an angelic creature. There is not one reference to mother

in the homely words in which he clothed his ballads but came direct from his heart and symbolized his own feelings. . . . He was always indifferent about money or fame. It was perhaps fortunate for him that he had several older brothers, who, being practical business men, advised him in matters which he would not have realized the importance of. . . .

Morrison's own solicitude for Stephen was indeed more practical than that of the sisters, who were tied to their homes with no access to cash. Yet despite Morrison's business sense and his love of song, he never thought of helping Stephen find instruction in his craft or experience in the world of music and poetry. Morrison's notion of his brother's "genius" looks, from a musician's point of view, more sentimental than the sisters' faith in the "gifts of God." None of the close group of brothers and sisters was capable of appreciating in "Jeanie" the outcome of Stephen's "great pains" to advance in his art, or his hope that "Jeanie" and "Ellen Bayne" (also written in 1854) would earn more money after 1857 than "Old Folks."

In the last years of his life Stephen put very great strains on all his family. Not only did he let Jane support herself and the child (she found a job as telegraph operator at Greensburg, Pennsylvania), not only did he look shabby and sometimes ill, but he associated with New York theater people unknown to the family, he strayed from the wing of the Democratic party that defended slavery, and he drank rum—according to his closest friend of the time, George Cooper, he drank constantly but was never intoxicated. When we are ready to consider the songs the friends wrote together in those last years, George Cooper will concern us again, but for our present interests we may note simply that Cooper did not go to Pittsburgh for the funeral; his letter and telegram to Morrison sound as if the two had not yet met.

During the Civil War, Morrison, Henrietta, and Ann Eliza all disagreed with Stephen's support for the Union armies, as it was expressed in his songs "That's What's the Matter," "I'll Be a Soldier," "We've a Million in the Field," and "Nothing but a Plain Old Soldier." This disagreement affected their view of "Jeanie" and other songs, even after Morrison and Ann Eliza had responded to the surprising postwar revival of "Old Folks." Ann Eliza's interest in politics was simply that of the loyal, submissive sister-in-law of President James Buchanan, and mother of a young lawyer named for his uncle. Henrietta's interest was more fanatical; she and her husband supported the Ohio Democratic senator Clement L. Vallandigham, who was convicted of treason in 1863 and banished by President Lincoln behind the Confederate lines—he ran for governor of Ohio *in absentia* that fall, and when he lost the election retired to Canada.

Morrison was a quieter Copperhead, sympathizer with Vallandigham, but supporter of the Union Democrats. Morrison's wife Jessie had a young brother, Isaac Lightner, who fought in the Confederate army from 1861 until he was killed in 1864. Jessie Lightner had known Stephen and sung his songs in the early 1850s, when for several months Morrison was engaged to Julia Murray; Jessie and Morrison were married only in 1860. Jessie's death in 1882 permitted Morrison to forget all political differences with Stephen, which he naturally omits from his book of 1896. Yet their effect on his interpretation of Stephen's work as a whole lingered in the back of his mind, together with his feelings about Jane, whose political positions remain unknown.

The scandal of Stephen's addiction to drink hurt the family more than his politics. Did the drinking affect the family more directly? None of their documents prove that it did. Henrietta gave the opinion to her granddaughter that drink was the "sole reason" for the failure of his career, but she supported this opinion with no evidence whatever. Did she or Morrison hear George Cooper's testimony that Stephen was never intoxicated? Probably not, for Cooper never tried to profit from his friendship with Stephen, and his testimony comes to us only because he was sought out by a biographer, Harold V. Milligan, about 1919. The family may have known more than Cooper knew, or more than he told, but it may have known less, only to suspect more. Whatever it knew or suspected in 1864, it had to endure the scandal beginning in 1867 when two long articles about Foster were published.

The two articles dealt with Stephen's drinking in very different ways. The first was outspoken and cruel, the second evasive and apologetic. The first, by George Birdseye, provoked Morrison to scribble on a copy, "This fellow is evidently a fraud." Birdseye claimed to have known Stephen Foster from 1862 (when Birdseye was a boy of eighteen), to have heard him tell about his earlier life, and to have heard him sing "with the pathos that a state of semi-inebriation lends the voice." Birdseye speaks of Foster's "well known passion for drink," his "insatiable appetite for liquor," and, worse yet, a history of alcoholism dating back to the "serenading expeditions" of friends in Pittsburgh:

> He sometimes said that he believed that it was in these parties, and the feelings of social good fellowship generated by them, that the germs of his love for strong drink were first planted, to be the bane of his whole future existence.

The second article of 1867 is by a friend of the family, Robert P. Nevin, written for the *Atlantic Monthly* with some help by letter from Morrison. Nevin had known Stephen since 1850 or earlier, for in that year Stephen dedicated to him the duet in slow waltz time, "Turn Not Away." Nevin, as druggist, amateur singer, member of the Buchanan Glee Club of 1856, and correspondent in 1859 for the New York *Evening Post*, could back up his claim to authority concerning the nameless habit:

> . . . a habit grown insidiously upon him—a habit against the damning control of which (as no one better than the writer of this article knows) he wrestled with an earnestness indescribable, resorting to all the remedial expedients which professional skill or his own experience could suggest, but never entirely delivering himself from its inexorable mastery.

The accounts of Cooper, Birdseye, and Nevin are easily reconciled in 20th-century terms: up to about 1855 Foster was a moderate social drinker; if his drinking occasionally disturbed his family, it was in connection with more disturbing questions of money, of moving, of finding the rhythms of life for an unusual business. By about 1856 Foster was worried enough about addiction to consult the druggist; by 1862 he sometimes blamed the habit for his poverty or his melancholy or his changeableness. Still he seldom if ever got drunk, and if alcoholism contributed at all to his death it was only by way of malnutrition and neglect of his "ague and fever." The immediate cause of his death was loss of blood from an accidental fall in his hotel room when he was ill with the fever.

To Morrison all this was shameful. He argued privately that it was irrelevant to the public. He wrote the editor of an article derived from Birdseye's:

> . . . If my brother had been distinguished as an orator, an actor, appearing before the public in person, references to the only failing he ever had might perhaps be relevant, but the public knew not him but only of him, his poetry and music being the only visible sign that such a being really existed at all; reference to certain peculiarities is not only out of place, but is a cruel tearing open of old wounds, which the grave should close forever.

But the editor knew that scandal can help to arouse and sustain public interest in a man and his work, perhaps a songwriter's work especially. Readers who wish they could write a song can console themselves in pity for the drunk who did write. So Birdseye's description of the "well known passion for drink" would be endlessly repeated. Morrison's public silence on this topic leads some readers to dismiss all his flattering interpretations; this is as foolish as accepting them uncritically. His refusal to reopen the wounds becomes part of a more comprehensive account of his brother's char-

acter, and, for many a 20th-century reader, all that can be known
about the character affects the meanings of the work.

Drink, in the view of the Fosters, was likely to lead to worse
"failings" like gambling and adultery, and eventually to violence,
not to speak of opium, sodomy, or incest, which, after all, they knew
were part of the wide world. Liquor, in the eyes of Ann Eliza and
Henrietta, was no gift of God but the Enemy's first trap. If they said
"failing" they meant sin. The sisters were ready to forgive such a
sin, if the sinner would repent. But again, drink, in other views,
is an attempt to escape frustration in work and love and friendship.
Morrison's attitude betrays the family's limited perception of Stephen's songwriting business, of his high hopes and his "great pains"
to write better songs. If Morrison could have joined his brother in
a few drinks, he might have helped more to spread the fame of
"Jeanie," helped more to produce more of Stephen's best work, as
well as to keep him healthy enough to live longer. Such thoughts
as these, repressed from Morrison's own mind, may be the wounds,
deeper than any scandal, that he wished to bury.

Morrison was no prohibitionist, no activist in the temperance
movement, like William B. Foster, his father, back in the 1830s and
'40s. But Morrison probably heard more than Stephen did about
their father's efforts in those days, as mayor of Allegheny, to reform some of the town drunks. Morrison had his doubts about the
"nice young men" of 1845, and especially about Charles Shiras, the
poetical abolitionist son of the prosperous brewer, for once more
Morrison's book has a significant omission: Shiras' name is left
out of the list. Morrison may well have enjoyed sipping the Catawba
wine that had made Nicholas Longworth of Cincinnati rich enough
to be the nation's greatest patron of painting and sculpture in the
1850s. Morrison must have accepted a mint julep from a business
associate on his travels. But he never drank whiskey out of the same
jug with Billy Hamilton, the member of the Buchanan Glee Club
who later claimed to have drunk in this style with Stephen. And
Cooper's rum could not tempt him. Nor the niggers' gin. When
Morrison sang "Auld Lang Syne," his "cup o' kindness" did not extend to the "gude-willie-waught." He would not sing Burns' song
of the "big-belly'd bottle's a cure for all care," or "Gude ale keeps my
heart aboon," though he must have heard both, or at least read
them in a book that he treasured.

Morrison's book was an 1849 edition of *The national melodies of
Scotland, united to the songs of Robert Burns, Allen Ramsey, and
other eminent lyric poets, with symphonies and accompaniments
for the piano-forte by Haydn, Pleyel, Kozeluch, and other celebrated
composers.* In October 1858 Stephen asked Morrison to lend him

the book, presuming he had taken it along to Philadelphia where he was working for two years. Stephen wrote:

> If you have the book containing scotch melodies I wish you would send it to me, I will return it to you. I have sent to F.P.& co the Song "Sadly to mine heart appealing" (Lines suggested on hearing an old Scottish melody) and would like to select an old tune for the introductory symphony. If you have not the book probably you can tell me where to find one.
>
> S. C. F.

Morrison did not send it. Stephen made do for his "symphony" with the last phrase of "Robin Adair," which is not included in the book, though Burns had used it for his "Phyllis, the Fair." But Morrison had taken the book to Philadephia; he left it there in 1860 with Ann Eliza, as Evelyn Foster Morneweck discovered in 1938.

Of all the Burns songs, there is one especially likely to have hovered in the minds of Stephen and Morrison: "Fair Jenny," to the tune, "The Grey Cock." Burns' first stanza sets a mood that Stephen wrote of again and again:

> Where are the joys I have met in the morning,
>   That danc'd to the lark's early song?
> Where is the peace that awaited my wandring,
>   At evening the wild-woods among?

Two more stanzas dwell on the "sorrow and sad-sighing care" of the present moment. Then comes an answer:

> Fain would I hide, what I fear to discover,
>   Yet long, long too well have I known:
> All that has caused this wreck in my bosom,
>   Is Jenny, fair Jenny alone.—
>
> Time cannot aid me, my griefs are immortal,
>   Nor Hope dare a comfort bestow:
> Come then, enamour'd and fond of my anguish,
>   Enjoyment I'll seek in my woe.

Robert Burns did not hide his feelings as Morrison Foster did. Burns came out with the fact that his wife Jean "Jenny" Armour caused a wreck. Morrison suspected, at least, that Jane "Jennie" Foster had caused a wreck. (The word "wreck" was used by Stephen at least once: when an admiring musician, Mrs. Parkhurst Duer, in New York in 1863, put out her hand and asked "Is this Mr. Foster?" he took her hand and replied, "Yes, the wreck of Stephen Collins Foster.") But Morrison was too much the gentleman to say such a thing then or later. He silently refused to give Stephen any assistance in the most delicate public hint of such a fact. The forthright Burns further confessed that he was sometimes "fond of my anguish." Morrison knew that "sentimental" Stephen was just as fond. Burns proceeded to seek enjoyment, often in the "big-belly'd bottle," and Morrison knew that Stephen did the same. When Morrison sang "Jeanie," all these associations, conscious or unconscious, contributed to the meaning of the song for him. He hid them, if not from himself, certainly from his innocent daughter.

Stephen Foster dared once to sing about drinking. In 1854 the temperance movement was at a peak: the State of Maine had enacted a prohibition law in 1851, and a nationwide campaign now raged, with fury on both sides. A Pennsylvania referendum narrowly defeated a similar law in 1854. T. S. Arthur's novel of the same year, *Ten Nights in a Bar-room and What I Saw There,* was enormously popular. Now Stephen wrote "Comrades, Fill No Glass For Me." The song does not appear in his manuscript notebook. Its copyright, 1855, is by the Baltimore successors to F. D. Benteen, Miller and Beacham, presumably with permission from Firth and Pond, whose name appears in smaller print on the title page; this makes it an exception among all the songs from 1852 to 1860. Some biographers, like J. T. Howard, have supposed that "Comrades" was a potboiler for use in the temperance movement, but the full text fits no such use. Rather, it tends to confirm the apologetic testimony of the druggist Nevin, who knew Stephen well enough to have heard him sing the song soon after he wrote it:

> Oh! comrades, fill no glass for me
>   To drown my soul in liquid flame,
> For if I drank, the toast should be—
>   To blighted fortune, health and fame.
> Yet, though I long to quell the strife
> That passion holds against my life,
> Still, boon companions may ye be,
> But comrades, fill no glass for me.
>
> I know a breast that once was light,
>   Whose patient sufferings need my care,
> I know a hearth that once was bright,
>   But drooping hopes have nestled there.
> Then while the tear drops nightly steal
> From wounded hearts that I should heal,
> Though boon companions, &c.
>
> When I was young I felt the tide
>   Of aspirations undefiled,
> But manhood's years have wronged the pride
>   My parents centered in their child.
> Then, by a mother's sacred tear,
> By all that memory should revere,
> Though boon companions &c.

Foster is no Burns. The singer of "Comrades," if not Foster himself, is much like him, as we have come to see him from the letters of his family. He sings not to a big public at a theater or a temperance meeting, not to his patiently suffering wife, not to God, but to his drinking companions. He apologizes for his abstinence on this occasion. He begs in the name of his dead mother that his friends let him abstain. He admits that he still longs "to quell the strife," and makes no plea for forgiveness, no promise for the future. The rhythm for this song is that of a slow mazurka, lingering on the syllables "fill . . . drank . . . long . . . holds . . . breast . . . suff(erings) . . . hearth . . . hopes . . . tear . . . young . . . years . . . moth(er)." Far as Foster is from Burns, he is nearly as far from Morrison.

Henry Baldwin Foster sang his brother's songs and appreciated some of them in ways that Morrison never demonstrated. Though Henry was never the close companion to Stephen that Morrison was in the 1840s, nor the paternal helper that Morrison tried to be in the '60s (when their eldest brother William had died), still Henry knew Stephen all his life and expressed affectionate concern in many letters. That Stephen recognized Henry's concern is shown by the fact that in his final illness he commissioned George Cooper to send a telegram first to Henry; somehow it was delayed two days and did not arrive at Lawrenceville until Cooper had wired Morrison that Stephen was dead, so that Henry received Morrison's summons to meet in New York at the same time as the first message.

Henry could never forget the amazing day Stephen was born. All of America that day was celebrating the fiftieth anniversary of independence; General Lafayette had come to Washington to bring reminders of worldwide hopes for the maturing republic. At Lawrenceville the ten-year-old Henry, mothered by fourteen-year-old Ann Eliza, was kept out of the house at a picnic table in the grove, where their father took a leading part in a political jubilee, with thirteen prepared toasts, followed by twenty-three impromptu ones —the party was well reported in the Pittsburgh *Mercury*. When news came a few days later that the republic's two founding fathers, Adams and Jefferson, had died on the same day, friends proposed that the Foster baby should be called Jefferson Adams Foster, but he had already been named Stephen Collins, in honor of a family friend recently dead.

Ten years later, Henry was on a business trip with Dunning, down the river as far as Nashville. He reported some of his adventures in a letter to his mother, March 10, 1836:

> . . . While at Nashville, the Bar Keeper & myself (for want of a better companion) Hired a Horse each and Rode out to the Hermitage which

is a very neat Building . . . Tell Mit & Stevy to be good boys and go to school regularly, and when they have time what kind of fellers they have for playmates and how they spend their time, will be thankfully recd. in a letter from either.

Give my best respects to Brother William. I will ever remember him for his kindness shown to us all.

In haste, yours affectionately,

Henry B. Foster

The haphazard spelling and colloquial diction of Henry's letters add to their value. These traits persist to the end. So does the imaginative concern for the younger brothers, and the respect for the eldest, who more and more acted as father, while the real father floundered in his business and political enterprises.

From 1838 to 1840, according to Evelyn Morneweck, Henry strayed from the Episcopal church to the more zealous Presbyterians. But soon he returned to the fold and, from 1840 on, he regularly sang in the Episcopal choir. In 1841 he found a good job in the Treasury Department at Washington, which he held until the Whigs turned out the Democrats in 1849. A letter of December 20, 1841, reports to brother William about the city of Washington:

. . . Now, I don't consider this any great scratch of a place after all. There is one thing certain that it contains about as many fools as any place I was ever in. . . . We keep Bank Hours at the Treasury working from nine in the morning until three in the afternoon, Really! . . . There are four clerks in the room I write in, two of whom are old Gentlemen with nine & ten in family and receiving the same salary as Pa, ($1,000). We are all engaged at the same business which is very simple, recording certificates of land sales and making out patents, which I can do as well as any of them. . . . I suppose you have seen accounts of the House of Representatives having elected Moffett, the great Kentucky Methodist preacher their chaplain. . . . ever your

affect. Broth.

Henry

in haste   would like to hear from you soon.

In March 1842 Henry entertained his mother in Washington. He introduced her to President Tyler at the White House, and refreshed her acquaintance with the Pittsburgh politician for whom she had named this son, now Judge Henry Baldwin of the Supreme Court. (The family received many letters from her, written at leisure in an elegant style quite opposite to Henry's.) Mother and son went together to Baltimore, then to more parties in Washington, as Henry reported to William, March 25, 1842:

. . . he had the East Room thrown open and splendidly illuminated by five large Chandeliers, attended by a large concourse of People & a fine band of Music. . . . There has been one [party] during my absence which was attended by Chas. Dickens & Washington Irving, so I missed the best one of all.

In three years Henry saw enough of Washington to be ready to return to Pittsburgh, if by doing so he could provide Stephen with a starting point for a career. Stephen's letter about this proposal, written to Ann Eliza, September 19, 1845, is the only letter of his between 1841 and 1849 that survives; it provides an invaluable perspective view of the "nice young man" of nineteen, as well as evidence about his easy relation with Henry:

My Dear Sister,

In one of your letters you expressed a desire that I should compose for you some organ music, but as I have no knowledge of that instrument I have thought it advisable not to expose my ignorance. I have, however, seen Mr. Mellor who has promised to lend me some music that he thinks will suit, which I will copy and send to you.

Henry has written home saying that he would like to change places with some person until he may have time to come to Pitt. and rest himself, and as it would be a very pleasant change I have thought of taking his place in Washington. If I do so I will, no doubt, have an opportunity of visiting you. He seems to think that there is no chance of advancement in the office which he now holds and if he can get a good situation here he will let me make a perminent [sic] stay at Washn.

We have received one letter from Dunning since he left us—I suppose he visited Paradise on his way east—he had not, when he wrote, visited Philadelphia, where (as you must know) his true-love is staying.

I am writing amidst the bustle of the Hope warehouse—you must therefore forgive my haste.

We are all well excepting little Tom, who has had quite a fever but is now getting better.

Love to all—,

Your affectionate brother
Stephen.

By 1846 Henry's position in Washington made him the advocate of Stephen's application to West Point. On this he reports to Morrison —since William and Dunning are both away from home, Morrison is the temporary head of the household:

March 16, 1846

Dear Brother,

I received your acceptable letter of the 12th inst. & it seems that the appointment to West Point resulted (I can scarcely believe it possible that there is so little justice in our Government) in that of young McK. . . . However, I make no complaints, hoping that it may result for the best, as I doubt very much whether Steve's health would have permitted him to remain at the Point had he received the appointment. . . .

Tell Steve not to be discouraged & to try to get at some employment as soon as possible.

Calhoun spoke today in the Senate—was for giving the notice & compromise.

With much love to Ma, Etty, Steve, Pa & the children, in hopes that God may permit us all to meet again before another year passes over,

I remain

Your affect. Brother Henry.

P.S. How was Dunning's health when you last heard?   In haste

The stiff beginning of this letter may well reflect the awkwardness of reporting to the younger brother, as much as it does the possibly disappointing content of the report. In any case, Henry's practical concern for Steve goes beyond mere hasty reporting.

Before he returned to Pittsburgh and Lawrenceville for work, Henry visited Allegheny often, and in 1847 he married his old friend Mary Burgess. Their daughter, "Birdie," was born soon, their second and last in 1854. "Birdie" often stayed with her uncles and grandparents, and she could report to Henry observations that may have escaped Morrison.

Stephen's visits to Henry's house in these years were recalled in family legend and finally recorded by Jessie Welsh Rose in 1934. A cousin had told her how

. . . he would arrive at his brother Henry's home at any hour of the day or night, filled with a burning purpose to write some new music. Henry's distracted wife finally presented him with the piano, more to get rid of her nocturnal and importunate visitor than because she really wanted to part with the piano.

About the same time as this recollection was recorded, one of Henry's descendents, Henry Butterfield, presented to Foster Hall a collection of 117 of Stephen's songs bound in two volumes, probably by Henry.

The next surviving letter from Henry to Morrison, though it does not mention Stephen, tells a story that Morrison himself would not have recorded or preserved for posterity. Its nature and its telling may affect a reader's sense of the whole family, and thus of Stephen's songs. The date is July 5, 1858.

. . . By the bye, did you hear of Tom Holmes Baby & marriage? If not, I will inform you that one gloomy day not long since, a carriage stoped at the door of the Rev. Vand Dusen, out of which alighted J. N. Duncan and Robert Finney, who informed the Rev. Gent. that they would like him to accompany them to a house not far distant and baptize a *Baby*. The Revd. complied & was ushered into a room containing about half a dozen Gents. when the *Baby* was handed in, not a female to be seen.

Some of the Gents. informed the Revd. its name which he gave it . . . About a week after, the same Gents. called again . . . they wished him to bury that *Baby* which he did—not a female to be seen on this occasion either.

When they returned, the Revd. Gent. considered it necessary to have some explanation of this misterious affair & called the Gents. into his parlor, where it was divulged that Mr. Thomas Holmes was the Father of the infant at whose house it died & that the mother was kept by him as his mistress, but was quite an educated & pretty woman, at which the Revd. expressed his regret at so sad a prospect & determined to use his exertions to have the parties married, which he did, & Mr. Holmes gave him a check for $500 for his church.

Henry adds no comment. He proceeds to other news, ending, as ever, "in haste."

In 1864 Henry wrote two accounts of the death and funeral of Stephen. The first, January 23, is to a friend who seems not to have known the family but only admired the songs and asked Henry for information about their author. The second, February 4, is to Ann Eliza. The first reports on Henry's receiving the news, his trip to New York, and the "particulars of his [Stephen's] death," as far as Henry has learned them. Then he ends:

. . . owing to the desire of his musical friends to manifest their appreciation of his talents, we had him buried from Trinity Church where the ceremonies were exceedingly solemn, & at his grave I was completely overcome by *his loss*, and the beautiful music of the Brass Band performing his quortett [sic], called "Come where my love lies dreaming."

My anxiety about him is *now all over*. He was a firm belivere [sic] in the gospel of Christ. & ever had an abiding confidence in his mercy.

In hopes you are all well,—

I remain your friend
Henry B. Foster

To Ann Eliza, Henry's report is more intimate, less confident:

My Dear Sister

I received your very welcom letter of the 1st inst to day and hasten to reply, in hopes I may in some measure relieve your sorrow by the assurance that we found everything connected with Stevey's life and death in New York much better than we had expicted [sic], he had been boarding at a very respectable Hotel and did not owe the Landlord a cent or any one else that we knew of, had retired early to bed on Saturday evening, the following morning opened his door and spoke to the chaimbermaid and turned to go back to his bed when he fell as if he had been shot striking his head on the chamber, a surgeon was procured immediately and his wounds dressed, he then sent for his friend Mr. Geo Cooper (as fine a little gentleman as I ever met) who telegraphed to Morrison and I, and persuaded Stevey to go with him in a carriage to the Hospital where he would be better attended to. on Tuesday he was much better, and Mr. Cooper was with him. on Wendesday, he was proped up and after having taken some soup was quite cheerful. when they commenced dressing his wounds and just as the person was washing out the rag, without Stevey saying a word he fainted away and never came to again.

There is something particularly sad about his life and death, yes! poetically Sad, and I shall never again admire the beauties of nature without being reminded of some of his beautif songs, such as

> When Spring time comes Gentle Annie,
>   and the wild flower scatters oe'r the plain.
> we shall never more behold thee
>   or see thy lovely face again.

or

> I see her still in my dreams,
>   in my dreams,
> By the meadow and the streams.

Our dear Mother said she could not endure it, in case Stevey was taken from her, to hear his songs. and we now realize what she sadly anticipated, oh! my dear sister it was heart rending to hear the band play "Come where my love lies dreaming as they lowered him into his grave, oh! I hope he is now happy, and that our prayers in his behalf have been heard in Heaven.

Henry's memory of "Gentle Annie" and "I See Her Still," with a line transposed in one song and a word changed in the other, pays a tribute to his brother such as no one else recorded. Both these songs lament the death of a friend, with melodies similar to that of "Jeanie." Everything known about Henry makes it likely that these melodies did indeed come back to his inner ear when he admired the beauties of nature, throughout the remaining six years of his own life.

All the brothers and sisters were devoted to their parents. Stephen, to his credit in the estimation of Morrison, carried devotion to their mother to the point of "adoration." Morrison's portrayals of the parents emphasize the father's patriotism and generosity (leaving a critical reader room to guess that he failed as provider) and the mother's piety (which sounds preachy), her interest in "the best authors" (Scott and Irving? surely not Burns or Bryant or Dickens, who must have offended her in various ways), and even her "musical and poetic genius," bequeathed in the genes to Stephen (to compensate for neglect of cooking, washing, and other "perplexities of housekeeping," as she called them?). All Morrison's efforts cannot make the family match the 19th-century middle-class ideal. The parents, like the children, were more complicated, more interesting than any type.

To Stephen the parents were like grandparents. By the time he was born, their adopted son, William, was beginning to be chief breadwinner, for they themselves were nearly exhausted with the predictable rigors and the unpredictable changing social pressures of their lives. They continued to face life bravely, but their predominating attitude was resignation—in the mother's case devoutly hopeful, and in the father's case with a wry touch from Robert Burns' song of conjugal fidelity, "John Anderson My Jo." When Stephen was six, his mother had recently buried his little brother James, the last of her ten children, and the beautiful, musical Charlotte, her oldest. On May 14, 1832, she wrote to the valorous adopted son, William:

> As I have written one letter to Ann Eliza the only time I have had a pen in my hand that I can recolect, for two years or more, in fact I felt fearful of making unpardonable mistakes, which prevented me from makeing the attempt . . . my mind was restored to that tranquility which a perfect reconciliation to the will of that omnicient power which regulates and rules, and although the vessels are all broken which I hew'd out to hold the sources of my earthly joys, and all my goneby hopes are nothing but a dream, the song of joy, the delightful cottage, and the sound of the deep toned instrument still comes danceing on in the arrear of memory, with pain, and sorrow, at thought of how it closed, with the departure from this transitory stage of her we loved so dearly. . . . the sincere prayer of one who proudly clames the name of Mother to the best of sons.

Much of Eliza Clayland Tomlinson Foster's character shows through these strained lines. Most of the qualities that Stephen saw—the fear of mistakes, the striving for tranquility, the stumbling over religious formulae, the dwelling on "goneby hopes," the association of music with pain and sorrow—come together and lead to the pride in motherhood. A few years later, March 24, 1840, William Barclay Foster, Sr., wrote to his eldest son:

> Your mother is quite composed and resign'd to her destiny, and I still look forward to the time when we can have a permanent situation, where we may "Totter doon the Hill together" in peace and quietness, and sleep together at the foot, and be forgotten by all the world except our dear children.

The tune of "John Anderson" fit the father's fiddle as the stanza he alluded to fit his prevailing mood:

> John Anderson my jo, John,
>> We clamb the hill the gither;
> And mony a canty day, John,
>> We've had wi' ane anither:
> Now we maun totter down, John,
>> And hand in hand we'll go;
> And sleep the gither at the foot,
>> John Anderson my Jo.

The old man, listening to his son Stephen's songs of 1844 to 1855, cannot have been much impressed. There is no record of his disapproving them, but no hint that he responded as did Morrison or Henry. As he tottered on down, he let each of the sons take a part in mothering him—in 1840 William was entrusted with all responsibility for Stephen's education, while Henrietta gave the parents a temporary refuge; even the baby, Stephen, took his share of filial responsibilities in the last year, and especially the last month, July 1855.

"Jeanie," in 1854, like "Susanna," in 1847, seemed a small thing in the perspective of a couple married in 1807. Both songs belonged to the unmanageable age of railroad and telegraph. Old William Foster and his wife belonged to that of the Conestoga wagon and the great canals. Their heritage was divided between young William's career with the Pennsylvania Railroad, which left him no time for music, and baby Stephen's music, which constituted his dubious business; neither could represent the whole of the old couple's bygone hopes.

Despite his prevailing weakness, the old man could burst forth as a true disciple of his heroes of 1812, James Lawrence and Andrew Jackson. When Foster served a term as mayor of Allegheny in 1842, he stood up for justice and music at once, and fourteen-year-old Stephen was either an excited witness or an eager listener to first-hand reports. But this incident relates to "Old Folks" more than to "Jeanie." Morrison suggested the right connection when he wrote:

> Stephen was attentive and devoted to his sick father as long as the latter lived. The sentiment of the poetry in the song of "Massa's in de Cold Ground" expresses his own experience and feelings.

"Massa" was composed in 1852, closer to "Old Folks" than to the death of the father, but well after the father was a confirmed invalid.

The aging Eliza perked up when her husband was mayor. A long letter of hers to William, Jr., dated October 18, 1841, reassures him that his vain efforts to educate Stephen have at least done no harm, and describes her own state with lively ambiguity. Old William is away for the weekend on business in Erie.

. . . Stephen and I have the house to ourselves and lonely enough it is, so much so that it has induced a very pretty (girl, you think I am about to say, no they like gay places where there is some stir on foot,) tortoise-shell collour'd cat to take up her boarding and lodging with us . . . Stephen gives her all the little bits he is permitted to gather for the sake of her company . . .

He is not so much devoted to musick as he was; other studies seem to be elevated in his opinion. He reads a great deal, and fools about not attall. . . .

The new Christ Church takes up the most of our attention at this time, as it is now completely under way; fine Preacher, fine musick, fine stoves, plenty of room, and people flocking.

. . . What will I tell you about myself; a haknied [sic] stale story. You know what I am doing very well at this season, turning old clothes into new ones, looking after the baking and the cooking, and brushing about the house, and sometimes taking a comfortable rest in a rocking chair, by a pleasant coal-fire to read the Cronicle in the forenoon, and the daily American at four o'clock in the afternoon, going to bed at nine o'clock that I may rise at six to have breakfast for Morrison who is off to his business the moment it is over. We have ever and anon a quiet and peacible and temperate house, exactly such a one as I have always been longing for.

Oh, my dear William, I trust we shall all see a happy day at one smileing board, all in health and good spirits, and Pa the hapiest of us all. . . .

Stephen requests with Pa that I will give their love to Henry and yourself.

Eliza C. Foster

There is shrewdness along with some affectation in Eliza Foster's character. She indulges Stephen with the cat and not the music. She tries to take satisfaction in the peace and temperance of the house, but she hopes Pa will settle down and be happy—she never writes about the affairs of commerce and politics that continually upset him. She refers everything to God except her own "haknied stale" work. She adjusts herself to whatever joys and sorrows come, while she always longs for the stable happy home of her dreams.

By 1847 Eliza complains that her eyes are preventing her from writing often, but she writes a long letter to Morrison, August 23, to report on her impressions of Youngstown:

. . . The neighbourhood is the best I have ever liv'd in, and nothing can excede the beauty of the spot for shade and verdure. If I had some of my boys here, I would not wish to do better than to make my home here the rest of my days, but this may not be, as Pa says he is trying to sell it.

I am glad you had a pleasant trip. Have you been well since you came home? Poor dear Duning [sic], what perils is he going through by this time, when shall we hear from him again. [So much for the Mexican

War.] Was Henry quite well looking when you parted with him? [So much for Washington.] Have you seen any one who has seen Stephen since you came home? [Enough for all the business and music of Cincinnati.] . . .

May every happines attend you, that can be realized from the knoledge of your worth, be as religious as you are moral and dutifull [did Morrison ever understand this?].

Eliza's intelligence tends to be abstract and to work sporadically; her sons may have supposed that every mother's mind should resemble hers. Stephen in particular, mothered by such a large family, and looking to Eliza as the model, was ill prepared to see pretty nineteen-year-old Jane McDowell become a mother before he had known her very long.

Stephen's first song in the group of nine or ten whose titles include the word "mother" appeared in March 1851, a month before the birth of Marion: "Mother, Thou'rt Faithful to Me." In 1861, when he has partially abandoned wife and child, and has mourned his dead mother for six years, there are three: "Oh! Tell Me of My Mother," in August; "Farewell Mother Dear," September; "Farewell Sweet Mother," October. Then in April 1862 comes "A Dream of My Mother and Home," the most elaborate of the group in its musical development. In 1863, published in Sunday School booklets, there are three more: "Leave Me with My Mother"; "Tell Me of the Angels, Mother"; and "Bury Me in the Morning, Mother." Published posthumously there is "Kiss Me, Dear Mother, Ere I Die"; a setting by Foster of a poem by Mrs. M. A. Kidder, "Oh! Meet Me Dear Mother"; and a doubtful song advertised as Foster's "last musical idea," "Give This to Mother." Any reader who goes beyond the titles to the repetitious contents must acknowledge that the first five of these songs sound as thoroughly honest as "Jeanie" and that even the last of the group, though doubtless more hurried and perhaps not entirely authentic, are far from crass bids for a supposedly scorned audience's readiest response. (Though publishers took a chance on these songs, there is no record that anyone sang them before about 1940.) Taken as a whole, the group tends to confirm Morrison's report of Stephen's "adoration." Several songs show the singer desperately trying to believe in a happy reunion with his dead mother after his own death. He does not claim assurance; he does not even pray for the mercy that Henry Foster hoped for, but rather he dreams obsessively of his mother.

The mother songs, though repetitious, make a group less coherent than the minstrel songs from "Susanna" to "Ring de Banjo." There are no cross references in the texts of the mother songs, so there is less reason to think of a single character as singer of them all. And if the similarity of theme and tone is enough to unite the mother songs, it unites them with many more of the "Jeanie" type. The dreams of dead mothers and the dreams of absent "Jeanie," "Lula," "Queen of My Song," "Nell," dead "Gentle Annie," "Lena, Our Loved One," and the nameless dead beloved of "I See Her Still in My Dreams" all blend together, as dreams typically do. In the very first song of this subgroup, "Where Is Thy Spirit, Mary?", Foster wrote of Mary Keller, to whom he had dedicated his "Good Time Coming," in 1846. Mary had died that same year, and the new song was dedicated to her sister Rachel, who published it only in 1895. In the text of "Laura Lee," which Foster worked over through nine pages of his notebook in 1851, there is a repeated question:

> Why has the happy dream,
> Blended with thee,
> Passed like a flitting beam
> Sweet Laura Lee?

The dreams blend with the women who inspire them. The women blend with each other in Foster's mind and his listeners'. All the women are gone from the singer's life; they linger in his dreams. Whether they were once his Laura, his wife, his sister, his mother, or his grandmother makes little difference to him. He has depended on them. Now he is abandoned. He dreams on.

Though neither Morrison's book nor any family document connects other songs closely with particular women, we may be tempted to do so. The first published song of the "Jeanie" type with words by Foster himself, in 1847, is "What Must a Fairy's Dream Be?" It is dedicated to the daughter of the Allegheny judge Thomas Irwin, friend of the "nice young men." The song, instead of answering its repeated title-question, offers dreamlike speculations that should have won a smile from the girl as she swayed to the pastoral 6/8 rhythm. "Stay Summer Breath" of 1848 is dedicated to a Cincinnati belle, a doctor's daughter, who is mentioned by Morrison as a fine soprano. This song, too, is full of fanciful questions, unanswered; the breeze is gently bid to desist from any wooing; the rhythm has a trembling kind of syncopation. "Ah! May the Red Rose Live Alway!", dedicated to the sixteen-year-old daughter of an old family friend in Allegheny, 1850, repeats the question "Why should the beautiful die?" with another lilting 6/8 rhythm. (The melody has won the affection of several antiquarian performers in the 20th century.) "Mary Loves the Flowers," in 1850, has no dedication. Stephen may be recalling Mary Keller, four years dead, when the singer pleads:

> Let no elfin finger
> > Blur from memory's sand
> Her name—ah! let it linger
> > While my airbuilt castles stand . . .
> To die beneath her tender care
> > Were life to me.

About the same time as this last song, there is one that might be an appeal to Jane—"Molly Do You Love Me?":

> . . . Let my dreamy rapture
> > Turn to waking joy. . . .
> Molly do you love me?
> > Love as I love you? . . .
> Can that voice's music
> > Flow from heartless glee?
> Must I read no feeling
> > In that melody?

These questions to "Molly" were copyrighted in May 1850. In June, still a month before the marriage, a song is copyrighted that seems to hark back to Mary Keller—"The Voice of By Gone Days":

> . . . Youthful fancy then returns,
> > Childish hope the bosom burns,
> > Joy, that manhood coldly spurns,
> Then flows in memory's sweet refrain.
> > Ah! the voice of by gone days
> > Will come back again. . . .
>
> Ah, the voice of by gone days
> > Bids my memory rove
> To the fair and gentle being
> > Of my early love.
> > She was radiant as the light,
> > She was pure as dews of night,
> > And beloved of angels bright,
> She join'd their bless'd and happy train.

Worse yet is a song copyrighted in April 1851, just before the birth of Marion. For this song, "Once I Loved Thee," the words are attributed to William Cullen Crookshank—probably a tribute to W. C. Bryant and the illustrator George Cruikshank—but they sound like Stephen Foster:

> Once I loved thee, Mary dear,
> > O how truly! . . .
> I loved thee, when in early youth
> > Lovely ever—
> Virtuous pride and honest truth

Ne'er could sever . . .
Sinning never . . .
O that dream hath passed away,
. . . And the tale of life is told
Passions blighted, withered, cold . . .
Though I drain my cups apart,
May, like mine, a saddened heart
Ne'er distress thee— . . .
May the passing moments roll
Bliss eternal to thy soul,
Holy, holy— . . .

About the time he wrote this song, if Jessie Rose's report is true, Stephen paid for an "artistic headstone" at the grave of Mary Keller. But worst of all is a cheerful song, copyrighted in October 1853 and destined to sell more copies than any other song in the series, including "Jeanie." This is "Maggie by My Side," dedicated to a Pittsburgh girl, Eliza Denniston, about whom nothing is known. The rhythm is vigorous and marchlike:

The land of my home is flitting,
Flitting from view;
A gale in the sails is sitting,
Toils the merry crew.
Here let my home be,
On the waters wide:
I roam with a proud heart;
Maggie's by my side;
My own love, Maggie dear,
Sitting by my side. . . .
Roll on ye dark waves,
O'er the troubled tide:
I heed not your anger,
Maggie's by my side.

Such defiant good cheer is unique among the Foster songs. If Eliza-"Maggie" brought it to expression for only a moment, she deserved a share of the $278.01 the song earned by 1857. (Stephen estimated that "Maggie" might earn another $75 after 1857. In 1968 his manuscript of "Maggie" was sold at auction for $4500—enough to have supported both author and dedicatee for some years.) If an almost irresistible guess about "Maggie" is indulged, then once more the meaning of "Jeanie" is modified: an affair with Eliza called for more than sad dreams of "Jeanie" to bring Jane and Stephen together.

Three songs of 1860–62 refer to "Jenny" or "Jenny Dow": "Jenny's Coming O'er the Green," 1860; "A Penny for Your Thoughts," 1861; and "Little Jenny Dow," 1862. Two men who knew Foster in those years reported contradictory interpretations of the name. George Birdseye, in an article of 1879, claimed that "Jenny Dow" meant Jane McDowell; that Stephen often sang "Jenny's Coming" "so tenderly and earnestly that the effect was always pleasing," and that he spoke of his wife "in the fondest terms" in connection with this song, "yet why they thus lived separately he never mentioned, always avoiding the subject." John Mahon, on the contrary, testified that Stephen told him of another "Jenny Dow," whose age of seventeen, originally mentioned in the first line of the song, he had deleted at Jane's request. We shall return to these songs in another context. They are more interesting in themselves than as inconclusive evidence about Stephen's biography.

Any of our unflattering guesses about the relations of husband and wife, based only on the songs and their dedications, must be weighed with less cynical guesses: possibly "Mary" as well as "Molly" means Jane; possibly even "Maggie" is Jane, and the married couple knew at least a moment of shared pride and joy in the face of the "troubled tide" of their life. Our knowledge permits either kind of guessing. It requires neither.

The group of songs addressed to a woman, like "Jeanie," "Mother," and "Maggie," can be stretched to include one song that tells of a family as a whole and of the singer's longing, not for one beloved person so much as for the thronging group that sheltered him in childhood. Such is "Farewell Old Cottage" of 1851. The singer's loneliness here is the same as the loneliness of the singers who address the women of their dreams.

> Farewell! old cottage,
>   You and I must part:
> I leave your faithful shelter
>   With a poor breaking heart.
> The stranger, in his might,
>   Hath cast our lot in twain;
> The term of our delight
>   Must close in parting pain.
> Farewell! &c.
>
> Farewell! old cottage,
>   Memory still enthralls
> The loved ones of my childhood
>   In your time-beaten walls.
> Here my brother played
>   In pride of health and youth,
> Here my sister prayed
>   In purity and truth.
> Farewell, &c.

Farewell! old cottage,
    Oft times from afar
Yon window light hath served me
    As a loved guiding star,
And cheered a heart that longed
    To join the household mirth
Where happy faces thronged
    A hospitable hearth.
Farewell! old cottage
    You and I must part: &c.

The White Cottage in Lawrenceville where Stephen Foster was born was abandoned by his family soon after his fourth birthday, with mingled regrets, hopes, and fears. When he was thirteen he parted from his parents in their boarding house, to go to school under the protection of William. At about twenty he parted to go to work in Cincinnati with Dunning. At twenty-four, with his new wife, Jane, he parted from his parents again to try his fortune in New York at his "business of song-writing." At twenty-seven he parted temporarily from Jane. At twenty-nine he parted from his parents for ever, unless they might meet in Heaven. From 1851, when he wrote "Farewell! Old Cottage," till he died, he continued to dream of the "faithful shelter," the "guiding star," the "hospitable hearth." His dreams of "Jeanie" and "Mother" blended with his own and his mother's dream of the "Old Cottage."

So many partings! If Stephen had never smiled, he might have been excused. If he had put on blackface to smile, he might have reconciled the family to such an indignity. He did not test their tolerance. His writing for blackfaced actors, for the sake of a smile and a little money, they accepted, uneasily. His asking the actors to put aside the smile and express the "pathos" of his best "plantation songs," we can understand. His sharing in the widespread literary trend of his age to dream of departed ladies seems now almost inevitable. That he never sang of love fulfilled, or of an overwhelming passion, or of remorse and fresh resolve is not surprising.

In one exceptional song the singer is a woman, thinking of a man. This is "The Wife," copyrighted 1860. The complete text of this song invites interpretation in the light of the Foster couple's life:

He'll come home, he'll not forget me,
    for his word is always true.
He's gone to sup
The deadly cup,
    And while the long night through.
He's gone to quaff,

And talk and laugh,
    To while the drear night through:—
He'll come home, &c.

He'll come home with tears and pleading words,
    and ask me to forget.
Can I be his
While he is mine
    And cause him one regret?
My heart may break,
But for his sake
    I'll do all I can do;—
He'll come home, &c.

He'll come home with sorrow on his heart
    that none but he can know,
With pangs of thought,
How dearly bought!
    And fears of coming woe;
He'll feel the cost
Of days now lost
    That time can ne'er renew.
He'll come home, he'll not forget me,
    for his word is always true.

The absent husband resembles Stephen. The Jane we have seen in
her letters and the family letters about her resembles "The Wife"
more than "Jeanie," who is one of Stephen's dreams. Here, in 1860,
about the time that Stephen and Jane last lived together, his song
seems to match more of his real life than most of his previous songs
do—the real attitude of another toward him he sees clearly, and
this attitude leaves room for the sorrow "that none but he can
know." Dreams are dismissed. The dream-songs are not false, but
their truth is cloudy and weak, whereas in "The Wife" there is
extraordinary force behind the refrain—"his word is always true."
Such a force can be felt in the extraordinary contour of the melody,
even without the words. It is still a simple "dulcem" melody but it
moves forward over the steadily pulsing accompaniment, through
the gasps of the short lines, up the scale to a steadily swinging, descending final phrase.

Stephen and Jane set out in 1850 to "climb the hill together." They
did not manage as well as their parents, "toddling down." When
Jane found that Stephen could not replace her father, she did not
resign herself to an inscrutable God, nor indulge herself with dreams
of childhood, but coped with her own life as best she could; she accepted temporary mothering from Morrison and Henrietta; she gave

the baby Marion a mothering sufficient for her to grow up to motherhood in her turn. When Stephen found that Jane could not play the part of a mother to him as well as the baby, nor the part of a companion on a carefree adventure, and that his work paid too little to maintain the family, he withdrew, by fits and starts, into lonely childish dreams. He rallied for a rare moment to express Jane's truth in "The Wife."

The best intentions of the Fosters contributed to keeping Stephen a child, more childish than any of their dutiful daughters or their daughter-in-law, more childish than the "niggers" he sometimes sang about. The attitude of Morrison most of all, demanding respectable prudence, conformity, and public achievement from any man, yet making allowances for an exceptional "musical and poetic genius" as if he were always to be a child—this attitude, in which Morrison merely represented many more powerful people and overpowering impersonal tendencies familiar all over the world, thwarted Stephen Foster.

More gifted men than Foster suffered similar stunting: Thoreau, for one, surrounded by an indulgent mother and mothering sisters, convinced of his own genius and the desperate corruption of society, could never take responsibility for a household, could never join in a chorus of singers, could neither join nor desert his hero John Brown, could not find readers for *Walden*, could not survive to complete the successors to *Walden* for which his Journal was full of materials. Foster's shortcoming is less deplorable than Thoreau's.

Having observed Stephen Foster and his songs from the viewpoints of many members of his family, we know him more than did the minstrel singers, publishers, critics, or groups of working people who put his melodies to use. We know some of his songs, like "Jeanie," more nearly as he himself knew them than do most singers and listeners. We can turn to a song like "Jeanie" that we have not heard before, able to understand its words in the context of Foster's life with and without his family and to attach concrete meanings to his "dreams."

Yet we are far short of a complete knowledge of Foster and his songs. We have postponed making any close acquaintance with Foster's best friends outside the family—Charles Shiras, Billy Hamilton, and George Cooper—who shared in his work and play in ways that none of the family could share. Their perspectives too are relevant to "Jeanie."

These companions and collaborators, moreover, might have laughed at our patience with people so different from Stephen Foster as his family, so little able to share his life, so ignorant of the traditions of music and poetry that he tried to animate. Of course he made use of his personal experience in his work, but that experience does not provide *the meaning* of "Jeanie" or of any song. Each song must organize selected meanings, evoke multiple meanings, accommodate meanings unsuspected by the author himself, not to speak of his family.

CHAPTER 7

Foster
and his public
in the tradition
of "home songs"

STEPHEN FOSTER worked in an international tradition of popular song. His dreams of "Jeanie with the Light Brown Hair,"
"The Old Cottage," and other people and places that can be associated with his family connect the same songs also with the public
tradition; for singers and listeners familiar with the tradition, these
connections constitute a meaning more important than private associations. Throughout the twenty-year span of his songs, 1844–64, he
tried steadily to participate in the international tradition; in the central years 1853–59, while the earlier "plantation melodies" like
"Susanna" and "Old Folks" continued spreading around the world,
Foster wrote no more of them but only songs like "Jeanie."

Foster's contribution to the broad tradition was most clearly represented, for the public after 1853, by "Old Dog Tray." "Tray"
sold more copies than most of the "plantation songs" and far more
than "Jeanie" or any other "sentimental song." "Old Dog Tray"
was sung by the Christy minstrels. It was sung by Henry Russell and
other concert soloists. From these performances it spread quickly
and widely. It was often parodied. Its tune was used for new words,
not so often as "Susanna," but more often than "Old Folks," not to
mention "Jeanie," which remained little known. Unlike "Susanna"
and "Old Folks," "Old Dog Tray" was advertised from the start as
a song by Stephen Foster; together with "My Old Kentucky Home,"

"Old Dog Tray" represented Foster to millions of his contemporaries, who knew and shared his tradition as no later generation can do.

Later admirers and critics of Foster, knowing something of him as author of "Susanna" and "Old Folks," but ignorant of most of the international tradition in which "Jeanie" and "Old Dog Tray" competed, give less emphasis to "Old Dog Tray" than did Foster's contemporaries. Some 20th-century readers find the song unfamiliar, while others remember it only in fragments. The full text will help some recall the catchy tune. Readers who remember all three stanzas by heart will be surprised, in turn, to learn of a song about "Poor Dog Tray" by the Scottish poet Thomas Campbell (1777–1844), whose name was illustrious in Foster's time. A comparison of the two poems can bring out at once several debts of Foster to the international tradition. First Foster's words:

> The morn of life is past,
> And evening comes at last;
> It brings me a dream of a once happy day,
> Of merry forms I've seen
> Upon the village green,
> Sporting with my old dog Tray.
> CHORUS: Old dog Tray's ever faithful,
> Grief cannot drive him away,
> He's gentle, he is kind;
> I'll never, never find
> A better friend than old dog Tray.
>
> The forms I call'd my own
> Have vanished one by one,
> The lov'd ones, the dear ones have all passed away,
> Their happy smiles have flown,
> Their gentle voices gone;
> I've nothing left but old dog Tray.
> Old dog Tray's ever faithful, &c.
>
> When thoughts recall the past
> His eyes are on me cast;
> I know that he feels what my breaking heart would say;
> Although he cannot speak
> I'll vainly, vainly seek
> A better friend than old dog Tray.
> Old dog Tray's ever faithful, &c.

Foster's "dream" of the past is not so vivid as Campbell's, nor his desolation so complete, nor his lines so long, nor his stanzas so logically knit together; but the mood is the same, as well as the name of the dog, his fidelity, and his kindness. The title of Campbell's poem is "The Harper."

On the green banks of Shannon, when Sheelah was nigh,
No blithe Irish lad was so happy as I;
No harp like my own could so cheerily play,
And wherever I went was my poor dog Tray.

When at last I was forced from my Sheelah to part
She said (while the sorrow was big at her heart),
"Oh! remember your Sheelah when far, far away,
And be kind, my dear Pat, to our poor dog Tray."

Poor dog! he was faithful and kind, to be sure,
And he constantly loved me, although I was poor.
When the sour-looking folk sent me heartless away,
I had always a friend in my poor dog Tray.

When the road was so dark, and the night was so cold,
And Pat and his dog were grown weary and old,
How snugly we slept in my old coat of gray,
And he licked me for kindness—my poor dog Tray.

Though my wallet was scant I remembered his case
Nor refused my last crust to his pitiful face;
But he died at my feet on a cold winter day
And I played a sad lament for my poor dog Tray.

Where now shall I go, forsaken and blind?
Can I find one to guide me so faithful and kind?
To my sweet native village, so far, far away,
I can never return with my poor dog Tray.

Campbell's "Harper" sings all too fluently. The extra syllable in the line of "sad lament" sounds like carelessness, not syncopated emphasis. The sudden revelation that the harper-minstrel is blind sounds like a trick. The neglect of Sheelah's memory after the second stanza diminishes her "big sorrow." There are other faults in Campbell's poem that account for its obscurity since his death. But in its day it was an acceptable song. Foster was bold to compete with it, lucky to supersede it for his own generation.

Morrison Foster, when he came to write about his brother in 1896, could assume that Campbell's poor dog was forgotten. Morrison's readers wanted a portrait of Stephen Foster, not literary history. Morrison provided a paragraph about a favorite dog, the gift of a distinguished Pittsburgh lawyer, neighbor of the Fosters in Allegheny. Morrison avows that Stephen "put into verse and song the sentiments elicited by remembrances of this faithful dog." Then in the next paragraph, as if to undercut his own sentimentality, Morrison tells how Stephen was once so upset by a strange dog's barking at night that he dashed out "partly dressed, with a poker in his hands" and chased the dog away. "The family had a good laugh at the author of 'Old Dog Tray' the next day." Morrison's assumption about "sentiments" in song, as neatly demonstrated here, provokes smiles in the 20th century more commonly than it seems to have done among readers and listeners in the 19th; but the smiles are readier when the object of the sentiments in question is a dog, rather than a wife or a mother, in the 20th century as well as the 19th. In Stephen's relation to the tradition of song, of course, "Old Dog Tray" and "Jeanie" and many more belong together.

Evelyn Foster Morneweck adds an anecdote about "Old Dog Tray." Stephen began the song, she says, at a friend's house, and thought it so silly that he left it there unfinished. On his next visit the friend persuaded him to finish it, but even when he sent it off to the publisher he had no high opinion of it. In 1857, however, he estimated that it might produce another $150, better than the $100 for "Old Folks," though well below his hopeful estimates for "Jeanie" and "Gentle Annie." "Old Dog Tray" was part of his central effort—a doggedly persistent effort.

If the theme of "Old Dog Tray" was less heartfelt than the obsessively repeated dreams of absent mother and wife, prospective customers in the music shops and their audiences in parlors and picnic groves and the new music halls of London still preferred the dog. Many competing songwriters held these audiences with dreams of other ladies, whereas Campbell's "Harper" offered poor competition. "Old Dog Tray" helped win only a small part of its audiences for "Jeanie," a larger part for "Gentle Annie," "Come, Where My Love Lies Dreaming," and "Beautiful Dreamer," but none of these songs rivalled the successful "plantation songs" and "Old Dog Tray." The friend in Morneweck's anecdote could understand this more readily than Morneweck could. We may go so far as to imagine the friend encouraging Stephen to finish his song, not by any remark about the faithfulness of the old dog, but rather by some remark about the old song of Campbell—little Steve could do better than that with half a try!

In the 1840s and '50s, the fame of Campbell and scores of writers like him was still vigorous. Criticism was increasing, but a struggle was required for even the best younger writers to supersede the old favorites, to transform their tradition. In 1850 Alfred Tennyson succeeded Wordsworth as poet laureate and alert critics began to hail Tennyson "the poet of the age." By the end of the century, when Tennyson himself was being roughly pushed aside, the older tradition survived only in a few songs whose authors' names were all by that time obscure like Campbell's. Tennyson's "Sweet and Low" (1850), with the tune by Joseph Barnby (1838–96), was a similar remnant. In the 20th century we must rely on specialist historians of literature and music to recover anything of Foster's tradition. We sift the specialists' work and coordinate it in relation to Foster, without necessarily wishing to restore the prestige that the tradition still commanded in his youth.

Tennyson's wife once wrote of her husband that "since Burns he is almost the only poet who has been able to do a song." Aware that hundreds of people between Burns and Tennyson tried, we may agree that none of them reached the supreme heights, yet we can suppose that their efforts made a sort of range among whose foot-hills we may place most of Foster's songs.

Some poems of Tennyson became favorites of Stephen, Morrison, Charles Shiras, and the other "nice young men" and their musical wives during their twenties and thirties. Burns belonged to their fathers and grandfathers. The songwriters between Burns and Tennyson were those that the young people shared in childhood and adolescence with their mothers and elder sisters. George P. Morris, Charles Mackay, and Henry Russell, directly connected with Foster and with each other, were typical of these songwriters, but several others made more serious contributions. When Morris edited a first anthology of *American Melodies,* 1840, he had to include two hundred writers.

A chronological list of contributors to the tradition enables us to see at a glance something of its extent, variety, and continuity. The list is a selective one, as specialists will recognize. Names are chosen not merely to represent various aspects of the tradition, but particularly to show Foster's many links with it. A few remarks about each writer on the list will demonstrate more—the density and power of their tradition and its narrowing development of a central theme. Among these writers, various 20th-century readers and singers may find various appeals to further study; every student of Foster can benefit from an acquaintance with the whole group in their interrelations.

POETS	MUSICIANS
1748 Hugh Henry Brackenridge, d. 1816	
56	(W. A. Mozart, d. 1791)
59 (Robert Burns, 1796)	
63	(Stephen Storace, d. 1796)
70 James Hogg, 1832	
71 Walter Scott, 1832	
74	John Braham, 1856
76 Carolina Oliphant, Lady Nairne, 1845	
77 Thomas Campbell, 1844	

POETS	MUSICIANS
1779 THOMAS MOORE, 1852	
81 Ebenezer Elliott, 1849	
84 Alan Cunningham, 1842	
Samuel Woodworth, 1842	
86	Henry Rowley Bishop, 1855
	Charles Edward Horn, 1849
87 Barry Cornwall	
(Bryan Waller Procter) 1874	
88 Sara Josepha Hale, 1879	
89 Richard Henry Wilde, 1847	
90 Fitz-Greene Halleck, 1867	
91 John Howard Payne, 1852	
92	Frank Johnson, 1844
93 Felicia Hemans, 1835	
James Hall, 1868	
96 Alfred Bunn, 1860	
97 Thomas Haynes Bayly, 1839	
Samuel Lover, 1868	
98	John Broadwood, 1864
1801	John Hill Hewitt, 1890
02 GEORGE POPE MORRIS, 1864	
06 Nathaniel Parker Willis, 1867	
08	Michael William Balfe, 1870
09 ALFRED TENNYSON, 1892	William Richardson Dempster, 1871
10	Alicia Ann Spottiswoode,
	Lady Scott, 1900
12	HENRY RUSSELL, 1900
	John Pike Hullah, 1884
14 CHARLES MACKAY, 1889	
17 Denis Florence McCarthy 1882	
25 Adelaide Ann Procter, 1864	
26 James Madison Bell, 1902	STEPHEN FOSTER, 1864
?	Richard Milburn, active 1855
27	Septimus Winner, 1902
31 Metta Victoria Fuller, 1886	
36 (William Schwenk Gilbert,	
1911)	
42	(Arthur Sullivan, 1900)

The pioneer American novelist, and founder of Pittsburgh's intellectual life, Hugh Henry Brackenridge, disliked and disapproved most music; he ordinarily left poetry to his Princeton classmate, Philip Freneau. But he once paid tribute to Burns, in a poem so good that the Foster family must have known it, "Whiskey":

I'm mair among unletter'd jocks
Than well-lern'd doctors wi' their buiks;
Academies and college nuiks
           I dinna ken;
And seldom wi' but kintra folks
           Hae I been benn.
Ye canna then expect a phrase
Like them ye get in poets' lays;
For where's the man that now-a-days
           Can sing like Burns,
Whom Nature taught her ain strathspeys
           And now she mourns.
I dinna like to sign my name
By that o' Whiskey, fie for shame!
I had a better ane at hame;
           In town or city
Where a' were glad to get a dram
           O' aqua vitae.

Brackenridge's novel *Modern Chivalry*, finished in 1815, was of course more important to the Fosters. Its hero, Captain John Farrago, and Teague O'Regan, his servant, paved the way for all the more Romantic fictional knights, squires, and minstrels of the next generation, and for the mock-chivalry of Morrison Foster's "Knights of the Square Table."

The supreme Romantic novelist, Scott, began his career as translator of German ballads (1796), editor of a three-volume collection of *Minstrelsy of the Scottish Border* (1802–03), and poet of "The Lay of the Last Minstrel" (1805). His use of the word "minstrel," approximating usages in earlier centuries that were archaic by his time, repopularized it, so that the Christys and others of the 1840s could count on its Romantic connotations. Scott's worldwide prestige continued all through the century. Balzac called him "the Homer of the novel." Though Scott's poetry naturally had a smaller audience than his fiction, it too was popular; its popularity lasted longer in America than in England, and especially in the Southern states. The bardic stanzas "Hail to the Chief," from his long narrative *Lady of the Lake* (1810), led to the adoption of their old Scotch boat-song as a theme of American presidents, beginning with Polk, in 1845. The pleading mood of Scott's "Minstrel's Request," softer than anything by Burns, is more typical of the mood that came to dominate the tradition:

I have wandered all the day,
Do not bid me farther stray.
Gentle hearts of gentle kin,

> Take the wand'ring harper in!
> . . . All my strength and all my art
> Is to touch the gentle heart.

The words pencilled on the scrap of paper found in Stephen Foster's purse when he died sound like a reminiscence of Scott: "Dear friends and gentle hearts." The name "Scott" is one of eleven in a list on the inside cover of Foster's sketchbook, indicating that he possessed a volume of the great author. He knew that Scott was more than a songwriter and that his participation in the tradition of song added much to its glory.

James Hogg, "the Ettrick shepherd," on the other hand, made the tradition laughable to sophisticated critics right from the start. Hogg's *Scottish Pastorals,* 1801, and *The Forest Minstrel,* 1810, were such pale imitations of Burns that they attracted little attention. Only when he was taken under the wing of the witty young journalist William Maginn (1793–1842) and made the hero of Maginn's largely fictional column in the new *Broadwood's Magazine,* "Noctae Ambrosianae," did Hogg's name win fame. As Maginn portrayed him, he was a caricature of the rude rustic bard. Hogg himself accepted this exaggeration and played up to it; he called his own works "ranting rhymes." Whatever Foster knew of Hogg would encourage his hope that he too, with his gentler manners, might find enough patronage to live as a songwriter.

R. H. Cromek was an English exploiter of the fashion for Scotch songs. He compiled a volume of *Reliques of Burns,* 1808, and he sponsored the publications of the honest young stonemason Alan Cunningham as if they were ancient anonymous lyrics: *Remains of Nithsdale and Galloway Song,* 1810. Cunningham had walked in Burns' funeral procession. He had walked miles to Edinburgh just to look at Sir Walter Scott. His testimony to Robert Southey in 1822 shows how the growing tradition absorbed energies from underprivileged people:

> I was bred in a lonely place, painting and sculpture seemed something like the work of sorcery and unattainable, and as my trade presented nothing to please my ambition I was fain in my twenty first year to wooe the more accessible muse of homely country rhymes.

Cunningham's words sound much like Foster's.

Lady Nairne published her songs anonymously too, but not with the pretense that they were old—rather because she thought it unbecoming a lady to put her name before the public and because she hoped that peasant singers would accept her words for their old tunes. Her most famous poem, "Land o' the Leal," 1798, was followed by a steady thin stream of excellent work in the serial publications such as *The Scottish Minstrel,* while the poet never told her husband the baron what she was doing for fear he would "blab." When she died, her complete works were published with her name at last, as *Lays from Strathearn,* 1846. Foster doubtless liked "Land o' the Leal" all the better for the sake of the romantic story, regardless of how many of the other songs he knew.

The poems treated in their consistent style a variety of subjects— some vigorously comic, some patriotic, most of them succinctly and joyously religious. For Lady Nairne, "religion is a walking not a talking concern." Around 1820 she undertook a "purified" edition of Burns, but gave it up as impossible. She had been in youth an enthusiastic dancer, praised by the great fiddler Neil Gow (1727– 1807). For his son Nathaniel she wrote "Caller Herrin'," based on the cries of fishmongerwomen. She was an able amateur performer on several instruments and a reader of French and German literature as well as the classics, but she wrote nothing but her songs and some fine private letters. If Foster had studied her work thoroughly, he could have improved his own.

The much younger amateur, Lady Scott, was composer of one immensely popular song, "Annie Laurie," 1838. Its words may be as venerably anonymous as any that she collected as a girl in 1827 from illiterate singers (her manuscript is in the National Library of Scotland) or any that Burns or Lady Nairne refined, but the tune, often imagined to be old, is the work of Lady Scott. It is especially similar to many Foster tunes and different from older ones in its insistent use of an upward-leaping octave in the middle of a phrase.

The poet who more nearly than any other came to dominate the international tradition was Thomas Moore, from Dublin. His *Irish Melodies* and assorted *National Airs,* appearing serially from 1808 to 1834, went through many editions. Selections from them were printed in newspapers and magazines everywhere; they filled half the pages of countless anthologies, such as *The Book of English Songs, from the 16th to the 19th Century,* 1851, whose anonymous preface hailed Moore as "the best writer of English [sic] songs whom our literature has produced." A study of all such collections published in the United States, 1825–50, by George S. Jackson, finds Moore by far the leading contributor. When he died in 1852, there were fulsome tributes in all newspapers and magazines. Americans forgave him his early drinking songs and even his satirical verses about America, written during a visit in 1804–05, for the sake of such lasting gems as "Believe Me If All Those Endearing Young Charms" (1808), "The Last Rose of Summer" (1813), and "Oft in the Stilly Night" (1818). Fewer Americans had paid attention to Moore's monumental exotic cycle of poems, *Lalla Rookh;* Edgar

Allen Poe and his friend Thomas Holley Chivers had both independently found inspiration there, as had Vigny, Stendhal, Berlioz, Schumann, and others in Europe. Moore was loved chiefly as a specialist in songs, a provider of words for the melodies of many nations, suitably arranged for the piano.

Moore was such a charming singer that he could easily have succeeded in the theater if this had not been beneath his dignity. He was enough of a musician to compose his own tunes for some of his early verses. And when he used other tunes he fitted their rhythms and intonations with rare skill.

But Moore's "national airs" showed little concern for the values that his German contemporaries were exalting in the name of the *Volk*. His poems were not, like many of Burns', classic versions of verses that had long circulated in variable forms. Moore knew nothing of the original words to most of the tunes that he used. In particular he knew no Gaelic. He knew little of peasant life. He came to regret his "boudoir education." He sang of feelings that suited the refined parlors with their pianos, and when he sang of rustic virtue, it was from the point of view of city people to whom rural life was almost as exotic as *Lalla Rookh*. When he sang of Ireland, to be sure, he expressed an ardent patriotism; sometimes he even dared hope for Irish liberty, but more often he simply lamented Irish oppression and consoled himself with the timeless beauty of the green isle and "The Harp That Once Through Tara's Halls. . . ." It never occurred to him to seek a distinctive Irish style of poetry, or to make a stylistic distinction between the Irish music and the other music he used.

Moore's most frequent subject was a "dream" of sweet security, of a "home" not too precisely defined, now lost forever in the busy, friendless, risky life of a crowded cosmopolitan city. Moore was the first writer to harp on this theme.

Among his late songs one has the title, "The Dream of Home":

> Who has not felt how sadly sweet
>   The dream of home, the dream of home,
> Steals o'er the heart, too soon to fleet,
>   When far o'er lea or land we roam?
> Sunlight more soft may o'er us fall,
>   To greener shores our bark may come;
> But far more bright, more dear than all,
>   That dream of home, that dream of home.

Moore's repetition dins in his vague theme. His context keeps it vague, applicable to the widest range of singers and listeners. His choice of words and his smooth arrangement of them in the flowing lines maintain the "sadly sweet" relish of the "dream."

In some of Moore's poems on the same characteristic vague new theme motifs were borrowed from older traditions—not so much from any Irish or other local tradition as from the Biblical image of Eden and the Greek myth of a primitive Golden Age. But Moore's "dream" was different. He did not imagine the human race deteriorating to an Iron Age, nor did he worry about original sin. He shared fitfully in the rational hopes of political reform, science, education, and naturally expanding sympathies. Only he found these hopes often disappointed. He wearied of the effort to realize them. He dreamed of escape. Unlike the most profound of his contemporaries, he never tried to measure the limits of "reason" and "nature" or to identify the sources of disappointment. He simply exploited the contrast and indulged his dreams. This indulgence suited growing numbers of insecure city-dwellers for many generations.

Moore knew what he was doing. One of his poems, for a Swedish air, explains:

> My harp has one unchanging theme,
>   One strain that still comes o'er
> Its languid chord, as 'twere a dream
>   Of joy that's now no more.
> In vain I try, with livelier air,
>   To wake the breathing string;
> That voice of other times is there,
>   And saddens all I sing.
> Breathe on, breathe on, thou languid strain,
>   Henceforth be all my own;
> Though thou art oft so full of pain
>   Few hearts can bear thy tone.
> Yet oft thou'rt sweet, as if the sigh,
>   The breath that Pleasure's wings
> Gave out, when last they wanton'd by,
>   Were still upon thy strings.

This "languid strain" echoes in the poems of dozens of later authors, including Foster. Whether or not Foster knew this particular poem, he knew enough of Moore to absorb the "voice of other times." "Old Dog Tray" shares Moore's dream, its voice, its heartbreak.

Moore's song "There's Nothing True But Heaven" was a favorite of Stephen's sister Charlotte who died when he was three years old. Their mother recorded how the girl "walked modestly to the piano" and sang "in a manner that touched the feelings and moved the hearts of all those present."

"Oft in the Stilly Night" and "The Last Rose of Summer" were staples in the singing school at the Third Presbyterian Church of Pittsburgh about 1840, when Stephen's brother Henry was a temporary Presbyterian. Their neighbor William Graham Johnston, who sang as a boy in that chorus of hundreds, recalled these songs of Moore along with "John Anderson" and "Robin Adair" and one hymn, as "songs which grow old, and will not die." Johnston was once soloist at a concert of this singing school, winning applause with Moore's "Canadian Boatmen's Song."

In 1847 "The Last Rose" was transplanted to Vienna by Friedrich von Flotow (1812–83) for use as a recurring theme in his most famous opera, *Martha;* the tune is ostensibly a *Volkslied* of 18th-century England, *Martha*'s scene. When *Martha* brought the old favorite back to London and New York, its fame and dignity were now immense.

Stephen Foster used the name "Milton Moore" as a pseudonym for one of his own songs of 1850, "I Would Not Die in Springtime." Morrison identified the reference to Thomas Moore in a marginal note on the manuscript. In an autograph of the "Old Folks at Home Variations" the same pseudonym appears again, though Stephen decided, by the time of publication, 1853, to use his own name here. Moore's name might have been equally appropriate for "Jeanie" and dozens of other songs of Foster.

Moore was represented in the little book of song texts that appeared in 1862 as *The Love and Sentimental Songster; a Choice Selection of Popular Love and Sentimental Songs by Stephen C. Foster and Others.* Along with five of Foster's recent pieces identified by copyright and three more Foster pieces not identified, Moore's "Harp that once" and Tennyson's "Come into the Garden, Maud" provided a chronological frame. Even if Foster himself did not make the "choice selection," it was appropriate and he doubtless approved it.

Foster remembered Moore in the last months of his life, when he wrote the "Song of All Songs." The text of this song is almost entirely a collage of sixty-one song titles, including Moore's "Oft in the Stilly Night" and Foster's "Jenny's Coming O'er the Green." Authorship of the text was claimed by several obscure versifiers; it has been claimed for Foster too, but this claim seems unlikely since "Jenny" is the only one of his titles mentioned. Moore's was probably the oldest title in the sixty-one.

One of the most impressive singers of Moore's songs, as well as an imitator of them in a few compositions, was John Braham, the brilliant Jewish tenor, protégé of Stephen Storace, who won fame in France and Italy around the turn of the century. His career was unusually long and varied; in 1811 he produced one of his more ambitious works for the stage, *The Americans;* a song from it on "The Death of Nelson" was his most enduring piece. He played the leading part in the first English performance of Weber's *Freischütz,*

1821, and created the part of Weber's *Oberon,* 1826; in 1838 he made Rossini's *William Tell* a success in London; the next year, becoming a baritone at last, he was a memorable *Don Giovanni.* In 1840–42 he visited America and astonished many listeners with the power of his arias from Handel's oratorios, the florid luxuriance of the cadenzas he inserted, and the tenderness of his modern songs, including some by Moore. He sang his last concert in London in 1852.

Moore's chief musical collaborator was Henry Rowley Bishop, arranger of the last three volumes of *National Melodies,* adapter for the London stage of nine of Scott's novels and of eleven operas from Italian, French, and German composers of 1814–33. Bishop also collaborated with the old James Hogg in his *Select and Rare Scottish Melodies,* 1829. Bishop was knighted in 1842; he was awarded the D.Mus. degree at Oxford in 1853. No other English musician before Arthur Sullivan became so famous; if Sterndale Bennett (1816–75) was more nearly worthy of the "age of Tennyson," he never reached so wide an audience at home or abroad as did Bishop. When he died in 1857, Dwight's *Journal* in Boston paid tribute to the great representative of "English national melody."

Charles Edward Horn, after an auspicious beginning in London with adaptations of Moore's *M.P., or the Blue Stocking,* 1811, and *Lalla Rookh,* 1818, and a memorable performance as Caspar in *Freischütz,* 1824, emigrated to America, where he continued to perform and to compose a few songs. In 1848 he became director of the Handel and Haydn Society of Boston.

The names of Braham, Bishop, and Horn loomed for Stephen Foster as likelier models than Mozart or Beethoven. The prestige of the English musicians reinforced that of Moore and other Irish and Scottish song writers.

In at least two poems of Moore there is a rhyme that Foster and others used again and again: roam/home. Moore probably noticed its use by Oliver Goldsmith, in "The Travellers," 1764, where the strong couplet is balanced by a more judicious one:

> Such is the patriot's boast, where'er we roam,
> His first, best country, ever is his home.
> . . . Though patriots flatter, still shall wisdom find
> An equal portion dealt to all mankind.

Moore's lines differ characteristically from Goldsmith's; most typical of the sentiments that Moore made so popular is the dreamy final couplet of "The Last Glimpse of Erin," 1807:

> In exile thy bosom shall still be my home
> And thine eyes my climate wherever we roam.

The poet continued to enjoy London, claiming only sympathy for his dream of Ireland. Equally typical of Moore himself, though less popular in his lifetime, are the following lines from his epistles from the city of Washington:

> 'Tis evening now; beneath the western star
> Soft sighs the lover through his sweet segar.
> . . . The patriot, fresh from Freedom's councils come,
> Now pleas'd retires to lash his slaves at home;
> Or woo, perhaps, some black Aspasia's charms,
> And dream of freedom in his bondsmaid's arms. . . .

In the same poem Moore reflects on the challenge of the American landscape:

> Were none but brutes to call that soil their home
> Where none but demigods should dare to roam?

And in another of the same time, Moore sums up his own feeling about America:

> Who can, with patience, for a moment see
> The medley mass of pride and misery,
> Of whips and charters, manacles and rights,
> Of slaving blacks and democratic whites,
> And all the piebald piety that reigns
> In free confusion o'er Columbia's plains?
> . . . Away, away—I'd rather hold my neck
> By doubtful tenure from a sultan's beck,
> In climes where liberty has scarce been nam'd,
> Nor any right but that of ruling claim'd,
> Than thus to live, where bastard Freedom waves
> Her fustian flag in mockery over slaves.

These lines, which few Americans of the 19th century could face, may paradoxically give some 20th-century readers a sense of the poetic power that Moore's consoling songs exercised in his own time. And some hints of these lines of Moore may echo in the roam/home rhyme of Foster: the home of Foster's "Old Folks" has all too often seemed a mockery.

A last quotation, in a more songlike rhythm than the heroic couplets, concerns the function of music amid the turbulent social changes that Moore knew. These lines end the poem "When Thro' Life Unblest We Rove," 1810:

> Music! oh how faint, how weak,
>   Language fades before thy spell!
> Why should Feeling ever speak
>   When thou canst breathe her soul so well?

> Friendship's balmy words may feign,
> > Love's are even more false than they.
> Oh! 'tis only Music's strain
> > Can sweetly soothe and not betray.

While poetry, in the more inclusive sense of the word, could serve for protest, this was not the function of music, as Moore and his followers liked it; their songs were for soothing.

Thomas Campbell, whose "poor dog Tray" so resembled Foster's "Tray," was handicapped in his rivalry with Moore and Scott by an utter lack of charm. Carlyle described him: "There is a smirk on his face which would befit a shopman or an auctioneer." But Campbell's skills in various kinds of poetry, in criticism, and in editorial work won him eventually the post of rector of Glasgow University, for which Scott was a candidate. Campbell's anthology, *Specimens of the British Poets,* 1819, was a standard text for several decades. His own long poems were respected: "The Pleasures of Hope," 1799, and "Gertrude of Wyoming," 1809; the latter, a romantic narrative of earlier frontier life in America, which Washington Irving had edited in 1810, naturally held American readers longer than others, and thus indirectly helped bring Campbell's dog Tray to Foster's attention. Two specimens of Campbell's more fugitive lines are especially useful in our survey of Foster's tradition as a whole. First, from an unfinished "Ode to Music," 1794, a clear statement of the technical relation between words and simple, songful music, together with an exaggeration of the central theme of dreams:

> Come, in thy native garb arrayed
> > And pour the sweetly simple song,
> And all the poet's breast pervade
> > And guide the fluent verse along.
> . . . What time the softening zephyr flies
> > My notes shall aid the gentle theme
> That lonely meditation tries,
> > And grateful soothe her placid dream.

The "placid dream" of the lonely meditator needs the soothing of music; though Campbell here says nothing about disappointed hopes, it is clear that his dream is a refuge from a life not at all placid. He withdraws from life into his dream more wholeheartedly than does Moore into his. Like Moore, however, Campbell can be cutting about American hypocrisy. His "Epigram to the United States of America," 1838, shows Campbell's sharpest style:

> United States, your banner wears
> > Two emblems—one of fame;

> Alas! the other that it bears
>   Reminds us of your shame.
> Your banner's constellation types
>   White freedom with its stars;
> But what's the meaning of the stripes?
>   They mean your negroes' scars.

The famous critic of American manners Harriet Martineau overlooked this poem when she dismissed Campbell with her concise
judgment: "His sentimentality was too soft." When Campbell died
in 1844, earlier than Moore, Braham, Bishop, and Horn, his passing
was not much noticed. Yet three of his songs continued to appear
in anthologies for another generation: "The Exile of Erin," "The
Wounded Hussar," and "When Jordan Hushed."

An American exactly contemporary with Alan Cunningham,
swayed by the fashions for Burns and Moore and Campbell, then
swept on by the fashion for Byron, was Samuel Woodworth, printer,
occasional journalist, Swedenborgian, playwright, and author of two
songs that won wide popularity: "The Hunters of Kentucky," about
Andrew Jackson at the battle of New Orleans, and "The Bucket,"
about the common dream of childhood security:

> How dear to this heart are the scenes of my childhood,
>   When fond recollection presents them to view!
> The orchard, the meadow, the deep tangled wild-wood,
>   And every loved spot which my infancy knew! . . .
> And now, far removed from the loved habitation,
>   The tear of regret will intrusively swell,
> As fancy reverts to my father's plantation,
>   And sighs for the bucket that hangs in the well—
> The old oaken bucket, the iron-bound bucket,
>   The moss-covered bucket that hangs in the well!

Woodworth wrote both his successful poems to airs that came from
the English theater: the anonymous "Miss Bailey" and "The Flower
of Dumblane"; the "Bucket" was adapted in 1843 to another tune,
composed in 1822 by the Swedish conductor in London, George
Kiallmark, to fit the stanzas about "Araby's Daughter" from Moore's
Lalla Rookh. Its popularity was thereby renewed and extended—
in 1864 a picture of the bucket by Currier and Ives insured its continued fame. For the other songs in Woodworth's collection of
*Melodies, Duets, Trios, Songs, and Ballads, Pastoral, Amatory, Sen-
timental, Patriotic, Religious, and Miscellaneous* (3rd edition, 1831),
he used tunes from Scotland, Ireland, and France, and tunes newly
composed by such obscure musicians—E. C. Riley and John Davies—
that their tunes failed to carry his words to any wide audience or
even to make his name much noticed. But "The Hunters of Ken-

tucky" and "The Bucket" held places in American anthologies for several generations. Singers like Henry Russell, who picked them up in America, made them popular in Britain too. Stephen Foster could not have escaped these two songs.

An American poet of utterly different character, just five years younger than Woodworth, was Richard Henry Wilde. Born in Dublin, he went with his family to Baltimore in 1797, then to Augusta, Georgia, in 1802, where he acquired the solid classical education that fitted him for a term as Congressman. Subsequent studies in Italy culminated in his *Conjectures and Researches Concerning the Love, Madness, and Imprisonment of Torquato Tasso,* 1842. He wrote one song that became his best-known work, "My Life Is Like the Summer Rose," 1814; it owes as much to Italian models as to Moore's "Last Rose of Summer." Foster must have known this poem long before he set it to music in 1860; he used its refrain as his title, "None Shall Weep a Tear for Me." Foster gave the accompaniment the unusual rhythm of a polonaise. His melody is one of his most graceful ones, perfectly fitted to the grammatical and logical structure of the poem. He could not have achieved this combination without the experience of a decade of songwriting. But Foster's setting never reached as wide an audience as the poem itself. An anonymous reviewer in *Clark's School Visitor,* 1860, recommended it in vain, as "A sweet song":

> Mr. Foster has recently composed a song which we think is one of his very best. It is touching, tender and soul-elevating. Its melody drops on the ear and heart like honeyed dew-drops on flowers. To all lovers of sweet song, we say, buy it.

That later admirers of Foster, including Morrison and Evelyn Morneweck, knew nothing of Richard Henry Wilde and overlooked the distinction of this song is an ironic confirmation of its sad sentiment.

Ebenezer Elliott was a Yorkshire poet who called himself a disciple of Robert Southey but who won his widest audience with songs imitating Burns, some of them written to tunes like "Robin Adair," "Scots Wha' Hae," and "The Land o' the Leal." Elliott's theme in nearly all his works was the outrage of the Corn Law; his collection of songs, 1831, he called *Corn-Law Rhymes,* and he was often dubbed "the Corn-Law Rhymer." Though his protests naturally lost as much interest as they gained when the law was finally repealed, their impassioned power held the respect of critics even after the popularity of Moore had declined. When Elliott died, a *Life* by John Watkins, 1850, and an American edition of the *Poems,* by Rufus Griswold, brought him to the attention of young men like Shiras and Foster. They could hardly miss the relevance of Elliott's protest to Moore's dream: the cottage homes such as Moore dreamed of Elliott saw being destroyed by the social process in which the Corn Law was a specially cruel phase. In Elliott's best longer poem, "The Splendid Village," a narrator returns to his Yorkshire home after some years in America, to see the ugly "splendor" of newly rich tradesmen, bankers, and lawyers, amid the squalor of the dispossessed peasants; he decides to go back to America.

> Yes, I have roam'd where Freedom's spirit fires
> The stern descendents of self-exil'd sires;
> But tir'd, at length, I seek my native home,
> Resolv'd no more in gorgeous wilds to roam. . . .
> Oh, welcome once again black ocean's foam!
> England! Can this be England?—this my home?
> This country of the crime without a name,
> And men who know no mercy, hope, nor shame?
> Fall'n country of my fathers! fall'n and foul!
> Thy body still is here, but where the soul? . . .
> The mocking-bird, where Erie's waters swell,
> Shall sing of fountain'd vales, and philomel;
> To my sick soul bring, over worlds of waves,
> Dew-glistening Albion's woods, and dripping caves;
> But—with her linnet, red-breast, lark, and wren—
> Her blasted homes and much-enduring men!

In his "Epistle" to a critic, Elliott defends his political poetry with a singing rhythm and an effectively developed metaphor:

> My pious Friend! what shall I say
>   To one so wise and grave?
> I got your letter t'other day;
>   It bids me be a slave.
> The poor man's joys, the poor man's pain
>   You bid my Muse discard;
> "Such themes," you say, "true bards disdain";
>   I, then, am no true bard.
> Because your dog obeys you well,
>   And well by you is fed,
> Must I obey the dogs of hell
>   Who growl, and snatch my bread?
> Slaves fawn; but do they fawn for nought?
>   Yes, slaves there are, indeed,
> Who bribe themselves with their own groat,
>   And lick the dogs they feed!
> A better aim will I prefer,
>   Nor fawn on fool or knave,
> Like—many a tyrant-homager;
>   Immortal! yet a slave!

Elliott's proud scorn hits home at the popularity of Moore and Campbell and most of the later singers in their tradition.

The first Englishman who could rival the Irish Moore and the Scottish school of song was Bryan Procter, using the pen name "Barry Cornwall." He specialized in song and theorized about it. His *English Songs*, collected in 1832, and his memoir of his friend Charles Lamb, 1866, were the chief works of a safe, modest career as editor, bon-vivant, and family man. (Carlyle called him a "pretty little fellow.") In the preface of 1832 Procter apologized:

> It may be said that a song is necessarily a trifling matter: but, if good, it is a trifle, of at least a different sort.

He referred to Campbell, Scott, Moore, Hogg, Cunningham, and Burns as challenging an English equivalent. He acknowledged the supremacy of Burns:

> The sentiment in some of Burns's songs is as fine and as true as any thing in Shakespeare himself.

Procter explained Burns' achievement as a result of his "earnestness and directness of purpose" and his "exquisitely tender and beautiful" sentiments, contrasting with the "verbiage" characteristic of too much modern verse. His own work is restrained in diction and sing-song in rhythm. But Procter indulges the dream of Moore without restraint; rarely is there a song with anything like Burns' scope and power, never anything so direct as Ebenezer Elliott, whose work he ignores. Even when Procter celebrates Wine (always with a capital letter) as source of "Truth divine," he falls into moping before the song is finished. When he pays tribute to his dog, the mawkish sentiment makes both Campbell and Foster seem restrained. Procter's dog is "The Bloodhound":

> Men tell us, dear friend, that the noble hound
> Must for ever be lost in the worthless ground,
> Yet, 'Courage'—'Fidelity'—'Love'—(they say)
> Bear *Man*, as on wings, to his sky away.
> Well, Herod,—go tell them whatever may be
> I'll hope I may ever be found by thee.
> If in sleep,—in sleep; if with skies around,
> Mayst thou follow e'en thither, my dear bloodhound.

Procter's preference for doleful sentiments is the subject of one typically neat, "pretty" "Song":

> Let us sing and sigh!
> Let us sigh and sing!
> Sunny haunts have no such pleasures
> As the shadows bring!

> Who would seek the crowd?
>   Who would seek the noon?
> That could woo the pale maid Silence
>   Underneath the moon?
> Smiles are things for youth,
>   Things for merry rhyme;
> But the voice of Pity suiteth
>   *Any* mood or time.

To praise his native land, Procter imagined himself losing it, with no explanation of why he must leave. Here, in "The Exile's Farewell," he finds his characteristic use of the favorite rhyme—roam/home.

> O'er lands and the lonely main,
>   A lonelier man, I roam,
> To seek some balm for pain,—
>   Perhaps to find a home:
> I go,—but Time nor tide,
>   Nor all that tongue may tell,
> Shall ne'er from thee divide
>   My heart,—and so, farewell!
>   Old England, fare thee well!

Some forty of Procter's songs he deleted from later editions of his book, as of "inferior quality." All these were retained in the American edition of 1851, which Stephen Foster probably knew, for some of them were "favorites in this country."

Procter showed little interest in traditional tunes, much less traditional texts. His favorite tunes were those written for his finished poems by the indefatigable conductor, organist, pupil of Haydn, composer of music in every form, Sigismund Neukomm (1778–1858). From Neukomm's instruction Procter learned to revere Handel, Haydn, "great Beethoven and thou, sweet, sweet-souled Mozart!"

Several of Procter's songs are about his prodigious daughter Adelaide, who was to surpass him in popular acclaim when her "Lost Chord" was set to music by Sullivan. "Golden-Tressed Adelaide" pretends to be addressed from the daughter to the mother:

> . . . Childhood should be all divine,
>   Mother dear!
> And like an endless summer shine;
>   . . . Therefore bid thy song be merry:—
>   dost thou hear, Mother dear?

In other poems Procter's paupers and beggars sing merrily, like children, while his charitable mothers and fathers go on sighing. The sweet, sonorous diction and the jingling rhythms go on regardless of the moods.

To compare Foster with Cornwall-Procter was to honor Foster, in the view of friend R. P. Nevin in 1858. Procter was "immortal," alongside Burns and Moore. Foster might hope to approach his loftiness only with much labor and luck.

The three oldest notable American contributors to the international tradition of song were not specialists like Procter, but versatile and competent writers of many kinds of poetry and prose. Sara Josepha Hale became notorious as editor of the ladies' magazine published by Godey, beginning in 1837, and then as supporter of the movement for women's rights. Among her most popular songs was "The Light of Home":

> My boy, thou wilt dream the world is fair,
>   And thy spirit will sigh to roam,
> And thou must go; but never, when there,
>   Forget the light of home.

Through three more stanzas the mother warns the boy of false pleasures, false hopes, and probable griefs and woes, always to console him with the refrain about remembering home. In *Godey's Magazine* and in the annual gift books that she also edited, Sara Hale excluded all drinking songs and nearly all controversial political themes, so that little remained but the vague dreams of lost loves and homes. At the same time Hale explored the great issues of slavery and Blackness in a novel, *Northwood; or, Life North and South: Showing the True Character of Both*, 1837, new edition 1852. Her critical equilibrium in this book made it appealing to people like the Foster family.

Fritz-Greene Halleck was a firm friend and witty colleague of Bryant, Irving, and Cooper, more active as editor than original writer, and more famous for two poems than for all the rest of his work: one of these was a tribute to "Burns," the other a lament "On the Death of Joseph Rodman Drake" (1795–1820), who had been Halleck's closest friend and collaborator, sharing in his hopes for American songs fit to follow the songs of Burns and their favorite, Campbell.

John Howard Payne had enjoyed a moderate success as playwright in London when his third play, *Clari*, 1823, provided the setting for the song that made him truly famous, "Home, Sweet Home." Bishop arranged the tune—said to be Sicilian—for a poem by Haynes Bayly, "To the Home of My Childhood," 1821, and Payne adapted it to his slightly different words. In *Clari* the song is a dominating theme. So it became in Payne's life. By the time he died, 1852, though all his plays were forgotten, this song was more celebrated than ever. Mrs. Anna Bishop had made it the key work of her concert career, which took her to Africa, India, and China, as well as repeatedly to America, North and South.

For some reason, Stephen Foster disliked "Home, Sweet Home." Perhaps the extraordinary inversion of the sentence offended him:

> 'Mid pleasures and palaces though we may roam,
> Be it ever so humble, there's no place like home.

Or did he notice the incongruity between the dependent poetic tags " 'mid" and "be it" and the vacuous, homely principal clause? Whatever he disliked, it was not the emphasis on home—the essential theme of the tradition of song.

Payne's song endured alongside Foster's most similar songs in the same contexts. In the 1920s Payne's manuscript was sold to the Sibley Library of Rochester for $1590. Foster collectors were not yet paying so much.

While Payne's one song kept his name alive, Felicia Hemans was more widely admired for many songs and for her more elaborate "lays," "ballads," and other forms. Her name ranked next to Moore's in the anthologies. Her popularity persisted in America longer than in England: "The Landing of the Pilgrim Fathers" outlasted "The Stately Homes of England" and "The Cliffs of Dover." Most of her poems dealt with the "domestic affections," not as dreams but rather as duties, with occasional satisfactions as well as many griefs. Death and the graveyard fascinated her as they did Procter, but she always went on, as he seldom did, to thoughts of heavenly reunion and reward. Her religiosity, however, lacked the delight of Lady Nairne's faith: the Hemans tears seemed never to dry. Her poems were surely favorites of the Foster ladies. When Stephen in his last year began to write for Sunday Schools, he remembered Mrs. Hemans. With all due respect, we may forebear quoting her here.

The foremost resident literary spokesman of the American West before Mark Twain, admired though hardly celebrated in Cincinnati, New York, and London as more "American" than Irving or Cooper, was James Hall, a versatile writer and editor, hero of the War of 1812, lawyer, judge, and banker. Some of his songs were written for the Pittsburgh *Gazette* when he was a lawyer there, 1816–20, and friend of the Foster family; these songs include parodies of Moore and show in other ways, too, Moore's dominating influence. Some later songs show Hall's increasing skill. Though none of them are so distinctive and influential as his story of the boasting illiterate frontiersman "Pete Featherton," several are as smooth as Campbell's or Procter's soft sentimental songs, and more convincing. Hall's sober use of the roam/home rhyme occurs in

"The Emigrant," which he published in his *Western Souvenir: A Christmas and New Year's Gift for 1829:*

> Pride and folly only
> Enticed me far from home,
> Friendless, sad, and lonely,
> Through distant lands to roam.

Another song in the same collection depicts "Wedded Love's First Home in the West":

> Far, far we left the sea-girt shore, endeared by
> childhood's dream,
> To seek the humble cot, that smiled by fair Ohio's
> stream . . .

When Stephen Foster began his brief career as clerk in Cincinnati in 1846, the eminent Mr. Hall, now more a historian than fiction writer, helped him with a recommendation. Stephen's poetic efforts were hardly fit for Hall's editorial eye. His "Ethiopian songs" could not amuse Hall, who had taken a leading part in Cincinnati's quarrel with Lyman Beecher and his pupil, the abolitionist Theodore Weld. Hall was now a stanch defender of "the business community" and an ally of John Calhoun in efforts to link Cincinnati and Charleston by rail. When Foster thought of Moore and Procter, he would naturally link their gentility with that of James Hall, who loomed so close over his own horizon. Foster's dream of making a business of songwriting was nourished by his glimpses of some such figures as Hall.

In his *Letters from the West,* 1828, Hall confessed that

> . . . I neither fiddle nor sing, and can scarcely distinguish "God save the king" from "Hail Columbia," though I have often felt the sweetness, and acknowledged the power of a "dulcet voice."

Foster's "dulcem melody" aims at the kind of vague "power" that Hall acknowledges.

The Philadelphia violinist, band-leader, and composer, Frank Johnson, set to music the verses of his gentlemen patrons, suitably for performance as serenades. By 1850, when Johnson had been dead six years and his band dispersed, his songs and his international reputation were forgotten; the fact that he was of African descent hastened his passing into near oblivion and made difficult the recovery of any information about him in the 1970s. But Johnson had a triumphant moment of recognition in London in 1835. The queen presented him with a silver trumpet. And he had traveled widely with his band in the northern states. One of his songs, "If Sleeping

Now, Fair Maid of Love," shows a thorough command of a somewhat old-fashioned style, with Mozartian appoggiaturas and trills.
More tantalizing is the report by the Philadelphia scholar and poet
Robert Waln, in his book *The Hermit in America*, 1819, of Johnson's
"remarkable taste in distorting a sentimental, simple, and beautiful
song into a reel, jig, or country-dance." Waln's chapter on "The
Cotillion Party" has a native Philadelphian describe Johnson to his
visiting English friend as

". . . a prominent character in the gay world, and happy the lady, in
whose ear at the midnight hour, he pours the dulcet notes of love!"
"Sir?" said I, starting.
"Be not alarmed. Music, you know, is the food of love. . . . This fiddler
is the presiding deity on such occasions . . . leader of the band at all balls,
public and private, sole director of all serenades, acceptable or not
acceptable. . . ."

When the dance ends, the gentlemen settle down to drinking and
gambling, then to "winey melody," first a series of solos, then choruses, while Johnson goes off with one of the party to serenade his
lady, perhaps with the song "If Sleeping Now."

Johnson's visit to Pittsburgh with his band in 1842 will concern us
in Chapter 10. His participation in the international tradition of
song, which will, for the sake of Johnson's whole career, concern
other students as more information becomes available, even now
shows something about that tradition's scope and complexity.

If we are tempted to connect Johnson's "taste in distorting a sentimental . . . song into a reel . . ." with his African ancestry, we must
consider similar accounts of what was done in London. One such
account will remind us of the master of our tradition, Tom Moore,
and the other will introduce one of his most skillful disciples,
Thomas Haynes Bayly. Moore's "Summer Fête"—eleven songs strung
together on a poetic narrative thread about a fashionable dancing
party—has a stanza about the quadrille music:

> Working to death each opera strain,
>   As, with a foot that ne'er reposes,
> She jigs through sacred and profane,
>   From "Maid and Magpie" up to "Moses";—
> Wearing out tunes as fast as shoes,
>   Till fagg'd Rossini scarce respires;
> Till Meyerbeer for mercy sues,
>   And Weber at her feet expires.

(In his journal for January 9, 1822, Moore remarked that "the ease
with which all Rossini's lively songs and choruses may be turned
into quadrilles and waltzes, shows the character of his music.")

Haynes Bayly has a French flutist in charge of the dance band, in his characteristic song, "At Home":

> Invitations I will write,
> All the world I will invite.
>   I will deign to show civility
>   To the tip tops of gentility;
>   To the cream of the nobility
> I'm "at home" next Monday night. . . .
> Oh! the matchless Collinet,
> On his flageolet shall play;
>   How I love to hear the thrill of it!
>   Pasta's song [,] think what she will of it,
>   He will make a quick quadrille of it
> "*Dove sono,*"—dance away.

The great soliloquy of the Countess from Mozart's *Figaro,* in which she wonders where the beautiful past has gone, needs some distortion as well as mere speed to fit a quadrille. Haynes Bayly, in this poem and others, shows ample knowledge of how such things are done, and a taste to enjoy them; his own most popular "sentimental songs" are outweighed in his collection of 1844 by "airs of *haut ton,*" "songs of fashionable life," "songs of the boudoir," and "lunatic lays." Among the airs of the boudoir, one is "My Harp of Sighs," followed immediately by "My Harp of Smiles." Haynes Bayly's first song was a huge success in 1826: "I'd Be a Butterfly" ("living, a rover, Dying when fair things are fading away"). For this he composed his own tune; Mrs. Haynes Bayly helped with the accompaniment and "symphonies." Another of his most famous songs had music by Bishop, "Oh, No, We Never Mention Her" (". . . But if she loves as I have lov'd, she never can forget"). Braham, Horn, and other composers loved to set Haynes Bayly's words, and to arrange the "melodies of various nations" that he sometimes used—impartial as to which nations, ranging to the "Hindoostanee." Unlike Procter, Haynes Bayly made no attempt to be specifically English. But his irony could hide a defense of English song behind a witty attack on it—"Don't Sing English Ballads":

> I hate English ballads, don't sing them . . .
> The English words seem so phlegmatic,
> Italian is aristocratic,
> I know that the sound is ecstatic
>   Whatever the meaning may be.

Haynes Bayly made fun of the dream theme, in "They Have Seen Better Days, You Say" ("Oh, tell me when and where"). But his humor and irony could seldom win the audiences who loved his

"Long, Long Ago" ("Tell me the tales that to me were so dear"). He could use the roam/home rhyme in both ironic and sentimental contexts. The gentle irony of his popular "Gaily the Troubadour Touch'd His Guitar" probably escaped most listeners; a sighing maiden remembers the troubadour and echoes in a refrain:

> Singing "in search of thee, would I might roam,
> Troubadour! troubadour! come to thy home."

Closer to the center of the song tradition is "The Old House at Home" in which the absence of irony is enough to madden Ebenezer Elliott:

> The old house at home where my forefathers dwelt,
> Where a child at the feet of my mother I knelt . . .
> My heart, 'mid all changes, wherever I roam,
> Ne'er loses its love for the old house at home. . . .
> But now the old home is no dwelling for me,
> The home of the stranger henceforth it shall be . . .
> Yet still, in my slumbers, sweet visions will come
> Of the days that are pass'd, of the old house at home.

Haynes Bayly's rhythm in this song, as well as his sentiment, is very close to Stephen Foster. Though no evidence proves that Foster knew this song in particular, his general knowledge of Haynes Bayly is not in question. According to Evelyn Morneweck, he could recall his sister's singing "I'd Be a Butterfly" when it was new. And according to his friend John B. Russell, writing about Foster in the Cincinnati *Gazette*, 1857, Haynes Bayly was, with "Tom" Moore, a model for the "intimate connexion between his poetry and music that gives such a charm to his compositions." Both Russell and Foster himself would have been astonished to think that for his sake anyone in a later time would need to search out Haynes Bayly from dusty library shelves. Did Foster know how Haynes Bayly would have the last laugh at anyone venturing to write about him? His poem titled "Biography" assures him that. It begins, in a sentimental tone, to tell of Mother Hubbard's dog. Gradually, through seven stanzas, a wealth of sharp detail destroys the sentiment, and the eighth makes a climax that bars this poem from the home magazines and gift books:

> In truth he was a naughty dog,
>   Of habits very wild;
> He never yet was known to care
>   One jot for wife or child.
> His wives were countless, each produced
>   Nine bantlings at a birth,
> And some were drown'd, and some were left
>   To rot upon the earth.

The point of the "Biography" arrives in the twelfth and last stanza:

> But now to take away a life
>   Each man of letters strives;
> The undertakers thrive by deaths,
>   Biographers by Lives.
> O'er new made graves, thro' murky mists
>   Of prejudice he jogs;
> And so it seems biography
>   Is going—to the dogs!

Something of Haynes Bayly's ironical *"haut ton"* was brought to bear on American scenes by Alfred Bunn in 1853. "Poet Bunn," as he was called, had made his most famous contribution to the song tradition ten years earlier with his libretto for Balfe's opera *The Bohemian Girl,* including "I Dreamt I Dwelt in Marble Halls" and "Then You'll Remember Me." (His heroine does remember; her dream comes true: for when she discovers her noble birth, she can bring her gypsy lover to the marble halls and go on singing and sighing forever.) Bunn was manager of London theaters for several decades, translator of Italian and French libretti, author of several hasty farces and a gossipy account of *The Stage: Both Before and Behind the Curtain,* 1842. Now he was gathering notes for a sequel, *Old England and New England, in a Series of Views,* 1853. At a music shop on Broadway he found the "counters strewn with American copies of almost every ballad we have been guilty of publishing." When he remarked on the crass piracy, one of the firm explained, in words Bunn thought worth preserving:

> "Oh, we live in a country where it is not necessary to ask any one's permission but our own."

Bunn made sure that he got paid for the American edition of his lively new book. Bunn's patronizing praise of Foster's friend Charles Shiras and his report of a concert by Elizabeth Greenfield will concern us in chapters 8 and 9. Here we may leave him with the explicit comparison of himself to Haynes Bayly's butterfly that he makes on the last page of his book:

> Roving forever from flower to flower,
> And kissing all things that are pretty and sweet.

A man of the theater, like Bunn, but a closer disciple of Moore was the Irish author Samuel Lover. When Lover toured in America with his "entertainments" and "Irish evenings," 1846–48, he was already known for his *Songs and Ballads,* collected in 1839, and even more admired for two novels that contained some of his most popular songs, *Rorey O'Moore, a National Romance,* 1837, and

Handy Andy, 1842. Lover not only sang his songs, but also composed some of the tunes, as well as collaborating with other musicians like Balfe, the composer of Bunn's *Bohemian Girl.* Among Lover's most popular songs were "The Widow Machree," 1842, to his own tune, and "The Low-back'd Car," 1846, to an old Irish tune. His most lasting success was a revision of the old anonymous song—presumably Irish—"The Girl I Left Behind Me," 1855. By the time Stephen Foster set Lover's "Oh! There's No Such Girl As Mine," 1863, Lover's career was declining—he retired to Dublin and brought out a last edition of his poetical works, with a preface exalting the songs of Burns and Moore above those of "great" Milton, Byron, and Shelley.

One Englishman of the generation of Haynes Bayly, Bunn, and Lover took the trouble to listen to illiterate rural singers in Sussex and record their songs—words and tunes. This was John Broadwood, an eccentric member of the family of the leading English piano manufacturers. In 1843 he printed privately the sixteen songs he had heard at Christmas and harvest festivals; he had played them on his flute, and got the village organist to write them down with the modal anomolies as he had learned them, despite the organist's distress. Only much later, when his niece Lucy Broadwood had founded the English Folksong Society and devoted a lifetime to its work, did these songs reach a wider reading public through her edition of them. In the 1840s and '50s the idea was still generally taken for granted that England had no living store of traditional song to compare with that of Scotland, Ireland, and other nations. Between the Sussex farm laborers and the ladies and gentlemen of *haut ton* there remained a firmer barrier than the distance of the Atlantic or the differences of French, German, and Italian language.

John Broadwood was stimulated, no doubt, by the work of another piano manufacturer and music publisher, William Chappell (1809–88), who devoted his leisure to antiquarian research in the history of British song before Burns and Moore. He reclaimed for England some of the tunes that those poets had associated with Scotland and Ireland, especially the jigs and other 16th-century dances. Chappell's first publication was a *Collection of National English Airs,* 1838–40; he expanded it into a richly illustrated treatise on *The Ballad Literature and Popular Music of the Olden Time . . . Also a Short Account of the Minstrels,* 1855–59, which was to exert a complicating influence on many later developments in England. Chappell extolled the Elizabethans like John Dowland. He preferred the *Beggar's Opera* and other 18th-century theatrical music to the sweetened modern style of Moore and his successors. But he showed his own time-bound taste when he insisted that "The great test of whether a tune is good or bad is, will it admit a good base?" If Chappell glanced at the discoveries of Broadwood, he probably condemned their crudity just as he condemned the artificiality of the modern songs he knew. If Foster was acquainted with Chappell's work, he was equally remote from Broadwood's.

The long career of John Hill Hewitt as journalist; biographer of Davy Crockett; drillmaster of Confederate troops; and composer of operas, cantatas, plays, and an oratorio *Jephtha* made his *Miscellaneous Poems,* collected in 1838, seem slighter than they did when they were new. Several were so popular that he was sometimes called "the father of the American ballad." Among them "The Minstrel's Return from the War," 1825, with Hewitt's words and music, was striking: the simple-minded minstrel has tried to use his guitar as a shield, so he returns dead, to be mourned by the fair lady. Hewitt's occasional later songs show various new adaptations of the common themes. One of these is "Carry Me Back to the Sweet Sunny South" which Foster could hardly have avoided. Another, which may have spurred Foster to surpass it, is "Rock Me to Sleep, Mother," 1860. And a last one, more enduring than the rest, is "All Quiet Along the Potomac To-night," 1861, with words attributed to Lamar Fontaine, music by Hewitt. Hewitt's technical musical equipment shown in these songs was no more than Foster's; to see the combination of their simplicity and Hewitt's reputation doubtless encouraged Foster in his hopes. But Hewitt was responding with speed and flexibility to his changing situation, while Foster persisted in his narrower interest.

The American poet most prominent in the international song tradition was George P. Morris, the one whose words Foster used in his first publication, "Open Thy Lattice, Love," 1844. Morris worked primarily as journalist and editor; he founded a series of magazines, from the *New York Mirror and Ladies' Literary Gazette,* beginning in 1823, to the *Home Journal,* 1845–64. He edited the first collection of *American Melodies,* 1840, with samples of two hundred writers, and later, with the composer Charles E. Horn, a collection with tunes, *National Melodies of America.* Morris was an early sponsor of Halleck, Bryant, and other writers more durable than he himself proved. His "Woodsman, Spare That Tree," 1837, and "My Mother's Bible," 1841, both set to music and sung by Henry Russell, represented Morris and America for many commiserating audiences. He himself preferred his "Jeanne Marsh" ("of Cherry Valley, at whose call the muses rally"), 1854. Foster's "Jeanie" may owe something to "Jeanne." The Philadelphia critic Horace Binney Wallace, writing in 1845, claimed that Morris surpassed Moore with his "vigorous simplicity, and genuine grace." The New Yorker Thomas

Ward, in 1855, compared Morris with Theodor Körner, whose *"Leier und Schwert,"* 1814, had inspired Weber and a generation of German students.

Morris' good friend and colleague Nathaniel Parker Willis was almost as prominent, first as poet and then as journalist and arbiter of taste. In his *haut ton* he resembled Haynes Bayly enough to elicit from an anonymous English critic the comment that he was "more like one of the best of our peers' sons than a rough republican." Willis' few songs appeared when he was still at Yale in the class of 1827. He went to England and met the old masters, Moore and Procter. He wrote a fine description of Moore's singing "When First I Met Thee" so as to bring tears to every eye at a fashionable party. Willis' collected *Poems: Sacred, Passionate, and Humorous,* 1848, were followed by a series of collections from his *Home Journal* pieces —*Hurrygraphs,* 1851, and *The Rag Bag,* 1855—just as Foster was striving most vigorously to win some fraction of Willis's respected position. Foster doubtless read his notes on propriety in the opera box, and his appeal for more space in the pit for impecunious music-lovers.

Morris and Willis could look indulgently at the songs of the rival group in New England—Longfellow, Holmes, Lowell, Whittier— all too partisan about slavery to qualify as "national melodists" until a generation after the Civil War. Morris and Willis could patronize the classicizing Wilde, the outré Southerner Poe, and the Westerner Hall, and ignore the "barbaric yawp" of Whitman. If as early as 1848 Whitman dared to call Willis a "humbug," Stephen Foster could not do so.

Boston had a concert singer, composer, and editor in William R. Dempster, who disdained Morris and Willis and Hewitt and Russell. An immigrant from England in the early 1830s, he judged his own works worthier than any native American's to stand alongside Burns, Moore, Scott, Bayly, Lover, and Bishop in his anthology, *The Beauties of Vocal Melody,* 1842. Dempster toured through Pittsburgh in 1846; Stephen Foster and his friend Charles Shiras heard him sing. For them, all his "pure" and "elevated" older songs were overshadowed by his cantata, "The May Queen," 1844, a setting of Tennyson. Both Foster and Shiras were inspired to write additional stanzas. Morrison Foster remembered ever afterward how Stephen recited the poem and sang the Dempster melodies. But Morrison failed to observe that Stephen never published anything of his own so elaborate as this cantata.

Dempster's "May Queen" was censured by John Sullivan Dwight as severely as Foster's "Susanna." Dwight reviewed Dempster in the *Harbinger,* 1846:

Poetry like that does not need music; and music should not trust to poetry to cover its own nakedness of ideas. It should be an equal, honorable match, wherein the music should give as much as it receives.

Dwight felt strongly because he had loved Tennyson from his undergraduate days. In his commencement oration on "Poetry in an Unpoetical Age," 1832, he had defied the Harvard professors by ranking Tennyson with Spenser. He had lent a copy of Tennyson to his friend Higginson and discussed Tennyson with Lowell and Fuller. In 1838 Dwight wrote the earliest comprehensive review of Tennyson's two volumes; according to the modern expert on Tennyson in America, John Eidson, this was a wise and understanding review. When Tennyson's "Princess" made a sensation in 1848, Dwight reviewed it for the *Harbinger*, with praise for the "flesh and blood existences in true functions of life." He recognized a danger in Tennyson's work that he thought the poet was warding off, the danger "of becoming spell-bound, as all must, who serve the ideal without grappling with the real." Dwight, with rare insight, valued Tennysonian realism, by contrast with Poe and many others—like Dempster? and Foster?—for whom Tennyson was, as Poe wrote, "the noblest of poets" because "the most ethereal," and "so little of the earth, earthy."

Dwight relented somewhat toward Dempster in his mellower years. He refers to him in an *Atlantic* article of 1872 on "Improvement in Popular Song Writing" as a model for the imitation of folksongs, an American model comparable to the German Franz Abt (1819–85). Dwight could think now of the "old Dempster ballads," as younger people were beginning to think of "old Foster songs."

The divergent tastes of Dwight, Dempster, Morris, and the rest constitute a complex environment for Foster's songs like "Jeanie" and "Old Dog Tray." Those divergences, which might be traced farther than Foster knew them, were apparent enough to present him with multiple choices—not the simple choice that some of his admirers have imagined between the vital, vulgar Ethiopian minstrels and a solid phalanx of refined musicians and poetasters, but rather with a whole range of possible models, interrelated with each other. He was not faced with any simple choice between American and British tastes for, as we have seen, the divergencies cut across national and regional divisions, while the underlying agreements embraced all the divergencies.

Within the variety and complexity of the tradition, the trend observed in Lady Nairne and Moore, then intensified in Procter and Hemans, continues and reaches a climax in the 1850s. The trend, as viewed from a distance, is to narrow the range of concerns, especially to avoid political issues in favor of safe domestic themes and dreams. The trend trims away from the tradition all praise of wine, all irony, much humor, and most gaiety, until there seems to be only a stagnant pool of grief and memory. If religious faith and hope are still approved, they are often confessedly weak or else suspiciously shrill. The same trend, viewed more nearly from within, is described by Charles Mackay in the preface to his anthology, *The Home Affections Portrayed by the Poets*, 1858:

> To Poetry . . . belongs the duty of celebrating the beauty and purity of Affection. . . . Love of Home, of Country, and of Kind—Love in innocent childhood, Love in courtship and youth, Love in matrimony and middle age, and Love on the confines of the tomb. . . . The poets of the last sixty or seventy years may be truly said to have surpassed all their predecessors —Shakespeare and Milton alone excepted—in the tenderness and beauty of their illustrations of this great passion. . . . The Lyre of Affection yields not only its sweetest but its most constantly recurring tones to the hand of Affliction.

Mackay's collection is a sumptuous publication, intended to be "the GIFT-BOOK OF ENGLISH LITERATURE." It includes elaborate poems as well as songs, but songs predominate. The writers range from Burns to Tennyson and younger poets; Scott, Campbell, Procter, Hemans, Morris, Willis, and Lowell are well represented, together with Wordsworth, Coleridge, Byron, Keats, Shelley, Poe, and many lesser names. There are notable omissions: Moore and Haynes Bayly. There is an appropriate page of free verse from the *Proverbial Philosophy*, 1842, by Martin Tupper, whose popularity in America was still rising—he had made a triumphal tour in 1851. Mackay found ample room for a young poet, not songwriter, who concentrated on the domestic theme: Coventry Patmore (1823–96) had published only the first part of his chief work, *The Angel in the House* (1854–63), but Mackay was alert to it. He misses Charlotte Yonge (1823–1901) whose song "Hearts and Homes" would have fitted in perfectly, and whose whole career as Sunday School teacher and chronicler of family life in 160 books made its characteristic beginning in *The Daisy Chain*, 1856. The trend that Mackay's gift-book glorifies is not confined to poetry, not to literature, but rather is covertly connected with the very social and political changes it seeks to escape. (Home is cozier because the market is more vast and impersonal than ever before.)

Mackay remembered "Old Dog Tray" and also Foster's "Willie, We Have Missed You," 1854, when he wrote the chapter on "Musical Epidemics in London" in his last book, *Through the Long Day, or, Memorials of a Literary Life During Half a Century*, 1887. He recalled Haynes Bayly's "I'd Be a Butterfly" among the "epidemics" of his youth; then Horn's "Cherry Ripe" and Procter's "The Sea," in 1833; Rice's "Jim Crow" reigning from 1836 to 1841; his own "Good Time Coming" and "Cheer, Boys, Cheer"; then the anonymous "Pop Goes the Weasel," followed in 1854 or 1855 by "Old Dog Tray" and "Willie," "good tunes in their way, but strikingly deficient in originality, and founded upon Scotch airs . . ." Mackay continued his survey down to the 1880s, with many generalizations, which he expressed with all the assurance of a successful contributor to the tradition. Though he ignored Foster's name, he acknowledged Foster as having been a colleague in the same tradition.

One of the youngest poets in Mackay's anthology is the Irish scholar Denis Florence McCarthy, whose "Summer Longings" Foster found in the *Home Journal* and set to music in 1849 before it appeared in McCarthy's collection of *Ballads, Poems, and Lyrics,* 1850. McCarthy's patriotism kept him from fully sharing the trend that Mackay celebrated; the topical "national poems and songs" that he published in the *Nation,* 1843–49, are more vigorous than the song Foster chose, or the one Mackay chose. McCarthy accordingly, unlike Mackay, was loyal to Tom Moore, "the Prince of all the Minstrels." In some of his best songs he was more militant and hopeful than Moore, urging his compatriots to be worthy of their heroic leader Daniel O'Connell, whereas Moore was only pleading that the English have mercy. None of McCarthy's patriotic songs won much attention outside Ireland; the international trend was too strong. What appealed to Foster was what appealed to an overwhelming number of his contemporaries—in McCarthy's own words, a "longing to escape," a sense that even summer is "dark and dreary," while "man is ever weary, weary, waiting for the May." Once McCarthy managed to combine his patriotism and his weary, dreamy mood; in this poem he provides his characteristic use of the roam/home rhyme. "Oh! Had I the Wings of a Bird," he sings, only to reject the escape:

> Ah! no! no! no! They have no charms for me.
> I never would roam
> from my island home,
> though poor it be!

In fact McCarthy left Dublin in 1864, to find in London a more suitable place for his chief work, the translation of Calderón. And singers everywhere who repeated the vow of his song were all likely to treat such a vow as a dream, as unreal as having the wings of a bird.

A poet exactly contemporary with Foster, a near neighbor of his in his Cincinnati years, and like him an admirer of the young

Tennyson, was James Madison Bell, a plasterer and a pioneer of Black letters. Bell's use of the home/roam rhyme appears in his words for the tune of "God Save the King," or "America":

> God hasten on the time
>   When slavery's blighting crime
>   And curse shall end:
> When man may widely roam
>   Beneath the arching dome,
>   And find with man a home,
>   In man a friend.

In 1854, with such a prayer, Bell went to Canada to help enlist men for John Brown's campaigns. If Foster was aware of him, he could not sympathize. If Bell was aware of Foster, he doubtless blamed him for contributing to the delay of God's liberation. Yet the two shared more than a language and a citizenship—their poetry was part of a single tradition, they aspired to the same cultural ideal.

The last poet of our list, Metta Victoria Fuller, was a native of Erie, Pennsylvania, then a resident of Wooster, Ohio. She began to publish regularly in the *Home Journal* when she was a child of thirteen; at twenty, she published, with her sister Frances, a volume of *Poems of Sentiment*. In 1856 she married Orville James Victor, inventor of the "dime novel," who encouraged her to continue her writing of popular verse and prose. Her poem set to music by Foster in 1850 personifies the tradition as "The Spirit of My Song"; it neatly symbolizes Foster's relation to the tradition, with an unanswered question:

> Tell me, have you ever met her—
>   Met the spirit of my song?
> Have her wave-like footsteps glided
>   Through the city's worldly throng?
> You will know her by a wreath,
>   Woven all of starry light,
> That is lying mid her hair—
>   Braided hair as dark as night. . . .
>
> Often at her feet I'm sitting,
>   With my head upon her knee,
> While she tells me dreams of beauty
>   In low words of melody:
> And, when my unskilful fingers
>   Strive her silvery lyre to wake,
> She will smooth my tresses, smiling
>   At the discord which I make.
> Tell me, &c.

> But of late days I have missed her—
>   The bright being of my love—
> And perchance she's stolen pinions
>   And has floated up above.
> Tell me, &c.

Foster searched "through the city's worldly throng" for the spirit of song. He often sat at her feet, hearing her dreams, striving unskillfully to wake the lyre. When he lost track of her, he wondered whether she came from heaven and now retired to heaven.

Fuller's words need a more flexible melody than Foster was able to provide. His tune, if heard with no words at all, could not be distinguished from the group of tunes like "Susanna" that we considered in Chapter 5. He manages some appropriate details of rhythm, such as the snapping "spirit" and "city," but when these snaps are smoothed out in succeeding stanzas, the rise and fall of pitch is not interesting or especially appropriate. When he writes his own words, as in "Old Dog Tray" and "Jeanie," he avoids such difficulties.

From 1847 to 1850, Foster in Cincinnati worked his way into the tradition of song with his settings of Mackay, McCarthy, and Fuller. In 1851 he turned once to Shakespeare (adapted), once to his Pittsburgh acquaintance H. S. Cornwell, and once to the Vermont journalist C. G. Eastman. In 1852 he used a poem of another Pittsburgher, G. F. Banister; in 1853 one by his friend Shiras. From then until 1859 he was his own poet in all his songs, as he had been in most of them already and continued to be until 1863. This record indicates an earnest self-conscious relation to the tradition. It fits precisely the words of Fuller's "Spirit." It enhances the meaning of "Jeanie": the object of the singer's dream in "Jeanie" is as much the "spirit of song" as a wife.

In 1860 Foster returned to the theme of inspiration: the muse is no longer a motherly spirit soothing a childish singer, but instead a "Beautiful Child of Song" who answers the lonely singer with flutelike fragments in the piano accompaniment.

> Come, I am longing to hear thee,
>   Beautiful child of song.
> Come, though the hearts that are near thee
>   Around thee devotedly throng.
> Come, I am longing to hear thee,
>   Beautiful child of song.

The first two lines make a graceful phrase in the minor scale, rising to the high keynote and gliding down to the low one. No other phrase of Foster is like this. The next two lines rise beyond the first, to move forward in a modulation, crescendo, that suggests a big development. Then there is a surprise: suddenly soft, the melody returns to the original octave, but transformed so that the high and low notes lead to a new keynote—the song is in the major scale after all. A listener attached to theories of tonal unity, or merely habituated to such unity, may think Foster's modulation is absurd; a 20th-century listener willing to take the words seriously may find it admirable. The song pauses here for the length of a single line, while the accompaniment presents the new motif, almost a trill. Then the song resumes, to rise twice more to the high note of the second phrase and bring it down gracefully to a reinforcement of the major tonic:

> Beautiful child of song,
> I'm longing to hear thee carol thy lay, sweet
> child of song.

The accompaniment now presents a variant of the trilling motif and a repetition of the singer's last phrase, as if the child consented to join the singer. The second stanza describes the child:

> Come, for the spell of a fairy
> Dwells in thy magical voice,
> And at thy step, light and airy,
> E'en cold hearts enraptured rejoice.
> Come, I am longing &c.

The description is no more than a token, but the right performance of this song can make the presence of the child vivid.

But "Beautiful Child of Song" found few singers. Foster's contemporaries preferred "Old Dog Tray." They accepted into the tradition a contribution that Foster himself thought little of, while they rejected his best efforts. His name was missing from the hundred-fifty-two identified in the 1860 cyclopedia of *Poets and Poetry of the West, with Biographical and Critical Notices*, though it was Fuller's "spirit" that dominated here.

The contemporary English musician and historian John Hullah demonstrates the further development of the tradition that brought about the welcome of "Old Dog Tray." The more closely contemporary American Septimus Winner demonstrates that Foster's indifferent reception by his contemporaries was a common one.

Winner kept a music store in Philadelphia. From 1847 to 1857 he played the violin in the Music Fund Orchestra, but he preferred playing in little groups, alternating his fiddle with piano, guitar, and banjo. For his songs he used the pseudonym "Alice Hawthorne" to keep this enterprise separate from the rest. He published also a stream of arrangements and teaching manuals and a few dances for piano—three of them polkas. His first song that achieved some success was "What Is Home Without a Mother?" composed 1850, published 1853. The next year he published his arrangement of a "sentimental Ethiopian ballad," "Listen to the Mocking Bird," that he attributed to Richard Milburn, a Black Philadelphia guitarist and virtuoso whistler; this was a more enduring success: "I'm dreaming now of Holly . . . And the mocking bird is singing o'er her grave." In 1864 Winner made the guitar arrangement of Foster's "Beautiful Dreamer," published by Firth and Pond. Winner's most elaborate piece that won wide use was a duet, "Whispering Hope," 1868, rather like Foster's "Come, Where My Love Lies Dreaming." But the piece that was sung and whistled far more widely, through more generations, was the simple version he made in 1864 of a German waltz of 1847, "Zu Lauterbach hab' ich mein Strumpf verloren"; Winner transformed it into "Der Deitcher's Dog":

> Oh, where, oh, where ish mine little dog gone?
> Oh, where, oh, where can he be?
> With his tail cut short and his ears cut long,
> Oh, where, &c.

Winner's lost dog appealed to the same interests as Foster's Tray. How many other dogs were more hopelessly lost? Foster's earnest "Spirit," his sweet "Jeanie," "Gentle Annie," and the rest would be as obscure in the 20th century as Winner's "Home Without a Mother," and "Susanna" would mean little more than the "Mocking Bird," if it were not for the more distinctive interest of "Old Folks." Foster and Winner were very nearly alike in their relation to the tradition of song they knew. That tradition attracted hundreds of competitors, so that the chance of a continuing success was tiny. Foster and Winner differed in that Winner kept his store and his teaching manuals, while Foster risked everything in his effort to be a songwriter. Though Winner never won critical respect, he kept up his creative work all his life: in 1901 he wrote a short operetta with guitar accompaniment; in 1903 a volume of his poems was published, *Cogitations of a Crank*, in which his good sense and good humor outweigh the crankiness.

John Hullah made a new kind of career. Its center was the Singing School for Schoolmasters, which he established under the auspices of philanthropists and government bureaus, and which he guided throughout the 1840s and '50s. He served as professor of vocal music at King's College, London, from 1844 to 1874, and his lectures on *The History of Modern Music* were published and widely read, (1862, 7th edition 1896). For the prestigious *Golden Treasury* series he compiled *The Song Book*, 1866, and finally, in

1877, he wrote a short treatise on *Music in the House*. These sum up the tradition that concerns us; before looking at them, we need to know a little more about Hullah. His educational work depended on a modest degree of competence as performer and composer. He had studied organ and continued to play all his life, though never as a virtuoso, nor an important participant in the revival of Bach; after 1858 he held the organ post at Charterhouse. He conducted choruses. He sang: in 1847, when Hullah was becoming famous, old Thomas Moore came to visit him at his home and asked him to sing some of Moore's songs; when he ended, Moore remarked, "Ah, I see you've found out it doesn't do to sing them as they are written."

Hullah's student efforts in composition, when he was about twenty, had won him the encouragement of Sigismund Neukomm and the friendship of Fanny Dickens, musical elder sister of the young novelist. In 1836 Hullah persuaded Charles Dickens to write the libretto for his first big work, the ballad opera, *The Village Coquettes*. He was still so inadequately equipped as a composer that when he took the score to John Braham he could not play it—Braham took his place at the piano, read it easily, and agreed to play the part of Squire Norton, corresponding to the Count in *The Marriage of Figaro*. The opera was produced and had some success. Then a fire in the theater destroyed all the music. Only two songs, published separately, survive: the dejected hero's "Autumn Leaves," and the pert heroine's "Some Folks." (Foster's "Some Folks," 1855, though its words are as far from Dickens as its tune from Hullah, may indicate a debt more than mere coincidence, in the light of evidence to be seen in a moment.)

Hullah married an heiress, who took him off to travel in Europe. He came back imbued with the doctrine of the singing teacher Guillaume-Louis Wilhem (1781–1842) and set to work applying the new "method" in London. From now on his compositions were few; he never returned to the theater, but several songs won some popularity: for example, a setting of Charles Kingsley's "Three Fishers," 1857, and two songs by Adelaide Procter, "The Storm" and "O Doubting Heart," 1860. Thus he was a participant in the tradition that he surveyed. Though his *Song Book* included none of his own songs, his judgment was that of a composer as well as historian-educator with concerns like those of Dickens.

Hullah's school was described in an early issue of Dickens' magazine, *Household Words*, 1850. An anonymous article on "Music in Humble Life" proclaimed hopefully:

Music—that is, classical music—has of late years been gradually descending from the higher to the lower classes. The Muse is changing her associates; she is taking up with the humble and needy, and leaves nothing better to her aristocratic friends than their much-loved Italian Opera. It is to the masses that she awards some of her choicest scientific gifts.

The writer went on to describe several bands organized in factories, several educational choruses, and the new hall built for Hullah's Singing School for Schoolmasters. These new institutions for the thronging city were to help make homes more than refuges from real life, and "home music" more than a vapid dream. They fitted the program that Dickens himself had announced as he launched *Household Words:*

> We aspire to live in the Household affections . . . [to] bring into innumerable homes . . . the knowledge of many social wonders, good and evil . . . [to] cherish that light of Fancy which is inherent in the human breast; which, according to its nurture, burns with an inspiring flame, or sinks into a sullen glare. . . . To show to all, that in all familiar things, even in those which are repellent on the surface, there is Romance enough, if we will find it out.

There are enough direct links between Dickens and Foster to indicate that Foster shared Dickens' aspirations. On a lecture tour of America in 1842, Dickens fell sick at Pittsburgh and prolonged his stay there a few days. Dr. McDowell, Jane's father, attended him. Mayor Foster of Allegheny sent Morrison to call on him, then the next day took sixteen-year-old Stephen along to pay his own call. In 1855 Foster wrote his "Hard Times, Come Again No More"— an allusion to Dickens' latest novel, *Hard Times.* Also in 1855, *Household Words* printed a satirical article by Dickens, "The Great Baby," protesting the way politicians speak to their constituencies:

> Is it because the People is altogether an abstraction to them; a Great Baby, to be coaxed and chucked under the chin at elections . . . ?

Foster picked up the phrase "great baby" and used it in his campaign song of 1856 to protest the abolitionists' abstractions. The fact that "Some Folks" was composed in 1855 increases the likelihood that it reflects Dickens. In 1860 Foster listed Dickens' *Bleak House* as first of the eleven items in the penciled catalog of his sketch book. In 1863 Foster set to music a poem by Dickens, "The Pure, the Bright, the Beautiful" ("These things never die"). Though Dickens' name was omitted from the publication, and though Foster in this year published so much that he may not have known the words came from Dickens, still it is possible that he paid closer attention to Dickens than ever before; in Chapter 8 we can weigh this possibility. What interests us now is that Foster's connections with Dickens help us imagine more vividly the hopes he felt in 1850 and help us understand how "Old Dog Tray" fitted the needs of Hullah.

Hullah's *Song Book* is subtitled *Words and Tunes from the Best*

Poets and Musicians, selected and arranged. There are 264 songs—
nearly half are English; the rest are mostly Scottish (Burns) and
Irish (Moore); and at the end there are five songs of America. Hullah's preface explains that he has chosen

> ... exclusively *National* songs—songs which, through their truth to nature,
> their felicity of expression, and the operation of time, have sunk "deeper
> than did ever plummet sound" into the hearts of the people among whom
> they have sprung up and circulated. . . . Everything, however, in America
> comes quickly to maturity, and the flavour which, in the Old World, can
> be given to national melody only by age, seems to be communicable in
> the New, through other agencies.

For the British songs Hullah cites his sources; for the American he
does not. His English ones come chiefly from the collection by Chappell, both words and tunes from "olden times." The words of Burns,
Moore, and others Hullah presents with melodies in the older versions published by Edward Bunting. Hullah dispenses with all accompaniment, for he disagrees flatly with Chappell: the songs he
thinks most beautiful can stand by themselves, as they did, he
believes, in the "olden times." So his version of "Old Dog Tray,"
the final song of his treasury, is austere and anonymous, thoroughly
assimilated to the tradition of "Auld Lang Syne."

The British-American song tradition is part of a broader current
of European social, cultural, and political change in which the songs
of Pierre Jean de Béranger (1780–1857) and Franz Schubert (1797–
1828) are monuments—Schubert's the more enduring. Thomas
Moore's dream, though less frequent as a theme for Béranger or
Schubert than for Moore, had a name that was becoming familiar
in Europe: *Heimweh, nostalgie*. (When Felicia Hemans wrote her
song about the "Homesick Swiss Boy," she still referred to the
peculiar disabling malady, observed by doctors since the 17th century, of Swiss soldiers abroad hearing the *ranz des vaches*.) Coleridge and Wordsworth were among the first to generalize the use
of the English word "homesick," while Heine and Baudelaire and
others were exploring the metaphorical uses of the idea. "Homesickness" belongs to the vocabulary of the "avant-garde," along with
"folk," "proletariat," "alienation," and "repression"—all terms foreign to Stephen Foster. For him and the tradition he knew, the
dream of home was thought to be altogether wholesome. For later
19th-century singers, the home songs that survived from the old
tradition, like "Old Dog Tray," would take on new shades of meaning. In the 20th century, our study of the tradition as Foster knew
it enables us to set aside later meanings, if we wish, and to recover
as much as we wish of what his songs meant to his contemporary public.

(CHAPTER 8)

Foster
among his friends,
to 1864

"JEANIE" meant to Stephen Foster and a few friends his continuing effort to take part in the tradition of "home songs." Songs meant to him more of the world than his own home, though they meant that too. He wanted to contribute to the world something more serious than "Old Dog Tray" and the "plantation songs." He reached beyond his family and closest personal acquaintance with an expression of "dreams" as intimate and sincere as he could produce. "Jeanie" and almost every other song that carried this meaning fell short of success. Yet no matter how discouraged and distracted he was, Foster kept up the effort all his life. Contrary to what is said of him in many accounts, he came closer to the contemporary success he longed for after "Jeanie" than before, with "Come, Where My Love Lies Dreaming," 1855, "Gentle Annie," 1856, and "Beautiful Dreamer," 1864. His many failures in the years 1858–63 included songs just as good as the earlier failures, or indeed the earlier success, "Tray," and half-successes, "Ellen Bayne" and "Willie, We Have Missed You." The feelings he wished to express changed little; his dreams were similar throughout his life. If there was a perceptible change, it was no deterioration. His effort led to a few successes by chance, and to repeated failure.

The friends who could understand and even assist Foster's effort included two of the "nice young men"—Charles Shiras and Andy

Robinson—and Susan Pentland Robinson. Then, from 1855 to 1858, there was a younger friend, Billy Hamilton. And finally, from 1862, the much younger George Cooper, friend and collaborator in at least twenty-one songs. With all these friends, though our evidence is more fragmentary than the documents of the family, we can watch Foster "straying" from his family and aspiring to the most genuine fellowship that nourished the song tradition. With Shiras and Cooper we can see Foster's approaches to theatrical forms other than the minstrel show; with Cooper we can see his contact with school and Sunday School and his concern with the Civil War. Through these friends and a few others, and through selected songs, studied in relation to them, we can learn more of the meaning of "Jeanie" and Foster's work as a whole.

Andy Robinson's friendship extended from early childhood to the last years of Stephen's life. In 1835, when Stephen was nine, the boys sang "Jim Crow" and "Zip Coon." In 1845 Andy was the "nice young man" who felt, in Foster's joking poem, "jealous" of the fugitive slave Latimer. During the ten years between, the two boys, neighbors in Allegheny, watched the younger neighbor girl Susan Pentland grow up. She was still no older than fourteen when Stephen dedicated to her the song "Open Thy Lattice." In 1849 Andy married her. In 1850 their son John was born. In 1851 Stephen dedicated to Mrs. Robinson a ballad, "Willie, My Brave," in which the piano imitates the waves of the sea that drown Willie while his faithful fair maiden continues to call for him. In 1851, when old General William Robinson had died, the young couple planned a cruise to New Orleans, with the widow Robinson and her daughter Anne as important members of the party. Stephen and Jane and the baby Marion were invited, probably as guests. Two more friends completed the party: Richard Cowan, one of Morrison's most devoted "Knights of the Square Table," a veteran of the Mexican War with Dunning Foster, and a former rival of Stephen's for the attentions of Jane; and Jessie Lightner, who was to marry Morrison in 1860. Jessie and Susan were Stephen's favorite singers. Richard Cowan sang too, though not so well, if his own letter to Morrison in February 1853 is as accurate as it seems:

> . . . I was out visiting tonight and some of the musical members of the family sang "Old Folks at Home" and the duet from Romeo & Juliet. These songs were favorites of our party last winter on our trip to Orleans, and I was vividly reminded of our delightful journey. When we reach'd the warm latitudes, we used to sit on deck to enjoy the moonlight and the sight of the negros [sic] burning brush & cotton stalks at the plantations. Tell Miss Jessie that the duet was well sung tonight, but the second was very different from hers. Indeed, I used to think that Steve must have

written that piece of music for Miss Jessie & Mrs. R.—they sang it so well.

The Robinsons' party was a memorable success. At Cincinnati, on the way back, Morrison and three more friends, two brothers and a sister, joined them. Morrison's paragraph about the trip in his book of 1896 emphasizes the magnificence of the boat and the refined manners of the captain. An incidental statement by Morrison, taken out of context, has been cited by innumerable later writers:

> On this voyage Stephen observed a good many incidents of Southern life, which he afterwards utilized as points for poetical simile in songs.

Morrison himself mentions no Black music in this connection—only later writers imagine Stephen hearing work songs and field hollers. As far as any evidence indicates, the "observations" that Morrison refers to were no more than the picturesque "sights" recalled by Richard Cowan, viewed in the moonlight from the deck of the ship, in the company of the Robinson party. The party is at least as closely connected to "Jeanie" as to "Old Folks." From what we know of the opposing views on slavery held by Andy Robinson and Jessie Lightner, it seems probable that any curiosity about the Blacks was checked, any discussion avoided, so as to make the most of the moonlight and of songs like the *Romeo* duet.

A letter from Stephen to Morrison, November 11, 1858, gives assurance that his friendship with the Robinsons continued to flourish:

> . . . Siss [Susan] gets along very well since her mothers death. We had a nice duck supper with her the other evening. She had plenty of jokes about Andy, as usual. . . .

Finally there is the testimony of John Robinson about a trip he took with his parents to New York to visit Stephen, early in 1861, when John was eleven. He told H. V. Milligan that Stephen called for them at the St. Nicholas Hotel on Broadway, took them out to the theater "in the oldtime way," and had "a happy evening." The boy saw nothing to indicate that Stephen was in trouble; presumably his parents were reassured that Stephen's troubles had been exaggerated by family rumor. In any case, their friendship held firm.

Susan Robinson in later days was annoyed by rumors that Stephen had been in love with her. Morrison Foster, in 1898, introduced his daughter Evelyn to the old lady. She seemed to the girl "kindly, forthright, and most emphatic." Repeatedly Evelyn heard her explain:

> We were the best of friends, but I was good friends with every member of the family. Steve and I had no love affair at all.

Morrison enjoyed "hobnobbing" with Susan, but neither of them left any record of her "forthright" comment on his book.

From Stephen's early years a few glimpses of him venturing away from his family are worth noticing. The family had a remarkable old uncle, John Struthers (1759–1845), who showed the boy a wider world than he knew at home, and who recognized something special in the boy's response. The family let Stephen stay alone with "Uncle Struthers" for a few days in 1837 and for some weeks in August and September 1839. Struthers, when he was only a few years older than Stephen was now, had served in the Revolution as a scout and ranger. Then, in his twenties and thirties, he had hunted, fought Indians, and surveyed and cleared land on the frontier in the Northwest Territory; in 1799 he settled near the town of Poland, which after 1802 was part of the new State of Ohio; here with Mary Foster he brought up a family. In 1819 Mary Foster Struthers died, and the old man lived on alone, enjoying the woods and streams, smiling tolerantly at the bustle of new settlements, roads, canals, and industries. When Henrietta Foster Wick came to live in Youngstown, Struthers' bonds with the whole Foster family were tightened. It was Henrietta who reported to William Foster on September 29, 1839:

> . . . it is five long miles to Uncle's. Stephen enjoys himself finely at Uncle Struthers. He never appears to have the least inclination to leave there, and don't seem to feel at all lonely. Uncle just lets him do as he pleases with the horses and cattle, which makes him the greatest man on the ground.

The contrast between Struthers' life and that of the Fosters in Pittsburgh must have been enormous for the thirteen-year-old boy. Morrison knew this contrast too; his paragraph about it shows a slightly wistful doubt about modern "improvement" and "refinement" that is rare in Morrison:

> Old Uncle Struthers had dogs and rifles, and himself would lead the hunt at night for 'coons, opossums, and such like nocturnal game. It was tame work to the old pioneer, who had been used to bears, panthers and hostile Indians. These hunts and the stories of adventure told by his aged relative, of course gave great pleasure to Stephen, and kindled the flame of his vivid fancy. One cold day, he was missed from the house, and was hunted for everywhere outside. At last his uncle discovered him sitting up to his neck in a pile of chaff, watching the movements of the chickens and other barnyard animals—"just thinking," as he briefly explained. The old gentleman always prophesied that Stephen, who even then displayed great originality and musical talent, would be something famous if he lived to be a man.

The prophecy cited by Morrison is found in a letter from the boys' father to the eldest brother, William, March 24, 1840:

... We think it time to receive another letter from Stephen. I hope he is attentive to his studies, give much love to him from his mother and myself. Tell him his old Uncle Struthers looks to him to become a verry great man. He says he is confident that he is possess'd of superior talents for one of his age. I hope Stevy will not disappoint the fond hopes of so good an old man.

If the prophecy so impressed the family, how much more must it have meant to the boy himself! And what a loss must Stephen have felt when Struthers died in 1845, before there had been time to begin fulfilling his hopes. In 1863 Stephen wrote a song in which he imagines Uncle Struthers (or someone very like him) talking about the problems of Lincoln and his generals: "I'm Nothing but a Plain Old Soldier," "an old revolutionary soldier . . . You've had many generals . . . you're still at a stand . . . we had *one* in command . . . Washington."

The glimpse provided by Struthers is complemented by a recollection of William Wallace Kingsbury, classmate at the Towanda Academy in 1841. Kingsbury was a lifelong resident of Towanda, Pennsylvania, and his recollection was recorded by his son in the annals of the Bradford County Historical Society, 1910:

Well do I remember that inimitable Stephen C. Foster. He was my special friend and companion; being a year older than myself and considerably larger, he used to defend me in my boyhood antagonisms with belligerent schoolmates. We often played truant together, rambling by shady streams or gathering wild strawberries in the meadows or pastures, removed from the sound of the old academy bell. One mutual luxury, in which we jointly indulged in those excursions without leave, was in going barefoot and wading pools of running water that meandered through Mercur's farm and down Mix's Run, in the village of my nativity. Foster wore a fine quality of hose, and I remember how it shocked me to see him cast them away, when soiled by perspiration or muddy water. His was a nature generous to a fault, with a soul attuned to harmony. His love of music was an all-absorbing passion, and his execution on the flute was the very genius of melody, and gave rise to those flights of inspired pathos, which have charmed the English-speaking world with their excellence from cabin to palace.

Several traits in this portrait make it valuable, though the tribute to "passion" and "genius" naturally come from the old man's reflection as much as from his boyhood memory. The extravagance with socks, the impatience with disciplined study, and the protective attitude toward a younger friend–all these ring true as characteristic of the man in his later years. The flute, no matter how impassioned or how mediocre the "execution" of the fifteen-year-old, fitted the character. Here in the meadows was a setting for Stephen's music more to his taste than either the minstrel show or the gas-lit parlor of home.

Both Struthers and Kingsbury help us picture a Stephen Foster that should have read Thoreau, one that somehow appealed to those later readers of Thoreau, Charles Ives and his father. But Foster's life did not often allow for "rambling" and "gathering wild strawberries." Once he had begun to work in an office, he supposed that even his songwriting was to be office work. And once he had married, his proper diversions were cruises and dances and theater parties rather than barefoot luxuries. His music found only a little opportunity for outdoor expansion.

Charles Perry Shiras (1824–54) was a more important part of Stephen Foster's life than Andy Robinson, Uncle Struthers, or any teacher or classmate. Just how important can never be known, though there is always a possibility that further information may turn up to bring us closer to the full truth. Soon after Foster's death, in 1866, one reporter made unsubstantiated claims for Shiras that were sharply denied by Morrison Foster, but Morrison's total omission of Shiras from his biography of 1896 suggests that Morrison knew both too much and too little to define the relation. The Shiras family kept its knowledge and opinion mostly to itself until 1953, when Winfield Shiras published a biography of his most distinguished ancestor, U. S. Supreme Court Justice George Shiras, Jr., (1832–1924), nephew of Charles. The 1866 reporter, John Hull, writing in the *Chicago News,* credited Charles Shiras with the words of "Susanna," "Uncle Ned," "My Old Kentucky Home," "Willie, We Have Missed You," "Hard Times," "Come, Where My Love Lies Dreaming," and "Gentle Annie." Morrison's comment on Hull's claim was solicited by a reader who saw the story reprinted in Rochester, Pennsylvania, in 1886:

> I thank you for your favor of 12th inclosing a newspaper article cut from Rochester Pa Herald originally published in the Chicago News.
>
> The author of the article evidently knows nothing personally about what he writes. My brother Stephen C. Foster and myself, being nearly of the same age, were intimately associated together from infancy until the time of his decease . . .
>
> I had personal cognizance of every song he ever wrote, at home. I mean in Allegheny County. His regular practice was to compose the music first, and then write the words afterwards, to suit the music. In writing the words his practice was to write a verse or two at a time, submitting them to me verse by verse for my opinion or to his mother, who possessed a fine poetic fancy. At rare intervals he wrote music to the words of others, but he always prefered [sic] to write his own words in order to harmonize them with the previously written music. Charles P. Shiras was an intimate friend of ours. We all esteemed him highly and admired his genius. He and his mother lived on Hemlock St. Allegheny

City in a two story brick house which stood out flush with the sidewalk and the house I suppose still stands there. They did not live in Pittsburgh during my recollection. Shiras' style of poetry was too heavy and sombre for Stephen's muse. The only words of Shiras published to which Stephen ever wrote music were a song called "Annie my own love." It was published about a year before Shiras' death and Shiras' name is printed on the title page as the author of the words. Shiras had half the royalty on this song but it did not have a very large sale.

It was a subject of regret with Stephen as well as myself that Shiras (notwithstanding his undoubted genius) could not write suitable words for Stephen's music. Stephen would cheerfully have given publicity to them through his music for the purpose of aiding Shiras, who (though possessing some little unremunerative real estate) was dependent entirely upon his literary labours for his support and needed money. . . .

Does Morrison, in this private letter, reject Hull's claim more sweepingly than the full truth would warrant? One strange fact arouses suspicion: in many letters to Morrison from Richard Cowan, though there is no mention of the Shiras family, Cowan calls himself "Shiras," as he calls Morrison "Sir George Armstrong." The full truth of the relations among all these friends was tangled.

Stephen's poem about the "nice young men" puts Charles Shiras first, with his groaning laugh. A family portrait, according to Winfield Shiras, shows Charles as "dark, intense, cadaverous." At this time he was the chief executive of the family brewery, his father having died and his older brothers retired. Morrison, busy with the cotton trade, must have known Charles through Stephen more than otherwise. In 1846, when Charles and Stephen were inspired by Dempster's singing of Tennyson's "May Queen," Morrison was not with them. In 1847, after Stephen had gone off to Cincinnati and Charles retired from the brewery to begin his weekly antislavery magazine, *The Albatross*, Morrison had no reason to keep in touch with Shiras. Then in 1850, when Stephen returned to Allegheny, Morrison was not so much interested as Stephen in Shiras' latest poems: "The Bloodhound's Song," a response to the Fugitive Slave Act; "My Mother, I Obey," a song set to music by Henry Kleber; and "The Popular Credo," which was quickly to prove Shiras' most famous work:

> Dimes and dollars! dollars and dimes!
> An empty pocket's the worst of crimes.
> If a man is down, give him a thrust—
> Trample the beggar into the dust!
> Presumptuous poverty's quite appalling,
> Knock him over! Kick him for falling!
> If a man is up, oh! lift him higher—
> Your soul's for sale, and he's a buyer!
> Dimes and dollars! &c.

The Shiras family believed that Stephen set this poem to music; though no other trace of a setting has been found, their belief warrants at least the idea that Stephen knew and liked the poem. It must have been in the back of his mind, along with the works of Dickens and other sources of inspiration, when he wrote his "Hard Times," 1855.

Shiras was married soon after Stephen and Jane were married. His daughter, Rebecca Shiras, was born in 1852; in 1899 she wrote her recollections about Stephen in a letter to her son Shiras Morris, who had doubtless noticed Morrison Foster's silence of 1896.

> My grandmother, like all mothers, did not want my father to associate with him nor put his name on the "Nigger songs." . . . I can faintly remember him coaxing me to call him Uncle, and I still have a toy he bought for me.

Charles' mother and daughter talked to an anonymous reporter for the Pittsburgh *Leader* in 1879; their memories of the young men's many hours together were vague, but Mrs. Shiras hummed "Oh! Susanna" and said:

> Well, Stephen composed that song anyhow, because Charles thought it was so foolish; he told me about it and said it was great trash. . . . Right in that front room yonder he and Stephen would sit night after night.

The Shiras family was never anxious (as Morrison was) to command public respect; George Shiras, Jr., and George III, a promising student at Cornell at the time of the interview, soon to be a successful lawyer and a pioneer of wildlife photography, far outshone Charles and his friend of dubious fame.

In 1852 Charles published his collected poems in a volume titled *The Redemption of Labor.* In May 1853 Stephen's setting of Charles' "Annie" was copyrighted. The poem has no distinction; it seems an entirely conventional example of the international tradition, in contrast to the liveliness of "The Popular Credo." We may imagine that Charles, having heard Foster's recent "Melinda May" and "Ring de Banjo" and his settings of Mackay, McCarthy, and Fuller, said "I can provide something as suitable."

> There's a wound in my spirit,
>> No balm can e'er heal;
> In my soul is a sorrow,
>> No voice can reveal.
> And deeper the furrows
>> Will sink on my brow,
> For Annie, my own love,
>> Is gone from me now. . . .

By Death, unrelenting,
        She's freed from her vow. . . .
Oh! seek not to sooth [sic] me,
        To earth let me bow. . . .

The fit of words and music is more satisfactory here than in Foster's earlier settings of more ambitious poems, but not yet so close as in "Susanna" or "Jeanie" or "Old Dog Tray." The collaborators needed more time if they were to achieve any memorable success.

In the spring of 1853 the English poet Alfred Bunn stopped at Pittsburgh and enjoyed a visit with Shiras. Bunn thought him "a delightful poet" and quoted some lines from another of Shiras's conventional poems:

Oh, life! it is far too brief,
And you waste its spring in bowers of ease,
And its autumn in cells of grief!

Then, in a condescending footnote, Bunn adds:

MR. SHIRAS.—It is not often the case that a manufacturing town can boast of great literary pretension; but, without forgetting our own renowned bard of Sheffield, and the famous Corn Law Rhymer, the genius of Mr. Shiras, of Pittsburgh, is one that any city, in any country, may be proud of.

Foster's "Annie" was written very close to the time of Bunn's visit. If, as Morrison claimed, Stephen wished to aid Shiras, he wished at least as much to benefit from what seemed Shiras' growing fame. Neither wish was as strong, in all probability, as the immediate pleasure of collaborating with a friend in the exercise of complementary abilities.

In the fall of 1853 Shiras produced a play, *The Invisible Prince*, based on one of the fairy tales of the Countess d'Aulnoy that had been used for burlesque extravaganzas by J. R. Planché in London in 1846, New York in 1847. According to advertisements for the performance, Stephen provided some incidental music. Probably this means simply that he chose instrumental "symphonies," for Shiras' play, unlike Planché's, needed no songs. Reviewers in the Pittsburgh *Post* and other papers, when they praised Shiras' wit and "skillfully woven" plot, left the music unreported. The public supported four performances of *The Invisible Prince*, but the next week's unprecedented excitement over the first dramatization of *Uncle Tom's Cabin* swept the *Prince* into oblivion. Morrison Foster, who sold to his friends sixty-five tickets for *The Invisible Prince*, at fifty cents each, seems to have forgotten it in later years. The modern investigator of this play, Edward B. Fletcher, in 1935 wonders why Morrison never mentions it in his letter of 1886, cited above. Fletcher remarks that the "silence about the play is somewhat peculiar."

Soon after the collaboration on the play, Stephen went to New York. While he was there he learned that Charles Shiras died of consumption.

The record is tantalizing. Whatever the extent of the friendship and collaboration, surely Stephen learned more from Charles Shiras than from his own family about poetry and a career as writer. The dream of "Jeanie," blended with so many dreams, could easily refer also to Charles. The smooth fit of words and music in "Jeanie" might have been impossible without Charles' contributions to Stephen's development. Most important, however, is the sheer fact that Stephen and Charles—minstrel songwriter and abolitionist—remained friends through the years 1845–54. What would be the most desirable addition to our knowledge is a clue as to how the two discussed slavery and Blackness. On this point not only Morrison but every other source is silent.

Two songs of 1854 won a gratifying degree of popularity, though not yet all that Foster hoped for: "Ellen Bayne" and "Willie, We Have Missed You." These, more than any earlier song, showed Foster's mature craftsmanship, and these, more than "Jeanie" or "Old Dog Tray," were models for many later songs. Their rhythms and chords are as simple as those of "Old Dog Tray" or the "plantation songs." Their melodies range through a tenth ("Ellen") and an eleventh ("Willie"). Their words fit the rhythms and melodies very well, and express with some intensity the central theme of the tradition of "home songs." "Ellen" dreams, while the singer soothes her:

> Soft be thy slumbers,
>   Rude cares depart,
> Visions in numbers
>   Cheer thy young heart.
> Dream on while bright hours
>   And fond hopes remain,
> Blooming like smiling bowers
>   For thee, Ellen Bayne.
> CHORUS: Gentle slumbers o'er thee glide,
>   Dreams of beauty round thee bide
>   While I linger by thy side,
>   Sweet Ellen Bayne.
>
> Dream not in anguish,
>   Dream not in fear;
> Love shall not languish;
>   Fond ones are near. . . .

> Scenes that have vanished
>   Smile on thee now,
> Pleasures once banished
>   Play round thy brow,
> Forms long departed
>   Greet thee again
> Soothing thy dreaming heart,
>   Sweet Ellen Bayne.

Foster piled up the rhymes more densely in this song than in most. The rhymes sustain the dream, much as the melody does. They make no pretense of developing an idea, no claim for attention apart from the melody.

"Willie" is more dramatic and more intimate. The singer seems to be a wife welcoming her husband home from a journey; no chorus joins in—but a family of children sleeping in the next room is essential to the scene:

> Oh! Willie is it you, dear,
>   Safe, safe at home?
> They did not tell me true, dear;
>   They said you would not come.
> I heard you at the gate,
>   And it made my heart rejoice;
> For I knew that welcome footstep
>   And that dear, familiar voice,
> Making music on my ear
>   In the lonely midnight gloom:
> Oh! Willie, we have missed you;
>   Welcome, welcome home!
>
> We've longed to see you nightly,
>   But this night of all;
> The fire was blazing brightly
>   And lights were in the hall.
> The little ones were up
>   Till 'twas ten o'clock and past,
> Then their eyes began to twinkle,
>   And they've gone to sleep at last;
> But they listened for your voice
>   Till they thought you'd never come;—
> Oh! Willie, &c.
>
> The days were sad without you,
>   The nights long and drear;
> My dreams have been about you;
>   Oh! welcome, Willie dear!
> Last night I wept and watched
>   By the moonlight's cheerless ray,

> Till I thought I heard your footstep,
>   Then I wiped my tears away;
> But my heart grew sad again
>   When I found you had not come;
> Oh! Willie, &c.

By 1857 "Ellen" and "Willie" together had earned royalties equal to those of "Old Dog Tray." Foster expected each of the two to earn more than "Tray" or any "plantation song" in the future. He counted on "Willie" for as much as his latest effort, "Gentle Annie." His expectations were not realized. By 1860 he could see that "Ellen" and "Willie" were fading, while "Tray" continued to prosper. But "Ellen" and "Willie" had spurred him to the more elaborate musical efforts of "Jeanie" and "Come, Where My Love Lies Dreaming." They had encouraged him to discontinue the "plantation songs." They were the foundation of what he supposed was his true vocation.

Singers who knew "Ellen" and "Willie" in the summer of 1854 when "Jeanie" appeared would notice how the first phrase of "Jeanie" resembles the first phrase of "Willie" and the second phrase of "Jeanie" the first phrase of "Ellen." "Jeanie" combines the two immediately preceding successes. For this very reason, perhaps, the singers of the Christy minstrels found "Jeanie" unattractive. If they had gone on to study the whole form of "Jeanie," they would have recognized a distinctive advance of technique in the phrase "happy as the daisies that dance on her way"—this modulates to the key of the fifth degree of the scale, making room for two phrases of contrast, about "many wild notes" and "many blithe birds," so as to bring the return of the opening phrase with a fine sense of satisfaction. With this smooth modulation and return, Foster achieves for the first time a firm unity embracing memorable musical variety. His contemporaries did not notice. Foster himself, while he knew that "Jeanie" was somehow better than its sales indicated, probably did not recognize the working of chords and form. His next efforts, ambitious in their own ways, miss the coherence of "Jeanie."

"Come with Thy Sweet Voice Again," copyright September 19, 1854, uses a flowing accompaniment in 6/8 time; some syllables of the text last through four of these flowing subdivisions, while a few others subdivide further into pairs of 16th notes. The accompaniment includes at one point a brief imitation of the melody—a rare thing in all Foster's works. These complexities against the poverty of the chords—almost entirely the two main chords of the key— make a grotesque incongruity. The words too have some incongruities: "soft, soothing pain" and "lulled in the lap of thy sighs." Foster is not complacent.

The unaccompanied quartet, "Come, Where My Love Lies Dreaming," copyright June 28, 1855, is the climax of musical complexity in all Foster's works. Its interwoven melodies and varied rhythms make several fine phrases, but they are strung together loosely—almost any random ordering of them would make as coherent a whole as the order prescribed; an ordering that put first the phrase we here call "a" would be easier to grasp than the actual order:

introduction (?) for three voices, two phrases: x, y;
entrance of high voice, phrase beginning and ending on the dominant: z;
concluding phrase, louder: z′;
opening phrase (?): a, answered by z′;
new staccato accompaniment for a′, then again z′;
three-voice contrasting phrases: b, b′;
z, z′; a, z′; a′, z′;
"finale ad lib." with ritard, crescendo, and high note.

The phrases here labelled y and b indicate that Foster was not content to stay in a single key for so long a piece but that he had no control of modulation as a means of shaping form. Possibly, to be sure, the loose form is what he wanted; it satisfies many singers and listeners. But its relation to "Jeanie" and the intervening "Come with Thy Sweet Voice," together with the fact that no later song is so long and complex, makes "Come, Where" seem freakish. Its words, on the other hand, fit easily between "Ellen Bayne" and "Beautiful Dreamer"; the singer's love is asleep, "dreaming the happy hours away" with thoughts that "dance through her dreams like gushing melody"; listeners are invited to come, "with a lute, with a lay," simply to prolong her dream.

By 1857 "Come, Where" had not yet won the degree of popularity it was to reach soon afterward. Foster's estimate for its future earnings was $100, the same as "Old Folks," much less than "Ellen," "Willie," and "Jeanie," though more than "Come with Thy Sweet Voice." In fact, "Come, Where" eventually earned more for the publishers and Foster's widow than any other song except for the four "plantation" favorites—"Old Folks," "Massa's in de Cold Ground," "My Old Kentucky Home," and "Old Black Joe." An arrangement of "Come, Where" for piano, by the English concert pianist and composer Brinley Richards (1817–85) was published by Pond in New York in 1860, and helped to spread its use. It gradually superseded "Old Dog Tray" as the best known of the "sentimental" songs; only in the middle of the 20th century did "Come, Where" yield to "Jeanie."

Foster's development from "Ellen Bayne" to "Come, Where My Love Lies Dreaming" was the kind of development that his friend

Shiras, had he lived, would have appreciated in detail. Andy Robinson and Susan, lacking a professional concern, doubtless appreciated the direction of the development without following its details. Foster's closest friends of later years knew only the fruits of this development and showed no curiosity about its course.

The memories of Billy Hamilton, Stephen's friend from 1855 to 1858, were recorded by careful Pittsburgh reporters in 1891 and 1895, independent of Morrison. Hamilton was now Superintendent of Allegheny Parks; the journalist Erasmus Wilson, calling Hamilton a "naturalist and weed-ologist," wrote to James Whitcomb Riley in 1891:

> He [Stephen] and Billy Hamilton steamboated together, sang together, went courting together and got drunk out of the same jug.

The anonymous reporter of 1895 put the story in Hamilton's words:

> I first met Steve, as we always called him, in 1855. He was such a genial young man, so kind-hearted and genteel in his manner, that I liked him from the start and we became firm friends. Both of us loved music, and hardly a week passed that we did not have some concert, musical or serenade on hand. During the summer and fall of the campaign in which Buchanan was elected president of the United States, in 1856, I saw much of Foster, and my recollections of this period are most vivid, perhaps, on account of the exciting times we had. I was a Democrat then, and so was Foster, and together we organized a Glee Club for the purpose of booming the campaign in Allegheny. Among the members of the club were Stephen C. Foster, Morrison Foster, Thomas Smith and myself. There were other vocalists, but their names have escaped my memory. Then we had a body-guard of sometimes 50, sometimes 100 men, who joined in the chorus of the songs. We would march through the streets singing campaign songs, and had many interesting conflicts with the Whigs and other political clubs. . . .
>
> On our way home from one of these trips to East Liberty, we stopped at a residence this side of the forks of the road, Lawrenceville, to serenade a family with which some of us were acquainted. We sang a Foster song on this occasion, and I had the solo part. Some stranger joined the crowd, and persisted in singing the solo part with me, although he was not familiar with it. He annoyed me, and I motioned to a member of the body guard to tell him to sing only the chorus. The guardsman misunderstood me. He thought the fellow had insulted me in some way, and promptly gave him a blow on the left ear, knocking him down. . . . In a twinkling our peaceful body of serenaders was transformed into a howling mob. Foster, his brother, myself and other vocalists hastened out of the crowd. We were all too small for our ages and had no business around where any fighting was going on. We always left that to our body guard, and they protected us most effectually in that case. . . .
>
> I think it was in 1858 . . . I was clerk of the steamer Ida May, plying

between this city and Cincinnati, and one day invited Stephen and his wife to take a trip to Cincinnati with me. They accepted my invitation, and we had a very enjoyable time. On the way down the river, Foster wrote and composed the song, "Ingomar to Parthenia," which was afterward published and enjoyed quite a season of popularity in concert circles. He had written some of the melody before, but most of it was composed on that occasion.

Hamilton's qualifications on this point show a closer knowledge of Stephen's procedures than Morrison himself shows in all his testimony. Hamilton has no interpretive slant; his memory can be trusted.

. . . During our brief stay there [in Cincinnati], we called on several friends . . . [We] went to the office of the "Commercial Gazette," on Third Street, to see Cons Miller, river editor of that journal, with whom we were both well acquainted. After a pleasant chat, we bade him good-by and started back to the boat to make preparations for our return to Pittsburgh. On our way down Broadway, we heard music, and discovered a party of serenaders . . . We stopped and listened. The melody was strangely familiar.

"Why, they are singing my song, 'Come, Where My Love Lies Dreaming,'" exclaimed Foster.

"It is a bungling effort they are making, too," I replied. "Let us go over and help them out."

We had some time to spare, and Foster accepted my proposition. We crossed the street and joined the party. They had not yet finished the song and we chimed in. Naturally they regarded us as intruders, and when the song was finished demanded what right we had to interfere with them in their enjoyment. I asked them if they knew the composer of the song they had just sung. They replied that they knew Stephen C. Foster composed the song, but they were not personally acquainted with him. I then introduced Foster, but the young men refused to believe he was the composer of the song, and declared we were imposters.

The situation began to grow alarming, and we were in danger of having a lively set-to with the young serenaders, when a happy thought struck me. I asked the leader of the party if he knew Cons Miller, of the "Commercial Gazette." He said he did, and I proposed that we all go over to the Gazette office and see Miller. The young men agreed to this, and in a few minutes Miller established our identity in the eyes of the serenaders beyond any question. Nothing was too good for us after that, . . .

Hamilton's ability to do more than "chime in" is signficant. He knew Stephen's most difficult song, "Come, Where My Love Lies Dreaming," well enough to "help out" in unbungling a performance. He did not merely chime in on a chorus, like the bodyguard of 1856 in easier songs. But neither did he think of the operatic quartet as confined to a stuffy parlor or a concert room—with the right skill and spirit, it was fit for an outdoor serenade. Hamilton's narrative of 1858 matches perfectly with Stephen's letter to Morrison, November 11:

> Mary Wick, Jane, Marion, and I start tomorrow for Cincinnati on Billy Hamilton's boat, the "Ida May." We all went to see Miss Davenport last night at the "old" theatre. We will stirr old John McClelland up in Cincinnati, make the children sing and bring in Billy's bass voice. The trip will be a recreation and variety for me. . . .

Hamilton saved a letter from Stephen to him, written in the time between the Glee Club and the Cincinnati trip, when Hamilton was clerk on the "Clara Dean," ice-bound at Point Pleasant, [West] Virginia.

Pittsburgh, Jan. 16, 1857

> Dear Billy
>
> Your letter from Point Pleasant has been received, and I am glad to know the whereabouts of the great North American ballad singer. When can you promise to appear again before a Pittsburgh audience? Masonic Hall can be had now. I have also had an engagement tendered me, but I declined. Kleber is going to give a concert and he has offered me the post of first *anvil* player in the "Anvil chorus" from a new opera. I was unwilling to go through the course of training and dieting requisite for the undertaking, and consequently declined. I understand he has sent to Europe for a "first anvil." We have had another little political brush in the election of Mayor, but there was very little excitement.
>
> I have not yet received the Cincinnati Gazette and suppose that puff has not appeared. [John Russell's article was printed January 22.] I will send you by this mail a copy of "Jeanie with the light brown hair" if I can find a copy. Mit is now living with us. . . .
>
> Your Friend
S. C. Foster

If Billy Hamilton received the copy of "Jeanie," he did not find it an outstanding song, for he left no comment about it. For him many of its meanings were obvious. Stephen's thought of sending him a copy, nearly three years after its publication, shows us more of its meaning to Stephen. "Jeanie," like "Come, Where," could suit this "naturalist" and practiced bass.

Even more suitable for Billy Hamilton, as for some 20th-century students of Foster, is the song of 1855, "Some Folks." Copyrighted the same day as "Come, Where," this song makes a contrast in mood. It harks back to the polka rhythm of "Susanna," now treated with more variety of accent; it tends toward a galop—the climax of a series of polkas in a dancing party. Its words are thoroughly subordinate to the dancing rhythm, but their literal meaning, dif-

ferent from any other poem of Foster's, fits a side of his personality
that Billy Hamilton brought to expression in the letters just quoted:

> Some folks like to sigh,
>   Some folks do, some folks do;
> Some folks long to die,
>   But that's not me nor you.
> CHORUS: Long live the merry, merry heart
>   That laughs by night and day,
> Like the Queen of Mirth,
>   No matter what some folks say.
>
> Some folks fear to smile . . .
> Others laugh through guile . . .
>
> Some folks fret and scold . . .
> They'll soon be dead and cold . . .
>
> Some folks get gray hairs . . .
> Brooding o'er their cares . . .
>
> Some folks toil and save . . .
> To buy themselves a grave,
>   But that's not me nor you.
> Long live &c.

In Foster's manuscript notebook there are some lines that were
omitted from the published version:

> Some folks toil and plod
>   Money is their God.
>
> Some folks preach and whine
>   This they call divine.

Billy Hamilton probably sang these and others that never got into
print.

Firth and Pond in 1856 issued the "Some Folks Polka" in an
arrangement "expressly for young pupils" by James Bellak, along
with the "Old Folks at Home Schottisch," similarly arranged. But
piano teachers were not interested. "Some Folks" found no success
in Foster's lifetime. It was neglected by Morrison. In later collections
of Foster's songs, it turns up as a relief from the sentimental dreams
and laments, but how many singers or readers of "Old Folks" or
interpreters of Foster's work as a whole pay attention to "Some
Folks"?

To suppose that "Some Folks" reveals more than "Jeanie" about
Foster's character and his intention throughout his work would be
unwarranted. But to see "Some Folks" and "Jeanie" as complementary is reasonable. The tradition of song is broad enough to in-

clude both. The personality of Foster, as seen in all the documents together, is complex enough for both. "Jeanie" and all the other songs for folks who "like to sigh" are balanced by "Susanna," "Nelly Bly," "Camptown Races," and "Some Folks," for times when guileless laughing appeals to "me and you."

After "Some Folks," down to 1860, no new song reflected so much of the cheerful tone of Billy Hamilton. From summer 1855 to summer 1858 there were fewer new songs than at any other time in Foster's career, and all were sad songs: "Comrades, Fill No Glass" is one; the rest are almost like a single song—"The Village Maiden" begins "merrily" with bells and a choir in the chapel for the maiden's wedding day, but mysteriously "joys have faded" and "hopes have flown" and the choir is singing a requiem; "Gentle Annie" is in her tomb, and the singer consistently laments her memory, whether he "ponders" there or "wanders" elsewhere; in "I See Her Still in My Dreams," the same singer seems to continue the same lament, with a melody that stretches out the title-refrain twice as slow as the lines of the verse; "Lula Is Gone" repeats the wander/ponder rhyme, and, until the final stanza, seems to repeat the whole situation; then, though Lula may return in the spring, it is too late in the song for anything but a dreamlike "longing."

One more song continues this cycle, "Where Has Lula Gone?" The singer imagines her "far in some distant land," and "roaming in rapture wild," while his own "dreams of hope have flown" and he must continue to ask his question. The tune has a steady motion except for some held high notes; it seems to fit the "roaming" Lula more than the "longing" singer. The cycle is thus framed in mystery. The two central songs of the group, "Gentle Annie" and "I See Her Still," are musically more like "Jeanie" than the first and last. Those central songs are the ones that Stephen's brother Henry associated with the beauties of nature.

For singers of the 20th century, familiar with "Jeanie," all these similar songs of 1855–58 serve not so much to specify particular meanings as to reinforce the position of "Jeanie" itself as representing Foster's central and continuous effort.

From the more numerous and more varied songs of 1858–60 a group of three stand out as an effort to reconcile the cheer of "Some Folks" with the wistfulness of "Jeanie." In "Fairy Belle" the singer describes a happy muse; in "Thou Art the Queen of My Song" he appeals to her, with a fairly wide range of feeling that he is able to hold together; in "Poor Drooping Maiden" he calls her away from "toiling hours" in "a dreary home" to "roam the laughing hills." The rhythm of "Fairy Belle" is almost that of a polka—once more the spirit of "Susanna"—but two polka measures are combined into one measure of this song, the accompaniment is smoothed into a quiet march, and the title-refrain, as in "I See Her Still," is spread out over a whole long measure. Fairy Belle is identified in the first stanza as "queen of my song." In the last stanza the singer exults that "her eye full of love is now beaming on my soul." The "Queen of My Song," however, has deserted the singer, who calls her to return "from the throng" and fulfill his dream amid "fields and flowers." His rhythm is varied, over a steady pulsing accompaniment; he alternates slower and faster motifs throughout the song, and these alternations fit the words perfectly, with emphasis on "I long," "I sigh," "welcome," "rejoice," and, at the climax of each stanza, "pride." There is no chorus. If the stilted "thou" and "queen" did not alienate listeners, this song would win at least as many admirers as "Jeanie." "Poor Drooping Maiden" also has an admirable variety of rhythmic detail over a steadily pulsing accompaniment, and a distinctive form in which every stanza begins with the same words as the chorus, "Poor drooping maiden sighing on a bright bright summer's day"; the melody for the opening line, after four intervening phrases, is answered by the chorus's two phrases, repeating the same words. Thus there is an intricate balancing of contrasts, with a convincing drive to the final phrase—the only phrase that ends on the tonic note. The slow motif of "poor drooping maiden" is tightly bound together with the quick "sighing" and the staccato "bright." In "Jeanie" the word "bright" is staccato, but not repeated; "light" balances "bright" but the effect is almost too subtle. In "Poor Drooping Maiden" the effect is unmistakable—the composer has given his idea a genuine development.

If these three songs are juxtaposed with "The Wife" ("He'll come home . . his word is always true") they make a touching dramatic sequence. The three seem to link Jane with Stephen's work as songwriter more closely than does any other evidence, including that of "Jeanie." No matter how closely they are connected with the real Jane, these songs link the poetic dream of secure affection with the outdoor world of movement and cheer. They avoid the word "dream." They show the persistence of the dream as more than mere repetition—rather an intelligently flexible effort.

In relation to the development from "Ellen Bayne" to "Come, Where My Love Lies Dreaming," 1854–55, the further developments of 1855–60 are broader and some of them more realistic.

Foster's development was confined, to be sure, within limits so narrow by the standards of John Sullivan Dwight or Walt Whitman or Henry Rowland Bishop or Alfred Tennyson that to discover the development at all requires a patiently sympathetic study, more than can be expected of biographers motivated by the fame of "Old

Folks." Yet by the standards of John Hill Hewitt and George P. Morris, of John Hullah and Charles Mackay, this development is measurable, genuine, meshed with the real world.

A vivid glimpse of Foster in 1860 is provided by the reminiscence of John A. Joyce from the Washington *Post* in 1900. Joyce had moved to Pittsburgh from his home in Kentucky in the spring of that year, to take a course in bookkeeping:

> After spending a few days between the college, the hotel and social resorts about town . . . I imagined that my mission in life was . . . the theatrical stage, where as a minstrel song and dance man and Shakespearean poetical "prodigy," I would fire the town.
>
> I went to a printer and had struck off a thousand small hand bills for a "Musical Entertainment" . . . [at] the Lafayette Theater.
>
> A few nights before the performance, I met the musical genius, Foster, in the tavern where I was staying, and he seemed particularly friendly, perhaps for the reason that I was announced to sing a number of his "Darky Songs," and on account of my youth. He introduced to me some of his "boon companions," who indulged in social cheer till after the noon of the night. And while Foster did not indulge very much himself in Bacchanalian eccentricities, we youngsters made up for his conservative conduct.
>
> He played on the banjo and piano and sang for us many of his noted melodies, and occasionally he played the flute with a sweetness I never heard before or since.
>
> He had a sweet, low barytone voice, and when playing the piano swayed backward and forward with his rhythmic numbers, like the sighing surges of a summer sea. . . . Foster was about thirty-three years of age when I met him, but with the settled melancholy look that occasionally swept over his charming face, like a passing cloud over a field of wild flowers, he seemed older.
>
> The night for my entertainment finally arrived. . . .
>
> Foster and a few of his friends occupied the front bench, and were, from the start, lavish in their applause, leading off with hands and feet when I made a hit with one of his own songs, or danced a shuffle or a jig to the music of a small string band that volunteered for my benefit.
>
> The more I danced, sang, and spouted, the wilder grew that impromptu audience, and after an hour and a half, from sheer exhaustion, I bowed myself out through the wings, rang down the curtain, and left the house for the tavern. . . .

Joyce later joined the army. By 1900 he was a colonel. His picture of Foster fits well with that of Billy Hamilton. The "passing cloud" of melancholy does not overshadow the spontaneous gaiety and generosity that motivate him still in his last years.

In Cincinnati and Pittsburgh Foster could count on groups of friends. In New York he was more nearly alone in the crowd, with single friends who themselves were lonely individuals, struggling to find their places. One was a reporter, John Mahon, born in Ireland in 1815. According to his memoir of Foster in the New York *Clipper*, 1877, the two met at a restaurant early in 1861; Mahon took Foster home to meet his family and try out his piano. For some months they saw each other often. Mahon helped Foster find a new publisher, John Daly, when Firth and Pond had rejected one of his songs, "Our Bright Summer Days Are Gone." Foster helped Mahon by arranging the accompaniment for a song of his, "Our Darling Kate." At the time of Foster's death, Mahon and his wife were seriously ill and out of touch with Foster, but less than a year before, at the wedding of the Mahons' daughter, Foster "played and sang several of his own pieces." Mahon was proud to have Foster's participation in this festivity, along with the attendance of "several theatrical lights" whose names no longer shone in 1877.

A group of four songs from 1861–62 brings to a climax the theme of "home." In each of these a solitary singer reflects on his distant home; in all but one a chorus joins him, but since it is never identified it may be only hollow echoings of his loneliness. The rhythms of all but one are slow and simple; the exception is another polka, *moderato*. "Why Have My Loved Ones Gone?" pictures the singer "plodding" while "dear departed friends" are "calmly gliding"; the singer expects to "battle in the strife" and "struggle in the fray" until he too dies; his plodding song hints that his struggle cannot last long. "No Home, No Home" is the bleakest of the group, with no chorus; the singer "wanders" on a "weary way" and "roams o'er the wide world" through its "busy scenes" with no friends, no hope; his self-pity overflows in a final phrase that stretches out the "drooping heart" to a high note and then leads down with an unusually jagged line of melody. From this depth of despair, the remaining songs look up. "I'll Be Home Tomorrow" is the polka; music more than the words confirms the resolution of the title, for the words mostly concern yesterday and today:

> I've wandered far from those I love, and many years have pass'd.
> Since in my dear old cherish'd home I saw their faces last . . .
> How dear the hearts that dwell within that sweet domestic realm!
> I know that they have long'd for me as I have long'd for them;
> The thought that I am near them makes my lonely spirit yearn
> To hear the burst of gladness that will welcome my return!
> CHORUS: Farewell, farewell! ev'ry cloud of sorrow,
>   All my heart is fill'd with joy for I'll be home tomorrow!

The last of these songs is a musing on "Happy Hours at Home" that never loses sight of the lost past and the demanding future:

I sit me down by my own fireside
  When the winter nights come on,
And I calmly dream as the dim hours glide,
  Of many pleasant scenes now gone;
Of our healthful plays in my schoolboy days,
  That can never come again;
Of our summer joys and our Christmas toys,
  And rambles o'er the streamlet and plain.
CHORUS: Happy hours at home! happy hours at home!
  How the moments glide by the bright fireside,
    In the happy hours at home.

. . . While the clear young voice of our household pride
  Makes melody . . . [to] allure my cares away,
To prepare my soul as the swift hours roll,
  For the duties of the bright coming day.
CHORUS: Happy hours &c.

The happiness is in the "calm dream," not in any homely exchange.
The music of the singer, like the melody he hears or dreams of
hearing, soothes care and fortifies the soul for unwelcome duties.

These songs had so little chance of finding customers that Firth
and Pond accepted only the lively one. Horace Waters took "Why
Have My Loved Ones Gone?" with a dedication to the Tremaine
family, singers imitating the Hutchinsons, one of whom was a clerk
in the Waters store. Waters went on to publish altogether forty-
seven Foster songs, twenty of them in booklets for Sunday Schools.
"No Home" and "Happy Hours" were published by John Daly, the
friend of Mahon, whose total was eventually sixteen. Neither
Waters nor Daly could disseminate the songs to singers like the
Christys. Waters could not afford to give Foster copies of "Why
Have My Loved Ones Gone?" George Birdseye recalled in 1867
going to the store with Foster to ask for the copies:

> They were refused him, and he left the store with the tears rolling down
> his cheeks, for he was very sensitive, and weeping came to him far more
> easily than smiling.

Birdseye's vignette does not name Waters, but generalizes that

> it was not seldom, . . . that a publisher would take advantage of his
> miserable condition, paying him a paltry sum for what other composers
> would demand and receive fair compensation. It may be that such small
> transactions were deemed to be all for his good, in order not to minister
> to his well known passion for drink. . . .

Birdseye's combination of vague but vivid pictures led to a widespread image of Foster as victim of publishers' exploitation throughout his life. The biography by J. T. Howard thoroughly acquits the

chief publisher, Firth and Pond, and moderates the charge against even Waters. But no one has observed that the particular song in Birdseye's tale is one that makes the dream of home too blatant for the singers and listeners addicted to that dream.

Sometime in 1862 Foster met George Cooper, a native New Yorker (1840–1927) who was about to enlist in the Army. Cooper was a desultory student of law and writer of verses, some for the theater, some for schools, some for churches. The two met in the back-room bar of a grocery shop. They quickly became friends and "partners" in songwriting. While Cooper was serving in the Army for some months, ending in July 1863, at least five songs were published with words by Cooper and tunes by Foster; three more appeared later in 1863 and five more at an unknown part of the same year. One of the first five was "Willie Has Gone to the War," the only one that Cooper referred to in particular when he talked with H. V. Milligan in 1920. This song, Cooper recounted,

> was written one morning, and after it was finished, Stephen rolled it up and tucking it under his arm, said, "Well, where shall we put this one?" Cooper says that he remembers it was a cold, raw, winter day, snow falling drearily, and the pavements covered with slush. Stephen's shoes had holes in them and he had no overcoat, but he seemed oblivious to discomfort and misery. As the author and composer proceeded up Broadway, they passed Wood's Music Hall [minstrel theater], and the proprietor, standing in the lobby, hailed them as they passed with the question, "What have you got there, Steve?" The song was sold then and there, Wood paying $10 cash, $15 more to be paid at the box-office that evening.
>
> Stephen called Cooper "the left wing of the song factory," and most of their songs were written and sold in very much the same manner as "Willie Has Gone to the War." They sold all of their songs for cash, receiving no royalties on any of them. . . .
>
> He wrote with great facility and without the aid of a piano. If no music-paper was handy, he would take whatever paper he could find, and, ruling the lines on it, proceed without hesitation to write. He seemed never at a loss for a melody, and the simple accompaniment caused him no trouble. These first drafts were taken out and sold to a publisher or theatre manager, practically without correction.

Cooper's lines for "Willie Has Gone" are glib; the singer "pines like a bird for its mate, till Willie comes home from the war." The melody suggests a military tone: many pairs of syllables are set as dotted eighth and sixteenth notes; but neither the detailed setting nor the general mood seems a good fit. Considered without the words, the tune has nothing to betray haste in composition, but nothing to indicate unusual care. The tune might have been written first and the words hastily added. Thus Cooper's account of the "song factory" is believable. Yet the dates listed above show that

Cooper's generalization about "most of their songs" cannot correctly be simplified to mean "all," nor "exactly the same way."

A one-line note from Foster to Birdseye, February 11, 1863, raises a question: "I will arrange Mr. Cooper's melody when my hand gets well." Did Cooper sometimes make up tunes as well as words?

Cooper himself gave a different account of the collaboration in 1869, when he published "Dearer than Life":

> Some three weeks before his death, Mr. FOSTER called upon me, and, as was usual with him commenced improvising on the Piano, during a social chat, and, dotting down this melody, presented it to me as a memento of our friendship. I have treasured it as such; but, feeling that the public had a right to *any* composition of their favorite song-writer, I have endeavored to express the sentiment of the melody in the words thereto, and present it to the readers of Demorest's Magazine.

"Dearer than Life" is a waltz—perhaps the smoothest of the several waltzes scattered through Foster's works. The words fit the smooth melody better than those of "Willie Has Gone"; Cooper spent more than an hour on these words, which Foster never saw. Cooper's procedure for "Dearer" may be as nearly a norm as the procedure for "Willie."

Several of the Cooper songs—especially lively and interesting ones—look as though a still different procedure was known to the partners, for in these the words are distinctive and the music in some ways subordinate to the words.

The first Cooper song to be published, before the end of 1862, is "There Are Plenty of Fish in the Sea." The title-refrain inspires a jigging rhythm, which Foster marks *vivace;* the words vary the jig, as they tell of a scornful lady who through many "merry years" sang the refrain—adding, "as good as ever were caught"—until she grew old and learned "the lesson time has taught": "But, oh, they're hard to be caught." The wit is theatrical. Foster never before chose anything like this; never before or after did he himself invent words like these. But now he responds to them with a wit of his own. The refrain provides a high note for "sea" with a surprising minor chord, so that the last phrase comes with a twist; the instrumental introduction runs up the scale one note beyond this high note; the epilog caps the same climax with a still higher note to place the whole final motif an octave above its normal position. Cooper has brought out a new side of Foster's character.

Wit of a similar brash quality is characteristic of the duet, "Mr. and Mrs. Brown," and the song "If You've Only Got a Moustache," both of which appeared ten days after Foster's death.

Not wit, but a disingenuous smile is combined with traditional motifs of home and "gliding hours" in "Kissing in the Dark."

A more surprising combination is found in "My Wife Is a Most Knowing Woman." The theme that Foster treated with utmost truth in "The Wife" and with delicacy in "Willie, We Have Missed You," "I'll Be Home Tomorrow," and "Poor Drooping Maiden" is treated here facetiously, with another jig:

> My wife is a most knowing woman,
>   She always is finding me out,
> She never will hear explanations
>   But instantly puts me to rout. . . .
> She says that I'm "mean" and "inhuman"
> Oh! my wife is a most knowing woman. . . .
> She would have been hung up for witchcraft,
>   If she had lived sooner . . .
>
> Now often I go out to dinner
>   And come home a little "so so,"
> I try to creep up through the hall-way,
>   As still as a mouse, on tip-toe,
> She's sure to be waiting up for me
>   And then comes a nice little scene,
> "What, you tell me you're sober, you wretch you,
>   Now don't think that I am so green!
> My life is quite worn out with you, man,"
> My wife &c.
>
> She knows *me* much better than *I* do . . .
> Yes, I must give all of my friends up
>   If I would live happy and quiet;
> One might as well be 'neath a tombstone
>   As live in confusion and riot. . . .
> I'll stay at home now like a true man,
> For my wife &c.

The grudging irony of these words is more remote from the gentlemanly personality portrayed by Morrison Foster than any "plantation song." Yet not so far from "Some Folks." The "witch"-wife portrayed in this song is not so different from the wife of other songs, nor from what is known of Jane, as the henpecked husband is different from the yearning dreamer. Can this knowing wife be identified with "Jeanie"? If not, then one or both must be detached from Jane. In any case, the author of "Jeanie" and all the other dreams is incompletely known until he is identified with the companion and collaborator of Cooper, the author of "My Wife Is a Most Knowing Woman." Cooper made him laugh; Birdseye's testimony that "weeping came to him far more easily than smiling," like all of Birdseye's exaggerations, needs the qualification provided by Cooper.

Six of the Cooper songs of 1863 in addition to "Willie Has Gone" refer to the war. Four of these have tunes with Foster's favorite *moderato* polka rhythm; the other two are slow and plodding. A soldier sings farewell to his "darling" in "When This Dreadful War Is Ended" ("I will come again to you"). Someone left at home sings "Bring My Brother Back to Me When This War Is Done," and a chorus joins: "Bring him back! bring him back!" until in the third, and last, stanza the plea becomes a prayer. In "The Soldier's Home," a detached observer-singer and chorus describe the hero on leave:

> O! joyful is the soldier's heart to be once more at home,
> To meet his wife and children dear and cease awhile to roam,
> What bliss beneath his cottage roof with Hope and Love and cheer,
> To pass the happy moments by with all that life holds dear.
> CHORUS: How happy is the soldier to be once more at home!
>   But sorrow falls on those he loves when parting time has come.

In the third and last stanza the soldier returns to battle and dies. Rhythmic and melodic details fit the words in this song as closely as in any song with Foster's own words; there is an unusually effective accented and repeated dissonant note in the chorus, combined with an appropriately severe dotted rhythm, which is answered in the last phrase by a smooth motion down the scale. "My Boy Is Coming from the War" makes an astonishing contrast, for here the mother's words seem mismatched with the polka; in the third and last stanza, all her words are suddenly put into quotation marks by a previously invisible reporter:

> My boy is coming from the war
>   The mother fondly said,
> While on the gory battle field
>   Her boy was lying dead!
> His comrades came with lightsome steps
>   And sound of martial drum,
> But now that Mother sadly waits
>   For one who'll never come!

The piano's introduction develops the second phrase of the tune into a striking evocation of a fife; the epilog recalls this development and adds syncopation. The mismatching is evidently an intentional irony, though the brief song does not escape unintentional pathos. "For the Dear Old Flag I Die!" is still different: the refrain is the exclamation of "the wounded drummer boy." A note claims that Cooper heard the boy at Gettysburg. In the three stanzas of the song the dying boy comforts his mother with visions of the "angel band calling" him. The chorus joins the boy: "Mother, dry your weeping eye; For the honor of our land And the dear old Flag I die."

Introduction and epilog, both alike, present the bravely dancing
first phrase of the chorus answered by a phrase with gasping silences
and snapping syncopations.

"A Soldier in de Colored Brigade" has six stanzas all in minstrel
dialect. The soldier, reinforced by an unidentified chorus, consoles
his "honey" as he sets off to war:

> . . . Wid musket on my shoulder and wid banjo in my hand,
>> For Union, and de Constitution as it was I stand.
> Now some folks tink de darkey for dis fighting wasn't made,
>> We'll show dem what's de matter in de Colored Brigade.

With "what's de matter" he alludes to Foster's song "That's What's
the Matter," 1862. He goes on to remind listeners of Black heroism
in the Revolution and the War of 1812, and then to reject emancipation:

> Some say dey lub de darkey and dey want him to be free,
>> I s'pec dey only fooling and dey better let him be.
> For him dey'd break dis Union which dere forefadders hab made,
>> Worth more dan twenty millions ob de Colored Brigade.

The final stanza follows:

> Den cheer up now my honey dear I hear de trumpets play,
>> And gib me just a little buss before I go away.
> I'll marry you when I come back so dont you be afraid,
>> We'll raise up picanninnies for de Colored Brigade.
> CHORUS: Ninnies! Ninnies for de darkey Brigade.
>> We'll raise up picanninnies for de Colored Brigade.

To what extent does this soldier express the opinions of Cooper and
Foster? His opinions do not conflict with any of theirs on record.
His cheerful tone sounds more like Cooper than like most of Foster's
words, but the tune harks back to "Susanna," with no hint of irony
or reserve.

All these songs concerning the war show a kind of collaboration
both more spontaneous and more craftsmanlike than the "song
factory" that Cooper's late account describes. They show that Foster
in the last year of his life was still developing his powers, not just
frantically repeating himself for the sake of a few dollars.

Cooper and Foster collaborated in two religious songs that were
published by Horace Waters: "Onward and Upward," November
20, 1863, and "We Will Keep a Bright Lookout," sometime in the
same year. In later years Cooper's more than two hundred songs
included several similar ones, of which the most famous was "God
Bless the Little Church Around the Corner." There is no reason to

suppose that his religious concern was mercenary. There is fair reason to suppose that Foster's was not.

Foster's most interesting "hymns," naturally enough, were the seven published in 1863 with his own words. (There were thirteen in 1863 with words by others, and, after his death, about four more advertised as his own, plus many adaptations.) The first group of five appeared in Waters' collection, *The Golden Harp*, April 14, and the remaining two in his *Athenaeum*, December 9. Though the order of appearance in the collections may be unrelated to the order of composition, this order seems to indicate a progression of thought, from a shy and noncommittal starting point through prayer to faith and a positive resolve to "work for the Lord." There is a corresponding musical progression, from limitations narrower than those of any other Foster song to a confident variety greater than Foster's average norm.

The first piece is just two phrases, in four-part harmony for congregational singing, with a rhythm untouched by any dance. The title is "Tears"; there are three little stanzas:

> Blame not those who weep and sigh
>   When to sadness given;
> Kindly view the tearful eye—
>   Tears bring thoughts of Heaven.
>
> When in death our friends depart,
>   When our hopes are riven;
> Tears bring comfort to the heart—
>   Tears bring thoughts of Heaven.
>
> To the suffering child of earth
>   Unto madness driven,
> Hallowed hours when tears have birth—
>   Tears bring thoughts of Heaven.

Foster knew that he himself might be blamed for his ready tears, or pitied or ridiculed for them, as George Birdseye soon invited the reading public to do. He often thought of death, he sometimes thought of madness, and now he was ready to think of Heaven, not only alone but in a group of worshippers.

The first musical prayer is "Give Us This Day Our Daily Bread." Here a more complicated stanza fits a melody of two long phrases and a short concluding one: The first three lines of the text make the first musical phrase.

> Father of love,
> Father above,
> Send down thy blessing upon each head;

> Shield us from pride
> While we here bide,
> Give us this day our daily bread,
> Give us this day our daily bread.

Three more stanzas ask for resignation and for God's care in spite of our thoughtlessness. The same music fits—not quite so well—three stanzas on a different theme, printed in *The Golden Harp* on the same page with Foster's prayer. These stanzas, by the New England Baptist Mary Ann Kidder (1819–1905), were probably Foster's model:

> Shepherd, we stray—
> Show us the way,
> Safe thro' each valley and mountain steep;
> Helpless we roam,
> Gather us home;
> Jesus, our Shepherd, lead thy sheep!
> Jesus, our Shepherd, lead thy sheep!

In Mrs. Kidder's refrain the commas interfere slightly with the melody, whereas Foster's line from the Lord's Prayer fits perfectly. But Mrs. Kidder's use of the roam/home rhyme makes Foster's second phrase wonderfully poignant: "helpless" falls back on the opening chant of repeated notes; then "gather" brings a fine unexpected high note and a smooth descent. The Waters books include many hymns by Kidder, three of them with Foster's music for which he wrote no words of his own, and several more with Foster tunes originally set to secular words. Mary Ann Kidder eventually wrote over a thousand hymns; a few of these, as sung by Ira Sankey and published in his *Sacred Songs*, 1878, became more famous than her Foster hymns.

Foster's next prayer begins as a duet, with piano accompaniment; questions and exhortations lead to the choral assurance: "Seek and Ye Shall Find" ("Every prayer is heard in heaven That is breathed from a truthful mind.")

"We'll All Meet Our Saviour" ("if we keep his sacred word") has chorus throughout, singing four short phrases in a bouncing cheerful rhythm. "We'll all live with the angels . . . in a fair and happy home . . . we'll sing heavenly praises . . ."

The last of the *Golden Harp* series unites prayer with cheer, individual concerns with the solidarity of a group, faith with dreams; also it emphasizes song—"The Angels Are Singing unto Me." It begins as an unaccompanied duet, so as to burst forth in a four-part chorus with a long high note:

> When my mother's hands are o'er me spread,
>   As I kneel, humbly praying by her knee;
> When her gentle voice is round me shed,
>   Then the angels are singing unto me.
> CHORUS: Music from above!
>   Strains of joy and love!
>   When my soul is fill'd with melody
>   Then the angels are singing unto me.

In the second stanza "birds gaily singing" remind the singer of God above. In the third, stars and soft winds lift him "on high." In the last, the singer descends again, and dreams:

> When I hear the laughing, gurgling stream,
>   Or the waves of the deep and plunging sea,
> Then I'm lull'd into a pleasant dream
>   And the angels are singing unto me.

The *Athenaeum* songs, almost certainly later than those of the *Golden Harp*, go beyond dreaming. One of these is Foster's setting of the four stanzas by Dickens, "The Pure, the Bright, the Beautiful," with an alternate text of two stanzas by Foster himself, "We'll Tune Our Hearts." The music, in a slow mazurka rhythm, fits Foster's words best. The verses are for solo voice with piano; then the chorus condenses the melody of the verse into two phrases, as if to confirm what the soloist has said on behalf of the group he belongs to:

> We'll tune our hearts to harmony
>   In praise of Him who died
> That we might not be cast away,
>   Our Saviour and our guide.
> His ways were full of gentleness,
>   His voice brought peace and love,
> And if we keep his holy word,
>   We'll hear that voice above.
> CHORUS: We'll tune &c.

> He quietly received affronts
>   As gently as a child,
> And pitied those who could assault
>   A soul so pure and mild.
> And when He chided, 'twas in grief
>   That we could sinful be;
> Then raise our voices to the Lord
>   In grateful harmony.
> CHORUS: We'll tune &c.

These lines are grammatically and logically connected more tightly than any others by Foster. No matter how their value may be measured, they are surely no product of a perfunctory moment—they are not shoddy. Skeptical readers may doubt whether these songs testify to an integrated growth of technical and spiritual strength, but to dismiss them without study is unjust.

The last song is a march; its short choral refrain, "While We Work for the Lord," answers a duet within the stanzas, as well as summarizing at the end. The middle lines of the stanzas are a solo, almost like a yodel, "O'er the mountains . . . shades of sorrow fly . . . raise a grateful voice." There is no reference to death or the angels or Jesus or an individual wanderer. The duet, growing out of the solo lines, declares that our hymns are "nature's" and that "gladness" is "around us" as long as "we work for the Lord." "*All* around" is emphasized at the beginning of the song and the beginning of the chorus.

Something like the ripe cheerfulness of the *Athenaeum* songs can be found united with Foster's older themes in "Beautiful Dreamer" and three more songs that were published soon after his death: "Sitting by My Own Cabin Door," "When Dear Friends Are Gone," and "Voices That Are Gone." These songs tend to reinforce our interpretation of the explicitly religious songs, while they indicate also that Foster was not simply converted from old attitudes to a fanatical religiosity. These songs, moreover, are musically varied and sustained—at least equal in craftsmanship to "Jeanie."

"Beautiful Dreamer," "Sitting By," and "Dear Friends" are solo songs. "Voices That Are Gone," sung by Wood's minstrels, has a chorus, *pianissimo*, "like music heard when dreaming."

"Beautiful Dreamer" resumes and completes a development of the flowing triplet rhythm that can be traced through several songs from "Come with Thy Sweet Voice," just after "Jeanie," 1854. It is a favorite dreaming rhythm of Donizetti, from whom many other composers learned it as well as Foster. "Linger in Blissful Repose," 1858, has several lines, like the first, that fit the measures marvelously, lingering on the first syllable: "While round thee melody flows . . . Mu—sic will flow from my heart." Toward the end, for a contrast, the word "dreaming" is set off by silence, and repeated, before the last rounded phrase, "I'll breathe my soul away." "My Loved One and My Own," or "Eva," also 1858, is more operatic, with sobbing dissonant notes and a very broad curve of melody including the sustained high note of the last phrase; the singer is inconsolable, for Eva first spurned him, then died. A duet of 1861, "Mine Is the Mourning Heart," is outstanding for its shifts of rhythm; the singers alternate long lines of melody in 6/8 measures, then overlap and finally parallel each other in 9/8. But this interesting feature cannot redeem the two from their competitive self-pity. Much simpler and more satisfactory is the lullaby "Slumber My Darling," 1862; in the traditional rocking rhythm, 6/8, a mother watches her baby, and invokes "sweet visions" and "angels" to help "fill the dark void with thy dreamy delight." "The Love I Bear to Thee," published January 14, 1863, is the song of a deserted lover, dreaming of the past and wishing for an angel to tell the absent one his love. The rhythm emphasizes syllables that are held on the second beat of a 9/8 measure, while the first and third beats have melodic motion within the syllables, so that the first beats are heavier than the sustained second beats. The same pattern of weights and durations fits more easily the words of "Beautiful Dreamer," which was probably written soon after "The Love I Bear," for "Beautiful Dreamer" was advertised on the title page of "Willie Has Gone to the War," July 1. The singer of "Beautiful Dreamer" at last asks "the queen of my song" to wake up and be happy with him. Though his rhythm seems likely to keep lulling her, the singer does not ask to prolong any dreams or take pride in the sorrows that he hopes to leave behind. Unlike the singer of "Jeanie," the singer of "Beautiful Dreamer" forgets his own dreams. The dream of the listener may even be thought to serve a purpose, if the listener responds to the invitation.

"Sitting by My Own Cabin Door," a solitary singer asserts his serenity:

> Through varied scenes of care and strife,
>   I've roam'd the wide world o'er,
> But now I calmly glide through life,
>   While I'm sitting by my own cabin door.
>
> I feel as happy as a king,
>   And free as the birds that soar,
> No sounds of battle round me ring,
>   While I'm sitting by my own cabin door.
>
> My time of life is waning fast
>   Upon this troubled shore,
> But still I smile on days gone past
>   While &c. . . .
>
> The blooming hopes of early days
>   May come to me no more,
> Yet memory sings me pleasant lays,
>   While &c.

The melody begins and ends with suitably calm phrases, but in the middle it dips and soars quickly through its full range of a tenth, with the accompaniment softly repeating full chords, so that the ending, where the accompaniment slows to regular beats and then to two-beat chords, makes the serenity convincing.

The lament for "Dear Friends" is purified from complaint, from family favoritism, and from dreams. The singer neither denies nor dwells on his grief but rather urges: "Let us turn from grief to mirth . . . We can make each other happy." His rhythm is steady and mild, accommodating both the griefs and the joys "quickly flown."

The tranquil recollection of "Voices That Are Gone" includes a line for the family and a line for Uncle Struthers or William Kingsbury:

> Voices heard in days of childhood
>> Softly at the hour of prayer,
> Or loud ringing through the wildwood
>> When the young heart knew no care.

The third and last stanza becomes a prayer:

> So when life's bright sun is setting
>> And its day is well nigh done,
> May there be no vain regretting
>> Over memories I would shun;
> But when death is o'er, to meet me
>> May some much-lov'd forms come on,
> And the first sounds that shall greet me
>> Be—the voices that were gone!

The prayer is much "like music heard when dreaming." But this dream is only a part of a simile. The waking singer appeals to friends alive and dead together. The whole waltzing song must be soft, the chorus as soft as possible. The main melodic phrase sweeps down and up in an unusual curve—no stale formula, but as fresh and sweet a melody as any of Foster's. In this song he most comprehensively portrays himself in his dreamy singing character, dedicating himself and his work to his friends.

CHAPTER 9

The public
of publicity
and Foster
in his maturity

WHEN Foster died, some of his songs were known to a bigger public than knew his name. He was likely to be identified, if at all, as author of "Old Dog Tray," "Come, Where My Love Lies Dreaming," "Old Black Joe," and a vague group of older "plantation songs." The public that recognized his name was interested in "Beautiful Dreamer," advertised as his last song, "composed but a few days previous to his death." It ignored "Jeanie." It ignored most of his work. It ignored his family and friends and the continuous effort that he had devoted to songwriting. People who sang the older songs, including "Susanna" and "Old Folks at Home" (different but overlapping groups of people), mostly neither knew nor cared who had written them.

The 20th-century public that knows "Jeanie with the Light Brown Hair" knows the name of Foster. It knows that he lived in the 19th century, and imagines that he lived unhappily, dreaming of an ideal Victorian woman in the intervals between his listening to Black singers. The public has heard that he drank a lot and died alone, penniless. Just where and when he lived is hard to remember. What "Jeanie" means to individuals of the 20th-century public depends on what the whole 19th century means.

Morrison Foster, in 1896, was distressed to see the growing image of his brother as an ignorant drunken pauper and nigger-lover.

Morrison tried to substitute an image of genius and gentleman, who "sounded the profoundest depths of musical science" and "founded a new era in melody and ballad," who needed, deserved, and always held the affection of his very respectable family. Morrison's image was closer to the truth than the one he opposed, but not convincing. It modified but never replaced the more vulgar one. Morrison was ineffective in the art of public relations. For some 20th-century readers his effort seems typical of 19th-century innocence or hypocrisy.

Morrison simplified when he wrote that Stephen was "always indifferent about money or fame." His testimony is confirmed, to be sure, by Jessie Rose's recollection of what Jane told her—that when pressed for his reaction to "the plaudits of the world" he would exclaim, "Oh! It's all 'hocus-pocus.' " But besides the careful record and discriminating estimate of royalties that Stephen made in 1857, to which we have referred several times, there are more documents to be considered, indicating that he cared very much about his "reputation." Not so deeply, steadily, as he cared about friendship and truth, but enough to make some efforts to manipulate publicity.

Morrison, though he knew that times were changing, knew too little of the world of music and poetry to describe his brother more precisely than he did. Morrison understood the changes in social structure that affected his own work: in 1861 he spoke up intelligently about the national importance of cotton exports from the South to England. He recognized that a national and international economic structure was superseding the older patterns of family farms and independent crafts, and that the railroad and telegraph were transforming the relations among cities, all of which depended on the Southern cotton farms. But how these changes affected song was no concern of his. For him, music and "poetic sentiments" were a refuge from change.

Stephen himself knew too little of either business or song to keep up with the rapid changes. He was swept along by what happened to "Susanna," and baffled by what failed to happen to "Jeanie."

"Publicity" was one of the many new ideas that emerged from the French Revolution. *Publicité* was thoroughly analyzed by Balzac in the 1840s. In America of the 1850s, though the arts of advertising and "working the press" did not yet evoke the name "publicity," these arts advanced rapidly, beyond what was developed by then in Europe. Foundations were laid for what became, in the 20th century, the special office of "public relations," indispensable to all bureaucracies. The Napoleon of publicity was Phineas Taylor Barnum (1810–91). His greatest triumph in "working the press" was the American reception of "the Swedish nightingale," Jenny Lind

(1820–87), who came under his management for a tour in 1850–51. This tour, far more than the songs of Foster, inaugurated a new era in American musical life. It gave new meaning to "America" in the world of concert music. It confirmed the character of Barnum as "typical American" in the estimate of many Americans and foreigners. Though Jenny Lind's direct connections with Foster are slight, if not apocryphal, her indirect connections with "Jeanie" and its history form a web worth examining. Only when "Jeanie" at last helped to make for Foster more publicity than that of Jenny Lind did his work fulfill any large part of his own hopes or Morrison's.

P. T. Barnum claimed no knowledge of music. But he recognized in the English reports of Lind the possibility that she could earn a million dollars in America. He had first won some national fame as brave liberal editor of a Connecticut newspaper, willing to go to jail in defense of truth. Then, in 1835, he had begun his career as showman by buying the slave Joice Heth from her Kentucky master, who was exhibiting her in Philadelphia as the 160-year-old nurse of George Washington. Barnum treated Heth generously, left unresolved all doubts of her authenticity, and left unchanged her "act"—including occasional hymns that she sang. For several months he built up her audience by a vigorous campaign in the newspapers; the challenges of the skeptics could do as much as anything to bring people to look, listen, form their own opinions, and tell their friends about her. When she died the next year (her age was estimated by doctors as closer to sixty than 160), Barnum went on to use his growing skills with the press as a means of acquiring the American Museum in New York. Here he flourished for a decade. He took the "dwarf" Tom Thumb to England. He read about Alfred Bunn's difficulties in managing the prima donna Lind, about the furor of her English public, and about her religious scruples: she was ready to quit the theater, of which her parents had always disapproved, but she wished to earn enough money to endow a hospital. Barnum sent an agent to offer her an unprecedented contract, paid in advance. She bargained. They agreed. Then Barnum launched the publicity campaign that made possible well over a million dollars and earned him the title "Prince of Humbugs."

Lind was in fact an outstanding soprano of the age. Idolized by the Swedish public for her perfect acting and singing as Agathe in *Der Freischütz*, she went to Paris in 1840 and studied for a year with the unique teacher Manuel Garcia. She refused to sing publicly in Paris because the French were, in her opinion, so immoral. But Chopin and Berlioz heard her sing Bellini and Donizetti and they praised her as "pure and true." Meyerbeer wrote his *Feldlager in Schlesien* especially for her in 1844. She made it a sensational success in Berlin and Vienna. Mendelssohn declared that she was "as great an artist as ever lived and the greatest I have known." For her and the English public Mendelssohn wrote his oratorio *Elijah* in 1847; together they gave new vitality to the notion of an angel. Mendelssohn confessed, on the other hand, that Lind "sings bad music the best." Her *Volkslieder* and *volkstümliche Lieder*, from Sweden, Italy, Scotland, Ireland, and, eventually, America, won the most rapturous applause from the most enormous audiences. Carlyle, who heard her only in Bellini's *Sonnambula*, said that she "sang, acted, etc. with consummate fidelity, but had unfortunately nothing but mere nonsense to sing or act." Many critics agreed that with all the sweetness, power, and agility of her voice, the predominating and distinctive quality of her performances was a unique "purity" or "chastity," unsuitable for most operatic roles. A few noted that her careful pronunciation of Italian, French, German, and English gave them all a specially clean and dispassionate connotation that no native singer could have found, and that few would have sought. These very qualities made her the supreme favorite of many of her contemporaries and a legend to connoisseurs of singing for many generations after. Her fame reached levels of society far from the audiences of opera or concerts: one of the street singers studied by Henry Mayhew sang about her, to the tune of the minstrel song "Lucy Long":

After Jenny signed the paper, she repented what she'd done,
And said she must have been a cake, to be tempted by A. Bunn.
The English language she must decline, it was such awkward stuff,
And we find 'mongst our darling dames, the one tongue's quite enough.
> So take your time Miss Jenny,
> Oh, take your time Miss Lind,
> You've only to raise your voice,
> John Bull will raise the wind.

The ship that brought Lind to America was greeted at the dock by a crowd of 30,000. A band marched up Broadway to her hotel, to greet her with "Yankee Doodle" and "Hail Columbia." Tickets for her first concert were sold at auction—4000 people bid; the first ticket brought $225. Proceeds from this concert, $10,000, were given to the mayor for distribution to charitable organizations. The program included a "Greeting to America," for which the words had been chosen in a contest that attracted 753 entries; the winning one was Bayard Taylor's, set to music by Lind's conductor Jules Benedict, with the lines:

> Cradle of Empire! though wide be the foam
>   That severs the land of my fathers and thee,
> I hear, from thy bosom, the welcome of home,
>   For song has a home in the hearts of the Free!

Taylor said he was worried about the effect of this poem on his reputation—he had submitted it because he needed the money. It did him no harm. His travel books probably sold a few more copies because of it. The Lind tour was magnificently launched.

Under Barnum's management she sang ninety-two concerts in eighteen American cities and three in Havana. Barnum was generous, tireless, and the soul of dignity. Everywhere the crowds came out to greet Lind, the auctioneers sold tickets, and charities benefitted—all producing more publicity. Jenny Lind dolls, scarfs, gloves, and handkerchiefs were sold. Barnum occasionally feared that the momentum was too great. But Lind everywhere gave intense satisfaction to her audiences and to nearly all critics. In Washington President Fillmore called on her; Clay and Webster paid tribute. For them she sang "Home, Sweet Home." In Boston, J. S. Dwight distinguished her excerpts of the sublime works of Handel, Mozart, and Mendelssohn from the merely pretty displays of Bellini, Donizetti, Meyerbeer, and others, but he ranked Lind's version of "Home, Sweet Home" with the sublime classics—she made it "joyful, hearty, vigorous." In Cincinnati her stay was extended to five concerts. In Pittsburgh an angry mob locked out of the Masonic Hall disrupted the 1850 concert with noise and rocks through the windows; in 1851, when she returned, an equally big crowd kept order.

Did Foster hear Lind? Possibly not, if he was like Septimus Winner who recorded in his diary, October 17, 1850, "Saw Jenny Lind accidentally, there had the gratification of seeing her at any rate, could not hear her, tickets 7, 6, and 5 dollars apiece." Foster at this point needed every cent for Jane and the expected baby.

One chronicler of Lind, Gladys Shultz, 1962, reports that Foster visited her in New York and presented her with a collection of his songs; she is said to have sung "My Old Kentucky Home" on several occasions, sometimes with the audience joining in. If these reports are true, first-hand evidence should support them. But if they are only guesses or fiction, they indicate at least a possible relation between the two. Even if Foster missed hearing her, he could not avoid Barnum's publicity. The lack of any mention of her in his letters and those of his family would be consistent with a wish that he had been famous enough in 1850–51 to command her attention, or with a dream that in the next years, when she was semiretired in England, she might sing his songs there. "Jeanie" in particular, especially if pronounced "Jenny" in accordance with Morrison's recollection, must have brought memories of Lind to the minds of some people who heard or only saw this song in 1854. More than that, the whole bevy of angelic ladies in Foster's songs must owe something to the reputation of the angelic Lind as greatest singer of the age.

Lind wrote to an admirer in Germany, shortly before her American tour:

> . . . Life has quite as much joy as it has sorrow: but I, for my part, prefer the sorrow: for there is something exalted about it . . . we first feel how poor we are on earth, how rich in heaven.

Foster, as we have seen, could sympathize with Lind's preference. To a close friend, in 1846, Lind wrote about her "homesickness":

> . . . though I may justly say that I am at home everywhere, I really feel quite homeless.

After she married her pianist, Otto Goldschmitt, pupil of Mendelssohn, in 1852, Lind devoted herself more and more to domestic life and religion, only rarely singing in public for a new charitable cause. For many of her American and English devotees this was the right fulfillment of her career; it made what they had heard before 1852 all the more precious. For Foster too, Lind's retirement was at least understandable, perhaps exemplary.

Barnum in later years seldom sponsored music. At his Museum in 1853 he competed unsuccessfully with the National Theatre's production of *Uncle Tom's Cabin*. He proceeded to acquire the circus, which was his main interest for the rest of his life—he made it not only the world's biggest circus, but a kind of entertainment approved by clergymen for respectable families. Barnum wrote his autobiography in 1855, and expanded it in later editions. He saw it prosper in French and German. He wrote also a survey of *The Humbugs of the World*, 1865, in which he hoped to teach readers how to discount publicity attached to religion and politics while they went on enjoying what was harmless in connection with entertainment. His point was that the "trade" of entertainment needs "only notoriety to insure success, always provided that when customers are once attracted, they never fail to get their money's worth." He condemned deceit even in entertainment. "Humbug" as he defined it was distinct from cheating; in the modern world a lot of it was needed, to bring people away from degrading entertainments to innocent ones. For him all claims of poets and tone-poets to prophetic inspiration were humbug; their trade was entertainment and their advertising was naturally extravagant. If he had taken seriously the claims for Jenny Lind that his advertising agents disseminated, he would have left her to the clergymen. He had foreseen how those claims would appeal and how the actual singing would satisfy; he supposed the claims would be forgotten, as he himself forgot about the music. He was a true liberal, opposed to bigotry and stinginess; he was a moralist, opposed to art that was lewd or intemperate; he was confident in ignoring any art that demanded too much knowledge or effort for a large public. If a few critics saw that he trivialized the arts and corrupted them to reinforce unjust social structures, he could reply: "Humbug."

One of the writers hired by Barnum to glorify Lind was George G. Foster (1801–56). Stephen Foster may have read one of his earlier books, such as *The Gold Regions of California*, 1848, or *The French Revolution of 1848*, on which he collaborated with the poet of "Ben Bolt," Thomas Dunn English, or *New York in Slices: By an Experienced Carver, Being the Original Slices Published in the New York Tribune, Revised, Enlarged, and Corrected*, 1849. After the *Memoir of Jenny Lind*, 1850, George Foster produced at least three more alluring short books on the city: *New York by Gaslight, with Here and There a Streak of Sunshine* (this earned him the nickname "Gaslight" Foster); *Celio; or, New York Above Ground and Underground;* and *New York Naked*. Undoubtedly Stephen knew about "Gaslight" Foster in 1855 when the latter was convicted of forging small notes and was rescued from prison by a campaign to raise his fine, led by the distinguished critic Rufus Griswold who never forgot the year's education in life and literature that George Foster had given him in 1831–32.

The publicity of "Gaslight" Foster, in contrast to the obscurity of Stephen Foster before 1852, may help account for the lack of evidence about direct connections between Stephen and Jenny Lind. It probably helps account for the lack of any advertising of Stephen's name before 1853. It surely helps account for the dimness of Stephen's reputation through the rest of his life. Only after the public had forgotten "Gaslight" Foster (and the abolitionist Stephen Symonds Foster) was there room for much publicity about the dead author of the songs that survived from the '50s.

Stephen C. Foster deliberately sought to preserve some of his obscurity. Only by exception, in 1852–53, did he try to promote his fame. In early years he occasionally used pseudonyms. He sold to E. P. Christy the privilege of claiming authorship for "Old Folks at Home," and probably for "Farewell My Lilly Dear," both 1851. Then he changed his mind. He wrote to Christy, May 25, 1852, a letter asking Christy to withdraw:

Dear Sir:

As I once intimated to you, I had the intention of omitting my name on my Ethiopian songs, owing to the prejudice against them by some, which might injure my reputation as a writer of another style of music, but I find that by my efforts I have done a great deal to build up a taste for the Ethiopian songs among refined people by making the words suitable to their taste, instead of the trashy and really offensive words which belong to some songs of that order. Therefore I have concluded to reinstate my name on my songs and to pursue the Ethiopian business without fear or shame and lend all my energies to making the business live, at the same time that I will wish to establish my name as the best Ethiopian song-writer. But I am not encouraged in undertaking this so long as "The Old Folks at Home" stares me in the face with another's name on it. As it was at my own solicitation that you allowed your name to be placed on the song, I hope that the above reasons will be sufficient explanation for my desire to place my own name on it as author and composer, while at the same time I wish to leave the name of your band on the title page. This is a little matter of pride in myself which it will certainly be to your interest to encourage. On the receipt of your free consent to this proposition, I will if you wish, willingly refund you the money which you paid me on that song, though it may have been sent me for other considerations than the one in question, and I promise in addition to write you an opening chorus in my best style, free of charge, and in any other way in my power to advance your interests hereafter. I find I cannot write at all unless I write for public approbation and get credit for what I write. As we may probably have a good deal of business with each other in our lives, it is best to proceed on a sure basis of confidence and good understanding, therefore I hope you will appreciate an author's feelings in the case and deal with me with your usual fairness. Please answer immediately.

Very respectfully yours,
Stephen C. Foster

Christy never agreed. His name continued to appear on the music until the copyright ran out in 1879. If he read Foster's letter carefully, he recalled that in fact Foster had not omitted his name from a majority of his Ethiopian songs. He naturally supposed that Foster's true motive for asking Christy to take credit was simply to sell more copies. He naturally resented Foster's inconsiderate argument about building up a taste among refined people, for Christy's own career was dedicated to that very effort and his success was widely recognized. Christy could reasonably dismiss the appeal as typical of the dreamy backwoodsman. In fact, he scrawled across the back of the letter: "vacillating skunk."

The amount of money involved has been established beyond

reasonable doubt by J. T. Howard: Christy was accustomed to pay $10 for the right to perform a song before publication. He paid an additional $5 for "Old Folks" and "Farewell."

In September of the same year, 1852, the publishers Firth and Pond began to advertise and to inspire anonymous news items about Foster's songs in the New York *Musical World*. In January 1853 Foster's name began to appear in these columns. His visit to the office of the *Musical World* was the basis for the first mention:

> We were recently visited by a celebrated Pittsburgher, namely, Stephen C. Foster, Esq., the author of most of the popular Ethiopian melodies now afloat—such for example, as Nelly Bly; Oh! boys carry me 'long; Uncle Ned; the Old Folks at Home, and many others. Mr. Foster possesses more than ordinary abilities as a composer; and we hope he will soon realize enough from his Ethiopian melodies to enable him to afford to drop them and turn his attention to the production of a higher kind of music. Much of his music is now excellent, but being wedded to negro idioms it is, of course, discarded, by many who would otherwise gladly welcome it to their pianos. We were glad to learn from Mr. F. that he intends to devote himself principally hereafter to the production of "White men's" music.

The *Musical World* followed up this story in its issue of February 19, 1853, with an "Answer to correspondents":

> Harry:—S. C. Foster is the author of the "Old Folks at Home." E. P. Christy probably bought the song and the right to be considered its author at the same time, and the publishers of course put his name to it, thinking he was the composer; but such things always "come out" sooner or later.

The editor of the *Musical World* was well informed. Firth and Pond took notice; in the issue for March 5 their advertisement honored the composer, while evading the question about "Old Folks":

> "MY OLD KENTUCKY HOME, GOOD NIGHT"
>
> This beautiful plantation melody, sung with great success by Christy's Minstrels, is this day published by the undersigned. The words and music are by Stephen C. Foster, the well known author of "Nelly Bly," "Massa's in de cold ground," etc.

An interested but impartial reader of these three excerpts from the *Musical World* must picture Foster having taken the initiative to "work the press" regardless of both publisher and performer. A more astonishing column in the *Musical World* fits into this context: on February 26 there is a letter from Foster, written from Pittsburgh on the 14th, in response to a column of January 8 that dealt with "the fundamental laws of harmony." Foster pretends that one of these laws needs clarification, which he is happy to provide; the point is a mere pretext for facetious wit:

Dear Sir:—In your "Musical Study" of the 8th ult. you say that the seventh of the scale must resolve upwards to the eighth. Is this not too briefly stated? Many persons might not give due emphasis to the phrase "seventh of the *scale*," and thus erroneously take the term "seventh" in its common acceptation, namely, with regard to the chord in which it stands, which would, in most cases, resolve itself downwards, being almost necessarily a minor seventh, as the *large* seventh is, I believe, rarely, if ever, used in harmony except as a transition note, or when heralded, or—more technically, when *prepared.*

By the way, botanists have divided the vegetable kingdom into genders, and I observe that Mr. Fry, taking the French cue, has given even to words, a distinction suggestive of matrimony. Might we not have a musical gender? Thus, for instance, in the tones of a four-fold chord, take the sturdy prime and the valorous *fifth,*—which, when sounded together, to the exclusion of the others, suggests trumpets, and "the big wars that make ambition virtue,"—and they might stand for the masculine, while the conciliating *third,* and the complaining, though gentle (minor) *seventh,* as they seem to lean for support on the sterner notes, might represent the feminine notes of the harmonic family. Then we might very appropriately lay down musical rules in this style. The males, though noisy and boisterous, may be doubled or reinforced with propriety, while the females (bless their dear hearts) can *speak for themselves*—a rule which you have already given, though in different words. In support of this idea, is the fact that the seventh has a natural *penchant* for the *third,* or sister tone of the succeeding chord, where it usually resolves itself in order to unfold its sorrowful story; a proverbial weakness of the sex, confiding their secrets to each other.

It will probably not weaken my hypothesis to admit that the aforesaid *seventh* can sometimes be used to great advantage in creating *discord,* but it would be ungallant to dwell on this branch of the argument.

Respectfully, yours, etc.

S. C. Foster.

Humbug, with no deception but no skill. Foster never again attempted anything of the sort. From this time on he let his publishers and two friends provide all the publicity he was to receive. He signed his name to all his work after "Old Folks," as far as is known, and while his efforts as songwriter went forward continuously to the end, he abandoned his brief effort to manipulate his reputation. The whole sequence of columns would be forgotten by his admirers if it were not for the sad fact that these columns in a single trade magazine constitute the biggest flurry of press notices that his name drew throughout his life.

Firth and Pond made a new contract with Foster on May 5, 1853. His share of royalties advanced from 8 percent (two cents a copy) to 10 percent (two and a half, or, for a few pieces, almost four cents). He agreed to discontinue sending work to any other publisher. About the same time the company commissioned a portrait by the respected painter Thomas Hicks; working from a single sitting, Hicks painted a conventionally prosperous handsome face that hardly resembles the face of Foster as captured on daguerreotypes. The company never collected the picture; reproductions of it reached the public only in 1935. Evidently the company's effort to promote Foster took no high priority.

A letter from Stephen to Morrison—the earliest one that Morrison preserved—shows a little of Stephen's activity during the months alone in New York while he had reason to hope that Firth and Pond would promote his whole list of songs:

> New York, July 8, 1853
>
> My dear brother
>
> Your letter of the 6th is received. The vest arrived safely, I am glad you sent it. I wish you could send me Mess. F. P. & Co's note for 125$ which I gave you. In my anxiety to pay you I rather stinted myself expecting to be able to live modestly at home, but circumstances have increased my expences as you know since that time. They have just rendered my account which is over five hundred dollars, and that for the dullest season in the year, so you see my prospects are good but I dare not claim any money until these notes are all paid, though full amt of my a/c current is passed to my credit, & bal. due to be claimed after that time. If you will let me have the note I will take the first occasion to pay you. I am not living expensively, and I hope it will not be long before I can pay you back the amt. I made it payable to your order, so if you send it don't forget to indorse it.
>
> I am getting along first rate, with plenty of work to keep me busy.
>
> Hippodrome no humbug—races there very exciting. Taylor's new saloon *great*. Sontag in opera with Salvi Seffanoni &c next week. Crystal Palace in a week.
>
> Fourth of July here good for nervous sick people I dare say, cleared myself out of town, went over to Staten Island and saw Vin Smith. Gilliad and wife at Niagara—home next week.
>
> I am about bringing out a couple of good songs.
>
> > Love to all
> > Your affectionate broth
> > Stephen

Firth and Pond's account with Foster was at its peak when he wrote this letter. Five hundred dollars was well above the average for a quarter-year through the years.

The advertising of new works by Foster from November 1853 to 1854 is interesting. An advance notice of *The Social Orchestra*, in the *Musical World* for November 12, 1853, begins a campaign:

Will be published on the 1st November
THE SOCIAL ORCHESTRA
a collection of the most popular operatic
and other melodies, arranged as
SOLOS, DUETS, TRIOS, and QUARTETTES
for Flutes, Violins, and Violoncello (or pianoforte)
and particularly adapted to
Evenings at Home, Serenades, &c.
It is arranged by
STEPHEN C. FOSTER
The well known composer
Price $1.00

From this time until February 1854, when the publication was actually delivered to customers, there were several short inquiries about it, apologies for the delay, and assurances that it was nearly ready. Then in the issue for May 27, 1854, comes an offer for special package sales: for one dollar, readers may choose any four songs from a list of five, of which three have lithographic title-page pictures and are listed at 38 cents each. The titles are "Old Memories," "Little Ella," "Ellen Bayne," "Willie, We Have Missed You," and "Jeanie with the Light Brown Hair." Stephen's pride in "Jeanie," as an example of his most advanced work, led finally to the advertisement of June 17:

Jeanie with the Light Brown Hair. Ballad
Words and music by S. C. Foster, 38 [cents]
   Mr. Foster's popularity as THE SONG WRITER OF AMERICA is too firmly established to require particular mention of any of his compositions. The above song fully sustains his reputation.

And this opinion is restated in the advertisement of September 9:

The publishers recommend this as one of the most beautiful of Mr. Foster's melodies. No song writer of the present day can approach Foster in the originality, beauty and simplicity of his melodies, and "Jeanie" is not an exception.

But these superlatives for Foster reached too small a part of the public to challenge the reputations of John Hill Hewitt and George Pope Morris.

The campaign for "Jeanie" failed. In November, "Jeanie" is omitted from the boasting advertisement of the more successful songs:

OUR CATALOGUE OF SHEET MUSIC IS
one of the largest and *by far the most popular in the country.*
. . . We have printed and sold of
"OLD FOLKS AT HOME," more than 130,000 copies.

"MY OLD KENTUCKY HOME," by Foster, 90,000 copies.

"MASSA'S IN THE COLD GROUND," by Foster, 74,000 copies.

"OLD DOG TRAY," in 6 months, by Foster, 48,000 copies.
  And of Foster's new songs

"OLD MEMORIES," "ELLEN BAYNE," and "WILLIE, WE HAVE MISSED
  YOU";
  (The last recently issued)

Large Editions are Daily Printed and Sold.

Firth and Pond here delete the name of Christy and imply that "Old
Folks," like all the rest of the songs, is Foster's. "Willie" is presented
as if it were the latest, most advanced product, but in fact its copyright date is March 4, and by September 2 it has needed a third
printing of 1000 copies. "Jeanie," copyrighted on June 5, is no longer
expected, in November, to do so well.

Foster, meanwhile, between the last two advertisements, abandoned New York. He was back in Allegheny by October 19. Then
on December 21 he revised his contract with Firth and Pond, deleting their exclusive right to his new work and spelling out many
details; the new contract survives in two copies, both in Foster's
writing.

Accordingly, it appears, Firth and Pond abandoned Foster to his
luck on the market. While they continued to publish his work, their
advertisements ceased. "Come, Where My Love Lies Dreaming"
made its way gradually, without publicity. "Jeanie" went into
oblivion.

The Social Orchestra was never followed up by another instrumental work. Though this collection has some interest beyond its
connection with the short-lived publicity campaign (see Chapter 10),
its publication fits neatly into the campaign.

By 1856 W. C. Peters, the publisher of "Susanna" and "Uncle
Ned," must have noticed the lack of publicity, for he provided to
the writer John B. Russell the "main facts" of an article on "Foster's
music" for the Cincinnati *Gazette*, January 22, 1857. Russell lists
sales figures for the same songs that Firth and Pond had advertised
two years previously; the figures are different, as though to allow
for the passage of time, but as though no new facts were available:

"The Old folks at Home" . . . has reached a sale of upwards of one hundred thousand copies in this country, and about as many in England.

Of his later pieces, there have been sold eighty thousand copies of "My
Old Kentucky Home,"—seventy thousand of "Old Dog Tray"—and about
the same number of "Massa's in de cold Ground."

Of the ballad style, "Willie, we have missed you" is the most popular.
"Maggie by my Side," and "Jeannie with her light brown hair," have also
had a great run. His last song is "Gentle Annie."

Foster's letter to his good friend Billy Hamilton, January 16, 1857, reveals his eager interest in Russell's "puff." When copies of the article arrived, Foster acknowledged them gratefully in a letter to Russell. He is explicit here about the value of publicity:

Pittsburgh, Jan. 28/57

Dear Sir

I have received the Copies of the Gazette which you sent me also your letter inclosing one copy of your complimentary notice of me and my music. I am beginning to think, since reading it, that I am "some punkins" and that the Nation will have to put on crape when I take my flight to a higher (or lower) sphere. I gave a copy to the editor of the "Dispatch," (the largest circulation here) and he was in the same fix that your Gazette has been, expecting a new dress, when that is received, he intends to make your article the basis of an editorial, as suggested by the notice in the Gazette.

Your humble servant, the gentleman with the "amiable character" will send two or three copies to his publishers in New York, for insertion in any paper, or papers that will not place over the article those diabolical words "New Advertisements."

"Contents noted" as regards sending Miss Eliza anything new that I may bring out. It will be attended to, although I have nothing "in press" at present.

How a man likes to show these little flattering testimonials to his wife! If it were not for that, the benefit to me of your kind and friendly action would be half lost.

With my best regards to all,

Your Friend
S. C. Foster

The would-be worldly tone of this letter clashes with Foster's blithe indifference to the fact that Firth and Pond were sure to be offended by the prominent mentions of their rival Peters. Foster sent off his copies in vain. The article was not reprinted.

In 1858 the family friend R. P. Nevin tried to be helpful, with an unsigned article in the New York *Evening Post* that was copied by several magazines, including the *Art Union*, Littell's *Living Age*, the *Western Fireside* (Madison, Wisconsin), and Dwight's *Journal*. The provocative title is "Who Writes Our Songs?" Nevin begins with the paradoxical situation:

The musical composer who really furnishes the great majority of our songs, and whose productions have the widest popularity among the masses of our people, is known to very few of them, even by reputation.

He goes on to inform his readers that numerous Ethiopian songs, with their "wide though, after all, evanescent popularity," are in fact the work of Foster, a "gentleman" whose family is distinguished in Pittsburgh. He quotes Foster's letter about "Susanna" and Peters, as we quoted it in Chapter 2. He then quotes an anonymous private letter from a traveler in Britain:

> I spent several weeks amid the poetic hills of Ettrick, along the braes of Yarrow, so famed in Scottish border minstrelsy, and here I found some of Foster's earlier melodies were almost displacing, in the estimation of the shepherd boys and cottage girls, the songs of Burns and Ramsey.

Nevin's traveler is unusual, not in hearing "Susanna" in the Burns country, but in identifying it as Foster's. But now Nevin turns to Foster's more recent work:

> Ethiopian minstrelsy, as it is called, has, however, culminated, and is now in its decline. Appreciating this fact, Mr. Foster has lately somewhat changed his style, and abandoning the use of negro jargon, he now writes songs better adapted for general use. We do not say that Mr. Foster's "melodies" can be compared with those that have immortalized the names of Burns, Barry Cornwall, or Thomas Moore; but we do maintain that the composer who produced such popular and pleasing songs as "Gentle Annie," "Willie, we have missed you," "Maggie by my Side," "I see her still in my dreams," "Old dog Tray," "Jeanie with the light brown hair," etc. deserves an honorable mention, as one of those who has enlarged the pleasure of thousands.

If the article had stopped here, it would have enlarged the pleasure of Foster himself. But Nevin went on, to criticize in a way that made his essay more attractive to Dwight and less so to the song-writer:

> The reason for the popularity of Mr. Foster's songs lies in their easy, flowing melody, the adherence to plain chords in the accompaniments, and the avoidance of intricacy in the harmony or embarrassing accidentals in the melody. They have a family resemblance, but not greater than the simpler melodies of Bellini and Donizetti, and the composer is no more truly open to the charge of self-plagiarism than are those Italian melodists. And as Mr. Foster is still young, he may improve and elevate his style, till he attains a musical reputation that will be more than ephemeral.

Nevin's encouragement is patronizing. Foster was too proud a man to thank him for that. Besides, at thirty-two he was not so young. When he read Nevin's words in the back columns of various periodicals, Foster perhaps decided to prove him mistaken by returning to his minstrel character once more—"The Glendy Burk" and "Old Black Joe" were issued in 1860. Nevin had not deigned to mention "Come, Where My Love Lies Dreaming"; Foster tried no more to "improve and elevate his style," though he continued his effort to develop his thought, as we know. Was he sure enough of himself to label Nevin's article "humbug"? Or did he rather recall, from the Psalms, that every reputation is "ephemeral"?

All the little efforts on behalf of Foster's reputation, by Firth and Pond, by Russell, and by Nevin, reached too small a portion of the public to sell such works as "Jeanie," "Some Folks," "None Shall Weep a Tear for Me," "The Wife," "A Dream of My Mother and My Home," "The Angels Are Singing to Me," "My Wife Is a Most Knowing Woman," and "The Voices That Are Gone." The genteel part of the public that sang "Ellen Bayne," "Willie, We Have Missed You," and "Come, Where My Love Lies Dreaming" had little more curiosity about the composer and his later works than the overlapping parts of the public that sang "Susanna," "Old Folks," and "Old Dog Tray."

John Mahon recalled that when he got acquainted with Foster in 1860 Foster was self-conscious about his small fame. He often boasted about his relationship to President Buchanan. He was always, according to Mahon,

> . . . pleased when I introduced him to people of note; but agreed with me on a signal, by which I understood when he did not wish to be known. This signal was a careless clapping of the hands three times, and when I heard that I simply introduced him as Mr. Foster.

Once the two attended a Temperance meeting and Foster consented to sing "Hard Times." The response of the crowd was an ovation, which "seemed to embarrass him." But then he relaxed and allowed Mahon to "introduce me in my true character." When Mahon explained that the moving performance was that of the composer of the song, the crowd was so enthusiastic that "something stronger than lemonade was improvised somewhere for Foster and myself during the recess." On another occasion, at a variety show in Newark, the two friends heard a performance of "Fairy Belle" that made Foster "wild with delight." He urged Mahon: "You must introduce me," and again there was good cheer. From both these incidents, it is easy to imagine Foster's sensitivity and his mute longing for a wider fame than he ever enjoyed.

If Foster's name had won even an ephemeral glory by 1860, then at least his songs about the war would have found more singers than they did. With his own words, he published one in 1861, three in 1862, two in 1863; with words by Cooper, six in 1863; and with words by James Sloane Gibbons, still another in 1862, "We Are Coming, Father Abraam [sic]." None of them won popularity, though "Old Dog Tray" and "Come, Where" maintained their places in many repertories and took on some associations with the war, just as did "Annie Laurie" and "Home, Sweet Home." The great new song of the Yankees in 1861 was "John Brown's Body," based on an older hymn. The rallying song of the South was Emmett's "Dixie," copyrighted by Firth and Pond in 1860. Out of Chicago came the songs by Henry Clay Work (1832–84): "Kingdom Coming," "Babylon Is Fallen!" "Wake Nicodemus!" and "Marching Through Georgia"; and those of George Frederick Root (1820–95): "The Battle Cry of Freedom" and "Tramp! Tramp! Tramp!" Both Root and Work quickly became more famous than Foster, though their names too remained unknown to most of the singers of their songs. Septimus Winner won some notoriety when his song of 1862 about General George McClellan so distressed Secretary Stanton that he had Winner arrested, accused of treason, and released only when his publishers agreed to destroy all copies—"Give Us Back Our Old Commander, Little Mac, the People's Pride." Songs were important in the war. Foster could not have missed any of those of 1861–63. According to H. V. Milligan, Foster believed that "John Brown's Body" was derived from his own "Ellen Bayne"; the resemblance is clear enough, once it is pointed out, but probably a coincidence, and in any case an indication that "Ellen Bayne" was superseded. One more song of 1863 must have puzzled him: the tune with a jigging rhythm and an archaic modal scale, "Johnny Fill Up the Bowl Again," transformed into "When Johnny Comes Marching Home Again" by the Boston Irish band leader Patrick Gilmore (1829–92). This song seems to belong to a new generation, for whom all of Foster's songs will fade into the vague company surrounding "Auld Lang Syne." Both G. F. Root and Patrick Gilmore were becoming masters of Barnum's arts of publicity. No one foresaw how their later work was to enhance the meanings of "Old Folks at Home." Their fame in the 1860s kept Foster's name obscure.

R. P. Nevin's long article for the *Atlantic* in 1867 never mentions "Jeanie." Under the title "Stephen Collins Foster and Negro Minstrelsy," Nevin now hopes to rescue the "plantation songs" from neglect and lend them dignity. He hopes to establish a "reputation that will be more than ephemeral" for his fellow Pittsburgher, not through any supposed improvement or elevation of style, but through an assertion that the plantation songs themselves are edifying: Foster's work, according to Nevin, "taught us all to feel with the slaves the lowly joys and sorrows it celebrated." This new well-intentioned humbug achieved its aim. It discarded "Jeanie" and all the bulk of Foster's work.

Mark Twain waited until 1906 to write his recollections of the "nigger shows" he had loved as a boy in the 1840s in Hannibal, Missouri. Even then he left the memoir unpublished; it appeared at last in a volume edited by Bernard DeVoto in 1940. Without mentioning Foster's name, Mark Twain takes a stand in favor of "Camptown Races" against the later "Sweet Ellen Bayne" and "Nelly Bly." He describes the comical acts, the audiences, the atmosphere of the shows, with all his skill. By confessing how he has been exhausted by Wagner's operas, he establishes several layers of irony between his 20th-century readers and himself as a boy. Thus he can fondly approve the comedy of "Camptown" along with the older "Buffalo Gals" and "Dan Tucker"; he suggests that these songs have a native strength even "Nelly" cannot match. He avoids the term "folk." He avoids the "pathetic" songs. But he joins the trend to attribute lasting value to "Camptown."

In 1914 scholars at the Library of Congress arranged an exhibition of Foster's works; the next year they published a detailed *Catalogue of First Editions of Stephen C. Foster*. In the preface, by the brilliant chief of the Music Division, Oscar G. T. Sonneck (1873–1928), all the songs like "Jeanie" are curtly dismissed:

> Many of Foster's songs, of course, belong to the mid-nineteenth century type of sentimental American parlour "ballad," not exactly distinguished by either beauty or skill, but some of his songs possess the beauty and power of imperishable folksongs.

Sonneck and his assistants were patient and meticulous in their bibliographic work, but this sweeping, undocumented judgment added something to the difficulties of later investigators. "Folksong" for Sonneck and others like him meant much. Reverence for "folksong" often reinforced a scornful impatience with "Jeanie."

When H. V. Milligan (1888–1951) published the first full-length book on Foster in 1920, "Jeanie" and all the other songs like it meant little to him or his readers. Foster was now generally regarded, as Milligan's subtitle put it, as "America's folk-song composer." Milligan gave some attention to the early songs "Open Thy Lattice" and "Ah! May the Red Rose," but he made no pretense of sympathy with Foster's continuous effort; his brief criticism of what Foster took most seriously is more condescending than Nevin's or Sonneck's:

> "Ellen Bayne," "Hard Times Come Again No More," "Jeanie with the Light Brown Hair," "Willie, We Have Missed You," and "Come, Where My Love Lies Dreaming," belong to the past, along with the crinoline and the daguerreotype.
>
> In many of the contemporary references to Stephen Foster, found in old newspapers and magazines, he is described as "the author and composer of 'Willie, We Have Missed You.'" The popularity of this song is difficult to account for, as it is one of his poorest. "Jeanie with the Light Brown Hair" and "Come, Where My Love Lies Dreaming" have more to recommend them. In the latter song he attempted a more elaborate con-

struction than was his wont, but it cannot be said that he succeeded well in handling it, for the song is overly long and rather wandering.

. . . if Stephen Foster had written nothing but these songs of his later years, his name would have been forgotten long ago. Most of them are extremely commonplace, and obviously are pot-boilers. Stephen had never mastered sufficiently the technic of composition to be able to produce interesting music on demand, and his vocabulary was so small that of necessity he repeated himself over and over again. He could usually find a melody of some sort without much trouble, but after a bar or two they are all apt to follow the same pattern. Many of his melodic ideas are worthy of better treatment, had he been able to handle them with greater skill. But even in these miserable days when he was drawing deeper and deeper into the shadow, now and then the pure ray of his earlier inspiration shines out in a melody as fresh and innocent as the clear voice of a child. Such are "Little Belle Blair" and "Nell and I" (1861), and "Jenny June" and "Katy Bell" (1863).

A few of the songs refer to the war, but they are among the poorest and were evidently produced in a vain effort to find the way to the public purse, rather than to the public heart.

Milligan's criteria of "musical interest," common though not universal in 1920, are irrelevant to Foster's effort. Milligan's purely subjective valuation of "inspiration" and "innocence" led him to rank the four late songs he lists above "Jeanie," "Come, Where," or "Beautiful Dreamer"—the last he omits altogether. His statement about Foster's "evident" motive for the war songs is unjust.

Milligan was an organist, composer, college teacher of organ, and lecturer on American music, who came from Oregon to New York in 1907. His motive for studying Foster is clear from his summary judgments:

> Stephen Foster's career is a good example of what happens when a musical soul is placed in an unmusical environment. Nothing ever takes the place of instinctive and intuitive culture, and this is absorbed unconsciously during the early years of life. No amount of study and industry can develop to its fullest possibilities the talent of one whose childhood is barren of music. Neither poverty, nor the material conditions surrounding his early life, thwarted the development of Stephen Foster's genius. The answer is to be found in the mental atmosphere in which he found himself.

Milligan's lament is as much for himself as for Foster. It reveals Milligan's ignorance of the actual music that Foster knew, in its actual social context. The difference between Milligan and Morrison Foster is striking; though both mean to praise Stephen, Milligan means also to blame Pittsburgh for its thin "mental atmosphere," whereas Morrison had tried to show that Stephen enjoyed ample cultural fare. Milligan goes on to another thought, as if he senses that the paragraph above is one-sided.

> It may be seriously doubted whether greater technical facility would have improved his music or achieved for him a greater name in history. The general average of his work might have been higher, but his best songs might have lost something of the sincerity and naive charm which are their greatest attribute. Limited as it was, his technical equipment was exactly suited to the production of such a song as "The Old Folks at Home."

And in a peroration Milligan exalts the meaning of "Old Folks" to cosmic proportions:

> Stephen Foster touched but one chord in the gamut of human emotions, but he sounded that strain supremely well. His song is of that nostalgia of the soul which is inborn and instinctive to all humanity, a homesickness unaffected by time or space. It is a theme which has always made up a large part of the world's poetry, and will always continue to do so as long as human hearts yearn for love and aspire toward happiness. Among all the poets who have harped the sorrows of Time and Change, no song rings truer than that of Stephen Foster. We have traced, as best we may, the story of his life from a bright happy childhood into the dismal shadows of failure and death. From the unpromising soil in which he grew, he was able to distill by some strange alchemy of the soul such sweet magic of melody as to win an immortality far beyond his dreaming. These wildflowers of music which blossomed, unwatched and untended, from unsuspected seeds, have found for themselves a spot which is all their own, where they may bloom forever in Fields Elysian.

The element of humbug here is palpable. Yet Milligan's judgment has been accepted, preserved, and disseminated through countless reference books. Though often qualified by skeptics, it has not been corrected until now, for most writers on Foster are not ready to probe their own assumptions about the growth of a musician in "unpromising soil." Milligan's "Elysian Fields" are set aside, but his "homesickness unaffected by time or space" is swallowed, often with no recognition of the tradition of "home songs," no notice of the religious songs, and no application of the theme to "Jeanie."

"Jeanie" acquired new meaning in 1926, the centennial of Foster's birth, when Earl Hobson Smith used the facts provided by Milligan in his *Stephen Foster, or Weep No More my Lady: A Biographical Play on Stephen Collins Foster, Father of American Folksongs.* Smith's play is a well-made entertainment, incorporating seventeen songs. It does not claim to be a serious interpretation of Foster's personality or his work, but rather something like Sigmund Romberg's musical comedy *Blossom-time,* based on the life of Schubert, 1922. The dramatic conflict is posed between Stephen's ambition in music and the claims of prudence, represented chiefly by his eldest brother, William; simultaneously Jane and Stephen are learning to love each other despite his continuing love for Susan Pentland Robinson. The action is compressed into about a year. At the end, in 1852, William is convinced by the glory of Christy, Barnum, Lind, and many more that Stephen's songs prove him right; Jane is ready to endure whatever troubles may come for the sake of art and love: she turns aside from a Christmas gathering of the families to gaze at a vision of Stephen, in New York, singing to her "I dream of Jeanie"; she joins the song; the curtain falls on their dreaming embrace. The audience disperses, smiling through tears and humming "Jeanie." Smith's play, as produced by the Foster Players of Knoxville, Tennessee, was widely popular through the 1930s. It was successful again in 1973 as produced with a few additional songs by the Minnesota Center Showboat at Minneapolis.

Soon after Smith's play first appeared, "Jeanie" was sung, apart from the play, by singers like the Irish-American operatic tenor John McCormack (1884–1945) and the pioneer of sound film, the "Jazz Singer," Al Jolson (1886–1950). Both of these singers recorded their performances for the phonograph. Both took some liberties with the notes as Foster had written them, especially with respect to the accompaniment, which their arrangers enriched with thicker chords and more frequent changes of chord than Foster's. In his own accompaniment for the title-line there is no change of chord at all; the arrangers' contribution was perhaps needed to make possible any wide popularity for the tune. Even the simplest of modern arrangements move the harmony once or twice in the first line.

An album of twenty-three Foster songs in the performance of the Jubilee Singers and the Victor Salon Group directed by Nathaniel Shilkret included "Jeanie." These records, heard in 1930, awoke the interest of the retired Indianapolis manufacturer Josiah K. Lilly, who commissioned James Francis Driscoll to collect first editions of the songs. Soon he was sponsoring a national enterprise, to which all later studies of Foster are indebted in many ways. Foster Hall, on Lilly's estate, stimulated and coordinated the work of many specialists and disseminated their work rapidly to many amateurs. Most important, Foster Hall printed facsimiles of the first editions of Foster's works and donated copies to libraries. The presence of "Jeanie" at the start of this enterprise, despite its neglect until so short a time before, affected all the later studies and many later unstudious celebrations of Foster. In 1935 Lilly told an interviewer, John G. Bowman, writing for *Atlantic*, that his generous work for Foster's fame was in repayment for the solace that he had found as a lonesome child: "Foster's songs—Jeanie with the Light Brown Hair and others—made me feel better." Lilly attributed to "Jeanie" all the personal meaning that Foster's work had for him; he avoided the questions that "Old Folks" evoked by his emphasis on "Jeanie," the only song he named.

A film of 1940, *Swanee River*, gave a subordinate place to "Jeanie" among the nine songs that it used. This version of Foster's biography, according to a review by the Foster Hall expert Fletcher Hodges, Jr., develops a leisurely plot-line from Foster's childhood to his death, taking many liberties with the facts in order to present his famous songs in the most picturesque settings and to make both him and Jane as appealing as possible. "Jeanie" represents Jane as a Kentucky belle. The action depends more on Christy, as played by Al Jolson, and on a wholly fictional war-theme: New York audiences suspect Foster of Southern sympathies until he tries to enlist in the Union Army and is rejected because of a weak heart. "Ring de Banjo" and "Beautiful Dreamer" provide the main motifs for continuity. The famous plantation songs are all featured; "Old Folks" is reserved for a triumphant finale, with the Hall Johnson Choir. Millions of viewers of this film, in America and abroad, when they next heard "Jeanie," attached to it all their memories of the film's version of Foster's life.

Wider popularity came for "Jeanie" as a result of radio broadcasters' need for music in the public domain when their contract with the American Society of Composers, Authors and Publishers expired at the end of 1940. ASCAP banned all broadcasts of the music it controlled, in order to win a new contract. "Jeanie" was one of the songs that benefitted indirectly from the bureaucratic contest. To many musicians and listeners "Jeanie" was new in the 1940 movie. To even more it was new on the radio. The fact that it was Foster's added to its interest for some listeners, but to others the tune became familiar as if it were the work of a contemporary.

A "transcription" of "Jeanie" for piano solo, by Elinor Remick Warren, 1940, was typical of the time. Reprinted in the magazine *Etude* in 1941, this version reached thousands of pianos across the United States. Though few amateurs could manage its widespread chords and lush chromatic chord-changes, more frequent than those of any "standard" arrangement, still a vague apprehension and memory of these accessories entered into the meaning of the tune for most of the people who learned it by heart. For them, any performance that restored the pristine purity of Foster's own accompaniment was likely to seem awkward. In a foreword to her transcription, Warren extolled the melody as combining "the folksong feeling with one of classic beauty." She thought the words "failed to meet the standard of the music."

In 1952 a film called *I Dream of Jeanie*, the third full-length Hollywood treatment of Foster's life and work, renewed the popularity of the song, with its words and their connotations. By this time television was ready to make use of it too. *I Dream of Jeanie* was a series title that loaded more associated meanings onto the tune for many listeners. Jeanie's hair blended with that of models advertising shampoos.

Interference among these meanings became common. A teacher who hoped that "Jeanie" would arouse interest in Foster's life needed to know that most students in the 1960s would quickly interpret a snatch of the tune as representing TV commercials.

"Jeanie" is too fragile a work to continue representing alone the main efforts that occupied Foster throughout his life. Any student who cares about Foster's intentions with respect to "Jeanie" enough to scrape away the associations that accumulated around this song between 1926 and 1960 cares also about at least a few of the other songs like "Jeanie."

One of them is a unique confrontation between a seller of the songs and a possible customer. This is "The Little Ballad Girl," 1860:

> Ho! little girl, so dressed with care!
> With fairy slippers and golden hair!
> What did I hear you calling so loud,
> Down in that heartless, motley crowd?

The accompaniment answers with its own fragment of melody before the singer, *con espressione*, explains:

> 'Tis my father's song,
> And he can't live long;
> Everyone knows that he wrote it;
> For I've been down at the hotel door,
> And all the gentlemen bought it.

The second stanza mocks:

> Ho! little girl, let me light my cigar!
> Where are you going tonight so far?
> What are you hiding under your arm?
> If I burn a sheet, will it do any harm?

There is no answer but the repetition of the girl's refrain. The third stanza offers only a modicum of sympathy:

> Ho! little girl, what makes you cry?
> Come, dry up the tears in that bright blue eye!
> What's all this that is blowing around,
> All soiled and scattered and strewn on the ground?

Foster's songs were "soiled and scattered and strewn on the ground." He knew it. His daughter was too young to work as a "ballad girl" when Jane took her away from the "heartless, motley crowd," but Foster could imagine her, sooner or later, mocked and pitied on his behalf. In his picture of the "ballad girl" he revealed his own relation to the public. Each line of the poem has its own melody; the music harmonizes the questioning stanzas and the answering refrain, without softening the bleak picture, without straining to increase its pathos, and without distracting from it in any way. The "Ballad Girl" does not blend with "Jeanie" and the other dream figures, but rather testifies to something wide awake that may be a more satisfactory meaning than publicity can touch.

The "Ballad Girl" is one of about twenty songs that Morrison left out of his collection in 1896. Was it unknown to him? Or did he think it so sentimental that it would make bad publicity? No matter; in either case, its absence from his collection shows the extent of Stephen's failure. After Josiah Lilly made the "Ballad Girl" accessible in a thousand libraries, the public could judge—everyone for himself—the extent of Stephen Foster's achievement.

PART THREE

"THE OLD FOLKS AT HOME" AND OTHER "PATHETIC PLANTATION SONGS"

CHAPTER 10

Foster
and other
contemporaries
of Uncle Tom

"JEANIE" and "The Little Ballad Girl" are two among eleven
Foster songs whose words depict someone's hair. "Jeanie's"
famous hair, "floating like a vapor," is not unique. The list of eleven
songs, encompassing a variety of colors and textures, extends from
1847 to 1862.

The theme of hair is worth tracing not so much for its own sake
as because it connects Foster's work with Harriet Beecher Stowe's
novel, *Uncle Tom's Cabin*, in which hair is an important symbol.
Along with this theme (if not looming above it) readers of *Uncle
Tom* can easily find other connections with Foster's work. The connection with "My Old Kentucky Home," documented in Foster's
sketchbook, is only one of the connections, which can all mean
more when we approach them by way of Stowe's book as a whole
and several groups of Foster's songs, including, particularly, the
eleven that touch on hair.

Uncle Tom was published serially, from June 1851 to April 1852,
and as a book in two volumes, March 1852. Foster almost certainly
read the book and saw at least one dramatization of it by the time
he wrote "Jeanie," which appeared in June 1854. And "Jeanie's"
hair resembles that of the child Eva in *Uncle Tom* more than any
earlier character's. The four earlier characters show that Foster was
ready to notice the hair in *Uncle Tom*.

"Uncle Ned" (1847) is famous for his lack of "wool." "Lemuel," the less famous leader of the field slaves' dance, is called "my woolly headed boy." The poem of Meta Victoria Fuller that Foster set to music in 1850, "The Spirit of My Song," celebrates a wreath on the lady's "braided hair as dark as night," and tells how "she will smooth my tresses" when I, the poet, fall short of learning her song. The poem of Charles Eastman, set in 1851, "Sweetly She Sleeps, My Alice Fair," exclaims that "her Saxon hair, like sunlight, streams o'er her breast," while she dreams. "Jeanie's" hair, with the distinctive rising line of melody that fits the words describing it, means much more than any of the hair in Foster's earlier work.

In *Uncle Tom's Cabin, or, Life Among the Lowly* the vivid array of interacting and changing characters, the violent action, passionate argument, and prophecy of the wrath of God looming over America make possible some readings that neglect the angelic child Evangeline St. Clare. But the plot could not hold together without her. When the book was adapted for the stage, her part was almost always central, no matter how the other parts might be cut, combined, extended, or debased. Hair makes a climactic halo for Eva. For many other characters hair is more subtly symbolic; it anticipates the glory of Eva's and it contributes to the unity of the narrative's beginning and end.

At the outset, when Tom's Kentucky master is beginning to bargain with a slave trader, he introduces a five-year-old quadroon boy whose "black hair, fine as floss silk, hung in glossy curls." Then the boy's mother, Eliza, appears, identified by "the same ripples of silky black hair." In the second chapter, "The Mother," Eliza and her husband, George Harris, resolve to flee; they are seen in their cabin with the boy—Eliza lifts his curls and George passes his hands through them. Many pages later George dyes his own brown hair black, as part of a Spanish disguise to escape fugitive-hunters in the towns of Ohio. Still later, on a wild rocky hill, when George has made an eloquent speech defying the federal law, a bullet of the slave hunters grazes his hair. Near the end of the book Eliza cuts her hair, to disguise herself as a man. Their son's hair is cut by the time they are reunited in Canada, but now they have a daughter, whose curls are again like her mother's. Meanwhile Uncle Tom, in the Kentucky cabin with his wife and children, has resolved to do his duty as he understands it and submit to being sold away from them, hoping that God will somehow eventually bring him back. The baby plays in Tom's lap, "burying her fat hands in his woolly hair, which last operation seemed to afford her special content." Tom's new master is Eva's father, Augustine St. Clare, wealthy planter in Arkansas. Tom observes that the child's hair and the father's are alike. He notices nothing about the hair of the neurotic mother, Marie, who decks herself in jewels and wears a lace scarf "enveloping her like a mist," and nothing about the hair of St. Clare's spinster cousin Ophelia visiting from Vermont, neat and stiff. But Ophelia remembers how when Augustine was a boy she used to comb his hair. She loves him and is ready to learn new duties. St. Clare challenges her to educate the motherless Black child Topsy, whose hair is braided in tails that "stuck out in every direction." Ophelia begins by having Topsy cleaned up, with hair "cropped short to the head" to "look more Christianlike." Only after angelic Eva has shown Topsy the possibility of love and has shown Ophelia that love is prerequisite to education, does Ophelia overcome her disgust at the touch of Topsy and her hair; only then can Ophelia gain the strength to win Topsy's freedom from St. Clare.

Eva's whole appearance is "such as one might dream of for some mythic and allegorical being," and her most distinguishing feature is "the long golden-brown hair that floated like a cloud." Tom sees her at once as "almost divine . . . he half believed that he saw one of the angels stepped out of his New Testament." But at first Eva is ignorant of her mission; she is as spontaneous as Topsy, but spontaneously good—loving, generous, and sensitive to Nature in all its beneficence. She learns from Tom to interpret the pages of the Bible that she reads for him, and to sing his songs about the angels. When he tells her that heaven is in the clouds, she points to the clouds and predicts that she will soon go there; at this moment the sunset "lit her golden hair and flushed cheek with a kind of unearthly radiance." When she is about to die she calls all the Blacks of the house to her bedside to hear her prayers and to receive her almost sacramental gift—a lock of hair for each. She wins her father's promise to free Tom. St. Clare now begins to draw legal papers for Tom's freedom and to plan more vaguely for a general emancipation; he reads the Bible to Tom and asks Tom to pray for him. Tom begins to plan his return to Kentucky; he thinks of Eva among the angels and dreams of her "with a wreath of jessamine in her hair . . . a golden halo seemed around her head." But before St. Clare's conversion is complete, he is fatally wounded in an attempt to separate two fighting drunks; he dies grasping Tom's hand and remembering his mother. Tom and Ophelia, preparing the body for burial, find a locket containing a lock of dark hair, which they bury with him.

The heartless, hairless Marie St. Clare sells Tom. He goes to Simon Legree, ruthless New Englander, now a cotton planter in Louisiana, whose hair is "stiff, wiry, sun-burned." Along with Tom, Legree buys Emmeline, a fifteen-year-old quadroon, whose "curling hair is of a luxuriant brown." At the slave warehouse, Emmeline's mother instructs her to brush her hair back straight, because "respectable families would be more apt to buy you, if they saw you looked plain and decent, as if you wasn't trying to look handsome." But the auctioneer overrules her: "Where's your curls, gal?" Cracking his whip, he compels the mother to undo her work: "Them curls may make a hundred dollars difference in the sale of her." Emmeline's curls must blend, for the reader, with Evangeline's. For Tom is driven to disobedience in order to protect Emmeline from Legree, and Legree's revenge tempts Tom to abandon God, until Eva appears and assures him, in words that "seemed to melt and fade, as in a divine music." Then, "as if wafted on the music, she seemed to rise on shining wings . . . was it a dream?" Tom now holds fast, even when Eva's lock of hair is taken from him by Legree's most degraded, superstitious, "savage" Black overseers, Sambo and Quimbo. They present it to Legree, as a conjuring device. It works as a curse on him. Legree is reminded of his mother, for he has burned the lock of hair she gave him, wrenching himself free of all her influence. "It would be a joke," says Legree, "if hair could rise from the dead!" His concubine, Cassy, half-converted from her cynical despair by Emmeline's shy faith and Tom's steadfastness, takes command, haunts and foils Legree, and leads Emmeline in escaping to the North. Legree tortures and finally kills Tom for refusing to reveal Cassy's plan of escape. Tom's martyrdom converts Sambo and Quimbo. When Cassy strokes Emmeline's hair, her conversion is complete. Finally Cassy is reunited in Canada with her lost daughter, Eliza Harris; she meets her new grandchild, whose "every curl" reminds her of Eliza at the time they were separated. In the author's "concluding remarks" all the mothers of the book, except Eva's mother, Marie, are like a chorus, echoing the direct appeal to the "mothers of America . . . I beseech you, pity those mothers that are constantly made childless by the American slave-trade!"

How did Foster read *Uncle Tom*? How did he discuss its characters with his family and his friends? Like many readers, of his time and later, he doubtless thought at first glance that he recognized the self-righteous author in Ophelia. He knew that the Reverend Lyman Beecher had brought his daughter Hattie as a girl from Connecticut to Cincinnati, where she had married the Reverend Calvin Stowe and borne seven children. She had helped fugitive slaves and tolerated abolitionists like Stephen Symonds Foster, while she relied on one Black domestic servant. She had written only a few short pieces of fiction before *Uncle Tom*. Suddenly she entered world literature. The book's sales broke all records within a year, in England even more conspicuously than in America. In translation it won ardent admirers in every civilized country. (Germans could choose among thirteen competing translations in 1852, another seventeen in 1853.) It won pious readers who had spurned all fiction until then. It won the praise of hundreds of statesmen, clergymen, poets, and novelists. The publishers quickly made use of all this excitement as publicity in the Barnum style, to feed further sales. Naturally the book and the author were also vilified by defenders of slavery; publishers made use of this too. More subtle critics, who protested that Stowe expected Blacks to be more Christlike than whites, that Uncle Tom's passive resistance actually strengthened slavery, or that the idealization of religious Blackness intensified white prejudice, were drowned out. Foster was inevitably involved in controversy about the book, and his attitude probably vacillated. He could not have persisted in the simple identification of Stowe with Ophelia. He could not have missed Stowe's identifying herself with the mothers. He could see that she required the "mythical" figure of Eva to unite all the tensions of her plot. Surely the image of Eva and her halo affected his vision of his own child and of all inspiring women and children.

If Foster discussed *Uncle Tom* in the Shiras household, he could identify himself to some degree with the young George Shelby, son of Tom's first master, who, when his father dies, proceeds to free all his slaves, offers them wages to continue working for him, and urges them to emulate Uncle Tom.

If Foster read and pondered alone, he identified himself more fully with St. Clare, who confesses that he is "a dreamy, neutral spectator of the struggles, agonies, and wrongs of man, when he should have been a worker." No reader could fail to admire St. Clare's agile and penetrating wit, which refutes every argument for slavery and skeptically challenges every argument for reform. If Foster did not skip over whole episodes, he was touched by the first change in St. Clare that Tom's love brings about: Tom helps him to bed, drunk; next day, on St. Clare's invitation, Tom expresses regrets and reproaches; St. Clare resolves never again to yield to this temptation, and he keeps his resolution. Foster may have found further parallels between his own and St. Clare's cool fidelity to their wives and their warm, brotherly concern for their daughters. If Foster read closely, he noticed that Stowe compares St. Clare with Moore, Byron, and Goethe, though she has named him after the disciple of St. Francis. Foster's mind, as we have come to know it, was capable at least of recognizing that Stowe portrayed more of herself in St. Clare than in any one of the mothers, much less Ophelia. However far Foster's thoughts were developed in this direction, they strengthened the appeal of Eva and her hair.

"Jeanie" could be a song for the dreamer St. Clare, dreaming of

Eva. Nothing in the song makes Jeanie old enough to be a wife. All of it fits a child. It fits the same child as "Little Ella," "cherub coming nearest to my dreams of forms divine," and this song, more obviously, could be sung by St. Clare. The six later songs too, with one exception, refer to someone whose age is either unspecified or definitely immature. "Fairy Belle," 1859, with "hair like the thistle-down . . . upon the air," is a "queen," but so playful, both in the words and the springing musical rhythm, that she may be as young as Ella or Eva. "Fairy Belle" is the song that John Mahon remembered hearing with Foster in Newark, a performance that made the author "wild with delight." The next song is the lullaby of a "lone mother" whose child is dead: "Under the Willow She's Laid with Care," 1860; the mother longs "to linger forever Near to my angel with golden hair In lands where there's sorrowing never," and her refrain, with three-voice chorus, repeats, "Fair, fair, and golden hair." When John Mahon recalled "Under the Willow," he remembered that Marian Foster "had her mother's auburn hair" and that the song had frightened him a little until Stephen explained that "the words are poetical, and may be understood either of death or of sleep, or of both."

"Little Belle Blair," 1861, is a serene recollection of a dead child. The singer is not alone, but rather surrounded by family and friends; beginning with "We have made a grave," he is joined in the refrain by a four-part chorus:

> Happy as the live long day was she,
> And flowing was her dark glossy hair,
> We will hear no more her winning melody,
> For we've parted with our little Belle Blair.

"A Penny for Your Thoughts," 1861, is the exceptional song in the series, and exceptional among all Foster's songs in its dramatic structure: the singer teases a dreamer, accuses him of "sighing now for Jenny Dow," and finally in the third stanza wakes him up:

> I have something worth revealing:
> Fair maids, though full of vows, are fickle and untrue;
> Now throw those flattering hopes away,
> Tomorrow's Jenny's wedding day . . .
> On your mind a change is stealing;
> What think you now of Jenny Dow, that lives beyond the mill?

The description of Jenny, so unlike Eva, brings her close to Jeanie: "Fair are her wavy locks as vapors on the hill."

The last song of the group is the simplest, the closest to Eva's name, and perhaps the closest to the image of a living child: "Gentle Lena Clare," 1862:

> I'm thinking of sweet Lena Clare,
> With deep blue eyes and waving hair;
> Her voice is soft, her face is fair,
>   My gentle Lena Clare.

The rhythm is Foster's old favorite, the *moderato* polka. A four-part chorus slows this down somewhat, with short lines stretched out, and a *fermata* before the last line:

> Gentle Lena Clare,
> My dear lov'd Lena Clare;
>   Her heart is light,
>   Her eyes are bright,
> My gentle Lena Clare.

Two more stanzas sustain the mood without development:

> I love her careless winning ways,
> I love her wild and birdlike lays,
> I love the grass whereon she strays. . . .
> Her home is in the shady glen,
> When summer comes I'll seek again,
> On mountain height and lowland plain,
>   My gentle Lena Clare.

The rhyme of "Little Belle Blair" and "Gentle Lena Clare" is one more reason to connect these songs with Eva St. Clare.

In the whole series of songs there is no return after "Jeanie" to the woolly hair, the braided hair, or the streaming hair of the earlier songs. The "thistledown" of "Fairy Belle" is the only fresh invention. But floating, flowing, waving, and vapor unite the later songs with each other and with Eva's halo.

The songs of Uncle Tom himself are the central thread of a broader musical strand running through the whole of *Uncle Tom's Cabin*. In the first chapter of the book, the little boy sings and dances, and Mr. Shelby calls him Jim Crow. In the first scene for Tom, before he sings, Tom responds to his baby girl's love by setting her on his shoulders and dancing with her; the dance expands through the cabin, "till every one had roared and tumbled and danced themselves down to a state of composure," which prepares for a religious "meetin'." Music pervades the meeting. Four hymns are described—the clapping and hand-shaking that accompanies them is not quite a dance, yet it blends the earlier family dance with the ritual. At the end of the meeting, Tom alone continues singing hymns. A few days later, when Tom leaves the Kentucky home, almost despairing, he finds lines from the Bible that "stir up the soul from its depths, and rouse, as with trumpet call, courage, energy, and enthusiasm":

> We have here no continuing city, but we seek one to come; wherefore God himself is not ashamed to be called our God; for he hath prepared for us a city.

The hymns that he sings to Eva and to himself are chosen to point forward to the home of souls and angels. When he arrives at Legree's plantation, Legree confiscates Tom's hymnbook: "I have none o' yer bawling, praying, singing niggers on my place . . . *I'm* your church now!" At the last, Tom defies this rule; he sings, alone in the night, two more hymns; Legree hears and beats him for it. When Tom is finally too weak to sing, his speech to Legree is "like a strange snatch of heavenly music, heard in the lull of a tempest":

> . . . Do the worst you can, my troubles will be over soon; but, if ye don't repent, yours won't *never* end!

From the dance, through all the hymns, to this trumpeting speech, Tom's progress is complete. When George Shelby arrives to see him die and to take his last consoling message back to his family in Kentucky, there is no music. But when George has freed his Kentucky slaves, they thank God in a chorus like "the peal of organ, bell and cannon" and then sing a Methodist hymn, "The Year of Jubilee Is Come,—Return, Ye Ransomed Sinners, Home."

The hatred of Legree and others like him for hymns meets different kinds of resistance from the other slaves. At the slave warehouse, before Legree enters, there is enforced dancing:

> . . . because some incline to pine, a fiddle is kept commonly going among them, and they are made to dance daily; and he who refuses to be merry —in whose soul thoughts of wife, or child, or home, are too strong for him to be gay—is marked as sullen and dangerous, and subjected to all the evils which the ill will of an utterly irresponsible and hardened man can inflict upon him. Briskness, alertness, and cheerfulness of appearance, especially before observers, are constantly enforced upon them, both by the hope of thereby getting a good master, and the fear of all that the driver may bring upon them, if they prove unsalable.

This is Stowe's only reference to a fiddle. There is none to a banjo. Her source for this vignette is no minstrel show, but rather the *Narrative* of the escaped slave Lewis Clarke, 1845. Clarke tells about a "slave-prison" he knew, where one or two fiddlers were hired to play continually, while the slaves "danced over and upon the torn-off fibres of their hearts."

When Legree is bringing his new slaves back to his plantation, he calls "Strike up a song, boys,—come!" He quickly stops Tom's "Jerusalem, My Happy Home." "I say, tune up, now, something real rowdy,—quick!" And he is satisfied with "one of those unmeaning songs, common among the slaves," "Mas'r See'd Me Cotch a Coon":

> The singer appeared to make up the song to his own pleasure, generally hitting on rhyme, without much attempt at reason; and the party took up the chorus, at intervals,
> > "Ho! ho! ho! boys, ho!
> > High—e—oh! high—e—oh!"
>
> It was sung very boisterously, and with a forced attempt at merriment, but no wail of despair, no words of impassioned prayer, could have had such a depth of woe in them as the wild notes of the chorus. As if the poor, dumb heart, threatened,—prisoned,—took refuge in that inarticulate sanctuary of music, and found there a language in which to breathe its prayer to God! There was a prayer in it, which Simon [Legree] could not hear. He only heard the boys singing noisily, and was well pleased; he was making them "keep up their spirits."

Stowe's insight in this scene doubtless owes more to Frederick Douglass' *Narrative* than to her own observations; she was unique among white authors in the use of this insight, and altogether unique in disseminating it. Foster's leaving off the merry blackface songs after "Ring de Banjo" could have been a result of his reading this passage. But there is a more dramatic confrontation of opposing uses of music: Emmeline's hymn-singing joins with the curse of Eva's hair to make Legree "shiver and sweat" and he calls Sambo and Quimbo to join in a drunken orgy of "hell dances . . . shrieking . . . singing, whooping, upsetting chairs." Emmeline, who has sung, in the slave warehouse with her mother, the funeral hymn, "O, Where Is Weeping Mary? 'Rived in the Goodly Land," now, alone and fearful, sings, in a wild, sweet, loud voice:

> O there'll be mourning, mourning, mourning,
> O there'll be mourning, at the judgment-seat of Christ!
> Parents and children there shall part!
> Shall part to meet no more!

Legree knows he is parted eternally from his mother. He drowns out Emmeline's song and his own fear with the bestial music of Sambo and Quimbo. After this, Legree hears nothing but the "confused noise of screams and groanings" in his dreams and the uncanny "voice, smothered far down . . . yet like the fore-warning trumpet of doom!"

The songs and dances of Topsy, part of her wild charm when she first appears, may have given Foster a ground for complaint about Stowe's vast structure, for the novel never names a particular song for Topsy and never discloses whether she learns to sing hymns, even after she grows up to become a missionary in Africa. Like the author, the characters surrounding Topsy neglect her music. As if in revenge, the Topsy of the dramatic versions of *Uncle Tom* expands her music and dance to rival all Tom's hymns and to exclude such complex uses of music as Stowe had built up around Legree.

The music of St. Clare, likewise eliminated in most dramatizations, is as important in the novel as all the music of Black characters. St. Clare sings to Eva, plays the piano, and has "a decided genius for music." He whistles a tune once, but desists because Marie complains that it gives her a headache. On the evening before he dies, while Marie sleeps and Ophelia knits and Tom listens at the door, St. Clare hunts up his mother's copy of the "Dies Irae" from Mozart's *Requiem*. He sings and plays "Recordare Jesu pie," and Stowe dwells on the performance:

> St. Clare threw a deep and pathetic expression into the words; for the shadowy veil of years seemed drawn away, and he seemed to hear his mother's voice leading his. Voice and instrument seemed both living, and threw out with vivid sympathy those strains which the ethereal Mozart first conceived as his own dying requiem.

Soon St. Clare, on his deathbed, is murmuring softly the "Recordare"; Tom recognizes that he is praying. When the doctor thinks, "His mind is wandering," St. Clare arouses himself to say, energetically: "No! it is coming HOME, at last!"

Did Foster observe that Tom listens to St. Clare more than St. Clare listens to the music of Tom or any other character? That no one else listens to St. Clare? That St. Clare approves Tom's songs for Eva, but needs Mozart for himself?

Did Foster observe that Tom rejects the paternalism of St. Clare, as well as George Shelby's, with as much energy as he defies Legree? When St. Clare, seeing his joy at the prospect of freedom, asks, "Why, Tom, don't you think, for your own part, you've been better off than to be free? . . . you couldn't possibly have earned, by your work, such clothes and such living as I have given you," Tom corrects him: the higher value of freedom is "natur." Then St. Clare supposes Tom will go back at once to Kentucky. "Not while Mas'r is in trouble . . ." "And when will *my* trouble be over?" "When Mas'r St. Clare's a Christian. . . . Why, even a poor fellow like me has a work from the Lord; and Mas'r St. Clare, that has larnin, and riches, and friends,—how much he might do for the Lord!" When George Shelby finds Tom on his deathbed, he commands, "You shan't die! . . . I've come to buy you, and take you home." Tom reproves him, with power: "The Lord's bought me, and is going to take me home,—and I long to go. Heaven is better than Kintuck."

Foster, like St. Clare and George Shelby, respected the force of faith, without quite endorsing it. Foster, like St. Clare, came closer to it at the end. But Foster's "dream of home" on earth held him; his own work was bound up in this dream; it was only in his last years that he sang of waking and working and finding a home with the angels. For Foster in 1853 Kentucky was still better than Heaven.

The song Foster is known to have begun for Uncle Tom, published in January 1853, was composed about a year earlier, while the novel was still appearing in the *National Era.* "My Old Kentucky Home" does not fit the character of the novel. Rather it fits the long dreamy tradition from Tom Moore. It uses the black mask to intensify the pathos, with no shred of Stowe's realism. Foster's deleting the name of Uncle Tom can be explained as a recognition that the song was unsuited to the novel after all:

> The sun shines bright in the old Kentucky home,
>   'Tis summer, the darkies are gay,
> The corn top's ripe and the meadow's in the bloom
>   While the birds make music all the day.
> The young folks roll on the little cabin floor,
>   All merry, all happy and bright:
> By'n by Hard Times comes a knocking at the door,
>   Then my old Kentucky Home, good night!
> CHORUS: Weep no more, my lady, oh! weep no more today!
> We will sing one song for the old Kentucky Home,
>   For the old Kentucky Home, far away.

> . . . The time has come when the darkies have to part
>   The head must bow and the back will have to bend
>   Wherever the darkey may go:
> A few more days, and the trouble all will end
>   In the field where the sugar-canes grow.
> A few more days for to tote the weary load,
>   No matter 'twill never be light,
> A few more days till we totter on the road,
>   Then my old Kentucky Home, good night!
> Weep no more, &c.

In his sketchbook are the original lines to end each stanza: "Poor Uncle Tom, Good Night," and a chorus that fits no extant melody:

> Then my old Kentucky Home, good night!
>   Poor Uncle Tom
> Grieve not for your old Kentucky home
> You'r bound for a better land
>   Old Uncle Tom.

The sketchbook has dialect spelling—"de" for "the.'" Two minor changes may affect the meaning: "sugar-canes" replace the original "cotton bud"; " 'twill never be light" reverses "it soon will be light." Both phrases of the early version are closer to Tom than the final ones. A field of sugar-cane in Kentucky is rare, and there is no hint that Tom's time in Louisiana is meant. Endless night is for Legree, not Tom. A vague sympathy had initiated the song; a little work had shown that its meaning was vaguer than Stowe's. Like eight other songwriters in 1852, Foster attached the name of Uncle Tom to vaguely suitable words: unlike those other eight, Foster acknowledged the vagueness by removing the name.

In 1860, with "Old Black Joe," Foster is closer to Stowe's Uncle Tom:

> Gone are the days when my heart was young and gay,
> Gone are my friends from the cotton fields away,
> Gone from the earth to a better land I know,
> I hear their gentle voices calling "Old Black Joe."

Joe's voices of friends "gone from the earth" are like the "Voices That Are Gone" which we examined in Chapter 9, but "Old Black Joe" does not develop the idea as the later song does. Joe's voices are not associated with dreaming. Rather they resemble the angels of Eva's doctrine in *Uncle Tom.* Eva declares to all Blacks: "Each one of you can become angels, and be angels forever." Tom tells Ophelia how Eva knows that she is within a few hours of death: "Thar's them that tells it to the child, Miss Feely. It's the angels— 'it's the trumpet sound afore the break o' day.' " And Ophelia assures Topsy about Eva: "She is an angel." Stowe herself, as we know from the account of Tom's vision, leaves an open question. But she doubtless preferred Eva's unorthodox doctrine to all the angelology that Tom Moore had accumulated from Patristic, Moslem, Jewish, and Zoroastrian lore. So did Foster. Yet the questions that he gives "Old Black Joe" in the second and third stanzas of his song resemble Moore's dream of home more than Uncle Tom's faith:

> Why do I weep when my heart should feel no pain?
> Why do I sigh that my friends come not again,
> Grieving for forms now departed long ago?
> I hear &c.

> Where are the hearts once so happy and so free?
> The children so dear that I held upon my knee?
> Gone to the shore where my soul has longed to go.
> I hear &c.

In the second line of each stanza, with the words "cotton," "come not," and "upon," there is a poignant dissonance as the melody comes down the major scale while the bass rises, more slowly, by half-steps; the natural and sharp fourth degrees sound together, pulling toward the chord on the fifth for the end of the phrase. This dissonance is extraordinary in Foster's whole work. It is closer to St. Clare's Mozart than to the hymns sung by Tom. But Tom could have listened to "Old Black Joe" with appreciation, whereas "My Old Kentucky Home" would have provoked his dissent.

Both these songs, nevertheless, were sung by Uncle Toms and choruses on the stage. Dramatizations of Uncle Tom broke more records than the novel. Harriet Beecher Stowe discouraged the first applicant who wanted to dramatize the story—Asa Hutchinson of the Hutchinson family singers. She told him she respected "the barrier which now keeps young people of Christian families from theatrical entertainments." Other dramatizers went ahead without asking permission. By December of 1852 there were nine versions flourishing in New York, eleven in London. The "barrier" was broken; clergymen led whole congregations to the theater, and some of them noted that the theater had now become more moral than most of the churches throughout the nation. The most successful script was that of George L. Aiken, playwright for the George C. Howard family troupe of actors. Aiken's work was modified by them in the course of its long run; its full-evening length was an innovation in American drama as revolutionary as any of its other features. Aiken's script, full of nonspecific cues for music, called for "Old Folks at Home," sung by Tom in the last act; the Howards added "My Old Kentucky Home" as soon as it was available to them— probably before its publication. Their production ran a hundred days in Troy, New York; then in July 1853 moved to Purdy's National Theatre in New York City, where it maintained its supremacy in competition with Barnum, Wood's Minstrels, Samuel Sanford, and Thomas "Jim Crow" Rice, among many others. In 1857 Barnum sponsored the Howards in a successful tour of England, Scotland, and Ireland. The Pittsburgh version, November 1853, included "Old Folks," sung by Tom, "My Old Kentucky Home," by Topsy, and "Massa's in de Cold Ground," by a chorus. During the Civil War new versions appeared and old ones were refurbished: "Old Black Joe" was sung in many of them. There can be no doubt that all four of Foster's most characteristic "plantation songs" owe much of their fame to *Uncle Tom*.

The *Tom* shows borrowed from the whole repertory of the minstrels, just as the minstrels parodied and adapted scraps of *Uncle Tom*. The two theatrical traditions overlapped and nearly coalesced; both affected every other kind of theater in the English-speaking world. The absorption of early materials into the *Uncle Tom* shows naturally applied to "Uncle Ned" more often than "Susanna," for

"Uncle Ned" could fit into the narrative with less stretching than "Susanna." Most of all, the expansion of *Uncle Tom* involved "Old Folks at Home" and thereby transformed Foster's relation to Christy and all the other minstrels. When "Old Folks" in an *Uncle Tom* show drew tears from audiences more respectable than those that Christy could attract to hear Foster's "Maggie," "Willie," and "Old Dog Tray," Foster's sense of his work as a whole was thrown into some confusion. When, in the spring of 1854, Christy's troupe joined with Wood's to present an opera of *Uncle Tom's Cabin, or Hearts and Homes,* with a finale of "Pop Goes the Weazel," Foster was in New York, dreaming of Jeanie and Little Ella; the chronology adds to the likelihood that "Jeanie" and "Ella" refer to Eva. But there is no record that the *Tom* shows used these songs. Nor that they used the "pathetic" "plantation" songs Foster had sent Christy in 1851, except for "Old Folks." The old songs they used, from "Jim Crow" to "Old Folks," were those that had already won popularity, not songs that had to be sought out.

Besides increasing the musical and comical aspects of *Uncle Tom,* the dramatizations all simplified the conflict into a melodrama: Legree's whippings, George Harris' gunfight, and especially Eliza's flight across the icy Ohio River (with bloodhounds after her—a grim borrowing from reality rather than the novel) roused audiences to the utmost excitement. Eva's apotheosis in the clouds exploited their piety. Aiken's version ends with Eva looking down to bless Tom, and also St. Clare, who has recovered from his wound and presumably goes on living as a "good" slavemaster. Aiken's version accommodates Topsy with a scene in Vermont, where she protects Ophelia from the advances of a new character, Gumption Cute, a caricature of Barnum. Many later versions twist the plot to bring Topsy into the final benediction as well. No matter whether a version stresses the atrocities or the beneficence of slaveholders, its picture of good and evil is sure to be simpler than Stowe's, and the final triumph of good is reassuring, rather than menacing to a Northern audience. The simplification of the theater, as well as its hospitality to music, makes Foster's songs fit the dramatized *Uncle Tom* better than the novel.

"Old Black Joe" was no favorite of the Foster family. Morrison left no comment on it. Jane, according to the late testimony of her granddaughter, Jessie Rose, forbade the singing of it. She connected it with her father's servant named Joe. Earl Hobson Smith and later fiction writers built up the character of this Joe as a principal inspirer of Foster's songs, though, in fact, Foster could have had only a brief acquaintance with him; Joe was dead long before "Old Black Joe" was written. The connection with *Uncle Tom,* on the contrary, was noticed in a German publication of the song, which simply retitles it *"Der alte Tom."*

The list of Foster's "plantation songs" between "Ring de Banjo" and "My Old Kentucky Home" is short:

"Oh! Boys, Carry Me 'Long," copyright June 12, 1851
"Old Folks at Home," copyright October 1
"Farewell My Lilly Dear," copyright December 13
"Massa's in de Cold Ground," copyright July 7, 1852

Each of these has its distinctive interest, though all are alike in the "pathetic" mood. The list of "plantation songs" after "My Old Kentucky Home" is equally short:

"The Glendy Burk," copyright May 29, 1860
"Old Black Joe," copyright November 8
"Down Among the Canebrakes," copyright November 15
"Don't Bet Your Money on de Shanghai," copyright March 9, 1861

Of these the first and last revert to comedy. All the least familiar songs on both these lists can contribute to our understanding "Old Folks," though not so profoundly as "Old Black Joe" contributes.

"Oh! Boys" is the song that Foster recommended to Christy as "certain to become popular, as I have taken great pains with it." Its rhythm is that of a lullaby. Its chords are the three primary chords. Its melody rises only once to the high keynote, at the beginning of the chorus; otherwise it stays within six notes of the scale, like "Susanna." The words pile up all the "plantation" clichés in a dying slave's appeal to fellow workers:

Oh! carry me 'long,
Der's no more trouble for me,
I's guine to roam
In a happy home
Where all de niggas am free;

The singer is still only vaguely attentive to his group; he wants the group to soothe his last pains, like a mother or a nurse. The group that can soothe is as dim as the group he will join when he dies. His concern is more with himself.

I've worked long in de fields,
I've handled many a hoe,
I'll turn my eye
Before I die
And see de sugar-cane grow.
CHORUS: Oh! boys, carry me 'long,
Carry me till I die,
Carry me down
To de buryin' groun':
Massa, don't you cry.

The single line for the master can be sung in various tones, with or without irony. The solo singer goes on, with two more stanzas about himself, the land, and the beasts—especially a dog, the only creature that will miss him.

All ober de land
I've wandered many a day,
    To blow de horn
    And mind de corn
And keep de possum away;
No use for me now,
So darkeys bury me low:
    My horn is dry
    And I must lie
Wha de possum nebber can go.
Oh! boys &c.

Farewell to de boys
Wid hearts so happy and light,
    Dey sing a song
    De whole day long
And dance de juba at night;
Farewell to de fields
Ob cotton, 'bacco, and all:
    I's guine to hoe
    In a bressed row
Wha de corn grows mellow and tall,
Oh! boys, &c.

Farewell to de hills,
De meadows cover'd wid green,
    Old brindle boss
    And de old grey hoss
All beaten, broken, and lean;
Farewell to de dog
Dat always followed me 'round;
    Old Sancho'll wail
    And droop his tail
When I am under de ground.
Oh! boys, &c.

Christy did not make "Oh! Boys" popular. Its "pathetic style" was too direct and monotonous. Its swaying rhythm is its only musical distinction. Was it this rhythm or the words or the way they fitted each other that cost Foster such "great pains"? Morrison Foster names "Oh! Boys" along with "Hard Times" in his dubious account of the family servant, Olivia Pise:

When Stephen was a child, my father had a mulatto bound-girl named Olivia Pise, the illegitimate daughter of a West India Frenchman, who taught dancing to the upper circles of Pittsburgh society early in the present century. "Lieve," as she was called, was a devout Christian and a member of a church of shouting colored people. The little boy was fond of their singing and boisterous devotions. She was permitted to often take Stephen to church with her. Here he stored up in his mind. "many a gem of purest ray serene," drawn from these caves of negro melody. A number of strains heard there, and which, he said to me, were too good to be lost, have been preserved by him, short scraps of which were incorporated in two of his songs, "Hard Times, Come Again No More" and "Oh! Boys, Carry Me 'Long."

Morrison's memories, in 1896, were dim and confused; if Stephen remembered Olivia Pise from his first three years, he remembered a lullaby that was as likely French as English or African; if he often attended one of the three churches in the "Haiti" district of Pittsburgh, it was as likely sedate as "shouting"; if he used a remembered "scrap" in "Oh! Boys," this does not distinguish the melody. Morrison's quotation from Thomas Grey's "Elegy" is as good a clue to Stephen's thought as the reference to Olivia Pise and the church. Morrison's linking the song of 1851 with the song of 1855 indicates that Stephen's statement was uttered long after "Oh! Boys" was written and had failed to become popular, at a time when Morrison and Stephen saw each other less than they did in 1851. Moreover, no one has found any confirming evidence of what Morrison thought he remembered. What the total evidence makes most likely is that Morrison, for the sake of brevity, fused several memories and a plausible supposition: he himself remembered Olivia; he remembered that Stephen had sympathized with Black suffering and Black religion, as shown in *Uncle Tom*, when he, Morrison, had scoffed; he remembered that Stephen had spoken of "Oh! Boys" and "Hard Times" as songs he had worked at with "great pains," songs that deserved more success than the public gave them; he supposed that Stephen had absorbed something from Black singers, though, in his own opinion still, Blacks had contributed nothing to "Susanna" or "Old Folks." The fused paragraph made good publicity. Morrison may or may not have composed it with that conscious aim. But he supplied what many readers wanted to believe. Skeptics were not likely to challenge his memory about songs so little known.

The singer of "Farewell, My Lilly Dear" is more like the singer of "Susanna" or "Nelly Bly" or "Melinda May" than the singer of "Oh! Boys." He sings to Lilly and she joins him in the two-part chorus. He must bid her farewell because "Old massa sends me roaming." In his third stanza he turns aside to tell an audience about Lilly and his wish to marry her; in his fourth and last stanza he turns back to her, for a last farewell. In all stanzas he tells more about himself than Lilly, but he never tells about his hopes or fears. He simply asks for sympathy in his grief; sympathy with his tears and his consoling banjo: Lilly must save *her* tears until after he is gone. The chorus suggests that he grieves as much for the home he is leaving as for Lilly:

> Farewell forever to Old Tennessee;
> Farewell my Lilly dear, Don't weep for me.

The melody ranges wide, like "Nelly Bly," but lacks the motivic interest and the rhythmic vigor of that melody. "Lilly" is meant to be pathetic, like "Oh! Boys." It indicates how ready Foster was to read about the partings in *Uncle Tom.* But it indicates how far he was from sharing Stowe's realistic concern for Black couples.

Even in 1860 Foster's imagination of Black people was flagrantly unreal. The text of "The Glendy Burk," if the singer is Black, includes some of Foster's most fatuous lines:

> De Glendy Burk is a mighty fast boat,
>   Wid a mighty fast captain too;
> He sits up dah on de hurricane roof
>   And he keeps his eye on de crew.
> I can't stay here, for dey work too hard;
>   I'm bound to leave dis town;
> I'll take my duds and tote 'em on my back
>   When de Glendy Burk comes down.
> CHORUS: (unison): Ho! for Lou'siana! I'm bound to leave dis town;
>   I'll take &c.
>
> De Glendy Burk has a funny old crew
>   And dey sing de boatman's song;
> Dey burn de pitch and de pine knot too,
>   For to shove de boat along.
> De smoke goes up and de ingine roars
>   And de wheel goes round and round,
> So fair you well! for I'll take a little ride
>   When de Glendy Burk comes down.
> Ho! &c.
>
> I'll work all night in de wind and storm,
>   I'll work all day in de rain,
> Till I find myself on de levy-dock
>   In New Orleans again.
> Dey make me mow in de hay field here
>   And knock my head wid de flail,
> I'll go wha dey work wid de sugar and de cane
>   And roll on de cotton bale.
> Ho! &c.

My lady love is as pretty as a pink,
    I'll meet her on de way
I'll take her back to de sunny old south
    And dah I'll make her stay.
So don't you fret my honey dear,
    Oh! don't you fret Miss Brown.
I'll take you back 'fore de middle of de week
    When de Glendy Burk comes down.
Ho! &c.

Foster's singer, discontented with the climate and the monotonous work in Pittsburgh or some similar town, forgets that he is supposed to be Black, or else he forgets all that *Uncle Tom* has taught the world about New Orleans and the "sunny old south." That this song was accepted for publication in 1860 by Firth and Pond is surprising; that it was seldom sung before the 1930s is less so. Without the words, however, it makes a good polka for fiddle or banjo, with a range like that of "Away Down South." Is it possible that Foster wrote "The Glendy Burk" around 1850, discarded it, and retrieved it only when he was becoming desperate about money? The boat named in the title was launched in 1851, at New Albany, Indiana. It was named for a New Orleans banker, Glenn D. Burke (1804–79), with whom Morrison had some business. After 1853, when the railroad offered a faster and slightly more reliable connection between Pittsburgh and Cincinnati than the river, Foster probably did not see the boat. But Foster's sketchbook shows that he worked on the song about 1860; he changed the fifth line, for example, from "I get no work" to "dey work too hard." Both phrases can be read as applying to Foster himself—his hard work failed to create a demand for most of his songs.

The line in "The Glendy Burk" about the "boatmen's song" has been seized by biographers as a pretext for imagining some unlikely scenes of Foster listening to Black workers in Cincinnati. In fact, steamboats on the Ohio and upper Mississippi employed few Blacks before the Civil War, and these few were free men—cooks, stewards, and barbers, not boatmen—more likely to sing "Jeanie" than "Go Down, Moses." One such cabin boy and steward was James Monroe Trotter (1842–92), who recalled, in his book of 1878 on *Music and Some Highly Musical People,* that his favorite school-days song was "A Captive Knight" by Hemans, and that in 1856 he had bitterly opposed any idea of a distinctive Black music. The crews and longshoremen in the 1840s and '50s were an important group of workers, mostly recent immigrants from Germany and Ireland. When slaves were used at all, notably for the worst work of firemen, they served only below Louisville, so as not to facilitate escape at Cincinnati. Thus Foster could rarely have heard any Black boatmen's songs. "The Boatmen's Dance" by Dan Emmett referred to the "keel-boat age" before steam, when the legendary Mike Fink (1790–1823?) terrified the landsmen as "half horse, half alligator." Foster knew the song, from the stage. Later legends are derived largely from the account of "Cincinnati Levee Life and Songs" that the poet Lafcadio Hearn contributed to the *Commercial* in 1876. Hearn's account is not legendary; he noted explicitly that " 'Before Freedom,' as the colored folks say, white laborers performed most of the roustabout labor on the steamboats" and that even in the '70s Blacks often imitated the accent of the Irish whose jobs they were taking over. Altogether the available facts suggest that Foster heard Black people singing outdoors less than in churches, and that he heard scattered individuals more than any sort of coherent group.

"The Glendy Burk" and the last of all the "plantation songs," "Don't Bet Your Money on de Shanghai," published in 1861, need no chorus at all. The word "chorus" simply marks the recurring refrain. The singer of "Shanghai" never identifies himself or his listeners. He comments at length on the fighting cock. His most interesting lines are a digression:

> De Shanghai fiddle is a funny little thing
> And ebry time you tune him up he goes ching ching.

The only hint of Blackness in this song is the dialect spelling. The tune harks back to the Scottish and Irish reels of Foster's childhood.

There is a four-part chorus joining the singer of "Down Among the Canebrakes," but the singer of the five stanzas ignores the group, to describe his own happy childhood, his mother, his "lovely one" who "might have been my own," and his wish to "return to die." The chorus reinforces his lament that "those happy days are o'er! . . . will come back no more!" with a final *ritardando* phrase. The languid mood of "Kentucky Home" and "Old Black Joe" is the whole subject of "Down Among the Canebrakes," but here there is less intensity, no distinction, and no saving qualification. The singer simply ignores slavery, which would stop any actual Black person from dwelling on a wish to return to "cane-brakes on the Mississippi shore."

A Pittsburgh writer and collector of local lore, Frank Cowan, pointed out in 1878 that some of the thousands of runaway slaves coming through Pittsburgh on their way to Canada in the 1850s "felt for the first time that they were strangers in a strange land." Cowan believes, "They inspired the sentiment which pervades the songs of Mr. Foster from beginning to end." But if Foster thought of the fugitives, he knew that they valued freedom above home.

How many fugitives valued their Southern homes at all? Lewis Clarke was one who answered with authority, in his *Narrative*, 1845. He stayed in the North to work for the antislavery cause, because he longed to be able to go home free.

> Could I make that country ever seem like *home*? Some people are very much afraid all the slaves will run up North, if they are ever free. But I can assure them that they will run *back* again if they do. If I could have been assured of my freedom in Kentucky, then, I would have given anything in the world for the prospect of spending my life among my old acquaintances, and where I first saw the sky, and the sun rise and go down.

Foster's songs never express the sentiment of Clarke. They do not try to do so. If people like Clarke "inspired" a song like "Down Among the Canebrakes," the inspiration was twisted. The songs that Cowan knew—"Old Folks," "My Old Kentucky Home," and "Old Black Joe"—can be twisted into a false meaning if their singers are imagined as fugitives, instead of characters in *Uncle Tom* or a similar fiction. "Down Among the Canebrakes," like the late comic songs, "The Glendy Burk" and "Don't Bet Your Money," is a weaker fiction than *Uncle Tom*. Its sentiment has sources enough in Foster's own life and the tradition of home songs to make Cowan's "inspiration" unnecessary. Foster's whole character and his whole career make the connection Cowan imagines unlikely.

The one song that more than any other evokes an imaginary Black group is "Massa's in de Cold Ground." This song, used in the *Uncle Tom* shows at the point where St. Clare has died, before Marie takes action, contributes as much as any other feature of the shows to conciliating some of their audience and offending others. A modern reader able to set aside his real sympathies for a moment, to share Foster's imagination, can admire the consistency of tone and the development of related images; a listener can admire the fit of words and drooping melody—again and again it descends from the high keynote through the octave leap, giving gentle emphasis to the feminine rhymes.

> Round de meadows am a ringing
>   De darkeys' mournful song,
> While de mocking-bird am singing,
>   Happy as de day am long.
> Where de ivy am a creeping
>   O'er de grassy mound,
> Dare old massa am a sleeping,
>   Sleeping in de cold, cold ground.
> CHORUS: Down in de cornfield
>   Hear dat mournful sound:

> All de darkeys am a weeping—
> Massa's in de cold cold ground.

The second stanza ignores the chorus, to concentrate on the feeble old master in a picturesque Southern scene. The third and last stanza reveals the singer as an individual after all, weeping for an unmentioned audience:

> When de autumn leaves were falling,
> When de days were cold,
> 'Twas hard to hear old massa calling,
> Cayse he was so weak and old.
> Now de orange tree am blooming
> On de sandy shore,
> Now de summer days am coming,
> Massa nebber calls no more.
> Down in de cornfield, &c.

> Massa made de darkeys love him,
> Cayse he was so kind,
> Now dey sadly weep above him,
> Mourning cayse he leave dem behind.
> I cannot work before tomorrow,
> Cayse de tear drops flow,
> I try to drive away my sorrow
> Pickin on de old banjo.
> Down in de cornfield, &c.

If the Uncle Tom of Stowe's novel had sung a lament for St. Clare, he would have prayed for his soul. (When Stowe's principal real model, the Reverend Josiah Henson, prayed for his master, he prayed at the same time for the rescue of his fellow slaves.) If Lewis Clarke had helped write a song for St. Clare, he would have made sure that it revealed some irony; his *Narrative,* frequently referred to by Stowe, includes a relevant paragraph:

> Loving master and mistress is the hardest work that slaves have to do. When any stranger is present we have to love them very much. When master is sick we are in great trouble. Every night the slaves gather around the house, and send up one or two to see how master does. They creep up to the bed, and with a very soft voice, inquire "How is dear massa?" . . . and go to the cabin with a merry heart. . . . When we got a stone to put on his grave, we hauled the largest we could find, so as to fasten him down as strong as possible.

Did such thoughts as Clarke's never enter Foster's mind? If not, his reading of *Uncle Tom* was far from Stowe's intention. But if he wrote "Massa's in de Cold Ground" shortly before he read *Uncle Tom,* and felt chagrin when his song was used in the dramatizations, then his revision of "My Old Kentucky Home" and the gap of more than seven years before "The Glendy Burk" and "Old Black Joe" make further sense.

Morrison Foster's surmise that "Massa" refers to Stephen's sick father more than to any other real person cannot do away with the questions of slavery and Blackness provoked by Foster's fiction. "Massa's" meaning to Foster himself in 1851, whatever it was, became absorbed in the public meanings of the song associated with *Uncle Tom.* The association, however coincidental, is close. "Massa" fits a stereotype of Uncle Tom that survives into the 20th century more effectively than the complex character portrayed by Stowe.

Between the old William Foster and a real group of Black musicians, Frank Johnson's band, there is an association that fits Stephen Foster's work as a whole better than any association with *Uncle Tom.* In May 1843, when William Foster was mayor of Allegheny, the Johnson band gave a concert there at the new Temperance Hall, for the benefit of the Temperance Society in which Mayor Foster was active. During the concert a mob assembled outside and nearly broke it up. The mayor had to help the bandsmen get from the hall to their lodgings. He showed remarkable courage and skill, as well as decency, for he had no police force to call on— police service was still rudimentary in Pittsburgh through the 1850s. Moreover, the mayor was persistent. Next day he got the ringleaders of the mob arrested. A jury acquitted them of crime but required them to pay the costs of their trial. The band stayed in town and played again a few nights later for a Grand Quadrille Party at Bonnafon's Saloon, as newspaper accounts testify. Foster family documents, though they show that Morrison had traveled on the same boat with the band, from Madison, Indiana, to Cincinnati, in April, omit any reference to the excitement of May. Whether Stephen heard the band is unknown. If he did, he heard no "Jim Crow" from them, nor any "plantation songs," but rather their advertised *pièce de résistance,* an arrangement of the hoary piano piece "The Battle of Prague" by Franz Kotzwara (1730–91), probably surrounded by arrangements of Rossini, Weber, and Bishop, perhaps supplemented by a piece of Johnson's like "If Sleeping Now, Fair Maid of Love." Regardless of whether or not Stephen heard the band, he knew that the mob had protested not its music but its mere existence. He knew that his father had shown not patronizing kindness but heroic concern for justice. If he meant "Massa" as a tribute to his father, then he may have meant his mourning "darkeys" to sing with self-respect more like Johnson's than Christy's or Uncle Tom's.

"Old Folks at Home" fits *Uncle Tom* only by a distortion of both the song and the novel, but this distortion was easy for George Aiken and other dramatizers. The singer of "Old Folks" is alone, roaming with no present attachments. His "chorus" is a mere refrain. There is no mention of fellow workers nor of a master. The lonely singer longs for his family and his childhood. His dialect and his placing of the old home on a plantation are arbitrary and dreamlike; he addresses his audience as "darkeys"; his whole idea is the common theme of the tradition of home songs. Foster's pathetic blackfaced singer of "Oh! Boys" and "Farewell My Lilly Dear" has now reached out to join all the lonely white singers of the dream of home. Listeners familiar with that dream were pleased at the slight novelty of attributing it to a Black man, for Swiss mountaineers and Irish patriots had worn out their welcome, while the general idea continued to gather strength; thus Foster's amalgamation renewed the theme:

> Way down upon de Swanee ribber,
> Far, far away,
> Dere's wha my heart is turning ebber,
> Dere's wha de old folks stay.
> All up and down de whole creation,
> Sadly I roam,
> Still longing for de old plantation,
> And for de old folks at home.
> CHORUS: All de world am sad and dreary,
> Ebry where I roam
> Oh! darkeys how my heart grows weary,
> Far from de old folks at home.
>
> All round de little farm I wandered
> When I was young,
> Den many happy days I squandered,
> Many de songs I sung.
> When I was playing wid my brudder
> Happy was I.
> Oh! take me to my kind old mudder,
> Dere let me live and die.
> All de world, &c.
>
> One little hut among de bushes,
> One dat I love,
> Still sadly to my mem'ry rushes,
> No matter where I rove.
> When will I see de bees a humming
> All round de comb?
> When will I hear de banjo tumming
> Down in my good old home?
> All de world &c.

The roaming singer makes no plan to return to his home, though he offers no account of anything restraining him wherever he is. Instead, he longs. He asks the listeners to take him home. He asks when. He expects no answer. His refrain, with a melody that rises above the rest of the song on the words "All de world," suggests that he and his sympathizers might still be "sad and dreary" even if the wish were fulfilled: the happiness of childhood cannot remain available; the most we can hope for is to die comforted by a mother.

In 1851 this weary sentiment was spreading to more and more people. It still carried some prestige from its association with Tom Moore and his followers. Many a listener, before "Old Folks," supposed that Black people were too crude to share such a sentiment. "Jim Crow" and "Susanna" strengthened the belief that Blacks were congenitally cheerful. "Uncle Ned" had persuaded some listeners that Blacks could be pathetic (though comical at the same time). With "Oh! Boys" Foster had taken "great pains" to make them more truly pathetic. Now with "Old Folks" he succeeded in making them pathetic in a surprisingly refined way. Christy understood. The song fitted Christy's shows perfectly. Christy's group made the song popular very quickly.

The weary sentiment was foreign to Harriet Beecher Stowe and the Uncle Tom that she portrayed; it was even contrary to her argument that slavery destroyed Black homes and families. But the pathos and the dignity matched her more general purpose of winning pity for the slaves.

George Aiken and others like him cared little either for the traditional dream or for the steadfast faith and passive resistance of Uncle Tom. Their political views were various. But they liked pathos and publicity. They combined the two fictions—Foster's and Stowe's—and brought millions of listeners to share in the vaguest, most general pathetic mood. To Aiken "Old Folks" seemed to fit *Uncle Tom*. It could be detached from its own tradition. Its unreal quality could be ignored, just as easily as Aiken ignored Stowe's preponderant realism. Vague sympathy for Blacks was enough. The memorable tune intensified the sympathy and left it vague. Most of Foster's words could be forgotten, while the refrain could specify just the mood—"sad and dreary . . . heart grows weary, far from the old folks at home."

Does the "Swanee River" in the first line of "Old Folks" mean the Suwanee in Florida? the "San Juan-ee" or Lesser St. John's? Though Foster intended to make only a vague myth, did he not know that there were in fact Black exiles who recalled a happy childhood in their own families' plantations on the Suwanee? From the time of Spanish rule in Florida this was Seminole country. The

Indian word "Seminole" meant "runaways" and applied to Blacks as well as Red men and others. Indians had bought a few Black slaves and had welcomed several hundred runaways, allowing them to bear arms as well as to manage their own farms. White settlers north and west of the Suwanee were not threatened by the Seminole nation itself, but they wanted to take over their slaves. They feared the brilliant leaders among the free Blacks, and most of all they feared the development of a center for wider Black action. As soon as the United States flag was raised over Florida, whites began to urge the Federal government to remove the Seminole nation, including those Blacks who could not be reclaimed, to the Indian Territory in the remote West. War raged from 1835 to 1842. One of the principal United States generals, Thomas Sidney Jesup, repeatedly called it "a negro, not an Indian war." Eventually Jesup guaranteed to Blacks willing to go West the protection of Federal force against any white claims: to do so he had to invoke War Department authority to cancel such claims, setting a precedent for Lincoln's Emancipation. The Seminole War was the longest American war before Vietnam; it was the costliest of its "Indian" wars. Did Foster hear about some aspects of it from his brother Henry, working in Washington at the end of the war? Or from Uncle Struthers, the old Indian fighter? or from Dunning or Morrison, serving in the Mexican War? or from Charles Shiras? Or only from the antiwar speeches by the Ohio Congressman Joshua Reed Giddings? From the book on the *Florida War* by John T. Sprague, 1848, in which there is a tribute to the Seminole's "love of home"? Or from Giddings' most persuasive speech, January 6, 1849, against Federal payment to Antonio Pacheco for the loss of his Seminole slave Louis? That Foster should not have heard of the war at all is very unlikely. But that audiences of Christy and the *Uncle Tom* shows would think of a connection with "Old Folks" seems unlikely too.

Morrison Foster tells how the name "Swanee" was chosen:

One day in 1851, Stephen came into my office, on the bank of the Monongahela, Pittsburgh, and said to me, "What is a good name of two syllables for a Southern river? I want to use it in this new song of 'Old Folks at Home.'" I asked him how Yazoo would do. "Oh," said he, "that has been used before." I then suggested Pedee. "Oh, pshaw," he replied, "I won't have that." I then took down an atlas from the top of my desk and opened the map of the United States. We both looked over it and my finger stopped at the "Swanee," a little river in Florida emptying into the Gulf of Mexico. "That's it, that's it exactly," exclaimed he delighted, as he wrote the name down; and the song was finished, commencing, "Way Down Upon de Swanee Ribber." He left the office, as was his custom, abruptly, without saying another word, and I resumed my work.

Nowhere else does Morrison attempt so much dialogue. He knows that his readers will be grateful for a circumstantial story about their favorite song. He does not imagine that many will ever consult the sketchbook, in which "Pedee" is written twice—the second time crossed out, with "Swanee" written in above it. Can readers who know that Morrison is simplifying the rejection of "Pedee" trust his account of the choice of "Swanee"? No matter: the possibility of a concrete meaning for "Swanee" is irrelevant to the public connections of "Old Folks" with the tradition of Tom Moore and the coincidental parallel of *Uncle Tom*. These connections, known well enough to Morrison and yet left unmentioned, reduce the possible connection with the Seminole to a private level equivalent to Morrison's finger on the map.

When Elizabeth Greenfield sang "Old Folks" in 1853, she and her listeners had never heard of Foster or his family; they ignored the Seminole War; they readily acknowledged the song as a new contribution to the song tradition, sponsored by Harriet Beecher Stowe. Greenfield had arrived in England just before Stowe. Finding the promises of her manager false, she appealed to Stowe for help on May 6. By May 23 Stowe had introduced her to the musical philanthropists of London, who had arranged a concert at Stafford House. Stowe's account of this concert, in her letters published as *Sunny Memories of Foreign Lands*, 1854, provides a unique picture of Greenfield and her use of "Old Folks":

The concert room . . . looked more picture-like and dreamy than ever. The piano was on the flat stairway just below the broad central landing. It was a grand piano, standing end outward, and perfectly *banked up* among hothouse flowers, so that only its gilded top was visible. Sir George Smart presided. The choicest of the *élite* was there. Ladies in demi-toilet and bonneted. Miss Greenfield stood among the singers on the staircase, and excited a sympathetic murmur among the audience. She is not handsome, but looked very well. She has a pleasing dark face, wore a black velvet headdress and white carnelian earrings, a black mohr antique silk, made high in the neck, with white lace falling sleeves and white gloves. A certain gentleness of manner and self-possession, the result of the universal kindness shown her, sat well upon her. Chevalier Bunsen, the Prussian ambassador, sat by me. He looked at her with much interest. "Are the race often as good looking?" he said. I said, "She is not handsome, compared with many, though I confess she looks uncommonly well to-day." . . .

Six of the most cultivated glee singers of London sang, among other things, "Spring's delights are now returning," and "Where the bee sucks there lurk I." The duchess said, "These glees are peculiarly English." It was indeed delightful to hear Shakspeare's aerial words made vocal within the walls of this fairy palace. The duchess has a strong nationality; and nationality, always interesting, never appears in so captivating a form as when it expresses itself through a beautiful and cultivated woman. One likes to see a person identifying one's self with a country, and she embraces England, with its history, its strength, its splendor, its moral power, with an evident pride and affection which I love to see.

Miss Greenfield's turn for singing now came, and there was profound attention. Her voice, with its keen, searching fire, its penetrating vibrant quality, its *"timbre,"* as the French have it, cut its way like a Damascus blade to the heart. It was the more touching from occasional rusticities and artistic defects, which showed that she had received no culture from art.

She sang the ballad, "Old folks at home," giving one verse in the soprano, and another in the tenor voice.

As she stood partially concealed by the piano Chevalier Bunsen thought that the tenor part was performed by one of the gentlemen. He was perfectly astonished when he discovered that it was by her. This was rapturously encored. Between the parts Sir George took her to the piano, and tried her voice by skips, striking notes here and there at random, without connection, from D in alt to A first space in bass clef: she followed with unerring precision, striking the sound nearly at the same instant his finger touched the key. This brought out a burst of applause. . . .

Lord Shaftesbury was there. He came and spoke to us after the concert. Speaking of Miss Greenfield, he said, "I consider the use of these halls for the encouragement of an outcast race, a *consecration*. This is the true use of wealth and splendor when it is employed to raise up and encourage the despised and forgotten."

"Old Folks" fitted this great occasion of *élite* patronage of the talented outcast. The kind audience's rapture was naturally vague. Stowe's pleasure in having arranged the scene was naturally mixed with the "captivating" interest of "nationality" and with all the excitement of her own sudden fame. The "occasional rusticities" of Greenfield in her French and Italian arias were "touching"; when she went on to the vaguely rustic and "national" "Old Folks," just as Jenny Lind had gone from foreign arias to a Swedish lullaby, an encore was appropriate. If some of the listeners associated the song with Christy, the presumed author, he was sufficiently rustic and "national," and now Greenfield could "raise up" the song to a "consecration." If others associated it with the theatrical *Uncle Tom*, better yet. Whenever these listeners heard the song again, from the stage or on the street or in the parlor, Greenfield's "gentleness" and her special *timbre* and her amazing range would all be remembered. Even the readers of Stowe's letter would share all these associations to some degree.

In the course of arranging for this concert, Stowe made a pleasing discovery; she confirmed what she had hardly dared hope: the liberal

English *élite,* when Greenfield took their hands, showed no "indications of suppressed surprise or disgust."

I never so fully realized that there really is no natural prejudice against colour in the human mind.

At the same time, Stowe progressed in her thinking about "nationality" to the point of acknowledging a paradox:

The highest class of mind in all countries loses nationality, and becomes universal; it is a great pity, too, because nationality is picturesque always.

The tension between liberal universality and picturesque nationality was not for her to resolve. She did not go so far as to connect the alleged "natural prejudice" with the "picturesque," nor to suspect that *Uncle Tom* and "Old Folks" could reinforce prejudice.

Stowe's rapture in London is offset by Alfred Bunn's cynicism when he attends a concert by Greenfield in New York a few months later. He tells about it, with his usual facetious tone, in his *Old England and New England:*

One day we visited Metropolitan Hall to hear the lady calling herself "The Black Swan" (recently arrived in "our own little village"), partly impelled to the adventure by a schoolboy's recollection of Ovid's line, "Rara avis in terris, *nigroque* simillima *cygno,*" and partly by the singular announcement of "No colored person will be admitted." Having heard, from the earliest moment we could hear and understand anything, that "a cat may look at a king," the idea of one nigger not being allowed to look at another, did strike us as the height of all human—impudence?—no, let us say, drollery. We did hear that the delicate distinction between "blackey" on the stage and "blackey" in the audience, ended by a place being set apart in the gallery of this huge assembly room for the especial accommodation of the people of Africa, who might desire to listen to the strains of their sisterhood.

Bunn does not deign to comment on the singing. His facts and his tone together are enough to show the prejudice that Greenfield could never break down. She soon gave up her effort to make a concert career and settled into a quiet life as teacher in Philadelphia. One of her pupils there, Carrie Thomas, was to become a leading singer in the Hampton Institute concert group. For Greenfield and Thomas and others like them, the meaning of "Old Folks" would always include something of the attitude of Alfred Bunn along with that of Harriet Beecher Stowe.

Not only "Old Folks," but the three other songs of Foster associated with *Uncle Tom* carried similar connotations. "Massa's in de Cold Ground," "My Old Kentucky Home," and "Old Black Joe," though each is different, all share the same kind of pathos. All combine the blackface mask with the tradition of home songs. All lend themselves to the patronage of a Stowe and the cynical attitude of a Bunn. "Old Folks" happens to have the strongest connections with the tradition, with Stowe herself, and with Bunn.

Martin Delany's *Blake* is a Black response to *Uncle Tom;* in Douglass' *Paper,* Delany criticized Stowe because she "knows nothing about us." An epigraph at the start of *Blake* is a hymn stanza by Stowe, "For the weak against the strong." The music in *Blake,* as we saw in relation to "Susanna," is more varied than that in *Uncle Tom.* Most distinctive of all the musical episodes is the one in which the hero listens to a song that resembles "Old Folks," sung by workers in the harbor at New Orleans. He hears them only at a distance, just after he has noted the great variety of songs hummed and chanted "along the private streets" of the city by individuals of both sexes and both races. To introduce the "Old Folks" song Delany writes two paragraphs of fascinating generalization:

> In the distance, on the levee or in the harbor among the steamers, the songs of the boatmen were incessant. Every few hours landing, loading and unloading, the glee of these men of sorrow was touchingly appropriate and impressive. Men of sorrow they are in reality; for if there be a class of men anywhere to be found, whose sentiments of song and words of lament are made to reach the sympathies of others, the black slave-boatmen of the Mississippi river is that class. Placed in positions the most favorable to witness the pleasures enjoyed by others, the tendency is only to augment their own wretchedness.
>
> Fastened by the unyielding links of the iron cable of despotism, reconciling themselves to a lifelong misery, they are seemingly contented by soothing their sorrows with songs and sentiments of apparently cheerful but in reality wailing lamentations. The most attracting lament of the evening was sung to words, a stanza of which is presented in pathos of delicate tenderness, which is but a spray from the stream which gushed out in insuppressible jets from the agitated fountains of their souls, as if in unison with the restless current of the great river upon which they were compelled to toil, their troubled waters could not be quieted. In the capacity of leader, as is their custom, one poor fellow in pitiful tones led off the song of the evening:

> Way down upon the Mobile river,
>   Close to Mobile bay;
> There's where my thoughts is running ever,
>   All through the livelong day:
> There I've a good and fond old mother,
>   Though she is a slave;
> There I've a sister and a brother,
>   Lying in their peaceful graves.

Then in chorus joined the whole company—

> O, could I somehow a'nother,
> Drive these tears way;
> When I think about my poor old mother,
> Down upon the Mobile bay.

Hearing this chorus, Delany's hero renews his resolution to proceed to Mobile with his message "of light and destruction":

> Light, of necessity, had to be imparted to the darkened region of the obscure intellects of the slaves, to arouse them from their benighted condition to one of moral responsibility, to make them sensible that liberty was legitimately and essentially theirs, without which there was no distinction between them and the brute. Following as a necessary consequence would be the destruction of oppression and ignorance.
>
> Alone and friendless, without a home, a fugitive from slavery, a child of misfortune and outcast upon the world, floating on the cold surface of chance, now in the midst of a great city of opulence . . .

the hero momentarily shares in the lament, only to redouble his determination to act. The author, ambivalent about such a "pathos of delicate tenderness" as that of "Old Folks," tries to rescue it from both the patronizing motherly sympathy of Stowe and the detached, theatrical, cynical attitude of Bunn.

For Delany and his hero, the chief value of any song is to unite a group in the struggle for its rights. Delany's elaborate description of the hero listening to the pitiful group of boatmen is exceptional. It is designed to win over readers remote from such a struggle, readers who may have found Foster's song vaguely "impressive" and may be persuaded to give not merely sympathy but some support to a heroic leader. The author implies that the group singing this song is more remote from the reader than is the hero; this group is too "benighted" to claim the hero's efforts—he sympathizes and moves on to more responsive groups who will never be "reconciled" to their wretchedness.

When Blake is aboard a river steamer, the songs he hears are the short, "harsh" chants of the firemen: "I'm Goin' to Texas" and "Natchez Under the Hill." When he hears Black seamen on the Atlantic, their songs are "merry" and defiant. When Blake himself sings, he stiffens his courage by a hymn, "Could I but Climb Where Moses Stood," or he encourages his fellow conspirators with a touching "Farewell, My Loving Friends," followed by "Insurrection Shall Be My Theme! My Watchword 'Freedom or the Grave.'" When other characters sing their parodies of "Susanna" and "Uncle Ned," there is no need for the apologetic description attached to "Old Folks."

When, on the contrary, a pitiable group of plantation slaves, in the first episode of the novel, "endeavored to ease their troubled souls by singing, 'Oh, When Shall My Sorrows Subside,'" Delany and his hero maintain a different kind of distance. These singers are too old and fearful to join Blake; rather they "Trus' to de Laud!" Blake is impatient: "Yes, the same old slave song—'Trust to the Lord.' Then I must go." As he leaves, they sing again trying to "soothe" their tears:

> See wives and husbands torn apart,
> Their children's screams, they grieve my heart,
>   They are torn away to Georgia!
> Come and go along with me—
>   They are torn away to Georgia!
> Go sound the Jubilee!

The whole scene, with its music, is like a revision of the first scenes of *Uncle Tom*. The hero's impatience with fatalistic religion and consoling music is Delany's too. Their exceptional sympathy with the distant boatmen's version of "Old Folks," with the "delicate tenderness" and hopeless loneliness, in the midst of all the novel's Black initiative and organized action, is all the more remarkable.

Did Delany in fact hear workers sing something like the song he cites? His modern editor, Floyd J. Miller, thinks "it is conceivable that Foster learned the song from Delany, or that both drew upon a common source." But Delany's placing of the song, his long commentary, and his footnotes about some of the other songs in the novel make this unlikely. If the faint possibility leads other investigators to further evidence, this would be welcome to friends of either Foster or Delany. But if further evidence should prove what is already probable—that Delany was borrowing from Foster—his unique commentary would be no less admirable than if he had independently learned from Black singers. The complex meaning he gives to "Old Folks" is more important than the question of its origins.

Some contemporary critics judged the origins of "Old Folks" to be more remote from any Black singers than "Jim Crow," and perhaps more remote than "Susanna" or "Uncle Ned"; these critics saw Foster's characteristic work as an adulteration of the minstrel tradition, which some of them wished to see restored while others wished it dead and buried. In *Putnam's* and in *Harper's* magazines, George William Curtis (1823–92) wrote frequently on music. He was a disciple of Emerson and J. S. Dwight; he had studied as a boy at Brook Farm and had contributed to the whole series of Transcendentalist journals. Now in 1853, addressing the wider and more heterogeneous audience of *Putnam's*, Curtis explained with assurance:

There is no people in the world so sentimental as we. Our only really popular songs are such negro melodies as those of Mr. Foster, ("Old folks at home," "Massa's in de cold ground," &c.) which are simply pathetic refrains adapted to what, in another sphere of literature, would be only extremely Laura-Matilda-ish poetry, mainly dirges and desperate love songs. The substance of the melody, which is very much the same thing in each of these songs, is purely Italian. . . .

Curtis developed his thought at greater length in *Harper's*:

It is remarkable that we, who are the most practical, are also the most sentimental people in the world. There is a kind of literature and art grown up among us, which is weak and unhealthy, and yet the most popular of all. . . . It is a favorite device of ordinary song-writers to harp much upon sickness and death; and the composer follows in the same strain by the most commonplace minor chords. The negro melodies are a ludicrous example of this peculiarity, to which the negro dialect only contributes. But we do not mean to deny the genuine pathos of the original negro-songs. They have a languid, tropical, wailing measure, which is very significant and characteristic. We condemn only the extravagant pursuit of the same effects through all gradations, until taste, offended by the base imitation, is almost willing to reject the original. Every lover of music will be a little jealous of his ear. He will feel alarmed if he feels himself pleased with inferior things. He will call himself to account if he prefers to hear König play *Old Folks at Home* upon his cornet, to hearing the entire orchestra perform a symphony. For he knows that a symphony is really best, and that he ought to like it.

The alliance that Curtis proposes, between the "genuine" songs of Blacks and the symphony, against the "base imitation" and "unhealthy" sentimentalism represented by Foster distinguishes this criticism from the attitude of Dwight or that of Douglass. Curtis recognizes the gentleness of Foster as a temptation to his readers. By claiming to prefer the rougher "original negro-songs" he aims to bring readers around to Beethoven.

In the *New York Musical Review*, 1854, an anonymous critic attempted the first survey of the history of the minstrel tradition in an "Obituary, Not Eulogistic: Negro Minstrelsy is Dead." He began even earlier than *Jim Crow* and came down through the career of Christy. In Christy's recent successes he recognized a *"bleaching process"* illustrated by "Old Folks at Home," "My Old Kentucky Home," and "Hazel Dell." This music, he thinks, "is Italian, German, English, or American. The mere fact that they continue to blacken their faces alters not its character." He concludes, personifying Minstrelsy:

> Let his winding sheet be the unsold copies of Uncle Ned, and let there be buried with him, as the emblems of his departed power, the Banjo and the Bones.

This article was reprinted in 1858 by Dwight. It was cited by many later writers on the subject, most of whom knew nothing of Elizabeth Greenfield or Martin Delany; though surely they knew something of Uncle Tom, they preferred to ignore any connection between Tom and Christy.

An anonymous writer in the New York Tribune, 1855, undertook a more sympathetic and hopeful survey, entitled "The Black Opera." His history goes back to English models. Before affirming that "minstrelsy has become a permanent institution" he pauses to approve such songs as "Uncle Ned":

> The homeliness, the truthfulness of these compositions established their popularity. There was nothing facetious in them; they filled a void in public amusement . . . their naturalness appealed to the sympathy of the multitude. Particularly was this the case with the younger portion of our population, most of whom have grown up to be men and women since then. . . .

This point is a new one. The history of the songs themselves must be related to the history of their reception by successive generations.

> Who has not often observed the tear of sensibility moistening the cheek of youth, while listening to the primitive strains of "Uncle Ned"? . . . Ah, those tears constituted one of the blessings of that youth, which has now departed. Sorrow and disappointment have doubtless weighed heavily upon many a heart since that spring of life passed away.

The writer connects the aging listeners with a supposed change in the "true originators of this music—the negroes":

> The gay laugh and cheerful song are not heard with former frequency. . . . The old, unmeaning songs of the plantation have fallen into disuse, and if they sing now there is memory in their songs. Plaintive and slow, the sad soul of the slave throws into his music all that gushing anguish of spirit which he dare not otherwise express. And yet the careless reviewer of events, observing not the causes or consequences, mourns what he terms the decadence of national negro minstrelsy!

The author is responding to the premature "obituary." He admits that there is "some truth in the assertion that the music has deteriorated." He condemns "sickly sentimentality" and "Miss Nancyism of vulgarity," but he cites no example. He mentions Foster as one of the four "most successful writers of Negro Songs," and he ends with a recommendation that he perhaps wishes Foster in particular to heed:

> Instead of adapting trashy words to some defunct Scotch or German melody, let the aspirants after this species of lyric fame mingle with its originators and draw inspiration from a tour through the South and West. There is plenty of material to work upon.

This article too was reprinted by Dwight in 1858, in the issue just preceding the "obituary."

Two more critical articles, though they fail to mention Foster, discuss the "plantation songs" in broad perspective. A writer for *Putnam's,* Y. S. Nathanson, in 1855, surveys "Negro Minstrelsy, Ancient and Modern." He compares the now "ancient" "Jim Crow" with the Scotch ballads. He finds a classic peak in "Ole Dan Tucker" that "reminds us of some of Donizetti's happiest efforts, while its simplicity and quaintness at times breathe of Auber." He deplores the later "glaring marks of barefaced and impudent imposition." He asserts that "a true Southern melody is seldom sentimental, and never melancholy," while in the debased "modern" products, "melancholy reminiscences of negroic childhood fill the places once allotted to the grand old ballads of former days." Nathanson disagrees with both the "obituary" and the "permanent institution." All three writers try to apply similar criteria of historical judgment, though which particular songs they like depends on more elusive affinities. Vague, shared attitudes toward social change may be more important, after all, than particular songs in determining what a song means to any one listener. A modern critic of Nathanson, Alan W. C. Green, has observed that Nathanson's preference for the "ancient" comic songs expresses the same yearning as the melancholy songs about childhood express.

"Songs of the Blacks" was an anonymous contribution to the New York *Evangelist* in 1856, reprinted immediately by Dwight. The author has listened a little to slaves singing at work and at worship. He reports almost no concrete detail, but he expresses admiration to the point of envy:

> The only musical population of this country are the negroes of the South. Besides their splendid organs of voice, the African nature is full of poetry. Inferior to the white race in reason and intellect, they have more imagination, more lively feelings, and a more expressive manner. In this they resemble the Southern nations of Europe.
>
> Americans, though surrounded with everything to make a people happy, do not show outward signs of uncommon cheerfulness and content. We are an anxious, careworn race. . . .

The author claims to have heard Blacks "sing their humble loves in strains full of tenderness," but his next sentence arouses the suspicion that he is only imagining a Black origin for a "dulcem" melody of Foster:

> We at the North hear these songs only as burlesqued by our Negro Minstrels, with faces blackened with charcoal. Yet even thus all feel that they have rare sweetness and melody.
>
> Mixed with these love songs are plaintive airs which seem to have caught a tone of sadness and pathos from the hardships and frequent separation of their slave life.
>
> . . . But it is in religion that the African pours out his whole voice and soul.

The one song cited, from a camp meeting, is "When I Can Read My Title Clear To Mansions in the Skies." The whole report may owe as much to *Uncle Tom* and "Old Folks" as to actual experience. It is valuable as testimony to a spreading vague sympathy.

None of these critics view "Old Folks" in a perspective that includes "Jeanie" and "Old Dog Tray." Though they try to write history, their unspoken motive is some concern about Blacks and slavery in the middle 1850s; this concern naturally overrides their concern for facts about Foster, for levels of craftsmanship, and for traditions intermediary between the minstrels and Italian opera or German symphony. Such narrow histories are further material for a broader history, not foundations for it.

Foster himself, in 1853, looked back at his "plantation songs" and gave new musical interpretations of several, including "Old Folks." His collection of instrumental solos, duets, trios, and quartets, *The Social Orchestra,* has an "Old Folks Quadrille," for quartet, a pair of variations on "Old Folks" appropriate for solo fiddle, and another pair, with the title "Anadolia," for flute. The quadrille is divided into five numbers:

"Old Folks at Home"
"Oh! Boys, Carry Me 'Long"
"Nelly Bly"
"Farewell My Lilly Dear"
"Plantation Jig."

The combination is surprising, for the dancers want no change of tempo in the set, whereas the words of the four songs suggest some contrasts of mood. But the surprise is mild: the three "pathetic" songs need only the slightest modification to fit the jigging dance. The one older song, "Nelly Bly," stands out in the group as both a natural lively dance and a driving melody; it makes "Old Folks" and "Oh! Boys" seem almost like introduction. "Nelly Bly" and "Nelly Was a Lady" (as a solo) are the only Foster songs earlier than "Oh,

Boys" in the collection—"Susanna" and "Uncle Ned," which would have made more effective publicity, are missing. The more recent songs, "Massa's in de Cold Ground" and "My Old Kentucky Home," are included as a simple duet and solo, respectively; "Old Dog Tray" is another solo, and there are five less known pieces of Foster mixed in with the "gems" and fragments from Donizetti, Beethoven, Schubert, Strauss, and others. But the most remarkable things are the "Old Folks" variations. The first set keeps the contour of the melody while it changes details so as to fit new rhythms—a rollicking 6/8 jig, then a jerky quick march with dotted sixteenths and thirty-seconds. All trace of "melancholy" is gone. There is nothing "weary" or "dreary" in these variations. The tune is brought closer to the vigorous spirit of "Nelly Bly" than in the quadrille.

"Anadolia" is both farther from the original "Old Folks" and closer to it. The name, a variant of "Anatolia," perhaps means something like "arabesque." The sinuous melody expands beyond the vocal range to two octaves plus a fourth; listeners not looking for a reference to "Old Folks" may never suspect one, though once alerted to the connection, they need no esoteric powers of analysis to find it. The tempo is marked *Andante cantabile*. There is no change of mood for the second variation—only a further elaboration of melody. The performer needs to accent the slow beats, because his irregular melodic motion obscures them—the melody is full of turns and swooping decorations, like an Andante of Mozart or Donizetti in which some dramatic pathos is isolated, sustained, and exalted. Such an exaltation of "Old Folks" (though he does not mention "Old Folks" here) Foster places at the end of the group of solos. Whereas the earlier variations he attributes to Christy, his own name is signed to "Anadolia."

All these instrumental interpretations suggest a weariness with the troublesome meanings of words—a longing to communicate through music alone. Perhaps with the *Social Orchestra* back in print since 1973, part of the series of *Earlier American Music* edited by H. Wiley Hitchcock, such a longing may occasionally be fulfilled. But after 1853 Foster never renewed the effort to write instrumental music.

The "Old Folks" fiddle variations and "Anadolia" together can represent Foster's whole work as he himself intended it to sound. The fiddle variations bring the "Old Folks" tune close to "Susanna" and "Nelly Bly"; "Anadolia" brings the same tune close to "Jeanie." The solo fiddle means dancing, young and old together, in a village hall or a country barn. The flute means a solitary dreamer, aware of dances, genteel parlors, concerts, and operas, but withdrawn from them preferring to roam the meadows and dabble in the brooks.

Foster's variations on his most famous tune pull it away from the national and international agonies with which *Uncle Tom* and *Blake* connect it; the variations cannot clarify the public meanings that trouble us and motivate our study. But the variations can bring us as close as we are likely to come to sharing Foster's own feelings and to understanding his character and work.

The connections of "Old Folks" with *Uncle Tom*, with Elizabeth Greenfield, with Delany's *Blake*, and with critics like Curtis, all contemporary with Foster's own development down to "Old Black Joe," "The Little Ballad Girl," "Beautiful Dreamer," and "Voices That Are Gone," help us more than the variations to follow the posthumous development of Foster's reputation and eventually to exchange with each other our own still various interpretations of "Old Folks."

{{ CHAPTER 11 }}

"People's song" writers following Foster

THE famous songs of Foster became models of the "people's song" as defined and cultivated by the prolific, prosperous, versatile musician George Frederick Root (1820–95). Foster's songs contributed to enlivening Root's broad tradition in the 1850s and then, for over a century, they kept a leading place in the repertory of that tradition alongside a few songs by Root and several by two of his protégés—Henry Clay Work and Philip Paul Bliss—who owed more to Foster than did Root himself.

Root's tradition is broader than "home song," "war song," "gospel song," "school music," or any other label by which later commentators identify him. His own label fits better. While his fading fame as author-composer of "Tramp, Tramp, Tramp, the Boys Are Marching" (1864) and as composer of the hymn tune "The Shining Shore" (1855) to words by David Nelson (1793–1844) would not alone warrant much attention to Foster's influence on him; yet Root's happy career and his sensible reflections on it, *The Story of a Musical Life* (1891), enable us to trace clearly several strands of continuous development in American and British music that affect the meaning of Foster's work. The broad tradition that Root represents, if its several strands can be grasped together, will provide a perspective relevant to our concerns with the Jubilee Singers, with Ives, with jazz, and with 20th-century "country music"—in short, with all the later developments affecting "Old Folks." Root had good reason to believe that he represented the musical interests of a majority of English-speaking people in his time. If no such majority interest can be identified in later generations, still Root's tradition continues to affect many minority interests.

Root grew up on a farm at North Reading, Massachusetts. Together with most members of his big family he sang in the village choir. At first their repertory was mainly that of native American composers like William Billings (1746–1800), but Root's parents had paid tribute to a higher foreign standard when they named their first son George Frederick, for Handel. They were gradually won over to the new repertory, predominantly German, that was arranged and promulgated most vigorously by Lowell Mason (1792–1872). Root recalled how he and his fellows clung to the old "fuging tunes" and the "fa-so-la" solmization until the smooth grandeur of Mason's music convinced them of the value of the "scientific" system of learning with seven syllables. Probably Root learned, for example, the several versions of "Antioch," Mason's tune derived from Handel for the hymn-text by Isaac Watts, "Joy to the World," as these versions appeared in Mason's successive hymnbooks from 1827 to 1839. The boy played the flute well and dabbled with other instruments, such as the bass viol that was the usual accompanying support for village choirs. He seldom saw a piano or organ until at eighteen (1838) he went to Boston as apprentice to a young disciple of Mason's, Artemus Nixon Johnson. Root learned so swiftly that Johnson soon put him to work as assistant teacher. He joined Mason's choir. He observed the classes that Mason was beginning to organize in the public schools. He studied singing with George James Webb (1803–87), the English organist and composer who had settled in Boston in 1830 and collaborated with Mason. In less than five years Mason and Webb adopted Root as their chief assistant, to help in their expanding "conventions" of teachers. In 1844, sponsored by the author and philanthropist Jacob Abbott, Root went to New York as apostle of the convention movement. In 1851 Abbott enabled him to spend a year studying language and singing in Paris; on his way home he stopped in London and heard *Messiah* and *Elijah* there. In 1853 Root brought Mason to New York for the summer institute that he founded, to teach alongside Mason's old collaborator (and rival) in editing hymnbooks, Thomas Hastings (1784–1872), and Mason's most distinguished pupil, the Baptist choir leader William B. Bradbury (1816–68), whose Sunday school choruses and cantatas were winning the praise of Walt Whitman. In 1856 Root took his summer institute back to North Reading, where he had built a fine house and had persuaded the town meeting to lend him support: he pointed out that the hundreds of singers and choir leaders from various states "would mean to the town some money." Root was now the peer of his former teachers, Mason and Webb, who joined him and Bradbury again at North Reading. It was Root more than any other who had made the movement nationwide.

In 1859 Root moved his national headquarters to Chicago, where he was a partner in the publishing firm that his brother, E. T. Root, and their friend C. M. Cady had organized the year before. He continued to lead conventions of teachers and summer institutes in cities throughout the country, but he was able to devote most of his time to composing and editing, freed from daily teaching by his prosperity. In the summer of 1860 Mason and Bradbury followed him to Chicago. In 1862 the seventy-year-old Mason joined him for the last time, at Wooster, Ohio. When Bradbury died in 1868, Root was the dean of active leaders in the movement. Among his younger associates was Mason's son William, concert pianist and teacher of piano preëminent among 19th-century Americans. Root's son Frederick Woodman Root (1846–1916) was one of William Mason's best pupils, an organist, composer of respected anthems and cantatas, writer of textbooks, and upholder of his father's institutions. In 1876 the Roots helped to establish the permanent Music Teachers' National Association.

George Root was proud that he had instigated the award of the first American doctorate of music, to Lowell Mason from New York University in 1853. Root's own doctoral degree, from Chicago in 1872, he spoke of modestly, regretting that he could never have passed the examinations for an English degree.

Root was modest too about his many compositions. He never felt "called" to composing and never had any instruction in music theory beyond the rudiments that were part of the choral tradition. He could improvise phrases of melody; he found this ability useful "before classes that could be kept in order only by prompt and rapid movements." When Bradbury and others encouraged him to try contributing to the collections they edited, Root was happy to find that he could answer the needs of the day, that his acquaintance with a broad variety of music enabled him to write in a simple style with ease and assurance. He wrote first, in 1851, choruses for a school play, *The Flower Queen*, with words by his pupil at the school for the blind, Fanny Crosby (1820–1915), who had just published her second volume of poetry. This was the first of about thirty cantatas by Root, all of which were performed by choirs throughout the United States, and many of which enjoyed even more success in England. Though no cantata by Root was so often performed as Bradbury's *Esther*, 1858, and none became permanent parts of a repertory, all were profitable and influential commodities. Root forebore to emulate the masters he most revered—Handel and Mendelssohn—not to mention the composer he recognized as the greatest contemporary genius—Wagner. In his modest, practical way, he surpassed dozens of his rivals who tried to come closer to *Messiah* and *Elijah*, or *Tannhäuser.*

As soon as he started to compose, Root was attracted in another direction: to compete with Foster. This attraction he kept secret at first, for he was not yet emancipated from the prejudice against theatrical life; he was not ready to take a stand about slavery, and he had only slight contact with the tradition of home songs. But he remembered thrilling concerts by John Braham and, especially, Henry Russell at Boston in 1839; more recently in New York he had heard all of Jenny Lind's performances (characteristically he bought enough tickets to resell them at prices that covered the cost of his own) and he knew how Lind enhanced the meaning of a Swedish lullaby or "Home, Sweet Home." So he adopted a pseudonym, Wurzel, and published two tunes, both with the words "The Old Folks Are Gone." The second tune was sung by Christy, but not often. Root resolved to try again, with help on the words from Fanny Crosby. In her *Memories*, 1906, Crosby printed her first contribution to Root's work, evidently an elaboration of his suggestion:

> Fare thee well, Kitty dear,
> Thou art sleeping in thy grave so low,
> Nevermore, Kitty dear,
> Wilt thou listen to my old banjo.

The collaborators still fell short of their generalized Foster model. But soon they succeeded, at least in terms of the market. "Hazel Dell," composed 1852, published 1853, was the first Wurzel hit. (Root's autobiography fails to credit Crosby with the words, but her *Memories* reclaim them.) The singer is grieving by the grave of his Nelly dear, in the hazel dell; he insists he is "all alone . . . friendless and forsaken," despite the four-part chorus that reinforces his refrain. His melody seems cramped in its octave range; it strikes its highest and lowest notes in every phrase, and treats most of the notes between them as mere decorations of the central keynote. A syncopated accent on "Nelly" seems an arbitrary deviation from the plodding rhythm, compared with the accent in Foster's "Lily Ray" (1850), which fits more smoothly into its melodic curve. In short, Root's song is a hasty and mechanical imitation of Foster's style. But for a few years "Hazel Dell" found many more singers than "Lily Ray" or most of Foster's efforts. Root's profits, though not so great as those of the hymnbooks of Mason and Bradbury, were enough to pay for his new house at North Reading.

Root's imitations of "Old Folks" set him apart from one older representative of Mason's tradition, Thomas Hastings, who wrote a long letter of protest about the adaptation of "Old Folks" itself to a Sunday-school text, in May 1853. Hastings told readers of the *Musical Review:*

> . . . A superintendent gave the music into the hands of a lady who had charge of about a hundred infant scholars. She saw the trick and remonstrated. "But," says the superintendent, "the children will never know it!" "Come and see," was her reply. She sang a line or two, and then said, "Children, have you ever heard anything like that before?" "Old folks at home! Old folks at home!" shouted the little urchins with such merry glances and gesticulations as showed them upon the very point of "Cutting up," when the experiment ended and the piece was abandoned. . . .
>
> It is an old trick, which many seem determined to "play off" every time they have an opportunity. No matter what is said against it; any thing will do for children: merry dances, street ballads, bacchanalian songs, and negro melodies, often tricked with parodies which, by a double power of association, bring wicked and irreverent thoughts to mind! . . . Christy has more melodies: and then "Yankee Doodle," "Frog and Mouse," and "Jim Crow," I believe, have not yet been appropriated.

Hastings could not stop the trend he deplored. Sunday-school repertories might discard the particular adaptation that roused Hastings to his attack, but they would also discard most of the thousand sober hymns of Hastings, which had had their day. His tune of 1831 for the words by Augustus M. Toplady (1740–78), "Rock of Ages," was an outstanding exception, carried on through the hymnbooks of most Protestant denominations into the 20th century. Root knew that Hastings was jealous, not only of adaptations, but also of the successes of Bradbury and even Mason himself. Probably Root knew that Mason was compromising with Root's own current trend to the extent of adapting the old tune for Tom Moore's "Oft in the Stilly Night" to words by Sarah Flower Adams, "Nearer, My God, to Thee," which Mason published with the title "Bethany" in 1859, and which was to keep its place along with some thirty of Mason's productions in the lasting repertory. Root was undoubtedly familiar with Bradbury's wide range of interests, as illustrated in his collection of 1850, *The Alpine Glee Singer,* in which he included his own setting of a rollicking ballad by Asahel Abbott, "The California Goldhunter," and a characteristic sweet tune for words of his own, "Think Gently of the Erring." Probably Root was a close observer of Bradbury's development, which led from the mournful hymn "Woodworth," 1849, (later combined with the words "Just As I Am, Without One Plea") to lively Sunday-school songs such as "Sweet Story of Old," 1859, "Savior, Like a Shepherd Lead Us," 1859, "Sweet Hour of Prayer," 1860, and "He Leadeth Me," 1864—these were Bradbury's most lasting works. Possibly Root not only observed but affected Bradbury's development, for beginning in 1864 Bradbury called on Fanny Crosby for hymn texts. At any rate, Hastings' strictures could not deter Root from his experiments.

In the next few years Root published nearly a hundred songs, about half of them with words by Fanny Crosby: typical titles were "Glad to Get Home," "Home Again Returning," "Dearest Spot of Earth to Me Is Home," "Home's Sweet Harmony," "Flying Home," "We Can Make Home Happy," "We Are Going Away from the Old Home," "My Cottage Home, Dear Mother," "Old Friends and True Friends," "Kind Friends, One and All," "Never Forget the Dear Ones," "Annie Lowe," "Jenny Lyle," "If Maggie Were My Own," "Dreaming, Ever Dreaming," "I Dreamt an Angel Came," and "Pictures of Memory." The most elaborate of these, like "Pictures," were the least popular. The most successful after "Hazel Dell" was "Rosalie, the Prairie Flower," 1855. The tune of "Rosalie" is livelier than that of "Hazel Dell," with a swinging dotted rhythm and a range of a tenth, so that the high note can be saved for just one appearance, in the first phrase of the chorus, where the rhythm is relaxed. The whole little form is exactly the same as that of "Hazel Dell"—a a' a a' b a' (it is the same as that of Foster's "Susanna" and "Old Folks" but not "Jeanie" or "Old Black Joe"). The words are sometimes crowded to fit the melody. They present Rosalie as "a lovely child . . . like a cherub" with "the wavy ringlets of her flaxen hair, Waving in the summer air," and surrounded by a grateful chorus for the first two stanzas:

> Fair as a lily, joyous and free,
> Light of that prairie home was she.
> Ev'ry one who knew her felt the gentle pow'r
> of Rosalie the prairie flower.

But she is doomed. The third stanza tells how "angels whispered . . . And they gently bore her, robed in spotless white, To their blissful home of light," so that new words are needed for the last chorus:

> Tho' we shall never look on her more,
> Gone with the love and joy she bore,
> Far away she's blooming in a fadeless bower,
> sweet Rosalie the prairie flower.

Root's treatment of themes dear to Foster is subtly different: Root's trust in the "blissful home" of the angels is complacent, while Foster's is only hopeful; Root's singer is not grieving, not self-conscious, not much involved; Root's matching of words and music is glib, compared with Foster's more careful use of almost identical words and phrases. But "Rosalie" earned nearly $3000 in royalties.

And "Rosalie" must have gratified Harriet Beecher Stowe, who paid a visit with her father, Lyman, and her brother, Henry Ward Beecher, to Root's institute at North Reading, just about the time "Rosalie" was composed.

The war inspired Root to original words, more closely fitting his most vigorous melodies. He dropped the pseudonym "Wurzel" and published songs under his own name, beginning at once in 1861 with "The First Gun Is Fired, May God Protect the Right," and continuing through 1864 with about thirty more. Among them three were widely used and long remembered: "The Battle-Cry of Freedom," "Just Before the Battle, Mother," and "Tramp, Tramp, Tramp." These are all very similar to "Rosalie" in rhythm, range, and form, though "Just Before the Battle" has its contrasting "b" phrase within the stanza, then again at the beginning of the chorus. "Tramp, Tramp, Tramp" excels the others because of its dramatic situation: the singer is a prisoner, encouraging his fellow prisoners to count on rescue:

> In the prison cell I sit
> Thinking, Mother dear, of you,
>   And our bright and happy home so far away,
> And the tears they fill my eyes
> Spite of all that I can do,
>   Tho' I try to cheer my comrades and be gay.
> Tramp, tramp, tramp, the boys are marching,
> Cheer up, comrades, they will come,
> And beneath the starry flag
> We shall breathe the air again
>   Of the free-land in our own beloved home.

Home and mother and tears, subordinated to the marching confidence in righteousness and victory, made this song easily win out over its competitors, including all of Foster's songs on the war. But clearly Root owes much to Foster in the very song that surpasses him.

When Foster died, Root wrote a tribute to him, in a letter to Clark's *School Visitor:* "He was the greatest melodist that America has produced." This was a rare judgment in 1864. By 1879, when George Birdseye wrote a series of articles on "America's Song Composers" for *Potter's American Monthly,* it was natural to devote the first article to Foster and the next to Root, as current leader among the "legitimate successors to the 'Song Writer of America' in the hearts of the people."

In Root's autobiography he referred often to Foster as a model and he explained his own development in relation to Foster:

I saw at once that mine must be the "people's song," still, I am ashamed to say, I shared the feeling that was around me in regard to that grade of music. When Stephen C. Foster's wonderful melodies (as I now see them) began to appear, and the famous Christy's Minstrels began to make them known, I "took a hand in" . . . It was not until I imbibed more of Dr. Mason's spirit, and went more among the people of the country, that I saw these things in a truer light, and respected myself, and was thankful when I could write something that all the people would sing.

. . . In all grades from the simplest to the highest—from Stephen C. Foster to Wagner, and in every kind of instrumental music, compositions divide themselves into two classes in another way. In one class are the comparatively few compositions having that mysterious vitality of which I have spoken; that power to retain their hold upon the hearts of the people after their companions of the same grade, and by the same composer perhaps, are forgotten. In the other class are those which create a temporary interest if any, and soon pass away. I do not think a composer ever knows when that mysterious life enters his work. If I may judge from my own experience, successes are usually surprises, and the work that we think best while we are doing it, is liable to be considered in very different light by the public.

Root implies that "Old Folks" and several other songs of Foster (as well as "Tramp, Tramp, Tramp" and possibly a few others of his own) have the "mysterious vitality" that may have "entered" them after they gathered connotations from the people who sang them.

Root defends simple music like Foster's and his own against the perennial complaints of musicians like Hastings who seek to elevate public taste. He counterattacks

. . . the absurdity of saying that simple music keeps the tastes and musical culture of the people down. You might as well say that a person is kept in addition, subtraction, multiplication and division by having around him more examples in elementary arithmetic than he needs. If he is interested in the subject, he'll go on after he has mastered the simpler to that which is more difficult. . . . If he is not interested, or is more occupied with other things, he may never go beyond those elementary mathematics which are needed for the common duties of life; but since he can not get higher *without going through them*, it is useless to put that which is higher before him *until they are mastered*. . . .

Those not in music, or not so musical naturally, do not get through the elementary state so soon [as Root himself, at nineteen, advanced from Henry Russell to the songs of Schubert]; in fact, many business and professional people, giving very little time or thought to the subject, never get through; they prefer the simpler music to the end of their days. . . . It is an axiom that emotional or aesthetic benefit by music can come to a person only through music that he likes. By that alone can he grow musically. . . . Since, therefore, there are always so many grown-up men and women, learned and strong in other things, who are still in elementary musical states, I keep, ready for use, the simple songs that helped me, and am always glad to sing them where they will do any good.

On this principle, Root's pupils who became supervisors of music in the public schools made use of the Foster songs that they had learned with delight in their childhood. And a modern student of "George Frederick Root, pioneer music educator," Mazie Corder, in 1972, praises his skill in establishing a repertory that is "realistic" in meeting the carefully classified needs of many teachers and pupils.

Did Root ever look at the bulk of Foster's work? Was he aware that Foster wrote some original music for the Sunday Schools? Did he ponder what little he could know of Foster's life and its frustrations? Probably not. Root's own life was too busy and successful. It is ironic that he won the very kind of reward and respect that Foster missed during his life.

Root and Foster were linked once more when singers of Hampton Institute, sometime before 1909, used the first phrase of "Susanna" and the first phrase of the chorus of "Tramp, Tramp, Tramp" to make a new Christmas song, "Go, Tell It on the Mountain." Root's phrase was likely to live longer in this form than anything else of his whole work.

Root recognized and respected the earnest craftsmanship of Henry Clay Work, whose life was mostly more obscure and more desperate than Foster's, though longer. Work was the son of a Connecticut abolitionist who had migrated to Illinois. The boy became a printer. He wrote his poetry and his tunes, apparently with even less instruction or experience as a performer than Foster. (He told George Birdseye that he had "no voice for singing.") In 1853, when he was twenty-one, his song "We Are Coming, Sister Mary" was performed by Christy, but it was soon forgotten. In the next year Work moved to Chicago. Here, until Root began to help him, he completed only half a dozen songs. At the same time he was inventing a knitting machine, a walking doll, and other devices. But when, in 1862, he brought "Kingdom Coming" to Root's office, Root was so enthusiastic that he advised Work to write more about the war and give up the printing business. In the next three years Work produced nearly thirty songs, of which at least four about the war became very popular: "Grafted into the Army," "Wake, Nicodemus" (with the chorus, "The 'good time coming' is almost here!"), "Marching Through Georgia," and "Babylon Is Fallen"; one more song, "Come Home, Father," took a place in the dramatization of *Ten Nights in a Bar-Room*, and was widely hailed as the greatest of all "temperance songs." Root testified that these songs of Work were composed very differently from his own:

> Mr. Work was a slow, pains-taking writer, being from one to three weeks upon a song; but when the work was done it was like a piece of fine mosaic, especially in the fitting of words to music.

Though Root took credit for giving Work "some musical help," he could see that Work's results owed more to patient effort. While Work's marching rhythms are close to Root's, his simple diction, colloquial grammar, detailed accents, and even intonations are closer to Foster's. "Marching Through Georgia" illustrates these similarities, though the triumphant partisan fervor that motivates Work's song is different from the more conciliatory loyalty of either Root or Foster:

> Bring the good old bugle, boys! we'll sing another song,
> Sing it with a spirit that will start the world along,
> Sing it as we used to sing it, fifty thousand strong,
>   While we were marching through Georgia.
> CHORUS: "Hurrah! hurrah! we bring the Jubilee!
>   Hurrah! hurrah! the flag that makes you free!"
> So we sang the chorus from Atlanta to the sea,
>   While we were marching through Georgia.
>
> How the darkeys shouted when they heard the joyful sound! . . .
> Treason fled before us, for resistance was in vain . . .

The syncopated accent of the final phrase fits perfectly with "fifty," "Atlanta," "resistance," and the corresponding word in every other stanza. The long high notes for "Hurrah" make a perfect climax in the rather complex but tightly coherent form: a, b, c, d, e, e', c, d. "Marching Through Georgia" kept Work's name alive longer than his other songs, though often it is merely mentioned alongside Root's "Tramp, Tramp, Tramp" and the anonymous "John Brown's Body," to whose tune Julia Ward Howe wrote "The Battle Hymn of the Republic." The distinctive quality of "Marching Through Georgia," typical of Work's whole character, might yet spur someone to learn more about him.

After the war, Work was not able to sustain his success. In 1866 his wife went insane, leaving him to care for a three-year-old daughter. In the rest of his life he composed only intermittently. His one later success was "Grandfather's Clock," 1876, which he gave to the Black minstrel singer Sam Lucas for first performance. He used some of the record-breaking $4000 this brought him to publish "The Upshot Family: A Serio-Comic Poem," 1878, which had no success at all. Did Root wonder what had become of him? Did Root or Work himself compare his fate with Foster's?

The fact is that Root and Work had a public disagreement on an issue that was beyond Foster's concerns, though it is not beyond our concern for Foster's songs. In 1863, from April through October, Work edited the new monthly journal published by Root and Cady, *The Song Messenger*. In the July issue Work criticized the editors of hymn books for altering the old tunes they included. In August Root overruled the criticism; he defended such "improvements" as he himself customarily made:

> I am sorry for the temporary inconvenience these changes cost, but I must put forth my work to the world as well as I can make it, and not entail upon the younger singers the faults and false tastes of their fathers. . . . [Cannot] the tunes of past time be improved in the light and greater knowledge of this age with its new and improved circumstances?

Work renewed his attack in September:

> . . . Now I am not opposing improvements in music. I believe in all kinds of real improvement . . . [But] it is a false notion that *everything* should be put through the mill of improvement. The people don't want the portraits of their fathers improved.

In November Work was no longer editor, for the boss, Mr. Root, had no sympathy with the "fa-so-la" singers who lingered in the villages of the West. His enterprise would soon confine the last of their tradition to the Southern hills, where they would survive to be discovered by 20th-century folklorists. Work, on the contrary, though younger than Root, never joined this uplifting educational enterprise. Though he wrote no religious songs of his own, he respected "the old tunes which are treasured up almost entirely by sincere worshipers." This respect fits with Work's painstaking procedure in composition. His obstinate opposition to Root on this point may account, more than his slow production or his personal troubles, for the frustration of his career. In any case, the disagreement between the two helps us define Root's broad tradition—a music for the supposed majority of Americans and a significant minority of people in other nations, but not for all Americans by any means.

There was a sizable minority audience for concerts in which "Old Folks at Home" was associated with hymns of Billings and other archaic New Englanders. These were the "Old Folks Concerts" of "Father" Robert Kemp and his troupe, which began to tour in 1856 and flourished through the 1880s. In Kemp's *Old Folks Concert Music: A Collection of the Most Favorite . . . Revised and Enlarged Edition*, 1889, the repertory is eclectic, extending from "Old Hundred" to the "Anvil Chorus" and comic songs *about* old Yankees by H. S. Thompson and M. S. Pike. If the program sometimes included Work's "Grandfather's Clock," there would be no greater incon-

gruity. "Auld Lang Syne" is retitled "The Song of the Old Folks."
Like most of the repertory, "Old Folks at Home" is presented in an
arrangement for four-part chorus. Its generally vague nostalgia made
it fit this context as well as it fitted Root's schoolbooks. Work's respect for the "sincere worshipers" who "treasured" the tunes of
Billings must have drawn his critical attention to the "Old Folks
Concerts," but no comment of his is known.

Philip Paul Bliss began to compose in 1864, when he was twenty-
six, a part-time singing-school teacher and still a farm laborer. He
sent his first composition to William Bradbury, who had led a
musical convention seven years before at Rome, Pennsylvania, the
first of many such meetings that Bliss attended. When Bradbury
rejected the offering, Bliss sent it to Root & Cady; Root recalled
that the covering letter was "entirely out of the run of literary or
musical aspirants" and that it proposed payment with a flute. "The
song needed some revising, but we took it and sent him the flute."
The song, "Lora Vale," according to Bliss' friend and biographer
D. W. Whittle, "enjoyed a sale of several thousands." "Lora Vale"
might be a parody of Foster's recent "Cora Dean" or Root's older
"Hazel Dell"—"Now she dwells, our darling Lora, In the home of
angels bright." Root and Bliss corresponded further. Soon the
younger man signed himself "Your Poor Pupil Bliss." In 1865 he
was drafted and served two weeks in the army. Then he went to
Chicago. For the next ten years he was a traveling singer, conductor, and representative of Root's publications at conventions in
towns from Ohio to Minnesota. He was so big, handsome, forthright, modest, witty, and constantly cheerful that he had no need
of much musical skill. He became more and more impressive as a
solo singer; his performances of the title part in Mendelssohn's
Elijah were memorable; but he preferred to lead the singing of big
groups in simple songs, and to write comic verses. At the same time
he was increasingly active as choir leader in church, Sunday School,
and the new institution for which Chicago was becoming world
capital—the Young Men's Christian Association. In 1874 he gave
up all his convention work to devote himself completely to revivals
of religion. In 1876, when he was planning a first trip to England,
he was killed in a railroad wreck.

In his ten-year career Bliss wrote words and music for more than
a hundred songs, and either words or music for several more. (There
is no complete list.) Many appeared in the collections edited by
Root in 1869 and 1870, while others were published separately. From
1871 to 1874 Bliss edited his own collections, the last of which was
Gospel Songs. In 1875 and 1876 he collaborated with Ira D. Sankey
(1840–1908) in editing the Gospel Hymns and Sacred Songs that by
the end of the century were to sell fifty million copies. Among the

most popular works in these collections were Bliss' "Hold the Fort,"
"Almost Persuaded," "I Am So Glad That Jesus Loves Me," "Dare
to Be a Daniel!," "Let the Lower Lights Be Burning," and "Wonderful Words of Life"; these and others continued to appear in many
later hymnbooks. Students of "gospel song" recognize Bliss' unique
achievement in providing both words and music for so many lasting
songs in so few years. But his earlier comic songs, never widely
known, have not interested his admirers. Thus, even though commentators have noted some resemblance between Bliss' and Foster's
rhythms, forms, and textures, there are still questions of just how
closely similar to Foster which of Bliss' works may be and of how
his work developed. Only a few clues are so far accessible.

One clue is a reference to "Old Dog Tray" in a facetious poem by
Bliss, one of several texts in which he calls himself "Pro Phundo
Basso." This one, printed in the *Song Messenger*, 1870, is "His
Courtshippe":

> 'Twas on a sunfull morning,
>> All in ye month of May
> When all ye birds and lambkins
>> Did skippe and eke did playe;
> A songful youth did saunter . . .
> His tuneful voice lamenting
>> Of "faithful ole dogg Traye,"
> Whose gentle, kinde attentions
>> Nor age nor grieffe could swaye. . . .

Foster's "Tray" and doubtless several more of his songs were for
Bliss what "Auld Lang Syne" and "Annie Laurie" had been for
Foster. When Bliss first attended the country singing schools, he
could refer to "Tray" as a standard of judgment and a symbol of his
poor honest family and small tight community. He did not accept
uncritically all the music he encountered at the conventions. Likewise, later, he did not wholly depend on Root to encourage and
instruct him; Bliss could laugh at both Root and himself, as he does
in another poem of 1870, "The Reverie":

> Down in the country we were first—here last;
> There king of toadies; here a toad 'mong kings.
> . . . Ah, what sickening grief,
> When Maestro Bassini said, Not so;
> . . . or when G. F. R.
> Urbanely smiled and drew with cruel skill
> The level of our teaching safety valve,
> And all the gas of self-esteem escaped. . . .
> What wonder we go home disconsolate,
> And fail to see wherein the 'vantage lies
> Of tending Normals thus? . . .

Bliss' songs up to 1874 are full of the fresh wit and humor illustrated by these poems. (The doleful "Lora Vale" is exceptional. The dream of home never appealed to Bliss.) His religious songs are full of a cheerful confidence and a personal intensity that belong to the same character. His letters in the last years are still full of wit, as he reports to his family about his revival tours. The concentration of interest and the increase of production at the end of his life constitute another resemblance to Foster, if our present picture of Foster's development is true. Bliss' cheer and wit distinguish him from some other writers, especially from Sankey.

Both Bliss and Sankey are linked indirectly with Foster by way of the pioneer gospel singer Philip Phillips (1834–95). Phillips was the first to make a career of solo evangelistic singing, accompanying himself on a portable reed organ. Since his own songwriting was a minor part of this career, his fame has faded with the memory of his performances. But his repertory and his style of performance had great influence. He kept in his repertory some songs older than Foster's, including several by Henry Russell and Asa Hutchinson, who had inspired him in his youth when he sang and taught in the music conventions throughout western New York and Pennsylvania. He also sang the solos from Bradbury's Esther, and he kept in touch with Bradbury's New York circle, so that after 1864 he came to rely on Fanny Crosby to produce words on given themes for his melodies. In 1866 and 1872 he made successful tours to England, paving the way for the enormous success of the Moody-Sankey tour in 1873. Phillips, in 1873, invented the "song sermon" with which he continued to tour all over the world for two more decades. His programs often included an "American Song Medley" that began with "The Sword of Bunker Hill," touched on "Columbia, the Gem of the Ocean," and dwelt at length on "My Old Kentucky Home," as well as mentioning "Old Folks" and "Massa." Phillips sang only a few of the newer "gospel songs" such as his own "Home of the Soul" and Bliss' "Hold the Fort." His way of dramatizing them was a model for Sankey, who most skillfully alternated his solos with congregational singing.

In several ways Sankey preceded Bliss by a few years, though Bliss was two years older. Then Sankey's career flourished for four decades after Bliss died. Thus Sankey's fame overshadowed that of Bliss, though the two had collaborated as equals and even though Bliss' songs proved the more lasting.

Sankey grew up in New Castle, Pennsylvania, northwest of Pittsburgh, but the Sankey family enjoyed economic and social advantages denied to the Blisses (advantages held by the Fosters insecurely and intermittently), so that a career in music was less likely for the

Sankeys' son. His father was active in politics and eventually banking; an uncle was a contractor for railroads and director of the New Castle Opera House. There was an organ in the house, which the boy learned to play. But not until his army service in Maryland in 1860 did he take much interest in home songs or church music. Back in New Castle, in 1867, he became secretary of the YMCA; gradually he devoted himself as a singer to its work. Sankey must have known, then or later, that the YMCA had originated in England; that its founder, George Williams (1821–1905), had been inspired by the foremost American urban revivalist, Charles G. Finney (1792–1877); and that Williams had studied music under John Hullah, overcoming some doubts about its religious justification. Sankey surely knew, in 1869, that the Hutchinson singers had sung for the YMCA for a few weeks. In 1870 Sankey went to Chicago to join the lay preacher Dwight L. Moody (1837–99) with whom he worked all the rest of his life. In their collaboration, Moody and Sankey set a pattern to be followed by revivalists for several generations. At first Sankey used the song books of Philip Phillips, Root's first gospel song, "Come to the Savior," then each of the books of Bliss and finally those that he and Bliss edited together.

Bliss' new career at the end of his life was the first of many careers to be modeled on Sankey's. In response to Moody's urging, after prayerful hesitation, Bliss formed a team with Daniel Webster Whittle (1840–1901). His gospel songs served primarily the immediate work of the team—the intense campaign for converting listeners and reinforcing the resolves of the converted. Bliss' songs were so effective, both in his own performances and in Sankey's, that they were quickly established in the repertories of the many thousands who heard them, they were imitated by several contemporaries, and they continued to be used by succeeding generations.

The most famous of all Bliss' songs was "Hold the Fort." Whittle, in a sermon at a Sunday School convention in 1870, had told the story of General Sherman's signal-flag message across the hilltops to the beleaguered defenders of Altoona Pass in 1864 and had compared Sherman to "Christ as our Commander . . . coming to our relief." Bliss soon put the thought to verse and music:

> Ho! my comrades, see the signal
> Waving in the sky!
> Reinforcements now appearing,
> Victory is nigh!
> CHORUS: "Hold the fort, for I am coming,"
> Jesus signals still.
> Wave the answer back to heaven,
> "By thy grace, we will."

> See the mighty host advancing . . .
> See the glorious banner waving . . .
> Fierce and long the battle rages,
>   But our Help is near;
> Onward comes our Great Commander.
>   Cheer, my comrades, cheer!
> Hold the fort, &c.

Bliss' piano accompaniment for the stanzas contributes an exciting rhythmic pattern of repeated chords. The tune makes its first two phrases out of a single motif, swinging back and forth in the range of an octave whose high note is only a lightly touched neighbor of the tonic and whose low note is needed only once, at the end of the first phrase. The second phrase, ending on the dominant note in the middle of the range, leads powerfully into the chorus. The chorus makes its contrast with repeated notes on the tonic, then a broken tonic chord, and a steady beat in the accompaniment. The climax comes with a single accented high note for the word "back." This is a melody of utmost simplicity and force. With substituted words, "Hold the Fort" rallied English labor unions in 1877, American Knights of Labor and International Workers of the World ("Wobblies") and other groups down to the United Fruit Workers Organizing Committee led by Cesar Chavez in 1967. The same tune became the national anthem of the Republic of Ghana. Its history was traced in detail by Paul J. Scheips, 1971. Probably this one song would sooner or later stimulate new interest in Bliss' whole work and his strong character.

"Hold the Fort" is more like "Susanna" than like "Old Folks" in its mood and music. When Bliss thought of the home/roam rhyme, it could have just one meaning: heaven and earth. In his *Gospel Songs* he included his arrangement of a hymn by one E. E. Rexford, "Welcome Home."

> Let us sing, let us sing, as on earth here we roam,
> Of the welcome that waits us in home, sweet home.

When Bliss died his place with Whittle was taken at first by another member of Root's company, George Coles Stebbins (1846–1945), who was to write the most detailed *Reminiscences* of the whole "gospel" school in 1924. Whittle's partner for a longer period was James McGranahan (1840–1907), composer of many gospel songs, including some with words by Bliss. The successors of Bradbury in New York, Robert Lowry (1826–99) and William Howard Doane (1834–1915), supplied music for some of the songs that Sankey, Stebbins, and McGranahan made famous, while Fanny Crosby went on supplying the words for many of them. The "Southern Moody," Samuel Porter Jones (1857–1916), formed a team with the composer and singer Edwin O. Excell (1851–1921), whose work continued the tradition within narrowing channels. A new development of the tradition was effected by another Southerner, Charles McCallon Alexander (1867–1920), who induced sluggish congregations to sing by coaxing, scolding, and drilling them, dividing them into competing groups, and supplementing or replacing the organ accompaniment by a piano or two, with percussive rhythms and enriched chords. Excell and Alexander maintained the favorite songs of Bliss, while expanding the repertory also with music by Charles H. Gabriel (1856–1932) and George Bennard (1857–1950): Bennard's "Old Rugged Cross," 1913, was among the last contributions that held place in the repertory for another generation. Excell, Gabriel, and Bennard were the chief composers associated with the "high tide" of urban revivalism in its "full accommodation" to publicity and administration, as the movement is described in the survey of the *Religious History of the American People* by Sydney Ahlstrom, 1972. The last great team was that of Billy Sunday (1862–1935) and the trombonist-song-leader Homer Rodeheaver (1880–1955). In the still later revivals of Billy Graham (b. 1918) there were able musicians like George Beverly Shea (b. 1909), but the repertory remained centered on the 1870s, with as many earlier as later pieces, as many of them English as American, and with nothing new winning popularity. Yet in some regions as late as 1960 a majority of voting citizens responded to a new gospel song: the singer Jimmy Davis, elected for a second term as governor of Louisiana, attributed much of the success of his campaign to his song "Someone to Care."

To millions of people who attended neither churches nor revivals, neither the YMCA nor Sunday School, gospel songs spread through the Salvation Army. Its founder, William Booth (1829–1912), had broken away from the Methodist church in 1861 and established his Christian Mission to the slums of London in 1865. With the new name that he adopted in 1878, the institution grew into a powerful worldwide organization. Its musicians played hymns on military band instruments, including bass drum and tambourine. Though they wrote new songs, none of them won popularity; their repertory gave a central place to the songs of Bliss and his contemporaries. It was from the Salvation Army, more than the revivalists, that working people borrowed the tunes for their various uses.

Beyond the cities, on the prairies of the West, cowboys sang songs from many sources in ways that attracted the attention of a folklorist from Texas, trained at Harvard, John Avery Lomax. His collection of *Cowboy Songs and Other Frontier Ballads*, 1910, marked a new stage in the development of ideas about American music.

Although Lomax knew the campmeetings and their powerful music in his own childhood, he minimized the connection between gospel songs and cowboy songs to claim a closer relationship to the academically respected, ancient, unwritten tradition of British ballads, as well as a distinctive American quality. But, in fact, what the cowboys sang often derived from gospel song, as the later historian Frank Dobie and others have observed. And through the work of Lomax, of the Chicago poet Carl Sandburg, the hobo ballad-maker Woody Guthrie, the country singer Johnny Cash, and many more 20th-century advocates of American "folksong," some of the late 19th-century "people's song" tradition was recycled. The continuity from "Old Folks at Home" to "Home on the Range" to "This Land Is Your Land" and "I Want to Go Home" runs straight through the songs of Root and Work and Bliss.

Gospel song thus represents a musical tradition more vitally coherent than most traditions in the fast-changing world of the late 19th and early 20th centuries. The historian Sydney Ahlstrom emphasizes its importance: "Few ties were there that bound American Protestants so firmly together in a popular tradition." Moreover Ahlstrom notes that the musical tie outlasted the ascendancy of the homogenized "Protestant establishment," which, around the turn of the century, "enjoyed special prestige and many privileges even though it was not supported or regulated by the government." By 1960, when the election of John F. Kennedy signaled "the crumbling of the Protestant Establishment," in Ahlstrom's words, "old-time religion was relegated to subcultural status," but its music still found many uses.

Within the churches and among musical scholars gospel song was continually attacked by advocates of more genteel, more demanding, and more ecumenical music. Editors of hymnbooks banned many of the most popular songs as trivial (if not corrupt) commercial products; beginning around 1900 they often recommended older, purer "folk songs" as replacements. At the beginning of the tradition, George Root had tried to lead singers through and beyond gospel songs, at least as far as his own cantatas and *Messiah*, if not so far as Wagner; he preferred, within his category of "people's songs," things that had stood the test of time for a few decades.

In the Eastern cities, and quickly spreading from them across the nation and abroad, the newer musical forms and media of David Wallis Reeves (1838–1900) and John Philip Sousa (1854–1932) largely superseded the tradition of Foster's followers, yet occasionally reinforced the "popularity" of their most popular songs in arrangements and medleys for band. Reeves made *Fantasia on Foster* songs. Sousa made recordings of "Old Folks" and "Kentucky Home" that were among his standard encores for concerts. Both these bandsmen viewed the Foster songs from a distance, almost as they viewed the songs of Tom Moore that Reeves edited and to which Sousa harked back in his collection of *National, Patriotic and Typical Airs of All Lands.* The style of Reeves and Sousa was closer to that of their European contemporaries, Strauss, Offenbach, and Sullivan, whose music they played more than Foster's.

The connection between gospel song and Foster, obvious to Root and Bliss, clear enough by now to us, was naturally obscure to many admirers of Foster's famous songs in the intervening generations. When admirers in the 1930s learned that he had written for the Sunday Schools, they were quick to excuse him because he needed money. They did not want to see his "classic" achievement associated with the vulgarity of Billy Sunday or the Salvation Army, or even Bliss and Moody. Evelyn Foster Morneweck, discussing her uncle's "religious hack-writing," insists:

> Knowing the family risibilities as I do, and especially those of Stephen's closest associate, Morrison Foster, I can assert positively that if Stephen actually wrote these barbarous compositions, he was far from being his normal self, or he wrote them with his tongue in his cheek.

Morneweck's disdain for a large group of her contemporaries prevented her from considering Foster's religious songs with an open mind and from recognizing the similarity of "Old Black Joe" to "The Old Rugged Cross."

The historic connection between school music and Foster, Root, Bliss, and Sankey likewise came to be ignored when, around 1930, high school marching bands throughout the country rescued the tradition of Sousa as it faded from the municipal parks. Foster's songs were taught in 20th-century schools as quasi-folksongs, more antique than the band music, more revered.

To what extent did the large minority of Americans who loved gospel songs overlap with the Black minority? When and where and how did this overlapping affect the performance and composition of songs? Too little is known about either group to measure their overlapping. And so much is at stake for all people in the efforts by Americans of African descent to identify and liberate Blackness that any white American's answer is subject to drastic revision. Yet the question naturally arises, and a few facts can be cited as evidence for a tentative answer. When Bliss, Sankey, Alexander, and Rodeheaver sang in Southern cities, a section of the hall or tent was customarily set aside for "colored" people. The same custom of segregation had prevailed in the camp-meeting revivals of earlier generations; it prevailed in Northern cities too, if any people of African descent attended there. (The Billy Graham revivals attracted very few.) In most American churches after the Civil War, however, racial segregation meant altogether separate institutions. Hence the revivals were an opportunity for acculturation more favorable than regular institutional worship. According to the modern student of revivalism W. G. McLoughlin, there was one occasion in Chattanooga when Moody and Sankey held a separate meeting for Negroes and the Blacks boycotted. McLoughlin quotes Sankey as reporting about Meridian, Mississippi:

> We have one side of *Tabernacle* for Blacks. D. L. [Moody] has them sing alone some times "just to show the white people how to sing."

Sankey's successor Charles Alexander is reported by James C. Downey to have used the piano in a style close to ragtime. In 1899 an investigator of the "Negro 'spirituals,' " Marion Alexander Haskell, reported in *Century* that Sankey songs were replacing the spirituals "wherever schools have sprung up." Homer Rodeheaver published a collection of *Negro Spirituals*, 1923, some of which were copied from earlier collections but some of which he claimed to have discovered at Columbia, South Carolina. The "gospel music" developed within some Black churches after about 1920 by Thomas A. Dorsey and others had more than its name in common with the tradition of Bliss and Sankey—the forms and the harmonies are similar, though the jazzlike rhythm and instrumentation of the new gospel music set it apart. When, around 1960, a growing number of white listeners to phonograph records began to appreciate the living, changing tradition of Black gospel music, especially as sung by Mahalia Jackson, most of these listeners were ignorant of white gospel songs; a few went on to discover them by way of the "country music" that now increasingly competed in the record stores. But such listeners were seldom ready to join in singing with either of the ethnic groups to whom the songs belonged. All these observations support provisional answers to our questions: some people of African descent participated in the cultivation of gospel song at all times, though most of the Americans who made and loved gospel song excluded Blacks from full participation; there was an interchange of music probably more continuous and more profound than any other sort of acculturation.

The comprehensive tradition that Root called "people's song" embraced many distinguishable subdivisions, not merely a spectrum of types from simplest to most complicated, but a network: patriotic songs, hymns, parodies, cantatas; solo songs, performances with and without instruments, performances by close-knit groups and by crowds of thousands; exclusively white groups, separate Black groups, groups segregated within one bigger group, and occasionally mixed groups integrated, especially in Britain or Canada. The Foster songs were adaptable throughout this range. They helped to unify it. It reinforced their popularity.

CHAPTER 12

Jubilee singers
and friends
of the "folk"

NEW meanings accrued to "Old Folks," "Massa," "Kentucky Home," and "Old Black Joe" in association with "Negro spirituals" and with ideas of "folk music," which gradually expanded from the 1860s to the 1960s. Many concrete connections, direct and indirect, can be traced between Foster's "plantation songs" and the various references of the modern terms that he himself never knew. First, there were singers and close students of the religious songs of Black Americans who also sang songs of Foster, Root, and Bliss. Next, there were interpreters of the Black "folk" who made incidental use of Foster's songs. Then there were interpreters of "American culture" and "American character" who idealized the four Foster songs as representative of America. Finally, simultaneously and partly in response to these things, there were Black songwriters for the theater—minstrel shows and Tom shows and later developments—who helped give the Foster songs classic status.

A repertory of choral songs with harmonizing parts for four or more voices became world-famous through the concerts of students from Fisk University in Nashville, Tennessee: the Jubilee Singers, beginning in 1871. The word "spirituals" usually suggests, somewhat vaguely, songs sung in the preceding decade or by preceding generations of slaves scattered through the South, but the word refers most precisely to the Fisk repertory and later extensions of it by singers from Hampton Institute in Virginia, and other groups, with necessarily unbounded connotations of their earlier sources. Even the most serious and sustained of the few earlier studies of words and melodies had barely touched the question of how individual singers or divisions of a chorus deviated from unison melody. Colonel Thomas Wentworth Higginson's article in the *Atlantic*, 1867, which established the name "Negro spirituals," described the freed slaves in the Port Royal Islands, South Carolina, singing at work and at worship, composing new songs and continually modifying old ones, but he did not attempt to analyze their polyphony. The chief editor of the first book-length collection of *Slave Songs of the United States*, 1867, William Francis Allen (1830–89), apologized in his preface:

> I despair of conveying any notion of the effect of a number singing together, especially in a complicated shout. . . . There is no singing in *parts*, as we understand it, and yet no two singers appear to be singing the same thing—the leading singer starts the words of each verse, often improvising, and the others who "base" him as it is called, often strike in with the refrain, or even join in the solo, when the words are familiar.
>
> When the "base" begins, the leader often stops, leaving the rest of his words to be guessed at, or it may be that they are taken up by one of the other singers. And the "basers" themselves seem to follow their own whims, beginning when they please and leaving off when they please, striking an octave above or below (in case they have pitched the tune too low or too high), or hitting some other note that chords, so as to produce the effect of a marvellous complication and variety, and yet with the most perfect time, and rarely any discord.

Allen was a classical philologist, trained at Harvard, Göttingen, and Berlin, and soon to be a brilliant professor of history at Wisconsin; his only acquaintance with the songs he edited was in 1863–66 while he served as a teacher in the Freedman's Aid Commission and the Charleston public schools; his perspective view, like that of his friend Higginson, derived partly from German concerns with *Volksmusik*. He played the piano and the flute enough to know his musical limitations. Allen's most musical collaborator, Lucy McKim Garrison (1842–77), who had begun writing down the melodies at Port Royal and reporting them to Dwight's *Journal* in 1862, was guided by Allen's prudent scholarly advice; her notations give no hint of the "complication and variety," though she too had observed "the curious rhythmic effect produced by the single voices chiming in at different irregular intervals." The Fisk repertory published in the 1870s is the earliest as well as the most influential record of the spirituals as polyphonic choral music. Though it does not attempt to record the improvised polyphony of a particular working community, still it does record how the students harmonized more than half of their songs; it is not so diluted with an outside arranger's "refinements" as some later commentators have supposed. Both the similarities and differences between the Fisk repertory and the songs of Foster, Root, and Bliss deserve attention.

The Fisk choir was formed under the leadership of the devoted white treasurer of the University, George Leonard White (1838–95), to sing first the music he had known in Ohio before his war service, when he was a teacher and Sunday School singing teacher. The choir's concerts at Nashville in 1867 and 1868 included only music learned from notes; in 1870 they advanced to Bradbury's cantata *Esther* for which the student pianist, Ella Sheppard, was better prepared than was the conductor, White. When the Hutchinson family gave a concert at Nashville in 1870, the Fisk singers learned something from them. In 1871, because the University desperately needed money, a group of eleven members of the choir began to venture on tour, singing in white churches and town halls. The first program, at Cincinnati, included "Old Folks" sung by Jennie Jackson, with Ella Sheppard at the piano. Audiences approved. But audiences were barely large enough to pay expenses. At Oberlin the singers sang a few of the unwritten hymns they had taught each other and worked out together, from diverse memories of their families and communities in various places. The response of a national Congregational ministers' group was enthusiastic. But was this right? Some of the singers objected to offering "slave songs" for entertainment; a few quit the choir rather than submit to what seemed degrading. The students were probably aware that the communities of the Port Royal Islands, as reported in letters by Elizabeth Pearson Ware, sang their old repertory less in 1867 than they had done in 1863. But George White and enough of his students shared the audience's enthusiasm. They agreed to expand the place of spirituals in their concert repertory, until little else remained except "Home, Sweet Home," "John Brown's Body," "Old Folks," and a "Grace Before Meat" by Bliss. One reviewer in 1873 noted that "Old Folks" now stood out somewhat on the program, as the "nearest approach to the conventional negro melodies of the drawing room." By this time White had named the group the "Jubilee Singers," and with replacements for all but Jackson, Sheppard, and Maggie Porter they were touring continuously. At H. W. Beecher's church in New York crowds of thousands loved them, while journalists were quick to label them "Beecher's Negro Minstrels." The publicity, now wisely managed by White and assistants, brought them engagements in New England that enabled them to buy new clothes and pay off the school's debts. A second tour took them to the Boston Peace Festival, organized by Patrick Gilmore, and on to England and Scotland, where Moody and Sankey gladly encouraged them. In 1877 German audiences welcomed them. In the course of six years they raised money to put the University on a firm footing.

As the modern compiler of "the available evidence on the spiritual" John Lovell, Jr., has observed, "Without these successes, it is quite possible that the spiritual, after a few years, would have relapsed into a state of mildly academic curiosity." The continuing performances of "Old Folks" in this context lent it new dignity. It was detached farther than ever from the comical associations of "Susanna."

George White enlisted a New York musician with more training than he himself ever had, Theodore Frelinghuysen Seward (1835–1902), to put the Jubilee songs on paper. Seward had studied with Mason, Hastings, and Root; he had served as an organist in Rochester, New York, and then as director of school music at East Orange, New Jersey. In 1872 he was chief editor of *The Coronation: A New Collection of Music for Choirs and Singing Schools*, as well as the sixty *Jubilee Songs As Sung by the Jubilee Singers of Fisk University*. By 1880 he had recorded over a hundred. In his introductory remarks he explains:

> Every melody was tested by being played on the pianoforte, and no line or phrase was introduced that did not receive full endorsement from the singers.

His transcriptions are enough to show a little of the characteristic integration of overlapping individual voices in the chorus. This is a fundamental trait of the style that had driven William Francis Allen to his "despair." It is a trait shared, according to later investigations such as the ethnomusicology of Richard Alan Waterman and the "cantometric" studies of Alan Lomax, with most of the music of central Africa.

An example familiar to most readers is "Swing Low, Sweet Chariot." Seward's transcription indicates that two singers in unison begin, then the full chorus in chords sings "Coming for to carry me home," ending the first phrase on a high note. The leaders repeat their call and the chorus responds with a variant that makes a concluding phrase, "home" on the keynote. The two phrases together constitute the refrain that from now on alternates with the changing stanzas. Within the stanzas the music is a variation of the refrain: there are new melodic motifs for "I looked over Jordan and what did I see?" and "A band of angels coming after me"; there is a climactic high note on "band"; the full chorus shapes the stanza

with its alternating phrase endings, "Coming for to carry me home."
Three more stanzas develop the idea of individuals supporting each
other:

> If you get there before I do,
>   Coming for to carry me home,
> Tell all my friends I'm coming too,
>   Coming for to carry me home.
> Swing low, &c.

> The brightest day that ever I saw,
>   Coming for to carry me home,
> When Jesus wash'd my sins away,
>   Coming for to carry me home.
> Swing low, &c.

> I'm sometimes up and sometimes down,
>   Coming for to carry me home.
> But still my soul feels heavenly bound,
>   Coming for to carry me home.
> Swing low, &c.

Whether "home" means freedom soon in Canada or later in Africa
or in the indefinite future throughout the United States, or in
eternal rest of a lively joyful Paradise, or even in a dream of
motherly protection on an "old plantation," may be determined in
particular performances or may deliberately be left to particular
listeners' interpretations, but the integration of the individual singers in the chorus may be the same despite all ambiguities of verbal
meaning. This integration of the chorus sets the spirituals apart
from Foster's songs. On the other hand, the chords and chord-
progressions of the chorus, blending the full seven-note major scale
with the main melody's five-note scale, bring "Swing Low" closer to
Foster than some of the Fisk spirituals like "Didn't My Lord Deliver
Daniel?" and "I'll Hear the Trumpet Sound" that Seward presents
without chords. In "Roll, Jordan" and "Go Down, Moses" there is a
further blending of distinctively modal melodies with a few firm,
Foster-like chords. A thorough study of the whole Fisk repertory
with respect to the way the chords function in the forms and textures would be rewarding. But the observations here are enough to
demonstrate both similarities and differences between the spirituals
and Foster's songs, more important than any similarities of melodic
motifs. ("Roll, Jordan" begins with a broken chord that has reminded some listeners of the refrain of "Camptown Races," but
such a similarity can well be mere coincidence.) "Swing Low" and
many other spirituals as sung by the Fisk students clearly reflect and
reinforce a kind of social behavior and concern that contrasts with

Foster's concerns as we have seen them in his life and all his work.

In 1872 the Hampton Institute in Virginia brought to its faculty from Providence, Rhode Island, Thomas Putnam Fenner (1829–1912) and his wife Ethie K. Fenner, to teach music and especially to organize a money-raising chorus like that of Fisk. Very quickly the Hampton singers were similarly successful on tour. In 1874 a book was issued including fifty "cabin and plantation songs" arranged by Fenner. His preface explains that the distinctive music of the former slaves is "rapidly passing away" and that the students show an "inclination to despise it, as a vestige of slavery," but he has managed to enable a larger group than White's—seventeen—to keep up studies during their tours. The Hampton singers dispensed with the piano. Their repertory seems never to have included anything like Bradbury's *Esther*. But at each concert, according to John Lovell, they included "some Stephen Foster song or other general favorite, such as 'Old Folks at Home,' and 'Massa's in de Cold Ground.'" Was it Fenner who arranged Foster's piano accompaniments for the chorus? Or did the chorus harmonize for itself? Available evidence suggests that the Foster songs, in whatever arrangements, fitted more smoothly into the Hampton repertory than into that of Fisk. All the Hampton music was arranged, rather than merely transcribed; Fenner acknowledged that there was some inevitable "loss in being transported" from its original functions; he thought the concert situation called on him "to develop it, without destroying its original characteristics; the only proper field for such development being in the harmony." Accordingly, his repertory makes more constant use of full chords than the Fisk repertory. Though some of the Hampton rhythms and modal scales are more remote from Foster than most of the Fisk songs, the group integration is less distinctive.

An individual singer could stand out from the Hampton group to make a more sustained theatrical appeal to an audience than in the Fisk group. One singer who did so was the tenor Joseph B. Tove, "shout leader" and author of a commencement essay on "the old slave music." Tove's favorite song was "In That Great Getting-Up Morning," which he had learned, he said, from an uncle who remembered the old slave who made this hymn. His long stanzas were chanted in a free rhythm, with choral responses reduced to "Fare you well!" If Tove was sometimes the soloist in "Old Folks," he doubtless gave it new dramatic values. At least he must have inserted between the lines a moaning "Oh, Lordy."

The interaction of the Fisk and Hampton singers would be a fascinating study, if documents survive to make it possible. The touring groups heard each other in 1873. By 1880 new editions of the Fisk songs included some from Hampton. From 1900 to 1916, under the direction of the Fisk graduate John Wesley Work (1873–1925), Fisk students toured in quartets like those of Hampton. One of the Fisk quartets made phonograph records, on which the selections from their repertory included "Old Black Joe." At both schools the singers taught their repertories to other students, so that singing by assemblies of the whole student body became an important tradition, noted by every visitor. The interaction of the whole Hampton chorus with spontaneously formed quartets and other groups, with individual singers and with some of the rural working and worshipping groups those individuals had grown up in, was most thoroughly studied and described by Natalie Curtis Burlin in her collection of *Negro Folk Songs*, 1916. Were the Foster songs included in assembly programs? If so, the visitors could enjoy the familiar tunes; the students could enjoy the visitors' innocence and benefactions. Did anyone here think of the contrast between "Old Folks" and William Wells Brown's and Harriet Tubman's version of "Susanna," "Star of Freedom"? If so, such thoughts were omitted from all publicity. Burlin gives a footnote to "ragtime," deploring its vulgarity and its exploitation by "commercial white song-writers," but she speaks more hopefully of "the popular song-life of America" bringing "Negro rhythms" to "the world at large."

The cultivation of spirituals at several other schools, on the model of Fisk and Hampton, brought forth additions to the total available repertory, further developments of the style, and at least one further link with Foster. At Calhoun Plantation in Alabama, Emily Hallowell, the editor of songs published in 1901 and 1907, paid special attention to the variable choral textures. At the Penn Normal, Industrial and Agricultural School at St. Helena Island, South Carolina, in 1925, the British-trained native of Freetown, Sierra Leone, Nicholas George Julius Ballanta-Taylor, transcribed choral songs with details such as had eluded previous editors. A student group from North Carolina State College for Negroes, Durham, was brought to the University of North Carolina, Chapel Hill, to record on the machine devised by Milton Metfessel for his book *Phonophotography in Folk Music*, 1928, the most precise graphs of microtonal pitch and offbeat rhythm. At Tuskegee Institute in Alabama, where Booker T. Washington had come from Hampton to be principal in 1881, an excellent choir was finally formed in 1931 by William Levi Dawson; Washington's policies of conciliation with white prejudice had discouraged "premature" efforts in the arts and sciences, while maintaining the hope that future Negro wealth and power would support their spontaneous development. At the Utica Normal and Industrial Institute of Mississippi, John Rosamund Johnson noted in 1930 that "Swing Low" and "Old Black Joe" fitted

together well; in Johnson's collection of *Utica Jubilee Singers Spirituals* there is a photograph taken in a radio studio where five of the
young singers surround an old lady at the piano—Marion Foster
Welch, Stephen's daughter. This picture symbolizes the social structure in which the songs like "Old Folks" were more and more commonly seen and admired through several generations.

The Hampton singers evoked the use of the term "Negro Folk
Songs" in 1873. An anonymous writer in the New York *Weekly
Review*, whose report was promptly reprinted in Dwight's *Journal*,
described their concerts with enthusiasm:

> At last the American school of music has been discovered. . . . Some of
> them [the songs] at once recall the "breakdowns" made familiar to us by
> the negro minstrel troupes. Others suggest ordinary Sunday School hymn
> tunes; but the majority are unique in construction, rhythm and melody.
> The cultivated musician will at once perceive that they are crude and
> childish, but he cannot deny their originality.

The term used in the title of this article, "Negro Folk Songs," won
general acceptance only gradually. Frédéric Louis Ritter (1832–91)
avoided the term in his pioneering historical survey of *Music in
America*, 1883, though he had lectured in 1869 on "Folk Songs, and
Piano-forte Compositions Founded on That Form." For Ritter, a
native of Strassbourg who had migrated to America in the 1850s
and become professor at Vassar College in 1867, "folk song" meant
such themes as Liszt used in his "Hungarian Rhapsodies"; he preferred G. F. Root's term "people's song" for the "songs of the colored
race" in America, which he mentioned only briefly in 1883. A more
snobbish attitude than Ritter's was that of Henry Theophilus Finck
(1854–1926), native of Missouri, graduate of Harvard, and frequent
contributor to the *Nation*. In his article for *Lippincott's*, 1878, on
"Music in America," Finck advised would-be composers that folk
songs were needed, but not "music for the feet" or dance music:

> In Germany—which perhaps has done more for music than all other
> countries combined—the foundation for musical culture is laid in the
> schools by the singing of folk-songs (*Volkslieder*) and chorals in three- or
> four-part harmony. . . . Of course it will not be necessary to confine our-
> selves to German folk-songs, although these are on the whole the best.

Finck admits some value to Italian, French, Scottish, and Russian
songs, but he sees no hope of native "foundations" in England or
America. The language of the enthusiastic reviewer of the Hampton
singers was still unusual in 1878. Before his term could come into
wide use, musicians had to learn more from literary men and from
foreign musicians.

The older term "national song," almost equivalent to *Volkslied*, prepared the way. It was now applied more and more to "Old Folks," while "Susanna," "Jim Crow," and the rest of the lively minstrel songs were neglected in literary discussion. Thus, in 1874, Constance F. Woolson wrote a survey of "Euterpe in America" for *Lippincott's* in which she pointed out that "American music is at present but a *pot-pourri*, possessing "no original national airs save the negro melodies, so-called." "Massa" and "Old Folks," she thinks, are "recognized as national airs by the musical world." Woolson is aware of a more authentic "wild and peculiar" music, but not yet of the spirituals:

> During the war some of the most stirring tunes came up from the South, particularly from the Mississippi River: they were wild and peculiar, the melody and time difficult to catch, and yet haunting the ear persistently. They seemed to have no names, they never appeared in print, but many a returned soldier whistles their fragments, and vainly tries to put them together or recall the minor chords with which they ended.

These tantalizing remarks indicate the process of nationwide dissemination of music by ear, going on unnoticed by the learned Ritter and Finck, and offering a basis for hope that Americans might some day share an authentic "national music," rooted in rural tradition, as European "folk music" was supposed to be. But Woolson did not develop the contrast between the "wild" tunes and "Old Folks." She used the old term "national air" to link "Old Folks" with the disseminating process.

Lippincott's printed an article on the "Folk-lore of the Southern Negroes" by William Owens in 1877, which encouraged the work that was soon to be most influential, that of Joel Chandler Harris (1848–1908). Harris began his reporting of "Negro folklore" in the Atlanta *Constitution* in 1879. The next year he published *Uncle Remus: His Songs and Sayings*, the first and most popular of his many books. In 1881, for the *Dial*, William Francis Allen reviewed *Uncle Remus* under the heading "Southern Negro Folk-lore." In 1883 Harris wrote for the *Critic* about "Plantation Music." He explains his own effort to give a realistic account, in contrast to the minstrels' stereotypes:

> The negroes of the South know little about the banjo and care a great deal less. . . . Sentiment is a very stubborn thing. It is sometimes stronger than facts; and the ideal and impossible negro will continue to exist in the public mind as a banjoist. . . . The stage negro is ground into the public mind, and he cannot be ground out. It is so in the North, and, in a great measure, it is so in the South. The first song the writer ever learned was a string of nonsense with this chorus:

"Oh, Susanna! don't you cry for me!
I'm going to Alabama with my banjo on my knee!"

Harris's childhood memory of "Susanna" suggests that he must have learned "Old Folks" and "Old Black Joe" as he grew up; more, that Foster's modification of the stereotype from comic to pathetic helped prepare Harris for his work just as did the work of Stowe. The combination of Foster's comic and pathetic moods fits the moral of *Uncle Remus*, as Harris sums it up in an introduction:

It is not virtue that triumphs, but helplessness; it is not malice, but mischievousness.

One of Harris's last volumes echoes Foster in its title, *Tales of the Home Folks in Peace and War*, 1898. By this time the connotations of "folks" and "folklore" and "folksong" had blended together. Variants of the *Uncle Remus* tales as told by the fiddler Prince Baskin had been published by A. M. H. Christensen as *Afro-American Folk Lore*, 1892. Hampton had its own Folklore Society; its singers had performed at Washington for the American Folklore Society, whose main efforts were devoted to the collection and literary analysis of the old British ballads catalogued by Francis Child.

Harris and most other students of folklore in his time kept their distance from their "folk" informants, no matter how they might strive to universalize the "triumph" of "helplessness." They were especially interested in the lore of the past. If their contemporaries of African descent wished to lessen the distance, to overcome the old "helplessness," the folklorists were quick to see and regret the decay of old folkways. Their work contributed both to the acknowledgment of a distinctive Black cultural tradition and to the repression of all people labeled Negro in their own time. To some readers the newly published folklore seemed to justify the political and economic measures of the decades after 1877 that were making the vast majority of Blacks more like a European peasantry, bound to the land, than most slaves had been before 1863. As the outstanding modern student of *The Black Image in the White Mind*, George M. Frederickson, has shown, a kind of "internal colonialism came to dominate national thinking" around 1900. No wonder, then, that the relatively few beneficiaries of Fisk, Hampton, Howard University in Washington, and other schools included some who questioned or rebelled against the "plantation songs." No wonder that the folklorists continually reported the increasing rarity of the songs they valued. There was not yet any recognition of an ongoing creative tradition among an oppressed group. The literary specialist on the "plantation myth," Francis Pendleton Gaines, emphasizes that the "new age" after 1870 is no new tradition but rather "a new appreciation" and "striking enlargement" of a traditional theme developed by several antebellum writers. Harris "perfects" the myth, and Harris is "most significant" for his emphasis on the Blacks' "strange musical sensitiveness and genius."

The songs of the dead Foster, written before Emancipation, and lamenting even then the dead master and the lost home, could be used more easily than the spirituals to define the Blacks as a help-less folk and to idealize a mythically self-contained, stable, agricultural society of genteel masters and contented servants, in contrast to the turbulent actuality dominated by national and international commerce. In *Harper's Weekly*, 1873, the words of "Old Folks" were printed with a memorable illustration by R. N. Brooke, under the title "Way down upon the Swanee Ribber." As the social historian Henry Nash Smith has observed, this "importation of the Foster song from its original context of the blackface minstrel show to the more genteel pages of *Harper's* . . . indicates the increasing currency of the plantation myth."

If a foreign musician looked for an American folksong, with or without the label, "Old Folks" was among the first things to come to his attention. It was adopted as a concert finale by Christine Nilsson (1843–1921), the Swedish soprano who had won fame as Violetta in Verdi's *Traviata*. For her American tour she needed something to correspond to Jenny Lind's use of "Home, Sweet Home." The story of how she found "Old Folks" was reported in *Harper's Bazaar*, 1871:

> Miss NILSSON's singing of FOSTER's little ballad of "The Old Folks at Home," constitutes one of the pleasantest features of her concerts. The way she chanced to do it was this. She was visiting Mrs. PARKE GOD-WIN, daughter of the poet BRYANT, at her country place. The little daughter of Mrs. GODWIN was the possessor of a banjo. Miss NILSSON invited her to sing. She did so, singing "The Old Folks at Home," which so touched the prima donna that she at once learned, and has since sung it with great applause. She is now learning "Willie, We Have Missed You," and will doubtless make a like hit with that.

The *Song Journal* in 1872 repeated the story and commented, "Her exquisite utterance of the melody will give renewed interest to a song which, in the last quarter of a century, has had an almost un-paralleled success." But "Willie" was no more mentioned. "Old Folks" served Nilsson's purpose partly because of the new contexts that it was given by the Fisk and Hampton singers and the *Harper's* illustrator; at the same time, it served their purposes partly because of the added dignity that Nilsson gave it. The combination made it seem more and more like the European "folksongs" that Ritter and Finck admired.

In 1878 the great violinist August Wilhelmj (1845–1908), having served as concertmaster at Bayreuth for Wagner's *Ring,* began a tour of America, South America, and Australia, in which his "Thème varié: Old Folks at Home" alternated with his Bach arrangement "Air on the G String" as a favorite encore. After Wilhelmj, many concert violinists played various arrangements of "Old Folks"— Efrem Zimbalist published his version in 1911.

Not only visitors, but also musicians settling in the United States, found the Foster songs useful. Thus, for example, Carl Busch (1862– 1943) dignified "Old Folks" with an arrangement for string orchestra, published in Leipzig as an *"Amerikanisches Volkslied,"* 1897. Busch had settled in Kansas City, Missouri, in 1887; he was to establish there a symphony and a conservatory like many others throughout the United States. His institutions were modeled as far as possible on those he had known in Copenhagen, looking always to Leipzig and Berlin for international ideals, but acknowledging a need for coordination with the local environment. Foster provided a convenient material for such acknowledgments, without provoking any actual concern for the rising schools of Black musicians in Kansas City, St. Louis, Memphis, and New Orleans, nor for the individual musicians of African descent who participated increasingly in international musical life despite every obstacle.

Literary appraisals of Foster's words rose higher and higher as the turn of the century approached. In 1887 Henry A. Beers' *Outline Sketch of American Literature* proclaimed that the songs like "Old Folks" were "the most original and vital addition which this country has made to the psalmody of the world, and entitle Foster to the first rank among American song-writers." In 1894 the eleven-volume *Library of American Literature,* edited by Edmund Clarence Stedman and Ellen Mackay Hutchinson, included "Old Folks," "Massa," "Nelly Bly," and "My Old Kentucky Home." When the Canadian poet Bliss Carman (1861–1929) edited the *Oxford Book of American Verse,* it was natural for him to take over three of the same songs; he dropped out the early, cheerful "Nelly Bly." An article in *The Literary Era,* 1901, by John Habberton was perhaps the first that called Foster "The world's greatest song-writer." These were not advertisers' humbug but testimonials of a growing reverence among men of letters, responding to a widespread development of taste.

The related trends were strongly reinforced among musicians and music lovers by Antonín Dvořák (1841–1904) when, in 1892, he came to the United States, not merely to conduct festive performances of his *Stabat mater* and other works as he had done in

England, but to stay for three years as director of the National Conservatory in New York and to compose, first among other works, his Symphony in E, *From the New World*. As soon as he arrived, he was prodded by the journalist, critic, piano teacher, and press secretary for the Conservatory, James Gibbons Huneker (1860–1921), to express opinions about American music, especially "Negro songs." The rival critic Henry Krehbiel (1854–1923) greeted Dvořák's arrival with an article in *Century* magazine, as signal for "the rise of a school of American composers" who would learn from him to exploit the "vast mines of folk music." Krehbiel linked Dvořák with Tchaikovsky and Rimsky-Korsakov in a "Slavonic school, which is youthful enough to have preserved the barbaric virtue of truthfulness and fearlessness in the face of convention." An anonymous Chicago reporter quoted Dvořák, in August 1893, as affirming that "in the negro melodies we find a sure foundation for a national school of American music."

Dvořák himself wrote more prudently and provisionally than the critics like Huneker and Krehbiel. His opinions on America he published only just before his return to Prague in 1895, whereas in 1894, prodded and assisted by Henry T. Finck, he contributed to *Century* an article on "Franz Schubert," crediting him with having absorbed a "Slavic trait" from his "residence in Hungary." The article on "Music in America," written with the help of Edward Emerson, Jr., for *Harper's*, begins with a disarming confession of ignorance about the vast land he has always admired. It pleads for state support to music and especially to music education. Most pointedly, Dvořák tells how his students impressed him immediately with their "American 'push,'" their patriotism, their enthusiasm, their eagerness to learn everything at once "as if a boy wished to dive before he could swim." At first this trait annoyed him, but he came to believe that it might be an advantage, provided that "people in general, however, begin to take as lively an interest in music and art as they now take in more material matters." He warned that "art that has to pay its own way is apt to become vitiated and cheap." Then, at last, he took up the question of a national style, still with caution:

> I suggested that inspiration for truly national music might be derived from the negro melodies or Indian chants. I was led to take this view partly by the fact that the so-called plantation songs are indeed the most striking and appealing melodies that have yet been found on this side of the water, but largely by the observation that this seems to be recognized, though often unconsciously, by most Americans. . . . The most potent as well as the most beautiful among them, according to my estimation, are certain of the so-called plantation melodies and slave songs, all of which are distinguished by unusual and subtle harmonies, the like of which I

have found in no other songs but those of old Scotland and Ireland. The point has been urged that many of these touching songs, like those of Foster, have not been composed by the negroes themselves, but are the work of white men, while others did not originate on the plantation, but were imported from Africa. It seems to me that this matters but little. One might as well condemn the Hungarian Rhapsody because Liszt could not speak Hungarian. The important thing is that the inspiration for such music should come from the right source, and that the music itself should be a true expression of the people's real feelings.

Dvořák had no way of judging whether "Old Folks" was a true expression. He trusted those who told him it was, though he acknowledged the doubt of Krehbiel. To him there was no important difference between "Old Folks" and "Swing Low" as they reached him in print or in performance of cultivated singers. He returned to the dubious parallel with Schubert that his earlier article had hinted at:

> Schubert . . . struck the true Magyar note, to which all Magyar hearts, and with them our own, must forever respond. . . . The white composers who wrote the touching negro songs . . . had a similar sympathetic comprehension of the deep pathos of slave life. If, as I have been informed they were, these songs were adopted by the negroes on the plantations, they thus became true negro songs. . . . Just so it matters little whether the inspiration for the coming folksongs of America is derived from the negro melodies, the songs of the creole, the red man's chant, or the plaintive ditties of the homesick German or Norwegian. Undoubtedly the germs for the best music lie hidden away among all the races that are commingled in this great country. The music of the people is like a rare and lovely flower growing amidst encroaching weeds. . . . It is discovered and clothed in new beauty, just as the myths and legends of a people are brought to light and crystallized in undying verse by the master poets.

Accordingly Dvořák had arranged "Old Folks" for two solo singers, mixed chorus, and orchestra, "clothing" it in luxurious garb. Foster's own chords are hardly changed, but the full orchestra builds a crescendo with trembling strings and rolling drums and Beethovenish brasses. When Dvořák conducted the performance, January 1893, he used a special baton of ebony. (The arrangement, apparently never performed again, was to be published for the first time in the Collected Edition of Dvořák's works, Prague. A manuscript copy was found at the New York Public Library in 1975.) Dvořák's essay offered advice to would-be composers, but not quite the advice that Huneker feared and Krehbiel hoped for:

> . . . the musician must prick his ears for music. Nothing must be too low or too insignificant for the musician. When he walks he should listen to every whistling boy, every street singer or blind organ-grinder.

Dvořák did not expect the busy professional to go in person to the plantations or the Indian reservations. Rather he urged an openness to all music and a special concern for what was closest at hand. Then Dvořák ended his essay with an appeal to civic pride and its possible justification:

> When music has been established as one of the reigning arts of the land, another wreath of fame and glory will be added to the country which earned its name, the "Land of Freedom," by unshackling her slaves at the price of her own blood.

Dvořák could hardly know that in 1895 Americans of African descent were meeting new legalized injustice and frequent violence in the South and smug racism in the North, while Northern commerce exploited Southern agriculture and any Northern effort at reform was blocked by Southern votes. He could not guess that his glorification of "Old Folks" served the self-deceiving beneficiaries of the reunited nation. He could not prevent Huneker, Krehbiel, and others from using his symphony and a few phrases detached from his essay to continue stirring a controversy about "nationalism in music." While Krehbiel went on eventually to a scholarly sifting of evidence about African sources of the spirituals, Huneker went on to argue, in 1920:

> . . . if we are to have true American music it will not stem from "darky" roots, especially as the most original music of that kind thus far written is by Stephen Foster, a white man. The influence of Dvořák's American music has been evil; ragtime is the popular pabulum now. I need hardly add that the negro is not the original race of our country. And ragtime is only rhythmic motion, not music.

Huneker had not "pricked his ears" to ragtime in 1895; no one else had shown ragtime to Dvořák, alas; no accidental evil effect of Dvořák's glorification of Foster could be so bad as Huneker's scorn for what he thought "too low or too insignificant." Dvořák made no arrangements of spirituals. He never sponsored a public performance of them. The "Largo" of his *New World* became associated with spirituals through the voluminous controversy. Scholars like John Clapham, who have traced the evidence in detail, conclude that any basis for the association must be less than the association with Foster. Naturally Dvořák's treatment of rhythm and polyphony remained closer to Foster than to the spirituals—or to Liszt or Brahms; though his chord-progressions owed much to Liszt and his forms a little to Brahms, Dvořák's favorite rhythms included the polka and his favorite textures were conventional accompaniments for songful melodies. What his work prompted was less a discriminating study of any music than an idealization of the comprehensive category of "plantation songs," in an association with the symphony that was startling for many people.

The singers in Dvořák's "Old Folks" arrangement were all of African descent. The chorus came from St. Phillip's Episcopal Church. The soprano was Sissieretta Jones (1868–1933), who had used "Old Folks," "Kentucky Home," and other Foster songs with the orchestras that accompanied her concerts of operatic arias. The baritone was Henry Thacker Burleigh (1866–1949), a native of Erie, Pennsylvania, and a student at the National Conservatory, whose later connections with both Foster and the spirituals were important. The manuscript was dedicated to him.

Burleigh became best known for his many performances at St. George's Episcopal Church and Temple Emanu-El, and, after 1916, for his concert arrangements of "Deep River" and forty-eight other spirituals for solo voice and piano. How far Burleigh and Dvořák affected each other is a question worthy of more disinterested study than it has yet received. Throughout his life, in his own eyes, Burleigh was primarily a composer of songs—ninety of them, plus two song cycles. He began to publish them in 1898. With "Jean," 1903, he won wide popularity; in a study of Burleigh's whole work by Janifer Ellsworth, in 1960, "Jean" is recommended as first-rate. Meanwhile Burleigh made his first arrangements of spirituals, not for voice but for violin and piano, in 1901. In 1904 he published a collection of Scottish folksongs. Then in 1909 he published an astonishing collection of twenty-one *Negro Minstrel Melodies* by Foster, Work, and others that was successful enough to call for a second, expanded edition in 1910. Nine of the songs are Foster's: "Old Folks," "Massa," "Kentucky Home," and "Old Black Joe" are supplemented not only by the earlier group of "Susanna," "Camptown Races," "Nelly Was a Lady," and "Nelly Bly," but also, characteristically for Burleigh, by "Come, Where My Love Lies Dreaming." A preface to this volume, by the journalist critic W. J. Henderson, laments the "decline" in popularity of these minstrel songs, "due to the rapid spread of the music hall." Henderson goes on, with the tacit consent of Burleigh, to declare that these songs were "not folk-songs, for we never had any folk-songs. . . . Yet they were distinctively American." Henderson makes no claim that the minstrel writers were distinctively Negro. In short, Dvořák's ideas have not been absorbed uncritically. Burleigh's piano accompaniments are far richer than those of Foster, with mildly dissonant chords, chromatically altered chords, and frequent change of chord—these arrangements match the dignity and sweetness that Dvořák gave to "Old Folks" without the bombast. Burleigh's masterpiece, "Deep River," is closer to his Foster arrangements than to the simple settings of spirituals he made for the scholarly book by Krehbiel in 1914.

While Burleigh pursued his career, thus varied, his classmate Will Marion Cook (1869–1944) worked as composer and conductor in the theater, where the cakewalk, ragtime, and the beginnings of jazz concerned him more than Foster and the spirituals. Cook had studied the violin at Oberlin Conservatory and in Berlin. Among his many contributions to music was the advice he gave to the young Duke Ellington (1899–1974). Together, in 1903, Burleigh and Cook inspired an anonymous writer in *The Colored Teacher* of Hopkinsville, Kentucky, and the *Negro Music Journal* of New York to a remarkable article on "Two Negro Musicians," in which their work is hailed with a new pride:

> It seems to be a poetic culmination, the law of compensation by which the negro element furnishes to the great American people the foundation of their national music, but this is the glorious prospect that awaits us. The Negroes, and the Negroes alone, have the songs of the American soul and soil, and Dvořák was not long in discovering the fact. . . . Burleigh and Cook are the men who lent Dvořák the opportune suggestion and it is whispered that they added their individual talents to their suggestions. . . . They form a shrine around which our future music must encircle.

From the Kentucky writer's point of view, Foster was negligible. Yet if Burleigh and Cook themselves did not reject Foster, then their admirer's "alone" must be read as an exaggeration.

What was the value of Foster for the several white students of Dvořák who tried to apply the advice he had given? Less than for Burleigh. Despite Dvořák's inclusive definition of the "plantation songs," such men as William Arms Fisher (1861–1948), Harvey Worthington Loomis (1865–1930), and Rubin Goldmark (1872–1936) could hardly fail to segregate the Foster songs from the spirituals and to pay more attention to the latter, while they tended to suppose that Burleigh and Cook were commercializing the music that they wished to glorify. Fisher waited until 1936 to edit a *Choral Book* of ten Foster songs in arrangements that imitate Burleigh's. Fisher's most memorable achievement was to supply the words "Goin' Home" for the largo theme of Dvořák.

Foster's songs in association with Dvořák's recommendations meant much to Henry F. Gilbert (1868–1928), pupil of MacDowell in Boston, 1889–92. Gilbert arranged "Old Dog Tray" and "Massa" with slightly elaborated accompaniments for publication under the pseudonym Frank Belknap, 1906. In 1910 he edited a collection of *A Hundred Folksongs* in which he included "Old Folks." His preface explains that this song typifies the

. . . important class of popular song which must be considered as folk-song inasmuch as it also expresses truly the spirit of the folk. These are simple songs composed in the style of the true folk-song which have immediately become popular and have retained their popularity. Many of them are true folk-songs in the making. "Way down upon the Swanee River" is a good example of such a song.

Gilbert's projected opera about *Uncle Remus* was never finished; the few orchestral works that were performed during his lifetime failed to hold interest; the survey of his whole work by Katherine Longyear, 1968, ends with a plea that some of the works be given a further chance, and Longyear seems to agree with Elliott Carter that the "Symphonic Piece" of 1925 may be especially deserving— in this piece, according to Gilbert's notes for the Boston Symphony program when it was performed in 1926, the second theme "has a slight Fosterian twang . . . a remote suggestion of 'Old Folks at Home'—a kind of family resemblance—interspersed with a couple of measures from 'The Arkansas Traveller.' "

None of Dvořák's students or admirers adequately realized the hopes that he encouraged. Yet the vague notions of the folk and of folksongs persisted and developed further, thanks partly to his encouragement and the surrounding publicity.

The classic literary expression of the idea of the spirituals is the book by William Edward Burghardt DuBois (1868–1963), *The Souls of Black Folk*, 1903. DuBois begins each chapter with an epigraph from a spiritual—a phrase or two of the melody with hints of the choral harmony. He devotes a whole final chapter to interpreting the spirituals in relation to slavery and racism: "Of the Sorrow Songs." DuBois first heard this music sung by a quartet from Hampton in a church at Great Barrington, Massachusetts, 1885. He had grown up there, little affected by prejudice, little aware of either city life or Southern life, but the songs immediately strengthened a sense of his identity with the slaves and their descendants. He went to Fisk as a student and learned to sing the repertory. In the summers of 1886 and 1887 he taught school near Alexandria, Tennessee, and heard the "sorrow songs" in the fields and at churches— heard through the depths of the sorrow to the "hopeful striving." In the summer of 1888 he was manager of the Fisk Glee Club at a resort in Minnesota. He went on to Harvard, where he was barred from the Harvard Glee Club, but encouraged by William James, Francis Child, and other great teachers. Then, during two years at the University of Berlin, he refined his understanding of the changing folk-character of Black Americans and of their relation to white America, to Europe, and to Africa. In Germany he heard many performances of Beethoven and Wagner; he also heard peasants in the

Rheinpfalz sing at work and at worship; he proceeded to grasp, better than Dvořák, the full meaning of the spirituals. His book, then, is an analysis and prophecy, addressed to all Americans. It makes vivid the huge past contributions and urgent present claims of the "Black folk" on behalf of an ultimate brotherhood of mankind. The songs are used as the strongest, most beautiful evidence for the argument. And Foster's songs fit into this argument. For Du-Bois presents a theory of gradual musical development, in which he specifies several steps:

> The first is African music, the second Afro-American, while the third is a blending of Negro music with the music heard in the foster land. The result is still distinctively Negro and the method of blending original, but the elements are both Negro and Caucasian. One might go further and find a fourth step in this development, where the songs of white America have been distinctively influenced by the slave songs or have incorporated whole phrases of Negro melody, as "Swanee River" and "Old Black Joe." Side by side, too, with the growth has gone the debasements and imitations—the Negro "minstrel" songs, many of the "gospel" hymns, and some of the contemporary "coon" songs,—a mass of music in which the novice may easily lose himself and never find the real Negro melodies.

DuBois illustrates each of the first three steps with an outstandingly fine example or two. He assumes that readers can supply the Foster songs. He classes them apart from the "debasements and imitations" and implies that they are valuable, at least when they lead listeners on to hear and heed "the articulate message of the slave to the world."

DuBois refined and expanded his argument in a less famous book, *The Gift of Black Folk*, 1924, with a chapter on "The American Folk Song" and one on "Negro Art and Literature." Here he brings Foster into closer connection with the minstrels, and makes use of the story of Olivia Pise:

> Around the Negro folk-song there has arisen much of controversy and of misunderstanding. For a long time they were utterly neglected; then every once in a while and here and there they forced themselves upon popular attention. In the thirties, they emerged in tunes like "Near the lake where droops the willow" [Morris' "Long, Long Ago"] and passed into current song or were caricatured by the minstrels. Then came Stephen Foster who accompanied a mulatto maid often to the Negro church and heard the black folk sing; he struck a new note in songs like "Old Kentucky Home," "Old Folks at Home" and "Nellie was a Lady." But it was left to war and emancipation to discover the real primitive beauty of this music to the world.

DuBois cites "Kentucky Home" and "Nelly Was a Lady" instead of

"Old Black Joe," doubtless aware that "Kentucky Home" is surrounded by questions and that "Nelly Was a Lady" is less familiar to most readers. "Old Folks" remains the central point of reference, but, even in a book hastily compiled, DuBois does not merely repeat himself. He no longer dismisses whole categories of music as "debasements and imitations." He deals with contemporary trends briefly and warily, referring once more to Foster:

> Out of ragtime grew a further development through both white and black composers. The "blues," a curious and intriguing variety of love song from the levees of the Mississippi, became popular and was spread by the first colored man who was able to set it down, W. C. Handy of Memphis. Other men, white and colored, from Stephen Foster to our day, have taken another side of Negro music and developed its haunting themes and rippling melody into popular songs and into high and fine forms of modern music, until today the influence of the Negro reaches every part of American music, of many foreign masters like Dvorak . . .

DuBois had modified his view of "gospel song" by this time, for on his first visit to Africa, 1923, he had heard marvelous derivatives of it there. In his *Dusk of Dawn*, 1940, he described what he heard:

> Christmas Eve, and Africa is singing in Monrovia. They are Krus and Fanti—men, women and children, and all the night they march and sing. The music was once the music of mission revival hymns. But it is that music now transformed and the silly words hidden in an unknown tongue—liquid and sonorous. It is tricked out and expounded with cadence and turn. And this is the same rhythm I heard first in Tennessee forty years ago; the air is raised and carried by men's strong voices, while floating above in obbligato, come the high mellow voices of women—it is the ancient African art of part singing, so curiously and insistently different.

Dusk of Dawn no longer refers to Dvořák or Foster. And there is no mention of them in the immense study of *Black Reconstruction in America . . . 1860–1880* that DuBois published in 1935; at the point where a mention might be expected, there is instead a linking of the spirituals with the "Hymn of Joy," Beethoven's text from Schiller. If a full account of the place of music in DuBois' thought is undertaken, more connections with Foster may come to light. But enough has been shown here to indicate the nature of those connections and their development.

The ideas formulated by DuBois in *Souls of Black Folk* affected every later interpretation of the spirituals, directly or indirectly. The songs of Foster continued to be associated with the spirituals in such influential books as John Wesley Work's *Folk Songs of the American Negro*, 1907, expanded 1915; Henry Krehbiel's *Afro-Amer-*

ican Folksongs: A Study in Racial and National Music, 1914; Alain Locke's *The New Negro,* 1925, and *The Negro and His Music,* 1936. Work called Foster's songs "the finest secular Negro Folk Songs in existence . . . in a class between all other imitations and the genuine Negro Folk Song." Krehbiel, distinguishing the *"volkstümliches Lied"* from the true *Volkslied,* merely mentions Foster; Krehbiel argues that there can be no all-American folksong; there can be no "American music" until "the work of amalgamation shall be complete." Locke calls Foster "the Joel Chandler Harris of Negro music, breaking its dialect bonds and smoothing it out palatably for the general American ear." In Locke's later judgment, if not earlier, this was no "unmixed blessing." Locke's work, completed by Margaret Just Butcher in *The Negro in American Culture,* 1956, 1972, includes an appraisal of the mixture:

> The ballads that Foster wrote in a straight sentimental vein, without Negro elements, are, in the main, completely forgotten. But "Uncle Ned" (1848), "Camptown Races" (1850), "Swanee River" (1851), "My Old Kentucky Home" (1853), and "Old Black Joe" (1860) are well known and will be known as long as American popular music has admirers. . . . Foster's ballads did more to crystallize the romance of the plantation tradition than all the Southern colonels and novelists put together. It is indeed an ironic tribute to Negro idioms that they inspired a popular balladry that reinforced and helped perpetuate the very system that kept Negroes enslaved.

Locke's choice of songs, omitting "Susanna" and "Massa," suggests that his judgment was based less on study of the songs and their uses than on concern for the future relations of individuals and groups in America; he emphasizes the fact that "the very musicians who know the folkways of Negro music" are the most exploited by "Tin Pan Alley," while "our musicians with formal training are cut off from the people and the vital roots of folk music." Locke knew that Dvořák's advice was not enough; he wanted to use Foster in the struggle for a better coordination. He knew also that some academic scholars were reacting against the ideas of DuBois with historical criticisms of the spirituals and new incidental references to Foster.

In the 1920s and '30s the folklorists Newman Ivy White and Howard W. Odum, the anthropologist Guy B. Johnson, and the professor of German literature and amateur musician George Pullen Jackson led in efforts to minimize the originality of Black musicians and their African heritage. By restoring to the word "spiritual" some of its archaic meaning among white singers, G. P. Jackson (1874–1953) had the greatest influence. In a series of three books he sought to show that the Negro spirituals were derived mainly from melodies in the hymnbooks of the early 19th century and from British oral tradition older than these. Jackson's books, *White Spirituals in the Southern Uplands*, 1933; *Spiritual Folk-songs of Early America*, 1937; and *White and Negro Spirituals: Their Life Span and Kinship*, 1943, brought to light many facts about the "fa-so-la" tradition, but they neglected questions of performing style—subtleties of rhythm and polyphony—and even Jackson's claims about melodic identities were only sometimes convincing to anyone who did not share his motivation. Yet he contributed positively, in addition to the facts, a readiness to find folk values in various groups and to study two or more groups comparatively over a long time. His essay on "Stephen Foster's Debt to American Folk-song," 1936, is a by-product of this continuing work; it shows similarities between twenty-seven Foster phrases and selected phrases from the fa-so-la repertory, together with "Annie Laurie" and "The Last Rose of Summer." He finds no debt whatever to any Negro source, but rather believes that Foster sometimes served as an intermediary along the way from the older white to the later Negro melodies. He regrets that he can find no source for "My Old Kentucky Home." He recognizes the incomplete and arguable status of his findings. He invites readers to pursue his search farther. But admirers of Foster preferred to pursue the interpretation of "Oh! Boys, Carry Me 'Long" and "Hard Times" put forward by Morrison Foster, even though Jackson's juxtaposition of "Hard Times" with the traditional Irish "Wearing of the Green" was his most persuasive exhibit.

The association of Foster with the spirituals was loosened in the 1920s and '30s less by Jackson's attitude than by the growing power of the spirituals themselves in the performances of the great Black concert singers Roland Hayes (b. 1887) and Paul Robeson (b. 1898), who had no need for Foster. Like DuBois, these singers could connect the spirituals more directly with Beethoven or Schubert or Moussorgsky. So could Marian Anderson (b. 1902), though she continued to sing "My Old Kentucky Home" and made a recording of it.

The association between the spirituals and the Foster songs was inevitably ambiguous. No evidence would suffice to end controversy about it. The ambiguity, however, could be used in ways that clarified the issue and challenged new response. Thus, for example, in the play *Purlie Victorious*, 1961, by Ossie Davis (b. 1917), there is a dialogue referring to "Old Black Joe" in which a Southern white boss reminisces:

> . . . how you and me growed up together. Had the same mammy—my mammy was your mother. . . . And how you used to sing that favorite ol' speritual of mine: "I'm a-coming . . . my heart is bendin' low," how

much it eases the pain . . . something absolutely sacred about that
spiritual—I live for the day you'll sing that thing over my grave.

The Black man, Gitlow, replies:

Me, too, ol' Cap'n, me too! (Gitlow's voice rises to a slow, gentle, yet
triumphant crescendo, as our LIGHTS fade away.)

When *Purlie* was filmed, the title referred again to "Old Black Joe"
with double meaning: *Gone Are the Days.*

The association of Foster with the spirituals was not peculiarly
American. In Germany, too, though scholars in the 1960s like Theo
Lehmann and Rochus Hagen studied the spirituals with exemplary
objectivity and concern, leaving Foster aside, the popular interest
in Black music was undiscriminating. Thus a questionnaire about
the most popular songs among students, sent by Heinz Benker in
1973 to ninety-five teachers in Bavaria, showed near the top of the
list—above any German folksong—the series: "Nobody Knows the
Trouble I've Seen," "Swanee River," "Swing Low." The Germans
who had most vigorously thought through their own long experience
of folksong advocacy, from Herder to Hitler, could not be surprised
by the results of the questionnaire. They knew, in the words of
Wolfgang Bruckner, that "folklorism means home at second hand,"
and further, in the words of Carl Dahlhaus, that "the 'genuine' is by
its own criteria phony."

The cult of Foster as American hero developed in part independently of the idea of the spirituals and the Black folk, in contexts where every other kind of music was disparaged as less American or less valuable, if not both at once. Though the cult focused
on the same four Foster songs, and though it rose and fell at the
same time as the idea of a Black peasantry, it was not merely dependent on that idea.

Beginning in 1893 the *Courier-Journal* of Louisville, Kentucky,
and other newspapers began to circulate legends about "My Old
Kentucky Home." A handsome old house at Bardstown, Kentucky,
south of Louisville, had been a summer home of Judge John Rowan
(ca. 1780–1842), a cousin of William B. Foster. According to the legend advanced in 1893 by the unreliable Louisville songwriter Will
Shakespeare Hayes (1837–1907), Stephen had written the song soon
after a visit to his relative and "evidently meant Judge Rowan's residence, known as 'Federal Hill,' for 'My Old Kentucky Home.'" In
1895 or 1896 Morrison Foster took his daughter Evelyn to visit Federal Hill; she remembered no more about it than a pleasant day; he
included in his book a picture of the house, captioned "The old Kentucky home," but without any comment in his text. In 1900 Morrison responded to an enquiry about the legend in the *Ladies' Home*

Journal, which by this time asserted that Stephen was a "protégé of Judge Rowan and made his home at Federal Hill most of the time." Morrison noted, "He was not a protégé of Judge Rowan but only an occasional visitor." On what occasions? Morrison never specified; no one else has succeeded in finding firm evidence, despite many efforts. Susan Pentland Robinson, in her interview of 1900 in the Pittsburgh *Press,* surmised that Stephen had visited Bardstown on the way home from New Orleans and had written the song just afterward. But she knew nothing of the discarded title "Poor Uncle Tom, good night." The song was probably written before the trip to New Orleans, as J. T. Howard argues from the evidence of Stephen's notebook. Howard, nevertheless, approves the legend as harmless publicity, "if those in charge of 'My Old Kentucky Home' are stimulating interest in the songs of Stephen Foster." But the publicity, involving (after 1922) a State museum and full-scale tourist exploitation, is better explained by Thomas D. Clark, who specialized in the questions related to "My Old Kentucky Home" and wrote in 1948:

> It is not the words which fascinate the modern Kentuckian, and it is not necessarily the melody which enthralls him. He is captivated by a dream.

The flourishing Kentucky legend overshadowed the facts of Pittsburgh and New York City in the most widespread public image of Foster. Not only Kentuckians but many other Americans could fondly associate Foster with Daniel Boone, Abe Lincoln, and the "frontier," all symbols of a native-born majority whose status was threatened less by the Blacks than by the new immigrants to the cities from Latin, Greek, Slavic, Yiddish, and Far Eastern cultures. Foster's songs were well adapted to the processes of "Americanization" in the "melting pot," and of preparation for the drastic limiting of immigration in the 1920s.

A German visitor, Martin Darkow, was first to explain these connections. In 1905, reporting on "Stephen Collins Foster und das amerikanische Volkslied" for *Die Musik,* he began with a long discussion of the "melting pot," which made impossible anything like German folksong. Foster's songs, however, were uniquely popular throughout the unique nation. Foster was not only "father of the American folksong—rather Father, Son, and Holy Ghost at once." Darkow finds "nothing specifically Negro" in the songs, but something of "the mood of the American autumn." He thinks "the feelings are those of poor oppressed people in general." He wonders at this "soft sentimentality," so unlike the prosaic optimism that he sees in the active American character. He understands its appeal to the Slavic Dvořák, for "melancholy" is a Slavic trait. He explains the contrast as "the breakthrough of a powerful individuality against the national character" and a "protest against the materialistic work of their compatriots." Similar "breakthroughs" and "protests" he has admired in Thoreau, Whitman, and Poe. Foster seems to him close to Poe. But Foster, more than these poets, has won the hearts of the people. To his own compatriots Darkow recommends especially an arrangement for *Männerchor* of "My Old Kentucky Home" by Frank Van der Stucken (1858–1929), who had conducted the first European concerts by a New York orchestra in 1892 and was now the dean of Cincinnati musicians. Darkow dismisses many of Foster's songs as *Modelieder* and *Gassenhauer,* in order to distinguish "Down the Swanee River," "Old Kentucky Home," and "Massa's in de Cold Ground" as worthy folksongs of the Americans.

The Bostonian author of *The History of American Music,* 1904, Louis Charles Elson (1848–1920), called Foster "as truly the folksong genius of America as Weber or Silcher have been of Germany." (Elson was oblivious of George P. Morris and John Hill Hewitt, not to mention any connection between them and Foster.) Elson's whole chapter on folk music shows him largely ignorant of the spirituals and uncomfortable about Dvořák; he relies on Morrison Foster for information to support the word "genius," which he does not dare apply to his fellow New Englanders and fellow graduates of study in Germany John Knowles Paine (1839–1906) and George Whitefield Chadwick (1854–1931). Elson praises "Kentucky Home," "Massa," "Uncle Ned," "Nelly Bly," "and above all 'The Old Folks at Home' " for expressing "the same tender melancholy" that he imagines is or was characteristic of plantation workers.

The more critical survey of *Music in America,* edited by Arthur Farwell and W. D. Darby, 1915, included a chapter by César Saerchinger on "The Folk Music of America," in which DuBois and Krehbiel are paraphrased for dealing with the spirituals, while Elson's reference to Silcher and Weber is copied for Foster, and both spirituals and Foster are used to deplore "degenerate . . . ragtime." Farwell's book failed to displace Elson, who brought out a second edition in the same year; his son Arthur provided a third edition in 1925, so that Elson's taste continued to dominate most of the rare academic discussions of 19th-century American music. Foster, partly by default, seemed to loom ever larger.

It was an interpretation like Darkow's and Elson's that motivated the cataloguing and the biographical research of the next decades and the interpretive judgments of several historians and literary critics.

John Tasker Howard (1890–1964) discussed Foster in relation to the "melting-pot" and folksong in 1921; he went on to compile his comprehensive book on *Our American Music* in 1931, in which he ranks Foster as "one of the summits of American music"; then, supported by Josiah Lilly, Howard wrote the biography of *Stephen Foster, America's Troubadour*, 1934, which superseded the earlier books by Morrison Foster and Harold Milligan. Howard also edited *A Program of Stephen Foster Songs . . . with New Accompaniments*, 1934; a *Foster sonatina* for violin and piano, 1934; and *From Foster Hall: Five Stephen Foster Melodies Transcribed for String Quartet*, 1938. The sonatina makes a first movement of "Ring de Banjo" and "Old Dog Tray," a second of "Jeanie" and "Come, Where," and a finale of "Camptown," "Massa," and "Old Folks." Howard's choices for the quartet transcriptions show a more personal taste: "Hard Times," "Oh! Susanna," "Massa," "Ring de Banjo," and "Gentle Annie." In his essay of 1921 on "Our Folk Music and Its Probable Impress on American Music of the Future," for the *Musical Quarterly*, Howard faces the paradox that "the great majority of us are merely the audience as far as American folksongs are concerned." The majority that "we" constitute is no "folk." Yet "we" claim as "our folk-tunes" what "really belong to only certain portions of our population with whom we never wish to be joined by ties of blood." Foster's songs can therefore be "ours" more thoroughly than the spirituals. "The American people from North, East, and West have joined the South in making them national." Howard wistfully hopes that future composers—like himself—may build a distinctive art-music on the foundation provided by Foster. "Did Dvorak show us the way when he wrote the 'New World' symphony?" he asks. The question baffles him. Howard sympathizes more deeply with Edward MacDowell (1861–1908), whose nearest approach to the recommended nationalistic art-music was in the exceptional piano pieces "From Uncle Remus," 1896, and "Of Br'er Rabbit," 1902. In *Our American Music* MacDowell has a bigger place than Foster. In the *Foster* book, Howard betrays uneasiness, not so much about race as about commerce in relation to individualistic art; he sees these issues only within America, as though people throughout the world looked only to America for their resolution, while American musicians—especially in New York—still needed European confirmation of the worth of their work. Howard supposes that commerce accounts for the fact that he cannot enjoy most of Foster's songs, while individual "genius" accounts for the response to a few of them that he shares with millions.

> He wrote for a market, but when he was at his best, the market never soiled his work—it merely gave him a voice that would be understood.
> Because the influences that moulded Foster's songs were so basically American his own songs are perhaps the most typically native product that had been produced up to his time. He was not like the composers in

seaboard cities who imitated foreign models; he was under the spell of the minstrel shows, the singing of the Negroes who came to Pittsburgh and Cincinnati on the river boats from the South, and of the Negro worshippers in a little church near his childhood home. His songs are distinctively American, and yet the thoughts they express are so basically human that they are sung throughout the world. Foster achieved a nationalistic expression that is at the same time universal in its appeal.

While they have a folk flavor, his songs are not merely a folk expression. They reflect the character and temperament of their composer, and in that sense they are truly an art product. . . .

Stephen Foster's fame rests chiefly on his great songs of the pre-Civil War South. These beloved plantation melodies were intended to portray one race of people, one section of our country, one period in our history, yet through his genius Foster succeeded in creating songs which have leaped the boundaries of space and time, and express universal thoughts and emotions.

Nearly every sentence of Howard's effortful summary can be contradicted on the basis of the facts that he himself assembled, with which we are now familiar. The market "soiled and scattered" Foster's songs, in his own words; it loaded meanings he had not intended onto "Susanna," "Old Folks" and eventually "Jeanie," so that his own voice was nearly lost and the "voices of old friends" never heard. The chief influences on his work included British and German products, more "basic" and pervasive than anything native. He chose to live in New York, rather than stay at home in Pittsburgh. The songs of Emmett and some other minstrel writers were more distinctively indigenous than Foster's. The songs of the slaves, whatever Foster knew of them, included things more distinctive still; there is no evidence that Foster knew them well. The thoughts he expressed are typical of an international current of nostalgia, strong in the 19th century but not necessarily "basically human," and more likely to repel than appeal to slaves. The ideas of a "folk" and of portraying a particular place and time were foreign to Foster. His "plantation songs" used a convention of the stage to express a traditional set of feelings in a way novel enough to make a modest commercial success, which Foster supposed would be ephemeral. Howard's interpretation depends largely on the ideas developed by Dvořák, DuBois, and others around 1900, though Howard has done nothing to develop them further. Howard was so conscientious and persistent in his fact-finding that he could smile at the humbug of Will Hays; he avoided the sheer fantasy of Martin Darkow. But he was distracted by words and ideas from considering "Anadolia" or the fiddle variations on "Old Folks." His half-hearted, second-hand interpretation encouraged more facile interpreters to develop the old ideas further.

Soon after Howard's book was published, the most elaborate "Americanizing" interpretation was provided by Bernard DeVoto's article on "Stephen Foster's Songs" in *Harper's*, 1941:

> He wrote well over two hundred songs, all potboilers, most of them quite dead now. . . . Art is mysterious, it is the miraculous and undefined, but if that should chance to be art which a people take most closely to their bosoms and hold there most tenderly and longest, then Stephen Foster is incomparably the greatest American artist. He made the Americans members of one another. . . . They were an inchoate people between two stages of the endless American process of becoming a nation . . . They were a people without unity and with only a spasmodic mutual awareness, at this moment being pulled farther asunder by the centrifugal expansion of the frontier and the equal explosiveness of the developing industry. . . . The way to understand the persons who were about to fight an unpremeditated war and by building new homes in the West push the nation's boundary to the Pacific—is to steep yourself in Stephen Foster's songs.

DeVoto's exhortation sounds remote in the 1970s; to recall its own historical context may make it reasonable. In 1941, when the American nation was about to fight again, in alliance with China and the USSR, and to take over imperial responsibilities from Britain, DeVoto was expressing a generous hope. As history or criticism of Foster, his interpretation is fatuous. As an eloquent document of the idealization of Foster, it maintains its value.

Like DeVoto, other literary Americanists reinforced the image of Foster—Van Wyck Brooks, E. Douglas Branch, Fred Lewis Pattee. None of them, however, either developed or criticized the underlying ideas.

The historian Henry Steele Commager developed and then criticized the ideas, yet kept his fondness for Foster. In 1950 Commager looked briefly at American music in his book, *The American Mind: An Interpretation of American Thought and Character Since the 1880's:*

> 20th-century America boasted a hundred symphony orchestras, but it still imported its conductors and its trios and quartettes, and it had not yet produced a single first-rate composer or even one to rank with Stephen Foster.

Commager could not be expected to take account of Henry Burleigh or Charles Ives or Elliott Carter; he was entitled to his own opinion of MacDowell and Copland; but he was certainly aware of Sousa, Ellington, and Gershwin, so that his naming of Foster is a tribute as well as a criticism. By 1965, when Commager wrote his essay on "The Search for a Usable Past," he turned some of his criticism against his fellow historians, while he kept Foster as most frequent if not favorite representative of music:

> The sentiment of American nationalism was, to an extraordinary degree, a literary creation. . . . The national memory was a literary and, in a sense, a contrived memory. . . . From "Swanee River" to "Ol' Man River" songs celebrating nature have usurped the place of formal patriotic music— "Dixie," for example, or "My Old Kentucky Home," or "On the Banks of the Wabash," or "Home on the Range," or best of all "America, the Beautiful."

Later in the essay Foster is named, though not Dan Emmett, Jerome Kern, Paul Dresser, nor Samuel A. Ward, composer of Commager's "best" tune, "Materna," 1882, for which Katherine Lee Bates provided the best-known words in 1904, firmly in the gospel tradition.

The "contrived memory" referred to by Commager was effective in the campaign that made Foster the first musician to have his portrait bust installed in New York University's Hall of Fame, 1941. (MacDowell waited until 1964 and Sousa until 1973.)

In 1950 a vast Stephen Foster Memorial at White Springs, Florida, was dedicated by the governor, and John Tasker Howard made a principal address, "The Hundredth Anniversary of 'Way Down Upon the Suwanee River.'" Here he claimed that Foster's songs "have in a century become true folk-songs" and that Foster "really expressed and typified our nation." His "greatest song . . . voices the American love of home, the unit of our civilization." The dedication should demonstrate "to all mankind that a free nation can give to the world a song-poet who has composed more folk-songs than any other man in history." Howard borrowed from the Memorial booklet his peroration:

> The real Suwanee River does not rise in any part of Georgia. It rises in the highest mountains of the human heart. It does not flow through Florida, but through the pleasant sunny lanes of memory.

The caution characteristic of Howard's book is gone. Pride celebrates. The Memorial, with the world's largest carillon added by 1960, commemorates the smug American power of 1950 better than Foster or any other reality of 1850.

American pride in Foster helped win him further recognition abroad. He became, in the words of a reporter for the Saturday Evening Post, R. Butterfield, "the real Voice of America." Butterfield tells how Josiah Lilly gave away more than two million copies of selected songs to prisoners of war during World War II, and how the songs were sung in many surprising places, by men of all the United Nations. Butterfield believes:

The warmth and kindly affection they express have probably spread more good will for this country than anything ever written by an American writer.

Soviet authorities agreed. In a survey of the *Paths of American Music*, 1965, for example, Valentina Konen gave Foster greater space than any other composer with "Old Folks," "Old Kentucky Home," and "Oh! Susanna," as arranged by J. Rosamund Johnson. In 1974 at a concert in honor of Richard Nixon in Moscow, "Way Down Upon the Swanee River" was sung by a Ukrainian chorus.

The humbug continued indefinitely. In 1967 Gerald Marks wrote on " 'Pop' and Posterity" for *ASCAP Today*, raving to outdo all his predecessors about

. . . "Swanee River," classic of classics and the most popular piece of music ever written, acclaimed *today* by all—the right and left, east and west . . .

In fact, protesting Blacks had long driven "Old Folks" out of many school books; in many more they had caused Foster's "darkies" to transform themselves into colorless "brothers." But Marks could count this attention as "acclaim" and use it to help maintain the vague "popularity."

Uncle Tom's Cabin had faded from the stage about 1930, and a revival of 1945 had to be abandoned, according to H. G. Nicholas, because of Black protests. But from 1852 to at least 1914, Tom shows had done more than all the literary and folkloristic praises to keep "Old Folks," "Kentucky Home," "Massa," and "Old Black Joe" constantly in the air. Beginning in the 1860s, touring Tom shows enlisted Black singers to make up a "jubilee chorus," and bandsmen to play in the street parades and outdoor concerts that attracted audiences to their theaters or tents. The outstanding singer and songwriter Sam Lucas (1848–1916) was the first Black man to play the leading role; he was touring with the C. H. Smith Tom show in 1881, when he published his *Careful Man Songster;* what careful double meanings did he lend to the Foster songs? More meanings than were recognized by most of his listeners. But for some time in the 1880s, according to Harry Birdoff, it was "almost fatal to stage the play without colored singers." One performance in Brooklyn used 800 in the chorus.

The minstrel show tradition, in which Sam Lucas was a prosperous "star," provided the chief medium for an outstanding songwriter of the 1880s who is often described in the 1970s as the chief successor to Foster: James Bland (1854–1911). Bland grew up in a family of free Negroes in Flushing, Long Island, and Washington, D.C. At Howard University he first encountered songs of the former slaves.

He dropped out of school to join the Georgia Minstrels, most successful Black troupe, managed by white impresarios George B. Callendar and then J. H. Haverly. In 1878 Bland composed "Carry Me Back to Old Virginny." When the troupe went to Britain, as Haverly's Genuine Colored Minstrels, 1880, Bland stayed there. He became a favorite in the music halls, and a special favorite in German theaters. Out of about 700 songs that he wrote, "In the Evening by the Moonlight" and "Oh, Dem Golden Slippers" most nearly rivaled "Old Virginny." In 1901 Bland returned to Washington, where his last works met no success; in 1911 he died in Philadelphia, ignored by the millions who sang his three hit songs. His sad end seemed a parallel to Foster's. How close the connection appeared to Bland himself has not yet been questioned: no one has studied all his songs in their own contexts; but wherever he is remembered, Foster's fame is reinforced.

The banjo, prime symbol of the minstrels, was cultivated especially by a Black musician, S. Swaim Stewart (1855–?), who published his own arrangements and instruction books in Philadelphia. *The Banjo: A Dissertation,* 1888, includes an advertisement for variations on "Old Folks" adapted for the banjo and piano. Stewart's work needs study even more than Bland's; when it begins to be recognized, it too will reinforce the fame of Foster.

Minstrel shows by blackfaced whites continued to flourish and to repeat the Foster favorites throughout the world longer than the Tom shows. The career of Al Jolson (1885–1950) in vaudeville, musical comedy, film, and television constantly renewed and glamorized the stereotype that he adopted as a boy street-singer in Washington, D.C., in the 1890s, when Foster songs earned nickels and dimes from the passersby. In England around 1950 the BBC's "Kentucky Minstrels" were enormously popular. In England, Australia, and New Zealand, 1957–69, *The Black and White Minstrel Show,* designed first for television and then for the stage, claimed unprecedented successes. In 1972 its successor, *The Magic of the Minstrels,* which I visited in London, came to a grand climax with a medley of "Golden Slippers," "Jeanie," "Susanna," "Some Folks," "Polly Wolly Doodle," "Dixie," and "Camptown," against a stage-filling backdrop of the United States flag. Though American television and city theaters found no room for such shows in the 1960s, there were still annual amateur performances of minstrel shows, most of which included "Old Folks," in towns like Trumansburg, New York. Their homely atmosphere contributed further meaning to the songs for people who remembered several such shows.

The minstrel shows were prime sources of the "country music" that developed through radio and phonograph, to the point where

Nashville, Tennessee, surpassed New York as a center of world music business. One of the most interesting country musicians, Uncle Dave Macon (1870–1952), grew up in the minstrel tradition. His repertory included not only "Old Uncle Ned," which he recorded, but also "Susanna," "Old Folks," and "Old Black Joe."

Meanwhile, in the decades around 1900, minstrel shows by Black performers for Black audiences in the South provided a chief institutional support for numerous musicians, including William Christopher Handy (1873–1958). They contributed, though less than the churches, to an increasingly homogeneous culture of Black people across the nation. What importance did the Foster songs have for these groups? Less than for the blackfaced whites, and different somehow. But more than might be supposed. Handy's autobiography, 1955, includes several references to Foster. He recalls that when he played in Mahara's Minstrels in 1896, "Brudder Gardner's picnic (a selection containing the gems of Stephen Foster) was always in order." He recalls meeting James Bland in 1897, and identifies Bland's songs as "second only to the work of Stephen Foster in the same field." Finally Handy philosophizes:

> Old Folks at Home (Swanee River) [is] dear to the hearts of all Americans. . . . It is my belief that Old Kentucky Home and Old Black Joe touched the heart of Lincoln and thus helped to make this book possible. . . . The well of sorrow from which Negro music is drawn is also a well of mystery. It's strange how the blues creep over you. I suspect that Stephen Foster owed something to this well, this mystery, this sorrow. My Old Kentucky Home makes you think so, at any rate. Something there suggests a close acquaintance with my people.

Handy's self-conscious belief is a tribute to Foster more important in the 1970s than all the tributes of Howard, DeVoto, Commager, the Soviet anthologists, and the British telly stars put together.

In popular theatrical music in New York, new influences from Black musicians appeared in every decade—the "cakewalk" of the 1880s, "coon song" of the '90s, "ragtime" around 1900, "blues" 1910, and "jazz" 1920. Though each new fashion met forms of resistance that exalted Foster and the spirituals in order to condemn modern vulgarity, yet at last there was an inescapable recognition of a strand of continuity, from Foster and the other minstrels of his time, to whatever was the latest fad.

Foster and the "black folk" were connected in a distinctive way by the leading composer of "ragtime" songs, John Rosamund Johnson (1873–1954), in his book *Rolling Along in Song: A Chronological Survey of American Negro Music,* 1937. Johnson was a versatile musician—not a scholar, but an independent thinker—who adapted the ideas of DuBois and Krehbiel and his brother, James Weldon Johnson, in the light of his own experience. His book is a first attempt to deal respectfully with the whole range of music made by slaves and their descendants down to a generation younger than Johnson's own. "Negro music rolls along," producing new forms and styles. "As the wheels of progress go speeding along, it is quite natural that other traditional forms of music should spring from such an inexhaustible source of rhythmic melody." Johnson was concerned with the living tradition more than with preserving or treating critically any of its old products. Moreover, he stressed the observation that "Negro characteristics in music are blending themselves into Negroid-American idioms with the verve of motion, speeding along on a rhythmic-streamlined vehicle." From this point of view, he credited Foster with "blending" some characteristic elements into a style basically distinct and valid in itself:

> It was undoubtedly the influence of Negro idioms in the musical mind of Stephen Foster that produced his best-loved songs. He was the writer of many songs that were not Negroid. In Pittsburgh he had written such beautiful ballads as "Open the Lattice, Love" and many other songs that were really worthwhile; but none of them seemed to have the "something" that would make them click into world-wide success. It was only after he had moved to Cincinnati, just across the river from Kentucky, that he caught the spirit of the slave songs and gave to the music world "My Old Kentucky Home" and "Old Folks at Home" (better known as "Way Down upon de Swanee Ribber").
>
> "Old Folks at Home" is built on the five-tone scale and its intervals are similar to those of "Deep River" in parts of its opening phrase. The second strain introduces the major seventh, used only once, as an innovation. The same treatment occurs with the use of the fourth.

Johnson's details prove no connection with "Negro idioms" in Foster's mind, but they show that Johnson thought for himself, that he was not merely repeating a conventional interpretation. *Rolling Along* includes Johnson's arrangements of "Kentucky Home" and "Old Folks," grouped with six other composers' "plantation ballads"; "Ring de Banjo" grouped with seven other "plantation and levee pastimes"; and "Susanna" and "Camptown" grouped with four other "minstrel songs." Johnson's arrangements are simpler than Burleigh's, but richer harmonically than the original versions, bringing the songs closer to the style of Johnson's young friend George Gershwin. Johnson wished to "encourage young musicians who are using characteristic Negro idioms to sound a distinctive note in a New World of Music." His generous treatment of Foster is incidental to his courageous optimism. Unfortunately, his knowledge of the living tradition does not extend to "gospel music," which might have showed then a stronger continuity of development within a more cohesive group of people than all the entertainment music. Naturally, if again unfortunately, Johnson ignores the "distinctive note" of his contemporary Charles Ives. Most regrettably, however, he neglects the distinctive musical irony that he might have recognized in Fats Waller, Louis Armstrong, Fletcher Henderson, and many more young men who jazzed Foster. Johnson's optimism, viewed in perspective with these contemporary developments, was too simple. Yet in the longer historical perspective we have surveyed, Johnson represents the nearest approach after George Root to a comprehensive American musical consensus in which Foster's songs are idealized as classic.

Does our far-ranging perspective that includes the international tradition of home songs, church and revival songs, and nationalistic "folklore," enable us now to probe more deeply? Foster's songs, like many others, may express both a languid homesickness and an active hope. The urban world tempts many of us, increasingly since the 18th century, to vain longings for a secure home, which we imagine as existing in the past, unrelated to our present actions. At the same time, the world of accelerating technology invites us to recognize that authentic art depends on truth and justice among increasingly interdependent groups, as well as on individual talent and technical practice guided by excellent models. When foreign models distract an artist from his neighbors, his talent is wasted or corrupted. Recognizing this, Herder and Burns proposed that we study the surviving art of rural neighborhoods, that we use it in preference to supposedly universal classic models, and that we use our various adaptations of it in striving toward the truth and justice that should animate our teeming nations. When "Old Folks" was hailed after 1870 as an example of neighborhood "folk" art, Foster's own homesickness fed a more insidious homesickness for "the old plantation," and a fragment of his life's work was used in attempts to unite all the people of the United States and proclaim their common distinctiveness from Europeans, though it always appealed as much in Britain and almost as much in Germany as at home. It was used also to help identify literate Americans of African descent with the "Black folk," segregated within the United States, among whom there actually flourished neighborhood arts, immensely vital and varied. Foster's work could be used for the increase of truth and justice among groups, or for many kinds of deceit and exploitation. To propose "Old Folks" as a "universal classic" is obvious humbug. To revere it as either American or Negro is likely to be worse. To connect it with the "dream of home" that obsessed some classes of people through some generations in many nations is an antidote. How good or bad "Old Folks" is depends on the circumstances of particular performances, and on the contexts of particular criticisms. Its history cannot guide but can help to clarify some present choices of individuals in interacting groups.

⦅ CHAPTER 13 ⦆

Composers
of "new music"

STEPHEN FOSTER, five of his famous songs, and especially a motif or a phrase from each of these songs had unique meanings for Charles Edward Ives (1874–1954). These meanings are among many elements that Ives used in composing his *Second Symphony;* his *Three Places in New England* for orchestra; his *Second Sonata,* "Concord, Mass., 1840–60," for piano; and several less famous compositions, including the "Elegy for Our Forefathers" that begins the *Second Orchestral Set,* which was first conceived as "An Elegy for Stephen Foster." Ives' intentions in these pieces have been obscured for some interested listeners (such as Elliott Carter, for example) partly because, for them, the Foster songs carry too many conflicting connotations. With a little study, however, listeners prepared by a survey of the songs' various changing meanings can pick out those valid for Ives and make use of them. The volume of Ives' *Memos* edited by John Kirkpatrick in 1972, together with his *Essays Before a Sonata,* 1920, and the music itself, enable us to learn what Foster meant to Ives more easily than earlier listeners could do.

Something as distinctive as the meaning of Foster for Ives is more relevant than Dvořák's *New World* for several younger composers who quote Foster's tunes, including Irving Berlin, George Gershwin, Aaron Copland, Francis Poulenc, and Lukas Foss. In the case of

Thea Musgrave's chamber concerto "In Homage to Charles Ives," there is no doubt that a Foster quotation calls for understanding in the context of all that listeners know of Ives.

In 1932 Ives wrote characteristically about his *Second Symphony*, composed in 1897–1902 and destined finally to be performed and published in 1951:

> Some of the themes in this symphony suggest Gospel Hymns and Steve Foster. . . .
>
> Some nice people, whenever they hear the words "Gospel Hymns" or "Stephen Foster," say "Mercy Me!", and a little high-brow smile creeps over their brow—"Can't you get something better than that in a symphony?" The same nice people, when they go to a properly dressed symphony concert under proper auspices, led by a name with foreign hair, and hear Dvorak's *New World Symphony*, in which they are told this famous passage was from a negro spiritual, then think that it must be quite proper, even artistic, and say "How delightful!" But when someone proves to them that the Gospel Hymns are fundamentally responsible for the negro spirituals, they say, "Ain't it awful!"—"You don't really mean that!"—"Why, only to think!"—"Do tell!"—"I tell you, you don't ever hear Gospel Hymns even mentioned up there to the New England Conservatory."

This passage from the *Memos*, characteristic in its animus against the "nice people," is likely to puzzle or put off a reader who associates Foster more with the spirituals than with gospel songs, whereas a reader who has traced some connections in both directions can recognize the particular "nicety" that Ives attacks and can accept, at least provisionally, Ives' emphasis on the gospel songs. (Most of Ives' listeners, unlike the "nice people," are unprejudiced about the gospel songs because they are ignorant of them. Henry Cowell, Ives' biographer, reported in 1951 that Ives himself had forgotten the names of many of his old favorites.) Ives continues for six paragraphs, with three musical examples, his "proofs" that the gospel songs are "fundamentally responsible" for the spirituals; he recounts some experiences of his own, his father's, and his grandmother's, and ends with a repetition of his claim:

> But the darkies used these things in their own native way, and made them somewhat different—"more beautiful and more artistic" says Rollo. [Rollo was the goody-goody hero of a series of didactic stories by Jacob Abbott, the patron of G. F. Root.] Yes, and so did some of the Yankees. I'm not trying to say that many of the spirituals, jubilees, etc. aren't in their own way natural, spontaneous, beautiful, and artistic—but some white Congregationalists or Methodists (drunk or sober) already had somepin' also natural, spontaneous, beautiful, and artistic—and that somepin' was to start the negro spirituals.

For Ives, Foster was associated with the many Yankees he had grown up with in Danbury, Connecticut, and with their singing of the gospel songs that were new in the 1870s and '80s. The spirituals Ives associated with "Rollo" and other "nice people" he had known at Yale, 1895–98, and in New York City ever since—people who refused his songs and symphonies—more than with any people of African descent; he knew nothing about the characteristic integration of Black choral singing, whereas he knew much about the "natural artistic" choruses at white camp meetings.

Foster was connected especially with Ives' father, George Edward Ives (1845–94). An unwritten family account that reached John Kirkpatrick through Amelia Merritt Ives Van Wyck, granddaughter of George's brother Joseph, testifies that George Ives met Foster in New York one Saturday evening in 1861 or early 1862. The sixteen-year-old made weekly trips from Danbury to take cornet lessons and attend orchestra concerts. He happened to encounter Foster at a moment when he could be useful; he helped Foster to his lodgings. So, fifteen or twenty years later, George Ives could pass on to his son a sense of a closer connection with Foster than any other such famous name in music. And Charles Ives testified often to the way his father played and taught the Foster tunes. In response to a questionnaire from John Tasker Howard, for use in *Our American Music*, Charles Ives wrote in 1930:

> My father was a musician and a teacher (in Danbury and neighboring villages) of the violin, piano (brass and wood instruments), harmony, sight reading (and ear training), etc. He played in and taught the brass band (and orchestra), led the church choirs, the music at the Camp Meetings, and the local Choral Society. He had a reverence, a devotion, and a talent for music which was unusual. His interest lay not only in what had been done but in what might be done. His study of acoustics led him to many experiments into the character of musical instruments and tonal combinations, and even into the divisions of the tone.
>
> He had a belief that everyone was born with at least one germ of musical talent, and that an early application of great music (and not trivial music) would help it grow. He started all the children of the family—and most of the children of the town for that matter—on Bach and Stephen Foster. (Quite shortly after they were born—always regardless of whether [they] had, would have, or wouldn't have any musical gifts or sense, etc.—) he put a love of music into the heart of many a boy who might have gone without it but for him.
>
> (I feel that, if I have done anything that is good in music, I owe it almost entirely to him and his influence.)

Foster here stands next to Bach in the most fundamental thoughts and feelings of Ives, most carefully expressed for a remote correspondent. In his *Memos* Ives recalls more about his father and Foster:

> Father could play, on his horn, a Franz Schubert or Steve Foster song better than many singers could sing it—he often taught songs and parts to singers or choirs, etc. by playing. But he always insisted that the words should be known and thought of, while playing. That, I suppose, gave me the idea of "songs with or without voices."

He recalls much more about his father and gospel songs:

> I remember, when I was a boy—at the outdoor Camp Meeting services in Redding, all the farmers, their families and field hands, for miles around, would come afoot or in their farm wagons. I remember how the great waves of sound used to come through the trees—when things like *Beulah Land, Woodworth, Nearer My God To Thee, The Shining Shore, Nettleton, In the Sweet Bye and Bye* and the like were sung by thousands of "let out" souls. The music notes and words on paper were about as much like what they "were" (at those moments) as the monogram on a man's necktie may be like his face. Father, who led the singing, sometimes with his cornet or his voice, sometimes with both voice and arms, and sometimes in the quieter hymns with a French horn or violin, would always encourage the people to sing their own way. Most of them knew the words and music (theirs) by heart, and sang it that way. If they threw the poet or the composer around a bit, so much the better for the poetry and the music. There was power and exaltation in these great conclaves of sound from humanity. I've heard the same hymns played by nice celebrated organists and sung by highly-known singers in beautifully upholstered churches, and in the process everything in the music was emasculated—precise (usually too fast) even time—"ta ta" down-left-right-up—pretty voices, etc. They take a mountain and make a sponge cake of it, and sometimes, as a result, one of these commercial travellers gets a nice job at the Metropolitan. Today apparently even the Camp Meetings are getting easy-bodied and commercialized. There are not many more of them here in the east, and what is told of some of those that still survive, such as Amy McPherson & Co., seems but a form of easy entertainment and silk cushions—far different from the days of the "stone-fielders." . . . In the summer times, the hymns were sung outdoors. Folks sang (as *Old Black Joe*)—& the Bethel Band . . . there were feelings, and of spiritual fervency!

A further recollection, especially relevant to Charles Ives' music, comes from a letter sketch of 1945:

> . . . at an outdoor meeting . . . with no instrumental accompaniment except a cornet . . . the fervor of the feeling would at times, especially on reaching the Chorus of many of those hymns, throw the key higher, sometimes a whole tone up—though Father used to say it [was] more often about a quarter tone up—and . . . Father had a sliding cornet made so that he could rise with them and not keep them down.

When Ives quotes either Foster or the gospel songs, he means his listeners to catch some such "fervor of the feeling" as he had known in the outdoor "conclaves." He means us to welcome the crowd's "throwing around" of words and music, to "rise with them," as his father did. Evidently his father's leading of the chorus was different from that of Bliss or Sankey, very different from that of Alexander or Rodeheaver or still later "silk cushion" revivalists. George Ives used the music as little for hastening religious conversions as for advancing himself. Rather he took an interest in every quarter-tone, as a measure of abstract "fervency," in order to "rise with" the group. His extraordinary attitude, which he passed on to his son, is shown wtih utmost clarity in the story of his sliding cornet.

A last recollection of George Ives and Foster involves a similar kind of listening. The full context from the *Memos* makes this story better than the context of Henry and Sidney Cowell's book about *Ives*, 1955, in which the story was also told:

> What my father did for me was not only in his teaching, on the technical side, etc., but in his influence, his personality, character, and openmindedness, and his remarkable understanding of the ways of a boy's heart and mind. He had a remarkable talent for music and for the nature of music and sound, and also a philosophy of music that was unusual. . . . For instance, he thought that man as a rule didn't use the faculties that the Creator had given him hard enough. I couldn't have been over ten years old when he would occasionally have us sing, for instance, a tune like *The Swanee River* in the key of E♭, but play the accompaniment in the key of C. This was to stretch our ears and strengthen our musical minds, so that they could learn to use and translate things that might be used and translated (in the art of music) more than they had been. In this instance, I don't think he had the possibility of polytonality in composition in mind, as much as to encourage the use of the ears—and for them and the mind to think for themselves and be more independent—in other words, not to be too dependent upon customs and habits.

"Old Folks," in this exercise for stretching and strengthening, serves as if it were a product of nature or an elementary geometrical shape more than a treasured relic of the personal and social past. Tunes of this kind can be neutral units of hearing and of musical thinking, not themes but rather the basic words of a language in which translation and dialogue and the hard work of thought can proceed. Did George Ives treat hymns in quite the same way? Or did the Foster songs have a special utility because for him they were free of partisan religious or political meaning? Nothing in Charles Ives' recollections calls attention to Foster's references to slaves or masters; rather he seems to assume that all his readers can relate "Old Folks" and similar songs to their own fathers and that the long familiarity of the songs makes them usable for dispassionate thinking and translating.

Ives presents something more than an exercise, yet something similar to his father's assignment, in his *Trio for Violin, Cello, and Piano,* composed 1904–11. In the middle of the second movement, the pianist plays the whole melody of "My Old Kentucky Home" with his right hand, while the other instruments and the pianist's left hand accompany in their own keys and rhythms, making a blurred background in which a listener's ear is invited to stretch, and his mind to strengthen.

"Kentucky Home" serves as a trio section also in the *Third March,* which was brought to a first performance only in the Ives centennial year, 1974. Here again there are ear-stretching counterpoints; the tune serves as a scaffolding.

The title-phrase of "My Old Kentucky Home" serves marvelously in the song "The Things Our Fathers Loved (and the Greatest of These Was Liberty)," composed in 1905 and 1917, published in the collection of *114 Songs* that Ives printed and distributed free in 1922. The text is Ives' own free verse:

> I think there must be a place in the soul
> all made of tunes,
> of tunes of long ago,

For the words "of tunes of long ago" the Foster phrase is recognizable in the voice's melody, "rising" in pitch and "fervency" to distort the key. Then the song continues:

> I hear the organ on the Main Street corner.
> Aunt Sarah humming Gospels;
> Summer evenings,
> The village cornet band, playing in the square.
> The town's Red, White and Blue,
> all Red, White and Blue,
> Now! Hear the songs!

Here the music is excited, complex, hinting at the title's parenthesis. Then it relaxes:

> I know not what are the words
> But they sing in my soul
> of the things our Fathers loved.

Again with the last line, the distorted Foster phrase appears. A singer who remembers something about George Ives and his sliding cornet, about his way of listening to the outdoor conclaves, and about his ear-stretching, mind-strengthening exercise, will do more than the notes on the page can indicate to evoke corresponding thoughts and feelings in his audience. A listener who recognizes the allusion as simply a "tune of long ago," whose original words are meaningless now, can respond to Ives' song, without necessarily knowing any biographical details. And a listener who has found the right response for this song can go on in the right attitude to Ives' bigger works.

The Foster allusions in the *Second Symphony* are mingled with the many other allusions, so that they are not so prominent as those of the *Trio* and "The Things Our Fathers Loved." On the other hand, there is room for much repetition and emphasis. Also there is an aptness about the words evoked along with the bits of the tunes: "Gwine to run all night, gwine to run all day" from "Camptown Races," and "Down in the cornfield" from "Massa's in de Cold Ground." A listener who thinks of the titles, rather than the particular words, may be worse off than one who cannot identify the tunes but senses only that they are vaguely familiar. "Gwine to run all night" booms out in the brasses at several points in the first and last movements; it is treated as a motif for development and contrapuntal combination, in which the feeling of boyish exuberance makes an effective contrast with more solemn passages. "Down in the cornfield" appears first unobtrusively in the first violins as counterpoint to the development of the principal original motifs of the first movement (measure 7). In the third movement, the wind choir, fortissimo, makes "Down in the cornfield" a memorable subordinate theme; the strings then, pianissimo, give the same phrase a mystical, pantheistic tinge. The last movement brings back this treatment of the phrase.

The finale of the symphony has another theme (measure 58) that may allude to Foster, though no listener yet has confirmed the suggestion that Ives included in his manuscript catalog of his works, 1937:

> The last movement is partly from an early overture called the American Woods (Brookfield). The part suggesting a Steve Foster tune, while over it the old farmers fiddled a barn dance with all of its jigs, gallops, and reels, was played in Danbury on the old Wooster House bandstand in 1889.

In the passage of his *Memos* of 1930, quoted at the beginning of our chapter, just after the name of Foster there is a parenthesis indicating that the fifteen-year-old's composition was quite different from the symphony:

> (The last movement was a kind of overture—played partly as a shorter piece by Father's Orchestra 1889, the Danbury Band—*The Red White and Blue* and old barn-dance fiddles on top.)

In the symphony the horn's theme under the fiddles is neither much like Foster nor at all like "The Red White and Blue," i.e., "Columbia the Gem of the Ocean" by Thomas à Becket, 1843. John Kirkpatrick wonders whether five notes at the end of the third phrase by the horns are a quotation from "Old Folks"—"far, far away." Though the possibility seems far-fetched to me, every guess by Kirkpatrick is worth further consideration. As the symphony comes to be played and heard and studied by more people, further possibilities may turn up. The possibility that now seems likeliest is that Ives' words "suggesting a Stephen Foster tune" mean that the symmetrical phrases of the horn melody constitute a clear unit, unlike the more open-ended symphonic themes; there may be nothing in this melody to evoke a particular Foster tune in the way "Gwine to run all night" and "Down in the cornfield" are evoked.

The two Foster phrases used in the *Second Symphony* are used in later pieces too. "Gwine to run all night" appears in the *Fourth Symphony* and in the orchestral "Washington's Birthday," but its appearances are fleeting; many other quotations of patriotic and popular tunes are more important. "Down in the cornfield" appears in seven pieces, and in some of them it is quite important. A short piano piece of 1908, "Some South-paw Pitching," carries the melody on to complete Foster's phrase—"hear that mournful sound"—and aside from this melody the piece concerns itself with rhythmic and percussive devices for commenting on a baseball game; the sense of the quotation must be that the ball has been hit into the "field." In the *First Piano Sonata*, 1902–10, quoted motifs overlap and merge and recur in the course of the five movements, as Dennis Marshall pointed out in 1968; the chorus of one of the principal themes, "I Hear Thy Welcome Voice" by Lewis Hartsough (1820–72), is like an ornamented version of "Down in the cornfield . . . the cold, cold ground," and the final four notes shared by these tunes are shared also by two others whose beginnings make a stronger melodic contrast. Marshall calls this a "musical pun." It is a favorite device in most of Ives' later large works. In the *First Sonata* vigorous ragtime accompaniments interfere with the comparatively slow-moving gospel songs; the outdoor atmosphere referred to by the "Cornfield" can help to reconcile them. A similar use of "Down in the cornfield" is found in the last movement of the *Theater* or *Chamber Orchestra Set*, composed mainly in 1906. The Foster phrase is a counterpoint to "Abide with Me," the most famous hymn of the English composer William Henry Monk (1823–89). The "Cornfield" phrase serves differently in the *Second String Quartet*, second movement, 1907–11: all four players abandon their contrapuntal wrangling near the end of the movement, to join in a common rhythm for a clear statement of "Down in the cornfield, hear that—" but then they proceed through ridiculously drooping chromatic chords to a pause, after which they resume the argument. The "Cornfield" phrase appears in the "Scherzo" for string quartet, 1903–14; the cello states it, loud, against a quasi-ostinato accompaniment of the upper parts; the cello goes on to quote "The sun shines bright on my old—" from "Kentucky Home," and at this point the violins break into a fortissimo suggestion of the "Sailor's Hornpipe," which distracts the cello into wild syncopations; all parts gasp for breath, then play a canon on the "Hootchie-kootchie Dance" that Sol Bloom had provided for the Chicago World's Fair. Ives was not reverent toward his Foster quotations.

The most important uses of "Down in the cornfield," however, are in the final movement, "Thoreau," of the *"Concord" Sonata,* composed mainly in 1911–12, and in the song "Thoreau," derived from the sonata, 1915. The text of the song is drawn from *Walden:*

> He grew in those seasons like corn in the night. Rapt in revery, on the Walden shore, amidst the sumach, pines and hickories in undisturbed solitude.

The singer chants these words while the accompaniment pursues a hypnotic ostinato in the bass and quotes Foster in the treble; aside from a newly adapted introduction, the accompaniment is the same as the end of the sonata. Ives' notes to the sonata provide a further interpretation:

> Sometimes, as on pages 62–65–68, an old Elm Tree may feel like humming a phrase from "Down in the Corn Field."

The pianist's melody is such a hum, rather than a direct utterance of the subject. In Ives' *Essays Before a Sonata* there are many more relevant notions, which the music can make more vivid if it does not accidentally distract a listener to thoughts irrelevant for Ives:

> Thoreau was a great musician, not because he played the flute but because he did not have to go to Boston to hear "the Symphony." . . . He sang of the submission to Nature, the religion of contemplation, and the freedom of simplicity—a philosophy distinguishing between the complexity of Nature, which teaches freedom, and the complexity of materialism, which teaches slavery.

A distraction is likely: if a listener thinks of Thoreau's defense of John Brown and then of Foster's fiction that "Massa made de darkeys love him, Cayse he was so kind," Ives' concern with Nature is likely to be overwhelmed. But if the listener can bind the melody with the image of growing "like corn in the night," he can follow the whole meditative program of the movement. Perhaps listeners who can recall, over the horizon, Foster's serene posthumous songs "Sitting by My Own Cabin Door" and "Voices That Are Gone" will agree that the "Cornfield" phrase, liberated from the "plantation" stereotype, fits the use that Ives makes of it.

A few lines of Thoreau to which Ives did not refer can provide further help for listeners of the late 20th century. In 1845, in a letter to the *Liberator*, Thoreau described Frederick Douglass

> . . . as superior to degradation from the sympathies of Freedom, as from the antipathies of Slavery.

In his *Journal*, 1853, Thoreau wrote one of his frequent entries on music:

> Many an irksome sound in our neighborhood, go a long distance off, is heard as music and a proud sweet satire on the meanness of our life. Not a music to dance to, but to live by.

And again in the *Journal*, 1854:

> Nothing is so truly bounded and obedient to law as music, yet nothing so surely breaks all petty and narrow bonds. Whenever I hear music I fear that I may have spoken tamely and within bounds.

Ives' musical portrait of Thoreau, with its use of the possibly "degrading," possibly "irksome" phrase about the "Cornfield," can be such a "proud sweet satire" as Thoreau heard; Ives "surely breaks all petty and narrow bonds," and his use of the "Cornfield" phrase can be an instance of his doing so.

Throughout the *"Concord" Sonata*, in the movements dedicated to Emerson, Hawthorne, and the Alcotts, as well as the Thoreau finale, Ives uses the four-note motif from the beginning of Beethoven's *Fifth Symphony*, which he labels, in his *Essays*, an "oracle." Its meaning for him he specified as not the well-known "fate knocking at the door" but rather "the soul of humanity knocking at the door of the divine mysteries," and this meaning, he says, is "the 'common heart' of Concord." Ives would have liked a passage from Thoreau's Journal of 1840, which waited for publication until 1958:

> There is as much music in the world as virtue.—At length music will be the universal language, and men greet each other in the fields in such accents as Beethoven now utters but rarely and indistinctly. It entails a surpassing influence on the meanest thing.

In the light of these words, Ives' use of the "Cornfield" phrase, subordinated to the Beethoven motif, fits Thoreau as nothing else could.

The two pieces of Ives remaining for consideration have much in common. In 1909 Ives began his "Elegy for Stephen Foster"; in 1913 he worked on this piece and, at the same time, the closely related

piece called "The St. Gaudens in Boston Common," which he sometimes referred to in his *Memos* as "The Black March." In 1914 he
completed the *First Orchestral Set, Three Places in New England,* in
which the "Boston Common" is first; in 1915 he completed the
Second Orchestral Set, in which the "Elegy" is first; the full final
name of the movement, "Elegy for Our Forefathers," may have been
added as late as 1947. The first set was performed in 1930, under the
direction of Nicolas Slonimsky; the score was published in 1935
and from then on won many friends for Ives. The second set,
recorded in 1967 by Morton Gould, still waited for publication in
1975.

Both pieces use the motif from the chorus of "Old Black Joe,"
"I'm coming." In the "Elegy" these few notes begin in the basses,
with a soft gong, and continue throughout the slow rise and fall of
the movement, as a foundation of the complex accompaniment to
a long melody. The same motif, in various registers, with conflicting
keys and irregularly coordinated rhythm, and combined with soft
jangling bell sounds, makes the accompaniment so complex that the
total effect for a listener is a blur, as if individuals are "coming"
from all directions to lose themselves in a crowd. Then the main
melody, begun by a soft trumpet and second violins, presents the
Foster motif once more, and continues into the phrase: "for my
head . . ." But now a pun takes over: all these notes belong equally
to the chorus of the Sunday-school hymn "Renar" by William Bradbury, "Yes, Jesus loves me, yes, Jesus loves me, the Bible tells me
so." As Ives' melody continues, Bradbury more and more dominates
Foster, as if all mourning for Foster or any other forefather were
dissolved in childlike faith. Yet when the melody ceases the blurred
accompaniment continues for the last third of the piece (measures
30–47). Faintly "Down in the cornfield . . . mournful sound"
emerges; it is repeated, transposed, shortened to "the cornfield" and
finally "cornfield," which puns with "I'm com-." The Sunday-school
assurance is perhaps no more than a memory of childhood, while
the mystery of Nature is endless. The sounds fade away into silence
without any resolution of the dissonant relations among them. Ives
asks that during the last seven slow measures the strings gradually
leave off, "until a distant effect is attained," as if he were thinking
again of Thoreau's "sweet satire."

There is another motif in the "Elegy," appearing soon after the
trumpet's beginning (measure 15), loud enough as played by second
trumpet and first violins to suggest that it is the beginning of an
expository countermelody, but disappearing quickly, never to return.
This motif is "Nobody Knows." Its players proceed smoothly into
another statement of "I'm coming," diminuendo. Nobody but Jesus

fully knows the individuals who come to a common death. Nobody knows who were the first singers of "Nobody Knows," nor whether Foster ever heard "Nobody Knows." Did Ives mean to suggest so much? It would be consistent with as much as is known of him.

"I'm coming" is the fundamental motif of the accompaniment in "The St. Gaudens in Boston Common." Again it forms an ostinato bass, which appears at the beginning and end of the movement, and also briefly just after the loud climax. At two points (measures 26 and 73) there is a further fragment of "Old Black Joe," "for my head is bending low." For Ives all the associations of the "Elegy" are relevant here. The sculpture by Augustus St. Gaudens commemorates the Black heroes of the 59th Massachusetts infantry regiment, led by Colonel Robert Gould Shaw, killed in 1863 as their surviving comrades captured Fort Wagner from the Confederates. At the dedication of the monument in 1897, the principal speaker was William James; for Ives as for James these heroes embodied "our American religion . . . the faith that a man requires no master to take care of him, and that common people can work out their salvation well enough together if left free to try." In his own words, printed as preface to the score, Ives exclaims:

> Moving—Marching—Faces of Souls!
> Marked with generations of pain,
> Part-Freers of a Destiny,
> Slowly, restlessly swaying us on with you
> Towards other Freedom!

He pays attention to the image of Shaw:

> The man on horseback,
> Carved from a native quarry
> Of the world's Liberty-rock
> Your country was made from—

Then he turns back to the Blacks:

> You—Images of a Divine Law,
> Carved in the shadow of a saddened heart—
> Never light-abandoned—
> Of an Age and of a Nation!

Then back to "swaying us on":

> Above and beyond that compelling mass,
> Rises the drum-beat of the common-heart,
> In the silence
> Of a strange and sounding afterglow—
> Moving—Marching—Faces of Souls!

The main melodic fragments, building up to the "drum-beat of the common-heart," Ives takes from Root's "Battle Cry of Freedom" and Work's "Marching Through Georgia." "I'm coming" surrounds these forceful marches with the shadow and afterglow of death. The Foster phrase lets Ives avoid any sectarian religious association. It lets him—and us listeners—"sway on" toward "other Freedom."

For Ives the Civil War and everything about it recalled his father. George Ives had led the band of the First Connecticut heavy artillery, 1862–65. According to the reminiscences of James R. Young, Ives' band won the praise of Lincoln when he visited Grant at Richmond. Grant's apology in reply to Lincoln was more famous than the praise: "It's the best band in the army, they tell me. But you couldn't prove it by me. I know only two tunes. One is 'Yankee Doodle' and the other isn't." During the war Ives employed the ten-year-old son of his company's laundress, Henry Anderson Brooks; he brought Brooks back to Danbury, guided him through school, and helped him start a career as cleaner and dyer; Brooks' letters to the Ives family, 1872–90, rarely mention music, but Charles Ives recalled stories of Brooks' whistling and humming pentatonic versions of the band's music. Among Ives' *Memos* there is a dialogue entitled "George's Adventure," 1919, in which he makes explicit the judgments of the Civil War and of Blackness that he shared with most of his associates:

> The circumstance of our Civil War of the '60s freed the slaves, but if that circumstance hadn't happened at that particular time, other circumstances perhaps more natural, perhaps more generous, perhaps with broader reconstruction feelings, etc., would have freed them. . . . Prejudice is the bad part of good traditions. . . . The difference between the negroe and the sun-browned white man is only of degree, not kind. . . . (. . . Mixture or social infusion has always of course been at work, we see it in all mythology and history and biology, we see the idea at least in the Tower of Babel, we see it in Herodotus.) Pure blood, if left to stand long enough alone, will like milk become sour and decomposed.

These opinions, like Ives' memory of his father, conditioned his choice of the Foster motif and his way of using it in the "St. Gaudens." Listeners who share the opinions may learn to "sway on" with the motif.

Conductors who admire Ives for the boldness of his innovations with sound and rhythm, more than for the associations of all his quoted tunes, may, nevertheless, find clues in some of the these associations for adjusting details of speed and loudness in their performances. Listeners may find in them means of keeping attention on the complex musical thought that Ives carries through his long movements. Above all, listeners who have been distracted by their own associations with Foster that Ives never intended may find the music sounding clearer and more coherent. Students of Ives will continue to contribute in various ways to keeping alive the fame of Foster; those who are patient enough to sort out Foster's meanings may avoid further confusing them.

Our concentration on Ives' use of Foster risks a new confusion: because Ives' other quotations are mentioned here only in their connections with Foster, it should not be supposed that the others are less important. George Root is quoted more often. The great majority of quotations come from gospel songs. An investigation of several of these might go farther toward clarifying Ives' music than all we have done with Foster. It might modify some of our findings, since Ives associated Foster so closely with gospel songs. But the Foster quotations call for clarification more urgently than others because these tunes are familiar to many admirers of Ives and because their multiple associations have obscured Ives' intention as much as they have served it.

Ives became familiar with something of the theatrical ragtime style during a few years in New York after he had given up his church organ post, 1902, and before he married Harmony Twichell, 1908. His memories of the characteristic syncopation of ragtime went back to blackfaced comedians at the Danbury Fair in 1892 and to the New Haven theater pianist George Felsberg. But Ives' use of ragtime in his own music was first encouraged after 1902 by Joseph Reutershan, a pianist who kept a music shop and was an insurance agent on the side—Ives' own insurance business as much as Reutershan's music brought them together. Reutershan persuaded friends in a theater orchestra to read some of Ives' ragtime pieces. But ragtime remained for him a kind of spice to be added to more solid musical materials. In his *Essays* he compares it to tomato ketchup and horseradish. He never referred to the ragtime of Scott Joplin (1868–1917). He left to others a close connection between ragtime and Foster.

Among the earliest records in music notation of the piano style that Joplin brought to a climax in his "rags," there is a version of "Old Black Joe," "Paraphrase de concert" by Charles Gimble, Jr., 1877, reprinted in Ann Charters' *Ragtime Song Book*, 1965. This piece, of no great interest in itself, may stand for many unpublished versions of the Foster favorites. A ragtime version of "Old Folks" by Joe "Fingers" Carr, 1953, is a fine representative of the tradition.

Irving Berlin (b. 1888) quotes four notes from "Old Folks" in the song that made Berlin and ragtime famous around the world in 1911, "Alexander's Ragtime Band." The next to last phrase of the song presents "Swanee River played in ragtime"—the four notes for "played in ragtime" are the notes Foster had set to the words "Swanee River." Berlin's words prepare a listener to recognize the notes; they stand out against earlier phrases because the second and fourth of these notes hit the high keynote for the first time; the smooth phrase containing them leads on to the final phrase, which ends on the same high keynote, contrary to Foster's tune. The Berlin tune uses its quotation not as basic material nor as a parenthesis but precisely as a climax, marvelously absorbed into its own continuity. Ives may well have envied him. "Alexander's Ragtime Band," however, lapsed into obscurity, like most songs that gain swift success. Its quotation implies that "Old Folks" is a classic that can be played in an endless series of replaceable modern styles.

Berlin's long career as writer of nearly a thousand songs, publisher, theater builder, and patriot sometimes led his admirers to compare him with Foster. Berlin himself, in an interview with Abel Green in 1962, compared some of his own songs of the 1940s with one of Foster's:

> . . . all I know is that some of the corniest and simplest songs have lasted, be they "White Christmas" and "Easter Parade" or "My Old Kentucky Home."

To develop these comparisons to their limits would be difficult. In the 1970s simply to take notice of them is enough to show one more of the ramifications of Foster's meaning.

George Gershwin (1898–1937) made his first success with the tune, "Swanee," 1919, in which there is more than one reference to "Old Folks." The title is the first. The words, by Ira Gershwin, include a "trio":

> Swanee, Swanee, I am coming back to Swanee.
> Mammy, mammy, I love the old folks at home.

The tune for the last line quotes Foster's "far from the old folks at home." Both text and tune contradict the singer's sentiment; his rush of cliché fragments indicates that he is already farther from Foster's old folks than Berlin and that he is likely to change direction several times before he reaches home; if, indeed, he really does plan to go back. The musical quotation is simply the final cliché. The song makes sense without the trio. The trio makes no sense by itself. What it adds to the song is probably a laugh. But "Swanee" adds to "Old Folks" another confirmation of classic status.

Gershwin's biggest work, the "folk opera" *Porgy and Bess*, 1935, brought him closer to the attitude of Dvořák, or even to that of Moussorgsky, for in preparing this work Gershwin learned more about the music of a Black community (in South Carolina) than

Dvořák and his immediate followers had done. Yet his libretto, by DuBose Heyward, kept him closer than he was aware to the stereo-types established by Foster and Stowe. Gershwin's success, however it may be measured, gave further plausibility to the interpretation of Foster as "father of American folk song." Gershwin's quotation, in "Swanee," is a clearer indication of the mythic unreality of both men's most famous work.

Gershwin's *Rhapsody in Blue* (1924), *Concerto for Piano* (1925), and orchestral suite, *An American in Paris* (1928), were played by American symphony orchestras for some decades more often than any other American works. By 1970, however, the music of Ives appeared on orchestra programs more often than Gershwin's. More often than either, there were works of Aaron Copland (b. 1900), and especially the work in which Copland quotes Foster—*A Lincoln Portrait*, for speaker and orchestra (1942).

The main lyrical melody of the *Lincoln Portrait* is the anonymous "Springfield Mountain," published in 1840. The chorus tune of "Camptown Races" is part of the lively contrasting material in the orchestral introduction. Both melodies are stretched, twisted, frag-mented, and developed in ways characteristic of Copland. And the whole musical development is subordinated to the spoken words, quoted from five of Lincoln's speeches. When the words are read with conviction, the work can urge listeners to "think anew and act anew." The Foster tune is well chosen for the purpose. Behind the choice and the treatment lie a lifetime's growth of craftsmanship and understanding.

Copland's three symphonies and his big orchestral pieces of the 1960s, *Connotations* and *Inscape*, still too seldom played, were as demanding as the works of Ives, while the *Lincoln Portrait* and four ballets and eight film scores brought Copland's thought successfully to most of the Americans who listened to Beethoven's *Fifth* or any other symphonic music. Both kinds of works were products of a single-minded effort that began when Copland studied in France. He looked back then at his youth in Brooklyn with surprise. As he ex-plained in his lectures on *Music and Imagination*, 1952:

> In my America, "classical" music was a foreign importation. But the foreignness of serious music did not trouble me at all in those days: my early preoccupations were with technique and expressivity.
>
> . . . My years in Europe from the age of twenty to twenty-three made me acutely conscious of the origins of the music I loved. Most of the time I spent in France, where the characteristics of French culture are evident at every turn. The relation of French music to the life around me became increasingly manifest. Gradually, the idea that my personal ex-pression in music ought somehow to be related to my own back-home

environment took hold of me. The conviction grew inside me that the two things that seemed always to have been so separate in America—music and the life about me—must be made to touch.

Back in America in 1925, Copland had expressed his growing conviction in his suite *Music for the Theater.* He had also spoken about "Jazz as Folk-Music," with a reference to Foster that was reported in *Musical America:*

> . . . the songs I heard when I was a child—rather commonplace jazz tunes and music of the "Old Black Joe" variety . . . are my material, and I must accept them for what they are . . . make the best of it.

Copland found no simple consistent way of bringing personal expression and commonplace material into touch. Rather, with each composition he did so in a new way—in some works more obviously than in others. He had not yet, in 1975, made use of "Old Black Joe"; he waited until 1942 to use "Camptown." Meanwhile he explored Mexican and Cuban materials, cowboy songs and the Shaker hymn "The Gift to Be Simple," which fitted his personal needs when jazz no longer did so. By 1952 he could speak of Foster in a different tone from that of the brash remark of 1925:

> We have our own national hero in Stephen Foster. He was a song writer rather than a composer, but he had a naturalness and sweetness of sentiment that transformed his melodies into the equivalent of folk song. His simplicity and sincerity are not easily imitated, but it is that same simplicity and naturalness that has inspired certain types of our own music.

The careful tone of this tribute in *Music and Imagination* matches the *Lincoln Portrait.* A reader aware of the range of Foster's work and the wider range of interpretations of it can appreciate Copland's tact, his deliberate emphasis and his successful avoidance of many traps. What Copland found to value in Foster was not merely "Camptown" but a delicate quality of the man among his friends. This quality is reflected in the way "Camptown" works with "Springfield Mountain" to portray Lincoln, "a quiet and melancholy man" able to "rise with the occasion" of his age and to inspire among some of his successors a "high resolve" for "a new birth of freedom."

Copland's success with the *Lincoln Portrait* overshadows similar efforts by many other composers of concert music in his generation. Each of these invites a similar study in the context of the composer's whole work, though the invitation goes unacknowledged in the 1970s, when music by younger composers, closer to *Inscape* than to the *Portrait,* barely fits into programs that are still filled mainly with

19th-century music. If we list these efforts together, they show merely that Copland, as he knew, was participating in a collective effort. The Swiss-born American, Ernest Bloch (1880–1959) quoted "Old Folks" together with "Dixie," "John Brown's Body," "The Battle Cry of Freedom," and "Tramp, Tramp, Tramp" in his epic symphony, *America*, 1927. The Pittsburgh church musician, teacher, and critic Harvey Gaul (1881–1945) wrote an interesting life of Foster, *The Minstrel of the Alleghenies*, 1934, and a composition for string orchestra, *Fosteriana*, 1935, using motifs of "Camptown," "Oh! Boys, Carry me 'Long," "Some Folks," and "The Glendy Burk." The Australian-born pianist and composer Percy Grainger (1882–1961) wrote an elaborate *Tribute to Foster* for chorus and solo singers with piano, harp, celesta, Glockenspiel, marimbaphones of steel and wood, and "a large army of wineglasses and glass bowls . . . rubbed by wet fingers." The second of three movements in this *Tribute*, a lullaby setting of "Camptown Races," Grainger arranged for piano solo in 1915. In his foreword he explained that his mother had sung the tune as a lullaby when he was an infant, and that for the full, unpublished version he had provided several stanzas of his own words, including these:

> Foster's songs weren't Darkie quite;
> Yet neither were they merely "white." . . .
> Deze songs dey trabble de worl' around;
> At las' dey come to Adelaide town.
> When I was young on my mummy's knee.
> She sang dat race course song to me.

Grainger's foreword hints that the other movements of the *Tribute* must be varied testimonies to

> . . . my ever-increasing love and reverence for this great American genius —one of the most tender, touching and subtle melodists and poets of all time; a mystic dreamer no less than a whimsical humorist.

But Grainger's public confined him to the old world "Country Gardens" and ignored his tribute.

The pioneer Afro-American symphonist, William Grant Still (b. 1895), wrote a piano version of "Old Folks" in 1939, sober and imaginative. The master of musical comedy Jerome Kern (1885–1945) used hints of Foster in his most ambitious work, *Portrait of Mark Twain*, 1945. The conductor Werner Janssen (b. 1899) wrote a *Foster Suite* for orchestra, 1937, in which "Old Black Joe" appears twice, to give some unity to the loosely connected "Jeanie," "Camptown," "Glendy Burk," "Susanna," and "Old Folks." The Seattle composer George Frederick McKay (b. 1899) wrote an orchestral *Homage to Stephen Foster*, 1950, without quotations but rather with evocations of three scenes—riverboat, summer dream, and village festival—by means of melodies and rhythms in McKay's own style. The versatile Morton Gould (b. 1913) wrote an orchestral *Foster Gallery*, 1940, followed by a suite of *Spirituals*, 1941.

The Parisian Francis Poulenc (1899–1963) included a fragment of "Old Folks" in the finale of his piano concerto, 1950. He explained to the journalist critic Claude Rostand that the whole concerto, commissioned by Charles Munch for Boston, was meant as a light souvenir of Paris and that the quotation was "a Negro Spiritual that was derived from an old song of the sailors of La Fayette—a nice friendly handshake with a country that is now by far my biggest and most faithful public."

All these composers of concert music in Copland's generation were making use of Foster in an attempt to reconcile three contending social interests: (1) the likeliest concert audiences were conservative; (2) the most respected performers, critics, and rival composers looked for innovation and individual style; and (3) the managers of concert institutions, publishers, and record manufacturers wished to attract moviegoers and radio listeners with music not too different from what was currently most popular. Copland's *Portrait* came close to the desired reconciliation because it transcended the contest—its motive was not only satisfaction of demands but also, much more, a positive incitement to "think anew and act anew." Ives, on the contrary, had rejected the demands of his musical environment altogether, without losing faith in the ultimate wisdom of a majority of mankind; he wrote music simply to satisfy his own need and to prophesy to anyone who might pay attention; he used Foster to formulate his thoughts about Nature and death and "other freedom."

All these composers, including Ives, seemed to take for granted the institution of public orchestral concerts as central in musical culture. They paid less attention than G. F. Root had paid to the older institutions—church and theater—from which the concert was derived; they paid less respect than did Berlin or Gershwin to the newer institutions—movies, radio, television, and phonograph—that were crowding the concert into a precarious position. Their quotations of Foster in concert pieces reflected their various hopes for a liberal citizenship in which a concert-going élite might lead the way. The hopefulness of all these composers is not unlike the young Foster's hopefulness about "The Good Time Coming."

When phrases of "Old Folks" fade in and out of the complex soft blur of sound in the vast concert called *Geod* by Lukas Foss (b. 1922), these phrases reflect a new attitude toward the institution, a new relation among performers, composers, listeners, and larger groups of people. Foss' score calls on certain performers to choose their own "folk tunes," so that when he conducts the piece at various times and places the tunes may be different. In the performance recorded at Buffalo, New York, where Foss was regular conductor of the orchestra, "Old Folks," was one of the choices, as it was again in a performance he conducted as a guest at Ithaca in 1973. For any listener acquainted with Ives, the tune seems appropriate; *Geod's* four independent orchestral choirs and their extremely loose coordination recall Ives' similar feats, so that the appearance of the Foster tune makes Foss still more Ivesian. But Foss, having learned also from Copland, John Cage, and many others, has gone beyond Ives. *Geod* offers many sorts of choices for the conductor as well as for some of the players; it presents choices and fanciful suggestions to the listeners; it proposes no fellowship but rather an unfamiliar range of tolerance and patience. The Foster phrases, if they show up, are merely representative of the numberless coexisting kinds of music in the world, available for our intermittent attention.

The English-Scottish composer Thea Musgrave (b. 1928) showed a relation among Foster, Ives, and herself closer than any American's. Musgrave was commissioned by the Summer School of Music at Dartington, England, to write her *Chamber Concerto No. 2, for Five Players,* 1966. The piece is subtitled "in homage to Charles Ives" and assumes that players and listeners are enough acquainted with Ives' music to recognize Musgrave's homage in her way of quoting "Old Folks." About half way through the piece, the violinist puts aside his violin and takes up the viola, to play three phrases of the 18th-century English dance tune "Smiling Polly," widely associated with Scottish words as "The Keelrow." Flute, clarinet, cello, and piano ignore the violist; they continue with dissonant trills and abrupt accents. The viola part is marked "Rollo's first appearance." Rollo and his British tune disappear. The violinist resumes participation in a *presto* passage. Then again he shifts to the viola for "Rollo's second appearance," beginning quietly with the notes for "I'm coming" from "Old Black Joe," which he has discovered in the hectic *presto;* he proceeds to use these notes for a pun: "—nee River" from "Old Folks" leading on through "far, far away, Dere's wha my heart is turning ebber—". Now the cello takes up the quoted motif, in the wrong key; next the bass clarinet and piano join the discussion. Then the viola converts a motif from the cello into the hymn tune by William Henry Monk for the words "All Things Bright and Beautiful." Eventually the bass clarinet adopts the "tempo di Rollo" and presents Monk's last phrase, "the Lord God made them all," which Ives might have read as "the Bible tells us so" from Bradbury's "Renar." When the flute takes up this phrase, the violin reappears, to play very slowly in harmonics almost two phrases of "Old Folks." The cello takes over "All Things," the flute "Old Folks" (with trills), the clarinet "All Things," and the violin "The Keelrow," distorted but easily recognizable. "The Keelrow" is derailed again and again, but at last its jerky rhythm is adopted by the clarinet for a final version of "Old Folks." Meanwhile the flute has punned "Way down up-" with "Three Blind Mice," which is cut off where "she cut off their tails," and the motif of "cut off their tails" returns with the clarinet's concession. The cello overwhelms the violin's last attempt at "The Keelrow" with "All Things Bright and Beauti-"; a wrong note, insisted on, provokes a shrill climax from the rest of the instruments; then the piano provides the right note, "-ful," and the concerto ends with all players united in soft sustained dissonant sounds; Rollo's tunes have all been used up in the counterpoint. Has Rollo been converted to Ivesianism? Surely there is no more "longing for the old plantation" in 1966. But perhaps Rollo's grandchildren are more subtle: has Ives been co-opted to support a continuing cosmopolitan elitism?

Though Foss and Musgrave are as different from each other as from Copland, yet they have much in common. Both Foss and Musgrave, unlike Copland, use the fragments of Foster in ways that cannot either hold conservatives or attract many new listeners from the mass media. For the younger composers, as for Ives, the Foster quotations are not themes but rather something like words, to be used in independent ear-stretching and mind-strengthening. Again, for Foss and Musgrave, unlike Ives or Copland or Thoreau, the hope of a "universal language" is attenuated, if it survives at all. More modest hopes are enough: for a few listeners ready to stretch their attention along with adventurous and thoroughly trained performers and composers.

Meanwhile the new medium of television was beginning to press movies, radio, phonograph, and taperecording into specialized minority markets, just as these media had pressed and continued to press the "legitimate" theater, the "classical" concert, and the music publishing trade. Now phonograph and radio brought to minority audiences of millions the work of more and more diverse and adventurous singers and songwriters. Several of these used Foster's most famous songs; a few gave them meanings newer and perhaps even more hopeful than those of Ives.

CHAPTER 14

New singers
and songwriters

R AY CHARLES traveled back and forth across the Suwanee
River in Florida dozens of times during his childhood,
1930–45. From the age of seven, when he was blinded by what was
probably glaucoma, until he was fifteen, when his parents died, he
attended the St. Augustine School for Deaf and Blind Children, in
Orlando, and returned to his home in the village of Greenville. In
1970 Charles spoke to the jazz critic Whitney Balliett about the
school and those trips:

> I was treated very fair in school. I was normal there, happy there. In
> September, the state bought your train ticket to get you there, and in
> June they bought you another one to get you home, but at Christmas
> your parents had to buy the tickets. Somehow my mother always got the
> money. I remember leaving at Christmas, and there would always be two
> or three kids left at school who wouldn't get home. I didn't want to leave
> them there alone and I also wanted to see my mother.

If Charles rode the Atlantic Coast Line, he crossed the Suwanee at
Old Town, more than half way home. If he rode the Seaboard Air
Line, he crossed at Ellaville, with Greenville only thirty more miles
to the West. "Old Folks at Home" was an inescapable song for him.
Official State song of Florida from 1935, it was taught in school. Its
meaning must have grown and changed with nearly every trip.

In 1957, with the band he had led since 1954 and would maintain without a lapse into the 1970s, Charles recorded "Swanee River Rock." Though not one of his biggest hits, it is typical of his whole work—technically perfect, stylistically fresh, and personally honest. Its perfection has room for spontaneity. Its freshness renews and blends traditions of numerous groups. Its honesty is that of a real man in 1957, turning his thought to "the folks back home" without romanticizing them. "Swanee River Rock" is more than a performer's interpretation of "Old Folks," more than an arrangement, yet less than a parody, less than a composition such as Thea Musgrave's. It is comparable to some of Bach's elaborations of chorales in his cantatas and passions. In Charles' own vocabulary, it is a song. In 1961 Charles told Ralph Gleason:

> There are lots of good songs, but I have to feel it myself. That's the only way I know. . . . I listen to all the music I can hear. There's some good in all phases of it. Music is so big. . . . I'm trying to get as many people as I can to listen to all kinds of music!

In 1970 he told Balliett:

> I've tried to find songs *I* can get feeling out of. I must please myself first before I sing a song in public. The song must strike me some way in my heart. Now, I love "Stardust," but I'll never record it. Every time I sing the song to myself, I can't get the feeling out of it. The same with the national anthem. . . . But I'd like to sing "America the Beautiful." The lyrics of a song are vital. You become the person the writer is talking about. It's like a dramatic actor. . . . The melody is your guideline, your radar, but music would mean very little to me if I had to sing it the same way day in and day out. What I do is try and improve on it each time.

"Swanee River Rock" improves on "Old Folks at Home." Foster's melody is hardly recognizable; its phrases and their chief accompanying chords are the framework for a new melody, yet the old one does constitute a "guideline." Charles explains:

> Change a note here and there, make a twist in your voice, bend a note— take liberties like that. You won't become stagnant if you can change a little each night. I'd have to *make* myself sing the same song the same twice a year, which some people do every night without any effort at all.
>
> I can't give any reasons why the public likes me. Of course, one time I might be up and the public might not feel a thing, and another time they might cry and I might consider myself down. The only thing is I have tried to be honest and I cannot be a disappointment to myself. I've felt that way all my life. I've often wondered, Who am I? What am I that people would spend the money to come out and stand in the rain to hear me, come out and spend the money on tickets and baby-sitters and carfare to hear me? But if I can tell myself I did my best, I know in my heart I feel satisfied.

The honest wonder, the habitual concern for baby-sitters and car-fare, and finally the deep satisfaction can all be recognized in "Swanee River Rock."

The lyrics that Charles and his answering quartet of women, the Raelets, make "vital" are only a few of Foster's, plus repetitions and interpolations that seem like spontaneous conversation, or, of course, like blues and like a sermon with a responsive congregation. The Raelets' responses are shown here in parentheses:

> Do you know? Way down (way down) down upon the Swanee (Swanee)
>   talkin' 'bout the River (River),
> You know, I'm so far (so far) so far away (so far away).
> Oh yeah, you know-a that's where (that's where)
>   where my heart is a-turnin' (turnin') oh, ever (ever),
> And-a that's where (that's where) that's-a where
>   my old folks stay (where the old folks stay).
> (Ah——) All the world is sad and lonely now,
> Everywhere I roam (roam, roam, roam).
> Keep-a tellin' you my darlin' (darlin')
>   how my heart is growin' sad (so sad) so sad and lonely (lonely)
> Because I'm so far (so far) I'm far from my folks back home
>   (the folks back home).

Instead of a second stanza of lyrics, a saxophone takes over, impro-vising an eloquent melody in which the contours of Charles' ver-sion are extended. The voices return for the "chorus" and then a coda:

> Yeah, I'm far from my folks back home (yeah)
> So far from my folks back home, yeah (yeah)
> Oh, far from my folks back home, yeah (yeah).

None of Foster's "plantation," "longing," "darkies," or "banjo." No appeal to "take me" back to mother, "let me die." Altogether noth-ing "dreary" or "weary." The fact that sometimes, in all places, the world grows "sad and lonely" is affirmed, and life goes on—you and I and our interacting groups "roam."

To anyone who asks for a particular place, "back home" can mean Greenville. Or it can mean any Southern community, remembered by people whose roaming has taken them to any city with an up-to-date recording studio. This vaguer meaning was clear enough to all the young listeners in America and England around 1960, whose unprecedented affluence was booming the record business and help-ing define "rock" and "soul." The more precise meaning enhances repeated listenings for me, a fellow-citizen ten years older than Charles; to know something of Charles' route from Greenville and

Orlando into the wide world may interest listeners not yet born when he sang "Swanee River Rock."

Charles left home and school to work as a musician first in Jacksonville, then in Orlando and Tampa. He played and sang with three successive groups. As soon as he had earned enough, he went farther away, alone, but not to New York or Chicago, which frightened him—rather farther still, to Seattle, Washington, where he formed a trio, made his first recording, married and had a daughter, and lost his wife to his mother-in-law, all within two years. In 1950 he went to Los Angeles, which was to be his headquarters from then on. He joined the touring band of blues singer Lowell Fulsom; when it reached the Apollo Theater in New York, Charles left it, to spend a year and a half as touring "single attraction" under the management of Billy Shaw; he sang and played—piano, clarinet, and saxophone—with many small groups addressing their mostly Black neighbors in cities up and down the nation. In 1954, at Dallas, Texas, he formed his seventeen-man band and made the recordings for the Atlantic label that began to win his national and international fame. His own tunes, including "What'd I Say?" and "Hallelujah, I Love Her So," were his biggest hits. In 1955 he married Della Antwyne. In 1956 their son Ray, Jr., was born. In 1957 they bought a house in Los Angeles. The band's travels and its recordings were more and more efficiently organized—"roaming" was continuous but thoroughly purposeful and extraordinarily successful. By the time he recorded "Swanee River Rock," Charles could be confident of further improvement. In 1959 he hired the pioneer Black radio announcer Joe Adams as master of ceremonies; gradually Charles adopted Adams as manager of the complex enterprise that came to control the recording and publication of his work as well as his concerts. In 1963 they built the office-studio in Los Angeles that Adams designed. Meanwhile Charles had two more sons, David, 1959, and Robert, 1960. In 1961 the band broke records for attendance and critical acclaim in Paris and New York. In 1963 the journalist Alfred Aronowitz reported that Charles was "the hottest property in the music business"; he was, in fact, no property but rather the master of the business—Irving Berlin at the same age, thirty-three, was only building a theater in his native city, whereas Charles was directing a worldwide conglomerate enterprise. Some hint of this power is implied in the "Yeah" of "Swanee River Rock." Moreover, whereas Berlin consciously exploited the "corny" Foster, Charles made "Old Folks" as honest as every song he sang. The power of the "yeah" is no boasting, no gloating. It is simply the satisfaction of knowing "I did my best." It combines this satisfaction with the wariness that Charles expressed to Balliett:

I'm only a small businessman. I'm content to let the business grow as long as I can see a little improvement each year. This is a very slippery business. You have to be careful. It's constantly changing, and you've got to move with it. I remember when there were only a handful of recording companies in the whole country. Now there are three or four hundred.

The carefulness as well as the confidence is suggested in the repeated "Yeah."

The words "sad and lonely," though they make a climax in the song, do not dominate it. The sadness is absorbed in the affirmation. The public record of Charles' career includes recurring evidence of sadness along with the steady, careful rise to wealth, fame, and control. His admirers know that in 1955, 1961, and 1964 Charles was arrested for possession of drugs. Though never convicted, he acknowledged his troubles; he told reporters like Aronowitz that he had used heroin, that he had not benefited, and that he had not hurt anyone but himself. The manager, Adams, told Balliett that the rules of the band forbade narcotics. And in a time when the songs of younger people, including Bob Dylan and the Beatles, often alluded to drugs, those of Charles never did so. But the miseries of which drugs may be a symptom were never denied. Charles described those miseries to Balliett, in his account of the first year after his parents died:

> We didn't work too often, and there were times when I was sustaining myself on beans and water and crackers, and it came to be a heavy proposition—a malnutrition thing. I can really understand how people get chained into situations like that, how people can get stuck in a web and can't get out. Men sit and stare and women become prostitutes. I was one of the fortunate ones. I had this little profession and I did get out of it. But it was total hell twenty years ago, with the race thing and being blind, too. It's easy for people who eat warm food and sleep in warm beds to talk about it, but it's detestable when you live it.

Charles' understanding of the "web" he barely escaped is in his voice when he sings "sad and lonely." The "folks back home" include many who are "chained," "stuck," as well as many like Charles' parents and his first musical friend:

> My father taught me if you ever get your hands on a dollar you always keep enough to get home on and you never let that dollar become your word. If your word is no good, your money isn't either. . . . My father was what they used to call a "good nigger." But he was no Uncle Tom. He just wanted to be left alone. . . . My mother was a sweet lady. She cooked and worked for white families, and she made all our clothes. And she had a strong feeling about independence. . . . I was brought up not to beg. Even now, I wouldn't beg nobody for nothing. . . .
> There was a little café next to us and it was run by a man named Wiley

Pittman. He had a piano there and he was of the boogie-woogie school—
Meade Lux Lewis and Albert Ammons and the like. When he played, I'd
run in and listen. He must of taken note. He would let me sit on the
piano bench next to him and bang on the keys. I didn't know *nothing*.
He would tell me, "Play it, play it. You're doing fine." I'll always love
that man for that. . . . Mr. Pittman had a jukebox and I'd hear those
blues by Big Joe Turner and Tampa Red and Big Boy Cruddup and Sonny
Boy Williams.

In Charles' voice, in his way of "twisting" and "bending" melodies,
in his rhythmic "liberties," adding and repeating words against the
steady beat of the accompaniment, and in the complete honesty of
his choice of words and emphasis on them in every song he sings,
he is loyal to the heritage of the blues singers he knew from earliest
childhood. However "far away" from those "old folks" he goes in
his "slippery" business, he brings with him both their "sadness" and
their "independence." He renews their tradition by improving old
songs and making new ones that delicately express his changing
relations with many groups of people. "All the world" he sings, but
without Foster's emphasis. Charles transforms the melody most
drastically just here, so that these words begin only one step up the
scale from "home," avoiding the very note that John Rosamund
Johnson had pointed to as Foster's departure from the pentatonic
norm. The phrase leads on to "sad," which takes a whole group of
notes, expanding from the one Foster specified, on up to the high
octave and back, like a cry. But the phrase continues, to "lonely
now," and this phrase pulls on to the ending "yeah." The Foster
melody has been converted to a blues.

The Raelets do not join the cry, as they do join the "yeah." Their
"so sad" is no echo of Charles; it is unlike any blues. All their responses to Charles are short, precise, and tough; they support his
phrases and will not let him prolong his sadness. Their only independent emphasis is on "roam." The group they most obviously
represent is the chief institution of Black American communities,
the church. Charles maintained a keen interest in the church's
"gospel" music, in which female choruses were characteristic. According to an anonymous interviewer for *Song Hits Magazine* in
1971, Charles continually listened to recordings of gospel music, and
some of these were tapes he himself made in churches. The tension
between blues and church music, through several generations, was
so strong that Charles' combination of the two seemed shocking.
This combination attracted more comment than any other aspect
of his music; it seemed to be the chief characteristic of a style that
claimed the new name "soul music."

Thus "Swanee River Rock" is more than the fresh combination of

Foster with blues. The Raelets' responses are indispensable parts of the complex reinterpretation of "Old Folks"; they give the leader the support and the limits that were typically absent from both blues and Foster's songs; the leader with his responding group make words and melody challenge listeners to go beyond pity or self-pity. The solidarity and brusqueness of the Raelets demand respect.

The band is indispensable too. When Charles was asked about the slogan "soul," he replied to Ralph Gleason:

> "Soul music" is like a cross between church music and modern jazz with a flavor of rhythm and blues mixed in.

And he explained to Alfred Aronowitz, "What you speak of as *soul* in jazz is *soul* in gospel music." The slogan had become current among such jazz musicians as Horace Silver and Art Blakey, whose style was also called "hard bop" in contrast to the "cool" style of Miles Davis and several other instrumentalists of the early 1950s. When Charles made recordings with the vibraphonist of the Modern Jazz Quartet, Milt Jackson, the records were entitled "Soul Meeting" and "Soul Brothers." Charles' music links him even more closely with the tradition of jazz than with church music or the self-accompanying blues singers. His band is a group of highly skilled, tightly disciplined players, who "swing" together like the bands of Ellington, Basie, Lunceford, Goodman, and Shaw, whose records Charles had studied in the 1930s; no doubt Charles' band is more skilled than the bands of Henry Washington and Joe Anderson with whom Charles began his career. He told Balliett:

> I've always wanted a big band to work behind me. I like the sound. You can make a small band from a big band, but you can't make a big band out of a small band. I'm a person who takes his time, and when I could afford a big band I put one together. And I've been fortunate enough to maintain everything new I've tried. It was my mother who taught me that patience.

Charles himself and the Raelets are part of the band. Though the band is literally "behind" them most of the time, Charles at the piano plays as part of his band, leading it as Ellington or Basie leads, while the Raelets are featured in a few songs, absent in some, and subordinate in most, as they are in "Swanee River Rock." When Charles occasionally shifts to the saxophone, he participates in another way, just as the other members of the band take their occasional solos. The normal sound is the full, brilliant blare of the whole band together.

Older jazz band arrangements of "Old Folks," though not memorable in themselves, were common enough to constitute a tradition

for "Swanee River Rock." Did Charles hear, for example, the one by
Jimmy Lunceford? Or possibly those by Tommy Dorsey, Bunny Beri-
gan, or Dave Brubeck? Or even those by the crooner Bing Crosby or
the sweet dance band of Louis Armstrong's favorite Guy Lombardo?

Within a year after "Swanee River Rock," 1958, a fine traditional
jazz performance was recorded in Brussels, where Sidney Bechet, the
New Orleans veteran, was joined by Buck Clayton, Vic Dickenson,
and others for a memorable concert. Their "Swanee River" begins
with a very slow solo for Bechet on soprano saxophone, with *sotto
voce* comments from Clayton on trumpet and Dickenson on trom-
bone. The "chorus" becomes more and more sentimental, until the
last phrase shifts to the minor mode and expands in a cadenza. Then
suddenly the key and tempo change, down a fifth and twice as fast,
for a second stanza in which everybody improvises counterpoint,
imitating the 1920s "hot" style of King Oliver or Ferdinand Morton.
No words are needed. The sure strength and exuberance of the ending clearly sweep away the moaning sentiment.

Charles' "Rock" unites its diverse elements in a tighter, more
complex unity than does Bechet's "Swanee River." Charles has gone
beyond the jazz tradition, building his own work on it, but affirming
all the diversity that has surrounded and fed into jazz.

Charles may have learned from the arrangements of "Old Folks"
for solo piano by Teddy Wilson, Art Tatum, and Claude Thornhill,
which appeared in a volume of "29 Modern Piano Interpretations
of 'Swanee River' " published by Robbins, 1939. These three musicians, all active in jazz, treated Foster's melody with sweetly dissonant chords in idiomatic piano figurations, more like the music
of Debussy than that of Bechet. Their interpretations betrayed
no irony. Their "sophistication" accommodated the "Old Folks"
nostalgia.

As jazz pianist and arranger, Charles roamed far away from the
church or the boogie-woogie pianists and blues singers and the responsive audiences, rural and urban, who had supported the blues
tradition in its segregation from majority audiences. ("Rhythm and
blues" was the euphemism for the segregation of recordings after the
1940s when "race records" became obsolete.) His roaming began in
school, despite all handicaps. He told Balliett about his music lessons:

> I studied Chopin and Mozart and Bach. Beethoven had a lot of feeling,
> but Bach was nervous, with all those lines running against each other.
> Classical music is a great foundation for playing jazz. You play correctly,
> with the right fingering. With classical music, you play exactly what the
> man wrote, but in jazz, when you get rid of the melody, you put yourself
> in. So every time I thought my teacher wasn't listening, I played jazz. . . .
> And of course my favorite pianist, then and now, my idol, was Art Tatum.

The way Charles contrasts Beethoven and Bach shows that they are more than names for him, though his contrast between "classical" and jazz shows that he had more to learn. His teacher sounds like many of the New Orleans Creole professors who made indispensable (if indirect) contributions to the jazz of Ferdinand Morton, Sidney Bechet, Louis Armstrong, and almost all younger New Orleans jazz men. Charles' appreciation of Tatum indicates that he could not be satisfied with a kind of jazz confined to the function of accompanying dance, nor a kind that advertised a superficial novelty, but rather that he was concerned with the dynamic advance of the style. All this sophistication contributes to the perfection and intensity of "Swanee River Rock." It makes the reaffirmation of blues and gospel sounds a deliberate one. The combination makes the very idea of "Old Folks" new. "Swanee River Rock" says "yeah" to both the distance roamed and the memory of the "folks at home." Its musical synthesis makes the "yeah" say so much, more convincingly than any argument. The final dissonant chord holds together the major and minor thirds above its root, which is the sixth degree of the scale.

Though Charles occasionally used the slogan "rock 'n' roll" that Elvis Presley and other white singers made famous in the 1950s, he seldom used the guitar in the style that these singers had learned from Chuck Berry and other Black singers. "Swanee River Rock" has no guitar. What justifies its title is the pattern of the drums, a single prominent pattern introduced as a solo and maintained throughout, in contrast to the rich rhythmic variety characteristic of modern jazz drumming. The pattern syncopates against a measure of four beats that the listener can recognize only after the song is underway: first and third beats silent, second beat divided, fourth beat whacked. By 1970 this pattern and other "rock" patterns like it had acquired their own nostalgia. For some young listeners the drumming might be enough to make Charles' work seem, if not quite so remote as Foster himself, yet more an "old folks'" music than their own, and open to an indulgent interpretation—even "camp." The "rock 'n' roll revival" of the 1970s, led again by Presley, obscured the complex affirmation of 1957.

Charles did not participate in the "free jazz" that was developed after 1958 by Ornette Coleman (b. 1930) and others. And this development too, as well as the various developments of rock, made Charles' daring comprehensiveness of 1957 seem faded and limited to some listeners. When Coleman used a motif from Foster, his way of doing so was more like Ives' than like Charles' "improvement" on a whole tune. For Coleman's improvisations were free from tunes, chords, scales, beats, measures, and formal patterns of every kind.

In one long piece that he played at a concert in Ithaca, 1968, Coleman included bits of "Old Black Joe," whereupon his bassist and master of ceremonies announced "That's our only political comment for tonight." Words and music were equally enigmatic to this listener.

Charles' own most popular work in the meantime contributed a further connotation to "Swanee River Rock": in 1962 he surprised old admirers and won new ones with a program of "Modern Sounds in Country and Western Music." He transformed tunes that until recently had been segregated for Southern white "hillbillies." His use of these tunes deeply affected the expansion of the "country" style. He had disregarded the doubts of record-company advisers about this program, just as he had declined their recommendation that he make a program of spirituals. He insisted, as he told Balliett, that he "always loved hillbilly music." He had listened to its radio programs from Nashville, Tennessee, as a boy:

> I never missed the "Grand Ole Opry." It was honest music, not cleaned up, and it still is. They don't sing, "I sat there and dreamed of you." They say, "I missed you and I went out and got drunk."

Charles' first job in Tampa was as pianist for a hillbilly group. So with this music in 1962, as earlier with the blues, he was recalling particular "old folks" in his own experience. His success on the nationwide market was an unprecedented reversal of the familiar "covering" by popular white performers of new songs introduced by Blacks. Charles' "country" songs were thus a complex affirmation of both distance and solidarity, like the "yeah" of "Swanee River Rock." If his "country" songs were destined to remain his most widely famous achievement, "Swanee River Rock" might be remembered as an anticipation.

Foster's "Uncle Ned," in various "country" fiddle or band performances, such as one by Dave Macon recorded in 1930, reached some listeners (such as me) thanks to the interest aroused by Charles. "Old Folks" had a lesser place in that tradition than "Uncle Ned."

What Charles played in 1972, for not quite so many listeners, added yet more connotations to "Swanee River Rock." This will be our final concern, after we glance at the uses that several more of his contemporaries found for Foster.

In 1960 "Old Folks" provided the theme for a long set of variations in a style comparable to Charles'—jazz? rock? soul?—by the organist and composer Johnny "Hammond" Smith, with important parts for his guitarist Eddie McFadden and guest vibraphonist Lem Winchester, accompanied by bass and drums. The improvised melodies of these musicians are closer to Foster than Charles'; the gradual building up of complexity through several stanzas makes an interesting piece. But there is no intensity like that of Charles' concise "Rock." Smith and his friends play in the recording studio much as they often play in public places to provide a mild background for diners and drinkers, rather than to improve on a song and its meaning. Their acceptance of "Old Folks," however, as worth a place at the beginning of a recorded program of Smith's compositions, may be meaningful. The whole program is named for one of the most churchy compositions, "Gettin' the Message." The end of the program is the jazziest piece, "Dementia." If Smith intended anything by this ordering of the program, it can only be that the "old folks" are receding ever farther "away."

In 1953, when Charles was preparing to organize his band, the Stephen Foster Memorial at White Springs, Florida, began to hold annual Florida Folk Festivals. They grew out of the "Jeanie" scholarship competition and ball for college-bound girls (wearing gowns from the 1850s), sponsored by the Florida Federation of Music Clubs beginning in 1951. While the competition continued as a prominent and characteristic part of the Memorial's program, the folk festival expanded to accommodate hundreds of amateur musicians, dancers, and craftsmen. The festival is supposed to teach "that the folk legacies of many lands have given America its national fabric of beauty and strength." Groups of Seminole Indians don beads and feathers. Slavic groups demonstrate their dances. The sponsors are careful to say that the Foster songs "might not be classed as folk songs, but some of his greatest have a folk song characteristic in that melodies and words are remembered and sung 'round the world." For the purposes of the festival, "Old Folks" can be sung as a solo with banjo, or by a massed chorus, or played on an accordion or balalaika. "Old Folks" is as welcome as "Susanna." "Swanee River Rock" would be out of place. There are few if any Black participants.

The State officials and legislators who support the Memorial can justify the festival as a tourist attraction, confident that the talk of "legacies" and "national fabric" is harmless humbug. But such a festival owes no more to the State or the tourists than to the nationwide, worldwide cultivation of folk music by individuals and groups who meant to organize protest or revolution or a "counterculture," and who accordingly rejected most of Foster's songs as commercial corruptions, or at least censored some of Foster's words.

At the center of this folksong movement was Pete Seeger (b. 1919), singer; master strummer and innovator on the banjo; casual player of the guitar (not amplified), the recorder, and occasional other instruments; composer of new songs; stimulator of younger songwriters; scholarly investigator of songs among people wherever he went, throughout the world, as well as through books and recordings; translator, teacher, editor; captain of the ship "Clearwater" on the Hudson River; yet still, as he claimed in his book of 1972, *The Incompleat Folksinger,* for his work was unending. When he sang a concert program he always included some songs that transformed the audience into singers and incited them to keep on singing as well as listening to each other when the concert was over. Often he enabled an audience to become a kind of secular congregation, sharing hopes of effective action for social justice, freedom, peace, and ecological harmony. His hero was "Johnny Appleseed"—John Chapman (1776–1847). His kind of patriotism was labeled treason by the House UnAmerican Affairs Committee of Congress in 1955, and through the next seven years Seeger was harrassed in the courts, while the folksong movement expanded; in 1962 the Court of Appeals set aside his case, and in 1964 his patriotism was acknowledged by *Life* magazine, which called him "A minstrel with a mission."

Seeger's versions of "Camptown Races," "Susanna," and "Old Folks" were published in his anthology, *American Favorite Ballads.* These versions claim no individuality. Rather they represent what Seeger calls in his preface "creative rearranging," such as takes place gradually when a song is carried through some generations of oral tradition.

Introducing "Camptown," Seeger says, abruptly, "By Stephen Foster. His best songs grew out of folk tradition and got taken back into it." Seeger puts the chorus first: "Goin' to run all night," but he omits Foster's four-part writing; Seeger's chorus may sing in unison or find parts by ear. His first "verse" is only half of Foster's stanza, and he neglects to mark the "Dooda" refrain as chorus. For a second verse he condenses Foster's little narrative into nonsense. Foster's words had related:

> De long tail filly and de big black hoss, Doodah! doodah!
> Dey fly de track and dey both cut across, Oh! doodah-day!
> De blind hoss sticken in a big mud hole, Doodah! doodah!
> Can't touch bottom wid a ten foot pole, Oh! doodah-day!

Seeger likes the mud hole for its own sake:

> Oh, the long tailed filly and the big black horse, Dooda, dooda,
> Come to a mud hole and they all cut across, Oh, de dooda day.

Seeger's third stanza is approximately the second half of Foster's first, but the change conceals a mild criticism. Foster's singer-narrator left geography vague, as in all his songs:

> I come down dah wid my hat caved in . . .
> I got back home wid a pocket full of tin. . . .

Seeger's "folk" version acknowledges a debt, without specifying who owes whom:

> I went down South with my hat caved in . . .
> I came back North with a pocket full of tin. . . .

Seeger modifies melody as well as words, but very slightly: where Foster's syncopated final line, "bet on de bay," accents the second degree of the scale, Seeger stays on the third degree for "on." Seeger's extra syllable for "oh, de dooda day" brings an extra note, the fourth degree, for "de," which makes a closer connection than Foster's with the final line.

Seeger calls "Oh! Susanna" "probably Stephen Foster's greatest song, a ditty children will always love." His first stanza makes only a minuscule improvement in the words: "a banjo" is easier to sing fast than "my banjo." The second stanza adopts a Bowdlerization from schoolbooks: instead of Foster's vivid line "De buckwheat cake was in her mouf," Seeger sings, "A red red rose was in her cheek." He omits the whole third stanza, with its reference to New Orleans, death, and burial. He smoothes the melodic line with several passing notes at points where Foster skipped from the keynote to the third degree; where Foster dipped below the tonic for a leading-tone, which would sound more genteel than folklike, Seeger stays above.

Seeger puts his version of "Old Folks" on a half-page following the nine stanzas of "John Henry," "noblest American ballad of them all," and a picture with boldface caption, "Nat Turner." He introduces his version, "Swanee River," with care:

> Stephen Foster's sentimental songs were typical of mid-19th Century America. But shorn of their minstrel show dialect and considered simply as melodies, it is no wonder they spread around the world. He had a genius for fitting syllables to tunes.

In the chorus Seeger uses another schoolmarmism: "Old brother" replaces Foster's "Oh! darkeys." (Seeger would surely not object to Ray Charles' answer, "Oh, darlin'.") Seeger's first stanza is only half of Foster's; he makes the second half a second stanza. Then he uses half the original second stanza and omits the lines about "brudder . . . mudder . . . die." He uses all of Foster's third (final) stanza, so that his total is five. While he preserves the fit of syllables and tunes that he admires, he changes a few of Foster's accompanying chords to make inconspicuous improvements. At the ends of lines "away" and "roam," where Foster's lack of chord change weakens the continuity of the whole tune, Seeger recommends appropriate changes that only a purist could find distracting. More questionable is Seeger's restlessness for change in the first measures of the second and last lines, where Foster plodded away at the tonic chord just as in the first line. But if listeners or guitarists are recalling the enriched accompaniments of H. T. Burleigh or J. Rosamund Johnson, then Seeger's will seem austere enough.

What "home" does Seeger picture when he ends the song with the question, "When will I hear the banjos strumming Down in my good old home?" Hardly his own childhood home in New York, for he is the son of Charles L. Seeger, one of the founders of the American Musicological Society, the Archive of American Folksong in the Library of Congress, the International Society for Music Education, the Society for Ethnomusicology, and other such organizations. In 1955 Charles Seeger was the best possible author of the article on "Folk Music: USA" in Grove's *Dictionary of Music*, and he had long understood what he wrote there:

> It may appear that a general integration of an American music—folk, popular, and fine art—is imminent. Perhaps it is. Pressure toward the casting of many diverse cultural functions into at least the *appearance* of a national art is very great. . . . The relationship between written and oral traditions . . . [is] the key problem.

Pete Seeger learned much from his father; for example, one of the songs in his anthology, which his father discovered about the time that Pete began to play the banjo in 1935; soon thereafter he found his vocation in a surprising relation to his father's work: Pete's music-making never yielded to the "pressure toward . . . *appearance*" but rather respected all the "diverse cultural functions" of his music and helped to perform new cultural functions. When he sang of Foster's "old plantation," he briefly indulged the tradition of nostalgic dreaming, as something too widely shared to be scorned. Quickly, however, he set it firmly in contexts that prevented his admirers from wallowing at length in any such indulgence. Likewise, when college audiences in the late 1960s, at Cornell and elsewhere, joined him most fervently in his own lament "Where Have All the Flowers Gone?" Seeger's banjo or guitar kept the tempo from dragging, and he followed up that song with something like his "Hammer Song" or "Waist Deep in the Mississippi." He urged his friends to put their dreams to work.

In *The Incompleat Folksinger* Seeger added a comment about "Massa":

> The best melodies will find a place in our grandchildren's hearts whether or not they bring with them any of their earlier lyrics.
>
> Just as well. Often the early lyrics deserve to be forgotten. The words of Stephen Foster's "Massa's in the de Col' Col' Ground" are weak and silly, but the melody is strong and great.

Seeger quotes the melody, beginning with "Down in the cornfield," as if to agree with Ives.

In Seeger's compendium, *The Incompleat Folksinger*, he pays tribute to two great predecessors. In this anthology, *Favorite American Ballads*, the same men are represented more often than Foster. These are Seeger's friends and principal teachers: Huddie Ledbetter, known as "Leadbelly" (1885–1949), and Woodrow Wilson ("Woody") Guthrie (1912–67). Ledbetter is Seeger's source for five songs in the anthology, Guthrie for seven. Neither of them sang of dreams like Foster's. When Guthrie sang about his Oklahoma home, it was a wry lament:

> So long, it's been good to know you,
> This dusty old dust is a-getting my home
> And I've got to be drifting along.

When Leadbelly sang about the girl in his dreams, "Irene, Goodnight," who "caused me to leave my home," the chorus emphasized:

> Sometimes I live in the country,
> Sometimes I live in town.
> Sometimes I take a great notion
> To jump in the river and drown.

Both singers sang more often of work than of dreams or homes. Guthrie made his principle explicit, in an essay of 1942 on "Ear Players," for the magazine *Common Ground:*

> Work is the thing. The biggest and best thing you can sing about is work. . . . Just learn where the work is: that's where you'll find real honest American music and songs being made up.

The folksong movement that Seeger carried forward was imbued with this principle. After Leadbelly's "Irene" made a first huge commercial popular success for such music in 1950, the movement began to rival jazz, then rock, until a younger disciple of Leadbelly and Guthrie, and of what he called "the saintliness of Pete Seeger," Bob Dylan, in 1964 combined folk and rock to become the foremost songwriter of his generation.

In 1960, at a conference of the Student Non-Violent Coordinating Committee and the Southern Christian Leadership Conference in Raleigh, North Carolina, Seeger led the song that was taken up as the hymn of the civil rights movement, "We Shall Overcome." Its melody was later traced back by James J. Fuld to the Sicilian mariners' hymn "O Sanctissima," first recorded in 1794 and published by Herder in his *Stimmen der Völker*, 1807. It was arranged by Beethoven, 1815. It was joined to the words "We will overcome" in 1945 and used by the food and tobacco workers of Charleston, South Carolina, in a strike campaign. One of the CIO organizers,

Zilphia Horton, spread it through unions throughout the South. She taught it to Seeger. The young California sociologist and singer Guy Carawan, who learned "We Will Overcome" from Horton, made it the theme song of the Highlander School in John's Island, South Carolina, beginning 1959. Carawan recalled in 1964, for Josh Dunson's book *Freedom in the Air: Song Movements of the Sixties*, some of his initial difficulties in using songs for the cause of civil rights:

> Civil rights movement gatherings [were] stiff and formal. It seemed most of the leaders running the meetings were those educated type of Negroes . . . afraid to sing a spiritual or gospel song that might cause a foot to tap, hands to clap, or bodies to sway.

Seeger, who is credited with changing "We will" to "We shall," got the conference of 1960 to sway with the melody. The possibility for many more songs to serve the movement was released at last. The meanings of many songs were transformed for many people from shame to pride. Continuities from old to new songs, and from old to new generations, were revealed, while confrontations between conflicting groups were dramatized. More and more individuals were challenged to identify themselves with the group resolved to overcome.

By 1965 Seeger had sung "We Shall Overcome" in twenty-five countries. "When I sing it," he wrote, "I think of the whole human race." By 1972 he had discarded the song from most concerts because "the disagreement on tactics between militant youngsters and compromising oldsters became too great." He acknowledged the "milky taste of 'so-omeday'." Still, he occasionally found himself "humming it at work when I feel low and pessimistic about the human species." In 1967 he observed:

> Singing in various countries overseas these days takes on a special poignant quality. I am glad to show them a different side of America than the one they may know of. But as much as I personally love the songs I sing, I can't fool my audience and say, "These are songs which 190 millions of North Americans also love to sing." Nor even a majority.
>
> It is interesting to see how the same song will take on new meanings when sung for different audiences. The most nearly universal songs I know are Negro spirituals and freedom songs. But even these can be misinterpreted and argued about.
>
> In 1967 I sang in Germany. I had sung in every country on its borders, and finally realized that only a psychological block was holding me back. I suppose I was afraid that every time I met someone my age or older I'd be wondering what they were doing in 1938 or 1942. Then I realized this was silly. In future years an American will receive the same glances: what was he doing in 1967?

In such surroundings Seeger would find few occasions to use "Susanna" or "Camptown," very few or none for "Old Folks." Yet in his varied work he continues to find some occasions for all these songs, without for a moment neglecting the commitment of "We Shall Overcome." Seeger's whole work and character stand behind each performance of the Foster songs and his careful recommendations of them. In his preface to *American Favorite Ballads* he addresses wise advice to his individual readers:

> Now, if you love one of these songs, you can make it your own by singing it; through the years it will become part of your life as little by little you change the tune in subtle ways, or add or subtract verses. . . .
> A good song is like a many-faceted jewel. Or a woman of many moods. Or a tool of many uses. Try these out, turn them over, look at them from several angles. Taste 'em.

Seeger's precept and example help bring millions of individuals to such active "tasting" of songs. While television, radio, phonograph, and film, like their old models theater and concert, too often induce a comparatively passive reception of music and a passive identification with social groups, the folksong movement encourages individuals to learn what they love in their own actual lives. "Susanna" and "Old Folks" are available for learning.

The expanding business of phonograph records, at the same time increasingly independent of other media, could incorporate "folksingers" as readily as jazz or "soul music," and in the business "Susanna" was as amenable a commodity as any song. In 1971 a new, enormously popular singer, James Taylor, included "Susanna" in a recorded program of his own songs, "Sweet Baby James." His version, with guitar, is complicated by many words added to each line of Foster's first two stanzas, so that it becomes almost as hard to learn as a song of Ray Charles. But the added words, the turns of melody, the soft husky tone of the voice—closely miked—reveal no complex social setting; the singer, dreaming of his girl, addresses each lonely listener at his or her hi-fi stereo set. The critic Harold Carlton, reviewing Taylor in the *Village Voice,* suggested that "Playing James Taylor on your record player is showing in the vaguest, least committed way possible, which side of the gap you're on. *Which* gap? Any one you'd care to name." Nothing prevented consumers from using Seeger's records in the same way, though he himself, in a wonderful witty "record review" of his own work, 1965, urged his fans to listen to the records of more traditional singers such as Horton Baker, Vera Hall, Gary Davis, and Mahalia Jackson, which would be hard to use as background or badge. Moreover, the same use was likely for recordings of very different selections from

Foster, such as the program of the "Jeanie" type that was prepared in 1961 by the concert folk singer Richard Dyer Bennett, or the scholarly program of Foster's "household songs" performed in 1973 by the concert singers Jan De Gaetani and Leslie Guinn with a group of authentic 19th-century instruments.

"Susanna" had a place on the 1972 recorded program of a singer and songwriter not yet so popular as Taylor but far more versatile and ingenious, at once more strongly individual and more attached to traditions. Taj Mahal, in his program called "Happy Just to Be Like I Am," transforms "Susanna" into a piece more than five minutes long, alternating flute and voice, accompanied by guitar, bass, and drums. The words begin in the middle of Foster's first stanza: "Rained all night the day I left." The chorus reverses Foster's geography: "I'm on my way to Alabama, baby." Foster's dreaming second stanza never shows up, much less Foster's dying finale. A whole new stanza appears after the flute's first interlude:

> Don't you laugh, baby.
> When I'm standin' near you, baby,
> You make me feel ten feet tall,
> Singin' Oh! Susanna. . . .

After two more interludes, a long coda includes more new lines:

> A banjo on my knee,
> Oh, on my knee, baby,
> Oh, woman on my knee,
> Oh, woman, you don't understand. . . .
> Say, set, set, set, set! . . .

The words are surpassed by the melodic excitement. When the flute returns and fades out at the end, at least one listener wants to hear and learn more of Taj Mahal, and can never again think of "Susanna" without his urgent cries, "don't you laugh" and "set!"

Music historians and critics who have grown up in the age of jazz, admiring the music of Ives, naturally reinterpret Stephen Foster, using the facts presented by J. T. Howard in the contexts of their own various interests. Thus Gilbert Chase (b. 1906) in his lively and scholarly survey of *America's Music from the Pilgrims to the Present*, 1955, argues that Foster's music is "a product of the urbanized frontier," and that its "appeal lies largely in this cultural dualism of his background, through which he was able to combine the vitality of the frontier and a certain element of primitive simplicity with the genteel tradition of the urban fringe, dominated by sentimentality, conventionalism, and propriety." H. Wiley Hitchcock (b. 1923), in his excellent textbook *Music in the United States: A*

Historical Introduction, 1969, treats Foster's "household songs" separately and more sympathetically than anyone before him, and challenges musicologists to study Foster's whole work yet more deeply. In 1973, reviewing the recording of "household songs" in authentic performances inspired by Hitchcock, the brilliant critic Jonathan Cott joins in the call for someone to "re-evaluate Foster's heretofore easily-dismissed role." If our patient study has led to no one clear and satisfying interpretation, it doubtless provides material for younger surveyers and interpreters to fit Foster into ever-changing historical contexts.

Whatever interpretations we choose, we use them to play our own parts in the world, in relation to each other. Our interpretations of Foster are important, if at all, only to the extent that they reflect and affect our interactions with each other, in all kinds of music and in more than music.

In 1972 Ray Charles recorded a program of ten songs entitled "A message from the people . . . by the people . . . and for the people," in which he confronted the issues of race, nation, class, and commerce more explicitly than he had done before. He took account of the past, present, and future. His adaptation of "Lift Every Voice and Sing," the "Negro national anthem" by the brothers James Weldon Johnson and J. Rosamund Johnson (1900), begins the program; his version of "America the Beautiful" ends it, with the "liberating strife" of the third stanza brought forward to the beginning, then with the "spacious skies" put in quotation marks, sung as remembered from school days, with chorus joining, and finally with the repeated prayer for "brotherhood" fervently straining. Between these two hymns are various newer songs, each different, each qualifying the claims of the two overlapping nations, each qualified by its subordination to the national prayers. Two of the new songs seem to me especially moving and especially relevant to Foster. In "Hey Mister" by Betty Lapcevic, with up-to-date wa-wa guitar and alternating fast and slow tempi, Charles calls on his listeners to "write a letter to the Congress of the United States, sayin' somethin' like":

> Hey mister, you better listen . . .
> The poor people know that they can't impeach you.
> They just hopin' that their cries will reach you.
> Now don't you hear 'em? . . .
> Many souls before me have sung this song,
> Tryin' to remind you to right this wrong,
> But what I'm wonderin', if you'll ever understan'—
> Rich or poor, a man's still a man. . . .
> Don't talk, get to doin' before it's too late.

"A man's a man," sang Robert Burns. Throughout the world, down through the generation of Foster, that of Ives, and that of Copland, "many souls" have used anonymous traditional songs and original songs growing out of local traditions in "tryin' to remind you"— distant, distracted listeners—to right their wrongs. Charles' blues and his hymns and "Swanee River Rock" are among these reminders, though of course they have other uses too. "Hey Mister" itself is more than a reminder. But its direct appeal is essential to Charles' "message" of 1972, it attaches the hopes of the hymns to a demand: "get to doin'."

In the whole "message" program there is another essential quali- fication. Charles acknowledges through Melanie Safka's "What Have They Done to My Song, Ma?" the limits of what any song can do; he recognizes and laments the likelihood that any song will be abused more often than it is used to right wrongs. The song's "they" are not defined. Whoever they are, they have made "my song" turn out all wrong: "put it in a plastic bag and turned the bag-a-da upside down." They picked my brain. They "stole everythin' I had, ma, and they made a million with it." Are "they" musicians? managers? whites? Americans? The song lets us define "them" variously, but it reminds us that such wrong does happen in the music business: it has happened to "Jim Crow," to "Susanna" and "Jeanie" and "Old Folks," to ragtime, to jazz, to blues, to "soul." It happens often enough to Beethoven, to Bach, to Ives. Is Foster one of "them" who stole from men like Charles? That small question can remain open while we agree that Foster's song has been turned upside down more often than Charles'. Larger questions remain open too, about the ever-renewed exploitation of the ever-renewed stream of song in- vented by Black Americans; within "Look What They Done" as well as through the context of the prayers, these questions are recognized as baffling and as subordinate. Charles precedes the song with an introduction, which changes Safka's "ma" to his own "mama," and asks listeners to picture her in the eloquent pauses, as if on the telephone:

> Hello, mama? Hello, mama, it's me.
> How ya feelin', mama? Um-hm, that's all right.
> I've got somethin' I want to talk to you about
> if you don't mind,
> and I ain't mad—no, no. Listen, mama,

Only after the first line of the song do we begin to hear "mama's" response, a further addition to Safka's song:

> Look what they done to my song. (Wait! what's the matter, son?)
> Look what they done to my song.
> The only thing I could do half right and nice,
> Turned out-a all wrong, ma.

We hear her again in the second stanza.

> Wish I could find the good book. (Read it!) . . .
> If I could find the real good book,
>   I'd never have to come out and look—

The pitch lurches up half a step to a new key for the third stanza:

> Look what they done to my brain.
> They picked it like a chicken bone
>   And I'm just about to go insane, mama.

Then Charles appeals to a chorus:

> If you don't mind, I'd like to hear this in French.

And immediately, a big chorus responds, fitting the tune neatly:

> Ils ont changé ma chanson.

Charles mumbles Safka's next two lines in French and apologizes that his French isn't good enough. But his point is made: the wrong is not merely an American one. The final stanza, about the "plastic bag," therefore suggests that the wrong is aggravated more by time than by place. And about "plastic" there is a challenging comment from mama: "Who cares?" Then comes a coda, nearly as long as the five stanzas, repeating many of their lines, incorporating a stanza of Safka's that she had placed before the French one and adding an essential new idea. Safka's lines cry:

> Maybe it's all right,
> Maybe it's OK, I don't know. . . .
> I'm insane, insane, goin' crazy, mama, that's what it is.

Charles' new idea, however, is utterly sane, an answer to mama's challenge:

> Lord knows, I don't care what they done to my song,
> But see, the main thing, mama, what they tryin' to do to me.

More than this, Charles adds as final statement a resolution:

> But oh, I'm gonna keep on workin' on the buildin'
> Just like you taught me, mama; oh, yes, I will, mama.

While the song slowly fades out with unconsoled repeated falsetto whines of "mama," the resolution to "keep on workin'" stands. What "mama" taught is a spiritual: "I'm Workin' on the Buildin' for My Lord." It is the same lesson taught by the "old folks" of Foster and all the "old folks" of all the other crazy singers: "Keep on Workin'." Charles' combination of lament and resolution fits our whole account of the meanings of Foster's songs. What "they done" to any song is not the "main thing" but rather a subject for a new song, which is a small but important part of the work on "the buildin'."

NOTES

INTRODUCTION

Page x

Every music library can provide the famous Foster songs to note-readers who may not remember them. Countless anthologies include the three songs here taken as typical. Versions of different editors may be worth comparing. *The Stephen Foster Song Book: Original Sheet Music of 40 Songs . . . Selected, with Introduction and Notes,* by Richard Jackson (New York: Dover, 1974), is my favorite collection (though I disagree with Jackson on some interpretations of admittedly incomplete evidence). This edition will be cited as "Dover."

A most convenient, cheap, and reasonably authentic collection of forty-one *Songs of Stephen Foster Prepared for Schools and General Use* by Will Earhart and Edward B. Birge (1934) is continually reprinted by the University of Pittsburgh Press; this edition will be cited as "U. of P." "Oh! Susanna" appears in U. of P. page 79; "Jeanie" 21; "Old Folks" 43, with a facsimile of Foster's manuscript of the words.

Hundreds of libraries have the Foster Hall Reproductions in facsimile of all the first editions that had been gathered by 1933. These I recommend to scholarly readers, but their format—loose pages in three big boxes—makes them clumsy for quick reference. A more handsome facsimile edition of some 40 songs, in two volumes, with an introduction by H. Wiley Hitchcock, forms part of his big series of *Earlier American Music* (New York: Da Capo); the series is indispensable to every American music library.

"Old Black Joe," U. of P., 61; "Kentucky Home" 12; "Massa" 72. Modern anthologies are likely to omit "Joe" and "Massa," whose words are especially offensive to many people, not only those of African descent. "Kentucky Home" still appears alongside "Marching through Georgia" and "Nobody Knows the Trouble I've Seen" and hundreds of older and newer songs in Charles Hansen's *Songfest No. 2: Folk Songs of Today* (New York: Folk World, 1973), hereafter cited as *Songfest.*

Page xiii

"Hard Times, Come Again No More," U. of P., 40. John Mahon's article about "The Last Years of Stephen C. Foster" in the New York *Clipper,* 27 March 1877, was reprinted in the *Foster Hall Bulletin,* 10 (1934), 2–6. The detail about "Hard Times," p. 5, has been overlooked by Foster's most devoted biographer, John Tasker Howard, who observes that Foster's notebook shows more work on words than on the music.

"Camptown Races," U. of P., 88, *Songfest,* 36, appears sometimes with the title "Gwine to Run All Night" or even the shorter refrain "Doodah!" "Nelly Bly," U. of P.; 48, *Songfest,* 132, provides the name adopted by Elizabeth Cochrane (1867–1922) for her famous career as journalist and feminist; both the song and the lady seem to be less known among my friends than they deserve to be.

"Come, Where," U. of P., 15, if unfamiliar, might ideally be heard first on a 78 RPM recording by the great Irish tenor John McCormack, with a male chorus, unaccompanied, Victor 64423. McCormack's "Jeanie," with piano, Victor 1700, is also touching.

"Old Dog Tray," U. of P., 75 and *Songfest,* 130; "Gentle Annie," U. of P., 65; "Beautiful Dreamer" 86. Pleasing performances of the last two songs by Leslie Guinn, with imaginative scholarly accompanists, are included in the program recorded at the Smithsonian Institution in 1972, Nonesuch H-71268. This program begins with "Jeanie" by the versatile soprano Jan DeGaetani, and includes also spirited samplings of the George Cooper songs. All these songs are included in the program recorded under the direction of Gregg Smith, again at the Smithsonian, 1974, Vox SVBX 5304.

Page xv

 Musical World, XLII (6 February 1864), 90.

Page xvi

 Biography, Songs and Musical Compositions of Stephen C. Foster (Pittsburgh; Percy F. Smith, 1896). The biography was reprinted with the title *My Brother Stephen* (Indianapolis: Foster Hall, 1932). I shall cite the latter simply as *My Brother*.

 Chronicles of Stephen Foster's family by Evelyn Foster Morneweck (Pittsburgh: U. of P. Press, 1944); I shall cite these volumes as *Chronicles*. Conscientious readers may be grateful for the page references, because Morneweck's documents are not always easy to find. *Chronicles*, I, 103, for example, presents a brief indication of Olivia Pise's time with the Fosters.

 "Slavery in Western Pennsylvania," by Edward M. Burns, *Western Pennsylvania Historical Magazine*, VIII (1925), 204, shows how the institution faded there from 1790 to 1845.

Page xvii

 Eliza Foster's letter to William Jr., 14 May 1832, is published in facsimile in *Chronicles*, I, 86. The lines about Stephen appear on its third page.

 "Tioga Waltz" first appeared in the *Biography*; see *My Brother*, 32.

 Letters of 1841, *Chronicles*, I, 210 and 215.

 "Open Thy Lattice," U. of P., 46.

Page xviii

 On Pittsburgh and its growth there are many attractive books. Leland D. Baldwin's *Pittsburgh: the Story of a City* (U. of P. Press, 1937), describes the life of Foster's time vividly. More recently Oscar Handlin has recounted how "The City Grows" in a richly illustrated volume edited by Stefan Lorant, *Pittsburgh* (Garden City, New York: Doubleday, 1964). Edward Park Anderson's study of "The Intellectual Life of Pittsburgh, 1786–1836" appeared in the *Western Pennsylvania Historical Magazine*, XIV (1931), 9, 92, 225, 288. Among many sources of information contemporary with Foster two are outstanding: Henry Moore Brackenridge, *Recollections of Persons and Places in the West* (Philadelphia, 1834; reprinted by the Lost Cause Press, Louisville, 1956) and Neville B. Craig, *The History of Pittsburgh* (Pittsburgh: J. H. Mellor, 1851).

 On Cincinnati I recommend especially James Hall's *The West: Its Commerce and Navigation* (Cincinnati: 1848; Lost Cause Press, 1956); Walter Sutton, *The Western Book Trade: Cincinnati as a 19th-Century Publishing and Book-Trade Center* (Columbus: Ohio State University Press, 1961); James F. Dunlop, "Queen City Stages: Highlights of the Theatrical Season of 1843" and "Sophisticates and Dupes: Cincinnati Audiences, 1851," in the *Bulletin of the Historical and Philosophical Society of Ohio*, XIX (1961), 128, and XIII (1955), 87; and Heinrich Arnim Rattermann, "Anfänge und Entwicklung der Musik . . ." in *Jahrbuch der Amerikanischen historischen Gesellschaft von Illinois*, XII (1912). 327.

Page xix

 The Social Orchestra is reprinted complete as Vol. XIII of the series *Earlier American Music*.

 The manuscript notebook is at Foster Hall, University of Pittsburgh, where I studied it, thanks to the curator Fletcher Hodges, Jr.

 "Science," *My Brother*, 33, 38. Morrison does not explicitly deny the report in Granville Howe's book, *A Hundred Years of Music in America* (Chicago: Howe, 1889), p. 96: "The advice of friends that he educate his musical talents, he rejected, from a fear that it might injure his originality."

 What music? Charles Hamm has investigated more thoroughly than anyone else the several traditions prevalent in Foster's surroundings and traced the similarities between his songs and his likely models; Hamm's work, not yet published in 1975, will complement my studies.

Page xx

 "*Freischütz* . . . followed me in America like a bad ghost," wrote Karl Bernhard zu Saxe-Weimar-Eisenach, in his *Reise . . . durch Nord-Amerika* (Weimar: Hoffmann, 1828), vol. II, p. 103.

"Auld Lang Syne," *Songfest*. 10; "Home, Sweet Home," 80. On these songs' histories, splendid, concise, critical accounts are provided by James J. Fuld in his *Book of World-Famous Music, Classical, Popular and Folk* (New York: Crown, 1966), where the order is alphabetical.

Page xxi

"Long-tail Blue," "Coal-black Rose," and "Jim Crow" have dropped out of popularity, unlike "Zip Coon," which appears in *Songfest*, 189 and in Fuld's *Book of World-Famous Music*. For the early models, see first Gilbert Chase's *America's Music* (New York: McGraw-Hill, 1955, 1966; [new edition in preparation for 1976 at the University of Illinois]) where words and tunes are presented with reliable discussion. Facsimiles of early editions are published by Harry Dichter, Philadelphia, and by S. Foster Damon at Brown University.

"Lucy Long" and "Dandy Jim" can be found in Damon's *Series of Old American Songs* (Providence: Brown University Library, 1936). Damon's facsimiles of the earliest known editions are fascinating, especially in connection with his article "The Negro in Early American Songsters," *Papers of the Bibliographical Society of America*, XXVIII (1934), 132. Libraries lacking these should have *Music in America: An Anthology . . . 1620–1865*, edited by W. Thomas Marrocco and Harold Gleason (New York: Norton, 1964); here "Jim Crow" and "Zip Coon" introduce the chapter headed "Minstrel Shows," which includes "Susanna," "Old Folks," and "Dixie" (Emmett's most famous piece, 1859).

"Boatmen's Dance" (with the whole work of Emmett) appears in Chase's *America's Music*. Some readers will know it best as one of Aaron Copland's *Old American Songs*, arranged for concert in 1950.

"Buffalo Gals" holds its place in the "folk" repertory of *Songfest*, 32. It is among the oldest songs in Pete Seeger's collection, *American Favorite Ballads* (New York: Oak, 1961).

Blacking Up: The Minstrel Show in 19th-Century America, by Robert C. Toll (New York: Oxford University Press, 1974), is an excellent account of the institution, based on thorough critical study of both primary and secondary sources. Though I wish Toll gave more attention to international aspects of his story, I can only admire his skill and tact in treating the more profound interracial aspect. His brief account of Foster, p. 36, makes no mistake.

"Blackface minstrelsy and Jacksonian ideology" are shown to have much in common by Alexander Saxton, in his article in *American Quarterly*, XXVII (1975), 3.

"Annie" appears in Volume XII of *Earlier American Music*, which has the comprehensive title given by Hitchcock, "Household Songs."

Page xxii

Agnes McDowell, *Chronicles*, II, 375; *Foster Hall Bulletin*; II (1935), 5.

New Orleans trip recalled, first, in a letter from Richard Cowan to Morrison Foster, 8 February 1853, *Chronicles*, II, 447; then by Morrison himself, *My Brother*, 51; then by Susan Pentland Robinson, for a reporter in the Pittsburgh *Press*, 12 September 1900, cited in Howard's *Stephen Foster* (New York: Crowell, 1934, 1953 [paperback 1966]), 169. These testimonies are worth study because every other account of the trip is still more remote from the events.

The duet adapted from *Romeo* is "Wilt Thou Be Gone, Love?" It can be heard, with flute and violin supplementing the piano, on the Smithsonian record Nonesuch H-71268; the music is in *Earlier American Music*, XII 22, and Dover, 66.

"Molly" and the rest of the list, except "Beautiful Dreamer," are missing from U. of P. and most other selections. In Chapter 7 here some of them will be discussed, with all possible evidence of Jane's point of view as well as Stephen's.

Page xxiii

"Down Among the Canebrakes," U. of P., 59.

"Ring de Banjo," U. of P., 35; "Glendy Burk," 106; "Don't Bet Your Money" is most readily available in Dover, 25.

Milligan, *Stephen Collins Foster* (New York: Schirmer, 1920), p. 105; repeated in Howard's *Stephen Foster* (1966 edn.), p. 318; and paraphrased in many shorter treatments of Foster's life and work.

CHAPTER 1   FOSTER, THE YOUNG AMATEUR

Page 3

Ice Cream Saloon advertisements, from the Pittsburgh *Daily Commercial Journal*, reprinted in *Chronicles*, I, 311 ff.

On the canals and railroads and their political ramifications, see Avard L. Bishop, *The State Works of Pennsylvania* (New Haven, Connecticut: Tuttle, Morehouse & Taylor, 1907); Joseph S. Clark, Jr., "The Railroad Struggle for Pittsburgh: Forty Three Years of Philadelphia-Baltimore Rivalry, 1838 [*recte* 1828]–1871," in *Pennsylvania Magazine of History and Biography*, XLVIII (1924), 1; Philip Shriver Klein, *Pennsylvania Politics, 1817–1832: A Game Without Rules* (Philadelphia: Historical Society of Pennsylvania, 1940).

Page 4

Facsimile of "The Five 'Nice Young Men,' " in *Chronicles*, I, 283.

Page 5

Knights, *Chronicles*, I, 316, 294, 366. A likely stimulus for the boys' name, because of its date, is the novel by William Alexander Caruthers, *The Knights of the Horse Shoe, a Traditionary Tale of the Cocked Hat Gentry in the Old Dominion* (Wetumpka, Alabama: 1845), reprinted often, most recently with an introduction by Curtis Carroll Davis (Chapel Hill: University of North Carolina Press, 1970). Caruthers depicts "a cunning banjo player" as foil for his gentle characters; songs turn up in several episodes.

"Open Thy Lattice," U. of P., 46.

Page 6

Abdy, *Journal* (London: J. Murray, 1835), vol. III, p. 104.

Page 7

"Star performer . . .", *My Brother*, 25.

On "Jim Crow" there is a vivid account, often quoted, by Foster's friend Robert Peebles Nevin in "Stephen C. Foster and Negro Minstrelsy," *Atlantic*, XX (1967), 608. "Traces of the Negroid in the Mauresques of the 16th and 17th Centuries," by Paul Nettl, *Phylon*, V (1944), 105, cites some of the earliest documented examples of blackface dancers, but the idea may be still older.

Page 8

Singing Schools of Pennsylvania, 1800–1900 are described in a dissertation by Richard Byron Rosewall (Minnesota, 1969).

"Yankee Doodle," *Songfest*, 210; Fuld's *Book of World-Famous Music*.

"Good Old Colony Times," about the "three roguish chaps" who "fell into mishaps because they could not sing," was published in Boston about 1800. Damon's *Series of Old American Songs* has an interesting note along with the facsimile.

The careful account of the "Polka" by William Barclay Squire in Grove's *Dictionary of Music* has not been seriously revised after the claims of Czeslaw Halski about "The Polish origin of the polka" in the volume on *Chopin*, edited by Zofia Lissa (Warsaw: 1963), p. 530. Barclay Squire traced it from Prague, 1835, to Vienna, 1839, to Paris, 1840, to London, 1844. The Philadelphia journalist-critic Horace Binney Wallace in 1846 reported the craze in Newport; he compared the polka with the dance of death; his article was reprinted in his *Art and Scenery in Europe* (Philadelphia: Parry & M'Millan, 1857), p. 353. On the polka in Berlin, I have been delighted to learn from my friend Lukas Richter in his "Tanzstücke des Berliner Biedermeier: Folklore an der Wende zur Kommerzialisierung," in *Deutsches Jahrbuch der Musikwissenschaft*, X (1969), 42. The parallels between Berlin and Pittsburgh are many.

"Lou'siana Belle" is in the *Treasury of Stephen Foster* (New York: Random House, 1946), p. 39.

Young America, 1830–1840, by Robert E. Riegel (Norman: University of Oklahoma Press, 1949), p. 212, connects the polka with political and social change.

Page 10

Spender, "Americanization," in *Partisan Review*, XXXIX (1972), 153. But

Europe is more and more "Americanized." Czech music-sociologists recently learned, from questionnaires and polls involving over 2,000 people, that "according to age we can see the sharpest differences in the field of folklore and its derivatives. . . . It is the point of view of generation that is decisive . . . not . . . the difference between country and town." Vladimír Karbusický and Jaroslav Kasan, *Výskum soućasné hudebnosti* (Prague: Svoboda, 1969), p. 159.

"The Good Time Coming" is in *Earlier American Music*, XII, 5; Dover, 130.

A list of the twenty editions of "Susanna," compiled by R. W. Gordon, appears in J. T. Howard's *Stephen Foster*, 1966 edition, p. 141.

Page 11

"Uncle Ned," U. of P., 25.

Nevin's article? The unsigned article of 1858, "Who writes our songs?" copied from the New York *Evening Post* in Dwight's *Journal of Music*, XV (1959), 51, may have had another author, but it is so similar to the article that Nevin wrote for the *Atlantic*, "Stephen C. Foster and Negro Minstrelsy," XX (1867), 608, that I attribute it to Nevin. In 1865 Nevin corresponded with Morrison about their recollections—his letter is quoted in *Chronicles*, I, 309. Morrison's account, *My Brother*, 35, may rely partly on Nevin.

"What Must A Fairy's Dream Be?" can be found only in the complete Foster Hall facsimiles.

"Away down South" is in the Random House *Treasury*, 35.

Page 12

"My Brudder Gum," U. of P., 31.

"Dolly Day," U. of P., 84.

CHAPTER 2   FOSTER AND HIS RIVALS IN THE INTERNATIONAL
MUSIC BUSINESS

Page 14

"Nelson Kneass: Minstrel Singer and Composer" finally found a biographer in Ernst C. Krohn. The article is in the *Anuario interamericano de musica*, VII (1971), 17.

"Samuel S. Sanford and Negro Minstrelsy," a dissertation by Jimmy Dalton Baines (Tulane University, 1967), is based mainly on Sanford's own recollections, recorded about 1885. It adds much to the picture of the tradition surveyed by Carl Frederick Wittke in his well-written and often-cited book, *Tambo and Bones: A History of the American Minstrel Stage* (Durham: Duke University Press, 1930).

Sanford's opinion of Kneass is found in Baines, p. 116.

Page 15

Foster's letter, *Chronicles*, I, 337.

Dean J. Rice, *Two Stephen C. Foster Songs* (New York: J. Fischer, 1931), cited in J. T. Howard, *Stephen Foster*, 125.

"Clare de Kitchen," Damon's *Series of Old American Songs*, unfortunately not copied into many other collections.

Page 16

Letter, *Chronicles*, II, 377.

Christy's life is recounted by Edwin Francis Edgett, in the *Dictionary of American Biography*, vol. II (1930), p. 98.

"Good Night, Ladies," *Songfest*, 70. James Fuld points out that the "Merrily" refrain was added later—the whole song was first published in 1867; *World-Famous Music*, 213, 295. Robert Toll, *Blacking Up*, p. 46, produces some evidence that Christy drew material from Black singers, including those at the Congo Square in New Orleans around 1827, and later a church singer in Buffalo, One-legged Harrison.

Page 17

An anonymous obituary of Henry Russell in the *Musical Times*, XLII (1901),

27 is the chief source of information, until John Anthony Stephens completes his dissertation at Illinois. Russell's own book *Cheer! Boys, Cheer! Memories of Men and Music* (London: Macqueen, 1895) is interesting. Gilbert Chase presents Russell as foremost representative of "the genteel tradition"—a label that Chase has adapted from Santayana—in *America's Music*.

Russell's songs dropped from most repertories too soon to be included in 20th-century popular anthologies; the historical anthology of *Music in America* by Marrocco and Gleason contains an extremely simple and sentimental example: "The Old Arm Chair," 1840. Large libraries may provide Russell's own *100 Songs* (London: Musical Bouquet, 1856), in which the Foster pieces appear, as well as older "Negro Songs" such as "Buffalo Gals."

Page 18

Foster's version of "The Good Time Coming" is sung too fast, too condescendingly, for the Smithsonian record Nonesuch H-71268. The music is in the *Stephen Foster Song Book* and *Earlier American Music*, XII. The song is neglected in *My Brother* and *Chronicles*.

Page 19

In "Stephen Foster, Democrat" Fletcher Hodges, Jr., assembles evidence on this point. His article, originally in *The Lincoln Herald*, 1945, was republished separately by the University of Pittsburgh, 1946.

"Susanna" and "The Good Time" appeared side by side in adaptations for the *Temperance Melodist* (London: F. Pitman, about 1850), p. 37.

Mackay, *Poetical Works* (London: Warne, 1876), p. 7, reprints the 1850 preface.

"Dixie," *Songfest*, 54; Fuld's account in *World-Famous Music* relies on Hans Nathan, *Dan Emmett and the Rise of Early Negro Minstrelsy* (Norman: University of Oklahoma Press, 1962), as I do too. (Nathan plans a new edition of *Emmett* soon.)

Page 20

"Juba and American Minstrelsy" is an exciting account by Marina Hannah Winter, in *Chronicles of the American Dance*, edited by Paul Magriel (New York: Holt, 1948), p. 39; the London reviewer's characterization is p. 50. A more accessible account, derived from Winter's, is in the book by Marshall and Jean Stearns, *Jazz Dance* (New York: Macmillan, 1968), p. 44. On the African Grove Theatre in New York around 1820, the Black Shakespearean actor Ira Aldridge, and others, see Loften Mitchell's *Black Drama* (New York: Hawthorn, 1967).

Page 21

Liszt's judgment of Herz, and other details, I take from Reinhold Sietz's article in the encyclopedia *Musik in Geschichte und Gegenwart*, vol. VI (1957), p. 293.

Mes voyages (Paris: Faure, 1866) has been translated by Henry Bertram Hill as *My Travels in America* (Madison: University of Wisconsin Press, 1963); I quote from the translation p. 91.

Page 22

Gottschalk's reminiscences, *Notes of a Pianist*, first published in a translation by Robert E. Peterson, 1881, were well edited, with an introduction, by Jeanne Behrend (New York: Knopf, 1964). I rely on Behrend, especially p. xxiv.

Gottschalk's *Piano Works*, in five volumes, edited by Vera Brodsky Lawrence, with a biographical essay by Robert Offergeld, became available at last in 1969 (New York: Arno). Offergeld compiled a *Centennial Catalogue of the Published and Unpublished Compositions* (New York: Stereo Review, 1970); numerous musicologists are contributing to the study of his work; there are recorded performances of a lot of it, though not yet the pieces using Foster tunes, unless the resemblance between Foster's "Camptown" and the main theme of Gottschalk's "The Banjo" is more than coincidental.

"Henry Kleber, Early Pittsburgh Musician," by Edward G. Baynham, in *Western Pennsylvania Historical Magazine*, XXV (1942), 113–120, assembles all the facts.

Page 23

Verdi's "Coro di zingari" became and remained so popular as the "Anvil" that it has a place in Fuld's *Book of World-Famous Music.*

Foster's letter. *Chronicles,* II, 481.

Page 24

The spectacular growth of the "sheet music" business was described with exact figures and dates by an anonymous reporter in the Washington *Globe,* whose article was reprinted in Dwight's *Journal of Music,* VI (1854), 43.

George Willig's career is described by John Hill Hewitt in his memoirs, *Shadows on the Wall* (Baltimore: Turnbull, 1877), p. 71.

Benteen's publications of Foster are thoroughly described by John Tasker Howard, *Stephen Foster,* 180–185.

Peters' Pittsburgh days and his earlier career are referred to confidently in a letter from the Kleber firm to Daniel Spillane, printed in his *History of the American Pianoforte* (New York: Spillane, 1890), p. 194. Peters' later career is summed up in Walter Sutton's *Western Book Trade* (Columbus: Ohio State University Press, 1961), p. 82.

Morrison's statement that Stephen had known Peters in Pittsburgh (*My Brother,* 35) must be doubted.

Peters' account to Russell is complete in *Chronicles,* II, 484.

Page 25

Foster's letter to Millet, 25 May 1849, *Chronicles,* I, 337; also in Howard, *Stephen Foster,* 139.

Facts about Firth and Pond were reported anonymously in the (New York) *Musical Review,* V (1854), 424.

On Steinway's system in the context of piano technology, see Alfred Dolge. *Pianos and Their Makers: A Comprehensive History* (Covina, California: 1911; reprinted New York: Dover, 1972), pp. 62, 71.

Letter to Foster, *Chronicles,* I, 354.

Page 26

Letter of 1851, reported by John Mahon to the New York *Clipper,* 26 May 1877, *Chronicles,* II, 586.

Contract, logically reconstructed by Howard, *Stephen Foster,* 237.

Advertisement, *Musical Review,* V (1854), 330.

CHAPTER 3   WORKING SINGERS

Page 28

"Arkansas Traveller—a Multi-parented Wayfarer," by Mary D. Hudgins, *Arkansas Historical Quarterly,* XXX (1971), 145, lists versions of this song earlier than the one published in Boston, 1860, and available in Dichter's facsimile: the earliest is from Peters in Louisville and Cincinnati, 1847, with the arrangement attributed to William Cummings—possibly a pen-name for Peters; in 1851 a version was published by Kleber; both of these bring the song close to Foster. Hudgins identifies Edward Washburn (d. 1859) as the painter whose "Traveller" was the model for the Currier and Ives prints of 1870, mentioned in Fuld's *World-Famous Music.*

The Keelboat Age on Western Waters, by Leland Dewitt Baldwin (University of Pittsburgh Press, 1941), p. 90.

Industrial Slavery in the Old South, by Robert Starobin (New York: Oxford University Press, 1970), pp. 92, 135.

Northrup, *Twelve Years a Slave* (Cincinnati: 1853). Relevant pages are included in Eileen Southern's *Readings in Black American Music* (New York: Norton, 1971), which should be in every American library and every German music library.

Northrup's whole book is edited by Sue Eakin and Joseph Logsdon (Baton Rouge: University of Louisiana Press, 1968), and by Gilbert Osofsky in *Puttin' on Ole Massa* (New York: Harper & Row, 1969).

Taylor, *Eldorado (or Adventures in the Path of Empire, Mexico and California)* 1849–50, in his *Works* (New York: Putnam, 1882–83), vol. II, pp. 13, 274, 314. *Bayard Taylor, Laureate of the Gilded Age,* by Richard Croom Beatty (Norman: University of Oklahoma Press, 1936), puts the reporter's early work in context.

Page 30

The Frontier Against Slavery, by Eugene H. Berwanger (Urbana: University of Illinois Press, 1967), p. 61.

"Who's agwan Souff?" *Songs of the American West,* edited by Richard E. Lingenfelter et al. (Berkeley: University of California Press, 1968), p. 16.

Page 31

Taylor, "The Magic of Music," in *National Intelligencer,* copied by Dwight's *Journal of Music,* III (1853), 131.

Sång under Segel, by Sigurd Sternvall (Stockholm: Bonnier, 1935), cited by Stan Hugill, *Shanties* (London: Dutton, 1966), p. 116.

Mormon Songs from the Rocky Mountains: a Compilation, by Thomas E. Cheney (Austin: University of Texas Press, 1968), p. 179. "Camptown" too turns up here, p. 84.

"Susanita," in *American Folklore* by Richard M. Dorson (Chicago: University of Chicago Press, 1959), p. 111.

Mayhew, *London Labour* (London: Griffin, Bone, 1861), vol. III, p. 179 ff. Selections from *Mayhew's London,* edited by Peter Quenell (London: Pilot Press, 1949), include much of the musical material, 477 ff.

Page 32

Putnam's Monthly, V (1855), 222.

MacGregor, *Our Brothers and Cousins: a Summer Tour* (London: Seeley, Jackson, & Halliday, 1859), p. 118.

"Folk Songs of an Industrial City [Pittsburgh]" by Jacob A. Evanson, in *Pennsylvania Songs and Legends,* edited by George Korson (Baltimore: Johns Hopkins Press, 1949, 1960), p. 423.

"Political Campaign Songs from Tippecanoe to '72" by Janet I. and G. Douglas Nicoll, in *Pop Music and Society,* I (1972), 193, starts correctly with "Auld Lang Syne"; notes the use of "Susanna" for Harrison in 1884, Landon in 1936.

Page 33

McCarty was his own publisher, Philadelphia.

"Hurrah!" *Chronicles,* II, 390.

Billy Hamilton, *Chronicles,* II, 477.

"Villikins" with original words is in Charles Hansen's *Songfest,* 194. Fuld's *Book of World-Famous Music* lists the earliest known printing of the music as 1853. Mayhew's play (London: J. Miller, 1834), gives the song to a character named Jem Bags, a clarionetist. Fuld cites the words of "Sweet Betsey" from San Francisco, 1858. Peter Seeger, in *American Favorite Ballads,* says that some of the lines of "Old Smokey" "go back to Elizabethan times." Both "Villikins" and "The White House Chair" are included in the Vox recording, 1974, SVBX 5304.

Page 34

Hutchinson's Republican Songster (New York: Hutchinson, 1860), p. 15. Another "Nelly Bly" campaign song appears in the collection of *Songs,* edited by G. W. Civis (New York: Tribune, 1860): "Ho! for Kansas," words by Lucy Larcom, p. 20.

On Harry McCarthy, the best article I know is Richard B. Harwell's "The Star of the Bonnie Blue Flag" in *Civil War History,* IV (1958), 285. "The Bonnie Blue" (New Orleans: Blackmar, 1861), is reprinted in Dichter's facsimiles.

Harps in the Wind: The Story of the Singing Hutchinsons, by Carol Brink (New York: Macmillan, 1947), is ample and accurate.

Page 35

"Get off the track!" was published separately (Boston: Henry Prentiss, 1844). Clark, *The Liberty Minstrel* (New York: Saxton & Miles, 1844); *The Harp of*

Freedom (New York: Miller, Orton & Mulligan, 1856), pp. 59, 295.

Brown, *The Anti-Slavery Harp* (Boston: Bela Marsh, 1849, 1851), p. 9.

Page 36

Narrative (Boston: Anti-Slavery Office, 1847); reprinted in the collection *Puttin' on Ole Massa*, edited by Osofsky. Here, p. 197, the "Better day" song is "said to have been composed by a slave." William Edward Farrison supersedes all earlier studies of Brown with *William Wells Brown, Author and Reformer* (Chicago: University of Chicago Press, 1969). But Brown's own last book, *My Southern Home*, 1880, reprinted by Gregg, 1968, cries out for study by an informed and critical musician.

Page 37

"Sojourner Truth" is described by Saunders Redding in the dictionary of *Notable American Women*, vol. III (1971), p. 479. The primary source is a *Narrative* compiled by Olive Gilbert (Battle Creek, Michigan: 1878), reprinted New York, Arno, 1968.

Stowe described "Sojourner Truth, the Libyan Sibyl" in the *Atlantic*, XI (1863), 473. Stowe's shock at hearing "Susanna" is imagined by Hertha Pauli, in *Her Name Was Sojourner Truth* (New York: Appleton-Century-Crofts, 1962), p. 184.

"John Brown's Body," *Songfest*, 94; *American Favorite Ballads*, 62; discussed in Fuld's *Book of World-Famous Music* under the title "Battle Hymn of the Republic." Sojourner Truth's words, "The valiant soldiers," are in Gilbert's *Narrative*, 126; "Possum" alludes to "Zip Coon."

"I Am Pleading," Gilbert p. 303.

"Harriet Tubman" in *Notable American Women*, vol. III (1971), p. 481, is by John Hope Franklin, relying largely on the biography by Earl Conrad (Washington: Associated Publishers, 1943). Conrad's information on music appears separately also in " 'General' Tubman. Composer of Spirituals: An Amazing Figure in American Folk Music," in *Etude*, LX (May 1942), 305.

Page 38

"Go Down Moses," *Songfest*, 68; "Swing Low," 182; both of these and also "Steal Away" are in the fine collection by John W. Work, *American Negro Songs and Spirituals* (New York: Bonanza, 1940), which can be found in most American libraries.

Page 39

Spaulding, "Under the Palmetto" in *Continental Monthly*, IV (1863), 188; also in *The Negro and His Folklore*, edited by Bruce Jackson (Austin: University of Texas Press, 1967), p. 64.

Higginson, "Negro Spirituals" in *Atlantic*, XIX (1867), 685; about the "minstrels," 693. Higginson included this article in his book *Army Life in a Black Regiment* (Boston: 1870); excerpts appear in Eileen Southern's *Readings in Black American Music*—here the "minstrels" appear on p. 192 (New York: Norton, 1971).

"Deep River," *Songfest*, 52.

White, *American Negro Folk-Songs* (Cambridge, Massachusetts: Harvard University Press, 1928), reprinted with a foreword by Bruce Jackson (Hatboro, Pennsylvania: Folklore Associates, 1965), p. 164. Compare also Eli Bowen, *Rambles in the Path of the Steam Horse* (Philadelphia: Brownell & Smith, 1855), p. 228 (Bowen heard *Uncle Ned* at a Virginia corn-husking); and Bruce A. Rosenberg, *The Folksongs of Virginia* (Charlottesville: University Press of Virginia, 1969), items 162, 506, 1047, 1064, 1447 ("Uncle Ned").

Lomax, *The Folk Songs of North America in the English Language* (Garden City, New York: Doubleday, 1960), p. 493. The International Folk Music Council agreed in 1954 that the term "folksong" is properly "applied to music which has originated with an individual composer and has subsequently been absorbed into the unwritten living tradition of a community. The term does not cover popular composed music that has been taken over ready-made by a community and remains unchanged, for it is the refashioning and re-creation of the music by the

community which gives it its folk character." I quote from Maud Karpeles, *An Introduction to English Folk Song* (London: Oxford University Press, 1973), p. 3.
Page 40
"A broad and quick diffusion of a work of art depends upon its 'poly-interpretability,'" in the view of H. de Jager, "Possibilities for Diffusion of Present Day Music from a Sociological Point of View," in *Interface*, 2 (1973), 55.

CHAPTER 4   CONTEMPORARY CRITICS

Page 42
Child edited *War-Songs for Free Men*, 4th edition (Boston: Ticknor & Fields, 1863), in which one of the tunes was "Long Time Ago"; for a blackface version of 1836 see Chase's *America's Music*, 279.
Busch's publisher was Cotta. The translation by Norman H. Binger titled *Travels . . .* was published at Lexington by University of Kentucky Press, 1971. Busch's application of the term "folk" was anticipated by Carl Friedrich Weitzmann, whose article "Volksmelodien" in the *Neue Zeitschrift für Musik*. XXXV (1851), 271, included "Lucy Neal" alongside two Scotch songs and one each from the Kazan Tatars and the Astrakhan Tatars.
Page 44
Busch in New York, I, 264; at Dunkirk, I, 50 (Binger 20); at church in Cincinnati, I, 82 (29); in Kentucky, I, 285 (153); recalling students, I, 172 (90); with Mormons, I, 225 (130); with Shakers, I, 144 (71); crier and band, I, 97 (38); at bar, I, 292 (159); cathedral, I, 112 (44); prison, I, 56 (25); steamboat, I, 265; on "pseudo-Negroes," I, 254. The chapter on songs is 250–280.
Unsere volkstumliche Lieder is the title of a famous collection by August Heinrich Hoffmann von Fallersleben, 1857, (4th ed., Leipzig: Engelmann, 1900). Franz Magnus Bohme's collection of *Volkstumliche Lieder der Deutschen* (Leipzig: Breitkopf u. Härtel, 1895), is still more famous and useful. Perhaps the earliest use of the term is in Karl Friedrich Erlach's *Volkslieder der Deutschen* (Mannheim: Hoff, 1836), vol. V, p. 5.
Page 45
Bremer's book was published in London by A. Hall, and in New York by Harper, 1853. The original title is *Hemmen i den nya verlden*. My quotations are from the London edition, I, 369 ff. Eileen Southern's *Readings in Black American Music* contain the more popular passages.
Herder: *His Life and Thought* by Robert T. Clark, Jr., (Berkeley: University of California Press, 1955) is my chief guide. Gene Bluestein's essays, collected as *The Voice of the Folk: Folklore and American Literary Theory* (Amherst: University of Massachusetts Press, 1972) have helped me connect Herder with many strands of culture, ever since Bluestein's dissertation (Minnesota, 1960). Walter Wiora's book on *Europäische Volksmusik und abendländische Tonkunst* (Kassel: Hinnenthal, 1957) helped profoundly to shape all my thoughts. Wiora's *Herder-Studien* (Wurzburg: Holzner, 1960), his debate with Ernst Klusen about Herder, and indeed all Wiora's writings are relevant to my work. Finally, my understanding of Herder is confirmed and refined by Isaiah Berlin's "J. G. Herder," *Encounter*, XXV/1 (July 1965), 29, and /2 (August), 42.
Page 46
About *Ossian*, Oisin, and St. Patrick, there is fresh information and wisdom in John Wain's "Alternative Poetry: An Oxford Inaugural Lecture," *Encounter*, June 1974, 26, with advice from which any future student of Stephen Foster could profit.
"The Opera" was reprinted in Carlyle's *Critical and Miscellaneous Essays* (New York: Scribner, 1901), vol. IV, p. 397.
Occasional Discourse on the Nigger Question (London: Bosworth, 1853; printed separately, omitted from most collections). I quote from pp. 14, 17, 43.
Page 48
"Charles Mackay: England's Forgotten Civil War Correspondent" is revived by George S. Wykoff in the *South Atlantic Quarterly*, XXVI (1927), 50.

Mackay's war reports were rated as deserving oblivion by an anonymous obituary writer in the London *Spectator*, 16 July, 1887.

Life and Liberty (New York: Harper, 1859), pp. 208, 299. In Mackay's *Memoirs of Extraordinary Popular Delusions and the Madness of Crowds* (London: Routledge, 1869), he is more particular about the "vile song called 'Jim Crow,'" vol. II, p. 248.

William Cullen Bryant by Charles Henry Brown (New York: Scribner, 1971) puts the tour in perspective.

Letters of a Traveller (New York: Putnam, 1850), reprinted in Bryant's *Prose Writings* (New York: Appleton, 1889), vol. I, p. 23. Bryant's report was called to the attention of modern specialists by Norris Yates in "Four Plantation Songs..." in *Southern Folklore Quarterly*, XV (1951), 251.

Page 49

". . . Schools," in *Orations and Addresses* (New York: Putnam, 1878), p. 285.

Page 50

James Russell Lowell by Martin Duberman (Boston: Houghton Mifflin, 1966) helped to organize my study of Foster, as well as to relate his age to ours. "Music in Lowell's Prose and Verse" by H. T. Henry, *Musical Quarterly*, X (1924), 546, helped me skim Lowell's voluminous works. I quote the *Papers* as edited by F. O. Matthiessen in *The Oxford Book of American Verse* (New York: Oxford University Press, 1950), p. 272.

The Pioneer, I (1843), 73.

"The Power of Sound," *Uncollected Poems*, edited by Thelma M. Smith (Philadelphia: University of Pennsylvania Press, 1950), p. 110. The 1896 edition, by Charles Eliot Norton, I have not seen.

Page 51

Fable, Oxford Book of American Verse, 261.

Page 52

"John Greenleaf Whittier: The Conscience in Poetry" by Perry Miller, *Harvard Review*, II/2 (September 1964), 8, is the critique most to my taste.

Proem, Oxford Book of American Verse, 152.

At Port Royal, 1861, Atlantic, IX (1862), 244.

"Samuel Atkins Eliot" is described by Claude M. Fuess in the *Dictionary of American Biography*. His *Address* was published in Boston by Perkins, Marvin in 1835; I quote from p. 14.

North American, LII (1841), 320.

Page 53

Life of Josiah Henson (Boston: A. D. Phelps, 1849); expanded with an introduction by Harriet Beecher Stowe (Boston: J. P. Jewett, 1858); here the story of the walnut for Chickering is told, p. 177; the remark on exhibitors and exhibited, p. 192.

North American, L (1840), 1. *A Selection from the Writings of Henry Russell Cleveland, with a Memoir* by George S. Hillard (Boston: Freeman & Bolles, 1844). I quote from the original, 11, 13 ff. Cleveland's ideas were expanded by Frederick William Sawyer in *A Plea for Amusements* (New York: Appleton, 1847), where music is treated especially in connection with national character, p. 145 ff. Another similar volume, typical of its time, is *The Connexion Between Taste and Morals* by Mark Hopkins (Boston: Dutton and Wentworth, 1841). Relevant in a different way is the essay on "Popular Music" by the English Swedenborgian Charles Lane, in *Spirit of the Age*, I/20–23 (1849), 310; 321; 353, in which America's need for a "national music" is deemed more urgent than England's.

Page 54

"Who Are Our National Poets?" in the *Knickerbocker Magazine*, XXVI (1845), 331, was attributed to "our 'salt-fish dinner' correspondent." The author is identified as Kennard by Hans Nathan, *Dan Emmett*, 153; as Kinnard by Bruce Jackson, who reprints the article in *The Negro and His Folklore* (Austin: University of Texas Press, 1967), p. 23. My quotations come from Jackson's volume, 25, 35, 33.

Page 55

Dwight's disciple George Willis Cooke wrote about him in *John Sullivan*

Dwight, Brook-Farmer, Editor, and Critic of Music (Boston: Small, Maynard, 1898; Hartford: Transcendental Books, 1973). A more critical first-hand account is the essay in William Foster Apthorp's *Musicians and Musiclovers* (New York: Scribner, 1894), p. 277. Helpful later studies include Irving Lowens, "Writings About Music in the Periodicals of American Transcendentalism," *Journal of the American Musicological Society*, X (1957), 2, reprinted in Lowens' *Music and Musicians in Early America* (New York: Norton, 1964); and Marcia Wilson Lebow, *A Systematic Examination of the Journal of Music . . .* (dissertation, University of California at Los Angeles, 1969). Dwight's letters in the Boston Public Library may well yield further insights to future scholars.

"On Music" quoted by Lowens, *Music . . . Early America,* 259; also in Perry Miller's *The Transcendentalists: An Anthology* (Cambridge, Massachusetts: Harvard University Press, 1950), p. 410.

The Pioneer, I/1 (1843), 26; I/2, 56.

The Harbinger, I (1845), 12, 44, 139, 154, 173, 236.

Page 56

Sartain's Magazine, VIII (1851), 406.

Dwight's Journal, I (1852), 86; on Moore 134; letter from Thayer 170.

Letter from Georgia, *Journal,* II (1853), 164.

Page 57

"City fathers . . . ," *Journal,* III (1853), 31; Strakosch, 70.

"Namby-pamby," *Journal,* III, 79; "Humanity," 156.

Page 58

"Clapping classes," *Journal,* III, 94.

Anna Zerr, *Journal,* III, 191; Gottschalk, IV, 21; "Yankee Doodle," IV, 30.

Gottschalk, *Journal,* IV, 44.

Page 59

"Popular amusements," VII (1855), 117.

"The strangest thing," XVII (1860), 174.

Atlantic, XXVI (1870), 321.

Dial, III/1 (July 1842), 46, especially 52. On Fuller, Thoreau, and others, there are useful indexes in Daniel Edgar Rider's dissertation, "The Musical Thought and Activities of the New England Transcendentalists," (Minnesota, 1964).

Page 60

Journal, edited by Bradford Terry and Francis H. Allen (Boston: Houghton Mifflin, 1949), vol. II, p. 379; vol. V, p. 294. Some of the most poignant musical references come from the long-lost journal volume of 1840, published at last by Perry Miller as *Consciousness in Concord* (Boston: Houghton Mifflin, 1958); e.g., p. 152: "When I hear a strain of music from across the street, I put away Homer and Shakespeare, and read them in the original." In the vast bibliography of responses to Thoreau, an outstanding volume is *Thoreau in Our Season,* edited by John H. Hicks (Amherst: University of Massachusetts Press, 1966); and a specially relevant essay is "Thoreau: The Ear and the Music," by Kenneth W. Rhoads, *American Literature,* XLVI (1974), 313.

Higginson's memoir, *Cheerful Yesterdays,* 1898, was reprinted in his five volumes of *Writings* (Cambridge, Massachusetts: Riverside, 1900); an early comment on the Hutchinson family singers, I 118; Lowell, 94; Whittier 132; Thoreau 216; S. S. Foster, 146.

Stephen Symonds Foster and Abby Kelley Foster are portrayed by Jane Hanna Pease in her dissertation, "The Freshness of Fanaticism" (Rochester, 1969). A letter from Pease to me confirms, alas, the lack of musical references.

Brotherhood . . . (New London, Connecticut: W. Bolles, 1843).

Revolution . . . (Boston: Anti-slavery Society, 1855).

Page 61

The Historic Whitman, by Joseph Jay Rubin (University Park: Pennsylvania State University Press, 1973), supersedes earlier biographies. Rubin's bibliography is especially helpful. The *Collected Writings* (New York: New York University Press, 1961) will supersede for scholarly purposes all earlier editions.

"Art Singing" is reprinted in the *Uncollected Poetry and Prose,* edited by Emory Holloway (Garden City, New York: Doubleday, 1921), vol. I, p. 104.

"True American Singing" is in *Walt Whitman Looks at the Schools,* edited by Florence Bernstein Freedman (New York, King's Crown, 1950), p. 216.

Rubin, *The Historic Whitman,* 279.

Page 62

"Mount's Negro . . ." *Uncollected . . . ,* I, 236.

"American Opera," cited in *Walt Whitman and Opera,* by Robert D. Faner (Philadelphia: University of Pennsylvania Press, 1951), p. 40.

An American Primer (Boston: Small, Maynard, 1904), p. 24.

"The English Opera . . . ," *Uncollected . . . ,* II, 97.

Page 63

"Salut au monde," NYU edition, IX, 633; "Our Old Feuillage," 173; *Proud Music,* 405. My understanding of the last poem owes something to Sydney J. Krause, "Whitman, Music and *Proud Music of the Storm,*" in *Publications of the Modern Language Association,* LXXII (1957), 705.

The Melville Log, by Jay Leyda (New York: Harcourt Brace, 1951), is my authority for biography. The superb edition of the works under way at Evanston, Northwestern University Press, supersedes earlier ones, but not yet Leyda's edition of the *Complete Stories* (New York: Random House, 1955).

Redburn, Northwestern edition, 248, 249.

Page 64

Whitejacket, Northwestern, 168, 275, 276.

Journal, edited by Eleanor Melville Metcalf (Cambridge, Massachusetts: Harvard University Press, 1948), pp. 23, 27.

Letters, edited by Merrell R. Davis and William H. Gilman (New Haven, Connecticut: Yale University Press, 1960), p. 126.

Page 65

W. R. Thompson, "Melville's 'The Fiddler': A Study in Dissolution," in *Texas Studies in Language and Literature,* II (1961), 492.

"Benito Cereno" provides the climax of a fascinating extended study, *The Intricate Knot: Black Figures in American Literature, 1776–1863,* by Jean Fagan Yellin (New York: New York University Press, 1972).

Page 66

Frederick Douglass, a Biography, by Philip Sheldon Foner (New York: Citadel, 1964), supplements Foner's edition of the *Life and Writings,* 4 vols. (New York: International Publishers, 1950–55), but Foner would not claim either work to be definitive. For the fact that Douglass took three music books in his baggage from Newport to New Bedford, 1839, I am indebted to Frederic May Holland, *Frederick Douglass* (New York: Funk & Wagnalls, 1895), p. 36.

Narrative (Boston: Anti-Slavery Office, 1845).

Tribune, reprinted in *Life and Writings,* I, 151.

Frederick Douglass' Paper, I/1 (3 December 1847), 2; I/5 (28 January 1848), 1; Charity Bowery's report, I/10 (3 March), 4; Ontario, I/23 (2 June), 1; Pittsburgh, I/37 (8 September), 1; Virginia Minstrels, I/44 (27 October), 2.

Page 67

North Star, 29 June 1849, p. 2.

"Black Swan," *North Star,* 23 October 1851, p. 2. "Elizabeth Greenfield" by Samuel R. Spencer, Jr., *Notable American Women,* II (1971), 87.

Page 68

". . . as a people," *Frederick Douglass' Paper,* I/39 (22 September 1848), 1.

Two biographers of Delany completed their books at the same time: Victor Ullman, *Martin R. Delany: The Beginnings of Black Nationalism* (Boston: Beacon, 1971), and Dorothy Sterling, *The Making of an Afro-American: Martin Robinson Delany, 1812–1885* (Garden City, New York: Doubleday, 1971). Both responded generously to my inquiries, but failed to learn much about Delany's musical interests.

Delany's sketch of the life of Vashon is in William C. Nell's book, *The*

Colored Patriots (Boston: Wallcut, 1855), p. 181.

 Condition . . . , Philadelphia, the author, 1852.

Page 69

 Blake (Boston: Beacon, 1970) is studied for the first time in relation to the fictions of Paulding, Kennedy, Simms, Hildreth, Stowe, and others in Jean Yellin's *Intricate Knot.*

 Douglass' Monthly, IV (1862), 695.

 Delany in *Douglass' Paper*, I/22 (26 May 1848), 2; I/25 (16 June), 1; *North Star* (6 July 1849), 1; (13 July), 4.

 In *Blake*, "Susanna," p. 143; "Uncle Ned," p. 105; "Old Folks," p. 100.

CHAPTER 5 FOSTER, THE CRAFTSMAN

Page 72

 Computer: Henry Ferdinand Olson, *Music, Physics and Engineering*, 2nd ed. (New York: Dover, 1967), p. 425 ff.; Wilbur Cross, "Machine Miltons," in *New York Times Magazine*, 4 December 1966, p. 59; Benjamin White, "Recognition of Distorted Melodies," in *American Journal of Psychology*, LXXIII (1960), 100.

Page 73

 "Nelly Was a Lady," U. of P., 90; altogether eight of the twelve songs are available in U. of P., with the choruses somewhat modernized. The same eight plus "Away Down South" and "Oh! Lemuel" are in the Random House *Treasury*. "Nelly" and three more of the list, with original accompaniments, are in the *Stephen Foster Song Book* published by Dover. Only "Melinda May" is hard to find. All these are naturally included in the *Minstrel Show Songs*, vol. XIV of *Earlier American Music*. The later songs referred to here are in most collections.

Page 76

 Manuscript memorandum, 27 January 1857, at the Library of Congress, published in J. T. Howard, *Stephen Foster*, 267.

Page 77

 Foster's accompaniments, with their irregular changes from measure to measure of instrumental figuration, seem to the pianist Neely Bruce to manifest a subtlety of thought similar to that of Charles Ives. Bruce spoke on this and other similarities at the Ives Festival Conference in New York, 19 October 1974. His observations will probably be set forth more amply in a future publication.

Page 78

 "Samuel S. Sanford," dissertation by J. D. Baines (Tulane University, 1967), p. 20.

Page 79

 Farmer's Register, VI (1 April 1838), 58. Foster could hardly have learned about "clapping juba" from the letter that Beverley Tucker wrote to Edgar Allan Poe, 1835, published in Poe's *Life and Letters*, edited by James A. Harrison (New York: Crowell, 1902–03), vol. II, p. 21. Nor from the studies of Poe's friend Thomas Holley Chivers, as reported in his "Papers," edited by George E. Woodbury in *Century*, LXV (1903), p. 555, and in S. Foster Damon's book, *Chivers* (New York: Harper, 1930), p. 235. But these reports indicate the possibility that Foster may have known more than the conveniently rhyming word.

Page 80

 "Comin' Through the Rye," according to James Fuld's *Book of World-Famous Music*, may have been printed for the first time in Burns' *Merry Muses of Caledonia*, about 1800. For a good brief survey of the relevant tradition, I recommend George S. Emmerson, *Rantin' Pipe and Tremblin' String: A History of Scottish Dance Music* (London: Dent, 1971).

 Du, du . . . , also according to Fuld, was first printed with both words and music in 1828, though it doubtless originated a few years earlier.

Page 81

 Nathan, *Dan Emmett and the Rise of Early Negro Minstrelsy* (Norman: University of Oklahoma Press, 1962), p. 174.

Page 82

"The Ole Grey Goose," Damon's *Series of Old American Songs.* The other songs of 1844 are in Nathan's *Dan Emmett.*

Foster's chords have been studied by Otto Gombosi, "Stephen Foster and 'Gregory Walker,' " in the *Musical Quarterly,* XXX (1944), 133. Gombosi notes patterns familiar to him from 16th-century dances, such as the *Passamezzo moderno;* he claims no continuity of style, merely notes the coincidence.

Page 83

Pope's article of 1895 is cited in Howard's *Stephen Foster,* 222.

Page 84

"Oh! Boys, Carry Me 'Long," U. of P., 55.

Letter of 1851, *Chronicles,* II, 396.

Page 85

Letter of 1851, *Chronicles,* II, 397.

CHAPTER 6   FOSTER AND HIS FAMILY

Page 89

"Sentimental," *My Brother,* 41.

"Jennie," *Chronicles,* II, 481. "Jennie" was the spelling also of an anonymous obituary, printed on the back page of the song "Lizzie Dies Tonight" (and probably others) published by Waters. The author presumably knew the song by ear, rather than from the Firth & Pond print. Did Foster or any of his associates hear the name as some of their Black contemporaries used it, to refer in a quasi-code to a kind of especially erotic dance? "Jenny's Toe: Negro Shaking Dances in America," by Chadwick Hansen, *American Quarterly,* XIX (1967), 554, provides no answer. My guess is that they were ignorant.

Page 90

"Choruses," *My Brother,* 40.

Page 91

"Sweet and kind," *Chronicles,* II, 426.

"My Grandmother's Memories," Pittsburgh *Post* and Louisville *Courier-Journal,* 4 July 1926, cited by Howard, *Stephen Foster,* p. 159 ff., complete in *Foster Hall Bulletin,* 10 (1934), 9–14, 22.

Washington, *My Brother,* 42.

Dunning's letter, *Chronicles,* I, 347; Stephen's, II, 375.

Page 92

Henrietta's letter, *Chronicles,* II, 429, supplemented from the manuscript at Foster Hall.

Dunning's letter, *Chronicles,* II, 453.

Page 93

Stephen's letter, *Chronicles,* II, 461.

Page 94

Elegy, *Chronicles,* II, 563.

"My Three Worlds," *Chronicles,* I, 24.

Page 95

Jane's letters, cited by Howard, *Stephen Foster* (1962 edition), 308 ff. are not yet published complete.

Page 96

Royalties are tabulated by Howard, 354 ff.

Page 97

Marion, Howard, 163.

"Little Ella" is found only in the Foster Hall facsimiles.

Page 98

My Brother, 8, 38, 39, 42, 44, 37.

Page 99

"That's What's the Matter" and "Nothing but a Plain Old Soldier" are in the *Stephen Foster Song Book,* Dover, 122, 84; and in the *Household Songs,* 74, 85.

Page 100

Henrietta gave her opinion to the music journalist Gustav Kobbé when he was preparing his book, *Famous American Songs* (New York: Crowell, 1906), p. 45.

"Fraud," Howard, 312.

"Serenading," Howard, 315.

Page 101

Habit, Howard, 316.

Morrison . . . old wounds, Howard, 307.

. . . pity for the drunk: compare James Hardin Wall's article, "Stephen Collins Foster, a Psychiatric Study," in the *Psychological Quarterly Supplement*, XV (1941), 327. Wall sees the "almost typical pattern of an alcoholic. . . . But . . . his weakness was his strength . . . that deep, abiding nostalgia for the comfortable, infantile state is the very quality which has given his songs their eternal appeal."

Page 102

"The Temperance Movement in Pennsylvania Prior to the Civil War" has been studied by Asa Earl Martin in the *Pennsylvania Magazine of History and Biography*, XLIX (1925), 195.

The Making of Nicholas Longworth: Annals of an American Family, by Clara Longworth, comtesse de Chambrun (New York: Long & Smith, 1933), is full of fascinating lore.

Page 103

Letter, *Chronicles*, II, 500.

"Fair Jenny," with the tune, can be found in James Kinsley's edition of Burns, *Poems and Songs* (London: Oxford University Press, 1969), p. 567.

Duer, "Personal Recollections of the Last Days of Foster," in *Etude*, September 1926, cited by Howard, 332.

Page 104

Ten Nights, published as a novel in 1854, has been edited with a fine introduction by Donald A. Koch (Cambridge, Massachusetts: Belknap, 1964). The dramatization by William Pratt, 1858, frequently revived, led Koch to his judgment that *Ten Nights* is "an enduring social document, one that seems to have gained rather than lost significance, as it passed through the transforming processes of burlesque and parody." Foster's "Old Black Joe" endures in similar transformations.

"Comrades" is omitted from most selective editions, but included in the Random House *Treasury*, 123. Howard, 253, echoed in Howard's note in the *Treasury*.

Page 105

1836 letter, *Chronicles*, I, 115.

Page 106

1841 letter, 219.

1842 letter, 233.

Page 107

Stephen's 1845 letter, 286.

1846 letter, 296.

Page 108

"My Grandmother's Memories" 14.

"Fine Fosteriana," *Foster Hall Bulletin*, 10 (1934), 22.

1858 letter, *Chronicles*, II, 498.

Page 109

January letter, Howard 338; February letter, 339.

Page 111

1832 letter, in facsimile, *Chronicles*, I, 86.

1840 letter, *Chronicles*, I, 178.

"John Anderson," in the Oxford *Burns*, 419.

Page 112

My Brother, 46.

1841 letter, *Chronicles*, I, 215.

Page 113

1847 letter, *Chronicles*, 307.

Page 114

Mother songs have repelled selective editors, so curious readers must go to the complete facsimiles, reprinted by Foster Hall. "Mother, Thou'rt Faithful" found a devotee in Frank Luther; in his *Americans and Their Songs* (New York: Harper, 1942), p. 142, Luther proclaims it "a song that some day will be recognized as one of the most beautiful songs ever written."

Page 115

"Gentle Annie" is in Dover, 33; *Household songs*, 53; and in the Nonesuch recording.

Laura Lee, U. of P., 99.

Page 116

"The Voice of By Gone Days," *Household Songs*, 14.

"Once I Loved Thee," Random House *Treasury*, 171.

Page 117

"Maggie," Dover, 59.

CHAPTER 7   FOSTER AND HIS PUBLIC IN THE TRADITION OF
"HOME SONGS"

Page 123

"Tray," U. of P., 75; *Songfest*, 130.

Page 124

Campbell, *The Complete Poetical Works*, ed. by J. Logie Robinson (Edinburgh, 1907; New York: Haskell House, 1968), p. 255. Compare Ecclesiastes ix, 4.

Page 125

My Brother, 48. Morrison is writing in the same year as Edward Noyes West-cott's *David Harum*, in which David advises a newcomer to join the village choir: "If this singin' bus'nis don't do more'n to give ye somethin' new to think about, an' take up an evenin' now an' then, even if it bothers ye some, I think mebbe it'll be a good thing fer ye. A reasonable amount o' fleas is good fer a dog—keeps him from broodin' over *bein'* a dog, mebbe." See the reprint of 1899 (New York: Appleton), p. 284.

Page 126

Chronicles, II, 449.

"Sweet and Low," Fuld's *Book of World-Famous Music*. The tune, 1863, is by Joseph Barnby (1838–96).

Page 127

Mrs. Tennyson is quoted in Harold Nicolson's *Tennyson* (London: Constable, 1923), p. 159.

Page 128

"Whiskey," in Frank Cowan's *American Story-Book* (Greensburg, Pennsylvania: 1881), p. 387.

Page 129

"Minstrel's Request," from the long narrative poem, *Rokeby*, edited by J. Logie Robertson in Scott's *Poetical Works* (London: Oxford, 1909), p. 355. One of the minstrel's listeners takes pity:

> Hard were his task to seek a home
> More distant, since the night is come.

Scott goes on to a critical portrait of the minstrel, p. 358, and then to the minstrel's self-pitying autobiography, p. 359, in which he claims his harp the "one solace to my heart."

Page 130

"Dear Friends," *Chronicles*, II, 560.

Sketchbook, Howard, *Stephen Foster*, 228.

Scott, Hogg, and Burns himself are viewed in new light by David Johnson, *Music and Society in Lowland Scotland in the 18th Century* (London: Oxford, 1972); reasons for the laughable aspects of the tradition are clearer than heretofore.

"Cunningham" by Miriam Allen de Ford in *British Authors of the 19th Century,* edited by S. J. Kunitz (New York: Wilson, 1936), p. 165, quotes the letter to Southey.

Page 131

"Caller Herrin'," *Songfest,* 35; "Annie Laurie," 8. On Lady Scott, David Johnson's *Music and Society,* p. 198, provides details.

English Songs (London: National Illustrated Library, 1851), p. 14.

G. S. Jackson, *Early Songs of Uncle Sam* (Boston: Humphries, 1933, p. 21. Compare also the advertisement by the publisher, O. Ditson, in Dwight's *Journal,* II (1842), 32: "No volume of music issued in the United States has been so freely welcomed or so much in demand."

"Believe Me" (the tune is also familiar as "Fair Harvard"), *Songfest,* 17; "Last Rose," 106.

A thorough and critical survey of Moore's life and work is Howard Mumford Jones, *The Harp That Once—* (New York: Holt, 1937). More recent and more ironically appreciative is the introduction by Peter Quenell to his edition of Moore's *Journal* (London: Batsford, 1964). Especially helpful are Neil R. Grobman's study of "The Ballads of Thomas Moore's Irish Melodies," *Southern Folklore Quarterly* XXXVI (1972), 103, and Richard Wilbur's reconsideration in "Poetry's Debt to Poetry," *Hudson Review,* XXVI (1973), 284.

Page 132

"The Harp," *Songfest,* 76.

"Dream of Home," in *Poetical Works,* edited by A. D. Godley (London: Oxford, 1910), p. 322.

Page 133

Swedish air, *Poetical Works,* p. 239.

"There's nothing true" is the refrain of the poem that Moore entitled "This World Is All a Fleeting Show," *Poetical Works,* p. 256.

Charlotte, remembered by Eliza, *Chronicles,* I, 40.

Henry, *Chronicles,* I, 137.

W. G. Johnston, *Life and Reminiscences from Birth to Manhood* (Pittsburgh: Knickerbocker, 1901), pp. 110, 169; Johnston claims to remember Stephen, p. 45.

Page 134

"Milton Moore was a nom de plume of Stephen C. Foster—it means John Milton & Thos. Moore." The note is cited by Howard, p. 185.

The Love and Sentimental . . . (New York: Dick and Fitzgerald, 1862).

"The Song of All Songs," Dover, p. 118. Details about the claims, *Chronicles,* II, 555.

"Jenny's Coming," only in the Foster Hall facsimiles.

"John Braham" by Frances Collingwood, *Musical Times,* XCVII (1956), 73, is my principal source of information.

Page 135

"Bishop" by William Barclay Squire in the *Dictionary of National Biography,* II (1921), 553, celebrates Sir Henry worthily.

Dwight's *Journal,* VII (1855), 70.

Charles Horn attracted rare attention from Neil Butterworth in his article on "The Songwriters of America" in *Music,* I/4 (1967), 24.

Goldsmith, *Works,* ed. by Peter Cunningham (New York: Putnam, 1908), vol. I, p. 13.

Moore, *Poetical Works,* 183, 116.

Page 136

Epistles, Poetical Works, 117, 115.

"When thro' life," 194.

Page 137

"Campbell" by Robert Woodman Wadsworth in *British Authors of the 19th Century* (ed. Kunitz, 1936), p. 112, includes the quotations from Carlyle and Martineau.

Campbell, *Complete Poetical Works,* "Ode," 368; "Epigram," 340.

Page 138
"The Hunters of Kentucky" is in Damon's *Old American Songs* and Dichter's facsimiles. "The Bucket" is still cherished in *Songfest*, 145, and countless other collections.

Page 139
Richard Henry Wilde: His Life and Selected Poems, by Edward L. Tucker (Athens: University of Georgia Press, 1966).
"A sweet song," *Chronicles*, II, 528.
Elliott, *The Splendid Village; Corn-Law Rhymes; and Other Poems* (London: Benjamin Steill, 1834–35), vol. I, pp. 17, 42, 44; vol. III, p. 93.

Pages 141-142
Proctor, *English Songs and Other Small Poems* (Boston: Ticknor, Reed & Fields, 1851), pp. vi, vii; "The Bloodhound," 25; "Song," 253; "Farewell," 13; ". . . Mozart," 227; "Adelaide," 174.

Page 143
Nevin, "Who Writes Our Songs?" in Dwight's *Journal*, XV (1859), 51.
Foster may have found Hale's "Light of Home" in her gift book, *The Poets' Offering* (Philadelphia: Grigg, Elliot, 1850), p. 236; this anthology was so successful that it was reissued as *A Complete Dictionary of Poetical Quotations*, 1870.
"The Story of 'Home, Sweet Home,'" is amply told by F. L. Bullard, *The Musician*, XVIII (1913), 227. Bishop's arrangement is included in Marrocco and Gleason's anthology, *Music in America*, 310.

Page 144
Foster's dislike, Howard, 213.
Sale price from Carl Engel, *Discords Mingled: Essays on Music* [1931] (Freeport, New York: Books for Libraries, 1967), p. 35.
James Hall: Spokesman of the New West, by Randolph C. Randall (Columbus: Ohio State University Press, 1964), is a fine study.

Page 145
Western Souvenir (Cincinnati: Guilford, 1828; Louisville: Lost Cause Press, 1956), pp. 15, 156.
Letters, (London: H. Colburn, 1828), p. 378.
Frank Johnson's career, as recorded in scattered sources, is carefully described by Eileen Southern, *The Music of Black Americans* (New York: Norton, 1971), p. 112. The earliest source, Waln's *Hermit*, is reprinted in Southern's *Readings*, 122. Additional confirmation can be found in James Silk Buckingham, *America* (London: Fisher, 1841), vol. II, p. 340; and Henry Simpson, *The Lives of Eminent Philadelphians* (Philadelphia: Brotherhead, 1859), p. 611. A new article by Southern on "Black Musicians and Early Ethiopian Minstrelsy," in *Black Perspectives in Music*, III (1975) 77, discloses that Frank Johnson in 1844 arranged "Dandy Jim."

Page 146
William Faulkner describes a serenading party similar to the Philadelphians' of a hundred years earlier, with "Home, Sweet Home" accompanied by "negroes" on clarinet, guitar, and bass viol, in *Sartoris* (New York: Harcourt Brace, 1929), p. 148.
Moore's *Summer Fête, Poetical Works*, 272.
Journal, edited by Quenell, p. 66; compare p. 90.

Pages 147-148
Haynes Bayly, *Songs, Ballads, and Other Poems* (London: Bentley, 1857), vol. I, p. 148; "Don't Sing," II, 228; "Gaily the Troubadour," I, 192; "The Old House at Home," II, 218; "Biography," II, 32.

Page 149
Bunn, *Old England and New England* (London: Bentley; Philadelphia: Hart, 1853), pp. vi, 315. A memorable modern English judgment of Bunn and Balfe is that of W. H. Mellers in his *Harmonious Meetings: A Study of the Relationship Between English Music, Poetry and Theatre, c. 1600–1900* (London: Dobson, 1965), vol. II, p. 285. Mellers calls the Bohemian girl's dream a nightmare.

Page 150

The life of Samuel Lover by Bayle Bernard (London: H. S. King, 1874), includes lively vignettes of his American success.

Elusive information on John Broadwood can be found in Frank Howes, *Folk Music of Britain* (London: Methuen, 1969). The *Sussex Songs*, edited by H. F. Birch (Reynarson, 1889; reprinted London: Leonard, 1914), are far from satisfying my curiosity. Lucy Broadwood's edition of *English Traditional Songs and Carols* (London: Boosey, 1908), may use some of the same sources; she describes (p. i) the cobbler and bell ringer Henry Burstow, Stephen Foster's exact contemporary but still alive in 1908, singing fifty or sixty traditional ballads, in a total repertory of over 400 songs.

Page 151

"The Minstrel's Return" is advertised in Dichter's facsimile edition as "the first American hit song." "All Quiet" is in Marrocco and Gleason's *Music in America*, p. 297. Hewitt's memoirs, *Shadows on the Wall* (Baltimore: Turnbull, 1877), may outlast his songs. But his claim is renewed in the survey of *Song in America from Early Times to About 1850* by Grace Yerbury (Metuchen, New Jersey: Scarecrow, 1971), p. 112.

The twenty pages on Morris in H. B. Wallace's *Literary Criticisms* (Philadelphia: Parry & McMillan, 1856), are unmatched in their informed sympathy for Morris as "classic." For the adulation characteristic of his own circle, sample a paragraph of Rufus Wilmot Griswold's essay in *Poets and Poetry of America* (1842), 16th ed. (Philadelphia: Parry & McMillan, 1855), p. 281.

Thomas Ward, "The Sessions of Parnassus: Or, the Bards of Gotham: A Day-Dream," in his *Knickerbocker Gallery* (New York: 1855), p. 224.

Page 152

Nathaniel P. Willis, by Cortland P. Auser (New York: Twayne, 1969), is a fine brief critical study. Willis and Morris together show up throughout Benjamin T. Spencer's helpful book, *The Quest for Nationality: An American Literary Campaign* (Syracuse, New York: Syracuse University Press, 1957).

The Beauties of Vocal Melody, new ed., revised and corrected (Boston: George P. Reed, 1846). "The May Queen" was published separately (Boston: Ditson, 1845). A rare modern mention of Dempster's work is included in Grace Yerbury's *Song in America*, p. 259.

Foster and Shiras, *My Brother*, 38; *Chronicles*, II, 439.

Harbinger, II (1846), 77.

Page 153

John Olin Eidson, *Tennyson in America: His Reputation and Influence From 1827 to 1858* (Athens: University of Georgia Press, 1943).

Harbinger, VI (1848), 158.

Poe, cited by Eidson, *Tennyson in America*, 61.

Page 154

The Home Affections (London: G. Routledge, 1858), pp. v, vi, vii.

Tupper: His Rise and Fall, by Derek Hudson (London: Constable, 1949), makes detailed comparisons between English and American Tupperisms.

Through the Long Day (London: W. H. Allen, 1887), p. 127; reference to "Tray," 137.

Page 155

McCarthy, *Ballads, Poems, and Lyrics* (Dublin: McGlashan, 1850); on Moore, p. 202, "Oh! Had I the Wings," 145.

Songs of the Irish Rebellion: Political Street Ballads and Rebel Songs, 1780–1900, by Georges-Denis Zimmerman (Hatboro, Pennsylvania: Folklore Associates, 1967), gives little attention to McCarthy, but provides many fascinating parallels to American trends. Zimmerman stresses, p. 108, the persisting lack of information about tunes.

Bell, *Poetical Works* (Lansing, Michigan: Wynkoop Hellenbeck Crawford, 1901, p. 196; reprinted Freeport, New York: Books for Libraries, 1970).

Page 156

"The Spirit of My Song" may lure a few readers to the libraries that keep the Foster Hall facsimiles.

Page 157
"Beautiful Child," U. of P., 63.

Page 158
Poets and Poetry, edited by William T. Coggeshall (Columbus, Ohio: Follett, Foster, 1860).

"Septimus Winner" is the sixth in the series of articles on American song-writers by George Birdseye (Foster was first) in *Potter's Magazine*, XII (1879), 433. Birdseye's information is only slightly supplemented by Charles Eugene Claghorn, *The Mocking Bird: The Life and Diary of Its Author, Septimus Winner* (Philadelphia, Magee Press, 1937).

Page 159
Cogitations of a Crank at Three Score Years and Ten (Philadelphia: Drexel Biddle Press, 1903).

A Life of John Hullah, by Frances Rosser Hullah (London. Longmans, Green, 1886); Moore's visit, p. 52.

Page 160
Household Words, I (1850), 161.

Page 161
"We aspire," Dickens, *Collected Papers* (Bloomsbury: Nonesuch, 1937), p. 223.

Learning and Living 1790–1960: A Study in the History of the English Adult Education Movement, by John Fletcher Clews Harrison (London: Routledge & Kegan Paul, 1961), provides perspective.

"Hard Times, Come Again No More," U. of P., 40; "Some Folks," 109.

"Great Baby," Dickens, *Collected Papers*, 610.

The Song Book (London: Macmillan, 1866), p. 6.

Page 162
La gloire de Béranger, by Jean Touchard (Paris: Collin, 1968), neglects the music but deals with the verse and its reception in ways that have helped me study Foster. Foster may have known something of Béranger in translation, for instance from the volume of *Two Hundred of His Lyrical Poems Done into English Verse* by William Young (New York: Putnam, 1850), or the *Songs of the Empire, the Peace, and the Restoration*, translated by Robert B. Brough (London: Addey, 1856); neither of these is listed by Touchard.

"Heimat- und Heimwehlied" is surveyed by Ina-Marla Greverus in the *Handbuch des Volksliedes* edited by R. W. Brednich (Munich: Fink, 1973), 899. Foster is correctly associated with "Heimatdichtung" by J. Wesley Thomas, *Amerikanische Dichter und die deutsche Literatur* (Goslar: Volksbücherei, 1950), p. 83.

Swiss "homesickness" is reported by Charles Burney in *The Present State of Music in Germany, Netherlands and the United Provinces* (London: Beldet, 1775; New York: Broude, 1969), vol. II, p. 126; Burney also describes an early collection of national tunes, II, 122.

The American twist in the international current is explored in detail by Fred Somkin, in *Unquiet Eagle: Memory and Desire in the Idea of American Freedom, 1815–1860* (Ithaca: Cornell University Press, 1967), p. 100: "In the lyrics of Stephen Foster, the pathos of nostalgia, set to music, became a favorite entertainment for a mobile people who couldn't be persuaded to stay at home."

In 1975, as observed by one of the graffiti in a New York subway, "Nostalgia ain't what it used to be."

CHAPTER 8   FOSTER AND HIS FRIENDS

Page 163
"Ellen Bayne," U. of P., 82.

Page 164
Cowan's letter, *Chronicles*, II, 446.

Page 165
My Brother, 51.
Letter, *Chronicles*, II, 503.
Milligan, *Stephen Collins Foster* (New York: Schirmer, 1920), p. 98.
Susan, *Chronicles*, II, 572.

Page 166

Henrietta's letter, *Chronicles,* I, 167.

My Brother, 50.

Page 167

Letter, *Chronicles,* I, 178.

Kingsbury memoir cited in *Chronicles,* I, 189.

Page 168

Justice George Shiras, Jr., of Pittsburgh (Pittsburgh: University of Pittsburgh Press, 1953); reference to Foster, 18.

John Hull's report cited in *Chronicles,* II, 588.

Morrison's letter, *Chronicles,* II, 408.

Page 169

The Albatross is mentioned with approval by Jane Grey Swisshelm in her memoir, *Half a Century* [Chicago, 1880] (New York: Source Book Press, 1970], p. 105.

Page 170

Shiras, 19; 18.

Page 171

Bunn, *Old England and New England* (Philadelphia: Hart, 1853), p. 101.

"Stephen C. Foster, Dramatic Collaborator," by Edward G. Fletcher, appeared in *Colophon,* I (1935); 33, and in a separate publication by Foster Hall.

Page 172

"Ellen Bayne," U. of P., 82. "Willie, We Have Missed You" is in the Random House *Treasury,* 115.

Page 174

Royalties listed by Howard, 354.

"Come with Thy Sweet Voice," U. of P., 53.

Page 175

"Come, Where," U. of P., 15; original versions in *Household Songs,* 42 and Dover, 18.

A piano arrangement by the American William Dressler was published by Pond in 1862, but it was clumsier than the English one.

Page 176

Letter from Wilson to Riley, *Chronicles,* II, 579. Hamilton, cited from Howard, 288.

Page 178

1858 letter, *Chronicles,* II, 503.

1857 letter, *Chronicles,* II, 481.

"Some Folks," U. of P., 109.

Page 180

"The Village Maiden," Dover, 139 and Random House *Treasury,* 175.

"Gentle Annie," U. of P., 65.

"I See Her Still," "Lula," and "Where Has Lula Gone?" only in the Foster Hall facsimiles.

"Fairy-Belle," U. of P., 69.

"Thou Art the Queen of My Song," Dover, 135; Roland Jackson's note calls attention to the uniquely extended piano coda.

"Poor Drooping Maiden," only in Foster Hall.

Page 182

Joyce cited by Howard, 297.

Page 183

"Our Bright Summer Days," U. of P., 51.

"Our Darling Kate," only in Foster Hall.

"Why?", Random House *Treasury,* 183.

"No Home," only in Foster Hall.

"I'll Be Home Tomorrow," only in Foster Hall.

"Happy Hours," U. of P., 57.

Page 184
Birdseye, cited by Howard, 315, 314.
Page 185
The "saga" of George Cooper is most amply recorded by James J. Geher in an article, "The Thankless Muse," *Variety*, CLXXXV (2 January 1952), 228. Geher interviewed Cooper in 1925.
"Willie Has Gone to the War," Dover, 161. Milligan, 104.
Page 186
Note of 1863, *Chronicles*, II, 554.
"Dearer Than Life," Random House *Treasury*, 163, with Cooper's note, which Howard needlessly discounts.
"There Are . . . Fish . . ." Dover, 126.
"Mr. and Mrs. Brown" and ". . . Moustache" are prominent in the *Household Songs*, 68, 65, and in the Smithsonian performances recorded by Nonesuch.
"Kissing," only in Foster Hall facsimiles.
Page 187
"My Wife Is a Most Knowing Woman," Dover, 72.
Page 188
"When This Dreadful War," Dover, 156.
"Bring My Brother," "Soldier's home," and "My Boy," only in Foster Hall.
"For the Dear Old Flag" and ". . . Brigade," only in Foster Hall.
Page 190
"The Hymns of Stephen Collins Foster" were first surveyed by Charles L. Atkins in *Hymn*, XII (1961), 52; a more thorough article is "The Gospel Hymns . . ." by Samuel J. Rogal in *Hymn*, XXI (1970), 7. None of the hymns are included in modern editions except for the Foster Hall facsimiles.
Page 193
"Beautiful Dreamer," U. of P., 86; *Songfest*, 16, and all other editions. The Nonesuch recording is fine. "Sitting by" and "Dear Friends," only in Foster Hall. "Voices That Are Gone," Dover, 143.
"His later works exhibit greater grace and tenderness than his earlier ones." This opinion by the anonymous writer of the obituary printed by Horace Waters —possibly John Mahon?—has seldom found support until now.
"Linger," "Eva," "Mine," and "The Love I Bear," only in Foster Hall.

Page 194
"Slumber," *Household Songs*, 71.

CHAPTER 9   THE PUBLIC OF PUBLICITY AND FOSTER IN HIS MATURITY

Page 197
My Brother, 32, 35, 37.
"My Grandmother's Memories," 14.
Commerce, Cotton, and Westward Expansion, 1820–1860, by William N. Parker (Chicago: Scott, Foresman, 1964), is a first-rate exposition of a complex subject; see especially p. 37: "In summary, a greater portion of people's working and consuming lives was transferred out of the family and local economy into the economy dependent on distant trade. In Central and Western New York, Pennsylvania, and the area just below Lake Erie, the effects were most apparent."
Page 198
Barnum, by M. R. Werner (New York: Harcourt, Brace, 1923), is supplemented but not superseded by later books, beginning with H. W. Root, *The Unknown Barnum* (New York: Harper, 1927). Especially lively and brief is *Barnum in London* by Raymund Fitzsimmons (London: Bles, 1969). Up-to-date is *Humbug: The Art of P. T. Barnum* by Neil Harris (Boston: Little, Brown, 1973). On Barnum's relation to the minstrel show, see Robert Toll's *Blacking Up* (New York: Oxford University Press, 1974) pp. 18, 136.
Jenny Lind, the Swedish Nightingale, by Gladys Denny Shultz (Philadelphia:

Lippincott, 1962), is the fullest account, though almost as uncritical as *Jenny Lind: Her Life, Her Struggles, and Her Triumphs* by Charles G. Rosenberg (New York: Stringer & Townsend, 1850). A recent specialized publication is *The Lost Letters of Jenny Lind* translated and edited by William Porter Ware and Thaddeus C. Lockard (London: Gollancz, 1966).

Page 199

Mendelssohn, cited by Werner, *Barnum*, 129; Carlyle, 132.

Mayhew, *London Labour*, II, 276.

"Greeting," cited by Werner, 144.

Page 200

Winner, in C. E. Claghorn, *The Mocking Bird*, p. 24.

Shultz searched her notes in vain for a source of this report, p. 277; she wrote me that she did not invent it. Unfortunately, she reports also that Lind sang "Old Black Joe," p. 312, and this is unlikely, because Foster's manuscript dates from 1860. Shultz confesses, p. 14, that in some details her "imagination supplements fact."

Page 201

Lind's letter, cited by Werner, *Barnum*, p. 196.

Homesickness, *Lost Letters*, p. 27.

The Humbugs of the World is reprinted (Detroit: Singing Tree Press, 1970). I quote from p. 8.

Page 202

"Gaslight" Foster is memorialized in *Rufus Wilmot Griswold* by Joy Bayless (Nashville: Vanderbilt University Press, 1943), pp. 8, 240.

1852 letter, *Chronicles*, II, 398. Gilbert Chase, in *America's Music* (1966 edition), p. 293, makes much of this "significant" letter, but neither he nor any other interpreter has tried to read it as Christy must have done.

Page 203

"Skunk," *Chronicles*, II, 400.

Page 204

Howard's careful discussion begins on p. 197.

Musical World cited by Howard, 212, 206.

Advertisement, Howard, 205.

Page 205

1853 letter, Howard, 220.

Page 206

Letter, *Chronicles*, II, 442.

1853 advertisement, Howard, 238.

Page 207

1854 advertisements, Howard, 206, 207.

Page 208

Contract, at the Library of Congress, summarized by Howard, 244.

Gazette article, *Chronicles*, II, 484.

Page 209

Letter, *Chronicles*, II, 483.

"Who Writes Our Songs?" is most accessible in Dwight's *Journal*, XV (1859), 51.

Page 211

Mahon's article of 1877, "The Last Years of Stephen C. Foster," is complete in the Foster Hall *Bulletin*, 10 (1934), 2. My quotation is neglected by other writers, though Milligan and Howard both rely on Mahon for some points.

"Hard Times," U. of P., 40; "Fairy Belle," 69.

"We Are Coming, Father Abraam," Dover, 153.

"War Music and War Psychology in the Civil War," by Jesse Stone, in the *Journal of Abnormal and Social Psychology*, XXXVI (1941), 543, is a fine short discussion of the subject. There are two anecdotal chapters on songs in Bell Irvin Wiley's elaborate study of *The Common Soldier in the Civil War* (New York: Grosset & Dunlap, 1943). A first musicological approach is Albert Luper's "Civil

War Music," in *Civil War History*, IV (1958), which contains an outstanding special study: Donald McCorkle's compilation of "The Repertory of the 26th Regiment Band," p. 234. Further gleanings are presented by the conductor Frederick Fennell in "The Civil War: Its Music and Its Sounds," *Journal of Band Research*, IV/2 (1968), 36; V/1, 8; V/2, 2; VI (1969), 46. An anthology for popular use is *Singing Soldiers . . . of the Civil War . . .* compiled by Paul Glass, arrangements for piano and guitar by Louis C. Singer, foreword by John Hope Franklin (New York: Grosset & Dunlap, 1968). All these have at least a brief mention of Foster.

Foster is absent from Frank Moore's *Lyrics of Loyalty* (New York: Putnam, 1863), and George Palmer Putnam's *Soldiers' & Sailors' Patriotic Songs* (New York: Loyal Publication Society, 1864). Foster's war songs found a place in an anonymous anthology, *Our War Songs, North & South* (Cleveland: Brainard, 1887).

Page 212

"John Brown's Body" is in the Hansen *Songfest*, 94; Seeger's *American Favorite Ballads*, 62, etc. The history of the song is carefully told by Boyd B. Stutler in *Civil War History*, IV (1958), 251.

"Marching Through Georgia," *Songfest*, 122; Marrocco and Gleason, *Music in America*, 304. The other songs of Work and Root are in *Earlier American Music*, XVII.

Winner's "Give Us Back," in Claghorn, *The Mocking Bird*, p. 32.

"Ellen Bayne" resemblance, Milligan, 80.

"When Johnny Comes," *Songfest*, 200; Marrocco and Gleason, 302; Fuld, *Book of World-Famous Music*.

Page 213

Milligan, 80, 96.

Page 214

Milligan, 112.

Page 215

Milligan, 112, 116.

E. H. Smith's play (Knoxville: The Foster Players, 1926), 4th edition, 1938. Among several later rival works are Paul Green's *Stephen Foster Story*, 1959, for the summer festival at Bardstown, Kentucky, and Myles Standish's *I Dream of Jeanie*, which had some success at the St. Louis municipal summer theater, 1963.

Page 216

McCormack, Victor record 1700 (matrix OEA 412); Jolson, Decca DL 5308.

Shilkret, Victor album M-1122-26.

Bowman, "A Singer to Pioneers," *Atlantic*, CLVI (1935), 83.

Page 217

Hodges, "Swanee River," Foster Hall *Bulletin*, 12 (1940), 5.

ASCAP ban: Deems Taylor, "Foreword" to the Random House *Treasury of Stephen Foster*, 1946, p. 7.

Etude, LIX/2 (February 1941), 104; and again, LXX/3 (July 1952), 28. Warren's *Concert Transcriptions* (Philadelphia: Ditson, 1940), include the foreword.

CHAPTER 10 FOSTER AND OTHER CONTEMPORARIES OF UNCLE TOM

Page 223

Stowe, *Uncle Tom's Cabin*, edited by Kenneth S. Lynn (Cambridge, Massachusetts: Belknap, 1962), supersedes hundreds of earlier editions. I shall cite it as *Tom*.

Page 224

"Uncle Ned," U. of P., 25.

Eliza and George, *Tom*, 18.

George dyes, *Tom*, 113. Eliza cuts, *Tom*, 394.

Tom's wool, *Tom*, 30. St. Clare, *Tom*, 154.

Page 225

Ophelia combs, *Tom*, 165. Topsy braids, *Tom*, 243. Eva mythic, *Tom*, 151; halo, *Tom*, 266, 323.

Legree wiry, *Tom*, 346. Emmeline curls, *Tom*, 339. "A dream?" *Tom*, 358. "If hair could rise from the dead!" *Tom*, 383, 387.

Page 226

Cassy strokes, *Tom*, 421.

Harriet Beecher Stowe: The Known and the Unknown, by Edward Wagenknecht (New York: Oxford, 1965), is my authority for biography. A fine survey of *The Novels of Harriet Beecher Stowe* is by Alice C. Crozier (New York: Oxford, 1969). An indirect connection between Stowe and Foster may be found in her volume of *Stories and Sketches for the Young* (Boston: Houghton Mifflin, 1896), especially p. 121, "Sir Walter Scott and his dogs."

Page 227

Mothers: perhaps Foster perceived, as did one reader, Mary Boykin Chesnut, that "Mrs. Stowe did not hit the sorest spot. She makes Legree a bachelor." *A Diary from Dixie*, edited by Ben Ames Williams (Boston: Houghton Mifflin, 1949), p. 122.

Page 228

"Fairy Belle," U. of P., 69; "Under the Willow," 104.

Mahon, "The Last Years of Stephen C. Foster," Foster Hall *Bulletin*, 10 (1934), 6.

"Little Belle Blair" and "A Penny," only in Foster Hall facsimiles.

"Gentle Lena Clare," Dover, 37.

Page 229

Tom dances, *Tom*, 30; sings alone, *Tom*, 42.

Trumpet call, *Tom*, 123.

Page 230

Legree confiscates, *Tom*, 345.

Tom's last songs, *Tom*, 404; speech like music, *Tom*, 423. Compare "Tom: a Ballet" by e. e. cummings, 1935, in his *Three Plays* (New York: October House, 1967), especially p. 169.

Jubilee, *Tom*, 451.

Warehouse dance to the fiddle, *Tom*, 335.

Narrative of the Sufferings of Lewis Clarke (Boston: D. H. Ela, 1845), p. 74.

Page 231

"Unmeaning songs," *Tom*, 351.

Narrative of the Life of Frederick Douglass, an American Slave (Boston: Anti-Slavery Office, 1845), p. 13: "They would compose and sing as they went along. . . . To these songs I trace my first glimmering conception of the dehumanizing character of slavery." P. 62: "the duty of raising the hymn generally came upon me." P. 74: "Christmas . . . fiddling, dancing, and drinking whiskey . . . to disgust their slaves with freedom."

Emmeline's "Weeping Mary," *Tom*, 339; "O There'll Be Mourning," 382. "Trumpet of doom!" 387.

Topsy, *Tom*, 253.

The World's Greatest Hit—Uncle Tom's Cabin, by Harry Birdoff (New York: Vanni, 1947), p. 325: "Music was such an integral part of the play . . ."

Page 232

St. Clare's genius, *Tom*, 182; sings, 284; plays Mozart, 318.

Tom and St. Clare, *Tom*, 312; Tom and Shelby, *Tom*, 429.

Page 233

"My Old Kentucky Home," U. of P., 12, *Songfest*, 130, etc.

"Poor Uncle Tom," facsimile of the manuscript, *Chronicles*, II, 408.

Page 234

Eight other songwriters: "Uncle Tom's Cabin, 1852–1952," by Herbert G. Nicholas, *Georgia Review*, VIII (1954), 143.

"Old Black Joe," U. of P., 61.

Angels, *Tom*, 295, 300, 305. "The Poets and the Angels," by Gustav Davidson, *Literary Review*, IX (1965), 90, helped me locate Stowe's allusions in relation to Moore. Davidson's *Dictionary of Angels* (New York: Free Press, 1967), though less relevant, is interesting.

Page 235

The comparison of "Old Black Joe" with Mozart was suggested to me by John Kirkpatrick.

Hutchinson's "barrier" is reported by Harry Birdoff in *The World's Greatest Hit*, p. 23. The relation of *Tom* to the "gradual breaking down of religious prejudice against the stage" is well explained by Foster Rhea Dulles in *A History of Recreation: America Learns to Play*, 2nd edition (New York: Appleton-Century-Crofts, 1965), p. 114.

George L. Aiken, *Uncle Tom's Cabin* (New York: Samuel French, 1858). In John Lovell's *Digests of American Plays* (New York: Crowell, 1961), p. 73, statistics back up this claim: "Though far from a literary masterpiece, *Uncle Tom's Cabin* is without question the most significant theatrical phenomenon in American, and perhaps in world theatrical history."

On *Uncle Tom* and the minstrels, first-hand sources have been carefully sifted and explained by Robert Toll, *Blacking Up*, p. 90.

Page 236

The simplification of *Uncle Tom* on the stage kept some generations of readers away from the novel, until Edmund Wilson pointed out differences in his article, "No! No! No! My Soul Ain't Yours, Mas'r!" *New Yorker*, XXIV (27 November 1948), 134, which he expanded in *Patriotic Gore* (New York: Oxford, 1962). Wilson began a continuing discussion, to which some important contributions are James Baldwin's "Everybody's Protest Novel," in *Notes of a Native Son* (Boston: Beacon, 1949); Severn Duvall's "Uncle Tom's Cabin: The Sinister Side of the Patriarchy," in *New England Quarterly*, XXVI (1963), 3; John William Ward's "Uncle Tom's Cabin, as a Matter of Historical Fact," in *Columbia University Forum*, IX/1 (winter 1966), 42; Cushing Strout's "Uncle Tom's Cabin and the Portent of Millenium," in *Yale Review*, LVII (1968), 375; and Jean Yellin's *Intricate Knot*, 1972. All these have encouraged my close reading.

"My Grandmother's Memories," Foster Hall *Bulletin*, 11.

Der alte Tom is reported in the Foster Hall *Bulletin*, 5 (1932), 5.

Page 237

"Oh! Boys," U. of P., 55; "Farewell," 67; "The Glendy Burk," 106; "Down Among," 59. "Don't Bet," Dover, 25.

Page 238

My Brother, 49.

Page 239

The French heritage in Pittsburgh is described in *A Century of Negro Migration* by Carter G. Woodson (Washington: Association for the Study of Negro Life and History, 1918), p. 12. French-speaking slaves from San Domingo are reported by Jessie Welles Murray in "Stephen C. Foster's School Days at the Athens Academy," Foster Hall *Bulletin*, 11 (1935), 1. According to Howard, p. 83, Olivia's father may have been Henry G. Pius, dancing master in Pittsburgh, 1815, from the West Indies.

Page 240

"The Glendy Burk," an anonymous article in the Foster Hall *Bulletin*, 11 (1935), 15, supplies information otherwise scattered.

Page 241

Steamboats on the Western Rivers: An Economic and Technological History, by Louis C. Hunter (Cambridge: Harvard, 1949), includes a valuable chapter on the crews and longshoremen. Even in New Orleans and Mobile, levee workers in the 1850s were predominantly Irish and German according to Richard C. Wade, *Slavery in the Cities: The South, 1820–1860* (New York: Oxford, 1964), p. 275.

Trotter, *Music* (Boston: Lee & Shepard, 1879; 8th edition, 1886), p. 274.

Page 242

Mike Fink was first glorified by Morgan Neville, "The Last of the Boatmen," in *Western Souvenir* (Cincinnati: 1828). A thorough study of the hero and his legend is *Mike Fink* by Walter Blair and Franklin J. Meine (New York: Holt, 1933).

Lafcadio Hearn's article is reprinted in his collection *An American Miscellany* (New York: Dodd, Mead, 1924), vol. I, p. 147.

Further facts about "The Negroes of Cincinnati Prior to the Civil War" are presented by Carter G. Woodson, *Journal of Negro History*, I (1916), 1.

Cowan, *Southwestern Pennsylvania in Song and Story* (Greensburg, Pennsylvania: the author, 1878), p. 225.

"The Operation of the Fugitive Slave Law in Western Pennsylvania from 1850 to 1860," by Irene Williams, *Western Pennsylvania Historical Magazine*, IV (1921), 150; especially p. 158: "Pittsburgh was renowned both in the North and South for the care it took of fugitive slaves."

Page 243
Clarke, *Narrative*, 39.
"Massa," U. of P., 72.
Page 244
Clarke, *Narrative*, 77.

"Massa" serves characteristically in the scholarly book on *American Negro Slavery* by Ulrich Phillips, 1918, reprinted with an introduction by Eugene Genovese (Baton Rouge: Louisiana State University Press, 1966), p. 330. Phillips intensifies Foster's dialect to "cawn fiel' . . . mo'nful soun'."

Page 245
Johnson concert, *Chronicles*, I, 262.
Page 247
"Pathetic—comical." Compare James Kirke Paulding's *Letters from the South* (New York: Easburn, 1817; 2nd edition, 1835), vol. I, p. 126: "Negroes of Maryland and Virginia, for some reason or other, have an invincible repugnance to being sold to the Southward. Whether this repugnance arises from an idea that they will be treated with more severity, or is only the natural dislike every human being, except our fashionable ladies, feels to going to live in a strange land . . . I cannot tell. I know not that these poor souls are worse treated in Carolina and Georgia, nor have I any reason to believe so; certain it is, however, that they discover an unwillingness amounting almost to horror at the idea of being sold there, and have a simple song which they sometimes, as I am told, sing with a mournful melancholy cadence, as they row along the rivers, in remembrance of home. It is merely the language of nature:

> Going away to Georgia, ho, heave, O!
> Massa sell poor negro, ho, heave, O!
> Leave poor wife and children . . .

There is something of the true pathetic in all this, were these people not negroes. This spoils all; for we have got such an inveterate habit of divesting them of all the best attributes of humanity, in order to justify our oppressions, that the idea of connecting feeling or sentiment with a slave actually makes us laugh."

Statistical confirmation from 260 song books is offered by Cecil Lloyd Patterson's dissertation, "A Different Drum: The Image of the Negro in the 19th-century Popular Song Books" (Pennsylvania, 1961).

Novelists more romantic than Paulding contributed much to the image of Black music before the Civil War; it seems likely that Foster, as well as his audiences, read several of the following, though I can find no proof; all of them provide tantalizing musical scenes:

John Pendleton Kennedy, *Swallow Barn* (New York: Putnam, 1832); *The Blackwater Chronicle* (New York: Redfield, 1853).

William Gilmore Simms, *The Yemassee*, (1835); edited by A. Cowie (New York: Hafner, 1962).

William John Grayson, *The Hireling and the Slave*, 2nd edition (Charleston: Russell, 1855).

John Eston Cooke, *The Last of the Foresters* (New York: Derby & Jackson, 1856).

James W. Hungerford, *The Old Plantation* (New York: Harper, 1859).

David Hunter Strother ("Crayon Porte"), "Virginia Illustrated," *Harper's*, 1854–

1856; *The Old South Illustrated*, edited by Cecil D. Eby, Jr. (Chapel Hill: University of North Carolina Press, 1959).

"Negroes and the Seminole War" by Kenneth W. Porter, two articles in the *Journal of Negro History*, XXXVI (1951), 302 and the *Journal of Southern History*, XXX (1964), 427, should be combined as a book. The quotation from General Jesup is from the later article. Porter's work is supplemented by John K. Mahon, *History of the Second Seminole War, 1835–1842* (Gainesville: University of Florida Press, 1967). A well-written shorter history is Henrietta Buckmaster's *The Seminole Wars* (New York: Collier, 1966). The most recent survey is perhaps best of all for most readers: Milton Meltzer's *Hunted Like a Wolf: The Story of the Seminole War* (New York: Farrar, Straus & Giroux, 1972); the title is quoted from one of the Seminoles, who said, "I have been hunted like a wolf and now I am about to be sent away like a dog." Meltzer gives due attention to the "Third Seminole War" of 1849. Further valuable perspectives are offered by Marjory Stoneman Douglas in *Florida: The Long Frontier* (New York: Harper & Row, 1967).

Page 248

Giddings, *Payment for Slaves* (Washington: Buell & Blanchard, 1849); *Speeches in Congress* (Boston: Jewett, 1853); *The Exiles of Florida* (Columbus, Ohio: Follett, Foster & Co., 1858). More information in George W. Julian's *Life of Joshua R. Giddings* (Chicago: A. C. McClurg, 1892); p. 264 begins an account of the 1849 speech.

Sprague, *Origin, Progress, and Conclusion of the Florida War* (New York: D. Appleton, 1848; reprinted with an introduction by John K. Mahon, Gainesville, 1964); p. 264 on the "love of home."

My Brother, 47, copied in countless program notes.

"Pedee," the river in Georgia, probably came to mind because of its appearance in the novel by John Pendleton Kennedy, *Horse Shoe Robinson*, 1835, revised 1852 and thus newly prominent (I have seen only the reprint, New York, Putnam's 1881). The hero's name is Stephen Foster.

Page 249

Did either Stephen or Morrison read the *Letters from the Slave States* by James Stirling (London: J. W. Parker, 1857)? From Florida, Stirling writes, p. 212, about a "resort of invalids from the North"; 222, about "white trash"; and 224, "Florida is the Paradise of an idle man. . . . This easy, lazy, good-for-nothing kind of life is very common among all the 'poor whites' of the seaboard Slave States, but it seems to have reached its climax in Florida." When Stirling heard "Old Folks," as he must have done, did he connect it with what he had noticed in Florida? Such a connection, once made, sticks.

Stowe, *Sunny Memories of Foreign Lands* (Boston: Phillips, Sampson, 1854), vol. I, p. 284; vol. II, p. 104. Stowe's report appeared also in the anonymous pamphlet, *The Black Swan at Home and Abroad* (Philadelphia: W. S. Young, 1855), in which Greenfield's performances of "The Last Rose of Summer" and "Home, Sweet Home" receive due attention.

Page 251

Sunny Memories, I, 44, 43, 69.

Bunn, 61.

Hampton and Its Students (New York: Putnam, 1874), p. 129.

Page 252

Delany explicitly comments on *Uncle Tom* in Frederick Douglass' *Paper*, 1 April, 29 April, 6 May 1853.

Blake, p. 100.

Page 253

Blake, 82, 124; at sea, 207; alone, 69; encouraging, 43; "Oh, when," 31.

Page 254

George William Curtis and the Genteel Tradition, by Gordon Milne (Bloomington: Indiana University Press, 1956), is a satisfactory study.

Page 255

Putnam's, II (1853), 572; "Old Folks" returns in III (1854), 563.

Harper's, VIII (1853), 132.

New York Musical Review and Choral Advocate, V (1854), 418.

"Hazel Dell" by George Root, see p. 264.

Page 256

Dwight's *Journal,* XIII (1858), 118.

Tribune, 30 June 1855, reprinted in the *Musical World,* XXXVI (7 August 1858), 502, and Dwight's *Journal,* XIII (1858), 107.

Page 257

Putnam's, V (1855), 72, reprinted in Bruce Jackson's volume, *The Negro and His Folklore* (Austin: University of Texas Press, 1967), p. 36.

Alan Green, " 'Jim Crow,' 'Zip Coon': The Northern Origins of Negro Minstrelsy," in *Massachusetts Review,* XI (1970), 385.

Evangelist, XXVII (1856), 1; Dwight's *Journal,* IX (1856), 51, and XV (1859), 178; this too is in Jackson's *The Negro and His Folklore,* 51.

Page 258

Social Orchestra, reprinted in *Earlier American Music,* XIV, and recorded by performers at the Smithsonian Institution, Nonesuch, 1974. The "quadrille" is well done. "Anadolia," though I imagine it on Foster's own instrument, the flute, is shown to be possible also for violin.

CHAPTER 11   "PEOPLE'S SONG" WRITERS FOLLOWING FOSTER

Page 261

"Tramp," facsimile in Dichter's collection of Musical Americana, and in *Earlier American Music,* XVII.

The Story of a Musical Life: An Autobiography (Cincinnati: John Church, 1891). An obituary article on "George F. Root and His Songs" by Lydia Avery Coonly, *New England Magazine,* XIII (1895), 555, provides supplementary details such as the fact of his parents' interest in Handel and the fact that "Tramp" earned more than $10,000. A more critical obituary is that by W. S. B. Matthews in *Music* (Chicago), VIII (1896), 502.

Page 262

Protestant Church Music in America: A Short Survey of Men and Movements from 1564 to the Present, by Robert Stevenson (New York: Norton, 1966), provides a uniquely impartial treatment of Billings, Mason, and other composers known to Root.

Page 263

"Some money," *Story,* p. 107.

"Before classes," *Story,* 95.

"The Secular Cantata in the United States, 1850–1919" by Jacklin B. Stopp, *Journal of Research in Music Education,* VI (1969), 388, studies 94 works from Root to Chadwick.

Esther appeared in *The Jubilee: An Extensive Collection of Church Music for the Choir, the Congregation, and the Singing-School,* new edition (Boston: Oliver Ditson, 1858).

Page 264

Crosby, *Memories of Eighty Years* (Boston: J. Earle, 1906), p. 112.

"Hazel Dell" is the first song in the musical appendix of Root's *Story.*

"Lily Ray," only in Foster Hall facsimiles.

Page 265

Hastings, cited from *Chronicles,* II, 467.

Page 266

"Rosalie," in the appendix to Root's *Story.*

Page 267

The tune of "Tramp" served the Japanese army, according to Motoyosi-Saizau, "L'armée japonaise," in *Le monde moderne,* I (1895), 568. The same tune was sung to interesting words by Ernst Busch, in the anonymous collection, *Mit Gesang wird gekämpft* (Berlin; Dietz, 1967):

"Go home, Ami, Ami, go home!
Spalte für den Frieden dein Atom!"
(Split your atom for peace.)

"The greatest melodist," cited from Foster Hall *Bulletin*, 10 (1934), 15.

Birdseye in *Potter's*, XII (1879), 28, on Foster; 145 on Root.

Root, *Story*, 83, 97.

Page 268

Story, 19.

Page 269

Corder, dissertation for the Ed. D. (Maryland, 1971), cited from *Diss. Abstracts*, XXXII (1972), 5252-A.

"Go, Tell It," in *Songfest*, 71.

A collection of Work's *Songs* was compiled by Bertram C. Work (New York: Little & Ives, 1895). This is reprinted in *Earlier American Music*, XIX. Birdseye's article on Work is the fourth in his series for *Potter's*, XII (1879), 284. A first scholarly study, based on forty of Work's letters and postcards, is "The Mysterious Chord of Henry Clay Work" by Richard S. Hill, *Notes of the Music Library Association*, X (1953), 211, 367.

Page 270

Root, *Story*, 137.

"Marching," *Songfest*, 122; Marrocco and Gleason, *Music in America*, 305, etc.

"Grandfather's Clock," *Songfest*, 72. Birdseye, in *Potter's*, XII, 286, tells about Lucas. It was Lucas who made the song famous, according to Eileen Southern, *The Music of Black Americans*, 269. The claim that Lucas composed the song, advanced by Orrin Clayton Suthern, II, "Minstrelsy and Popular Culture," *Journal of Popular Culture*, IV (1971), 658, is unsupported.

Page 271

Song Messenger, cited from Dena Julia Epstein's *Music Publishing in Chicago Before 1871: The Firm of Root and Cady* (Detroit: Information Coordinators, 1969), p. 50.

Kemp, *Old Folks Concert Music* . . . (Boston: Oliver Ditson, 1889). An undated earlier edition I have seen lacks "Old Folks." The study of the troupe by Judith T. Steinberg, "Old Folks Concerts and the Revival of New England Psalmody," *Musical Quarterly*, LIX (1973), 602, mentions the increase of popular songs in the repertory and the resemblance to a minstrel show, but omits to mention Foster.

Page 272

Memoirs of Philip P. Bliss, edited by his collaborator D. W. Whittle (New York: A. S. Barnes, 1878), provide almost all my information; a few additional bits I have gleaned unsystematically from the songbooks, a few more from the *Reminiscences and Gospel Hymn Stories* of George Coles Stebbins (New York: G. H. Doran, 1924).

Root, *Story*, 138.

"Lora Vale," in Bliss' *Memoirs*, 31.

"Cora Dean," in Foster Hall facsimiles.

Gospel Hymns, reprinted in *Earlier American Music*, V.

Page 273

"Hold the Fort," in Pete Seeger's *American Favorite Ballads*, 20. "Almost Persuaded," "Let the Lower Lights," "Wonderful Words," in *Billy Graham Crusade Songs* (Minneapolis: Cliff Barrows, 1960), 62, 27, 11.

"His Courtshippe," *Memoirs*, 212.

"The Reverie," *Memoirs*, 217.

Page 274

Phillips, *Song Pilgrimage Around the World* (Chicago: 1880; New York: Phillips Publishing Company, 1887); a brief memoir with a collection of songs. Alexander Clark's *Philip Phillips: His Songs and Tours* (New York: Phillips, 1887), is a little more ample: 48 pages.

"Medley" in *Song Pilgrimage*, p. 132.

"Home of the Soul," in Clark's *Philip Phillips*, 21.

Ira D. Sankey, *My Life and the Story of the Gospel Hymns* (Philadelphia: Sunday School Times, 1906); *My Life and Sacred Songs* (London: Hodder & Stoughton, 1906); I have seen only the British version. Two later publications add details: Charles Ludwig's *Sankey Still Sings* (Anderson, Indiana: Warner Press, 1941), and the collective volume. *The Ira D. Sankey Centenary: Proceedings . . . with Some Hitherto Unpublished Correspondence* (New Castle, Pennsylvania: Lawrence County Historical Society, 1941). For historical perspectives, I have consulted the excellent works of Sydney E. Ahlstrom, "A Bibliography of Religious History in Its American Setting," *American Studies*, XI/1 (autumn 1972), 3; and *A Religious History of the American People* (New Haven, Connecticut: Yale University Press, 1972). Ahlstrom discusses music, especially pp. 846, 1037, 1076.

Page 275

History of the YMCA in North America, by Charles Howard Hopkins (New York: Associated Press, 1951); on George Williams, p. 4; on Sankey, 181, 187.

The Life of Sir George Williams, by J. E. Hodder Williams (London: Hodder & Stoughton, 1906, 1918), especially pp. 79, 151.

Scheips, *Hold the Fort! The Story of a Song from the Sawdust Trail to the Picket Line* (Washington: Smithsonian, 1971), especially pp. 33, 35, 37, 43, 34.

Page 276

Gospel Songs, 82.

Stebbins, *Reminiscences* (New York: G. H. Doran, 1924).

Modern Revivalism and *The American Evangelicals, 1800–1900*, by William Gerald McLoughlin, provide a comprehensive picture. The former book (New York: Ronald Press, 1959), includes many details about the musicians in relation to the preachers. The latter book (New York: Harper & Row, 1968), is a selection by McLoughlin from the best sermons and writings of the leading preachers, from Charles G. Finney to Sam Jones.

"Revivalism, the Gospel Songs, and Social Reform," by James C. Downey, *Ethnomusicology*, IX (1965), 115, is a sample of the most sustained work on the subject. Downey's master's thesis (Southern Mississippi, 1963) led to his dissertation (Tulane, 1968), "The Music of American Revivalism." His *Ethnomusicology* article, p. 120, first alerted me to Charles Alexander.

Page 277

"Old Rugged Cross," in *Billy Graham Crusade Songs*, 9.

Ahlstrom, p. 740.

George Beverly Shea, *Then Sings My Soul* (Old Tappan, New Jersey: Revell, 1968), p. 15, tells how his career as radio singer began with "Old Folks" about 1936.

"The World of Religious Music," a special issue of *Billboard*, the entertainment trade magazine, LXXVIII/43 (22 October 1966), is full of anonymous reports of facts otherwise hard to find in libraries. "Gospel and Politics: They Mix for Jimmie Davis," p. 52, tells about "Someone to Care."

Lomax, *Cowboy Songs* (New York: Sturgis & Walton, 1910; revised and enlarged, Macmillan, 1938); *Adventures of a Ballad Hunter* (Macmillan, 1947).

Page 278

Dobie, "The Tempo of the Range," *Western Folklore*, XXVI (1967), 177. *The People's Song Book*, edited by Waldemar Hille, foreword by Alan Lomax, preface by B. A. Botkin (New York: Boni and Gaer, 1948).

Ahlstrom, *A Religious History of the American People*, pp. 846, 842, 875, 876.

"D. W. Reeves and His Music," by David L. Stackhouse, *Journal of Band Research*, V/2 (1969), 15, and VI/1, 29.

The Sousa Band: A Discography, by James R. Smart (Washington: Library of Congress, 1970), pp. 254, 619.

Page 279

Sousa, *National . . . Airs* (Philadelphia: H. Coleman, 1890).

Chronicles, II, 467.

Page 280

McLaughlin, *The American Evangelicals*, p. 25.

Century, XXXVI (1899), 577.

Rodeheaver's *Negro Spirituals* (Chicago: Rodeheaver, 1923).

Thomas A. Dorsey is the subject of a special issue of *Black World*, XXIII/9 (July 1974), with an interview, a selected discography, and an article by Horace C. Boyer, based on his dissertation about gospel music.

"As the Spirit Moves Mahalia," by Ralph Ellison, *Saturday Review*, XLI (27 September 1958), 41; reprinted in his *Shadow and Act* (New York: Random House, 1964), p. 213. This marvelous appreciative essay may be supplemented with Tom Bethel's "Mahalia Jackson: Good News, Bad Times; Reflections on Gospel Music and Black Culture," *Jazz Journal*, XXV/5 (May 1972), 4.

CHAPTER 12 JUBILEE SINGERS AND FRIENDS OF THE "FOLK"

Page 282

Black Song: The Forge and the Flame: The Story of How the Afro-American Spiritual Was Hammered Out, by John Lovell, Jr. (New York: Macmillan, 1972), is the most voluminous compilation of evidence and commentary.

"Slave Music in the United States Before 1860: A Survey of Sources," by Dena J. Epstein, in *Notes of the Music Library Association*, XX (1963), 195, 377, is more precise, complete within its limits, and well organized than any other study known to me. Epstein led me to many more sources than will be cited here.

Page 283

Slave Songs, reprinted (New York: Oak, 1965). The preface, table of contents, and directions for singing, with variants of eight songs, are included in Eileen Southern's *Readings in Black American Music*, 139. The passage quoted here begins in Southern's edition, p. 141.

Rehearsal for Reconstruction: the Fort Royal Experiment, by Willie Lee Nichols Rose (Indianapolis: Bobbs-Merrill, 1964), gives valuable new extramusical information and suggests questions for further musical research.

William Francis Allen, Essays and Monographs, edited with a biographical memoir by David B. Frankenburger (Boston: 1890).

"Lucy McKim Garrison" by Dena Epstein, in *Notable American Women*, II (1971), 23, is a fine summary of Epstein's article in the *Bulletin* of the New York Public Library, LXVII (1963), 529.

Dwight's *Journal*, XXII (1862), 254.

Page 284

Chariot in the Sky: A Story of the Jubilee Singers, by Arna Bontemps (Philadelphia: John C. Winston, 1951), gains readability and loses no authenticity by a fictional framework. Bontemps' sources will be cited here for details, but his full story must be recommended.

John W. Hutchinson, *The Story of the Hutchinsons* (Boston: Lee and Shepard, 1896), vol. II, p. 13.

Jennie Jackson's performance of "Old Folks" is described in *The Story of the Jubilee Singers*, edited by J. B. T. Marsh (London: Hodder & Stoughton, 1876), p. 20.

Letters from Port Royal (Boston: W. B. Clarke, 1960), p. 328.

1873 reviewer in *The Orchestra* (London), cited by Dwight's *Journal*, XXXIII (1873), 37.

Page 285

Lovell, *Black Song*, 427.

"Seward" by John Tasker Howard, in the *Dictionary of American Biography*, is my authority.

The Coronation and *Jubilee Songs* (New York: Biglow and Main [successors to W. B. Bradbury], 1872).

Lomax, "The Homogeneity of African—Afro-American Musical Style," in *Afro-American Anthropology*, edited by N. E. Whitten and J. Szwed (New York: Free Press, 1970), p. 188.

"Swing low," *Songfest*, 182; Seeger's *American Favorite Ballads*, 16.

Page 286

"Roll, Jordan," in Eugene Genovese's *Roll, Jordan: The World the Slaves Made* (New York: Praeger, 1974), foreword, and in Chase's *American Music*, p. 240. A vivid account of an 1864 performance of this song, with shuffles, claps, jerks, a circle dance, a trance, a double-shuffle, and, most important, with coordinated beats "at first with their feet, then with their hands," appeared in the anonymous article, "Worship of the Negroes," *Rebellion Record*, VII (1864), 21.

"Go down, Moses," *Songfest*, 68.

Page 287

Hampton and Its Students, by Two of Its Teachers. With Fifty Cabin and Plantation Songs Arranged by Thomas P. Fenner, was the excellent work of Mary Frances Armstrong and Helen W. Ludlow (New York: Putnam, 1874). Fenner's preface, p. 272.

Lovell, *Black Song*, 410.

Tove is memorialized in the anonymous book on *Twenty-two Years' Work of the Hampton Normal and Agricultural Institute* (Hampton: 1893), p. 55.

Page 288

Victor record 35097; the sound is too dim to be recommended.

Burlin, *Hampton Series of Negro Folk Songs* (New York: Schirmer, 1918–19). The combination of fine detail and broad perspective in this edition is extraordinary, worthy of more continuing notice than most students of the subject seem to grant. I quote especially vol. III, p. 6.

Hallowell, *Calhoun Plantation Songs* (Boston: C. W. Thompson, 1901), especially p. 69.

Ballanta-Taylor, *St. Helena Island Spirituals* (New York: Schirmer, 1925).

Phonophotography (Chapel Hill: University of North Carolina Press, 1928).

Page 289

Utica Jubilee (Boston: O. Ditson, 1930), pp. v, xiv.

Dwight's *Journal*, XXXII (1873), 411.

Ritter, *Music in America* (New York: Scribner, 1883), pp. 421, 426. Ritter's brief comment on Foster begins p. 437.

"Folk Songs, and Piano-forte Compositions," in Dwight's *Journal*, XXIX (1869), 24. For information about Ritter, I rely on *A Handbook of American Music and Musicians*, edited by F. O. Jones (Canaseraga, New York: 1886; reprinted New York: Da Capo, 1971), p. 144. Jones, incidentally, p. 59, claims that Foster's "Hard Times" was not only derived from Black camp-meeting songs but also "became exceedingly popular with the slaves." His access to facts about Ritter was better than to facts about either Foster or the slaves.

Lippincott's, XXII (1878), 630, especially 635. On Finck my information comes from Allan Nevins, *The Evening Post: A Century of Journalism* (New York: Boni & Liveright, 1922), p. 565.

Page 290

Lippincott's, XIV (1874), 627; I quote from 629.

Owens in *Lippincott's*, XX (1877), 748.

Harris, *Uncle Remus* (New York: Appleton, 1880; revised edition, 1908).

Allen, "Southern Negro Folk-lore," *Dial*, I (1881), 183.

Critic, II (1883), 505. See also Julia Collier Harris' reprint, p. 208, in her *Life and Letters of Joel Chandler Harris* (Boston: Houghton Mifflin, 1918).

Joel Chandler Harris—Folklorist is carefully examined by Stella Brewer Brookes in her book (Athens: University of Georgia Press, 1950); songs, p. 120. A more critical view is Darwin T. Turner's "Daddy Joel Harris and His Old-time Darkies," *Southern Literary Journal*, I (1968), 20.

Page 291

Uncle Remus, xiv.

Tales (Boston: Houghton Mifflin, 1898).

Afro-American Folk Lore (reprinted New York: Negro Universities Press, 1969), p. 1.

1877 compromise: see Arthur P. Davis and Saunders Redding in their *Cavalcade, *Negro American Writing from 1760 to the Present* (Boston: Houghton Mifflin, 1971), p. 229.

The Black Image in the White Mind: The Debate on Afro-American Character and Destiny, 1817–1914 (New York: Harper & Row, 1971).

Gaines, *The Southern Plantation: A Study in the Development and the Accuracy of a Tradition* (New York: Columbia University Press, 1924), pp. 62, 74, 76; see also Gaines' emphasis on music, p. 94.

Page 292

Harper's Weekly, XVII (1873), 552. Smith, *Popular Culture and Industrialism, 1865–1890* (New York: New York University Press, 1967), p. 231, includes a reproduction of Brooke's picture.

Harper's Bazaar, IV (1871), 51.

Song Journal, preserved in a "Scrapbook of Clippings About Christina Nilsson," compiled by Jaura Josephine Post, 1874, and deposited at the New York Public Library. A conflicting story is told by Henry Watterson in *"Marse Henry:"* *An Autobiography* (New York: Duran, 1919), vol. II, p. 28; "at Paris . . . let me teach you." But Watterson liked to improve his memories.

Page 293

Wilhelmj, "Thème varié" (Berlin: Schlesinger, 1880 [?]).

Zimbalist, "Old Folks" (Mainz: Schott, 1911).

Busch, "Amerikanisches Volkslied" (Leipzig: Breitkopf & Härtel, 1897). "Sir Carl Busch: His Life and Work As a Teacher" is the subject of a dissertation, University of Missouri at Kansas City, 1972, by Donald Robert Lowe; I rely on *Dissertation Abstracts*, XXXIV (1973), 2683-A, together with my memories of a Kansas City childhood.

Beers, *Outline* (Philadelphia: G. W. Jacobs, 1887), p. 228.

Stedman and Hutchinson, *Library* (New York: Benjamin), vol. VIII, p. 288.

Oxford Book (New York: Oxford, 1927), p. 244.

The Literary Era, 1901, p. 365.

Antonín Dvořák, Musician and Craftsman, by John Clapham (London: Faber; New York: St. Martin's, 1966), is the most reliable source in English for the whole life and work. But the Czechs are publishing more detailed information in English, German, and Czech. Jarmil Burghauser is editor of both the *Thematic Catalogue* (Praha: Státní nakl., 1960), and the *IX. Symfonie* (Praha: Pressfoto, 1972), with elaborate commentary.

Page 294

Krehbiel in *Century*, XXII (1892), 657, 660. Huneker's account, possibly doctored, appears in his memoirs, *Steeplejack* (New York: Scribner, 1921), vol. II, p. 65.

"Dvořák Has Arrived," Chicago *Tribune*, 12 August 1893, 4; "Music at the Fair," *ibid.*, 8; "Bohemia at the fair," 13 August, 2; "For national music," *ibid.*, 29. The quotation is from the last piece.

Dvořák's "Schubert," *Century*, XXVI (1894), 341; "Slavic trait," 345. "Music in America," *Harper's*, XC (1895), 428; also in Bruce Jackson's anthology, *The Negro and His Folklore* (Austin: University of Texas Press, 1967) 263. I quote from *Harper's*, 432, 434.

"Dvořák and American music" is the subject of persistent though biased investigations by Lionel Davis, reported in *Student Musicologists at Minnesota*, V (1972), 250. Davis thinks he finds in Dvořák's Quartet, op. 96, and Quintet, op. 97, something "Foster-like."

Page 296

Krehbiel, *Afro-American Folksongs: A Study in Racial and National Music* (1914; reprinted New York: Ungar, 1962). The sifting was under way by 1894, though Krehbiel may not have known of it yet and Dvořák naturally did not. In that year William Wells Newell, president of the American Folklore Society, brought the Hampton singers to perform at Washington. Nathaniel Dett recalled the program in "The Emancipation of Negro Music," *Southern Workman*, XLVII, (1918), 172. Such a program excluded Foster.

Huneker, 1920, *Steeplejack*, II, 67. Compare Arnold T. Schwab's *James Gibbons Huneker, Critic of the Seven Arts* (Stanford, California: Stanford University Press, 1963).

Page 297

"Sissieretta Jones: A Study of the Negro's Contribution to 19th-century American Concert and Theatrical Life," dissertation (Syracuse, 1968) by Willia Estelle Daughtry; Foster songs are mentioned pp. 53, 58, 111, 114, 226.

"New York Church Pays Tribute to Burleigh," an anonymous article in *Musical America*, 12 April 1924, p. 21, includes a speech by Burleigh that is unsurpassed as a primary source. The recollection that Burleigh attended the lectures of Henry T. Finck may be important; see Finck's book, *My Adventures in the Golden Age of Music* (New York: Funk & Wagnalls, 1926), p. 279.

Ellsworth, "H. T. Burleigh Ten Years Later," *Phylon*, XXI (1960), 144, is an outstanding study.

"Deep River," *Songfest*, 52.

Negro Minstrel Melodies (New York: Schirmer, 1909).

Krehbiel, *Afro-American Folksongs*.

Page 298

W. M. Cook is an important musician, not yet sufficiently studied. The best account of his work I know is in Eileen Southern's *Music of Black Americans*, p. 295.

The Negro Music Journal, I/7 (March 1903), 120.

"The Influence on American Musical Culture of Dvořák's Sojourn in America," dissertation (Indiana, 1965) by Merton R. Aborn, concludes that the composer did not teach nationalism; he was a poor conductor, mediocre teacher, made no changes in the curriculum at the National Conservatory. But he will continue to be praised or blamed for the ideas disputed by Krehbiel and Huneker.

William Arms Fisher's *Seventy Negro Spirituals* (Boston: O. Ditson, 1926), p. xii, tells his version of the Dvořák story; p. xiv gives credit to Burleigh. Fisher's *Choral Book* (Ditson, 1936) is a pitiful compromise.

"Henry F. Gilbert, His Life and Works," dissertation (University of Rochester, 1968) by Katherine M. Longyear, sent me to primary sources. *A Hundred Folksongs* (Boston: Birchard, 1910) is in many libraries, but its preface is generally neglected. The Boston Symphony program notes are fascinating. I quote from 26 February 1926, p. 1358.

Page 299

The Souls of Black Folk (Chicago: McClurg, 1903). The final chapter is reprinted in Southern's *Reader*, 193.

DuBois tells about the Hampton quartet in *Dusk of Dawn: An Essay Toward an Autobiography of a Race Concept* (New York: Harcourt, Brace, 1940), p. 23; his work at Alexandria, 31; Lake Minnetonka, Minnesota, 33; Harvard, 35. Additional memoirs about the Harvard Glee Club were published at last as "A Negro Student at Harvard at the End of the 19th Century," *Massachusetts Review*, I (1960), and in the review's anthology, *Black and White in American Culture* (Amherst: University of Massachusetts Press, 1969), 119. On the peasants in Germany, *Dusk of Dawn*, 47.

The indirect debt of DuBois and his successors to Herder has been investigated by Bernard W. Bell, *The Folk Roots of Contemporary Afro-American Poetry* (Detroit: Broadside, 1974).

Page 300

Souls, p. 256.

The Gift of Black Folk: The Negroes in the Making of America (Boston: Stratford, 1924; reprinted New York: Johnson, 1968), p. 275.

Page 301

Dusk of Dawn, 119.

Black Reconstruction (reprinted New York: Russell & Russell, 1963), especially p. 126.

Work, *Folk Songs* (Nashville: Work Bros. & Hart, 1907; reprinted New York: Negro Universities Press, 1969), on Foster, p. 28.

Krehbiel, *Afro-American Folksongs* (reprinted New York: Ungar, 1962), pp. 17, 27, gives credit to DuBois; I quote from p. 154.

Page 302

Locke, *The Negro and His Music* (Washington: The Associates in Negro Folk Education, 1936); on Foster, p. 2.

Butcher, *The Negro in American Culture, Based on Materials Left by Alain Locke* (New York: Knopf, 1972), p. 114.

White, *American Negro Folksongs* (Cambridge: Harvard University Press, 1928; reprinted with foreword by Bruce Jackson, Hatboro, Pennsylvania: Folklore Associates, 1965).

Odum and Johnson, *The Negro and His Songs* (Chapel Hill: University of North Carolina Press, 1925; reprinted with foreword by Roger D. Abrahams, Folklore Associates, 1964). Odum's early article, "Folk-song and Folk-poetry as Found in the Secular Songs of the Southern Negroes," *Journal of American Folklore*, XXIV (1911), 255, 351, despite its condescending tone about "ridiculous pathos," p. 273, presents unique findings relevant to the questions of acculturation.

Jackson, *White Spirituals* (Chapel Hill, 1933; reprinted with introduction by Don Yoder, Folklore Associates, 1964). *Spiritual Folk-songs* (New York: J. J. Augustin, 1937, reprinted New York: Dover, 1964). *White and Negro* (Augustin, 1943).

Page 303

"Stephen Foster's Debt," *Musical Quarterly*, XXII (1936), 154. Jackson's contributions are appraised by the professional folklorist D. K. Wilgus in an appendix of his survey of *Anglo-American Folksong Scholarship Since 1898* (New Brunswick, New Jersey: Rutgers University Press, 1959), p. 345. They are more thoroughly reconsidered by Dorothy D. Horn, in *Sing to Me of Heaven: A Study of Folk and Early American Materials in Three Old Harp Books* (Gainesville: University of Florida Press, 1970): Horn defines the group whose songs Jackson studied as "middle class folk," p. 159.

Victor record 18314, with orchestral accompaniment.

Davis, *Purlie* (New York: French, 1961); I quote from an anthology by P. Sterling, *Laughing on the Outside* (New York: Grosset and Dunlap, 1965), 247. The cultural lag between poets and most musicians in 1971 is illustrated by the confidence of the Black tenor, George Shirley, that "it was the spiritual that inspired Stephen Foster to cast many of his songs in the black idiom." Shirley's article on "The Black Performer," *Opera News*, XXXV/4 (30 January 1971), 6, might better have omitted Foster.

Page 304

Lehmann, *Negro Spirituals: Geschichte und Theologie* (Berlin: Eckart, 1965).

Hagen, "Abriss der Geschichte der Spiritualforschung," *Jahrbuch für musikalische Volks- und Völkerkunde*, IV (1968), 59.

Benker, "Bevorzugte Lieder," *Musik und Bildung*, V (1973), 473.

Bruckner, "Heimat und Demokratie: Gedanken zum politischen Folklorismus in Westdeutschland," *Zeitschrift für Volkskunde*, LXI (1965), 205; I quote from p. 213.

Dahlhaus, " 'Echt' und 'unecht,' " *ibid.*, LXIII (1967), 56. But perhaps a more generous idea is that of Marguerite Yourcenar, *Fleuve profond, sombre rivière: les "Negro Spirituals"* (Paris: Gallimard, 1964), p. 35 on Foster; p. 50: "We are all slaves."

The Bardstown legend is discussed thoroughly by Morneweck, *Chronicles*, II, 403, and Howard, *Stephen Foster*, 170. Thomas D. Clark participated in debunking, with "The Slavery Background of Foster's My Old Kentucky Home," *Filson Club Historical Quarterly*, X (1936), 1; his later article, from which I quote, is "My Old Kentucky Home in Retrospect," in the same journal, XXII (1948), 104. The remoteness of "folk," either Black or white, from "Kentucky Home" is noted by MacEdward Leach, *The Ballad Book* (New York: Harper, 1955), p. 31: "nowhere have folk singers re-created it in terms of a local or individual culture."

Page 305

Israel Zangwill's play, *The Melting Pot* (New York: Macmillan, 1909), made the image popular; the hero is a violinist-composer, but whether he plays "Old Folks" depends on the particular production.

Die Musik, IV/3 (1904), 268; I quote especially pp. 271, 277, 275, 276, 278, 277, 273, 271.

Page 306

Elson, *The History of American Music* (New York: Macmillan, 1904), pp. 134, 136. Dissent was not absent in 1904: the poet Rupert Hughes, introducing his collection of *Songs by Thirty Americans* (Boston: O. Ditson), wrote that Foster "at his best trembled on the razor-edge between the perfect simplicity of folk-song and the maudlin banality of streetsong."

Farwell and Darby, *Music in America* (New York: the National Society of Music, 1915), pp. 286, 318.

Howard, "Our Folk Music and Its Probable Impress on American Music of the Future: Casual Remarks by Way of a Survey," *Musical Quarterly*, VII (1921), 167. *Our American Music, Three Hundred Years of It* (New York: Crowell, 1931; fourth edition 1965); p. 187 begins a passage on Foster; p. 210: "it is as a poet of homesickness that he was greatest."

Page 307

Program (New York: J. Fischer, 1934); *Sonatina* (Schirmer); *From Foster Hall* (C. Fischer, 1938).

Howard, *Stephen Foster*, 2.

"John Tasker Howard" by George Kent Bellows, *Notes of the Music Library Association*, XIV (1957), 501, portrays the writer as "usually a sentimentalist."

Howard, 3. This paragraph, added in Howard's 1953 edition, quotes without acknowledgment from the essay by Fletcher Hodges, Jr., "A Pittsburgh Composer and His Memorial," in the *Western Pennsylvania Historical Magazine*, XXI/2 (June 1938) 3. Hodges' idea is exaggerated by Howard's context, whereas the original context smoothly qualifies it:

> . . . the last quarter century witnessed a marked revival of interest in both the music and the life of the composer.
>
> Foster's fame rests chiefly on his four great songs of the South, *Old Folks at Home, My Old Kentucky Home, Massa's in de Cold Ground,* and *Old Black Joe*. These beloved plantation melodies were intended to portray one race of people, one section of our country, one period in our history, yet through his genius Foster succeeded in creating songs which have leaped the boundaries of space and time, and express universal thoughts and emotions. The best of his sentimental ballads . . . recall the charm of an age which is past. *Oh! Susanna* and *Camptown Races* are proof that Foster possessed a sense of humor. . . . Altogether . . . his best works . . . form a remarkable contribution to the music of our nation and of all mankind.

Howard distorts his source as well as the facts.

Page 309

Harper's, CLXXXIII (June 1941), 109; quotations from pp. 110, 111; slightly revised, the article forms an "Interlude, Doo-dah Day," in DeVoto's book, *The Year of Decision: 1846* (Boston: Little, Brown, 1943), p. 136; my quotation ends with this, p. 139.

Brooks, *The World of Washington Irving* (New York: Dutton, 1944), pp. 410, 470; *The Times of Melville and Whitman* (Dutton, 1947), pp. 4, 88, 204, 260, 366, 409.

Branch, *The Sentimental Years 1836–1860* (New York: Appleton-Century, 1934), p. 181: "American balladry reached probably its high mark for all time."

Pattee, *The Feminine Fifties* (Appleton-Century, 1940), p. 318: "promise of outlasting all the American classics musical or literary."

Commager, *The American Mind*, (New Haven, Connecticut: Yale University Press, 1950), p. 421.

Commager, *The Search for a Usable Past, and Other Essays* (New York: Knopf, 1967), pp. 25, 21, 26. Another historian, David M. Potter, helped me come to grips with Commager and DeVoto in his essay on "The Historian's Use of Nationalism and Vice Versa," *American Historical Review*, LXVII (1962), 924.

Page 310

Howard, "Way Down Upon the Suwanee," *National Music Council Bulletin*, XI (January 1951), 16.

"Foster Memorial's New Bell Chime," by C. E. Wright, *New York Times*, 9 November, 1958, sec. 2, p. 29.

Florida's Memorial to Stephen Foster (White Springs: Board of Trustees of the Stephen Foster Memorial, Department of State, State of Florida, published sometime between 1967 and 1973) has lavish colored pictures of the carillon and other features.

The U.S. Congress, in a joint resolution, 15 October, 1951, paid tribute more ephemeral than Florida's or Tennessee's, but no less exaggerated: "a national expression of democracy . . . the father of American folk music."

Saturday Evening Post, CCXXVI (6 February, 1954), 30.

Hans Nathan complained, in *A History of Song*, edited by Denis Stevens (London: Hutchinson, 1960), 419, that "popularity is too weak a word . . . Foster's songs . . . have become part of the American way of life."

Page 311

Konen, *Puti amerikanskoi muzyki* (Moscow: Muzyka, 1965), p. 503. See also T. Matalaeva's anthology, *Pesni i tantsy S. Sh. A.* (Muzyka, 1968), p. 3.

ASCAP Today, I/2 (June 1967), 11, 28.

"Southern Solons Rap Censorship of Foster Lyrics," anonymous article in *Variety*, CCVII/9 (31 July 1957), 1, 110.

Nicholas, "Uncle Tom's Cabin, 1852–1952," *Georgia Review*, VII (1954), 148.

Careful Man Songster (Chicago: White, Smith & Co., 1881). My information comes from Robert Stevenson's article, "America's First Black Music Historian [J. M. Trotter]," *Journal of the American Musicological Society*, XXVI (1973), 400.

Birdoff, *The World's Greatest Hit* (New York: Vanni, 1947), p. 237.

Bland, *Album of Outstanding Songs . . . Arranged by Charles Haywood* (New York: Marks, 1946) belongs in every American music library, it includes a biographical sketch. "A worthy heir to Foster's laurels" is the phrase of Eileen Southern, *The Music of Black Americans*, 1971, p. 265. Possibly it derives from the article by Kelly Miller, "The Negro 'Stephen Foster' . . . James A. Bland," in *Etude*, LVII (1939). A somewhat longer study is John Daly's *Song in His Heart: The Life and Times of James A. Bland* (Philadelphia: John C. Winston, 1951). Still admittedly incomplete, but the best account so far of Bland's career, in historical context, is in Robert Toll's *Blacking Up*, p. 216.

Page 312

"Carry Me Back," *Songfest*, 39; "Golden Slippers," 69.

In Philadelphia, at the annual "mummers' parade," the theme "Golden Slippers" is said to be "an old Negro spiritual," according to Charles T. Welch in his book on the Philadelphia tradition, *Oh! Dem Golden Slippers* (New York: Thomas Nelson, 1970), p. 115. Welch himself believes the song to be a satire.

Mistah Jolson, as told to Alban Emley (Hollywood: House-Warven, 1951), p. 44. An interpretation of Jolson's work is included in "The Burnt Cork Illusion of the 1920s in America: A Study in Nostalgia," by Stanley W. White, *Journal of Pop Culture*, V (1971), 530.

The "Kentucky Minstrels" are pictured in the frontispiece of Reginald Nettel's excellent survey, *Seven Centuries of Popular Song: A Social History of Urban Ditties* (London: Phoenix, 1956). Nettel's discussion of Foster, p. 177, helped me locate his place in the international tradition.

Page 313

Uncle Dave Macon: A Bio-Discography, by Ralph Rinzler and Norm Cohen (Los Angeles: John Edmunds Memorial Foundation, 1970), pp. 13, 22. The recording is Vocalion E 3742-43.

Handy, *Father of the Blues: An Autobiography*, edited by Arna Bontemps (New York: Macmillan, 1955), pp. 35, 112, 149.

"Stepin Fetchit" was the stage-name of Lincoln Theodore Monroe Andrew Perry, born 1892. In an interview with Ralph Gleason, *Rolling Stone*, 18 January 1973, p. 18, Perry said, "I started in Plantation shows. They were Negro minstrel shows."

American Vaudeville As Ritual, by Albert F. McLean, Jr. (Lexington: University of Kentucky Press, 1965), sets ample facts in a persuasive interpretation. What is perhaps the most exciting strand in American theater is presented by Arthur Todd in "American Negro Dance, a National Treasure," *Ballet Annual*, XVI (1962), 92.

Rolling Along (New York: Viking, 1937), p. 24.

Page 314

"James Weldon Johnson's Theories and Performance Practices of Afro-American Folksongs," by Wendell Phillips Whalum, *Phylon*, XXXII (1971), 383.

Rolling Along, 26, 21.

Rolling Along, 27. Johnson's limitations were eventually outmoded when LeRoi Jones published *Blues People: Negro Music in White America* (New York William Morrow, 1963).

Page 315

"Gospel" . . . continuity . . . cohesive group: the clearest exposition I know is Alan Lomax's book *The Rainbow Sign: A Southern Documentary* (New York: Duell, Sloan and Pearce, 1959).

Among countless historians whose thoughts helped me shape those summed up here, one gave a particular push: Herbert G. Gutman, "Work, Culture, and Society, in Industrializing America, 1815–1919," *American Historical Review*, LXXVIII (1973), 531, partly because of his precise but tactful, impartial comparisons with Britain.

A psychologist helped too: Hildemarie Streich, "Über die Symbolik der Musik," *Jahrbuch für Psychologie*, XV (1967), 120, with a synthesis of the "dream of home" and many aspects of music.

CHAPTER 13   COMPOSERS OF "NEW MUSIC"

Page 317

Memos (New York: Norton, 1972).

Essays, edited by Howard Boatwright (New York: Norton, 1961); this careful edition, annotated and supplemented with some of Ives' other writings, belongs in every American library and every music library of the world.

Page 318

Memos, 52.

Memos, 34.

Page 319

Foster story, *Memos*, 246. Kirkpatrick's mention of this story to me, soon after he heard it, perhaps 1950, spurred my work.

Letter to Howard, *Memos*, 236.

Page 320

Memos, 127.

Memos, 132, 72.

Memos, 75, 72; letter sketch, 133.

Page 321

Memos, 114.

Page 323

Memos, 155, 52.

Page 324

Marshall, "Charles Ives's Quotations: Manner or Substance?" *Perspectives of New Music*, VI/2 (1968), 45.

Page 325
> Bloom, *Autobiography* (New York: Putnam, 1948), p. 135.
> *Essays*, 51.

Page 326
> Thoreau, *Correspondence*, edited by Walter Harding and Carl Bode (New York: New York University Press, 1958), p. 165.
> *Journal*, V, 294; VI 100.
> *Consciousness in Concord*, edited by Perry Miller, p. 100.

Page 328
> James, *Memories and Studies* (New York: Longmans, Green, 1911), p. 43.
> "Colonel Shaw in American Poetry: 'For the Union Dead' and Its Precursors," by Steven Axelrod, *American Quarterly*, XXIV (1972), 523, discusses works of William Wells Brown, Paul Lawrence Dunbar, James Russell Lowell, and William Vaughan Moody, which may have been read by Ives; may even have reminded him, though not explicitly, of Foster.

Page 329
> *Memos*, 45 fn.; 250 about Brooks.
> "George's Adventure," *Memos*, 214, 223.

Page 330
> *Essays*, 94.
> "Berlin," by Abel Green, *Variety*, 19 September 1962, cited in the article in *Current Biography*, 1963, p. 33.
> Theodore Dreiser, introducing his brother Paul Dresser's *Songs* (New York: Boni & Liveright, 1927), takes credit for guiding his career by asking in 1896, "Look at My Old Kentucky Home, Dixie, Old Black Joe—why don't you do something like that?"

Page 332
> *Music and Imagination* (Cambridge: Harvard University Press, 1953), p. 99.

Page 333
> *Musical America*, XLIII/9 (19 December 1925), 19.
> *Music and Imagination*, 81.

Page 334
> Grainger's *Lullaby* (New York: Schirmer, 1917). More connections between Grainger and Foster may be forthcoming in the studies of David Josephson and others.

Page 335
> *Entretiens avec Claude Rostand* (Paris: Juilliard, 1954), p. 133. In 1973 Morton Gould's arrangement for two pianos of "Oh! Susanna" was played by "Americans in China," Richard Hadden and Frances Roots, *High Fidelity-Musical America*, XXVII/6 (June 1973), 30. Chinese interpretations of Foster may be the best yet.

Page 336
> "Thea Musgrave" is the subject of a good introductory article by Norman Kay, *Music & Musicians*, XVIII/4 (December 1969), 34.

CHAPTER 14 NEW SINGERS AND SONGWRITERS

Page 338
> Balliett, "It's Detestable When You Live It: Ray Charles," *New Yorker*, XLVI (28 March 1970), 44; I quote from p. 58.
> School: compare "Cosby Promised His Teacher He'd Never Sing 'Old Black Joe' Again," by Joanne Stang, *New York Times*, 30 June 1968, sec. D, p. 17.

Page 339
> Gleason, "Ray Listens To All the Songs He Can To Get a Few Good Ones," San Francisco *Chronicle*, XXIV/52 (16 April 1961), 61, cited in *Current Biography*, 1965, p. 8.
> Balliett, 76.

Page 340

"Swanee River Rock," Atlantic record 1154 (45 rpm) and 8025 (LP, 1958). *Top Pop Records, 1955–1972*, by Joel C. Whitburn (Menomonee Falls, Wisconsin: Record Research, 1973), p. 48, shows the piece's rank on the market. Whitburn's *Top Rhythm & Blues Records, 1949–1971*, (1973), p. 25, shows its place on the black market.

Home: Social Essays, by LeRoi Jones (New York: William Morrow, 1966), reinforces the connotations of the word. A younger and more academic writer, Mike Thelwell, in "Fish Are Jumping an' the Cotton Is High: Notes from the Mississippi Delta," *Massachusetts Review*, VII (1966), 362, speaks for many others: "Although this is your first time there, you recognize when you have come home . . . safety in numbers, friendship, and some degree of security after the exposed vulnerability of the highway." But compare Charles himself, "I Don't Need To See," in *Music Journal*, 28 (January 1970), 3: "I've got to keep moving, keep trying to find something new."

Page 341

"I used to be a much better clarinet player than a saxophonist," wrote Charles in a brief article, "I'd Like to Work with a Small Combo Again," *Crescendo International*, 10 (November 1971), 14.

Aronowitz, "Blind Genius: What's So Great About Ray Charles?" *Saturday Evening Post*, CCXXXV (24 August 1963), 75.

Page 342

Balliett, 74, 62, 53, 61.

Cry: compare "The Romance of the Negro Folk Cry in America," by Willis Laurence James, *Phylon*, XVI (1955), 15.

Page 343

Song Hits, XXXV/59 (January 1971), 28.

Page 344

Gleason, cited in *Current Biography*, 1965, p. 81. My interpretation depends on much reading, from which I recommend the following works:

Arna Bontemps, "Rock, Church, Rock," *Common Ground*, III/1 (1942), 75.

E. Franklin Frazier, *The Negro Church in America* (Liverpool: London University Press, 1964).

Joseph R. Washington, Jr., *Black Religion: The Negro and Christianity in the United States* (Boston: Beacon, 1964).

Claude Hall and others, "Negro Gospel," *Billboard*, LXXVII/44 (23 October, 1965).

Arnold Shaw, *The World of Soul* (New York: Crowell, 1970).

Charles Hobson, "The Gospel Truth," *Downbeat*, 30 May, 1968, p. 17: "Gospel remains an underground music."

John F. Szwed, "Musical Adaptation Among Afro-Americans," *Journal of American Folklore*, LXXXII (1969), 112; reprinted in Whitten and Szwed's *Afro-American Anthropology* (New York: Free Press, 1970), p. 219.

Tony Heilbut, *The Gospel Sound* (New York: Simon & Schuster, 1971).

"Georgia Tom Dorsey," an interview by Jim and Amy O'Neal, *Living Blues* XX (April 1975) 17, adds fascinating new detail.

Aronowitz, *Saturday Evening Post* (24 August 1963), 75.

Jazz Masters of the Fifties, by Joe Goldberg (New York: Macmillan, 1965), is comprehensive within its limits. From the vast bibliography of jazz in general, the following works are especially relevant:

Arna Bontemps and Jack Conroy, *Any Place but Here* (New York: Hill & Wang, 1966), pp. 85, 248, 253, 345.

Charles Keil, *Urban Blues* (Chicago: Unversity of Chicago Press, 1966).

Theo Lehmann, *Blues and Trouble* (Berlin: Henschel, 1966), with a foreword by Martin Luther King, Jr.; "It is not surprising that in the struggle of the American Negroes for inner concentration so much has been accomplished by the jazz musicians. Long before modern journalists and scholars wrote about 'racial identity' as a problem for the multiracial world, musicians turned toward their roots."

Leslie B. Rout, Jr., "Some Post-war Developments in Jazz," *Midcontinent American Studies Journal*, IX (1968), 27.

George H. Lewis, "Social Protest and Self Awareness in Black Popular Music," *Pop Music and Society*, II (1973), 327.

Balliett, 48.

Page 345

Bechet, "Swanee River," Columbia record CL 1410 (matrix XLP 48444/5).

Balliett, 61.

29 Modern . . . (New York: Robbins, 1939), pp. 8, 6, 4.

Page 346

Bourbon Street Black: the New Orleans Black Jazzman, by Jack V. Bueckle and Danny Barker (New York: Oxford, 1973), pp. 43, 45.

Page 347

Country Music U. S. A., a Fifty-Year History, by Bill C. Malone (Austin: University of Texas Press, 1968), is a unique scholarly survey based on participation. On Charles' contribution, see especially Arnold Shaw, "The Sound Heard 'Round the World," *BMI World of Music*, November 1968, 4.

Balliett, 62.

Smith, Prestige record, PR 7217.

Page 348

" 'Down Upon the Suwannee': A Colorful Story of the First All Florida Folk Festival," *Etude*, LXXII/4 (April 1954), 12. Thelma Boltin, "The Florida Folk Festival: Activities . . . ," *Southern Folklore Quarterly*, XXV (1961), 223. Louise Wendell Carpenter, "The Stephen Foster Memorial, 1931–1969: A Socio-Cultural Force in a Rural Community," (Dissertation, Florida State, 1969).

Seeger, *The Incompleat Folksinger* (New York: Simon & Schuster, 1972).

Page 349

Life, LVII (8 October 1964), 61.

American Favorite Ballads (New York: Oak, 1961).

Page 350

"John Henry," also in *Songfest*, 95.

Page 351

"Hammer song," in *American Favorite Ballads*, 19.

Page 352

"So long," 92. "Irene," American Favorite Ballads, 48.

Common Ground, 7 (spring 1942), 43.

Dylan, "Eleven Outlined Epitaphs," with the record of "The Times They Are a-Changin'," Columbia CS 8905.

Fuld, *Book of World Famous Music*, (New York: Crown, 1966), p. 510.

Page 353

Guy and Candie Carawan, *We Shall Overcome! Songs of the Southern Freedom Movement* (New York: Oak, 1963).

Dunson, *Freedom in the Air* (New York: International Publishers [Little New World Paperbacks 7] 1965), p. 39.

The Carawans' book was expanded to *Freedom Is a Constant Struggle: Songs of the Freedom Movement* (Oak, 1968), with more details about "We Shall Overcome," p. 138.

Incompleat Folksinger, 112.

Page 354

Ballads, 9.

Taylor, Warner Bros. record 1843.

Village Voice, 23 December 1971, reprinted in *Rolling Stone* 17 February 1972, p. 63.

Page 355

Taj, Prestige record C 30676. Compare Bob Groom, *The Blues Revival* (London: Studio Vista, 1971), p. 106.

America's Music, p. 297. Chase's third edition, scheduled for 1976, may revise this "summing-up" of Foster. His insight enlightened me and every other careful student of Foster from 1955 on. The English scholar and composer Wilfrid Mellers, expert on many phases of American music, tried in vain to argue a paradoxical reversal of Chase's position on Foster in his survey, *Music in a New Found Land: Themes and Developments in the History of American Music* (London: Barrie & Rockliff, 1964). The cultural historian Carl Bode brought Chase's interpretation into relation with all the traits of "American character" that he saw defining itself in a "pivotal period": *The Anatomy of American Popular Culture, 1840–1861* (Berkeley: University of California Press, 1959).

Hitchcock, *Music in the U.S.*, p. 61. The challenge is presented forcefully in Hitchcock's article on Foster in *HiFi/Stereo Review*, XVIII/1 (January 1967), 48.

Page 356

Cott, "Our Musical Past Rediscovered—from Fuging Tunes to Sousa," *New York Times*, 11 March 1973, sec. D, p. 25, 35.

"Message," Tangerine record ABCX 755/TRC.

Lift Every Voice (New York: Marks Music Corporation); words and melody reprinted in Southern's *Music of Black Americans*, 301.

"America the Beautiful," in *The Hymnal* (Ithaca: Cornell University Press, 1952), p. 411.

"Hey Mister," copyright Racer Music Corp., I have not found in print.

Throughout the world: Compare James Baldwin, in *A Dialogue by James Baldwin and Nikki Giovanni* (Philadelphia: Lippincott, 1973), p. 72: "The crisis has something to do with identity, and that has something to do with buried history. When you look at the British, the English working class, that history has been buried too. . . . [See] what Ray Charles does with dreary little anthems one wouldn't dream of hearing until he got his hands on them and put our experience into them."

Page 357

"What Have They Done," words only in *Song Hits Magazine*, XXXV/59/60/65 (January to June 1971), copyright credit to Kama Rippa Music, Inc. and Amelanie Music. This printing enables me to distinguish the words added by Charles in his recorded performance.

Page 358

"I'm Workin'," in *American Negro Songs and Spirituals*, edited by John W. Work (New York: Bonanza, 1940), p. 97.

Index

Italic numerals indicate notes; the numeral refers to the page in the text, and this page number appears also with the note, though the notes are located pp. 359–402. Dates in parentheses after song titles identify the songs of Foster. Other songs indexed have in parentheses the names of authors (words-music). Following the alphabetical index there is a classified chronological list of all known songs and other music by Foster, with an index to their principal mentions here.